THE CAMBRIDGE HISTORY OF LATIN AMERICA

VOLUME I

Colonial Latin America

THE CAMBRIDGE HISTORY OF LATIN AMERICA

VOLUME I

Colonial Latin America

edited by

LESLIE BETHELL

*Reader in Hispanic American and
Brazilian History at University College London*

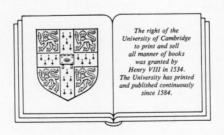

The right of the
University of Cambridge
to print and sell
all manner of books
was granted by
Henry VIII in 1534.
The University has printed
and published continuously
since 1584.

CAMBRIDGE UNIVERSITY PRESS

Cambridge

London   New York   New Rochelle

Melbourne   Sydney

Published by the Press Syndicate of the University of Cambridge
The Pitt Building, Trumpington Street, Cambridge CB2 1RP
32 East 57th Street, New York, NY 10022, USA
296 Beaconsfield Parade, Middle Park, Melbourne 3206, Australia

© Cambridge University Press 1984

First published 1984

Printed in Great Britain by the University Press, Cambridge

Library of Congress catalogue card number: 83–19036

British Library Cataloguing in Publication Data

The Cambridge history of Latin America.
Vol. 1: Colonial Latin America
1. Latin America – History
I. Bethell, Leslie
980   F1410

ISBN 0 521 23223 6

108220

UP

CONTENTS

PART ONE. AMERICA ON THE EVE OF THE
CONQUEST

v

MAPS

NOTE ON CURRENCY AND
MEASUREMENT

Various units of value and measurement are referred to in the text of the following chapters. It is not possible to give exact equivalents in modern terms, particularly as there were many local variations. The following explanations may prove helpful.

Peso	The silver peso of Mexico in the late eighteenth century was equal to the American dollar or 4*s.* 8*d.*
Real	The peso was divided into eight silver reales or twenty copper reales (*reales de vellón*).
Maravedí	The value of the maravedí varied widely and was often no more than an imaginary division of bigger coins, since for long periods there were no maravedí coins at all. The last ones to circulate, probably in the late seventeenth and early eighteenth centuries, were copper coins, often debased. One such coin was worth 1/34 part of a real de vellón.
Réis (sing. *real*)	Smallest Portuguese monetary unit; existed only as money of account.
Milréis	1,000 réis, usually written 1$000; worth 12*s.* in the middle of the seventeenth century.
Cruzado	The Portuguese cruzado was equal to 400 réis (480 réis in the first half of the eighteenth century); originally of gold, later silver
Conto	A conto equalled 1,000$000 réis (1,000 milréis).
Fanega	A dry measure for cacao, wheat, maize, etc. Usually equal to 1.5 English bushels, but there were local variations, e.g. in Mexico, where the fanega of maize could be either 1.5 or 2.5 bushels (or 55 or 90.8 litres).

ix

Quintal   Usually translated as 'hundredweight' and composed of
                4 Spanish *arrobas* or 100 *libras*.
Arroba   The Spanish arroba weighed about 11.5 kg (25 lb). The
                Portuguese arroba weighed 14.5 kg (32 lb).

ABBREVIATIONS

AESC	*Annales, Économies, Sociétés, Civilizations*
CHLA	*Cambridge History of Latin America*
HAHR	*Hispanic American Historical Review*
JGSWGL	*Jahrbuch für Geschichte von Staat, Wirtschaft und Gesellschaft Lateinamerikas*

GENERAL PREFACE

In the English-speaking and English-reading world the multi-volume
Cambridge Histories planned and edited by historians of established
reputation, with individual chapters written by leading specialists in
their fields, have since the beginning of the century set the highest
standards of collaborative international scholarship. *The Cambridge
Modern History*, planned by Lord Acton, appeared in sixteen volumes
between 1902 and 1912. It was followed by *The Cambridge Ancient
History*, *The Cambridge Medieval History* and others. The *Modern History*
has now been replaced by *The New Cambridge Modern History* in fourteen
volumes, and *The Cambridge Economic History of Europe* has recently been
completed. Cambridge Histories of Islam, of Iran and of Africa are
published or near completion; in progress are Histories of China and
of Judaism, while Japan is soon to join the list.

In the early 1970s Cambridge University Press decided the time was
ripe to embark on a Cambridge History of Latin America. Since the
Second World War and particularly since 1960 research and writing on
Latin American history had been developing, and have continued to
develop, at an unprecedented rate – in the United States (by American
historians in particular, but also by British, European and Latin
American historians resident in the United States), in Europe (especially
in Britain and France) and increasingly in Latin America itself (where
a new generation of young professional historians, many of them
trained in the United States, Britain or Europe, had begun to emerge).
Perspectives had changed as political, economic and social realities in
Latin America – and Latin America's role in the world – had changed.
Methodological innovations and new conceptual models drawn from
the social sciences (economics, political science, historical demography,
sociology, anthropology) as well as from other fields of historical

research were increasingly being adopted by historians of Latin America. The Latin American Studies monograph series and the *Journal of Latin American Studies* had already been established by the Press and were beginning to publish the results of this new historical thinking and research.

In 1974 Dr Leslie Bethell, Reader in Hispanic American and Brazilian History at University College London, accepted an invitation to edit the Cambridge History of Latin America. For the first time a single editor was given responsibility for the planning, co-ordination and editing of an entire History. Contributors were drawn from the United States and Canada, Britain and Europe, and Latin America.

The Cambridge History of Latin America is the first large-scale, authoritative survey of Latin America's unique historical experience during almost five centuries from the first contacts between the native American Indians and Europeans (and the beginnings of the African slave trade) in the late fifteenth and early sixteenth centuries to the present day. (The Press has under consideration a separate Cambridge History of the native peoples of America – North, Middle and South – before the arrival of the Europeans.) Latin America is taken to comprise the predominantly Spanish- and Portuguese-speaking areas of continental America south of the United States – Mexico, Central America and South America – together with the Spanish-speaking Caribbean – Cuba, Puerto Rico, the Dominican Republic – and, by convention, Haiti. (The vast territories in North America lost to the United States by treaty and by war, first by Spain, then by Mexico, during the first half of the nineteenth century are for the most part excluded. Neither the British, French and Dutch Caribbean islands nor the Guianas are included even though Jamaica and Trinidad, for example, have early Hispanic antecedents and are now members of the Organisation of American States.) The aim is to produce a high-level synthesis of existing knowledge which will provide historians of Latin America with a solid base for future research, which students of Latin American history will find useful and which will be of interest to historians of other areas of the world. It is also hoped that the *History* will contribute more generally to a deeper understanding of Latin America through its history in the United States and in Europe and, not least, to a greater awareness of its own history in Latin America.

For the first time the volumes of a Cambridge History will be published in chronological order: Volumes I and II (Colonial Latin

America – with an introductory section on the native American peoples and civilizations on the eve of the European invasion) in 1984; Volume III (Latin America, Independence and Post-Independence, *c.* 1790–1870/80) in 1985; Volumes IV and V (Latin America, 1870/80–1930) in 1986; and Volumes VI–VIII (Latin America, 1930 to the present) as soon as possible thereafter. Each volume or set of volumes examines a period in the economic, social, political, intellectual and cultural history of Latin America. While recognizing the decisive impact on Latin America of external forces, of developments within what is now called the capitalist world system, and the fundamental importance of its economic, political and cultural ties first with Spain and Portugal, then with Britain, France and, to a lesser extent, Western Europe as a whole, and finally with the United States, the emphasis of the *History* will be upon the evolution of internal structures. Furthermore, the emphasis is clearly on the period since the establishment of all the independent Latin American states except Cuba at the beginning of the nineteenth century, which, compared with the colonial and independence periods, has been relatively neglected by historians of Latin America. The period of Spanish and Portuguese colonial rule from the sixteenth to the eighteenth centuries is the subject of two of the eight volumes. Six are devoted to the nineteenth and twentieth centuries and will consist of a mixture of general, comparative chapters built around major themes in Latin American history and chapters on the individual histories of the twenty independent Latin American countries (plus Puerto Rico), and especially the three major countries – Brazil, Mexico and Argentina. In view of its size, population and distinctive history, Brazil, which has often been neglected in general histories of Latin America, written for the most part by Spanish Americans or Spanish American specialists, will here receive the attention it deserves. The editor of the *History* is himself, above all, a specialist on Brazil.

An important feature of the *History* will be the bibliographical essays which accompany each chapter. These will give special emphasis to books and articles published during the past 15–20 years, that is to say, since the publication of Howard F. Cline (ed.), *Latin American History: essays in its study and teaching, 1898–1965* (2 vols., published for the Conference on Latin American History by the University of Texas Press, Austin, Texas, 1967), and Charles C. Griffin (ed.), *Latin America: a guide to the historical literature* (published for the Conference on Latin American History by the University of Texas Press, Austin, Texas, 1971); the latter was prepared during 1966–9 and included few works published after 1966. The *History* will include some maps, but the reader is referred to John V. Lombardi (ed.), *Latin American History: a teaching atlas* (published for the Conference on Latin American History by the University of Wisconsin Press, Madison, Wisconsin, 1984).

PREFACE TO VOLUMES I AND II

The first two volumes of *The Cambridge History of Latin America*, which are close integrated, are devoted to the three centuries of Spanish and Portuguese colonial rule from the first contacts between the native American Indians and Europeans at the end of the fifteenth and beginning of the sixteenth centuries to the revolutions and wars of independence at the beginning of the nineteenth century.

Man first entered the continent through the Bering Strait, perhaps as long ago as 35,000 B.C. There is some evidence of the possible presence of man in what is today Mexico as early as 20,000 B.C., but the oldest certain human finds – for example, at Tepexpan, north-east of Mexico City, and Lagôa Santa in Minas Gerais, Brazil – have been dated no earlier than 9,000–8,000 B.C. Agriculture in Mesoamerica dates from around 5,000 B.C., and the production of pottery from around 2,300 B.C. The earliest evidence of societies with political and religious structures can be found, in Mexico, at the Olmec sites, notably La Venta, and, in the Andes, at Chavin, both dating from before 1,000 B.C. By A.D 1500 there were states with highly structured economies and societies and highly developed cultures and religions, like the Aztec empire in Mexico and the Inca empire in the Central Andes, as well as more or less stable chiefdoms of varying degrees of complexity throughout, for example, the Caribbean and circum-Caribbean and, still, hundreds of nomadic or semi-nomadic tribes in North America, southern South America and Brazil. Research on pre-Columbian America has advanced rapidly during the past twenty or thirty years, especially in Mesoamerica, but also most recently in the Andes – and elsewhere. Important contributions to knowledge have been made by archaeologists, but also by linguists and palaeographers, geographers and botanists, even by mathematicians and astronomers and, above all, by anthropologists, ethnologists and ethnohistorians. The invaluable *Handbook of Latin American Studies* (1936–) has since 1960 included a section on publications in the important new field of ethnohistory. The *Handbook of South American Indians*, ed. Julian H. Steward (6 vols., Washington, D.C., 1946–50), and the *Handbook of Middle American Indians*, ed. Robert Wauchope (16 vols., Austin, Texas, 1964–76), remain indispensable, although the former in particular is now seriously out of date. No attempt has been made in *The Cambridge History of Latin America* to present a full-scale account of the evolution of the various indigenous American societies – in isolation from the rest of the world – during the two or three thousand years before the arrival of the Europeans. This belongs to another Cambridge *History*. However, the five chapters which form the first section of the first of these two volumes on colonial Latin America survey the native American peoples and civilizations on the eve of the European invasion.

The expansion of Europe in the fifteenth and sixteenth centuries and in particular Europe's 'discovery' of America, although not entirely neglected, have been largely excluded from this history of colonial Latin America. They are subjects which belong more properly to the history of Europe. There is in any case a vast literature on European expansion: for example, John H. Parry's classic *The age of reconnaissance: discovery, exploration and settlement 1450–1650* (London, 1963); V. Magalhães Godinho, notably *Os descobrimentos e a economia mundial* (2 vols., Lisbon, 1965); Samuel Eliot Morison, *The European discovery of America*, vol. II, *The southern voyages 1492–1616* (New York, 1974); and, most recently, G. V. Scammell, *The world encompassed: the first European maritime empires c. 800–1650* (London, 1981), which examines Norse, Hanse, Venetian and Genoese maritime explorations before turning to the Portuguese and Spanish and finally the Dutch, English and French. The first three chapters of the second section of Volume I of this history of Latin America examine the European invasion, subjugation and settlement of parts of the New World during the period from 1492 to 1570/80. The viewpoint is not, however, exclusively European. Equally important is the 'vision of the vanquished'. And post-conquest relations between the Spanish and Portuguese and the native Americans are given particular attention. The remaining five chapters of this section, the central core of the volume, examine the political and economic structures of the Spanish and Portugese empires in America from the middle of the sixteenth to the end of the eighteenth centuries – to a large extent from a metropolitan perspective. There is some discussion of imperial rivalries, and the integration of Spanish America and Brazil into the new world economic system is also explored. The volume concludes with two chapters on the Catholic Church in colonial Latin America, but the reader is also referred to the *Historia General de la Iglesia en America Latina* which is being published in eleven volumes by CEHILA (Comisión de Estudios de Historia de la Iglesia en Latinoamérica) under the general direction of Enrique Dussel.

The second of these two volumes on colonial Latin America opens with two chapters on population trends and is then largely devoted to aspects of the internal economic and social history of colonial Spanish America (nine chapters) and colonial Brazil (four chapters) which have attracted most research interest during the past twenty years: for example, urban development; mining; land tenure and exploitation; labour systems, including African slavery; local economies and inter-colonial trade; social organisation and social change; Indians under colonial rule. Spanish America and Brazil have been for the most part treated separately. They have, on the whole, two different histories, two different historiographies. There are in any case few historians competent and willing to write comparatively about Spanish America and Brazil in the colonial period. The volume concludes with four chapters which survey the intellectual and cultural life – literature and ideas, architecture and art, music – of colonial Latin America.

A Cambridge *History*, as John F. Fairbank, one of the general editors of *The Cambridge History of China*, has written, is meant to be indebted to every single contributor to its field. More particularly in the case of these two volumes on colonial Latin America many of the historians who have themselves contributed chapters – nine American, eight continental European (two resident in the United States, one in Brazil), seven British (four resident in the United States) and seven Latin American (one resident in the United States, one in France) – also read and commented on the chapters of their colleagues. I am especially grateful in this respect to Dauril Alden, J. H. Elliott, Charles Gibson, Murdo J. Macleod, Richard M. Morse and Stuart B. Schwartz. In addition, Woodrow Borah, J. S. Cummins, Valerie Frazer, Olivia Harris and Enrique Tandeter provided critical assessments of several chapters. Most important was the advice and encouragement generously offered throughout the planning and editing of these volumes by my colleague John Lynch.

Patricia Williams at Cambridge University Press was largely responsible for initiating this project and continued to support it even after she left the Press. A number of editors at the Press have been involved in this *History*. I am particularly grateful to Elizabeth Wetton. The subeditors of the volumes were Cynthia Postan and Mandy Macdonald, after preliminary advice from Clare Davies-Jones. Nazneen Razwi at University College London offered invaluable secretarial assistance. The indexes were prepared by Alison Rowlatt.

Part One

AMERICA ON THE EVE OF THE
CONQUEST

1

MESOAMERICA BEFORE 1519

The first chapters of a history of Latin America belong to its inhabitants before their first contact with Europeans. This is especially true in Mesoamerica.[1] Mexico, Guatemala, El Salvador, Honduras and, to a lesser degree, Nicaragua and Costa Rica, like Ecuador, Peru and Bolivia in the Central Andes, have roots deeply embedded in the subsoil of their pre-Columbian civilizations. The aims of this chapter are, first, to outline briefly the development of the peoples and high cultures of Mesoamerica before the settlement of the Mexicas (Aztecs) in the Valley of Mexico (c. 1325); secondly, to examine the main features of political and socio-economic organization and artistic and intellectual achievement during the period of Mexica (Aztec) pre-eminence (fourteenth and fifteenth centuries); and, thirdly, to present an overview of the prevailing situation in Mesoamerica on the eve of the European invasion (1519).

Situated between the solid continental land masses of North and South America, Mesoamerica (an area of 350,000 square miles) has a distinctly isthmian character with several conspicuous geographical

---

[1] Some German scholars, in particular Eduard Seler (1849–1922), introduced more than 70 years ago the expression *Mittel Amerika* to connote the area where indigenous high culture flourished in central and southern Mexico and the adjacent territory of the northern Central American nations. Many years later, in 1943, Paul Kirchhoff in his 'Mesoamérica: sus límites geográficos, composición étnica y caracteres culturales', *Acta Anthropologica*, 1 (Escuela Nacional de Antropología, México, 1943), 92–107, focused attention on the geographical limits of what he called Mesoamerica. Mesoamerica is more than a geographical term. It relates also to the area where indigenous high cultures and civilizations developed and spread in various forms at different periods. At the time of the European invasion in 1519 its northern frontiers were the Río Sinaloa to the north-west and the Panuco to the north-east, while in the north-central part it did not extend beyond the basin of the Río Lerma. Its southern limits were the Río Motagua that empties into the Gulf of Honduras in the Caribbean, the southern shores of Nicaragua lake and the Nicoya peninsula in Costa Rica.

features like the gulfs of Tehuantepec and Fonseca on the Pacific side, and the Yucatan peninsula and the gulf of Honduras on the Caribbean side. This area, where the high cultures developed, probably exhibits greater geographical and ecological diversity than any other region of similar size in the world. The region has a complex geological history. In particular, recent mountain building and volcanic activity, including the formation of two volcanic axes (one running east–west along the southern limits of the Valley of Mexico and the other following a north-west, south-east orientation through Mexico and Central America), have played important roles in the formation of distinct natural regions. Although Mesoamerica is situated within the tropics, the complexity of its reliefs and the variety of its landforms, soils and drainage systems, combined with the effects of ocean streams and winds, result in a diversity of climates, vegetation and animal life. This diversity is very marked in the river basins, such as the Panuco, Coatzacoalcos, Grijalva, Usumacinta, Hondo, Motagua, Lerma-Santiago and Balsas, and in the lake areas of the Valley of Mexico or Patzcuaro in Michoacán, and it is not without significance that the most important cultural changes in Mesoamerica occurred in these regions. The truly tropical sub-regions of Mesoamerica comprise the well-watered lowlands of Veracruz and Tabasco; the scrub-covered Yucatan peninsula; the Caribbean rain forest area of Central America; the Pacific coastal plains of southern and central Mexico (Chiapas, Oaxaca, Guerrero, Michoacán, Colima) and of Guatemala, El Salvador, Honduras, Nicaragua, together with the Nicoya peninsula and the Huanacazte province in Costa Rica. The principal highland sub-regions – the Sierras (the Central American highlands, the southern Sierra Madre, as well as portions of the western and eastern Sierra Madre, and the transverse volcanic axis) and the two large southern and central mesas or plateaux – although falling within the tropics, are temperate in terms of the climate and vegetation. The vast region to the north of Mesoamerica, between the central plateau and the present Mexican–U.S. border, is ecologically very different and in many respects similar to the great North American deserts. The vegetation is generally limited to a variety of cacti and some clusters of shrubs, yuccas or palmillas and, near intermittent streams, mesquite trees. At times Mesoamerican high culture diffused in an attenuated form into some sub-regions of the northern plateau (as in La Quemada and Calchihuites in Zacatecas). However, in general the arid north remained the permanent home of the fiery Chichimecs who several times threatened the existence of the northern Mesoamerican settlements.

THE EARLY CIVILIZATIONS OF MESOAMERICA

Remote prehistory, in the case of the Americas, begins around 35,000 B.C., when apparently man first entered the continent through the Bering Strait. There is some evidence to indicate a probable presence of man in what is today Mexico around 20,000 B.C. Nonetheless, the oldest human remains, discovered at the site of Tepexpan, about 25 miles to the north-east of Mexico City, have been dated as no earlier than 9,000 B.C. Over a long period, only bands of food-gatherers and hunters inhabited the land. Three or perhaps four millennia still had to pass before man in Mesoamerica initiated, around 5,000 B.C., the process that ended up as agriculture. Discoveries in various caves within the Sierra of Tamaulipas and in Cozcatlán, Puebla, show how, little by little, the former gatherers began the domestication of squash, chili, beans and corn. The production of pottery started considerably later, around 2,300 B.C. In various parts of central and southern Mexico and in Central America, villages of agriculturists and pottery makers began to proliferate. Some of these villages, probably those established in better environments, such as on the banks of a stream or close to the sea, experienced an early growth in population. The inhabitants of villages scattered over such a vast territory often differed ethnically and linguistically. From among them, one group in particular was soon to stand out. Archaeological evidence shows that a series of extraordinary changes began to appear, commencing around 1,300 B.C. in an area close to the Gulf of Mexico, in southern Veracruz and the neighbouring state of Tabasco. That area has been known since pre-Columbian days as 'The Rubber Land', *Olman*, land of the Olmecs.

Excavations made in Olmec centres such as Tres Zapotes, La Venta, San Lorenzo and others have revealed great cultural transformations. La Venta, the largest centre, was built on a small island, a few feet above sea level, in a swampy area near the Rio Tonalá, ten miles before it empties into the Gulf of Mexico. Although available stone is more than forty miles away, a number of colossal stone sculptures (some of them ten feet high) and other monuments have been unearthed there.

In La Venta, as in some other Olmec sites, a sort of proto-urbanism began to develop. The agriculturist villagers who settled in the vicinity of La Venta had probably experienced, together with population growth, various stimuli to stir them from their old ways of subsistence. What they achieved also presupposes changes in their socio-economic, political and religious organization.

As far as we know, the Olmecs were, within Mesoamerica, the first to erect large complexes of buildings, mainly for religious purposes. Thus, the centre of La Venta, skilfully planned, included mud-plastered pyramids, long and circular mounds, stone-carved altars, large stone boxes, rows of basalt columns, tombs, sarcophagi, stelae, colossal heads of basalt and other smaller sculptures. The existence of large plazas seems to indicate that religious ceremonies were performed in the open air. Jaguar masks, formed of green mosaics, conceived probably as offerings, and therefore covered up with clay and adobe, have been found below the floor, as a sort of ancient pavement, in some of the open spaces in front of the religious buildings. What we will call artistic creations also included many pieces made of jade, figurines, necklaces and other objects in carved and polished quartz, obsidian, rock crystal and serpentine. A division of labour can be inferred. While many individuals continued with agriculture and other subsistence activities, others specialized in different arts and crafts, in providing defence for the group, in commercial enterprises, in the cult of the gods and in government, which was probably in the hands of the religious leaders.

Olmecs worshipped an omnipresent jaguar god. Elements attached to the symbolism of what later became the Mesoamerican rain god probably derived from the jaguar god's mask. Stelae and other monuments show various representations of fantastic birds, often in association with jaguars, serpents or human beings. The offerings found in burials are evidence of a cult of the dead with a belief in an afterlife. The beginnings of Mesoamerican calendar and writing ought probably to be linked to the Olmecs who lived along the Gulf coast, although it is Oaxaca (at places influenced by the Olmecs) where the earliest vestiges of these achievements have been brought to light.

All this, and the fact of the early diffusion of Olmec elements in different places, some far from the centres of origin, seem to confirm the character of a mother high culture. Olmec influence – probably through commerce and perhaps also by a sort of 'missionary' religious impulse – is manifest in many sites in the area close to the Gulf of Mexico and also in the Central Plateau, in Oaxaca, in the land of the Mayas and in western Mexico (Guerrero and Michoacán). Here were the antecedents of the Classic Period in Mesoamerica.

The extraordinary cultural innovations of the Olmecs did not mean the disappearance of some notorious limitations that continued to affect the development of the various peoples of Mesoamerica. These included, first, the permanent absence of any utilitarian application of the wheel, with its many consequences, as for instance, in transportation and pottery-making; secondly, the absence (until around A.D. 950) of even an elementary kind of metallurgy, and that was derived from the Andean area via Central America; finally, the absence of animals capable of domestication: no horses or cattle existed and, apart from turkeys (for eating), only the hairless Mexican dogs were the companions of man in his daily life – and in his after-life, since they were sacrificed to accompany their owners to the Land of the Dead.

However, these and other limitations were not insurmountable obstacles to further development in Mesoamerican groups. The influence of Olmec culture began to be felt around 600 B.C. in sites such as Tlatilco, Zacatenco and others in the vicinity of what centuries later became Mexico City. Parallel processes developed in other regions of central and southern Mesoamerica. Agriculture expanded and diversified; among other things cotton was cultivated successfully. Villages grew and larger centres arose.

Teotihuacan, the 'metropolis of the gods', is the best example of the culmination of Classic civilization in the central plateau. There recent archaeological research has revealed not only a large ceremonial centre, but everything implied by the idea of a city. It did not grow overnight. It took several centuries for generations of priests and architects to plan and realize, modify, enlarge and enrich what was perhaps originally conceived as an entity to exist forever. Besides the two great pyramids and the Temple of Quetzalcóatl, other enclosures, palaces, schools and different kinds of buildings have been discovered. Large suburbs, where members of the community had their homes, surrounded the more compact religious and administrative centre. Avenues and streets were paved and there was also a well-planned drainage system. Pyramids, temples, palaces and most of the houses of the rulers or members of the nobility were decorated with murals in which gods, fantastic birds, serpents, jaguars and various plants were represented.

The metropolis of Teotihuacan which, at its zenith, around the fifth or sixth century A.D., extended for around twenty square kilometres, had a population of at least 50,000 inhabitants. Differences of status related to divisions of labour, an efficient army, extensive agriculture, and well-organized commerce with merchants going to distant places, are some of the features that can probably be inferred as attributes of the socio-economic structure of the Teotihuacan state. The many vestiges of its influence in various remote sites, in Oaxaca, Chiapas and even in the Guatemalan highlands, seem to indicate that Teotihuacan was the centre of a large kingdom or of a confederacy of different peoples. Many of the members of the ruling class probably spoke the Nahuat language, an archaic form of the Nahuatl which was to be, centuries later, the official language of the Aztecs.

Teotihuacans worshipped several gods that were later invoked by other Nahua-speaking peoples: Tlaloc and Chalchiuhtlicue, Lord and Lady of the Waters; Quetzalcóatl, the Feathered Serpent; Xiuhtecuhtli, Lord of Fire; Xochipilli, Prince of the Flowers. As in the case of other institutions, the art that flourished in Teotihuacan was to influence, in various forms, other Mesoamerican peoples.

Parallel to the development of Teotihuacan, civilization appeared in other sub-areas of Mesoamerica. One very early instance is offered by the site of Monte Albán in Central Oaxaca whose beginnings can be traced back to around A.D. 600. There, besides the religious centre built on top of a hill, numerous structures visible on the slopes suggest the existence of a rather large urban settlement. More complex forms of writing, with dates, place-names and other hieroglyphs appearing in various inscriptions are also evidence of the high cultural level attained by the Zapotecs who had built Monte Albán and ruled over many other groups in what is today Oaxaca.

The Mayas were inhabitants of the Yucatan peninsula and of the lowlands and highlands of the Mexican states of Tabasco and Chiapas, and of Guatemala, Belize and parts of El Salvador and Honduras. Thanks to archaeology, we know about more than 50 Maya centres of considerable importance which were occupied throughout the Classic Period. Some of the most famous are Tikal, Uaxactún, Piedras Negras and Ouiriguá in Guatemala; Copán in Honduras; Nakum in Belize; Yaxchilán, Palenque and Bonampak in Chiapas; Dzibilchaltún, Cobá, Labná, Kabah and the early phases of Uxmal and Chichén-Itzá in the Yucatan peninsula.

Arguments have been put forward both for and against the urban nature of the Maya centres. Today it is generally recognized that settlements built on the banks of rivers, such as those close to the Usumacinta or, in general, within a dense tropical forest area, encompassed not only sanctuaries for the gods and palaces for religious leaders, but also residential quarters for the people.

From a political point of view it appears that some of these urban centres were associated in various kinds of 'confederations' or 'kingdoms'. In Classical Maya society two clearly different social strata co-existed: the ordinary people or commoners (devoted for the most part to agriculture and to the performance of various personal services) and the dominant group composed of the rulers, priests and high ranking warriors. To the priests and sages one has to attribute the extraordinary creations in the arts. Architecture, which featured the corbeled vault, sculpture, in particular the bas-reliefs, and mural paintings such as the famous ones of Bonampak in Chiapas, are all noteworthy. Thousands of hieroglyphic texts, inscribed on stone stelae, stairways, lintels, paintings, ceramics and books or codices confirm that the Maya priests and sages were in possession of an extremely sophisticated high culture. We also know that the Classic Mayas had various calendars of extreme precision. They also had a concept and symbol for zero, perhaps inherited from the Olmecs, several hundred years before the Hindus had developed the idea. Whoever succeeds in completely deciphering Maya writing will discover a universe of ideas and symbols, the core of the Maya cosmos. For the moment we can at least assert that civilization in Classic Mesoamerica, from which all further development derived, reached its peak with the Mayas.

Explanations of what happened to the Mayas, the Zapotecs, the Teotihuacans and, in general, to those who gave birth to and fostered civilization during the Classic Period are as yet mere hypotheses. The decline and final abandonment of the splendid ancient metropolises between the seventh and the tenth centuries probably took various forms. Archaeological evidence seems to indicate a sudden collapse in the case of Teotihuacan. Was the city put to fire, as some extant remains of walls, beams and other pieces of wood suggest? Or was destruction wrought by outside forces, who, perhaps realizing that decline had already set in, decided to take possession of the fertile lands of the Valley? Or was the ruin of the city a consequence of an internal political or religious struggle? Or, more simply, as some authors have insisted, was the abandonment of the metropolis an effect of climatic changes related to deforestation and the drying-up of the lakes, the consequence of natural processes or perhaps of man's own actions?

While it appears that Teotihuacan came to a sudden end around A.D. 650, we know that the Zapotec city built on Monte Albán entered a period of prolonged decline before it, too, was finally abandoned. In the case of the Maya centres it seems as if an irrevocable moment came when the priests raised no more stelae. Then, perhaps over a period, the old cities began gradually to be deserted. No traces of attacks from outside or of destruction by fire have appeared. The centres were just abandoned, their inhabitants seeking other sites to settle. And it would be difficult to prove that this was caused by a general violent climatic change, agricultural collapse or universal epidemics.

Conjecture apart, the fact remains that the period between A.D. 650 and 950 saw the downfall of the Classic civilizations in Mesoamerica. However, desolation did not mean the death of high culture in this part of the New World. We know now that other peoples inherited and developed many of the Classic achievements, and some deserve mention since they were to influence the following cultural evolution of those inhabiting Mesoamerica. Not a few survived the Spanish conquest and are still ingredients in the culture of many people in Mexico and Central America.

One of the main features of the Classic legacy was urbanism. No town, for instance, could be built without a close-knit religious–political core. Temples and palaces were surrounded by open spaces. Tradition and formal learning being a concern of the religious leaders, communal schools had to be erected in the various quarters of the town. Another important institution was the market-place. It was a place not only to trade but also to meet people. Dwellings for the ordinary people, which were very scattered, formed extensive suburbs around the central part of the town. Most of the inhabitants owned, besides their single storey house, a small piece of land where they grew some vegetables. Mesoamericans were in love with plants of all kinds. Thus, many of their towns, seen from a distance, looked like a combination of small forests and gardens with thatched roofs visible here and there and painted temples and palaces rising amidst the surrounding greenery. This form of urbanism remained typical of Mesoamerica. An extraordinary example greeted the *conquistadores* in the Aztec metropolis, México-Tenochtitlan.

As with patterns of urban life so in the artistic sphere we find later the strong influence of the Classic Period and the same is true of basic beliefs and forms of worship. A satisfactory explanation of the similar, at times identical, myths, rites and gods of different groups living in the Post-Classic Period (A.D. 950–1519) may be derived from a probable common origin, part of the Classic legacy. Other cultural elements belonging to the same heritage were the calendar, hieroglyphic writing, astronomical and astrological knowledge, a world view, basic forms of socio-economic, political and religious organization, the institution of the market and a commerce that stretched far afield.

Among the peoples who profited from this cultural legacy, some exercised considerable power until the arrival of the Spaniards. There were also the many groups in the north beyond the territories which submitted to Teotihuacan. Some already practised agriculture to a limited degree, like the present-day Coras, Huichols, Tepehuans, Cahitas and Pimas of north-western Mexico. Beyond the area inhabited by them were more groups, some particularly primitive, like the ones belonging to the Hokan linguistic family, but others who had reached more advanced levels, like the so-called Pueblo Indians of present-day New Mexico and parts of Arizona.

Archaeology has shown that the Teotihuacans had exerted, at least indirectly, some influence upon some of these groups. This appears to be particularly true in the case of the Pueblo Indians, the most advanced in the vast territories north of Mexico. Evidence also exists of the presence of some groups culturally, and perhaps also politically, related to Teotihuacan, who had settled in the north, as advanced outposts, to protect the frontier from incursions of those generically called Chichi-mecs, barbarian semi-nomads, gatherers and hunters.

Those later called Toltecs should be included among the settlers in the advanced outposts. When the collapse of Teotihuacan became known to them, they apparently decided to 'come back', as the native texts put it, to the land of their cultural origin, that is, Central Mexico. Various accounts tell of their wanderings before they reached small towns still inhabited by people of Teotihuacan origin. The Toltecs finally settled in Tula, a place about 50 miles to the north of present-day Mexico City. *Tula* or *Tollan* actually means metropolis; and that was precisely what the Toltecs were about to build.

A central figure in Toltec history is the famous Quetzalcóatl, a sort of culture hero who derived his name from that of a god (the Feathered Serpent) who had been worshipped since the days of Teotihuacan. Numerous native books and texts in Nahuatl tell of his portentous birth, life and deeds. It is said that while Quetzalcóatl was still young, he retired to Huapalcalco, a former settlement of the Teotihuacans, to devote himself to meditation. There he was taken by the Toltecs to act as their ruler and high priest. Palaces and temples were built and many towns and peoples accepted the rule of Quetzalcóatl (the god and his priest). What caused the end of the golden age of the Toltecs and the final collapse of Tula around 1150 is not wholly clear. However, the ruin of the Toltecs meant a diffusion of their culture and their penetration among various distant peoples. The presence of the Toltecs is recorded in annals such as those of the Mixtecs of Oaxaca and the Mayas of Yucatan and Guatemala.

The Mixtecs succeeded the Zapotecs in the Valley of Oaxaca after the latter's cultural and political decline. We can attribute to them the founding of new towns, such as those of Tilantongo and Teozacualco, as well as the partial rebuilding of famous Zapotec cities and strongholds. They also excelled in the arts, particularly as goldsmiths. Metal-work, gold, silver, copper and to some extent, tin, was introduced in Mesoamerica around A.D. 950. The Mixtecs are also well known for their books of historical content – a few have reached us with records that take us back as far as A.D. 692.[2]

The Mayas had not regained their former splendour. Nevertheless a few small kingdoms – Quiché and Cakchiquel in the highlands of Guatemala, Uxmal and Chichén-Itzá, Mayapán and Tulum in the Yucatec peninsula – showed some signs of prosperity. The arrival of groups of Toltec origin to Yucatan and Guatemala contributed to this revival. Those who entered Guatemala came as followers of Gucumatz, the Quiché and Cakchiquel translation of the name of Quetzalcóatl. In Yucatan the invaders' guide was called Kukulcán, a word with an identical connotation. These new Quetzalcóatls were more militarily than religiously inclined. In Guatemala – according to the Sacred Book of the Quichés – Gucumatz and his followers imposed themselves upon the Mayas. Thus, a new mixture of peoples and cultures occurred. The Guatemalans became, to various degrees, *Toltecized*. In Yucatan much the same thing took place. A so-called League of Mayapan was created, which comprised that town and Chichén-Itzá and Uxmal. Toltec influence was so strong there that in Post-Classic Chichén-Itzá pyramids and other temples and palaces were built imitating those of the metropolis of Tula. However, neither the new blood nor the cultural elements that had arrived from the central plateau of Mexico brought about a renaissance in the Maya world. Its destiny was to survive, but

[2] In a posthumous publication by the Mexican scholar, Alfonso Caso, an analysis is offered of the contents of several Mixtec native books containing biographies of a good number of rulers and noblemen from A.D. 692 to A.D. 1515. *Reyes y reinos de la Mixteca*, 2 vols. (Mexico, 1977–8), II.

without splendour, until the days of the Spanish conquest, which in Guatemala was completed in 1525 and in Yucatan in 1546.

The complete abandonment of Tula, as with the earlier collapse of Teotihuacan, facilitated the entrance into the Valley of Mexico of groups from beyond the northern frontier of Mesoamerica. This time barbarian Chichimecs were the first to penetrate what had been Toltec domains. Various native texts describe what happened. The Chichimecs, in trying to take possession of the abandoned rich territory, came up against some families and groups of Toltecs who had remained. Although first contacts were far from friendly, little by little things changed for the better. Processes of acculturation can be fully documented from various sources.[3] The food-gatherers and hunters began to settle in the neighbourhood of former Toltec towns. The Chichimecs dominated from a political and military standpoint. However, those in possession of Toltec high culture were to influence the Chichimecs deeply. Reluctantly at first and willingly later, the latter accepted agriculture, urban life, Toltec religion, the calendar and the art of writing.

Thus, by the end of the thirteenth century, new states or chiefdoms existed in Central Mexico. Some were the result of a kind of renaissance in towns of Toltec or even Teotihuacan origin. Others were strictly new entities in which the cultures of Chichimecs and Toltecs had merged. This was the situation in and around the Valley of Mexico when other groups from the north arrived. This time the newcomers did not speak a barbarian Chichimec language, but Nahuatl, which had been spoken by the Toltecs and by a good number of Teotihuacans. The various Nahuatlan groups – the so-called 'Seven Tribes' – resembled, in some cultural aspects, those Toltecs who had been living earlier in the northern outposts, on the frontier of Mesoamerica. Texts left by some of them, such as the Tlaxcallans and the Mexica (Aztecs), often repeat: 'We are coming back from the north, we are returning to where we used to live.'

Aztec penetration, or, as it is often described, their 'pilgrimage', had to overcome numerous obstacles. Many were the hardships, persecutions, attacks and so on, they had to face before they finally settled on the island of Tenochtitlan, among the lakes that covered a large part of the Valley of Mexico. This occurred, according to various sources, in 1325.

[3] See, Miguel León-Portilla, 'La aculturación de los Chichimecas de Xótotl', *Estudios de Cultura Náhuatl* (Universidad Nacional de México, 1968), VII, 59–86.

THE MEXICAS (AZTECS)

One of the achievements of the Mexica at the height of their political and cultural development (roughly speaking the last 60 years before European contact) was the forging of an image of their own origins, development and identity. Around 1430 their ruler Itzcoatl ordered the burning of the ancient books, both annals and those of religious content, on the grounds that: 'It is not necessary for all the common people to know of the writings: government will be defamed, and this will only spread sorcery in the lands; for they contained many falsehoods.'[4] In their place was developed and imposed a new tradition conveying an image of the past that would fit the requirements and ideals of the group whose dominance was in the process of rapid expansion. Consulting sources of Mexica provenance, we can reconstruct the new image that their elite produced.

They are explicit about the kind of existence they had to endure in Aztlan Chicomoztoc, the place from which they claimed to originate. Their descriptions reveal that in Aztlan (or at any rate before they entered the Valley of Mexico), they possessed numerous traits of Mesoamerican culture (an assertion confirmed by archaeological evidence). An important factor is that in their place of origin they were subordinate to a dominant group. They describe this group as the *tlatoque* (rulers) and *pipiltin* (nobles) of Aztlan Chicomoztoc. They refer to themselves as *macehualtin* (commoners, with the connotation of 'serfs'). They had to work for and pay tribute to the tlatoque of that place.

They left Aztlan Chicomoztoc and their former rulers because they were tired of them. Their priest, Huitzilopochtli, had told them that their god *Tetzahuitl Teotl* (a manifestation of Tezcatlipoca, the Smoking Mirror), had found them a privileged site. The purpose was to free 'his people' from subjugation and make them prosperous. The god had announced that 'there [in the promised place] I will make you pipiltin and tlatoque of all those who inhabit the land... Your macehualtin will pay you tribute'.[5] Simplistic as this may sound, the Mexica accounts and the paintings in their books, tell how, step by step, the prophecy was fulfilled. The priest through whom the god spoke was himself deified. The attributes of Huitzilopochtli and Tezcatlipoca show striking

---

[4] *Codex Matritensis*, ed. A. M. Garibay and M. León-Portilla (4 vols., Mexico, 1958–69), fo. 192v.
[5] Cristóbal del Castillo, *Fragmentos de la obra general sobre Historic de los Mexicanos* (Florencia, 1908).

similarity in iconography, as for instance in representations found in codices *Borbonicus* and *Matritensis*. A whole cycle of poems and myths developed, recalling the deeds of Huitzilopochtli (his portentous birth, his victory over the Four Hundred Warriors of the South, his taking their destinies upon himself, his identification with the Sun, Giver of Life...).[6] All these events fulfil prophecies and, since the destiny of the Mexicas is intrinsically linked to that of their god, foreshadow their ultimate fulfilment for the people themselves.

The Mexicas tell how in Aztlan Chicomoztoc, and during their wanderings in search of the promised site, they were extremely poor. In Aztlan they practised agriculture for the benefit of others. Later, they lived as gatherers and hunters. Only occasionally they interrupted their journey to cultivate some land. The Mexicas were following their guides (priests and captains). They formed groups which received the name *calpulli* (*calli*: house > *calpulli*: 'big house', with the sense of 'people belonging to the same house', perhaps (though this is by no means certain) groups of families related by kinship). One of the indigenous chronicles says that originally there were seven Mexica calpulli.[7] Another asserts that altogether they numbered 10,000 people.[8] Their legends claim that the god Huitzilopochtli, in making promises to them, gave his word he would protect all those belonging to the 'houses' (calpulli), those linked by blood: 'your children, your grandchildren, your great-grandchildren, your younger brothers, your descendants'.[9] Contrary to the doubts expressed by some scholars, the traditions insist upon the idea that, both in that remote past and in the present (right after the Spanish conquest), the members of a calpulli had a common ancestry.[10] Oral tradition and indigenous books largely coincide in numerous anecdotes about the many hardships overcome by the calpulli of the Mexicas guided by their priests and warriors. Occasionally some Mexicas disobeyed the commands of Huitzilopochtli with disastrous consequences. To follow the god's advice always resulted in the fulfilment of his promises.

The Mexicas (in their own version of their past) seem to enjoy describing themselves as a people at that time esteemed by no one. For

[6] See *Florentine Codex* (hereafter cited as *FC*), 12 vols. (Santa Fe, N.M., 1950–82), bk III, ch. 1.
[7] Fernando Alvarado Tezozómoc, *Crónica Mexicayotl* (Mexico, 1972), 22–7.
[8] Diego Chimalpahin Cuauhtlehuanitzin, *Second Relation*, facsimile reproduction in *Corpus Codicum Americanum Medii Aevi*, Ernst Mengin (ed.) (Copenhagen, 1949), III, fo. 28r.
[9] Castillo, *Fragmentos*, 66–7.
[10] Alonso de Zorita, *Breve y Sumaria Relación* (Mexico, 1942), 36.

their own part they already set themselves apart as having a unique destiny. Among other things, they depict themselves revering those forms of government and organization with a divine origin, directly linked with the high priest of the Toltecs, Quetzalcóatl. Other groups before or contemporary with the Mexicas had also realized the value (religious and political) of claiming the investiture of power from the same source of Toltec origin. Thus, various peoples of central Mexico, and of sites in regions as distant as Oaxaca, Guatemala and Yucatan, had received the insignia of government from the Lord of the East, one of the titles of Quetzalcóatl.[11] No wonder the Mexicas, already established on their promised island, decided to follow the advice of their former guides and to link themselves with Quetzalcóatl and the Toltec nobility. An Aztec nobility was begun by a descendant of the Toltec–Culhuacans who also had Mexica ancestry, lord Acamapichtli. He and other Culhuacan pipiltin married the daughters of the ancient Mexica priests and warriors. Members of the families of those who had led the Mexicas were also incorporated into the chosen group. When Mexica parents of the pipiltin stratum advised their children in their speeches (*Huehuetlatolli*), they repeatedly reminded them of their origin: they were descended from the Toltecs and, ultimately, from Quetzalcóatl himself.

Thus, the traditions and books of the Mexicas disseminated this 'true image'. At the time, the life of the Aztec nation as a whole was being transformed; there were many peoples paying tribute to the tlatoque and pipiltin of Tenochtitlan; the prophecy of Huitzilopochtli had been completely fulfilled; from among the descendants of those macehualtin, 'commoners and serfs' in Aztlan Chicomoztoc, Mexica tlatoque and pipiltin arose. So we learn from the oral accounts, books, poems and speeches of the elders.

We will now see how this 'true image' compares with what we can discover about the history, politics, economy, society and culture of the Mexicas (Aztecs) during the last chapter of their autonomous existence from the available archaeological, ethno-historical, linguistic and other documentary sources.

Around 1390 Acamapichtli, the first ruler (*huey tlatoani*) of Toltec lineage and founder of the ruling house of the *tlazo-pipiltin*, 'precious nobles', died. He, and his immediate successors, Huitzililuitl

---

[11] See, among others, the cases registered in *Anales de Cuauhtitlan* in *Codice Chimalpopoca* (Mexico, 1975), fo. 10–11; *Popol Vuh*, trans. by A. Recinos (Mexico, 1953), 218–19; *Anales de los Cakchiqueles*, trans. A. Recinos (Mexico, 1950), 67–8; Caso, *Reyes y Reinos de la Mixteca*, I, 81–2.

(1390–1415) and Chimalpopoca (1415–26), were still subject to the Tecpanecs of Azcapotzalco, a chiefdom in which peoples of Teotihuacan, Toltec and Chichimec descent had merged and which at that time exerted hegemony in the central plateau. The island of Tenochtitlan, where the Mexicas had settled, was owned by the Tecpanecs. Thus, in fact, the Mexicas for more than a century, since their arrival in 1325, had been paying tribute to and performing personal services for Azcapotzalco.

In 1426 Chimalpopoca died, probably murdered by the Tecpanecs. Some time after, war broke out between the Tecpanecs and the Mexicas. The latter succeeded in obtaining the help of several other peoples also subjugated by Azcapotzalco. The 'true image' underlines at this point an extremely significant episode. When the Tecpanecs were about to open hostilities, most of the Mexica people, i.e. the macehualtin or commoners, insisted it was better to surrender. In response, the pipiltin made a deal. If they were unable to defeat Azcapotzalco, they would obey the macehualtin for ever. But if the pipiltin succeeded in defeating the Tecpanecs, the macehualtin would pledge total obedience to them.[12] The victory over the Tecpanecs around 1430 laid the basis for the greatly enhanced political and socio-economic status of the Mexica pipiltin.

The victory also meant the complete independence of the Mexica chiefdom and the point of departure for their future achievements. Itzcoatl (1426–40), assisted by his sagacious adviser, Tlacaelel, initiated an era of changes and conquests. Moteuczoma Ilhuicamina, 'The Elder' (1440–69), consolidated the power and renown of the people of Huitzilopochtli. Under Axayacatl (1469–81), Tizoc (1481–5), Ahuitzotl (1486–1502) and Moteuczoma II (1502–20) Aztec rule was further extended. An extraordinary strengthening of their military powers, combined with their conviction about their own destiny, resulted in continued political and economic expansion. Numerous chiefdoms inhabited by peoples of many different languages, among others the Totonacas and Huaxtecs in the present-day states of Puebla and Veracruz and the Mixtecs and Zapotecs in Oaxaca, were in various ways subjugated by the Mexicas. And organized forms of far-flung commerce were responsible for the constantly growing prosperity of the Mexica 'empire'.

[12] Diego Durán, *Historia de las Indias de Nueva España*, ed. A. M. Garibay, 2 vols. (Mexico, 1967), I, 65–75.

The solid economic structure of the Mexica polity which was essentially formed by the end of Moteuczoma I's rule (around 1469), has been the subject of many divergent interpretations. Most of the Spanish chroniclers (and nineteenth-century historians, like Prescott, Bancroft, Ramirez and Orozco y Berra) had accepted that Mexica society was in many ways similar to that of the feudal European kingdoms. So, to describe it, they did not hesitate to use terms like those of kings and princes; royal court, *hidalgos* and courtesans; magistrates, senators, consuls, priests and pontiffs; members of the aristocracy, high and low rank nobles, landholders, plebeians, serfs and slaves. Critical revisionism was initiated by Lewis H. Morgan in terms of the ideas expressed in his celebrated *Ancient Society* (1877). 'The Aztec organization', he wrote,

stood plainly before the Spaniards as a confederacy of Indian tribes. Nothing but the grossest perversion of obvious facts could have enabled Spanish writers to fabricate the Aztec monarchy out of a democratic organization.
...
they [the Spanish chroniclers] boldly invented for the Aztecs a monarchy with high feudal characteristics... This misconception has stood, through American indolence, quite as long as it deserves to stand.[13]

The ideas of Morgan, accepted and expanded by Adolph F. Bandelier (1878–80), exerted a profound influence. Most researchers accepted that the Mexicas and the other peoples inhabiting southern Mexico and Central America had no differentiated social classes and had not developed forms of political organization like kingdoms or other kinds of state. It was accepted that the Mesoamerican peoples were merely groups linked by blood (various kinds of 'tribes' or 'clans'), sometimes associated as confederations.

Half a century later a more serious study of often previously-unknown indigenous sources led to a new revisionism. Manuel M. Moreno, Arturo Monzón, Paul Kirchhoff, Alfonso Caso, Friedrich Katz and others reached conclusions that coincided in the following points: the macehualtin, grouped into calpulli, constituted social entities linked by kinship; their socio-economic status differed so radically from that of the pipiltin that one had to accept the existence of social classes; among the many distinctions that prevailed between the macehualtin and pipiltin, a very important one related to the forms of land tenure; only the pipiltin could own land as private property. In addition, the existence of an authentic state (a kingdom) in the political organization of the Mexicas was recognized.

[13] Lewis H. Morgan, 'Montezuma's Dinner', *American Review* (April, 1876), 308.

The general acceptance of these conclusions made it seem for a while as if firm ground had been reached as to the character of the social and economic structures of the Mexicas. However, recent research by Pedro Carrasco and others, carried out within a Marxist theoretical framework and using the concept of the Asian mode of production as a key analytical device, has challenged many generally accepted conclusions. Briefly, it is argued that these societies are based upon primitive communal villages which collectively possess and work the land. Periodically, these entities become organized under the rule of a dominant and despotic group which appropriates surplus value and arbitrarily distributes the usufruct of the land among its own members according to their office. (Since they do not privately own the land there is some hesitation in using the concept of class: the terms 'strata', 'estates' or 'sectors' are preferred.) The people, or dominated stratum, continue to be integrated in communal entities working the land for subsistence and to support the growing demands of the dominant group. The latter justifies its existence by governing and leading the people and directing the realization of imposing public works, mainly the establishment of urban centres, roads and large irrigation works.

The central issue in the debate about the nature and structure of Mexica society and economy is the status and achievements of the ruling group, the pipiltin, once they effectively controlled not only Tenochtitlan but a vast part of Mesoamerica. By their own account the pipiltin were predestined by their god to free their people (those communal entities of villagers subject to the tlatoque and other pipiltin of Aztlan Chicomoztoc). Texts from the *Huehuetlatolli* ('the Ancient Word') exemplify this. These are the words of an elderly dignitary who, speaking for the city, answers a discourse of the supreme ruler.

O master, o ruler, o our lord, your commoners are here... [and also] the sons, the noble sons, the precious green stones, the precious bracelets, the sons of our lords, and the descendants of Quetzalcóatl,
...
So they came to life, so they were born, so they were created, where in the beginning it was determined, ordained that they were to command, to rule...[14]

Within the dominant group various ranks, positions and titles existed: the tlazo-pipiltin, 'precious nobles', were the descendants of those who had been the supreme rulers. From this select group the huey tlatoani was chosen. The pipiltin (not as a generic term, as previously used, but as a specific designation), were those related in other ways

[14] *FC*, Bk VI, ch. 16.

(not as direct descendants) to the same ruling group. They also claimed a lineage of Toltec origin. The _cuauh-pipiltin_, 'eagle nobles', were individuals somehow assimilated by the dominant group (an indication of 'social mobility') on account of their deeds, mainly in battle. The _tequihuaque_ (translated by Alonso de Zorita as 'hidalgos'), were children of those who performed important administrative functions, like the _teteuctin_ (lords), some of them pipiltin, and other distinguished members of a calpulli.

The pipiltin were extremely conscious of these differences of rank among themselves and of the possible positions open to them in the political and economic administration of the Mexica state. This is reflected in the following fragment of a speech addressed by a noble to his son:

> You know, you remember that there is only one ruler, the heart of the city, and that there are two assisting dignitaries, one from the military (_ce quappan_), one from the nobility (_ce pil-pan_). The one from the military is the _Tlacatecuhtli_. The one from the nobility, the _Tlacochcalcatl_... And the military one... Was he born to this position? Did perhaps his mother, his father bequeath it to him? No. For he is just elected on earth, is commissioned, endowed by Him, the Supreme Giver of Life.[15]

When Moteuczoma I began his reign the Mexicas and their allies were already the lords in a large territory embracing most of the Central Plateau. To cope with the new situation their political organization was enlarged to be more effective. Much more than in the past the huey tlatoani became endowed with supreme and absolute power. Although he was considered a representative of the divinity on earth, he was not taken to be an incarnation or son of a god. He was commander in chief of the army and a religious pontiff, as well as the highest judge and the lord whose will nobody dared to contradict. He held this supreme role not by hereditary succession but by election. The election of the huey tlatoani was the duty and privilege of a limited number of pipiltin. They represented the ancient nobility who had received a pledge of obedience from the commoners when they were all in danger of being annihilated by the Tecpanecs. To be elected as supreme ruler presupposed being a member of the tlazo-pipiltin. Personal attributes were carefully examined by the electors. They did not actually vote as their aim was to reach a unanimous decision, but spent several days consulting different people and deliberating among themselves. Finally they came

[15] _FC_, Bk vi, ch. 20.

to a point at which they all accepted someone who, even if he could in some ways be surpassed by others, satisfied their various interests in most respects and could also be considered sufficiently endowed to be the leader of the entire nation.[16] From Moteuczoma I until the Spanish invasion all huey tlatoani were chosen by this method, vestiges of which, in the opinion of some researchers, still somehow survive in the presidential elections of modern Mexico.

As a reflection, perhaps, of the belief in a supreme dual god, *Ometeotl*, the office of high ruler was complemented by that of an assistant and adviser, the *cihuacoatl*. Although the more obvious meaning of this title is 'female serpent', it can also be understood as 'female twin'. The most important duties of the cihuacoatl were to substitute for the high ruler in his absence or death and to preside over the council of electors and the highest tribunal.

Other prominent dignitaries were the *tlacochcalcatl* (lord of the house of the spears), and the *tlacatecatl* (commander of men). Acting also in pairs were two principal judges, two high priests and two guardians of the nation's treasure. All of these dignitaries presided over their corresponding high councils and participated in the supreme council headed by the huey tlatoani or his substitute, the cihuacoatl.

In all towns, whether those of the Mexicas and their allies (Tezcoco and Tlacopan), or those that had been conquered, there were governors, appointed by the high ruler. These were the *tlatoque* (plural form of tlatoani). In some instances the high ruler sent one of the pipiltin from the Aztec metropolis to act as governor of a subjugated chiefdom. In other cases members of the former ruling group of the conquered towns were allowed to remain after a new pledge of obedience had been made.

To administer some calpulli, the supreme tlatoani appointed officers known as *teteuctin*. As has been said, they were often pipiltin. At other times, not being nobles themselves, they were in the service of a family of pipiltin. The group of units of production administered by one *teuctli* was known as a *teccalli* (house of the people of the palace), that is, of those appointed by the huey tlatoani. The duties of the teteuctin were very important. They were responsible for production in the socio-economic unit 'entrusted' to them. Its production, in addition to supporting the macehualtin working the land, had to provide the tributes to the pipiltin and, ultimately, also to the huey tlatoani.

Most important administrative positions were reserved for the

[16] See the detailed description of this 'electoral process' in *FC*, Bk VIII, ch. 18.

pipiltin. Titles accompanying these positions were awarded to them, as well as the possession and usufruct of lands. The pipiltin paid no tribute. They could hire as many *mayeque* (workers) to till the land as necessary. Some of the pipiltin were also entrusted with the *teccallis*, which included both land and the macehualtin working it. Members of the dominant group could have as many wives as they could support and other privileges, such as special vestments and insignia, forms of entertainment and even some kinds of food and drink. In addition they were subject only to the jurisdiction of special tribunals.

The sons of the pipiltin attended the *calmecac* or centres of higher learning. There the ancient wisdom was carefully preserved, added to and transmitted. Those entering them, spent a number of years preparing themselves for the offices considered eligible for pipiltin as part of their destiny. The indigenous texts tell us what was taught in the *calmecac*. The young pipiltin learned elegant forms of speech, ancient hymns, poems and historical accounts, religious doctrines, the calendar, astronomy, astrology, legal precepts and the art of government. When the young nobles left the calmecac, they were ready to play an active role in public administration.

The education received at home and in the calmecac, as well as the experience gained as members of the dominant group, instilled in the pipiltin a sense of responsibility and dignity. Excerpts from some *huehuetlatolli* show us how conscious the pipiltin were of their status. The father tells his son:

And who are you? You are of noble lineage; you are one's hair, you are one's fingernail, you are a ruler's son, you are a palace nobleman, you are a precious one, you are a nobleman...[17]

The pipiltin attitude towards the macehualtin often appears in these speeches. In an anecdote about one who over-indulged in drinking we find:

It will be said: had he perhaps performed the role of a commoner?

Or, admonishing a noble daughter, words like these frequently occur:

Especially do I declare to you that you are a noblewoman...Do not in anything cause embarrassment to our lords, the rulers...Do not be a commoner (*maa timacehualti*), do not appear as a commoner (*maa timomacehualquixti*).

[17] *FC*, Bk VI, ch. 20.

In practically every aspect of the expected behaviour of those of noble lineage, the comparison is underlined:

You are to speak very slowly, very deliberately... Also you are not to cry out, lest you be known as an imbecile, a shameless one, a rustic (a cultivator of the land), a veritable rustic...[18]

The question of the pipiltin and the ownership of land is particularly complex and controversial. The first land distribution made by the Mexicas immediately followed their victory over the Tecpanecs of Azcapotzalco around 1430. The record of it is particularly interesting:

The first to whom lands were allocated was the ruling house; lands belonging to the chiefdom, for the high ruler's maintenance... Eleven pieces of land were then given to the ruler's adviser, Tlacaelel; and also two and three pieces of land were conceded to the various pipiltin, in proportion to their merits and offices...[19]

Through other sources we know the Nahuatl designation of the variously allocated lands: *tlatocatlalli*, 'lands of the ruler', *pil + tlalli* (*pillalli*), 'land of the pipiltin'. Closely related to the *tlatocatlalli* were other lands specifically reserved to cover the expenses of the palace (*tecpantlalli*), of the temples (*teopantlalli*) and of the wars (*yaotlalli*). The lands possessed in a communal form by the calpullis comprised of macehualtin were known as *calpul + tlalli* (*calpullalli*).

Were lands possessed as private property by the ruler and the pipiltin, or merely as privileges pertaining to particular offices held by the favoured? Those following Morgan and Bandelier maintain that all the lands simply belonged to the 'tribe' or 'confederacy of tribes'. Others, like Alfonso Caso, Paul Kirchhoff and Friedrich Katz, frankly admit that, in the case of the huey tlatoani and the pipiltin, their land was possessed as private property.

The extant sources, although not always precise on this point, seem to favour the idea that the possession of land was in direct relation to the office and administrative position of the favoured individuals:

...the lord [tlatoani] has lands in various places annexed to his chiefdom, and the macehualtin till them for him, and revere him as lord, and these lands are possessed by the one who succeeds him as ruler...[20]

[18] *FC*, Bk VI, ch. 14. [19] Durán, *Historia de las Indias*, I, 101.
[20] Sebastián Ramírez de Fuenleal, 'Carta al Emperador, de fecha y de noviembre de 1532', *Colección de Documentos Inéditos*, 42 vols. (Madrid, 1864–84), XIII, 254.

As in some cases the successor of a tlatoani was not a direct descendant, the meaning of the text seems to be that the land was possessed and transmitted as a function of rank. On the other hand, it is true that there were families of pipiltin some of whose members occupied the same administrative position for several generations. They thus enjoyed a continuous form of possession of the allotted lands. An episode that took place in the days of the Mexica ruler Ahuitzotl is of interest in this context. The Mexicas had conquered the chiefdom of Chalco and Ahuitzotl had installed a new local ruler there. The latter deprived many of the local pipiltin of their administrative positions. Consequently, he also took the lands they had owned. The deprived pipiltin complained to the Mexica ruler. The reaction of Ahuitzotl was ambivalent. He said to the dispossessed pipiltin: 'Take back your lands.' But when the lord he had appointed to govern in Chalco explained his point of view, Ahuitzotl told him: 'You know what to do. Destroy them, hang them...all of them, who want to be as pipiltin...'[21]

As for the undertakings and achievements of the dominant group within the context of the society they governed, Angel Palerm has argued within the theoretical framework developed by Karl A. Wittfogel, that 'the causal relation between the support offered to [an] Asiatic society and despotism by hydraulic agriculture, is clear enough...'[22] Looking for the existence of economically significant irrigation works in Meso-america, Palerm has listed numerous sites where there is some evidence of that sort of enterprise.

In the specific case of the Mexicas, Palerm recognizes that 'the economic life of the Tenochcas under their first three rulers does not suggest agricultural cultivation.'[23] This was due, among other reasons, to the small size of the island inhabited by the Mexicas and to the floods of salty water to which it was exposed. In his opinion the situation changed after the victory over Azcapotzalco. Then the Mexica rulers (with advice from Nezahualcoyotl, the wise lord of Tezcoco), introduced important hydraulic works. Dikes were built to separate the fresh from the salt waters of the lakes, and aqueducts to bring drinking water into the city. The *chinampas*, small artificial islands, built in a process of land

[21] *Anales de Cuauhtitlan*, fo. 39.
[22] Angel Palerm, 'Teorías sobre la evolución en Mesoamérica', in *Las civilizaciones antiguas del Viejo Mundo y de América*, Theo R. Crevenna (ed.) (Washington, 1955), 79.
[23] Palerm, 'La base agrícola de la civilización de Mesoamérica', *Las civilizaciones antiguas*, 177.

reclamation, where vegetables and flowers were cultivated, received the benefits of irrigation.

Accepting all this, one still wonders about the importance of the irrigated chinampas in comparison to the amount of resources (corn, beans, squash, vegetables and other kinds of agricultural products) obtained by Tenochtitlan as tribute from the many conquered towns and chiefdoms. It is true that the building of the dikes, aqueducts and causeways facilitated enormously the development of the Aztec metropolis. But can we say that these works were one of the key achievements of the dominant group justifying their despotic rule over the rest of the Mexicas?

If we insist on finding something that (in terms of the Asian mode of production) could be described as an imposing and effective enterprise, we have to look elsewhere. The pipiltin, as we have seen, had forged their own 'image' which, above all, confirmed their mission to maintain the life of their own cosmic age, of the sun and mankind. The offering of blood (re-enacting the primeval sacrifice of the gods when they created this cosmic age) helped to restore the divine energy, propitiating the gods, and obtaining from them the vital gift of the waters. To fulfil this destiny, the cult of the gods, human sacrifice and the fighting of wars to obtain captives and impose Aztec rule, became the primary concerns of the dominant group. In this respect the erection and restoration of the temples (in particular the great ensemble of sacred buildings in Tenochtitlan) and the organization and effectiveness of the army, supported by a complex ideology, were the most imposing achievements of the Mexica dominant group. Other achievements included urbanization and the embellishment of their metropolis, the administrative organization, the establishment of far-flung commercial routes, the functioning of local markets, the production of manufactured goods (arts and crafts), the maintenance of a school system and the propagation of Nahuatl as a lingua franca throughout Mesoamerica.

As already stated, the macehualtin were not only part of extended families but also formed the extremely important units known as calpulli. These socio-economic entities were common in Mesoamerica. We have already quoted some evidence supporting the idea that the members of a calpulli were, at least originally, linked by kinship. Although some authors have tended to consider the calpulli as a kind of guild or association for specific economic aims, available evidence seems to indicate that in the Mexica calpulli endogamic tendencies predominated.

Some calpulli were established as integral parts of large towns. This was the case in places like Tezcoco, Culhuacan and Mexico-Tenochtitlan. In the latter there were more than fifty calpulli at the time of the arrival of the Spaniards. As we will see, the members of most of these 'urban' calpulli did not till the land. They were dedicated to other forms of production. Among them groups of artisans, artists and merchants had achieved great economic importance. Other calpulli existed whose members comprised most of the population of smaller towns and also of many scattered villages. Some of those towns, surrounded by clusters of villages within territories of varying extent, constituted a chiefdom. A local nobility (with its corresponding administrative apparatus) governed these polities. At the time of the greatest Mexica expansion many of these entities in the central plateau and in other areas of Veracruz, Guerrero, Oaxaca and Chiapas, were subject in various ways through payment of tribute to the rulers of Mexico-Tenochtitlan. In some cases their local nobilities had been replaced by Mexica pipiltin. In others various forms of compromise were introduced. *Teteuctin* (official administrators) were often sent to the subject towns and villages to direct local production. Thus, many calpulli of areas under Aztec control were 'entrusted' to a Mexica *teuctli*. This kind of socio-economic unit constituted a *teccalli*. Its organization was structured to facilitate the exaction of tribute and personal services directly from the calpulli rather than merely through the conquered chiefdom in whose jurisdiction these calpulli fell.

This imposed structure did not suppress the internal socio-economic features of the calpulli. Each one had its local authorities, about whom Alonso de Zorita writes:

Two *principales* in each calpulli convoke the people to arrange the payment of tribute or to obey what the governor (teuctli) or other officials have commanded...and they [those of the calpulli] prefer that their 'heads' [the principales] belong to the same group...[24]

These two *calpulleque* (those in charge of the calpulli), in addition to responsibility for the subsistence of their own community, had to act as the intermediaries with the teteuctin. The calpulli, according to Zorita and other sources, had its own local institutions: a priest (or priests)

---

[24] Zorita, *Breve y Sumaría Relación*, 30.

in charge of the local temple; a *tlahcuilo*, a 'painter of books' or scribe, who mainly kept the records of its landed property, tributes and other facts related to the history of the group. A local treasurer (*calpixqui*), the chieftains of the calpulli's squadrons and the council of elders, were also key figures in the calpulli.

Land was owned communally by the members of the calpulli. Nevertheless, one ought to realize that the 'ultimate proprietor' of the agricultural resources, including the land and whatever was attached to it, was the political unit to which the corresponding calpulli was subject. Other calpullis existed without land. With the exception of those described as 'urban calpullis', people living in those lacking land had to work as *mayeque*, servants or labourers, tilling the lands of others (mainly of the prosperous pipiltin).

Under whichever specific circumstances non-pipiltin individuals lived, it can be stated that they belonged to a particular calpulli. The sum of the members of the calpulli (urban, semi-urban and rural), formed the social stratum of the macehualtin. For the most part the macehualtin form of life implied an economy of self-subsistence within their calpulli and total obedience to their internal authorities, to the teteuctin and to the other administrative officers appointed by the dominant group. In addition, they had to pay tribute, serve in the army, and perform a variety of other personal services to the state. These included manual labour in the building of temples and palaces or in other public works, or serving as porters carrying heavy bundles of merchandise to distant places.

In difficult times macehualtin conditions worsened in many ways. Thus, for instance, during famines they had often to sell themselves or their children as *tlatlacotin*, a term the Spaniards translated as 'slaves'. However, in Mesoamerica slavery was very different from that prevailing in the European world. In the days of the Mexicas a slave was sold for a limited time: the slave himself, or his relatives, could obtain his redemption. Children born to slaves were not considered slaves. On the other hand, to become a slave incurred the risk of being chosen as a human sacrifice, for the master had the right to offer his slaves for those rituals.

To summarize: it is clear that the way of life of the macehualtin differed radically from that of the pipiltin. The latter's relations to the available natural resources, their participation in production and in the fruits obtained from it, their function in the public administration and their privileges, contrast strongly with the status of the people, the commoners, so often described as the 'poor and miserable' macehualtin.

The Aztec economy is difficult to study due to the scarcity of sources which might permit quantification of the elements and forces affecting production. There is no agreement on the total population figure for Central Mexico, the states of Mexico, Hidalgo, Puebla, Tlaxcala, Querétaro, Guanajuato, Michoacán, Colima, Jalisco, Guerrero and Veracruz – recent estimates have ranged from 12 million to 25 million[25] – nor on the number of persons involved in each area of production in the various regions, towns and villages.

On the other hand there is at least reliable evidence about the principal forms of specialization within the labour force. Thus we are informed that there was a division of labour according to sex. The agricultural tasks and the majority of craft production fell to men. Women were assigned the household duties, including heavy work, like the making of dough for tortillas, the flat maize pancakes, which required long hours of labour over a grinding stone. Spinning and weaving were also women's tasks. We also know of other kinds of specialization, for example, fishing and mining, as well as construction (bricklayers, stone-dressers, carpenters and painters) and manufacturing (potters, basket-makers, makers of mats and sandals and tanners). There was a broad range of artisans producing utilitarian objects such as paper, stone and wooden implements, canoes, or luxury items, principally for members of the nobility and priesthood. Among the latter were goldsmiths, feather workers, sculptors and the famous *tlahcuilo* or book painters. It must be recalled that, while these specializations existed, the great majority of the macehualtin devoted most of their time to the land.

Information about the natural resources upon which the Mexica economy was based suffers from the same sort of limitation as that relating to human resources. Although some sources provide quantitative data, they are in the main merely descriptive. For example, in dealing with agricultural land, although measurements are occasionally given, it is more usual to find descriptions of type and use. *Atoctli* was a term used to describe land with adequate water and of value for agriculture, while *cuauhtlalli*, 'lands of trees', indicated the presence of vegetable residue or mulched land. In the rather limited areas blessed

[25] See Note on the native American population on the eve of the European invasions, *CHLA* I.

with water and organic material, the cultivation of basic crops – corn, beans, squash, chili – obviously prospered. There were also other lands designated for specialized use, such as those called *xochimilpan* for growing flowers. The variety of territories in one way or another under Mexica rule included uncultivated lands which supported plants used for medicine and others for food or for trees which provided wood for construction. The animal population included aquatic species found in the lakes and rivers and others obtainable for food either by hunting or through selective breeding, as in the well-known case of the turkey. The absence of other domestic animals (with the exception of the dog) was, to a large degree, an obstacle to the development of a more efficient technology. As there were no beasts of burden or other animals which could serve for pulling, the wheel was limited to use in some toys.

Gold, silver, copper, tin and, probably to a lesser extent, lead, were the metals known to Mesoamericans. Other minerals used were cinnabar (mercury sulphate) and calcite (calcium carbonate), as well as various mineral dyes, semi-precious and other types of stone.

The Mesoamericans, in spite of their achievements in art and calendrical computation, did not excel as producers of implements. Nevertheless, their tools were, in many ways, reasonably adequate. They included utensils made from stone, such as hammers, knives, scrapers, mortars, grindstones and other variously-shaped instruments. Others, such as hooks, needles and skin-working implements, were made of bone. Wood was used to make fire drills, arrows, darts, clubs and the *coa*, or digging stick, used in agriculture. Later on, when metallurgy was practised, copper axes, hoes, punches, knives and various weapons were produced.

Agricultural techniques were varied. Apart from seasonal farming, in which at times some kinds of fertilizer were employed, Mesoamerican societies made use of systems of irrigation, terracing and, above all, in the central region, introduced the famous chinampas, often described as 'floating gardens'. These were artificial structures of reed, covered with fertile mud, anchored to the beds of the lakes with wooden posts. Willow trees were planted on the chinampas to hold them in place. In the extremely good soil of the chinampas the Mexicas grew flowers and fresh vegetables in abundance.

Study of indigenous books like the *Scroll of Tributes* and *Codex Mendoza*, allows us to appreciate the amount of goods that the subjugated calpulli (the basic unit of production), towns and polities (considered as broader economic units) delivered to the rulers of Tenochtitlan. It is no wonder that the Mexicas, in order to obtain prompt and precise payment of tribute, developed such a complex administrative apparatus.

Other elements of major importance in the economy of ancient Mexico were the market places and the commerce carried out by the *pochtecas* or merchants. Greatly impressed, some conquerors have provided us in their chronicles with a picture of the principal market place of Tlateloco, the town incorporated into Tenochtitlan. Most of the products offered at the market were brought into the Aztec metropolis by merchants or as tribute. At the same time, other manufactured products were exported by the Mexicas. A factor that significantly contributed to the expansion of commerce was the need to satisfy the growing demands of a richer nobility and an extremely elaborate religious life.

The pochtecas, who, as commoners, belonged to calpullis, soon became aware of the importance of their functions. They transformed their organization into a social entity comparable to a guild. Each guild had its director (these were called pochtecatloque, 'chiefs of the pochtecas') and various categories of member. Among the latter were the *Oztomecas*, who were experts on far-off regions and spoke their languages. There were 69 different categories of trader including traders in slaves, precious metals, tobacco, cacao, animals, paper and corn.[26]

In addition to buying and selling, the merchants also dealt in various types of contracts and loans, in order to make their business possible. The ruler and members of the nobility, as well as some of the established merchants (including some women), made loan contracts with those who travelled to distant parts. Thus, an Aztec account records an occasion on which King Ahuítzotl granted 1,600 mantles as a loan to merchants on their way to the Pacific Coast. The mention of the small mantles, called *quachtli*, refers to a particular kind of symbol of exchange. They were, in fact, mantles of varying sizes, accepted as a sort of monetary symbol since they were backed by the wealth and authority of the Aztec huey tlatoani. There were also loans in the form of small tubes full of gold, as well as sacks of cacao of various sizes.

[26] Abundant information about the *Pochtecayotl* or commerce is included in Book IX of the *FC*. See also, Bente Bittman and Thelma D. Sullivan, 'The Pochteca', in *Mesoamerican communication routes and cultural contacts* (Provo, Utah, 1978).

The administration of the markets and the establishment of standards of exchange were two important functions of the merchants. Moreover, Ixtlilxochitl tells us that of the four supreme councils of government 'the fourth council was that of the Treasury, wherein all the stewards of the king and some of the most important merchants of the city met to discuss Treasury matters and royal tributes.[27] With the merchants acting as economic advisers to the ruler, it is not surprising that they acquired numerous privileges that made them almost equal to members of the nobility. Besides having their own tribunals, they collected tributes, frequently traded on behalf of the king, and acted as spies in distant regions. Through their agency, commerce and the economy generally expanded vigorously and contributed to the flourishing of religious and cultural institutions. Conversely, religious and cultural developments exerted considerable influence on society as a whole, including the economy.

The prevailing religion in Mexico–Tenochtitlan at the time of the Spanish conquest resulted from a long process of fusion and synthesis. Nevertheless, it was far from being a mass of heterogeneous elements, as the priests had worked hard to give it a functional order which incorporated the world view and ideals of the Mexicas.

The world had existed not at one, but at various consecutive times. The 'first founding of the earth' had taken place thousands of year-counts earlier. Four suns had existed. During these eras or 'suns', processes of evolution had produced forms, each more perfect than the last, of human beings, plants and foodstuffs. Four primordial forces (earth, wind, water and fire), with a curious similarity to classical thought, had ruled these ages until the arrival of the fifth or present epoch, that of the 'sun of movement'.

Perhaps evolving from the sun and earth cults, belief in an all-begetting father and a universal mother as a supreme dual deity, developed. Without losing his unity, in that the ancient hymns always invoked him in the singular, this deity was known as *Ometeotl*: 'the dual god', he and she of our flesh, *Tonacatecuhtli* and *Tonacacíhuatl*, who in a portentous cosmic union engendered all creation.

The dual god was also 'mother of the gods, father of the gods'. In a first manifestation of his own being his four sons were born: the white, black, red and blue 'smoking mirrors'. These gods constituted the primordial forces which set the sun in motion and created life on earth.

[27] Fernando de Alva Ixtlilxochitl, *Obras históricas*, 2 vols. (Mexico, 1891–2), I, 211–18.

They were also responsible for the four previous, cyclical destructions of the world.

Although cataclysm was foretold as the final destiny of this, the fifth age, the Mexicas did not lose interest in life. On the contrary, it spurred them on in a remarkable way. Since it was a primeval sacrifice of the gods that created and set in motion the sun, it was only through the sacrifice of men that the present age could be preserved. The 'people of the sun' took upon themselves the mission of furnishing it with the vital energy found in the precious liquid which keeps man alive. Sacrifice and ceremonial warfare to obtain victims for sacrificial rites were their central activities, the very core of their personal, social, military and political life.

There is good evidence that human sacrifices were performed in Mesoamerica prior to the Mexicas, but apparently never before in such great numbers. If the Mexica pipiltin believed that their mission was thus to maintain the life of the sun, they realized too that, through their wars to obtain victims, they also extended their dominion and satisfied their growing economic demands.

Several other forms of cult addressed to the many gods worshipped by the Mexicas are also described in the sources. A very special place was reserved for those rites and ceremonies in honour of the Mother Goddess, invoked with numerous titles, including the most generic Tonantzin, 'our Reverend Mother'. The importance of the *Dea Mater* of the Mexica (and Mesoamericans in general) was clearly perceived by the Spanish missionaries, some of whom did not reject the possibility of a synthesis of the pre-Columbian concept with the beliefs related to the Virgin Mary. A good example is the Virgin of Guadalupe, whose shrine was built where that of Tonantzin used to be.

Native books and sixteenth-century transcriptions in indigenous languages of numerous texts previously preserved by oral tradition are the repositories of Mesoamerican literatures. In them we find myths and legends, ritual hymns, a variety of poems, discourses, chronicles and historical accounts, the beginnings of dramatic composition, religious doctrines and government proclamations. Through these texts an image of the everyday life not only of the Mexicas but of several other peoples can be attained. The following hymn speaks about the dual god;

> In the place of authority,
> in the place of authority, we command;

> it is the mandate of our Principal Lord,
> Mirror which makes things show forth.
> They are already on the way, they are prepared.
> Intoxicate yourselves,
> the God of Duality is acting,
> the Inventor of Men,
> Mirror which makes things show forth.[28]

Sometimes the words of the sages declare their beliefs but frequently, also, their doubts. They recognize that life on earth is transitory and that, in the end, everything must vanish. The following is an example of these more personal forms of poetical composition:

> Truly do we live on earth?
> Not forever on earth; only a little while here.
> Although it be jade, it will be broken,
> Although it be gold, it is crushed,
> Although it be *quetzal* feather, it is torn asunder.
> Not forever on earth; only a little while here.[29]

On the eve of the Spanish invasion, Mexico–Tenochtitlan, the Aztec metropolis, was the administrative centre of a large and complex political and socio-economic conglomerate. Various authors have, in describing the political nature of this entity, employed terms like empire, kingdom or confederation of chiefdoms and even of tribes. Most of the old chiefdoms in the central plateau (like those of Chalco–Amaquemeca, Cuitlahuac, Xochimilco, Coyohuacan and Culhuacan) and many more in the areas of Hidalgo, Morelos, Guerrero, Puebla, Veracruz, Oaxaca, Tabasco and Chiapas acknowledged Aztec rule. They were subject to the Mexica metropolis in different ways. Nevertheless, even in the cases in which the local rulers continued to govern their chiefdoms, they recognized Mexico–Tenochtitlan as the central metropolis from which commands and exactions originated, including the payment of tribute and a variety of personal services, like the 'protection' of the commercial routes. The tutelary gods of the dominated chiefdoms shared in the fate of their peoples. In Mexico–Tenochtitlan a temple existed, the *coateocalli*, 'common house of the gods', in which the tutelary deities of the subject towns and provinces were kept: they were considered 'divine captives'. Their destinies (*tonalli*) (as in the myth of Huitzilopochtli who incor-

[28] *Historia Tolteca–Chichimeca*, Mexican Manuscript 46–58 bis, Bibliothèque Nationale, Paris, fo. 36.
[29] *Collection of Mexican Songs*, Aztec manuscript preserved in the National Library of Mexico, fo. 17.

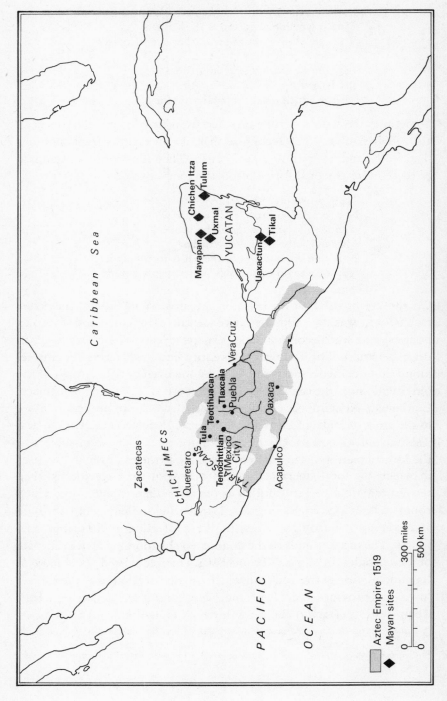

Caribbean Sea

Chichen Itza
Tulum
Mayapan
Uxmal
YUCATAN
Tikal
Uaxactun

VeraCruz
Teotihuacan
Tlaxcala
Puebla
Tula
Oaxaca
Zacatecas
CHICHIMECS
Queretaro
Tenochtitlan
(Mexico City)
Acapulco

PACIFIC

OCEAN

Aztec Empire 1519
Mayan sites

300 miles
500 km

porated into his own the destinies of the Four Hundred Warriors of the South) symbolized the prophesied destiny of the People of the Sun. Moreover, Nahuatl became the lingua franca over a vast area of Mesoamerica. The speakers of Otomi, Mazahua, Matlatzinca, Tepehua, Totonac, Tlapanec, Mazatec, Mixtec, Zapotec, as well as various Mayan languages like Chontal, Tzeltal and Tzotzil, agreed to employ the language of the rulers in Tenochtitlan.

At the same time there were chiefdoms which had managed to resist the penetration of the Mexicas. This was the case with the Purepechas or Tarascans of Michoacan and the Tlaxcalans in the Central Plateau. The latter, particularly, had developed a deep hatred of the Mexicas with whom they were forced to fight periodically in the famous 'Flower Wars', whose purpose was the supply of victims for sacrifice to the Sun–Huitzilopochtli. Beyond the territories of direct Mexica influence, in the southern and northern areas of what is now Mexico, a great number of peoples preserved their own distinct cultural patterns. In the south-east several chiefdoms of Maya language and culture (those existing in Campeche, Yucatán, the Petén, Guatemala and Honduras), or of Nahuatl tongue (in El Salvador and Nicaragua) maintained to various degrees many elements of their ancient high culture, despite their lack of any significant political organization. In the north-west, beyond the rim of Mexica–Mesoamerica, a good number of speakers of Uto-Aztecan languages had settled, among them, the Cora, Huichol, Tepecano, Tepehuano, Mayo, Yaqui, Tarahumara, Pima and Opata. Most of these groups lived in small villages, as sedentary agriculturists. Their patterns of culture can be compared to those of the inhabitants of central Mesoamerica in the Middle pre-Classic period.

Much-less developed groups lived in the bordering areas to the north of the Central Plateau and to the north-east of Mesoamerica. Generically, all the inhabitants of those regions were known to the Mexicas as the Teochichimecs, that is, the authentic Chichimecs, the 'wandering peoples of the bow and arrow'. The Teochichimecs, it was frequently recorded, had no villages, or houses, or cultivated fields. They were, indeed, fearsome *popolocas*, a word conveying a meaning very close to that of barbarians. In a distant past (during the Toltec age and perhaps also in the Classic Period), the Mesoamericans had extended their influence beyond the territories which became the possession of the Teochichimecs. In the days of Mexico–Tenochtitlan no attempt to expand into the north is recorded. It was left to the Spaniards (accompanied by Tlaxcalans and Mexicas) to conquer and settle the vast span of the territories beyond Mesoamerica.

Thus, a mosaic of peoples, cultures and languages possessed the land where Hernán Cortés and his 600 men were shortly to disembark. The conqueror was soon to hear of the existence of the Mexicas. References to them were made by the Mayas of Yucatán, the Chontals of Tabasco and the Totonacs of Veracruz. Through the latter, and also particularly through the Tlaxcalans, Cortés learned about the power and wealth of the Aztec metropolis and of its rulers, in particular Moteuczoma. In his writings (and in those of the other 'soldier–chroniclers') can be found numerous references to the most obvious aspects of the political, religious and socio-economic structures which supported the Mexica grandeur. Although at times superficial or erroneous, the comments of the Spanish conquerors coincide in several points with the evidence derived from indigenous sources and from modern archaeological research. The Spaniards certainly realized that in the middle of that mosaic of peoples, cultures and languages, the Mexicas stood out as the creators and rulers of a complex political entity, with as many contrasts inside as outside its great metropolis. On the one hand, there were the rich and powerful pipiltin served by the macehualtin; on the other, radical differences were noticeable between the Mexica tlatoque ruling in many towns and provinces subject to Tenochtitlan and the dispossessed and obedient pipiltin and macehualtin of the peoples under Aztec domination. Cortés soon understood the situation. Side by side with the magnificence of the Aztec metropolis (he visited as a guest in 1519) was the reality of imposed Mexica rule. He knew how deeply the Totonacs, Tlaxcalans and many others, hated the Mexicas. He took advantage of this and (without fully realizing it) played a key role in the last chapter of the history of autonomous Mesoamerica. The enemies of Tenochtitlan believed the Spaniards were siding with them. In this belief they succeeded in defeating the Mexicas, not knowing for a while that their foreign allies were the only ones to profit from such a victory. The Spanish order – political, religious, socio-economic – inexorably implanted was to affect equally Mexicas, Tlaxcalans and all other Mesoamericans.

2

THE INDIANS OF THE CARIBBEAN AND CIRCUM-CARIBBEAN AT THE END OF THE FIFTEENTH CENTURY

At the end of the fifteenth century A.D. the lands surrounding the Caribbean Sea were densely populated with people who were frequently organized into rank societies or chiefdoms of varying degrees of complexity. Among these polities two major spheres of political interaction can be delineated. The centre of one was the northern half of Colombia, with lower Central America (Panama and Costa Rica) and northern Venezuela as regional extensions to west and east, respectively. The centre of the other was the islands of Hispaniola and Puerto Rico in the Greater Antilles including Jamaica and Cuba. Geographically intermediate between these areas of higher political development, and in some ways linking them culturally, were the peoples of the Lesser Antilles, north-eastern Venezuela and the Venezuelan *llanos* (plains) north and west of the Orinoco river whose organization was less complex. On the periphery of the circum-Caribbean territories, that is, in eastern Nicaragua and Honduras, the Orinoco delta, and small portions of Cuba and Hispaniola, a few societies continued to exist at a still lower, tribal, level of cultural development.

Circum-Caribbean rank societies were composed of two social sectors of elites and commoners, hierarchically related. Hereditary membership in one or the other sector, together with additional distinctions in social status recognized particularly among members of the elite, conferred differential rights, obligations, and privileges on individuals and groups. For example, persons of high rank controlled select aspects of the production, distribution and consumption of resources. They supervised social relations within their group by periodic public admonishments and by authorizing sanctions for serious wrongdoing. They led squadrons of warriors into battle against external opponents. In these respects

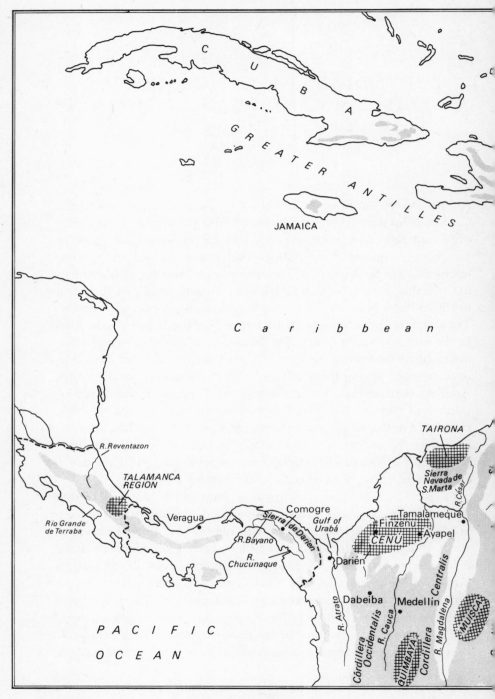

Indians of the Caribbean and Circum-Caribbean at the end of the fifteenth century

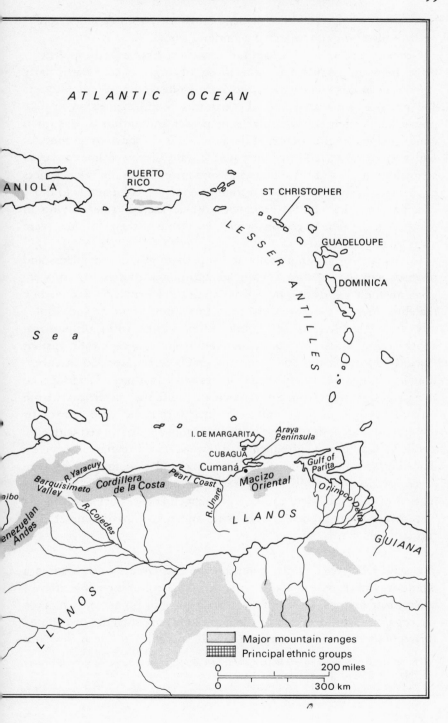

elite activities helped to unite all members of society into a single polity; perhaps also into an integrated economic whole.

Other aspects of elite behaviour, however, emphasized the distinctions between commoners and those of high estate. Particularly significant in this context were the more exclusive or esoteric interests and practices associated with the acquisition and expression of elite power and authority. The search for power and authority was often conducted within the context of the supernatural, for awesome contacts with deities and sacred forces in supernaturally distant realms conveyed an analogous aura of sacredness and supremacy upon the ruler. Rulers probably also sought equally prestigious contacts, comparable to those effected with the supernatural, with other 'sacred' rulers living in geographically remote regions which, by virtue of their distance, were also 'sacred' lands.[1]

Contacts with geographically and supernaturally distant places and peoples, and the superior knowledge and power they imparted, were given material expression by various sumptuary privileges assumed by the elite. Among these were the right to acquire, circulate and display rare and valuable 'luxury' goods, often in the form of personal adornments, which frequently derived from geographically distant 'sacred' realms. Elites and especially chiefs were also clad in exceptionally fine textiles, transported in litters and sometimes affected special 'languages' distinct from the vernacular. In life they dwelt apart from ordinary people in large and elaborately decorated elite centres or compounds and in death were buried in tombs richly stocked with elite goods including, not infrequently, a few sacrificed retainers or wives. The interests and activities of the common population, in contrast, were more localized spatially and were concerned with more mundane matters of daily subsistence and kin group well-being. Their adornments were fewer, their homes less elaborate and their burials simpler than those of their lords.

The cultural variety which characterized the circum-Caribbean as a whole was mirrored on a smaller scale in the cultural complexities of constituent regions. Colombia is a major case in point. By A.D. 1500 the organizational diversity of the numerous rank societies distributed throughout its three Andean cordilleras and the Caribbean lowlands

---

[1] The relationship between supernatural distance and geographical distance is discussed further in Mary W. Helms, *Ancient Panama: chiefs in search of power* (Austin, Texas, 1979).

was matched only by the heterogeneous topography and physiography of the country itself.

The highest levels of political development and regional influence were attained by a cluster of polities, including those of the Muisca or Chibcha, situated in highland basins of the Cordillera Oriental; of the so-called Tairona peoples, located along the Caribbean coast and in the adjacent foothills of the Sierra Nevada de Santa Marta in extreme north-eastern Colombia; and of the Cenú, established in the north Colombian savannahs. Possibly the chiefdom of Dabeiba, situated in the northern Cordillera Occidental, and some of the Quimbaya polities on the western slopes of the Cordillera Central in the middle Río Cauca region also held key positions of regional influence, although the level of political elaboration reached by Dabeiba and the Quimbaya societies was not as great as that achieved by the Muisca, Cenú and Tairona. Additional polities of comparable regional significance undoubtedly existed, including Tamalameque, on the lower Magdalena River not far from its confluence with the Río César and Thamara, somewhere on the Río César.

Surrounding these focal polities of highest political elaboration or greatest regional influence were relatively smaller, often rather militant, and perhaps less complex societies, whose leaders' prestige and authority may have derived to a considerable extent from their involvement in networks of elite associations which centred upon the focal polities. In at least one region, a rather secluded section of the middle Magdalena river valley, rank societies were apparently absent, possibly because of the inability of local tribal leaders to interact effectively in the association networks which sustained the high position of political elites elsewhere.

The powerful position enjoyed by rulers of the Muisca, Tairona and Cenú, and the prestige held by the lords of Dabeiba and the major Quimbaya polities, was heralded in part by these leaders' access to or control over certain scarce and highly valued resources, either naturally occurring or crafted, which were greatly desired by elites throughout the country and, accordingly, were widely distributed through the networks of elite associations. For example, the highland domains of the Muisca included emerald mines and the coastal domains of the Tairona yielded fine sea shells. The Spanish *conquistadores* found Muisca emeralds in Tairona, while Taironian sea shells adorned distant Muisca chiefs and hung before the doorways of their dwelling compounds. The Muisca, the Cenú and the Tairona were famous, too, for the fine textiles and delicate gold and tumbaga pieces crafted by skilled specialists working under the authority of the elite. These goods were also widely distributed, as was salt prepared by the Muisca from highland salt springs and by the Tairona and Cenú from coastal sources. Similarly, the lord of Dabeiba was renowned for the gold pieces crafted at his elite centre, which were distributed through elite networks as far away as Panama. In like fashion, the Quimbaya realm included productive gold fields and salt springs, and Quimbaya craftsmen were highly skilled in weaving and probably also in metallurgy. Once again, salt, textiles and gold and tumbaga objects were exchanged both with neighbouring peoples and with more distant groups.

The lords of lesser chiefdoms surrounding these focal polities were drawn into the elite exchange network in various ways. In some cases they were able to inject a vital resource, such as salt, into the distributional flow, receiving in turn valued elite goods produced elsewhere. Alternatively, these lesser lords controlled local production of raw materials required by craftsmen at major elite centres. Highland Muisca weavers, for example, depended on raw cotton grown in lower *tierra templada* and *tierra caliente* zones of the Cordillera Oriental and middle Magdalena river valley by non-Muisca peoples, who exchanged local raw materials for finished products from the highlands. Similarly, the populace of some Quimbaya polities produced raw cotton, while other Quimbayan groups specialized in spinning and weaving. Muisca goldsmiths acquired raw metal from mining peoples further south on the upper Magdalena river in exchange for salt, textiles and emeralds. The metallurgists of Dabeiba, of the lowland Cenú and of the Quimbaya acquired much of their raw gold from the *caciques* directing the famous Buritican mines high in the Medellín area of the rugged Central Cordillera in exchange for finished gold pieces, agricultural products, salt, textiles, dried fish and war captive slaves, all of which undoubtedly enhanced the power of the local lords.

The records also indicate logistical means whereby lords of the lesser domains played their part in operating the far-flung elite distribution networks. For example, at one point on the lengthy trail connecting the Buritican mines with the elite crafting centres of the northern lowlands local lords controlled a vital bridge across the Río Cauca and extracted a toll from those who wished to pass.[2] Other local lords, particularly

[2] Luis Duque Gómez, *Prehistoria*, tomo II, *Tribus indigenas y sitios arqueológicos* (Bogotá, 1967), 207–8.

those situated between major highland and lowland elite centres, may have benefited from roles as middlemen in the exchange of interior mountain goods and lowland products. A number of sites on the borders of contrasting ecological zones or between major watersheds served as central exchange points to which elite representatives, often termed 'merchants' in the European literature, brought valued products from interior mountains and from coastal or interior lowlands. Such exchange centres included Tahami on the Cauca river close to the Magdalena rivershed, where mountain foothills approach northern lowlands, Tamalameque on the lower Magdalena close to the confluence with the Río César, Sorocota on the northern borders of Chibcha territory close to the middle Magdalena, and Ibaqué in the heights of the Central Cordillera where Quimbaya peoples of the Cauca valley met with emissaries from the Magdalena valley and the Muisca domain. It is very likely that the local lords of these exchange localities benefited politically from the barter, particularly if they guaranteed the 'peace of the market' (for border zones could be places of warfare) for those who came from near and far to exchange goods.

Although the words 'merchants' and 'market' appear above, it must be emphasized that the regional and long-distance elite contacts which were given material expression in the exchange of valued resources had political and ideological, as much as, or perhaps even more than, economic significance. Many of the scarce and valued goods exchanged, not only the emeralds, gold pieces and fine textiles but also such products as salt, dried fish and war captive slaves, were most likely highly charged with political–religious symbolism signifying the sacredness, efficacy and authority of chiefship. There is evidence that the mining of gold and of emeralds was a sacred activity, requiring preparatory ritual; weaving was apparently regarded in this light too. Furthermore, at elite centres such as Dabeiba, the Cenú capitals of Finzenu and Ayapel, Guatavita in the Muisca realm and many others the dwelling places for chiefs and priests and the centres for the crafting of sumptuary goods were directly associated with shrines or temples. These sites also served as places of pilgrimage or as elite necropolises. Finally, to the extent that, in chiefdom cosmologies, geographical distance was correlated with supernatural distance, as was suggested in the introduction, sacred significance accrued to all goods derived from, and activities associated with, regions and peoples remote from a given political centre. Factors such as these should warn against a strictly economic interpretation of pre-Columbian long-distance exchange.

The densely populated and highly complex chiefdoms of the Muisca, Tairona and Cenú rested on an extremely productive subsistence base with intensive agriculture and fishing, and with hunting as a significant supplementary activity. The fertile and well-watered *altiplanos* inhabited by the Muisca produced a variety of agricultural products, including potatoes and quinoa, some of which were probably grown on ridged planting beds raised above the wet basin floors to regulate moisture. Hillsides may have been terraced or cultivated by slash-and-burn techniques. Rich aquatic resources, particularly fish and water fowl, were available in rivers and bodies of stagnant water, or *pantanos*, scattered throughout the valleys. Special fish ponds were constructed in *pantanos* and on rivers too. The Spaniards also commented on the abundance of deer in the Muisca territory, but deer hunting was an activity restricted to elites.

Both venison and the contributions of agricultural produce tendered by heads of local kinship and territorial groups (*uta*) to community leaders, and by them to higher lords, were kept in storehouses (which also held weapons and sumptuary goods such as goldwork) built in the enclosed dwelling compound of the lord. These foodstuffs supported priests and warriors on duty and probably provided comestibles for periodic ceremonies and celebrations. In addition to gifts of produce, the local populace accorded personal services to the local lord, cultivating his fields and building his enclosure and dwelling place.

The population and ceremonial centres of the Cenú chiefdoms were located near the major rivers which crossed the northern lowlands close to large *ciénagas* or seasonal lakes. Typically they were surrounded by grassy savannah which eventually gave way to wooded hill slopes. It is likely that slash-and-burn agriculture was practised on these wooded slopes at the outer margins of the savannahs. Possibly a more intensive and permanent type of agriculture was conducted on ridged fields situated on the margins of *ciénagas* and on the backslopes of natural levees along the major rivers. The rivers themselves provided extraordinarily rich fishing, and both rivers and *ciénagas* supported a tremendous diversity of edible land and water life, including turtles, manatee, iguanas, caimen, capybara, paca and waterfowl. The grassy savannahs supported deer, rabbits, peccary and ground birds. These abundant resources provisioned the general population living in small communities scattered over upland interfluves and the elite inhabiting the large crafting and ceremonial centres.

The inhabitants of the well-ordered towns and temple-filled ceremonial centres of the Tairona used ditch and canal irrigation to water the fields and stone-supported terraces that covered the lower slopes of the Sierra Nevada de Santa Marta for many miles. Arboriculture, hunting and, particularly, fishing augmented the diverse and abundant agricultural products.

Judging from the reports of the *conquistadores*, even the lands of smaller or relatively less important polities were well populated and well cultivated, sometimes by swidden techniques, sometimes by local irrigation or ridged field systems. Fishing and hunting were also cited as productive enterprises in virtually all regions. In the middle Cauca valley, to take one more example, the river proper and adjacent marshlands of the hot valley floor yielded excellent fishing, while the cooler mountain slopes provided well-drained and probably fairly permanent kitchen gardens close to comfortable and defensible house sites situated near streams and springs. Extensive field and tree plots and a variety of wild game were available farther upslope.

The basic culture patterns and political forms characteristic of the northern Colombian Andes and Caribbean lowlands were also found in lower Central America (Costa Rica and Panama) and in northern Venezuela. On the basis of the distribution of goldwork and other sumptuary goods it is further postulated that elites of both these regions engaged in long-distance contacts with the elite centres of those portions of Colombia closest to their territories. In this sense lower Central America and northern Venezuela may be regarded as part of a complex political–ideological interaction sphere affecting the diverse elite systems of much of north-western South America and lower Middle America.

The narrow stretch of land composing Panama and Costa Rica contains interior mountain ranges descending on both the Caribbean and Pacific versants to varying amounts of coastal lowlands. Frequently the domain under the control of a given chief included an ecologically diverse strip of land centring on one or more river valleys and extending from interior mountain heights to lowland littoral. In some cases these lands were divided, with interior mountain territory under the control of one lord while lower slopes and coastal shores were controlled by another. Available evidence suggests that a chief's domain tended to include the territory within one-half to one day's travel from the centre of power.

Judging from the Spanish accounts, the highest level of organizational complexity evidenced by the several dozen rank societies of lower Central America was closer to that attained by Dabeiba or by the larger Quimbaya chiefdoms in Colombia than to the polities of the Muisca, Cenú or Tairona, whose elite centres were significantly more elaborate than any described for Panama or Costa Rica. Furthermore, there are no indications of intensive irrigation or ridged field agricultural techniques for lower Central America. Instead swidden horticulture with digging sticks predominated on the open lowlands and slopes of the sierras. There is some evidence, however, that women and children captured in war were used as agricultural labourers. If so, even slash-and-burn agriculture might have been notably productive.

Additional foodstuffs derived from pejivalle palms and other fruit-bearing trees and from land game and wild fowl. River and ocean fish, manatee and sea turtle were particularly abundant too. Indeed, the rich aquatic resources of rivers and ocean were as fundamental as agriculture to the support of the sizeable populations indicated by the *conquistadores*. No regular chiefly tribute was collected in lower Central America, although personal services and labour were expected when the chief requested them for house building, for planting, fishing or hunting for his use and at time of war. On such occasions the lord distributed food and drink from storehouses replete with dried meat and fish, agricultural produce and various fermented drinks or *chichas*.

In Panama and Costa Rica, as in Colombia, a cluster of highly influential focal polities can again be discerned. Each regionally dominant lord was in turn supported by a political hinterland of allied or subordinate elites whose ties with the central ruler were sometimes strengthened by marriage, for polygyny was common among elites both here and in Colombia. The elite centres of the focal polities were situated at strategic locations on major travel routes by which long-distance contacts and the exchange of valued scarce resources were effected. In Panama, for example, the lord of the town of Darién on the Gulf of Urabá received gold from Dabeiba via the Río Atrato. Similarly, the elite centre of Comogre, strategically situated in the Sierra del Darién at the headwaters of the Río Bayano and Río Chucunaque, received pearls and raw gold from Pacific coastal regions and south-west Panama in return for textiles and war captive slaves. The capital town of Veragua, close to the Caribbean coast in north-western Panama, was another busy exchange centre where hammered gold pieces were crafted. In Costa Rica the renowned lords of the so-called Eastern Guëtar and Western Guëtar controlled domains strategically situated in or near the *mesa central*, in the mountainous heartland of central Costa Rica, close to headwaters of two major travelways, the Río Reventazan, which flows into the Caribbean, and the Río Grande de Terraba, which courses to the Pacific.

Although much of the raw gold, pearls, textiles and other products exchanged among lower Central American elites probably remained in the region, some undoubtedly moved into north-western South America through contacts between Panamanian regional elites and the lords of nearby Colombian centres such as Dabeiba and Cenú. Elite valuables, including cast gold and tumbaga ornaments, were probably received in return by lower Central American lords. This argument rests largely on the fact that, although quantities of elaborate cast gold and tumbaga pieces are known from pre-Columbian Panama and Costa Rica, there are no data in the sixteenth-century records clearly indicating the practice of complex metallurgy, including alloying or casting, in Panama or Costa Rica at that time, although this possibility cannot be dismissed.[3]

Both the culture patterns and the topography of northern Venezuela were not unlike those of lower Central America. The Colombian Cordillera Oriental extends into this territory, breaking into several smaller mountain chains. One range, the Sierra de Perija, extends along the western side of Lake Maracaibo, while a second, the Cordillera de

[3] For a fuller discussion of the author's position on this controversial question, see Helms, *Ancient Panama*. The documents do indicate that raw gold was available in lower Central America and that simple hammering was practised by craftsmen at the regional centres of Darién and Veragua and at mountain sites close to Comogre. Surface enrichment of tumbaga pieces by the acid bath process known as *mise-en-couleur* is noted, too, and could be interpreted as evidence for casting. Surface treatment of alloys by various methods was a separate and distinct development in South American metallurgy, however, and its use in lower Central America need not automatically indicate casting. See Heather Lechtman, 'Issues in Andean metallurgy', paper read at the Conference on South American Metallurgy, Dumbarton Oaks, Washington, 1975. Alternatively, it should be noted that data from the early seventeenth century give evidence of tumbaga-casting in the Talamancan region of south-eastern Costa Rica, and circumstantial evidence from the sixteenth century allows the possibility that more complex metallurgy was practised at a Talamancan regional centre at the time of initial European contact. See the report of Fray Agustín de Zevallos in León Fernández, *Colección de documentos para la historia de Costa Rica* (Paris, 1886), v, 158–9. Recently, too, a casting mould has been found in Guanacaste, Costa Rica.

Merida or Venezuelan Andes, stretches north-east along the southern
end of the lake and then, under the name of the Cordillera de la Costa,
runs parallel to the Caribbean coast of northern Venezuela. According
to sixteenth-century accounts, the Venezuelan Andes and the Cordillera
de la Costa were the most densely populated sections of the country.
The populace formed rank societies whose organization may well have
been more complex than is indicated by the ethnohistorical data
remaining to us, since massive European slaving had drastically reduced
most northern Venezuelan societies by the early sixteenth century.

In the high, *tierra fria* portions of the Venezuelan Andes intensive
agriculture utilizing terracing and irrigation and supplemented by
hunting supported a dense population. Weaving, salt production and
crafting of nephrite and serpentine provided sumptuary resources both
for local elite use and for regional exchange with the lowlands closer
to Lake Maracaibo. Textiles and salt also probably facilitated the
long-distance contacts which yielded rough stone for crafting and
finished golden pendants. The latter probably derived from adjacent
portions of Colombia, readily contacted by the Río Espíritu Santo, since
as yet there is no clear evidence of metallurgy in north-western
Venezuela. These activities, together with sacred shrines and complex
burials, suggest a general cultural pattern and, perhaps, level of political
organization broadly comparable to those of the Tairona of north-eastern
Colombia.

On the lower slopes of the Venezuelan Andes, in the *tierra templada*,
hoe agriculture, rather than irrigation, predominated and burials were
simpler than in the *tierra fria* zone. The general level of political
development here invites comparisons with the more modestly organized Panamanian chiefdoms or with the polities of the Cauca valley of
Colombia. Yet it is likely that the elites of these lower mountain regions
had achieved considerable status, perhaps benefiting politically from
roles as middlemen in the exchange of highland and lowland resources
between *tierra fria* groups and those residing in the Lake Maracaibo
lowlands or, for those resident on the southern slopes of the mountains,
between *tierra fria* peoples and lowland groups of the Venezuelan *llanos*.

Around Lake Maracaibo the main subsistence activities were fishing
in the lake itself and adjacent rivers and lagoons and agriculture and
hunting in the fertile lacustrine and riverine lowlands near the lake.
Although hunting, fishing, gathering and agriculture were all pursued
to varying degrees by the diverse peoples of the lake and interior

regions, nonetheless, notable economic symbioses existed both between lake fishermen and lowland agriculturists and between these agricultural groups and mountain peoples in the ranges to south and west.

East of Lake Maracaibo numerous rank societies apparently flourished along the coast and paralleling mountain ranges of northern Venezuela, each polity probably being composed of an ecologically diverse strip of land extending from mountains to sea, as was common in Panama. Marine products were abundant, and mountain agriculture included canal irrigation. Numerous fortified towns were also situated along the banks of the Yaracuy river, which facilitated travel between the coast and the irrigated Barquisimeto valley in the interior. The nearby Cojedes river extended travel routes to llanos peoples to the south. Sumptuary elite goods, including gold pieces and pearls, indicate that northern Venezuelan elite long-distance networks ultimately reached the llanos to the south, Colombia to the west, and the 'Pearl Coast' of Venezuela further east.

Spanish accounts indicate that warfare was conducted as actively as exchange in these northern reaches of Venezuela. Here, as in Colombia and lower Central America, militancy produced captives who could be exchanged for other valuables, such as salt or coca, and who were also expected to serve as labourers for the conquering community. The economic significance of this added manpower is not clear, but agricultural productivity could have been increased significantly. The data also strongly suggest, however, that warfare, like long-distance exchange, was conducted for the political benefit of war leaders and other elites as much as, or more than, for economic gain. Captives, like other valuable goods, carried political and ideological as much as economic significance. Such persons were not regarded as impersonal slaves. Indeed, captives were often incorporated into their captors' groups by marriage, and the children of these unions became fully legitimate members of society.

The richness and diversity of natural resources and the circumscribing factors inherent in rugged topography undoubtedly influenced the development of rank societies in the mountainous islands of the Greater Antilles, as they did elsewhere in the circum-Caribbean. Here, as in Panama, northern Venezuela and portions of Colombia, many chiefdoms centred on fertile mountain valleys traversed by rivers running from interior mountain heights to the sea and providing access to the

resources of the littoral, cultivable grasslands, and waterways. A few
polities seem to have been located on the upper portions of rivers in
mountainous, interior country away from direct contact with lower
savannahs and coastal reaches, but with equivalent benefits from small
yet well-watered highland basins.

The Spanish chroniclers emphasized the bountiful subsistence resources available to the islanders. River, lake and ocean fish, land birds
and water fowl, crabs, lobsters, sea turtles and manatee were all
abundant, although game, in contrast, was limited. Some of these wild
resources were husbanded; there is mention of artificial fish and turtle
enclosures and of large compounds for land birds. The islanders also
intensively cultivated the fertile river valleys and, to a lesser degree,
grassy savannahs, producing a number of food staples and useful
materials, including cotton and tobacco. Not surprisingly, given the
wealth of protein-rich fish, fowl and other aquatic animals, starchy root
crops formed the primary agricultural staples, although a range of other
foods were grown too. Plots were cleared by slash-and-burn techniques
and planted with digging sticks. Where conditions allowed, the soil was
heaped into rows of large flat-topped hills or *montones* which may have
improved and stabilized drainage. In valleys on the leeward side of
Hispaniola, however, where annual rainfall is low, ditch irrigation was
practised.

Some agricultural, fishing and hunting activities were directed by the
elite, probably to provision specific feasts and other elite-directed public
functions. At harvest the population also offered gifts of first fruits to
the chiefs. In addition, certain foods were reserved for the elite,
including iguanas and a particular type of cassava cake.[4] Most of the
sumptuary goods which identified and glorified the Antillean elite were
also produced within the islands, and it is not clear to what extent
Antillean lords were engaged in long-distance contacts. They did
exchange various prestige items among themselves in recognition of
alliances, such as marriage, and as tokens of respect and esteem. These
exchanges extended to nearby inter-island contacts, which were both
numerous and frequent.

The elite of certain polities exercised some control over local
production of specific valuables and, presumably, benefited politically

---

[4] Iguanas were symbolically associated with lordship by the ancient Maya and, probably, by
pre-Columbian Panamanians as well as the elites of the Greater Antilles. See Mary W. Helms,
'Iguanas and crocodilians in tropical American mythology and iconography with special
reference to Panama', *Journal of Latin American Lore*, 3 (1977), 51–132.

by their distribution to a wider region. For example, rich salt beds on the southern coast of Puerto Rico may have been associated with the domain of the highest chief of the island, who also lived on this particular coast because of its fishing advantages. Similarly, the domain of a leading *cacica* of western Hispaniola included the off shore island of Guahaba where women fashioned elaborately carved basins, platters, stools (*duhos*) and other items for elite use from a black wood, perhaps of the ebony family, which took a high polish.

Finely woven textiles decorated with coloured stones and small gold pieces were also used to indicate elite status. Placer gold, which existed in Hispaniola, Puerto Rico and Cuba, was hammered into thin sheets and leaves for helmets, ear and nose pieces, and other body ornaments. Since there is no evidence for casting or other complex metallurgical skills in the islands, the small amounts of tumbaga that are known from the Greater Antilles must have derived from mainland South America, presumably through a network of elite contacts. Similar associations may have provided the nephrite, jadeite, calcite and other stones made into strings of beads highly prized by elites.

Elite settlements were composed of twelve to fifteen large, conical structures each housing, probably, a kin group of several families most of whom may have been related to the chief whose large and elaborately decorated dwelling place formed the focus of the elite centre. (Commoners' house clusters were typically located near rivers or on the savannahs near fields.) In front of the chief's abode a flat or levelled plaza was generally located for public functions. Some of these plazas also served as playing courts for a team ball game called *batey*. At times *batey* games included contests between teams representing competitive and rivalrous chiefs. Formal warfare, ostensibly over such matters as trespassing on hunting or fishing rights, or a breach of marriage agreement between one lord and another lord's sister or daughter, also served as a vehicle for expressing chiefly power to elite rivals.

A successful chief was supported by a large consanguineous descent group and, through polygyny, had numerous affinal ties to other elite families. He was also a successful war leader and the proud owner of an elaborately decorated dugout canoe suitable for sea travel and capable of carrying as many as 50 men or more. A lord's expertise as war leader and canoe owner testified to his ability as an organizer and leader of men, whether into battle on land or into the hazards of ocean travel to near or distant lands. However, the sacred zöomorphic and anthropomorphic symbols (*cemis*) painted on warriors' bodies, beaten onto pieces of gold worn by elites in battle, and carved and painted on canoes and innumerable other objects, testified that these and other chiefly capabilities were thought to derive fundamentally from supernatural powers. They were therefore expressions of sacred forces as much as declarations of human rivalries and ambitions. Association with sacred esoteric powers, in turn, further legitimized the role of a chief as an anomalous being who stood between society and higher sacred realms. It is understandable, then, that in the Greater Antilles and throughout the circum-Caribbean a lord's responsibilities also included the obligation to 'travel' by means of trance to distant sacred realms above and below the earth to discourse with supernatural beings concerning the affairs of the populace under his charge and to gain prophetic insight into future events.

Evidence about the native cultures of the Lesser Antilles is primarily derived from early seventeenth-century observations on the islands of Dominica, Guadeloupe and St Christopher. This information indicates that the indigenous Callinago, or so-called Island Carib, did not achieve the complex hierarchical social and political organization characteristic of their Greater Antillean neighbours. Instead, the Callinago maintained a more tribal or egalitarian socio-political organization, although specific political and ideological elements elaborated in Greater Antillean culture are also found here, albeit in simpler form.

By virtue of their island habitats the Callinago also enjoyed access to the rich resources of the Caribbean Sea. Fish, lobsters and crabs, sea turtles and manatee were dietary staples. So were agoutis, the most important land animal. Sea products and land game were complemented by slash-and-burn root crop agriculture.

Callinago settlements were small, containing approximately 30 to 100 individuals and, typically, were located close to a freshwater river. A village was usually composed of the extended family of a leading 'man of importance' who resided virilocally with his several wives, for headmen practised polygyny and also received women captured in war. His married daughters and their children and husbands lived there, too, since men other than headmen lodged uxorilocally.[5] In physical form

---

[5] Virilocal residence refers to a pattern of marital residence in which the married couple become part of the husband's natal household or community. In uxorilocal marital residence the couple joins the natal household or community of the wife.

a village included a capacious community house set in the midst of a clearing where the headman, his sons-in-law and older boys spent their days when they were at home. Surrounding this large structure were a number of small sleeping and kitchen quarters, one for each wife and her daughters and young sons.

A village headman's position of leadership was largely expressed in the size of his family and particularly in his control over unmarried sons and resident sons-in-law, who cleared gardens, built houses and went fishing for him. Headmen were also likely to have wives in other villages, even on other islands, whom they periodically visited. Such ties presumably extended a leader's sphere of personal influence beyond his immediate community. Warfare, usually against other Antillean peoples far from home, even against groups on Trinidad or the adjacent South American mainland, was another avenue leading to political prestige for those few whose endurance and bravery on raids and wisdom as war counsellors led to their acceptance as war leaders. Men who owned and directed the large canoes in which the long journeys to opponents' islands were made also held positions of honour and influence.

Successful warfare, in the form of surprise raids, netted prestige for victorious warriors and valuable long-distance booty including captive women who were delivered by the young warriors to their fathers and grandfathers to serve as wives. The children of these women became fully legitimate community members, and it is likely that acquisition of captive women and control over their children assisted a village headman to develop his political base of sons and sons-in-law.

The three routes to political influence in Callinago society – direction of a large family with many sons-in-law, war leadership and canoe ownership – were considered separate activities and could be held by different men whose influence was restricted to those specific situations requiring their particular expertise. It may be assumed, however, that the most successful Callinago leaders, including those few who were accorded wider regional recognition,[6] were men who were able to achieve several of these positions. It is noteworthy that in the Greater Antilles the more developed role of chief combined all three of these leadership factors into a single position.

Successful Callinago leaders, like Greater Antillean chiefs, gave

[6] See Douglas Taylor, 'Kinship and social structure of the Island Carib', *Southwestern Journal of Anthropology*, 2 (1946), 181.

material evidence of their status through adornment with valued ornaments, although sumptuary goods were used on a smaller scale than was common in the large islands. The most valued and prestigious items derived from the distant localities where warriors ventured. Foremost among these were the crescent-shaped golden chest plates, or *caracoli*, worn by leaders and their sons and acquired by exchange and raid from the north-eastern South American mainland.

The travels of the Callinago led them to the general region of Cumaná, the Gulf of Paria and the Orinoco delta, where contacts could be made with mainland peoples of north-eastern Venezuela, the eastern llanos and the lower Orinoco, as well as with groups from the Guianas further south. The populace of the north-east coast and adjacent Macizo Oriental, sustained by abundant fish and productive agriculture, were again organized into rank societies, although the polities toward the Gulf of Paria appear to have been smaller and organized in a less complex way than those further west. The contrast is exemplified by comparing the annually elected war chiefs of the Paria area with the regional lord of the Unare valley, Guaramental, who maintained a large, well-fortified elite centre with streets and plazas, storehouses for food and weapons and dwelling compounds for his many wives and sons and their retainers.

The low, open Unare river valley joins the interior llanos or savannahs of eastern Venezuela to the Caribbean coast and the mountain ranges running parallel to it to west and east. Undoubtedly the prestige and power of the dominant lord of this valley reflected his strategic position on an important travel and exchange route. Evidence from north-eastern Venezuela in general, indicates that a number of regional products, including fish, coca-lime paste, salt from the Araya peninsula and pearls from the waters around Cumaná, Cubagua and Isla de Margarita, were exchanged with peoples of more distant areas who offered in return maize, slaves and small pieces of worked gold said to derive from a coastal country six days travel to the west.

Among those contacting the north-eastern exchange centres were Carib from the eastern llanos lying between the coastal Macizo Oriental and the lower Orinoco river. Here again, as among the Callinago or Island Carib of the Lesser Antilles, political leadership was based on prowess in warfare and on control of groups of kinsmen and war captives. The women conducted subsistence agriculture along streams and rivers, while the men hunted deer in the grassy *mesas* between river valleys and travelled widely to the Antilles, along the coasts of Guiana and Venezuela and along the Orinoco river system in order to raid and trade. Raiding and trading provided the Carib with a variety of useful resources including numerous war captives who, if men, were either ritually sacrificed or incorporated into Carib communities as sons-in-law, or, if women, were employed either in agriculture or as labourers on the long-distance excursions undertaken by Carib men.

The famed trading and raiding activities of the eastern llanos Carib were part of much larger and very complex networks of regional symbiosis and long-distance contacts which extended the length of the Orinoco river system. These associations involved the numerous sedentary populations of gallery forest and riverine floodplain agriculturists, the specialized river-fishing peoples resident along tributaries and the nomadic hunter-gatherers of the extensive interfluvial grasslands of the Venezuelan and eastern Colombian llanos lying north and west of the Orinoco. Distinctive bands of hunter-gatherers and particular communities of riverine agriculturists were linked in long-standing symbiotic relationships which provided agricultural resources for the hunter-gatherers and various palm products, wild fruits and meat for the horticulturists. These exchanges were effected at the agriculturists' villages through an elaborate system of somewhat strained hospitality frequently augmented by quick garden raids by the hunter-gatherers. Fishing communities entered this system by exchanging dried fish for agricultural produce. Such fish were particularly important for non-fishing groups during the rainy season when other foods were scarce.

Fishing groups also controlled dry season fishing camps at selected beaches and islands on the middle and upper Orinoco and its major tributaries where immense numbers of *arrau* turtles congregated annually to lay eggs. At such times thousands of other natives, both agriculturists and foragers, also travelled from near and far to the turtle beaches to collect turtle eggs and oil and to hunt the various forest animals which also came to the beaches to prey on the turtles. These immense gatherings of fishermen, horticulturists and hunters served also as large trade fairs, for a wide range of products from all sections of the Orinoco system and the llanos were exchanged on these occasions. The extensive bartering was facilitated by far-flung kin ties, which united specific families from various regions, by group specialization in craft and resource production, by widely used trade languages known throughout the Orinoco system, by attention to norms of reciprocity such that he who received an exchange gift reciprocated with an object of slightly higher value, and by strings of snail shell discs called *quiripa* which served as 'primitive money'. Highly valued lengths of *quiripa* were also worn as adornments indicating personal wealth and status.

Dry-season, turtle-beach exchange fairs on the middle and upper Orinoco attracted Carib from the lower Orinoco and the eastern llanos, peoples from the Guiana highlands and representatives from north-western Amazonia. Similar dry-season, fish-camp exchange centres on rivers of the northern and western edges of the llanos at places where grasslands met the northern Venezuelan ranges and the Colombian Cordillera Oriental linked llanos groups to these highland regions, too. In this manner turtle products, raw cotton or cotton thread, feathers, body paint, resins and oils, and *quiripa* moved from the llanos to the mountains, while salt, gold and cotton textiles moved into the llanos from the adjacent Andean territories. By means of llanos exchange networks Andean products then moved throughout the length and breadth of northern South America. Indeed, the central location of the Orinoco river system and adjacent llanos was instrumental in connecting peoples and resources from all the adjoining circum-Caribbean lands.

It is worth noting that llanos and Orinoco groups acted largely as intermediaries in this inter-regional exchange, for, of the diverse goods which passed along the llanos and Orinoco networks, only the shell money and, perhaps, the turtle products were exclusively produced by llanos and Orinoco peoples.[7] It is also significant that the goods received in the llanos from outside were not generally crucial to subsistence but were luxury items, such as elaborate textiles, finely woven hammocks and golden ornaments. Receipt of such 'political' materials suggests that activity within the exchange network conferred political benefits. Certainly the most complex llanos settlements and, probably, the most complex political organizations were located in restricted zones along the major Orinoco tributaries and along the lower slopes of the cordilleras to north and west, strategically placed for the northern South American spheres of interaction. Nevertheless, there is no clear evidence that rank societies existed in the llanos region. According to the

---

[7] Robert V. Morey and Nancy C. Morey, *Relaciones comerciales en el pasado en los llanos de Colombia y Venezuela* (Caracas, 1975), 29–30.

ethnohistoric data, much of which, however, post-dates initial contact by several centuries, most village societies were directed by community headmen alone, although control of numerous wives and captive women and displays of *quiripa* could testify to the high personal prestige and community status of individual leaders.

3

ANDEAN SOCIETIES BEFORE 1532*

When the Andean region was invaded by Pizarro's troops in 1532, 40 years had passed since the fall of both Granada and the first of the Caribbean islands to the Castilians and more than twenty years since the invasion of Mesoamerica. An entire generation of Europeans – almost two – were knowledgeable in the ways of 'heathens' and 'Indians'. The children they had fathered in the New World were now grown; they spoke the languages of their mothers. Fathers and sons heard tales of other, even more remote, places with richer peoples, south of Panama. Rumours of societies in the Andes were commonplace among the settlers on the Isthmus, some think even in Brazil. One Portuguese, Aleixo Garcia, heard enough to encourage him to join a Chiriguano raid against the highlands; marching in from the south-east, they attacked Inka[1] installations at least five years before Pizarro invaded from the north. Long after the Pizarro clan had enforced their claim to the Andes, other pretenders insisted that they had been first to hear of these kingdoms.

It is from such tales and the later accounts of eyewitnesses that our knowledge of the Andean civilizations in 1532 is primarily drawn. It is very incomplete knowledge; even the scholarly community is not

---

* The author and the editor wish to acknowledge the help of Ms Olivia Harris, Goldsmiths' College, London, in the final preparation of this chapter.

[1] Some ten million people speak Quechua and Aymara today. In 1956, the Congreso Indigenista Internacional, meeting in La Paz, decided on a standard orthography for the writing of these languages, and this spelling is used here. Since there are at least six phonemes all of which have been written with the Spanish *c*, the Congress urged that each of the six be carefully separated. Thus we write Inka, not Inca, *khipu*, not quipo. Ch, P and T can all lead to confusion since in Andean languages each can be glottalized, aspirated or plain, each with phonemic value. Thus, *mit'a*, to avoid confusion with similar words that lack glottalization. In 1975, the Peruvian government declared Quechua to be an official language of the country, to be used in schools, courts and other public places. Grammars and dictionaries using the correct or similar orthographies are widely available.

always aware how fragmentary the record remains. Archaeology could help but for the marginal position still held by archaeologists in the Andean republics (in sharp contrast to Mexico). Millions may have read Pablo Neruda's ode to Machu Picchu and millions more have visited the monument, but no one knows which segment of Inka society inhabited the site. This does not inhibit successive waves of architects from 'restoring' the settlement but few, if any, archaeologists earn a living working on the actual site embedded deep in the almost vertical landscape, or on the building techniques which distinguish Machu Picchu from other Andean urban centres.

Paradoxically, much earlier periods, some dating thousands of years before the Inka, seem more accessible and have been studied minutely for their ceramic detail; and the decorative aspects of other crafts, especially weaving – the major art of the Andes – have all been catalogued, photographed, preserved. But the closer we come to 1532, when the Andean state was brought down and splintered into hundreds of component ethnic groups, the less we are likely to learn from archaeology as it is practised today, and the more we have to depend on the written accounts left by those who 'were there'.

In some ways these accounts are remarkable: within two years of the disaster at Cajamarca where King Atawallpa was captured, two reports describing these events were published at Seville, at a time when transatlantic communications were slow and the printing of books dangerous. One of them was the official account of Pizarro's first scribe, Francisco de Xerez, who was at pains to establish that his was the 'true relation' (*Verdadera relacion de la conquista del Peru* [1534]) since another eyewitness had beaten him to it. Even earlier, at an annual fair held at Lyons, hawkers had peddled printed broadsheets describing Atawallpa's ransom to traders from the Rhine and the Piemonte.

Scholars tend to complain about the shortcomings of these accounts; each specialist has lists of major questions that remain unanswered. Although folk dances re-enact even today the meeting of Inka and European soldiers, no dynastic oral tradition can be recovered 450 years after the events. Some early accounts by foreigners have long been common knowledge, but there are not many. The nineteenth century was the great period of unearthing and publishing these early descriptions; even before most of them had been printed, W. H. Prescott had had access to them. It is remarkable how undated his *Conquest of Peru* (1847) reads today, more than 130 years after it was published. This is due less to Prescott's understanding of pre-Columbian civilizations than to the limited amount of time contemporary historians invest in looking for new sources, plus the superficiality of Inka archaeology referred to above.

The one important scholar in this field was Marcos Jiménez de la Espada, who was most active a hundred years ago while earning his living as a curator of amphibians at Madrid's Museum of Natural History. As a sideline he published the sources Prescott had used in manuscript form and others the New Englander had never seen. By 1908 when Pietschmann found something truly unprecedented at Copenhagen, a 1,200-page 'letter' to the king of Spain, written and illustrated around 1615 by an Andean 'Indian', the urgency Jiménez had felt about publishing primary sources was spent; it took 28 more years before Waman Puma's grievances (*Nueva Coronica y Buen Gobierno*) saw print. Since then occasional new texts have been located, most of them by Hermann Trimborn of Bonn, but it is notable how similarly Prescott reads to Cunow (1896), Baudin (1928), Rowe (1946), Murra (1955), or, most recently, Hemming (1970). All of them used pretty much the same sources, and if they differ it is in matters of interpretation and ideology.

In the last thirty years some of the mystery has been removed, particularly where the Inka state is concerned. Some progress has been made in understanding the articulation of local ethnic groups to the Inka, through the study of litigation, or demographic and tax records compiled in the early decades of European rule. Still, it is a fact that John H. Rowe's survey of the polities of the Central Andes, 'Inca culture at the time of the Spanish conquest', published almost 40 years ago (1946) in the *Handbook of South American Indians*, is still a fair statement of our ethnographic knowledge. Fathoming the daily life in, and the organization of, Andean states remains a long-term job to be seriously undertaken when archaeologists and ethnologists learn to work together, and when the five republics which are heir to the Andean tradition – Bolivia, Peru, Ecuador, Chile, Argentina – decide that heritage is truly theirs.

In the meantime, we note that the earliest sixteenth-century observers reached certain conclusions which have been confirmed by modern scholarship.

First, the landscape was like nothing they had ever seen or heard about before, though some had been soldiers who had fought in Italy,

Mexico, Guatemala, Flanders or North Africa. In the Andes the mountains were higher, the nights colder and the days hotter, the valleys deeper, the deserts drier, the distances longer than words could describe.

Secondly, the country was rich and not only in terms of what could be carried away. There was wealth in the numbers of people and their skills, the technological wonders observable in construction, metallurgy, road building, irrigation or textiles ('after the Christians took all they wanted, it still looked as if nothing had been touched').[2]

Thirdly, the realm had been brought under a prince's control only recently, some three or four generations before 1532. And from the earliest days after the Spanish success at Cajamarca, thoughtful people wondered how this authority, ruling so many people separated by their particular geography, had collapsed so easily.

While basically true, each of these conclusions can stand restatement. Although located entirely within the tropics, Andean geography has few if any analogues for man in other latitudes. For example, the regions having the densest population are also extremely high. In 1532 (as in fact today) there were more people on the high plateau around Lake Titicaca than anywhere else. This distresses not only international planners; even local economists frequently reveal their exasperation. They see a very large, poverty-stricken population, trying to scratch a living under what to the urban outsider look like the most unpromising circumstances. Why would so numerous an agricultural population insist on cultivating where 300 nights of frost or more can be expected in any given year?

A major step in the scientific understanding of Andean geography came in the late twenties when the German scholar, Carl Troll, did fieldwork in Bolivia. In 1931 he published what is still the single most influential discussion of the many and diverse 'pockets' in the landscape created by the close proximity to each other of high mountains, coastal deserts and wet Amazonian lowlands.[3] He noted that traditional rainfall and temperature charts were inadequate and misleading when compiled for this area. To record Andean extremes within any given 24-hour period, Troll invented new graphics. Early on, he discovered that

---

[2] Francisco de Xerez, *Verdadera relacion de la conquista del Peru* [1534] (Madrid, 1947), 334.

[3] Carl Troll, 'Die geographische Grundlagen der Andinen Kulturen und des Inkareichs', in *Ibero-Americanisches Archiv*, v (Berlin, 1931). See also *idem, The Geo-ecology of the mountainous regions of the tropical Americas* (Bonn, 1968).

scientific terminology developed elsewhere did not describe local climates; he borrowed much of his vocabulary from Andean ethno-geographical practice. Obviously one can shoehorn the Andean *puna* into a box marked 'steppe' or 'savannah', but this implies a serious loss of specificity. These tropical but cold and high grasslands have long been cultivated, maybe even at a time before all the trees had been cut; for millenia, most Andean peoples have lived here. Not only the Inka but earlier state structures (Tiwanaku, Wari) emerged in the puna; Troll took this to be a significant indicator of the potentialities most contemporary observers do not grasp.

Andean agriculture has only recently begun to attract the attention of agronomists. The easy adaptation by the peasantry of European and African cultigens – barley, sugar cane, the grape, bananas – has masked their attachment to hardy, locally domesticated crops, minutely adapted to Andean conditions. No one knows how many scores of such cultigens were grown in 1532; many have since been lost and others linger on, suffering from low status despite their proven nutritional values. As one studies the many tubers (of which the potato is only the most celebrated) or the *tarwi* (a lupine rich in fats) or the *kinuwa* (a high altitude grain, heavy with proteins) or the thirst-quenching coca leaf, one becomes aware how aboriginal, how pristine, was the Andean agricultural complex. Some of the crops (maize, sweet potatoes) were to be found throughout the continent, but in the south none were staples, although some were highly valued exotics.

However, in Andean circumstances it was not enough to have perfected local adaptation. There is too little land of any one kind. Good pastures can be far apart. Even if one compared the products of two or three neighbouring tiers, one could not provide the bases for a large population or for state formation. If the Andean peoples wanted to avoid famine, to fill their own granaries and those of their lords and gods, the abrupt changes in geographic conditions had to be faced, not only as handicaps or limitations but as potential advantages. This was achieved in the Andes even by small, quite early, human groups who in the course of a single year would fish, gather and garden on several tiers. As their population grew, they began husbanding resources further and further away – down on the dry coast if they lived in the western cordillera, or in the forest of the Andean slopes if their home base was in the eastern chain.

In Andean agriculture, adaptation confronted another handicap: the sudden changes in temperature from the glacial nights to the tropical days. On the *altiplano*, the most densely populated region, differences of 30°C and even more within a single 24-hour period are frequently recorded. This apparent handicap was also transformed into an adaptational advantage: at a still unknown date in Andean history, all vegetable tissue, but particularly the literally thousands of varieties of tubers, and all wild and domesticated flesh began to be processed: frozen at night and dried out in the tropical sun the next day. The freeze-dried tissues were many, but two names have lasted in more general use: *ch'uñu* and *ch'arki*. Most of them were not only light to transport but would also keep indefinitely under puna conditions.

Within such adaptations and transformations of the environment, the size of Andean polities varied from a few hundred households to as many as 25,000 or 30,000, with total populations reaching maybe 150,000; when pooled by a state like Tawantinsuyu of the Inka, the numbers could rise to five million or more.[4] Increases in the scale of the polity led to changes in the location and functions of the dispersed settlements. In the valley of the Huallaga, in what is today central Peru, the early European inspections identified several ethnic groups, the largest of which, the Chupaychu, claimed 4,000 households in the Inka system of decimal accounting. Others in that valley reported as few as 400 'fires'. Independent of size, in 1549, each group reported possessing coca leaf gardens three to four days' walk away, down from the main settlement:

asked if the Indians in the coca fields were natives of the area, [the local lord of the Queros] said that there were three Indians in the coca of Pichomachay – one of them from Pecta, another from Atcor and a third from Guacor and that they had been there since Inka times; and when one of their wives dies or they themselves die, they are replaced by others and in the coca of Chinchao they had two other Indians, one from Rondo and another from Chumichu.

This 1549 testimony was recorded only seven years after the local resistance to the invasion had been broken. The coca leaf of Chinchao is mentioned again:

on that same day we inspected...at Chinchao 33 Indians who are in charge of the coca leaf; they come here from all the settlements of the Chupaychu and twenty of them had [already] been enumerated in the very villages they were natives of.

[4] On the population of Peru in 1532, recent estimates of which have ranged from 2 to 9 million, see Note on the native American population on the eve of the European invasions *CHLA* 1.

From this testimony, unusual in Andean historiography in its thoroughness and early date, we see that colonists were sent from every highland settlement; they remained in the lowlands for the life of the couple – since a single or widowed person was not enumerated by the Andean census; although physically absent from their native area, they continued to be knotted onto its *khipu* records. In similar outliers, two to four days' walk away, other colonists herded camelids, dug for salt, cut timber or raised hot peppers and cotton. In the Huallaga valley, both the coca leaf and the salt were shared by people from outside the immediate neighbourhood: some of the salt miners were resettled six and eight days away from 'home'.

The main settlements in this area were located just below the 3,000 metre line, at a *tinku*, the meeting place of two ecological zones, where both tuber and maize lands can be reached easily, within less than a day's walk, above and below the village.[5]

Elsewhere geographic conditions made this easy access to maize impossible: where nuclear settlements rose to 3,500, even 3,800 metres – closer to the camelid herds – one could no longer work the maize field and return the same day. On the populated altiplano of Lake Titicaca,[6] maize as a ceremonial and hospitality grain was still indispensible but was now grown on plots several days away from home by permanent settlers, on the model outlined above for the coca leaf cultivators. The larger size of the polity made it possible to send out larger colonies and to settle them many more days' walk away. The Aymara kingdom of the Lupaqa had sent out swarms as far as the desert coast, ten, sometimes even fifteen days from the nucleus. Thierry Saignes has recently studied the access of all circum-Titicaca polities to lowland 'islands' east of the lake; there timber, coca leaf and honey, as well as maize, could be minded directly by one's own kin or subjects.[7]

Such complementary access to many and dispersed ecological[8] tiers has been termed the 'archipelago' pattern in Andean settlement. While

[5] Iñigo Ortiz de Zúñiga, *Visita de la Provincia de León de Huánuco* [1562] 1 (Huánuco, Perú, 1967), 44; *ibid.*, 303–4.

[6] Garci Diez de San Miguel, *Visita hecha a la Provincia de Chucuito* [1567] (Lima, 1964), 109.

[7] Thierry Saignes, 'De la filiation à la résidence: les ethnies dans les vallées de Larecaja', *AESC*, 33/5–6 (1978), 1160–81. This is a special issue of the *Annales* on the historical anthropology of the Andes, edited by John V. Murra and Nathan Wachtel.

[8] John V. Murra, 'El control vertical de un máximo de pisos ecológicos en la economía de las sociedades andinas' in J. V. Murra (ed.), *Formaciones económicas y políticas del mundo andino* (Lima, 1975).

in most places its reach has been eroded in colonial and more recent times, some highland populations still practise 'double domicile'.[9]

Archaeology asserts that this pattern is old, but few excavations have tested its age. Some have claimed that such multiple and simultaneous access to many micro-climates by a single polity could not occur until the peace-making umbrella of a state protected the annual caravans linking peripheral settlements with the power nucleus. States probably did favour this arrangement, imposing their authority on competing ethnic groups. But even in the centuries when no major political centre could claim hegemony, during periods archaeologists call Early or Late Intermediary, complementary access to a wide range of ecological niches was too important to be dropped from the economic repertoire of Andean local lords.

Independent of origin, one can state that increase in the scale of the polity had consequences in the complexity of arrangements at the peripheries. We saw above, in the case of the salt-miners, that their settlement was multi-ethnic; this feature became more common as polities grew. Simultaneous occupancy of a peripheral 'island' by colonists from several polities must have led to friction, squabbles, even temporary hegemonies of one contender over the other. But the evidence suggests that the drive for access to exotic products was so strong that periods of strife were followed by years in which access was shared, no matter how tense the truce.

How the colonists-for-life were selected, and how their loyalty to the group who sent them was maintained, have been subjects of inquiry. When the distance from the nucleus is short, the colonist, known in Quechua as a *mitmaq*, could readily maintain his ties at home. But when the distance grew to eight, ten days away or even more, institutional devices emerged to guarantee not only the colonists' access to products but also to sociability, marriage partners for their offspring and to ceremonial participation at the nucleus. European church records from the sixteenth century indicate that caravans moved freely from one tier to another; spouses are listed as coming from very far away.[10]

Craft specialization became implicit in the very pattern of dispersed settlement. The mitmaq in the wooded areas were also responsible for

---

[9] Olivia Harris, 'Kinship and the vertical economy', in International Congress of Americanists, *Actes* (Paris, 1978), IV, 165–77.

[10] Freda Yancy Wolf, personal communication, based on a study of church records at Juli, in the province of Chucuito.

wooden goblets and plates; the people at the beach might dry fish and edible algae, but they also gathered guano. In return, the caravan from the highlands would periodically deliver tubers, the main staple, but also meat, wool and other items, including maize from the middle levels. At some, still undetermined point in Andean history, the dispersed settlement pattern underwent qualitative change when it was extended to include artisan settlements which were not tied to the ecological relationship. In addition to the peripheral 'islands' listed above, the Lupaqa also reported a village of potters and another of metallurgists. Each lineage from the seven provinces kept a representative in the specialized villages, several hundred artisans in all.

Dispersed settlement patterns were a feature of Andean territoriality which Europeans noticed early. In 1538–9, five years after the invasion, the *encomiendas* awarded by Pizarro followed this principle. The bene-ficiary received not land but the persons of the two local lords plus all their subjects however *salpicados* ('sprinkled') across the landscape they might be. Thus, Lope de Mendieta, an early associate of the Pizarros, received whatever *estancias* of camelids, agricultural villages or fishing hamlets had owed allegiance to Chuki Champi and Maman Willka, lords of the Karanqa.[11] Their non-contiguous territories reached from well above 4,000 metres to sea level and were located in what are today Bolivia, Chile and Peru.

The same pattern was followed when an ethnic group had to be reserved for Charles V: the Lupaqa, near Lake Titicaca, were known as 'los yndios del Emperador'. In the 1550s the crown's attorney appealed to the viceroy against the grant of some of the Lupaqa's coastal outliers to private parties. He argued that:

when these private encomiendas were awarded...the [post-Pizarro] governors did not understand the order which ruled the Indians' life. When the marquis of Cañete governed these kingdoms the matter was taken up and it was established that the information which I provided was true...it was ordered that the Indians and the lands which the province of Chucuito [as the Europeans called the Lupaqa] had at the coast since Inka times had to be returned.[12]

The information provided by such European sources is better at documenting the patterns of 'vertical complementarity' at the ethnic

---

[11] Unpublished manuscript, Legajo 658 in Justicia section, Archivo General de Indias, Seville.
[12] Juan Polo de Ondegardo, 'Informe...a licenciado Briviesca de Muñatones [1561]', *Revista Histórica* (Lima), 13 (1940), 18.

level, since that was the reality they tolerated and dealt with in the early decades of the colonial regime. The macro-adaptation of this age-old Andean pattern by the Inka state (over thousands of miles, with millions of inhabitants, in what are today five Andean republics) crumbled so soon after 1532 that it is extremely difficult to reconstruct today.

However, this maximal dimension is important for an understanding of the changes which the pattern suffered when the polity in control went beyond a scale of some 20,000 households. At first, the state followed the prevailing Andean norms: its revenues were raised on acreage alienated from the local polities on the 'archipelago' model. These state lands were worked lineage by lineage, on rotation, by the local people, much as they had worked the fields of their ethnic lords or of the regional shrine. Eventually, state mitmaq were transplanted to the new territories to ensure Inka rule and revenues. But such rule was still 'indirect': it was exercised through the 'natural', pre-Inka lords. There was no tribute: no one owed anything raised on their own fields or stored in their own larders.

In the last decades before 1532 the scale of Inka administration grew to such an extent that the distance separating the nucleus from the outliers had no precedent. A ten, fifteen days' walk to their birthplace might be undertaken almost every year if the mitmaq wanted to reassert a claim at the centre, to worship at the main sanctuary, or just to visit their kinfolk. When moved during late Inka rule, the colonists could find themselves 60, even 80 days' walk away. Even if they continued to be enumerated with their original ethnic group, one wonders what substance was left in such affiliation.

There is no doubt that this attempt to claim Andean precedent was made: Don Pedro Kutimpu, a well-informed Lupaqa lord who had been a young adult in 1532, clarifies this attempt while explaining the discrepancies between the population khipu in his possession since before the invasion and the head count made by the colonial administrations:

when this province was inspected by the Inka many colonists were enumerated together with the other natives of this province... The colonists may have been in many other, faraway places...some in Chile and some in Quito...and together, all of them were the 20,000 Indians mentioned in the quipo. But now [1567] these colonists have been granted in encomienda at their distinct residences and have no longer been counted with those of this province...[13]

[13] Diez de San Miguel, *La Provincia de Chucuito*, 170.

How long could such residual affiliation and rights be effectively exercised in the original ethnic group? Transfers to Chile or Quito from Lake Titicaca seem a heavy burden, no matter how much precedent was claimed for it. Hints of an answer come from the frequency of rebellions against the Inka[14] and the ready siding of many local polities with the Europeans after 1532. But no statement of grievance on this account has reached us through the eyewitnesses of the invasion.

What can be asserted here is that the Inka state continued Andean complementary settlements, even if the new scale involved hardships. New functions were also assigned to the mitmaq: much as the Lupaqa had specialized artisan villages, the state ran a manufacturing installation near Huancané, on the north-eastern shore of Lake Titicaca.[15] It brought together 'one thousand' weavers and 'one hundred' potters. While the actual numbers need not be taken literally, the proportions of these state operations should not be doubted; being the major Andean art form, cloth also had many political, ritual and military uses which required its weaving for the state on what were truly industrial dimensions by sixteenth-century European standards. Full-time weaving occupied scores of 'chosen' women separated from their ethnic group and located at every state administrative centre, where soldiers expected rewards in cloth as they marched towards the frontier. What is new about the workshops at Huancané is that the weavers form domestic units; nor can we tell if this manufacturing centre was unique or a regular feature of Inka productivity that had remained unreported.

Another new, state-level, use of mitmaq was for military purposes. There is no evidence of full time, far-away garrisons in pre-Inka times, but in the decades before 1532 the constant expansion and the consequent rebellions required that the frontiers be manned on a full time basis:

he said that his ancestors were placed in this land [the Huallaga valley] to guard the fortress of Colpagua which is towards the eastern woodlands and the fortresses were three, one called Colpagua, the other Cacapayza, and one Cachaypagua and another [sic] Angar and the said colonists and the forbears of the speaker were taken out of the valleys near Cuzco and stationed in the said forts, 30 married men in each. And those who guarded the fortresses had

[14] John V. Murra, 'La Guerre et les rébellions dans l'expansion de l'état inka', *AESC*, 33/5–6 (1978), 927–35.

[15] John V. Murra, 'Los olleros del inka: hacia una historia y arqueología del Qollasuyu', in *Historia, problema y promesa, homenaje a Jorge Basadre*, 1 (Lima, 1978), 415–23.

no planted fields since they could not cultivate there so they received this town [Guarapa] where others of their group planted and supplied those guarding.[16]

Other late uses of mitmaq for non-agricultural purposes can probably be identified, but the artisan and military extentions of the archipelago strategy are sufficient evidence that what began as a means of complementing productive access to a variety of ecological tiers had become an onerous means of political control.

Tawantinsuyu, the Inka state, was not the earliest multi-ethnic polity to emerge in the Andes. In recent decades, archaeologists have distinguished several 'horizons' (periods when central authorities were able to control both highland and coastal polities), from 'intermediate' eras, when ethnic separatism flourished.

The Early Horizon, also known as the Formative in the Andes, centred on Chavin, a temple at 3,135 metres altitude in the eastern highlands; best known for its religious art, it was thought by Julio C. Tello, the dean of Andean archaeologists, to have been 'the womb of Andean civilization'. It reached its peak of influence some 3,000 years ago, 1000–300 B.C., when it affected other highland settlements and modified coastal art forms; it is uncertain if such influences imply domination. Donald Lathrap has recently stressed and documented the Amazonic roots of the art, first postulated by Tello. Through the tropical lowlands Chavin may have reached for much earlier sources of inspiration in Mesoamerica.[17]

No agreement exists among archaeologists about how such 'horizons' emerged and eventually disintegrated in the Andes. Some have suggested that the active ingredient was 'trade', enforced by military controls which usually stemmed from the highlands; others have detected religious zeal behind the expansion.

The Middle Horizon is dated from before A.D. 500 to about A.D. 1,000 and was centred on at least two places: Tiwanaku, near Lake Titicaca in Bolivia, and Wari, near the modern city of Ayacucho in Peru. Both were true urban settlements, thought to have been nuclei of large and

---

[16] Ortiz de Zúñiga, *La Provincia de León*, II, 197.

[17] See Julio C. Tello, *Chavín, cultura matriz de la civilización andina*, ed. Toribio Majía Xesspe (Lima, 1960); John H. Rowe, 'Form and meaning in Chavín art', in John H. Rowe and Dorothy Menzel (eds.), *Peruvian archaeology* (Palo Alto, Calif., 1967); Donald W. Lathrap, 'Our father the cayman, our mother the gourd: Spinden revisited', in C. A. Reed (ed.), *Origins of agriculture* (The Hague, 1977), 713–51; Thomas C. Patterson, 'Chavín: an interpretation of its spread and influence', in E. P. Benson (ed.), *Dumbarton Oaks Conference on Chavín* (Washington, D.C., 1971), 29–48.

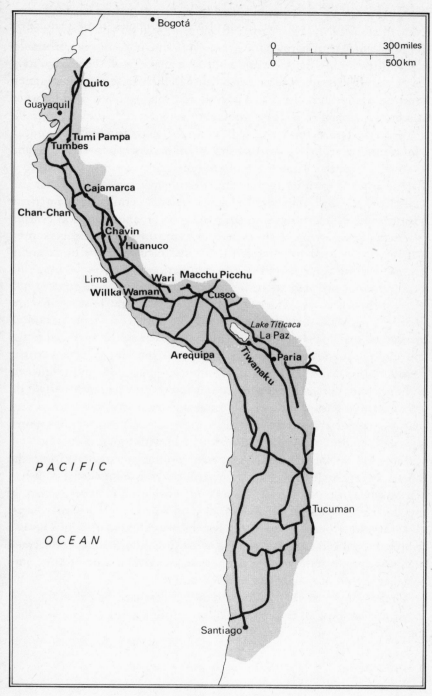

The extent of the Inka empire

Source: John Hyslop, *Inka road system: survey and general analysis* (Academic Press, 1984).

wide-ranging states. There is evidence of contemporaneity and even contact between the two; earlier in this century it was usual to consider both as a single polity whose capital was in the southern highlands. Recent research suggests that while Tiwanaku and Wari may have exercised their hegemony at the same time, their spheres of interaction were separate. Some have even suggested that a buffer zone between the two stretched from the snowline to the ocean.[18] In his *Peoples and Cultures of Ancient Peru* (1974), L. G. Lumbreras, the leading Andean archaeologist, argued that urbanism and militarism began with Wari and gradually affected all the Central Andean societies.

The impetus for inter-regional integration may have come systematically from the highlands, but the desert, coastal peoples frequently had centuries in which to develop their own, ocean and irrigation-centred potential. Most of the early archaeology on the coast, undertaken by foreigners, focused its interest on the spectacular adobe-brick architecture, or the ceramic and textile productions, samples of which fill museums and private collections the world over. In their guide to the Andean hoard at the American Museum of Natural History in New York, Wendell C. Bennett and Junius B. Bird refer to 'a period of master craftsmen'. Recent archaeology has attempted to provide the chronological and social organizational underpinning for such artistic manifestations. In the long run, the highlanders could, and frequently did, interrupt coastal florescence by cutting and diverting the irrigation canals bringing the waters of the Andean glaciers to desert plantations, but it is remarkable how many times local coastal groups could return to earlier traditions once the 'horizon' had withdrawn.

Similarly, in the highlands, the many polities incorporated into the Inka state maintained ethnic distinctiveness and self-awareness. While Tawantinsuyu expansion had been rapid, it achieved such despatch only by absorbing whole political entities, not separate villages or valleys. The local lords were fitted into a system of 'indirect rule'; it was they who enforced and administered the new order, which may have seemed less novel since its ideology claimed no more than a projection onto a wider screen of patterns of existing authority.

Oral tradition in the Andes agrees with archaeology that the Late Intermediate period, the centuries just before the Inka expansion, had been *awqa runa* (soldier times):

---

[18] Elias Mujica, personal communication (1980).

the towns were depopulated...fearing war, they had to leave the good places mentioned...They were forced to move from their towns to the higher places and now lived on peaks and precipices of the high mountains. To defend themselves, they had to build fortresses...ramparts and walls; the houses and hidden places were inside....

They fought and there was death...they took captives, even women and children. They took each other's lands and irrigation ditches and pastures... even the stones they had used for grinding.[19]

In the Late Intermediate Period each region produced identifiably distinct artefacts, free of pan-Andean manifestations like the earlier Tiwanaku or Wari. Research in the Lake Titicaca region has confirmed the archaeological presence in late pre-Inka times of 'houses and hidden places' inside heavy ramparts surrounding twenty hectares or more, at altitudes above 4,000 metres.[20] When conquered by the Inka, the population we know as the Lupaqa were moved or deported 'down' to 3,800 metres, on the lake's shore. The walls were no longer needed after *pax Incaica*; now the royal highway passed through the seven Lupaqa 'provincial capitals', some of which became Inka administrative centres. Some occupied up to 40 hectares of urban space and can all still be distinguished today. According to the khipu in the possession of Pedro Kutimpu, this Aymara-speaking group had comprised 20,000 households before 1532. The testimony of their two lords was recorded in 1567 by an inspector sent from Lima to verify a rumour that these 'emperor's yndians' were extremely wealthy. The inspector reported that they were, indeed, rich: in pre-European times they had controlled hundreds of thousands of camelids; even after 35 years of looting one Lupaqa admitted he still owned 1,700 head.[21]

The two testifying lords ruled Chucuito, one of the seven 'provinces'; they were also lords or kings of all the Lupaqa.[22] Each of the other six had its own two leaders, one each for the upper and lower moieties. Dual division was an almost universal feature of Andean social organization; there is no reason to attribute this to Inka influence.

Kin ties were the organizing principle inside the fourteen subdivisions. Each moiety reported some ten to fifteen *hatha*, sometimes translated as lineages. Since the European notaries and scribes preferred

[19] Felipe Guaman Poma de Ayala, *Nueva coronica y buen gobierno* [1615] (México, 1980), 63–4.
[20] John Hyslop, 'El área lupaca bajo el dominio incaico: un reconocimiento arqueológico', *Histórica* (Lima), 3/1 (1979), 53–80.
[21] Diez de San Miguel, *La Provincia de Chucuito*, 303–63.
[22] John V. Murra, 'An Aymara kingdom in 1567', *Ethnohistory*, 15/2 (1968), 115–51.

the Quechua terminology of Cusco, these were recorded usually as *ayllu*. The debate over the nature and functions of this social unit has a long history in Andean studies, much as the *calpulli* has in Meso-america. Each Lupaqa hatha was a named unit; it could hold land and herds but so did the kingdom as a whole, each moiety and each of the seven polities. Each had its own authorities; each included households from both the dominant Aymara population and from the oppressed Uru fishermen; we cannot tell in practice how successful this ideo-logical effort was in joining people from separate classes into a single kin group.[23]

There is no information about Lupaqa shrines since the inspection was undertaken so soon after the conversion of the Lupaqa lords to Christianity. They were warned not to worship the snow-covered mountain tops; pilgrimages to the monuments erected back in the walled-in, pre-Inka towns were prohibited. In 1567 there was still a minority of wealthy herders who remained unbaptized; some of the Aymara shamans and priests are reported to have been kept spinning in a lakeside concentration camp but were ordered to be freed by the second bishop of Charcas, Fray Domingo de Santo Tomas. Author of the first dictionary and grammar of Quechua, the bishop sat on the Royal Council of the Indies, but was also a confidant of Bartolomé de Las Casas; he argued that the shamans could not be kept prisoner since they had never been converted and thus were not apostates.

There is some information about temples of the solar cult built in Lupaqa territory by the Inka. A section of the Yunguyo 'province' was alienated and a pilgrimage centre erected. Members of the Cusco royal lineages were resettled at Copacabana and the islands immediately offshore.[24] Late in the sixteenth century the European church decided to re-utilize this pilgrimage centre; it is still in use today.

The Lupaqa are the best known of the many Aymara polities that emerged in pre-Inka times on the highest altiplano. Others are now receiving attention and their holdings, including those on the desert Chilean coast, have been mapped.[25] Their oral traditions have occasion-

---

[23] The scholar who has given most thought to ancient Andean kin ties and their manipulation by the state is R. Tom Zuidema. See *The Ceque System of Cuzco: the social organization of the capital of the Inca* (Leiden, 1964), and 'The Inca kinship system: a new theoretical view', in R. Bolton and E. Mayer (eds.), *Andean Kinship and Marriage* (Washington, D.C., 1977).

[24] See Adolph Bandelier, *The islands of Titicaca and Koati* (New York, 1910).

[25] Tristan Platt, 'Mapas coloniales en la provincia de Chayanta', in Martha Urioste de Aguirre (ed.), *Estudios bolivianos en honor a Gunnar Mendoza* (La Paz, 1978).

ally been recorded in the litigation papers filed by their lords with the *Audiencia* of Charcas; for a decade or so, the colonial administration encouraged such petitions for their own reasons. These claims for past and new privileges included recitations of genealogies by still practising keepers of knot-records. One such petitioner listed the names of his predecessors, including one who 'gave the obedience' to the Inka four generations earlier. In return he had received a wife from the court and their son, Moroco, was remembered in the genealogy as an 'Inka'; along with the wife came garments woven by the king's artisans and the privilege of using a litter.

Another special relation between Cusco and the Aymara lords was their military role. Early in the expansion of Tawantinsuyu, its armies were recruited on the same *mit'a* principle which mobilized energies for the other public works: men and women turned out for battle on rotation, ayllu by ayllu, one ethnic group after another. They came armed with their traditional weapons, led by their own ethnic lords. None of this freed them from the many other chores they owed Cusco.[26]

At some point in the history of Tawantinsuyu this military mit'a must have seemed inefficient: the Aymara lords claimed in a memorandum addressed to Philip II that their ancestors' military skill and loyalty had been rewarded and they had been freed from all other prestations:

we were soldiers only...excused from tribute...and all other taxes and personal services like herding...or from serving the mit'a at court, in the great city of Cuzco, or from being masons, weavers of cloth...and from farming, carpentry or quarrying – people accustomed to move a hill by hand to some other place...We were neither dancers, nor clowns accustomed to sing victory songs to the said ingas...[27]

We cannot tell what the consequences of such protracted military service may have been on the subsistence productivity of the Aymara population left behind. Elsewhere in the Andes those remaining in the ethnic homeland were obligated to work the soldiers' acreage, but long absences, overriding the agricultural calendar, must have put a strain on kin-based but politically exploited reciprocities.

Nor can we tell to what extent the dual division of the whole altiplano into an *urqusuyu* (the mountain half) and an *umasuyu* (the water side) reflected Aymara or later Inka realities. The dichotomy seems to have

---

[26] Waldemar Espinoza Soriano, 'El memorial de Charcas: crónica inédita de 1582', *Cantuta* (Revista de la Universidad Nacional de Educación, Chosica, Peru), 1969.

[27] Murra, quoted in 'La Guerre et les rébellions', 931–2.

been most pronounced in the Lake Titicaca region. There may have been a linguistic substratum behind the dual one, with the eastern half speaking Pukina, not Aymara. Unfortunately, the Inka filter through which many have been viewing Andean matters does not yet permit the unravelling of the ethnic context of dualism. Originally the moieties may have been centred or have 'met' on Lake Titicaca, a 'neutral' zone with its own micro-climate. *Urqu* and *uma* may have found themselves reorganized when Cusco became the nucleus.[28] When first encountered by the Europeans, both were ritually and administratively included in the same southern quarter, the *qollasuyu*, the most densely populated quarter of the Inka state.

The 'watery' component of dual division on the altiplano is also discernible in the presence among the Aymara of an occupational and ethnic minority, maybe even a 'caste' of Uru fishermen. The true significance of their presence is becoming clearer through recent research.[29] In colonial times the fishermen gradually joined Aymara ranks, but their reported Pukina speech and the widespread feeling that they were the aboriginal occupants of the high Andes require archaeological verification.

Correlating historical information with archaeological excavation is an approach that has been used only occasionally in the Andes. Many of the puzzles of Andean history are less inaccessible than it may seem. Continuities in ways of life and languages still exist despite the 450 years of colonial rule; they reach backward even to pre-Inka times. Both the dynastic and the demotic oral traditions are at least partially available in the records of European eyewitnesses and administrators; were they to be verified and expanded with the aid of archaeology, a much sounder, if less sensational, version of Andean society would become available.

It can be documented that in pre-colonial times Aymara speech reached much further than it does at present. The inhabitants of the antiplano north of Lake Titicaca are still perceived as Qolla (Aymara) by the Cusco-dweller, even though they shifted to speaking Quechua. It should not be too difficult to ascertain when the shift took place and under what historical circumstances, but the scarcity of philological studies in 1980 still limits us to conjecture. Many of the Pacific valleys

---

[28] Thérèse Bouysse-Cassagne, 'L'Éspace aymara: *urco* et *uma*', *AESC*, 33/5–6 (1978),' 1057–80.

[29] Nathan Wachtel, 'Hommes d'eau: le problème uru (XVIe–XVIIe siècles)', *AESC*, 33/5–6 (1978), 1127–59.

in what are today Chile and southern Peru were also Aymara-speaking; at the beginning of the twentieth century, towns at the latitude of Lima, in the province of Yauyos, spoke Kauki, an Aymara dialect.[30]

The Europeans referred to the language of the Inka as Quechua deriving it from the word for 'valley', *qhishwa*. The self-designation, used till today by the native speaker, is *runa simi*, 'the tongue of people'; it has not caught on in European and literate discourse. Before 1532 Quechua was the language of state administration and was understood by many bilinguals; colonial sources refer to it as the *lengua general* (Aymara and Pukina are sometimes also described that way). The linguist, Alfredo Torero, has suggested that Quechua was once the speech of the central coast, from where it spread both before and after the Inka.[31] Mutually intelligible variants were spoken from what is today Ecuador in the north to Tucumán in the south. The distinction between altiplano and valley dwellers was fundamental in Andean ethno-classification; this distinction was apparently identified by the Europeans with separate languages.

There is little serious archaeology in the Inka heartland: the Vilcanota valley and the circum-Cusco area. John Howland Rowe initiated the scientific study of Inka antecedents,[32] but has attracted few disciples.

What can be asserted with some confidence is that after a long period of conflict separating the 'Middle Horizon' from the Late or Incaic one, Cusco changed in the fifteenth century from being the nucleus of a local polity to being a major urban centre, capital of the Tawantinsuyu described by the Europeans. It was not only the administrative headquarters of the Inka realm but also a ceremonial centre, where a hundred pieces of fine cloth were sacrificed daily and scores of priests fasted while watching the movements of the sun from their palace-observatories. The state calendars here are not as well understood as those of the Maya because the results of the observations were not recorded on stone but, most likely, woven into perishable textiles.[33]

The capital stood at the hub of royal highways measuring 20,000 kilometres or more, connecting it to Chile, the Pacific Ocean and north

[30] Martha Hardman de Bautista, *Jaqaru: an outline of phonological and morphological structure* (The Hague, 1966).

[31] Alfredo Torero, *El quechua y la historia social andina* (Lima, 1974).

[32] John H. Rowe, *An introduction to the archaeology of Cuzco*, Papers of the Peabody Museum, 28/2 (1944).

[33] John V. Murra, 'Cloth and its functions in the Inca state', *American Anthropologist*, 64/4 (1962), 710–28.

to the equatorial line. The partition of the territory into four parts named *suyu*, again subdivided, has been studied, and it has been suggested that each 'line' radiating from the ceremonial centre linked particular royal kinfolk to the shrines for which they were the custodians.[34] Most of the royal lineages lived with their retainers either in the city or in the townships nearby. Garcilaso de la Vega, who was born in Cusco only a few years after the European invasion, provides us with a nostalgic description of his Inka mother's hometown, written in Andalusian exile many years later,[35] but no maps, either architectural or sociological, comparable to what is available for Tenochtitlan, the Aztec capital, can be drawn up for Cusco, despite the recent, decade-long effort sponsored by UNESCO.[36]

It is unclear to what extent the ethnic groups incorporated by the Inka were represented in Cusco. We hear that the Chimu, a coastal polity, were expected to deliver artisans and women to the capital. The silversmiths were still there in 1542, their presence noted by a European friar. The king of Chimu was not expected to provide troops, coastal soldiers being considered untrustworthy and probably also unfit to fight at an altitude of 4,000 metres. On ceremonial occasions, aliens were expected to leave Cusco.

There is no agreement on the amount of direct intervention by Cusco in the governing of the incorporated ethnic groups. Enemies of the Inka-like viceroy, Francisco de Toledo (1568–81), portrayed the traditional ethnic lords as 'tyrants', which in sixteenth-century Spanish meant they were 'illegitimate', bureaucratic appointees, sent from the royal capital and in that sense not 'natural rulers' at all. It is also alleged that the Inka ran out of royal kin, appointable as regional administrators, and were eventually forced to assimilate to Inka status the loyal inhabitants of certain circum-Cusco villages. Known as *allikaq* (those who were improved, promoted):

they were senior sons of the Papri and Chillque; these were inspectors sent all over the kingdom to check the administrative centres and the weaving nuns and the warehouses...some [others] were from Quilliscachi and Equeco...[37]

There is evidence that in some rebellious regions, particularly on the

---

[34] Zuidema, *Ceque System*.
[35] Garcilaso de la Vega, 'El Inca', *Primera parte de los Comentarios Reales* [1604] (Madrid, 1960).
[36] The best approximate map of what the city may have looked like before 1534 is in Santiago Agurto Calvo, *Cusco: la traza urbana de la ciudad inca* (Cuzco, 1980).
[37] Guaman Poma de Ayala, *Nueva coronica*, 363 [365].

coast, the Inka did appoint 'governors' to replace the 'natural lord'. These were usually kinfolk of the 'rebels', or neighbouring gentry whose regional hegemony was endorsed from Cusco.[38] However, most of our information comes from the highlands, since the coastal population disappeared soon after 1532: highland local rulers belonged to the ethnic community which they governed. They understood what was demanded of them since, at least in theory, the pre-Inka standards prevailed. The diagnostic, all-important, Andean trait characterizing these standards was that the larder of the peasant remain untouched. True, he now had not only to fill the storehouses of his own lord and of the local shrine but also to create revenues for the state by working its newly-alienated or recently-irrigated acreage and by herding the state camelid herds.

Still, there was a 'federal' bureaucracy: they were stationed in large administrative centres like Willka Waman, Huanuco Pampa, Paria or Tumi Pampa, all erected along the royal highway. Of these only Huanuco Pampa has been studied in detail: it covered almost two square kilometres and contained up to 5,000 dwellings and palaces, in addition to almost 500 storehouses. The city could have housed between 12,000 and 15,000 inhabitants, most of them serving their mit'a turns but some living there on a more permanent basis: the weaving and cooking women of the *aqllawasi*, their ageing guards, accountants responsible for the warehousing, religious specialists.[39] How many of these were 'Inka', either members of the royal lineages or *allikaq*? An Andean writer like Waman Puma, claimed that his non-royal kinsmen filled even such 'federal' posts in the administrative centres.

Whatever the proportions along the road, royal functionaries 'inspected' the subject, provincial lords and their territories. The best information about their relationship comes from a 1562 inspection of the Chupaychu, a small ethnic group in the Huallaga valley, some two days' march from Huanuco Pampa. Interviewed in their own region, they testified that before 1532 there had been:

a lord Inka who governed 10,000 households... [and] who came to inspect them once a year... and if he found a local lord or lesser authority guilty of five very

[38] Ortiz de Zúñiga, *La Provincia de León*, II, 46.
[39] Craig Morris, 'Reconstructing patterns of non-agricultural production in the Inca economy', in Charlotte B. Moore (ed.), *Reconstructing complex societies* (Cambridge, Mass., 1972); *idem*, 'Tecnología y organización inca del almacenamiento de víveres en la sierra', in Heather Lechtman and Ana María Soldi (eds.), *Runakunap Kawsayninkupaq Rurasqankunaqa*, I (México, 1981), 327–75.

serious faults like not having obeyed what the royal representative had ordered
or
wanting to rebel or
having been negligent in collecting and delivering what was due or
not performing the required sacrifices three times a year or
occupying the people at weaving in his own service or
doing other things which interfered with what they were meant to do and for
other similar things. If he committed five faults, they took away his office and
gave it to his son, if he was fit, and if not, they granted it to his brother or
the nearest relative...

if some ethnic lord [*cacique principal*] wanted to rise and rebel, they killed him
and all his lineage so not one was left. When the Inkas were still alive, this
witness was young and saw some of it and the rest he has heard from his elders
and other old men who talked of it. These were well-known facts....[40]

No European 'chronicle' has ever pinpointed the articulation of the
ethnic lords with the state in such explicit terms. Another witness, older
than the first, called Xagua and experienced in 'serving' before 1532
at Cusco, explained to the European inspector that when the local lord
died;

if he had a grown son, able to govern, he did not dare take over without going
personally to Cuzco, to gain the acquiescence of the Inka and the seat [*tiana*]
for his rank; then the Inka granted it. And if the son was a child and not fit
to govern, they took him to Cuzco and in his place appointed a kinsman, the
relative closest to the dead lord, to govern in his place and this he did as long
as he lived and they did not deprive him...

Another ageing witness could remember beyond Inka rule and referred
to the times:

before the Inka came to this country. When a lord died, they granted the
authority to someone else who was brave they did not give it to the son. After
the Inka ruled, he heard that they succeeded from father to son...

In this case the witnesses confirmed what some European writers had
also recorded about pre-Inka practice: a shift from 'selecting the brave',
in what were *awqa runa*, military times, in the direction of greater
rigidity along hereditary lines.[41]

The witnesses from the Huallaga valley did not elaborate on the
census conducted by the Cusco authorities as part of their 'inspections'.
Periodically, the households were enumerated and the results knotted

[40] Ortiz de Zúñiga, *La Provincia de León*, II, 45-9.
[41] John V. Murra, 'La visita de los chupachu como fuente etnológica, part II: las autoridades
étnicas tradicionales', in Ortiz de Zúñiga, *La Provincia de León*, 381-406.

onto the khipu record. According to Waman Puma, both men and women were classed into ten age-groups.[42] The census coincided with the state's recognition of recent marriages: the new couples were now listed in their own right. No single person, no matter what their age, owed personal mit'a services; she or he went as part of someone's household. To forge marriage, a familial rite of passage, into a device of statecraft was characteristic of Inka state ideology.[43]

There is evidence that late in Inka times an effort was made to go beyond the ethnic principle, whose recognition had governed the relations of the state with its component units. An administrative vocabulary was introduced, related to the decimal arrangement of the knots of the khipu strings. The ethnic lords and their 'provinces' could now be recorded for the census as so many thousands, hundreds and even smaller groups of households. The lords of the Wanka were said to govern 28 one-thousand units or *waranqa*; those of the Lupaqa, twenty. Xulca Condor, on the upper Huallaga, reported only three *pachaka* of 100 households each, while his downriver neighbour, Pawkar Waman, claimed to have ruled four *waranqa*.

To what extent this decimal effort went beyond census practice into the actual administration of the subject ethnic groups is uncertain. There was obviously no bureaucratic device that could maintain social and ethnic units within neat, decimal patterns. When the Huallaga material became available, it was possible to use the house-by-house figures to show that one *pachaka* corresponded to a cluster of five neighbouring hamlets.[44] Even in 1549, after a ten-year long resistance to the Europeans, the five reported a population of 59 households. Thirteen years later they had recovered up to 75. A Swedish scholar, Ake Wedin, has related the emergence of the decimal vocabulary to military needs. If accurate, one would expect it to be used most frequently among the Aymara, in the southern Andes. However, we find its widest use in the north, where some think the Inka adapted it from local practice.[45]

If one looks for Inka intervention into day-to-day local matters which might challenge the ethnic leader's authority, the information is sketchy. One witness stated that:

[42] Guaman Poma de Ayala, *Nueva coronica*, 196–236.
[43] John V. Murra, *The economic organization of the Inka state* (Greenwich, Conn., 1955; reprinted 1980), 98.
[44] Gordon J. Hadden, 'Un ensayo de demografía histórica y etnológica en Huánuco', in Ortiz de Zúñiga [1562], *La provincia de León*. I, 371–80.
[45] John H. Rowe, 'The kingdom of Chimor', *Acta Americana* (Mexico), 6/1–2 (1948), 26–59.

in civil causes, if one had invaded the lands of another and the latter complained, when the Inka came to inspect the country he investigated the matter and provided relief by returning the land to the aggrieved and punishing the invader. The same could be done by the ethnic lord in the absence of the Inka...

The last clause is in some ways the most significant one. Long before the Inka, but also today, the ethnic leadership in the Andes has confirmed annually the rights in land of lineages and households. While the state's representatives may have claimed to act on appeal, our vision of the Inka state would predict that local decisions about agricultural parcels would remain in ethnic hands.

According to the witnesses from the Huallaga valley, some limitations on the ethnic lord's authority to decide matters of life and death had been introduced by Cusco. In cases of murder, said one witness:

they brought the accused before him [the Inka] and in the presence of the local lord, in the public plaza the witnesses...described the crime...and if he had murdered but there was an explanation, they did not kill him but punished by whipping...and ordering him to support the widow and children...

The frequency of such 'inspection' trips cannot be stated. The Andean writer, Waman Puma, claimed they took place every six months: the witnesses quoted above, once a year. If true, such frequency would have required a large Cusco staff for which there is no independent evidence. So far as we can reconstruct it, the policy was set at the top and announced at public gatherings held at the *usnu* built in each of the large, urban-sized administrative centres along the royal highway. The implementation of any policy seems to have been left in the hands of the local ethnic leaders, familiar with the system, who decided whose mit'a turn it was to perform a certain task. The ability of the ethnic authority to mobilize and manage large numbers of cultivators, builders, or soldiers was taken for granted and was tested in the early days of the European invasion when Pizarro or Benalcazar could rely on their Andean allies to raise armies and the porters without whom the invasion could not have succeeded.

The variety of tasks covered by the pre-Hispanic mit'a was very large. We have an account, unique so far, dating from 1549, that claimed to list the tasks owed Cusco by a single, relatively small, ethnic group.[46] It was recorded only seven years after the Chupaychu of the Huallaga

---

[46] Ortiz de Zúñiga, *La Provincia de León*, II, 289-310.

valley had been brought under European rule. The informants were still using the decimal vocabulary in describing local organization. When the interrogators wanted to know what the '4,000' households had 'given' to the state, Pawkar Waman and his peers responded by reading from a khipu of some 25–30 cords. The record is most likely incomplete; the amounts claimed seem very large and are not confirmed by any other available source. However, the lack of a sample should not deter us from using it, if not for the numbers quoted, which may simply be mistranslated, then for the ethno-categories the khipu used to group kinds of obligations. In early colonial times, European courts, even the royal audiencias, readily accepted sworn testimony based on the khipu. One witness, who came to the Andes as Francisco Pizarro's trumpeter, testified in another case:

the Indians of this country keep records and accounts of the things they give their lords…using what they call *quipos*; everything given [even] for a long time back is also recorded there. And this witness knows that the said *quipos* are very accurate and true since on many and different occasions the witness has verified some of the accounts he has had with Indians, recording things they had given and owed him and others he had given them. He has found that the *quipos* held by the said Indians were very accurate…[47]

The first two cords read in 1549 by Pawkar Waman's accountant were probably out of order; he had been asked if they had any mines and if they did, to state how many 'Indians' were 'thrown' into the gold mines. The answer was three men and three women from each pachaka, 100 households; they served for one year each.

The record keeper was then allowed to proceed in his own way. First he listed eight obligations owed to the Inka crown in Cusco and beyond. One was to send 'four hundred Indians' to the capital, some 60 days' walk from their homes, 'to make walls'. Another 400 went to plant, raising food 'for those absent'. Even allowing for the probability that 400 refers to both sexes, even 400 pairs or couples out of 4,000 households is a very high percentage of the total Chupaychu population. Had all other ethnic groups sent such high proportions to Cusco, there would have been no place, physically, for them to stand. An easy way out is to assume a mistake in translation or copying, since the interpreter was a local man, whose Spanish arithmetic could have been tentative. The 400 masons may well have coincided with the 400 who farmed since

[47] Waldemar Espinoza Soriano, 'Los huanca aliados de la conquista [1560]', *Anales Científicos* de la Universidad del Centro, Huancayo, 1 (1971–2), 367.

frequently people sent out on mit'a duties had to raise their own food. Another explanation would be to assume that the lords had some reason to exaggerate their burdens in Inka times. These eight cords also included people who guarded the mummy of king Thupa; others were stationed in garrisons facing the rebellious Far North.

The next ten or so cords dealt with duties performed nearer to home, within the dispersed territory controlled by the Chupaychu, in what is today the department of Huánuco. They included herding the state camelids, weaving their wool and gathering 'earths and colours' for dyeing. Three cords enumerated mining salt and harvesting hot peppers and coca leaf. Cord 13 dealt with the main tier of the Chupaychu country, the broad bed of the Pillkumayu, the river known today as the Huallaga. Here Pawkar Waman's people provided 40 'Indians' who:

> guarded the fields which they [the Inka] had throughout this valley and the maize [harvested] went mostly to Cusco but also to the storehouses [at the administrative center of Huanuco Pampa, two days' away]...[48]

This is the only reference in the khipu to lands alienated by the state within the Chupaychu territory.

Cords 17–20 form a macro-category of skilled artisans who also remained in the home area. One referred to beaters for the royal hunt, another to sandal-makers, a third to 'carpenters to make plates and bowls' in the wooded areas downriver from their main settlements. This is also the tier on which coca leaf is grown but the two cords listing these duties were not contiguous on the khipu as recorded.

With cords 21–24 we return to activities connected with state installations, except that these deal with the regional Inka administrative centre at Huanuco Pampa, two days' walk from the Huallaga valley. Here 68 Chupaychu households provided 'guards', a job they shared with many other ethnic groups in the region – but so far archaeological research has been unable to determine from within what radius the 'guards' were recruited for this large, urban-like centre.

Eighty more households sent bearers, ready to carry burdens along the royal highway. Only two waystations are listed, one five days' march south, the other only one day away. The European chronicles had reported that bearers were responsible for only one day's carrying but

[48] Ortiz de Zúñiga, *La Provincia de León*, II, 306.

students of the Inka communications network, like John Hyslop, doubt this. Forty 'older' men were assigned to guard 'the women of the Inka' – these were the *aqlla*, the 'chosen' women who wove and cooked for the troops passing through, on their way north.

Number 25, the last cord read, returns us to both agriculture and the home valley: 500 households 'planted and did other things without leaving their country'. This is the largest single number reported on the khipu and refers superficially to the same kind of tasks as cord 13. Maize grows well here; it was an important sumptuary and ceremonial crop. The beer made from it was indispensable for ceremonies and institutionalized 'generosity'. We can assume that the 40 Indians of cord 13, one household from each pachaka, were those responsible, year around, while the 500 took turns cultivating.

All these many activities, no matter how diverse, can be subsumed under mit'a prestations: soldiering, planting, masonry, were all expenditures of energy on behalf of the state, owed in different proportions by virtually all ethnic groups incorporated by Tawantinsuyu. None of these cords imply giving or 'paying' anything from one's own resources – if we do not count the lands alienated originally and worked now for the benefit of the state, the crown and the Sun.

There was, however, one exception: cords 8 and 9 dealt with 'making feathers' and gathering honey. These were uncultivated products that were handed over (to whom?) by the unmarried young, as a by-product of their herding and scouting work on behalf of their households. It is in this sense that there was 'no tribute' in Inka society: the only items in kind actually turned over to the state were provided by those who had not yet formed their own household and the objects themselves were 'raw' in Claude Lévi-Strauss's dichotomy. Nothing 'cooked' was owed the authority, nothing that had been cultivated or manufactured for the individual's own storeroom.

The fact that the revenues of the state consisted overwhelmingly of prestations in energy, of time spent on the state's behalf in a wide range of enterprises, comes out very clearly from the Chupaychu khipu. The best of the European eyewitnesses understood this: Cieza and Polo make the point emphatically and contrast this burden with the tributes in kind exacted from the Andean populations in the 1550s. The very same inspection protocol of 1549 records also what the Chupaychu now gave to Gomez Arias de Avila, their *encomendero*. That khipu is a long list of sacks of coca leaf, finished garments, European footwear, roof tiles, exotic food and poultry, all of which they were expected to hand over in kind. The juxtaposition on neighbouring pages, recording revenues generated according to Andean and European principles, could not be more dramatic.

The rapid expansion of Tawantinsuyu over 4,000 kilometres from what today is Ecuador in the north to Chile and Argentina in the south, achieved in less than a century, implied changes in the basic and ancient dimensions of Andean organization. Administrative as well as religious ties were strained. Indirect rule through the ethnic lords and the local shrines became more difficult because common understandings could not be taken for granted. Ecological complementarity worked best where there were no large scale markets; state revenues based on mit'a prestations were easier to enforce where regional political authorities were used to such revenues. However, by A.D. 1500, many of these pre-conditions could no longer be taken for granted.

Cusco armies found themselves in unfamiliar, temperate or equatorial regions, hence new ecological circumstances. For example, north of Cajamarca, in Peru, puna conditions were replaced with rainier and warmer climates in which no one lived at 4,000 metres altitude; where *ch'uñu* and *ch'arki* freeze-dried reserves could not be made; and where ecological complementarity, if present at all, was practised on a minor and very local basis.

In the puna where the densest population lived, complementary exchanges remained in the hands of the ethnic group. Barter and trade, if present at all, were marginal since the caravans of a single ethnic group connected the political and economic nucleus with the outliers they controlled. Where distances were less and contrasts minimal, exchanges might remain in the hands of peasant households but could also have been left to outsiders, some of them professional traders. Roswith Hartmann has stressed that the southern patterns of 'no trade, no markets', did not apply to all of Tawantinsuyu;[49] Udo Oberem and Frank Salomon have shown that in the Pasto-Carchi area there were *mindala*, long- and middle-distance exchange specialists. One of the sumptuary commodities they marketed was coca leaf, grown in the

[49] Roswith Hartmann, *Märkte im alten Peru* (Bonn, 1968).

north by lowland dwellers who were not highland colonists; other items of light weight but high value are also listed. Salomon suggests that these traders enjoyed the political protection of highland ethnic leaders and could devote all their time to exchange activities.[50]

In the north, Tawantinsuyu encountered fiercer resistance than it had faced in more familiar country. The dynastic oral tradition records the need to 're-conquer' again and again the territories north of Tumipampa, the modern Cuenca. These military challenges presumably encouraged the Inka to experiment first with non-mit'a soldiers from the Aymara south; only twelve years before the European invasion they too were replaced by local ex-rebels, the Cañari, co-opted for military duties on a virtually full-time basis. Frank Salomon has traced the details of Inka expansion in the north and shown that the attempt to impose southern social and economic institutions was late and partial.[51]

The new long distances from Cusco also made it difficult, if not impossible, for the mitmaq to exercise their residual 'archipelago' rights in their original polity. By 1532 the people may still have been counted on the khipu of their original group, but if it was now too distant and their new duties very specialized, they tended to remain wherever they had resettled. Even the appearance and the victory of the Europeans did not persuade some mitmaq to return to their places of origin, unless they came from nearby ethnic groups, as happened with the 'thousand' state weavers at Huancané.

Another factor encouraging permanent settlement away from their ethnic base was the privileges granted to those relocated. In the Huallaga valley the inspections of 1549 and 1562 recorded complaints by the newcomers and their locally born descendants that as soon as the Inka regime had collapsed, the local people had taken back many of the fields which had been alienated for the benefit of the mitmaq. And yet there is no evidence that any of the plaintiffs returned to their own regions; they simply gave up guarding the fortresses to which they had been assigned and resettled among the natives.

Waldemar Espinoza has published records of severe Inka relocation

---

[50] Udo Oberem, 'El acceso a recursos naturales de diferentes ecologías en la sierra ecuatoriana (siglo XVI)', International Congres of Americanists, *Actes* (Paris, 1978), IV; Frank Salomon, 'Systèmes politiques verticaux aux marchés de l'empire inca', in *AESC*, 33/5–6 (1978), 967–89.

[51] Frank Salomon, *Ethnic lords of Quito in the age of the Incas: the political economy of north-Andean chiefdoms* (Cornell, 1978).

policies enforced in the Abancay region;[52] a high percentage of the local population was deported elsewhere and their farms granted to mitmaq, some from as far away as present-day Ecuador. Similar measures were taken along the coast, where the Inka had upon occasion met serious resistance: the local irrigation societies were dislocated, a higher percentage of coastal land was alienated for state use, lowlanders were not trusted in the army and temples of the solar cult were imposed. To what extent the highlanders interfered with the coast-wise traffic by raft to the warm waters of the Gulf of Guayaquil[53] is unknown, but it is not likely that it remained unaffected.

The most extreme cases of resettlement by the state go beyond any conceivable extension of the principle of ecological complementarity. They involve two ample, maize-producing valleys at Yucay and at Cochabamba. In both cases the aboriginal population was deported and new people brought in.[54] Apparently no effort was made to present this relocation in ideologically palatable terms: the regions emptied were too large and the deportations too thorough to be explained in terms of 'access to a maximum variety of resources'.

At Yucay, which is close to Cusco, the resettlement had to do with political factors: among those transferred here were the full-time soldiers co-opted from the rebel Cañari in the north. Their almost full-time dedication to military duties may have been without precedent in the Andes but, like the Charka whom they had replaced only twelve years before 1532, the Cañari were still recruited along ethnic lines and they were still expected to grow their own food when at home.[55]

At Cochambamba, the largest maize-growing valley in all of Tawantinsuyu, the local people were also expelled, but here an unprecedented step was taken to increase the productivity of the state acreage. In King Wayna Qhapaq's time, just before the European invasion, the newly emptied territory was divided first into quadrants and each of these into strips, reaching 'from cordillera to cordillera'. Each strip was assigned to a highland Aymara-speaking group living from as far north as Lake

[52] Waldemar Espinoza Soriano, 'Colonias de mitmas múltiples en Abancay, Siglos XV & XVI: una información inédita de 1575 para la etnohistoria andina', *Revista del Museo Nacional* (Lima), 39 (1973), 225–99.

[53] María Rostworowski de Diez Canseco, 'Mercadores del valle de Chincha en la época pre-hispanica', *Revista Española de Antropología. Americana* (Madrid), 5 (1970), 135–78; John V. Murra, 'El tráfico de *muelu* en la Costa del Pacífico', in *Formaciones economicas* (1975).

[54] Nathan Wachtel, 'Les mitimaes de la vallée de Cochabamba: la politique de colonisation de Wayna Capac', *Journal de la Société des Américanistes* (Paris, 1980).

[55] Murra, 'La Guerra et les rébellions', 933–4.

Titicaca to the desert of Atacama in the south; the cultivators they provided were not mitmaq settlers but *mit'ayuq* sent in temporarily on rotation. But for a few rows of maize in each quadrant, destined to feed the mit'a (which involved no less than 13,000 cultivators and 2,400 local storehouses), the bulk of the corn harvested was sent to the administrative centre the Inka had built at Paria, on the altiplano, and from there to Cusco.[56] The replacement of the mitmaq principle with a new kind of mit'a must have had ideological implications which have not yet been unravelled.

There was another change in late Inka times with ultimately far-reaching consequences: the emergence of populations whose affiliation and enumeration with the original group had been severed by the state. These people devoted full-time attention to royal, and possibly even state, business. The *aqlla* women 'chosen' to weave for the state and the kings have already been mentioned; Waman Puma heard that there had been six kinds of aqlla of differing status and responsibilities.[57] Virtually nothing is known about their internal organization because they were attractive to European soldiers (who identified them as 'nuns') and thus disappeared almost immediately after 1532. A male equivalent were the *yana*, who were also removed from the authority of their traditional settlements. Unlike the aqlla, they formed households; they worked full-time as artisans, herders and cultivators.

There is evidence of pre-Inka retainers assigned to the polygynous households of the ethnic lords. One minor authority in the Huallaga valley reported four such local *yana*: one, living above the main valley did the lord's herding; the second toiled below, in the coca leaf fields; the last two lived in the same settlement with their master and attended to his many interests. It may be simply a coincidence that the number of his yana was the same as that of his wives.[58]

Inka ideology, as reflected in the dynastic oral tradition, claimed however that the yana were their innovation. A royal 'brother', sent to inspect the realm and conduct a census, is alleged to have withheld some populations from the khipu, hoping to use them in a dynastic challenge to his reigning kinsman. The plot failed and the brother's skin was made into a drum; the people he had left unreported were also treated as rebels and were due to be killed. The queen is supposed to have stopped the massacre by suggesting to her husband that the

[56] Wachtel, 'Les Mitimaes'.   [57] Guaman Poma de Ayala, *Nueva Coronica*, 298–300 [300–2].
[58] Murra, 'La visita de los chupachu'.

'rebels' could profitably be put to work on royal estates. Since the place where it all happened was called Yanayaku, the retainers were thereafter named *yana* and sometimes *yanayakus*.[59]

European observers reported these populations as being 'free' from their kinship and ethnic obligations since they were no longer enumerated on their original khipu. While many have asserted that their service status was hereditary, the evidence for this is not conclusive: one of the few mentions of their fate in reliable, early accounts claimed that only the son of the yana who was 'fit' for it would succeed in the job. The others presumably returned to their ethnic home. There is much pressure on the evidence to make it read as if the *yana* were slaves.[60]

Attempts to present as privileges what were actually new onerous tasks and changes in status probably preceded the Inka. The name of the aqlla, lost to their ethnic group and to their potential husbands, came from *aqllay*, to select, to choose; the name of the yana came from *yanapay*, to assist fully, to help someone without strict calculation of return. The deported retainer was to view his new task as a variant of the most unselfish and emotionally fulfilling kind of reciprocal duties.[61] It is uncertain if anyone in the Inka state was taken in by such transparent verbal devices; there is much about these retainer populations that we still do not know. One of the more accessible dimensions of their status and functions should be their percentage in the population. While the total was apparently low (about 1 per cent of the total), this need not be the only consideration. If the trend was towards an increase, and if their status was affected by 'rebellions', the yana may have been the harbingers of the future. Tawantinsuyu in 1500 seems to have been moving away from fairly autonomous ethnic groups speaking their own languages, worshipping their own gods and able to provide, as an ethnic group, for most of their own needs. All this would be affected and, in the long run, threatened by the emergence of full-time retainers.[62]

---

[59] John V. Murra, 'Nueva información sobre las poblaciones *yana*', in *Formaciones economicas*.

[60] Emilio Choy, *Antropología e historia* (Lima, 1979). On the debate about the mode of production which prevailed in 1532, see the various articles reproduced in Waldemar Espinoza Soriano (ed.), *Los modos de producción en el imperio de los incas* (Lima, 1978).

[61] Murra, 'Nueva información sobre las poblaciones *yana*'.

[62] For further discussion of Andean societies before the European invasion. See *CHLA*, I, Wachtel, ch. 7, 215–19.

4

THE INDIANS OF SOUTHERN SOUTH AMERICA IN THE MIDDLE OF THE SIXTEENTH CENTURY*

At the time of the European invasion into South America, the southern cone presents at first sight a confusing array of different and shifting ethnic and social groups. To the north were the great Andean civilizations: complex, centralized state structures, astonishing techno-logical achievements, unique forms of economic organization, stable ethnic boundaries and well-defined rights to land, and long-distance communications stretching back for centuries. The cultures of the southern cone inevitably offer a pale contrast. The influence of the states to the north was, of course, felt in many areas. By 1532 the Inca empire extended as far south as what is today Santiago de Chile, but both archaeological and documentary records give evidence of movement, exchange and communication beyond the limits of a single political system. This chapter will suggest the ecological complementarity of different peoples, each in a particular environment, or establishing settlements in different niches; many of them nomadic, some trans-humant, at times co-existing peacefully with their neighbours, at times competing for particular resources and in some cases so specialized economically that their livelihood depended on a complex and far-reaching circulation of subsistence goods.

The very complexity of the Inca state was in part responsible for its rapid subjection to the king of Spain. In contrast, the less settled, less centralized societies in the southern and south-eastern periphery of the continent were not so readily subjugated. In some cases, for example the famous Araucanians, effective European domination came only after centuries of military pressure. Unfortunately for the historian such

* Translated from the Spanish and reduced in length by Mr John Palmer, Institute of Social Anthropology, Oxford; translation revised by Ms Olivia Harris, Goldsmiths' College London, and the Editor.

resistance has made our knowledge of these peoples extremely fragmentary. At present we can only offer a classification of the peoples of the southern cone, one that can do little more than establish the general configuration and possible historical links between different societies and different areas.

For present purposes the southern cone has been divided into three geographical areas, a classification which is based on economic differences. No system of classification is free of inconsistency, gaps and contradictions, but this general division offers a starting point for grasping the range and variation of cultures. The three main cultural areas are:

1. The southern Andean agriculturists;
2. Lowland hunter-gatherers and cultivators of the Chaco, inter-fluvial and littoral regions;
3. Hunters, gatherers and fishers of the Pampa, Patagonia and the southern Archipelago.

THE SOUTHERN ANDES

We refer here to all those societies whose economy was based on a mix of agriculture and camelid-herding, covering the area of what is today southern Peru and Bolivia, three-quarters of Chile and north-west Argentina, including the province of Mendoza. This area can again be regionally subdivided into:

i.   A central section, including the Aymara, Lipe, Chango, Atacama and Diaguita of northern Chile, and the Omaguaca and Diaguita of north-west Argentina;
ii. The south-eastern periphery, including lowland societies which had been the meeting ground of Andean lowland cultures: the Lule and Tonocoté of Tucumán, the Sanavirón and Comechingón of the hills of Córdoba and San Luis, and the Huarpe of San Juan and Mendoza;
iii. The southern periphery from the Aconcagua valley to the island of Chiloé where Mapuche and highland Pehuenche lived.

Although the Inca claimed credit for all the technological advancement in the area, in fact its historical roots lay thousands of years earlier. The population which the Europeans encountered after the invasion appears to have been fragmented into distinct ethnic groups in the wake of the decline of Tiwanaku culture – a period known as 'local-level

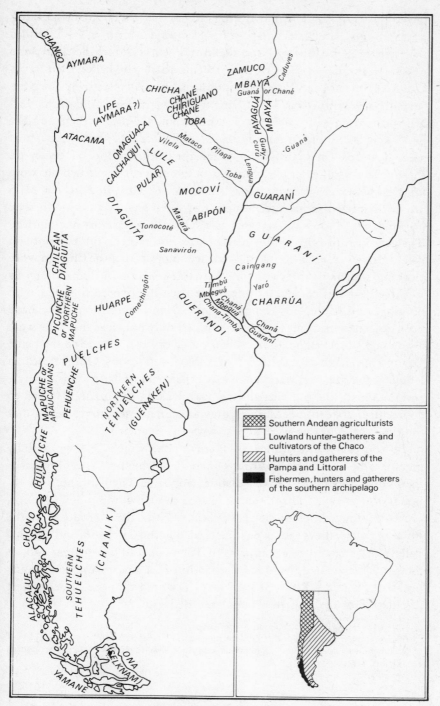

Indians of southern South America on the eve of the Conquest

development'. At its height during this period the Aymara-speaking population of Arica and Tarapacá has been calculated at 8,851.[1] Besides the Aymara agriculturists of the inland valleys, this figure included three groups of nomadic fishers of the Atacama coast who called themselves Uru, Camanchaca and Proanche, although known collectively since the seventeenth century as the Chango. By 1540, after the Incas had transplanted part of the Aymara population as *mitimaes*, their number had fallen, according to early *encomienda* title deeds, to about 5,000, plus some 600–700 Chango. The Aymara agriculturists looked down on these coastal fishing people, who, like others specializing in fishing, were known as Uru. An account of 1581 talks of 400 Urus in Atacama 'who are not baptized, nor concentrated, nor obey anybody although they give fish to the lords of Atacama as a symbolic gesture of recognition. They are very primitive, they neither sow nor gather, and feed only on fish'.[2] However, archaeological evidence suggests that the Chango wore clothing similar to that worn by Aymara: remains of domestic crops and of metal and ceramic objects have been discovered together with offerings and fishing instruments. The Chango were thought to have been descendants of the Atacama; it is certainly not clear that they were always a distinct ethnic group. Their mode of subsistence and the name Chango may have been the result of colonial conditions. Of the Atacama language, Cunza, only fragmentary wordlists, phrases and songs survive, and the size of the pre-Hispanic Cunza-speaking population is open to conjecture: sixteenth-century figures are unrepresentative, because at the time the Atacama were at war with the Spaniards.

To the east is the valley of Humahuaca, which was worked by members of many ethnic groups including Chichas. The Omaguaca themselves apparently spoke a distinct language. Their southern neighbours, the so-called Diaguita, comprised three main linguistic groups, each speaking a different dialect of cacana. These three groups were the Pular of Salta valley; the Calchaquí, settled in the Calchaquí and Yocavil valleys of Salta and adjacent parts of Tucumán and Catamarca; and, to their south, the Diaguita, inhabiting most of Catamarca and neighbouring districts of La Rioja. It has been calculated that the pre-conquest population of these three groups exceeded 55,000.[3]

[1] Horacio Larrain, 'La población indígena de Tarapacá, norte de Chile, entre 1538 y 1581', *Norte Grande* (Universidad Católica de Chile, Instituto de Geografía, Santiago), 1/3–4 (1975).

[2] Marcos Jimenez de la Espada (ed.), *Relaciones geográficas de Indias. Perú* (1881–97), 3 vols. (Madrid, 1965), II, 61.

[3] Antonio Serrano, *Los aborígenes argentinos. Síntesis etnográfica* (Buenos Aires, 1947), 20.

The inhabitants of the valleys to the west of the cordillera also came to be known as Diaguita. The extension was originally made on the grounds of linguistic and ceramic affinities. As to ceramics, recent archaeological research has demonstrated that local correlations between the two Andean areas do exist, in a way which indicates that the western groups had reached a stage of transition to Diaguita culture under pressure from a westward migration of Diaguita in the tenth century. Regarding linguistic affinities, though, comparative study of respective proper names and place names reveals very few traces of a relationship. That north-east Chile was ever a Cacana-speaking area is still more improbable, in view of the fact that, at the end of the sixteenth century, according to a contemporaneous Jesuit, Father Valdivia, Mapuche was spoken as far north as Copiapó. Bibar, in contrast, had maintained that five local languages were spoken in different valleys between Copiapó and Aconcagua.[4] It is not possible to determine whether Mapuche expansion was pre-Hispanic or whether the linguistic homogeneity which Valdivia perceived was due to the post-conquest transplanting of indigenous groups: in this instance, Diaguita were conscripted by the Spaniards to fight against the southern Mapuche, and captive Mapuche were sent to work in the northern gold mines.

Early documents allow for a reasonably accurate estimation of Chilean Diaguita population at different moments in history. In 1535 the population of the valleys of Copiapó, Huasco, Coquimbo, Limari, Combarbala and Choapa amounted to 25,000 inhabitants; by 1540 the number had dropped to 20,000 and continued to fall until it reached 10,900 in 1545. In other words, the population fell in ten years by more than half.

The geography of the central section of the south-central Andes is typified by high mountains, sea and desert. In Tarapacá, the desert between the west coast and the Andean foothills is generally unfavourable for agriculture, but there were pre-Hispanic farming communities living both on the coast by rivers and inland in valleys or by oases such as at Pica. Most permanent settlements, though, were found in the Andes from 2,000–3,200 metres above sea level.

The southern altiplano, or *puna*, from 3,300 to 4,200 metres altitude, has always been an area of transhumant pastoralism based on the exploitation of its limited resources. Agriculture is severely restricted

---

[4] Gerónimo de Bibar, *Crónica y Relación Copiosa y Verdadera de los Reinos de Chile* [1558] (Santiago, 1966), 27, 29, 32, 38.

because of salt deposits and the high frost rate. These conditions encouraged communication and exchange between groups, both neighbouring and distant, using llama caravans. To the east of the high plateau, and between the Humahuaca valley to the north and the Diaguita to the south, lies an extensive tract of intermontane valleys and gorges. Local vegetation includes two species of tree, the algarrobo (*Prosopis chilensis*) and the chañar (*Geoffrea decorticans*), which were of economic and cultural significance both here and in the oases of the Atacama desert.

In much of the area agriculture depended on the natural drainage system, and hence the population was scattered. In certain areas, however, forms of irrigation were used, though on a much smaller scale and of less complexity than the famous hydraulic feats of the states to the north. For example, in Quebrada del Toro in the valley of Calchaquí, swollen rivers were used to flood fields and terraces in succession. This irrigation system, using stone walls to protect against erosion, produced larger areas of arable land than the systems in use today. In other areas, for example the valley of the Mapocho, it was probably Inca technology that made possible the cultivation of land away from the river beds through the construction of irrigation canals. According to Cristóbal de Molina, Chilean Diaguita fertilized their maize crops by sowing each seed inside a sardine. More generally, though, the farmers of the southern Andes used the guano deposits of seabirds and llama dung to fertilize the soil, as they still do. Traditional indigenous systems of crop rotation and fallowing the land also survive.

Both archaeological and historical evidence suggests that each kin-based community engaged in a variety of subsistence activities; those who cultivated the land also kept flocks of camelids. Fishing groups appear to have been more specialized, concentrating on one species of fish or on sealing and manufacturing sealskin canoes for exchange. However, fishing people probably also farmed in addition to obtaining agricultural products through exchange. It is of interest to note that mollusc shells from the Pacific Ocean are found not only in the Atacama oases but also in numerous sites on the eastern slopes of the Andes. Despite the importance of farming activities, the subsidiary value of hunting and gathering must not be overlooked. The fruit of the algarrobo and chañar trees, both of which are well adapted to an arid environment, were the means of survival in times of drought: they were ground to a flour for making bread and fermented, as they still are today, to produce beer for festivals. The fruits were also used as fodder for llamas.

The socio-economic organization of this area was thus typically Andean: each domestic unit was minimally self-sufficient in food, textiles and pottery production. Metal-working was a domestic industry, too, judging by the frequent and widespread references that are made to pre-Inka foundries. Pedro Sande, for example, remarked with reference to the entire Lípez region that 'the Indians build small smelt-furnaces in their houses and on hilltops to catch the wind; in general, they all engage in processing and extracting silver'.[5] On the other hand, it has been suggested that specialist artisans must have been responsible for producing certain types of metal and textile objects associated with social status and religious or mortuary functions.

Settlement patterns among these agriculturists were adapted not only to ecological but also to historical circumstances. The first evidence we have of the administration of a hierarchically organized social system by an incipient elite dates from the period 300–900, when the Atacama culture was flourishing. During this period, some sites in north-west Argentina were colonized, evidenced by findings of artefacts in the San Pedro style, including polished black ceramics and objects associated with the so-called 'rapé-complex' used for the consumption of hallucinogenic drugs. A general shift in settlement patterns occurred in the area as a whole during the post-Tiwanaku period when it was subjected to Aymara pressure from the north. The *chullpas* (funerary towers) in the headwaters of the Río Loa which, it is thought, were built by Aymara from Lípez, are evidence of such pressure. The shift in settlement patterns consisted of a change from the dispersed residences in valleys or by oases to fortified towns (*pucara*). These stone edifices were built on strategically high ground, partly in response to a demand for resources and partly in response to the disruptive, often violent, effects of migration. Disputes and violence may also have resulted on occasion, from attempts to re-open old traffic routes or to re-colonize far-off territory.

Towards the end of the Late Intermediate period, with its predominantly local-level political organization, a sort of inter-regional equilibrium was achieved through the development of centralized

[5] Juan Lozano Machuca, 'Carta del factor de Potosí Juan Lozano Machuca al virrey del Perú, en donde se describe la provincia de los Lipes', in Jimenez de la Espada, *Relacions geográficas de Perú*, II, 61.

polities. This development must have facilitated regional specialization and access to far-flung resources; some of the more concentrated settlements could not have survived without access to such resources, since their immediate territory was insufficient to support a dense population. Even in the eighteenth century there were settlements from Atacama in the valley of Calchaquí; this pattern of dispersed settlement may have extended as far south as Santiago. This system must have been reinforced, directly or indirectly, by Inca government.[6] On the one hand, imperial peace would enable local lords to establish more secure relations with distant subjects; on the other, the Inka practice of redistributing the population afforded unprecedented possibilities of maintaining links with far-off areas. For example, Diaguita mitimaes were being sent to Cochabamba until as late as 1580, judging by archaeological discoveries there of funerary urns belonging to the Santamariana Calchaquí culture.[7]

As occurred elsewhere in the Andes, some land was probably allocated preferentially to the lords of the polity (*curacas*). The rights to land and resources conferred on curacas would have been supplemented by their claim to the services of the group's collective labour at certain times of the year. Otherwise the individual nuclear families probably had relative parity of access to fields and to water supplies. We know that in colonial times communities laid collective claim to both pasture lands and algarrobo groves. There is justification for thinking, however, that there were limitations and obligations attached to the use of communally tilled land; irrigated fields are an obvious case in point. Where conflict arose over access to basic goods and services, local leaders would have been prominent in the resolution of the conflict. They were also responsible for the distribution of public wealth and for the organization of labour. The gold mines in the Aconcagua valley, for instance, are known to have been worked by members of local communities during the Inca period, according to a system of rotating shifts arranged by the curacas.[8]

The ethnic lords were clearly privileged figures, marked out from the rest of the people, and their activities were regarded with veneration.

[6] John V. Murra, 'El control vertical de un máximo de pisos ecológicos en la economía de las sociedades andinas', in Iñigo Ortiz de Zuñiga, *Visita de la provincia de León de Huánuco en 1562*, J. V. Murra (ed.) (2 vols., Huánuco, 1967–72).

[7] Dick Edgar Ibarra Grasso, *Argentina Indígena y Prehistoria Americana* (Buenos Aires, 1967), 659.

[8] Pedro Mariño de Lovera, *Crónica del reino de Chile* [1595] (Santiago, 1867), 54–5.

They married many wives: sixteenth-century chronicles mention lords in Copiapó who had up to ten or twelve wives. They wore 'lustrous' robes of llama wool. A different writer describes as 'poor' those whose clothing is made of fibre from the cabuya plant. The lords were greeted in a special way, and their houses were conspicuous in size and appearance. Despite the prestige attached to their hereditary office, however, their authority rested at all times on consensus. In peace-time, this meant an assembly of heads of family amongst whom agreement was reached, we are told, only after lengthy deliberation and abundant beer-drinking; in war-time, young warriors also participated in the deliberations, and they were consulted on policy matters. Under Inca rule, the influence of such leaders probably increased to the extent that they collaborated with the invaders; we know that they spoke Quechua, and some had visited Cuzco where they exchanged gifts with the Inca. Their authority and social distinction extended to female kin. One woman of the curaca class was carried about in a litter and was able to save the lives of two Spaniards against the wishes of other leading men in Copiapó.[9]

In its general outlines, this model corresponds most closely to the political system of the Diaguita. With the exception of Calchaquí, these societies were normally autonomous and little centralized: that is to say, all the curacas in a locality exercised power on an equal footing, and separate local or ethnic groups were opposed, forming temporary alliances only under conditions of semi-permanent warfare when the most prestigious among the allied military chiefs was elected to head the rest. However, a military hierarchy did not exist as a separate socio-political unit: just as military leadership was connected with the office of curaca, warriors were not a separate group. Farmers working the soil, for instance, went armed with bows and arrows; those digging for salt kept watch at the same time.

In the case of the Atacama, the Humahuaca, and perhaps also the Calchaquí, by contrast, the power of a principal curaca extended beyond the radius of his own community to include not only distant colonies but also different ethnic groups. The Humahuaca town curaca is a case in point, since not only did he hold sway over the leaders of the numerous Humahuaca valley settlements, but his control also extended beyond the limits of the valley: a proportion of the Ocloya, for instance,

[9] Bibar, *Crónica*, 66.

were dependent on the Omaguaca, and may have been their mitimaes as well.[10] The southern territories of the Inca empire owed their allegiance to Cuzco, but they were in some cases also subject to more local control. Apo Cari, for instance, a lord of the Lupaca on the shores of Lake Titicaca, was, according to his grandson, second in person to the Inca, with command over an area stretching from Cuzco to Chile, in which 'lands were cultivated for him...and he was given clothes, silver, and Indian men and women servants'.[11] Finally, in the context of the internal and inter-ethnic political relations in this area, it should not be forgotten that the Spaniards took advantage not only of disputes and rivalries but also of existing relations of solidarity and dependence. When Almagro, for instance, undertook the conquest of the southern Inca empire, he had the backing of 10,000 bearers under the command of three high-ranking figures (two from Cuzco and one from Copacabana) with whose counsel and collaboration the way was cleared for the Spanish Army.

Only the earliest and most detailed Spanish documents provide us with even fragmentary data for the reconstruction of pre-Hispanic institutions. In much of this area a system of dual administration was in operation which Spanish descriptions of indigenous political systems often overlooked by emphasizing one curaca to the exclusion of the other. Chronicles do reiterate, nevertheless, that the Spaniards met two leaders in each valley of the Chilean Diaguita region. On the basis of such material we can reconstruct that each valley was conceived as a whole formed of an upper and a lower moiety: the mountain moiety and the coastal moiety. The former was governed by the principal curaca and the latter by a junior one. Each had under his leadership two military chiefs. It is uncertain if the moieties were endogamous or exogamous, or according to what principles of descent and residence they functioned. Although paired curacas in the valleys are described as brothers, this term was most probably symbolic of kinship ties uniting the two moieties which they represented. Their relationship was one of rivalry and competition; and they fought one another in ritual battles, which the chronicles interpreted as warfare in the European sense. On the other hand, they also co-operated with one another and frequently decisions were made by mutual consent.

The social structure of the Atacama, northern neighbours of the Chilean Diaguita, was based on this type of dual organization until the

---

[10] Serrano, *Los aborígenes*, 71–2.
[11] Garci Diez de San Miguel, *Visita hecha a la provincia de Chucuito* [1567] (Lima, 1964), 107.

beginning of the nineteenth century; that of the Aymara of Tarapacá, further north still, has remained so up to the present. In north-west Argentina the presence of dual organization is revealed both by historical sources and by archaeological remains. A notable exception was the early seventeenth-century Calchaquí valley, where, according to numerous accounts written at the time, one person held sway over the entire valley. This unitary command, though can be understood in connection with the necessities of war – specifically the war of resistance to European domination which the Calchaquí people had by then been fighting for a long time. Elsewhere, chronicles repeatedly mention that single villages had two leaders. Argentine Diaguita society had dual organization until the seventeenth century, as attested both by frequent references to *encomiendas* and *repartimientos* formed of paired residential groups, and also, even more significantly, by references to groups recognizing two leaders.[12]

A further example of dual organization in north-west Argentina is contained in Father Lozano's account of Piltipico and Diego Teluy, the two Omaguaca curacas in the last decade of the sixteenth century. Piltipico is presented as 'the most authorized and famous (*cacique*) in the whole province of Omaguaca...(a man) whose name was the dread not only of timorous Indians but even of the boldest Spaniards'. Yet, despite his having entered a period of peace after 'thirty years of fury spent depopulating several cities', he was incited to take up arms again by Teluy, who was 'cacique in the town, properly called Omaguaca, from which the whole valley derives its name'.[13]

The southern limits of dual organization coincide with the imaginary line that may be drawn between the Aconcagua valley and Mendoza. The founder of Mendoza was received by the two Huarpe curacas, Ocoyunta and Allalme, 'with others who came from those valleys, whose names are Gueimare, Anato, Trabalasto, and others, and who were obeyed by all the Indians in the neighbouring district'.[14] In the east, sixteenth- and seventeenth-century registers of curacas in Cordoba record the existence of settlements with two or three lords.[15]

Although there were no temples in the sense understood by the

[12] Anibal Montes, 'Encomiendas de indios Diaguitas documentadas en el Archivo Histórico de Córdoba', *Revista* (Universidad Nacional de Córdoba, Instituto de Antropología), nos. 2–3 (1961), 7–29.

[13] Pedro Lozano, *Historia de la compañía de Jesús en la Provincia del Paraguay* (2 vols., Madrid, 1754–5), I, 211, 215.

[14] Mariño de Lovera, *Crónica*, 251.

[15] Alberto Rex Gonzales, *Arte, estructura y arqueología. Análisis de figuras duales y anatrópicas del N.O. Argentino* (Buenos Aires, 1974), 133.

Spaniards in this area there were, for example in Calchaquí, special cult houses called *mochaderos*, buildings decorated with sticks, feathers and religious sculptures. There were also many sacred places where people worshipped; at Copiapó, Spanish captives were imprisoned in a sanctuary.[16] Andean houses have a religious significance beyond their function as dwelling-places. To this day, wherever Andean tradition persists, house-building is accompanied by a ceremony at which each of the inner corners is consecrated. Houses were also associated with ancestor cults, as attested both by historical and by archaeological evidence of burial of the dead inside, or very near, their houses.

Religion in the south-central Andes was closely linked to the socio-economic system. Lozano, for example, in describing Calchaquí beliefs, revealed their metaphorical correspondence between the ancestors, human society and the universe. He wrote that 'Venus and other more resplendent stars were deceased curacas, transformed at death into those stars; ordinary Indians and llamas were converted into an innumerable throng of less notable stars, and the most evil men became devils'.[17] The curacas' proximity to the divine ancestors conferred on them a sacred nature. For this reason, curacas are described sometimes as *huacas* (sorcerers).

In the absence of contemporary descriptions of ideas and religious beliefs, archaeological remains become a fundamental resource for their reconstruction, as do the folklore and religious practices of today. Thus, a correlation can be established between ancient Andean social structures based on dual leadership and a series of sculptural, ceramic and graphic representations of dualist conceptions, such as bird-men, or half-human, half-feline figures. Other archaeological pieces combine features of one or more animals which take on a quite different appearance when viewed as a whole; for example, the appearance of a human face. Sometimes opposition is represented realistically on the obverse faces of a piece; for example, the open-eyed anthropomorphic figure which appears from behind with its eyes closed, symbolizing life and death, vigilance and sleep, day and night. Other pieces depict two different aspects of a subject according to the angle from which they are viewed. Finally, there are many sculptured images of sexual polarity. Images of this nature are usually formed of a pair of human figures, though feline features may also be superimposed on the bas-relief at the junction of the knees

16 Mariño de Lovera, *Crónica*, 12.
17 Lozano, *La Compañía de Jesus*, I, 425.

and feet of the figures. Much of this art was connected with the use of hallucinogenic drugs and with myths about the metamorphoses of the shaman – his transformation, for instance, into a hunter-warrior endowed with feline qualities. It can also be seen, however, in the wider context of understanding reality in terms of sets of opposed but complementary categories which are used as classificatory concepts of social organization.

Among religious specialists the most numerous were herbalists or curers; the Hambi-Camayo were treated as sorcerers by the *cabildo* of Santiago which decided to persecute them in November 1552. Some 'spoke with the Devil' and lacerated themselves during rituals when the group gathered together for what the Spaniards called 'holy drunkenness'. On such occasions the shaman would beat a drum while others danced and sang. There was in addition a common motif, known as the 'sacrificer', of a human figure with an axe in one hand and a human head in the other. Spanish prisoners of the Diaguita in the valley of Copiapó reported being taken before an 'Indian who for many years had had the duty of sacrificing... clothed in a long robe reaching to his feet and in place of a staff carried a copper axe and what this Indian sacrificed was people'.[18] The cult of head-taking was associated with military culture throughout northern Chile and north-west Argentina.

Inca hegemony brought the imperial cult of the sun and moon to the area. It would appear that the state religion was blended with local traditions, since the 'sacrificer' of Copiapó performed rituals in worship of the sun in front of the Spanish captives. Other Inca forms of worship may have been restricted to immigrant mitimaes, for example the sacrifices made in sanctuaries on high mountain peaks; sites have been found on peaks between 5,000 and 6,000 metres altitude in Santiago, Coquimbo, San Juan, Jujuy and Atacama, where the extreme cold has preserved figurines of silver, copper, gold and spondylus shell, clothed in feathers and brightly coloured cloth, the wood to make fires and even the bodies of the victims.

At the time of the European invasion and during the first centuries of the colonial period, the south-east (that is to say, the forests and the Chaco of Tucumán) was inhabited by the 'Rhea' people, so-called from Quechua and in early chronicles because they wore rhea feathers. In fact, there were at least two distinct groups, the Tonocoté and the Lule.

[18] Mariño de Lovera, *Crónica*, 81–2; see also Bibar, *Crónica*, 66.

The Tonocoté were sedentary llama-herders, who kept domesticated rhea and cultivated maize, squash, beans and peanuts in the floodplains of rivers, which they also fished. Their language was described by several early authors as the 'general language' of the whole of Tucumán. The Matará of the Río Bermejo were a Tonocoté tribe with a total population of 20,000; in 1585, Alonso de Vera y Aragón, by his own account, had 2,000 in his service. Tonocoté lived in well-stockaded settlements of several thousand people.[19] This was to defend themselves against the Lule, nomadic hunter-gatherers of the tropical Chaco woodlands who invaded Tonocoté territory in order to raid their foothill villages. At the time of the conquest, Lule were centred between Jujuy and Santiago del Estero. Barzana says that they lived scattered 'without houses or gardens, but such warmongers, and in such numbers, that had the Spaniards not arrived when they undertook the conquest of the province of Tucumán, this nation alone would have done away with the Tonocoté, by eating some and forcing others to surrender.'[20]

The Lule, 'while they are a single people have diverse tongues because they do not all reside in a single territory'. However, they also understood Toconoté, which for them was the language of Christianity. Among these peoples death was the occasion for ritual dancing, chanting and beer-drinking, and for guests to give gifts which it was the host's obligation to reciprocate. Similar rites secured a good algarrobo harvest or a supply of honey, or a victory over adversaries.

In the central sierras to the south of the Tonocoté lived two societies, the Sanavirón and the Comechingón. The Sanavirón were settled in an extensive area south of the Río Dulce, including the Mar Chiquita depression. The Comechingón lived in the Sierra de San Luis and the Sierra de Córdoba. In the second half of the sixteenth century, the two groups together numbered 30,000 distributed in over 600 villages. Each village constituted a separate unit of between ten and 40 houses, with four or five married adults to a house. Each house was big enough to conceal a group of ten Spanish soldiers with their horses. They were built like underground cellars covered with grass roofs, and the village

[19] Bibar, *Crónica*, 162, 163.
[20] Alonso de Barzana, 'Carta del Padre Alonso de Barzana de la Compañia de Jesús al Padre Juan Sebastián, su provincial. Fecha en la Asunción del Paraguay a 8 de Septiembre de 1594', in Jimenez de la Espada, *Relaciones Geográficas de Perú*, II, 79.

was walled in with thorn defences;[21] these societies practised a mixed economy, in many ways like those of the south-central Andes. They were mainly agriculturists, with a staple crop of maize supplemented by beans and quinoa, but they also raised llamas and gathered algarrobo and chañar as additional sources of subsistence. They are closer to the Pampa dwellers, on the other hand, in their emphasis on hunting, the main species of game being guanaco, deer and hare.

Ayllus were the foundation of Comechingón social organization. Each ayllo owned land, some of which was divided into parcels allotted to the individual families of the community, while the rest was worked communally. Ayllu heads, themselves subordinate to leaders at higher levels of organization, were entitled to communal labour for the maize and algarrobo harvests; in payment, they organized beer festivals in their houses.[22] Factional sorcery accusations were a constant feature of ayllu life, leading to the dissolution and reformation of residential groups on community land.

Huarpe lands at the time of the invasion comprised the region which is delimited by the Río Zanjon in the province of San Juan, the Río Diamante in the province of Mendoza and lake Guanacache. An expedition returning from Peru under Villagra in 1533 found the area densely populated, though numbers dwindled considerably in the south. Bibar described the western Huarpe as skilled peasants with irrigated fields in which they cultivated maize, beans and quinoa.[23] He adds that they owned 'guanacos' by which he presumably meant llamas. The eastern Huarpe of lake Guanacache lived by hunting and gathering. In 1610, according to Father Diego de Torres, their main sources of subsistence were fish and the root of the totora reed, the stalk of which they used in the construction of large rafts.[24]

Huarpe social and religious organization was typically Andean, based as it was, according to Marino de Lovera's chronicle, on a system of dual leadership. In other words, it was not, as Bibar had claimed, typical

[21] Gerónimo Luis de Cabrera, 'Relación en suma de la tierra y poblazones que don Gerónimo Luis de Cabrera, gobernador de las provincias de los Juries, ha descubierto donde va a poblar en nombre de su Majestad una ciudad' [1573], in Jimenez de la Espada, *Relaciones Geográficas de Perú*, I, 388–9; Bibar, *Crónica*, 163; Pedro Sotelo Narváez, 'Relación de las Provincias de Tucumán que dió Pedro Sotelo Narváez vecino de aquellas provincias, al muy ilustre señor licenciado Cépeda, presidente desta real Audiencia de La Plata' [1583], in Jimenez de la Espada, *Relaciones geográficas de Perú*, 393.

[22] Antonio Serrano, *Los Comechingones* (Córdoba, 1945), 329–31.

[23] Bibar, *Crónica*, 164.   [24] Serrano, *Los Comechingones*, 154.

of the system of the Picunche of the Mapocho valley, which was based on individual leadership.

The western agricultural fringe of the central southern Andes was the home of the Mapuche. They can be divided into three separate areas: the Picunche ('northern people'), who had settled the lands to the south of the Chilean Diaguita, from the Mapocho valley to the Río Maule; the Araucanians between the Maule and the Toltén; and the Huilliche, the 'southern people' of the area between the Toltén and the island of Chiloé. These divisions are extremely fluid and appear to be mainly geographical. However they are also based on underlying economic and cultural criteria.

The northern Mapuche or Picunche were divided: those in the Mapocho valley had extensive areas of land under irrigation, using an Inca system of ditches which were noteworthy enough to be mentioned in Spanish chronicles and title-deeds. The Picunche were nicknamed 'wild wolves' (*promaucaes*) by the Quechua-speakers of Cuzco because of the simplicity of their agriculture, their reliance on gathering and their resistance to entering Inca service.[25] Although no detailed historical study of Picunche demography exists, it is possible to estimate the size of their population at the time of the Spanish invasion at between 117,500–122,500.[26] Further south, eye-witness accounts from the first expeditions into Araucanian lands express astonishment at the size of the population on the coast and central plains. In a letter to the king of Spain in 1551, Valdivia expressed his enthusiasm for the area, which he described as 'a single town, garden, and gold mine,...(in which) there is no space for more houses unless they are built one above the

[25] Bibar, *Crónica*, 135.

[26] Pedro de Valdivia wrote in a letter to Hernando Pizarro in 1545 that there were 15,000 Indians between Copiapó and the Río Maule valley; assuming then an average of five persons in each domestic unit, the total population would have been 75,000. Valdivia adds, however, that an equal number had died in the intervening years since the conquest of Chile began, which brings the total retrospectively to 150,000 in 1540 (Pedro de Valdivia, *Cartas* [1545–52] (Santiago, 1955)). If we exclude from this figure an estimated 20,000 Chilean Diaguita and the estimated Aconcagua valley population of 7,500, we arrive at 122,500 Picunche. Bibar writes that in 1558 the jurisdiction of Santiago (i.e. from the valley of Aconcagua to that of the Rio Maule) there were more than 25,000 Indians when the Spanish entered the land in 1540 (Bibar, *Crónica*, 213). If we make the same calculation as above, there would have been a total population of 125,000 in 1540, or, excluding once again the inhabitants of the Aconcagua valley, 117,500 Picunche. The earliest historical figures for the Picunche, therefore, can be amplified within a range of 117,500–122,500. According to both authors, however, population decline was devastatingly rapid: 50 per cent in five years, according to one, and 72 per cent in eighteen years, according to the other.

other'. Steward's estimate of 1,000,000 seems to be the closest approximation to the reality of mid-sixteenth century Araucania;[27] in the five years up to 1555, however, the upheaval in Araucanian society resulting from war combined with high mortality, drought, the destruction of crops, famine and a smallpox epidemic, slashed the population by over 60 per cent.[28]

Pre-Columbian Araucanian economies varied according to differences in ecology. In the dry, northern hinterland, ground above irrigation level served at best as seasonal pasture. In contrast, the central valley was wet and supported a population of llama-herders, practising rotation agriculture in open land and slash-and-burn techniques in the interfluvial woodlands. Swidden agriculture was extensive since at any one time it called for a number of gardens at different stages of cultivation and secondary growth. For this reason, it did not allow the degree of population density or stability which intensive hydraulic agriculture afforded, a constraint which was reflected in the characteristically dispersed distribution of Araucanian settlements and garden sites. Because swidden systems, being intensive, entailed competition for land, there was also a lack of political cohesion and the occurrence of warfare among and between settlements.[29] Central valley Araucanians cultivated most of the crops grown in the Andes, such as maize, beans, potatoes, quinoa and chillies, as well as certain gramineous plants, brome grass (*Bromus mango*), madia (*Madia sativa*) and the *teca* cereal. But if agriculture was less important to them than to other Andean societies, gathering was of proportionally greater value to their diet. In addition other groups occupied ecological niches unsuitable for agriculture. For example, the Pehuenche, inhabiting the high Cordillera, lived by hunting and by gathering Araucania pines 'with which they make bread, wine and stews',[30] and were in permanent exchange relations with the Mapuche; or seafaring people on the coast where excessive humidity made agriculture difficult. Some parts of the coast and the islands supported a dense population through marine resources.

---

[27] Julian H. Steward, 'The native population of South America', in J. H. Steward (ed.), *Handbook of South American Indians*, 6 vols., (Washington, D.C., 1946–50), v, 658.

[28] The demographic decline continued, judging from the fact that by 1870 the Araucanian population, including the inhabitants of those parts of Argentina which had come under Araucanian influence, barely reached 115,000. See Leonardo León, 'The Araucanian rebellion of 1867–72 in Argentina and Chile'. Unpublished MA thesis, University of London, 1979, 9.

[29] Tom D. Dillehay, *Estudios atropológicos sobre los Mapuches de Chile Sur-Central.* (Pontificia Universidad Católica de Chile, Temuco, 1976), 25–9.

[30] Mariño de Lovera, *Crónica*, 268.

Araucanian political organization was based on the *lebo*, a unit which comprised in turn seven or eight *cabi* or smaller divisions, each with its own leader. These offices were hereditary and therefore distinct from that of the military leader who was elected for the duration of a dispute or campaign. A hereditary leader was not however invested with the power of coercion, and what influence he had was a measure of his prestige and persuasive abilities. 'They had no recognized right to inflict punishment, to claim tribute or personal service, or to demand obedience from their kinsfolk or "subjects". The latter paid no attention to them and did as they pleased if the leaders showed themselves arrogant or domineering.'[31] Important decisions, therefore, were taken in council, when representatives met

to hear lawsuits and to discover causes of deaths; people marry there, and they drink in quantity...; if they are at war with another leader, all the lords and cabi are obliged to mobilize their people and take up arms on behalf of the group which council instructs them to support. If any one among them fails to do so, it is on pain of death and loss of estate. Disagreements between heads or any other members of the group are heard and settled, and buying and selling takes place every day while the meeting of the council lasts.[32]

Council met several times a year in a place called the *regua*. Headmen were given special burials: unlike other Araucanian dead who were buried in their preferred garden sites, holding different seeds to sow in the after-life, men of rank rested near their houses on wooden platforms supported by uprights, in coffins made of dug-out tree trunks.[33] After death, they lived in volcanoes or among the stars.

THE CHACO AND THE LITTORAL

The area which is now Paraguay, north-eastern Argentina and Uruguay was peopled at the time of the conquest by a heterogeneous mixture of ethnic groups; some were recent migrant agriculturists from Amazonia; the inhabitants of longer standing were in the main hunter-gatherers. To the south, the littoral peoples merged with those of the Pampa and Patagonia. The Chané or Guaná were settled mainly in the Paraguayan Chaco. They spoke an Arawak language, which in Susnik's view indicates the route along which they migrated. She also distinguishes three main groups, one to the south of the Chiquitos, a

---

[31] John M. Cooper, 'The Araucanians', in Steward, *Handbook*, II, 724.
[32] Bibar, *Crónica*, 160.   [33] *Ibid.*, 135, 156.

second near the Río Paraguay neighbouring with the Mbayá, and a third scattered towards the Andean cordillera by Chiriguano migrations. It appears that at the time of the conquest these latter had not established themselves in the upper Paraguay and sought refuge with other tribes using their established practice of alliance or integration through marriage. Those neighbouring on the Mbayá hunter-gatherers and fishers were, in the words of the German Schmidl in 1552, 'vassals and subjects of the aforementioned Mbayaes, just as in our countries peasants are subject to their lords'.[34]

Chané villages were large, with fifteen or more communal houses, arranged in two or three concentric circles and housing up to 1,000 people. In each house lived a family head with his kin, commoners and slaves; the size of a house, averaging 16 metres by $6\frac{1}{2}$ metres, testified to its significance as a socio-economic unit. Similarly, the size of a village was a symbol of its claim to prestige. It was divided into different quarters, the senior one being that of the leader and his immediate relatives. Chané society was divided into four classes: nobles, warriors, commoners and slaves. Marriage was based on class endogamy within a village moiety system. The noble lineage, whose ancestors guaranteed the success of the harvest, exercised leadership by heredity. Heads of the communal houses and lower-ranking war leaders belonged to the warrior class. Although preferentially endogamous, this class did not preclude social mobility: the commoners and slaves could acquire the status of warrior, and marriages between warriors and commoners were frequent. The ethnic heterogeneity of the *wahere-shane*, or commoners (literally, filthy people), was a function of Chané social integration; they cultivated the land and were recruited for service in Mbayá households. Slaves, captives from other tribes, performed economic services in the domestic group to which they belonged.

The Chané practised female infanticide by live burial, which together with the practice of abortion maintained a low population with a sex ratio of 2:1. As a result, few Chané men were able to marry within their own group. The ambiguity of the Chané marriage system is reflected in the myth of the twin sons of a cultivating woman; one son was possessive and endogamous, the other nomadic and exogamous. Some Chané men could form marriage alliances within their own group, but their brothers had no alternative but to steal women, which thus

---

[34] Quoted in Branislava Susnik, *El indio colonial del Paraguay. III: El chaqueño: guaycurúes y chanés-arawak* (Asunción, 1971), 141.

recruited new members to the group and made possible the establishment of new houses and settlements. Susnik argues that fertility control was an integral element in the reproduction of the Chané social system.

Two peoples of the Tupian language group were found in this area: the Guaraní lived in widely-scattered groups in the south-east Chaco on the islands of the Paraná delta and north of the interfluvial provinces of Corrientes and Misiones in what is today northern Argentina. The Chiriguano had migrated into the north-west Chaco from Brazil in 1521, led by a Portuguese named Alejo Garcia, forcing the local population into submission and presenting a challenge to Inka hegemony.

In common with other Amazonian cultivators, the Guaraní staple crops were maize and manioc; squash and sweet potato were also grown in all areas except the Paraná delta where the cold climate precluded them. The Guaraní also grew beans, peanuts, mate, cotton and urucu. Gardens were abandoned every five years; the clearing and preparation of new sites were men's work, while women had the tasks of sowing, tending and harvesting. This diet was supplemented by hunting, gathering and fishing.

As can be seen in the early drawings that were made of them, Guaraní villages consisted of up to eight communal houses surrounded by a stockade. Each house was the residence of a patrilineal kin group sometimes incorporating as many as 60 families. The village leader was the head of the principal lineage. His influence was most significant in creating external alliances; internally his powers were limited and decisions about village issues required the consensus of heads and elders. Unlike military leadership to which men were expressly elected, civil leadership was hereditary. However, succession could generate divisions and the establishment of a new settlement, where a new headman would be elected. Polygyny was a chiefly privilege, as were the services of the village work-force, who built the headman's house, cultivated his gardens and harvested the crops. Shamans had great prestige in Guaraní society, and after their death their remains might become objects of worship.

Chaco hunter-gatherers belonged to six language groups, the Guaycuruan, the Lule-Vilelan, Mascoian, Matacoan, Zamucoan and an unidentified group that included the Matará. The largest of these groups was the Guaycuruan, which included the Abipón, the Mocovi, the Pilaga, the Toba, the Payagua, the Mbayá and the Caduveo. The Chaco is an alluvial bed of clays which floods in the wet season between

February and April and is subject to severe drought in the dry season. The area was unfavourable both for cultivation and for European settlement. As a result, Tupi- and Arawak-speaking cultivators lived only on the edges of the Gran Chaco. Some Chaco groups practised simple horticulture, despite such natural disadvantages as 'dryness of soil, lack of chemicals and excessive floods...blight, locusts, tordo birds, parakeets, (and) peccaries'.[35]

Fish was an important subsistence base in the Chaco, and in April and May, when the fish came up the Pilcomayo and other rivers, bands would gather on the banks and use various fishing techniques. They would then dry and smoke some of the catch to exchange for maize and other products with non-fishing tribes. Gathering was also of central importance: some of the wild plants and fruits gathered by Chaco peoples are of rich nutritional value and were conserved for long periods. Tribes of the north-east Chaco, for example the Mbayá, gathered various species of palm, in addition to algarrobo. Family groups would spend a few weeks in the palm groves, returning to the village with several parts of the tree for which they had a use: its sap was drunk; the fruit, seeds and shoots were eaten in different ways; its pith was reduced to a flour; and grubs from the trunk were a delicacy. Rope was made from the leaves, and its thorns served as needles.

Hunting was also important in the Chaco, especially for those who had no access to the rivers. Changes in hunting patterns were brought by European encroachments. The efficiency of the bow and arrow was improved through the early adoption of metal arrowheads. The Guaycurú, who at an early date contracted to supply the Spaniards in Asunción, began to hunt a limited variety of game more intensively: each week they brought in roast deer and peccary, smoked fish, lard, jaguar hides and the skins of other animals, and dyed fibre cloth. The demands made by this increased pressure on the hunting grounds intensified intertribal disputes. Trade relations with the Asunceños themselves were peaceful, but there was violence between the Guaraní who were in the Spanish service and the Guaycurú who obtained from them maize, manioc, peanuts, bows and metal arrowheads. The Spaniards themselves began to get worried as the numbers of hunters involved in exchange reached 3,000–4,000.

In Métraux's view the Chaco peoples fell into two different groups in terms of political and social organization. Among non-equestrian

[35] Alfred Métraux, 'Ethnography of the Chaco', in Steward, *Handbook*, 1, 251.

Chaco tribes, like the Mataco, Choronti, Ashluslay, Macá, Lengua, Toba and Lule-Vilela, the basic unit was a band of between 50 and 200 people united through kinship. Separate territories were identified under the title of a chief, in some cases a shaman, whose position depended on his personal gifts and standing. He had no privileges, and the position was rarely hereditary. Among the horse-riding and marine (canoeing) groups, like the Mocovi, the Abipones, the Peyaguá and Mbayá, there was a degree of social stratification. As already mentioned, the Mbayá were overlords to some of the Chané. The introduction of European horses reinforced relations of domination over Tupi- and Arawak-speaking neighbours and intensified the degree of stratification within the nomadic groups themselves. It also enabled them to oppose and defeat the Spaniards.

The Mbayá were divided into four classes similar to those of their servants, the chané: nobles, warriors, servants and slaves. The Mbayá nobility, whose sons received special education, was formed of a stratum of hereditary chiefs and individuals of merit. Despite an ideology of purity of descent, cases are known of Mbayá chiefs who were sons of Chané women. Warriors were more numerous than nobles, and the approval of the more distinguished among them, as well as that of the lower-ranking leaders, was required before administrative agreements could be reached.

The master-servant relationship between the Mbayá and the Chané was established on the basis of affinal alliance; a Mbayá chief would marry a Chané noblewoman and thereby gain ascendancy over her subjects. The fact that the Chané addressed the Mbayá head as 'lord', while ordinary Mbayá were addressed as 'brothers', indicate that the Chané were servants of Mbayá chiefs only. At the annual harvest Mbayá villages visited subject Chané villages; their headmen received tributes and reciprocated with metal or glass objects of Spanish origin; in turn, the gifts which a leader received were redistributed among his own people. There were in addition Chané living as slaves in Mbayá villages: the men were put to work in the gardens, while women spent their time weaving. To own slaves or captives was a matter of pride and prestige for Mbayá men and women and, although inside the communal houses slaves were the furthest removed physically from the head of the kin-group, they were treated as kin, sharing meals, participating in sport and in councils of war. A slave could become free on grounds of merit.

In the river system framed by the middle and lower reaches of the

Ríos Paraná to the west and the Uruguay to the east, besides the Amazonian horticulturists and hunter-gatherers already mentioned were people who combined these two forms of subsistence and show mixed influences from the Amazon, the Chaco and the Pampa. These were the inter-fluvial Caingang and Charrúa, and the numerous but scarcely-known littoral group on both banks of the lower Paraná. The central Timbú and Carcará, who had come under Guaraní or Arawak influence, practised small-scale horticulture, growing maize, beans and gourds. The southern Chaná-Iimbú and Mbeguá were also cultivators: and their horticulture manifested Guaycurú traits, according to Lothrop.[36] The rest lived mainly by fishing, with supplementary hunting and gathering. Villages were built on high ground beside rivers and reservoirs, with rectangular houses made of matting. Very little is known of their political organization, except that one man was known to the Spaniards in Tucumán for his reputation as a leader. Polygyny was practised, and shamans had an important position.

The Caingang linguistic family occupied a wide area between the Paraná and the Uruguay rivers and extended into the present-day Brazilian states of Rio Grande do Sul, Santa Catarina and Paraná. The Cainaroes of Cabot's *mappa mundi* of 1554, located between two other groups who can be identified as Guaraní to the north and Mbeguá to the south seem to be the same as the Caingang. The term, meaning 'long haired', was that generally used by Caingang to refer to themselves. In 1536 Schmidl described the Caingang (whom he called Chaná) as 'short, thick-set men who eat nothing but meat and honey'; they lived away from the rivers in order to escape Mocoreta raids. Each village was organized in moieties, with five or six houses of the matted windscreen type found among the littoral societies. Villages were widely scattered around the hunting grounds of deer, rhea, peccaries and small rodents, and they also fished to a limited extent. Eastern Caingang gathered pine-cone seeds while those between the rivers gathered algarrobo and tubers.[37]

Groups speaking a Charrúa language lived among Chaná, Mbeguá and Yaro on the lower Paraná and in parts of the inter-fluvial region extending as far north as the Río Ubicuí, and south to the Río de la Plata. Charrúa bore very close resemblance, both physically and culturally, to

[36] S. K. Lothrop, 'Indians of the Paraná delta and La Plata littoral', in Steward, *Handbook*, I, 177–90.
[37] Ulrich Schmidt, *Viaje al Río de la Plata (1534–54)* (Buenos Aires, 1903).

the hunting societies of the Pampa and Patagonia. They lived in groups of ten to fifteen families under the aegis of a leader, and groups united for the purpose of defence. Their houses were typical of those of the littoral and inter-fluvial area: unroofed, matted walls supported by a rectangular frame of wooden house posts. Traditionally, the Charrúa hunted on foot, using bows and arrows, bolas and nets to kill deer and rhea; when they became equestrian in the seventeenth century, they also hunted with lances, several metres long, like those of the Araucanians. Riverine Charrúa fished from dug-outs.

THE PAMPA, PATAGONIA AND THE SOUTHERN ARCHIPELAGO

Societies of the Pampas, Patagonia and Tierra del Fuego depended generally on hunting for their subsistence, since the deep-rooted grasses of the Pampas were a natural deterrent to agriculture. The same vegetation, however, also fed rhea and guanaco, both prized game for which precise rules had been elaborated for the distribution of different parts of the animal. Several techniques were used in the hunt: the first European inhabitants of Buenos Aires were astonished at the Querandi's skills in chasing guanaco. The Tahuelche stalked rhea by disguising themselves in feathers and imitating the bird's head and neck with an arm.

The bewildering range of tribal names mentioned by the chroniclers and historical documents in this whole area probably conceals a considerable degree of ethnic identity. In terms of economic organization, two major types can be distinguished – the Ona and the Tehuelche. The latter adopted horses soon after the arrival of the Spaniards and thereafter concentrated on collective hunting of large game using bolas and lances. The Ona-type subsistence pattern relied more on smaller game and fishing. On the coast they hunted seals and gathered shellfish. Since the Ona never adopted horses, the accounts we have of their society may shed light on the pre-Hispanic organization of the Querandi who we know were also fishers.

The Ona inhabited the main island of Tierra del Fuego; the mainland was the home of the Tehuelches who are divided into the southern Tehuelche of Chanik, who lived between Magellan's Strait and the Río Chubut, and the northern Tehuelche from the Chubut northwards into the hills of the provinces of Buenos Aires and Cordoba. The latter grouping includes the Puelche-Guenaken, the Querandi, the Pampa of southern Buenos Aires, the Serrano and the Puelche. These divisions are not to be taken too rigidly, since all these groups were extremely mobile, and the languages they spoke probably belonged to a single language family.

Eighteenth-century accounts of the Tehuelche suggest that each village or clan consisted of between twenty and 80 tents, with three or four families to a tent, though previously they had probably been smaller. Each village had its own headman and its own hunting grounds, and to enter the grounds of another village without the headman's permission could lead to open conflict. Leadership became hereditary at a later stage: although all a headman's sons were eligible for the succession, many declined to take office because of the duties it involved. One of these was the intelligent conduct of the village's hunting activities, failure in which could lead to a man and his close kin being deserted by the rest of the village, leaving them exposed to outside invasion. A man who accepted the office, therefore, made every effort to ensure that he won the allegiance of the village.

When a Tehuelche man died, he was buried with all his possessions, and his livestock (particularly horses) were sacrificed and left as offerings in the grave. His wife and female kin observed a long period of mourning seclusion. A year or more after burial, the bones were disinterred, painted and given secondary burial.

The peoples of the archipelago and coast of the southern extremes of the continent included the Alcaluf, the Yahgan and the Chono. The Alcaluf lived between the Golfo de Penas and the western Fuegian islands. The Yahgan who dwelled on the coast of the Beagle Channel and on the islands to the south spoke an unaffiliated language with five distinct dialects. Each local group had its own waters, but territorial divisions lapsed in times of scarcity and during hunts before a festival. Mainly nomadic, the Yahgan would at some periods of the year build more permanent conical houses from branches covered with skins. They also used skins for clothing.

The Chono, on the other hand, wove cloth from dog fur and a fibre taken from the bark of a tree. They lived in the archipelago that bears their name, and on the Guaytecos archipelago. There is no record of the language they spoke, but it is known to have been unaffiliated. The society was never large: at the beginning of the seventeenth century there were some 200 families (that is to say, over 500 individuals) on a Jesuit mission in the Reloncaví gulf; Jesuit records of the period register 220 baptized and 50 unbaptized Chono. Captives taken by the Chono from among their southern neighbours were sold by them to the inhabitants of the island of Chiloé to the north, who themselves raided the Chono from time to time.

These southern coastal canoeists have rightly been called sea nomads. They travelled in beech tree dugouts, skilfully caulked and balanced to make them seaworthy. Each nuclear family occupied a canoe; the wife paddled and steered while the husband fished and hunted sea mammals; children sat amidships by a fire built on a bed of stones covered with earth. The wife also gathered shellfish from the rocky shore: mussels (*Mytilus chilensis* and *Mytilus edulis*) were staple foods. For Fuegians, penguins, cormorants, wild geese and other birds were game, while a shoal of herring provided an abundant supply of food not only from the fish themselves but also from other animals and birds that swarmed around the shoal. Seals and sea-lions were hunted with harpoons; a whale could feed a fleet of canoeists for weeks, so that any that were sick or wounded coming close to land were killed with harpoons and towed ashore.

Among the hunting societies of the Pampas and Patagonia, the social organization of the seafarers was egalitarian. Elders with a reputation for intelligence and integrity could exercise moral influence, but extended families looked after the interests of their own members, as in the event of conflict or revenge. These were all shamanic societies. It was the shaman's duty to help the local kindred, not only by curing the sick but also by influencing the weather and predicting the future; he was instructed by spirits with which he had contact through dreams. Society was organized on the basis of patrilineal descent; men were heads of families, but the autonomy and independence of women were well respected. Yahgan initiation for boys and girls consisted of moral instruction on matters such as respect for elders and the evils of spreading scandal. This advice was proclaimed as the will of the Supreme Being, the father of animals and plants, life-maker and life-taker, *Watavineva*. The Ona celebrated a secret rite of male initiation known as *kloketen*, similar to the *yinchihava* of the Alacaluf. It alluded to male domination of women, but this was not a reflection of any hostility towards women in everyday life. In the canoeist *kina* ritual, youths learned from a shaman the secret myth which spoke of the time when men rebelled against women, by whom they have previously been dominated; in the guise of spirits, they successfully imposed themselves on the weak and disobedient women who were filled with fear. Initiates were forbidden to disclose the myth to women on pain of death.

The hunting, gathering and fishing peoples of the south had no products of interest to the Europeans and they could not be enticed off their lands by the colonizers by means of economic incentives. Their lands were however suitable for sheepfarming, which developed on a huge scale in the nineteenth and twentieth centuries. The aborigines were forced to settle on missions where they were decimated by disease and converted into sheep-stealers, leading to their persecution and total destruction. Their long history ended abruptly, even if that end, in comparison to that of other native American groups, was for a time delayed.

5

THE INDIANS OF BRAZIL IN 1500

The most satisfactory way of classifying the many hundreds of Indian tribes living in what is now Brazil when the Europeans arrived in 1500 is by language group and by geography and habitat. There were four main language families (in probable order by population): Tupi (or Tupi-Guaraní), Gê, Carib and Aruak (Arawak). (Other language families were only represented at the edge of the frontiers of modern Brazil: Xirianá and Tukano in the north-west, Panoan and Paezan in the west, Guaicuruan and Charrua in the south. Some surviving tribal languages are classified as isolated, or only slightly linked to the main language trunks: Nambicuara (Nambikwara), Bororo, Karajá, Mura, Aripaktsá, and doubtless many others among the hundreds of tribes who died out before their speech was studied by linguists.)

The Tupi-Guaraní were established along most of the Atlantic seaboard. They may have originated in the Andes foothills or the plateau of the middle Paraguay and Paraná rivers and been in the process of a gradual northwards invasion of the Brazilian coast. Other Tupi-speaking tribes occupied the south bank of the Amazon river, moving up the southern tributaries near its mouth, and upstream on the main river almost to the modern Peruvian border. The Gê occupied the vast, relatively open, plateau of central Brazil. The Gê may be descendants of the original inhabitants of Brazil – the oldest human fossil finds at Lagôa Santa in Minas Gerais, which are over 10,000 years old, correspond physically to modern Gê types. These central Gê-speaking tribes cover an enormous arc of land from Maranhão to the upper Paraguay. Other Gê-speakers lived in the hills inland from the south-eastern coast and in places descended to the ocean itself. These might have been remnants of tribes displaced by the Tupi invasion, although they showed little affinity with the sea.

The Amazon basin which was inhabited and contested by three of the main language groups – Tupi, Aruak and Carib – had seen the most sophisticated pre-conquest cultures in Brazil. Pottery excavated on Marajó island at the river's mouth, and at Santarém and other sites along its banks, bear witness to societies more advanced than the tribes encountered by the Europeans in the sixteenth century. Some of these finds are dated 2,000 years B.P. or more. The Omagua of the upper Amazon – who spoke a Tupi-related language – were still making elaborate pottery at the time of their first contact in 1542. Tupi tribes occupied riverine islands such as Tupinambaranas and much of the right bank of the lower river. Many of these Indians may, however, have invaded these areas only shortly before, or even after, the arrival of the Portuguese. The Aruak were well established on the Negro and Orinoco, along the banks of the middle Amazon and on the headwaters of the Madeira. There were isolated Aruak-speaking tribes near the sources of most of the major southern tributaries; and the populous Parecis tribe was across the watershed on the plains of the upper Paraguay. The Aruak are, of course, one of the largest language families. They are found throughout Central America and in Florida and the large Caribbean islands. One theory is that the Aruak had migrated south-eastwards, moving into the Amazon basin from Colombia. A more recent theory is that their culture originated on the river itself, at the confluence of the Negro and Amazon near modern Manaus. Aruak tribes could then have radiated outwards from this nucleus. These riverine, canoe-transported tribes were highly mobile. Apart from pottery they left very few datable artefacts; and little archaeological work has been done on the Amazon. It is therefore impossible to determine with certainty the direction of movement or precise geographical disposition at the time of the conquest.

Spanish *conquistadores* soon became aware of the enmity between the more settled Aruak and the aggressive, often cannibalistic, Caribs on the north coast of South America and in the lesser Caribbean islands. This rivalry appears to have carried over into the Amazon. Carib-speaking tribes were firmly in possession of the Guiana highlands and most of the northern tributaries of the lower Amazon. Isolated Carib tribes are found today far up some of the southern tributaries – but it is difficult to say how recently they migrated there. Early Spanish, Portuguese and French chroniclers mentioned tribes of exotic speech – languages with which they were unfamiliar – on Marajó and around

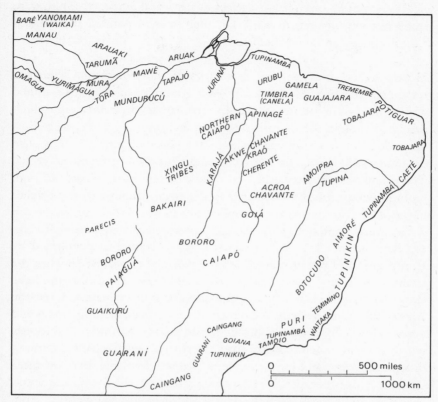

The Indians of the Amazon basin and Brazil, *c.* 1500

the mouth of the great river. It is possible to see these as survivors of the more sophisticated Amazon valley cultures. The Portuguese did not subdue these 'Nheengaiba' ('strange tongue' in Tupi) of Marajó until the mid-seventeenth century. As with almost all tribes of eastern Brazil, they have disappeared, victims of European disease and invasion. There are records of Carib attacks on these peoples at the mouth of the Amazon. A Carib thrust into the lower Amazon – both across the Guiana shield and around the Atlantic coast – was apparently still in progress in the sixteenth century.

Before examining in greater detail what is known of Brazilian Indians on the eve of the European conquest, it is important to note some of the historical problems. The Indians themselves were, of course, pre-literate and innumerate. Their legends and oral traditions, although rich in invention, are almost useless as historical evidence. They were craftsmen of consummate skill, but they built, decorated and painted almost entirely in perishable materials.

Most Brazilian Indians lived in villages of short duration. The main reason for this was that lowland South America had no native animal which could be domesticated – unlike the llamas and guinea-pigs which provided protein for the great Andean civilizations. There were thus no pastoralists in Amazonia. Its peoples were condemned to hunt, fish or gather wild game and insects to augment their agricultural crops. The result was a society based on village communities, people of high mobility who could move their few possessions rapidly to areas richer in game or fish, or whose annual cycle often included migrations to gather fruits, nuts or eggs at the appropriate place and season. It is no accident that much of Brazil was scarcely inhabited or penetrated by Europeans until recent years. Both the Amazon rainforest between the rivers and the dry *campo*, *campo cerrado* and *mato* of the plateaux have always been very difficult environments for human beings. Even the Amazonian river system, teeming with fish, manatee and turtle and whose *várzea* (floodplain) is highly fertile, floods regularly. The forests which cover so much of Brazil have always been unsuitable for farming other than slash-and-burn clearings planted for only two or three seasons. This is because the laterite soils beneath the forests are weak, predators and parasites are constantly on the attack, competition from other vegetation is intense and unremitting and powerful sun and rains, coupled with a lack of seasonal temperature change, inhibit repeated planting of the same ground. All these factors operated against permanent settlement, except for the fortunate tribes who were strong enough to occupy stretches of large river banks or sea coast.

Brazilian Indians have left no monuments because their only building materials were the woods, lianes and grasses found in such abundance, but which perish so rapidly from tropical decay and the depredations of termites and a myriad other insects infesting Brazil. Historians can, therefore, expect little help from archaeologists. The *sambaqui* shell mounds along the Atlantic coast and on Marajó, some 'black earth' sites on the upper Amazon river banks and a few inhabited caves are the only archaeological remains.

With so little help from native sources, a student of pre-conquest Brazil is forced back to the writings of the first Europeans. Some of these wrote vividly and recorded honestly what they saw, but they were untrained observers. Most were missionaries intent on imposing Christianity; the rest were soldiers or adventurers. They wrote almost exclusively about the Tupi, since by geographical accident these were occupying the Atlantic coast when the Europeans arrived. There was great curiosity about American natives during the first decades of the sixteenth century, but Brazilian Indians lost their place in the intellectual limelight with the discovery of more exciting civilizations in Mexico, Peru and New Granada. By the time the Europeans pushed inland and contacted the Gê, Aruak, Carib and other language groups, there was little interest in Brazilian Indians. The quality of observation declined markedly in the seventeenth and eighteenth centuries. In addition, throughout the centuries of colonial conquest and rule, the tribes of Brazil suffered an appalling demographic catastrophe. They died in untold thousands from imported diseases, and the pattern of settlement was totally disrupted by the invasion from the east. All the tribes described by the first chroniclers have disappeared, along with hundreds that were virtually unrecorded by the Europeans.

On the credit side, however, enough tribes have survived into the present century in an uncontacted state to provide a good model of the way of life of their vanished ancestors. Indians are very conservative, so that uncontacted tribes have presumably changed little during the intervening centuries. Some tribes contacted and studied by anthropologists in recent times are survivors of peoples who retreated from the colonial frontier; others had the good fortune to be living in parts of Brazil far from the Atlantic coast or the accessible rivers.

Furthermore, sixteenth-century literature about the coastal Tupi is reasonably full. The most important contributions from Portuguese or Italian sources begin with the letter from Pero Vaz de Caminha to the king, 1 May 1500, describing the first landfall in Brazil and the first contact with its tribes. This was soon followed by the widely-published letter from Amerigo Vespucci to his Medici patron, the so-called *Mundus Novus* letter that did so much to arouse philosophical debate about the noble savage, and which resulted in the new continent being called America. Another Italian, Antonio Pigafetta, who sailed on Magellan's cirvumnavigation in 1520, added to Vespucci's idealized picture of Brazilian Indians. The next important Portuguese source was the account of Pero Lopes de Sousa's fleet which established the first colony in Brazil in 1530–2. The Jesuits arrived in 1549, and the letters and writings of these intelligent missionaries rapidly provided an important corpus of information about the Tupi. Many Jesuits described their experiences, but the works of José de Anchieta, Manuel da Nóbrega and at the end of the century, Fernão Cardim are outstanding. The only other major Portuguese sources from this early period are the chronicles of Pero de Magalhães Gandavo and of Gabriel Soares de Sousa (dated 1576 and 1587 respectively) and Vicente do Salvador's early seventeenth-century history of the conquest of north-eastern Brazil.

Authors from other European nations provided far more detail about Indian society and a more sympathetic understanding of Indian outlook and philosophy. Two German soldiers – Hans Staden, who survived capture by the Tupinamba near Santos in 1552, and Ulrich Schmidel, who was on expeditions to the upper Paraguay in the 1530s and 1550s – provided admirable insights into tribal life. So also did the young English adventurer, Anthony Knivet, who lived among the tribes of the southern Paraíba at the close of the sixteenth century. But the palm must go to the French. Their short-lived colony at Rio de Janeiro, 1555–65, produced two splendid chroniclers, the Calvinist, Jean de Léry, and the Franciscan cosmographer, André Thevet. A later, even shorter, attempt to colonize Maranhão produced fine chronicles from the missionaries, Claude d'Abbeville and Yves d'Évreux.

The Europeans' first impression of Brazilian Indians – in particular of the Tupi inhabiting the eastern seaboard – was of simple, egalitarian tribal groups living in internal harmony but obsessed with inter-tribal feuds. The Indians were physically perfect, for, unknown to the explorers, any abnormal infant would have been killed at birth. Their active way of life, with every member of the community taking part in hunting, fishing or farming, kept them fit. Vespucci started a false belief that Indians lived to extreme old age, with many aged well over a hundred. Since they were in a tropical or semi-tropical climate they had no need of clothing. This nakedness, combined with Brazil's luxuriant plant life and abundance of game, gave the impression of people living in an earthly paradise. Vaz Caminha wrote to his king: 'I infer that they are bestial people, of very little knowledge...and yet they are well cared for and very clean... Their bodies are so clean and plump and beautiful that they could not be more so....'[1] Vespucci wrote: 'I fancied myself to be near the terrestrial paradise.'[2]

---

[1] William Brooks Greenlee (ed.), *The voyages of Pedro Álvares Cabral to Brazil and India*, Hakluyt Society 2nd Ser., LXXXI (Cambridge, 1937), 23.

[2] Amerigo Vespucci to Pier Francesco de' Medici, Lisbon, 1502 (The Bartolozzi Letter), trans. Samuel Eliot Morison, *The european discovery of America. The southern voyages* (New York, 1974), 284.

A typical Tupi village consisted of four or more long, barrel-vaulted thatched houses arranged around a parade ground and surrounded by a circular rampart or pallisade. Every long hut sheltered many families, each one with its hammocks slung near its own cooking fire. Early visitors were impressed by the tranquillity inside these huts. The Indians' lack of personal possessions and their communal attitude to land and food also made a deep impression. 'In every house they all live together in harmony, with no dissension between them. They are so friendly that what belongs to one belongs to all. When one has something to eat, no matter how small, all his neighbours share it.'[3] Each family group was essentially self-sufficient, with the father responsible for hunting and fishing, fighting and, if necessary, clearing forest for plantations. Women planted and gathered manioc and the other plants cultivated by these coastal peoples – notably peanuts, cotton and some fruits and nuts. The women also prepared food and tended the young. Both sexes made their own personal belongings: baskets, hammocks, bows and arrows, feather and bead ornaments, simple tools, utensils and traps, canoes and, of course, the straw huts themselves. This meant that all Indians were skilled artisans. Being so dextrous themselves, they assumed that each European had made his own clothing and equipment, and they were enormously impressed by the cutting power of metal knives and axes. This misapprehension meant that Indians initially attributed almost supernatural skills to their foreign visitors. The powerful attraction of metal tools continues to be the most potent means of persuasion available to attraction teams or missionaries pacifying uncontacted tribes.

Indian creative expression was largely devoted to personal adornment. Apart from a few tribes of the upper Amazon, all Indians of Amazonia and central or coastal Brazil went largely naked. Decoration, therefore, consisted of body painting and of feather or stone ornaments worn at the neck, wrists, earlobes, nose, ankles or waists. Tupinamba men of the Atlantic seaboard wore polished plugs of green jadeite in their cheeks and lower lips. Such stones were greatly prized and were carefully traded from tribe to tribe. Many Gê tribes wore wooden discs in their earlobes and particularly in their lower lips. Among the Kayapó today, for instance, boys have their lips pierced at puberty and wear increasingly large discs as they grow older. The discs flap up and down

---

[3] Pero de Magalhães Gandavo, *Tratado da terra do Brasil*, trans. John B. Stetson, *The histories of Brazil*, Cortes Society, 2 vols (New York, 1922), I, 87.

as the wearer talks or eats and they make him look terrifying, which was apparently their original purpose.

The most commonly available decorative material was the plumage of the countless birds of South America. Amazonia has more species of bird than any place on earth, and the Indians perfected special blunt arrows to stun birds so that their feathers would not be damaged. Different tribes used elaborate combinations of feathers to make head-dresses, chaplets, armlets, pectorals and to adorn their arrows, clubs and gourd rattles. Some Tupinamba shamans wore spectacular cloaks of scarlet feathers from the *guara* ibis; warriors hung on their buttocks balls of resin surrounded by clusters of great ostrich feathers; and most wore bonnets of parakeet and macaw feather with the crown 'of a feathered fabric so daintily made with a fillet of barkwood that', so it seemed to Thevet, 'it could scarcely have been better if made entirely of silk thread'.[4] Present-day tribes of the upper Xingu make head-dresses of red and blue macaw feathers or white egret feathers fixed on basket frames. Similarly, Gê-speaking Chavante and Caiapó favour green and yellow parrot feathers or the tawny browns of falcons and shining jet blacks of *mutum* curassows. Amid the myriad of creative designs, three tribes among those that survive to the present day excel in the brilliance of their featherwork: the Bororo of central Mato Grosso, the Karajá of Bananal Island on the Araguaia – whose feathered tiaras rival in fantasy anything concocted in the European *belle époque* – and the Urubu-Kaapor of the Gurupí on the Maranhão–Pará border, whose jewel-like creations of hummingbird and other miniatures have deservedly been the subject of art books.

The other common outlet for Indian creative expression has always been body painting. Two vegetable dyes are abundant in most of Brazil and Amazonia: red *urucum* or anatto and black genipap. Whites and yellows are also used, but black and red predominate in most tribes. The first Indians seen by Cabral's men in 1500 included warriors quartered in red and black and a group of attractive girls, one of whom 'had her thighs and buttocks all painted with that black dye, but the rest of her in her own colour. Another had both knees and calves so painted, but her privy parts so naked and exposed with such innocence that there was no shame there.'[5] In some tribes age groups of the same

[4] André Thevet, *La Cosmographie universelle* [Paris, 1575] in Suzanne Lussagnet (ed.), *Les Français en Amérique pendant la deuxième moitié du XVIe siècle: le Brésil et les brésiliens* (Paris, 1953), 162.
[5] Greenlee, *Voyages of Cabral*, 21.

sex paint one another. Among Xinguano tribes, the men paint each other before wrestling; Caiapó women finger-paint with genipap on bodies and anatto on the lower faces; the Kadiwéu of southern Mato Grosso and Tirió of northern Pará paint or tattoo elaborate geometric patterns on women's faces; some tribes have standard markings—circles on the cheeks for the Karajá, a horizontal line across the cheeks for the Cintas Largas or Suruí, black around the mouth for the Juruna, vertical tattooed lines for the Asurini, and so forth; the Bororo and others have elaborate codes of body paint to differentiate moieties, clans and age groups; whereas for the Yanomani colours and patterns can denote moods or aggression. Caiapó war parties use black dyes as camouflage in the gloom of the forest. One early observer noted that Tupi women 'paint their men and make a thousand delights on their bodies, such as figures of birds or waves of the sea...and the women paint their own legs, so that from a distance you would think that they were dressed in very fine black worsted stockings...'.[6]

Other ornaments worn by Brazilian Indians include a wide variety of bead, shell and nut necklaces, girdles and anklets of rattling nuts, and – particularly among the Karajá and the Tukuno of the upper Solimões – masks made of straw thatch, pumpkins or balsa and barkwood, for ceremonial use by shamans. The Pareci of Mato Grosso–Rondônia used to have stone cross pectorals. There is a variety of musical instruments, many kinds of rattle and a range of wind instruments, from circular nose flutes of the Nambikuara, to pan-pipes, long trumpets of the upper Xingu, and propeller-like bull-roarers of the Bororo. The weapons of each tribe have individual characteristics, with variations in such details as the length, head and feathering of arrows, type of wood and profile of bows, ingredients of curares, blow pipes generally among tribes north of the Amazon, manatee-hide shields of the Omagua, different types of trap and a wide range of styles of club.

Gourds and baskets are, and were, common as containers in most tribes, although the weave and pattern of the basketry varies from tribe to tribe. Pottery is now rarer. The magnificent ceramics of the early Amazonian Marajó and Santarém cultures seem to have been lost by the time of the conquest, except among the Omagua and Machiparo of the upper Amazon. Early Spanish explorers noted Omagua pottery that rivalled Chinese wares in delicacy and wealth of polychrome decoration. Among surviving modern tribes, the Xinguano are famous

[6] Thevet, *Cosmographie*, 162.

for their wide basins for manioc *beiju* and for red and black zöomorphic dishes, the Karajá have for some centuries made doll-like figurines slightly reminiscent of early Aegean Cyclades ware, and the Kadiwéu decorate their pottery with incised geometric designs similar to those that they use for facial tattooing. Indians made their pottery by shaping and sometimes by moulding or coiling, but never on a wheel in a continent in which the wheel spinning on its axis was unknown.

Inter-tribal relations took various forms. Some tribes were so isolated that they rarely came into contact with other Indians. Other tribes were constantly at war, either through vendettas with rival groups of their own people or against neighbouring tribes. Early explorers noted that, although the banks of the Amazon and other large rivers were densely populated with a succession of Indian villages, there were buffer zones – stretches of unoccupied river bank – between the territories of large, hostile tribes. In more sparsely occupied land between the rivers, tribes lived far apart but occasionally organized long marches through the forests to launch surprise attacks on their enemies' villages. There were, and still are, exceptions to this pattern of inter-tribal warfare. Some groups of tribes learned to live peacefully with one another. Such amity could well depend on trade. Early chroniclers noted trade of such items as jadeite, which passed from tribe to tribe along the coast of Brazil, or of golden objects brought down to the Negro and Solimões by the energetic Manaus, or of wood for bows that the Waitacá of the mouth of the Paraíba acquired from inland tribes in return for their dried fish. The most famous modern examples of trade between tribes of different language stock are among the tribes of the upper Xingu, first contacted by Carl von den Steinen in the 1880s and cared for in recent decades by the Villas Boas brothers; and between the Baniwa and other tribes of the Uaupés and Içana rivers. Different Xinguano tribes specialize in the manufacture of such items as broad earthenware pots for making manioc *beiju* or necklaces of river shells. Such trade, together with reasonably amicable inter-tribal sporting competitions or festivals, must have helped to calm the tension and occasional violence always present between different tribes living in close proximity.

Social organization varied considerably from tribe to tribe. Among the Tupinamba, girls had to undergo ordeals and seclusion at puberty, after which they were allowed considerable sexual licence. A young man had to prove himself in battle or by killing prisoners before being considered sufficiently valiant for marriage. He had to serve and provide for his future father-in-law. Once married, a couple would remain faithful to one another. The marriage was generally matrilocal, with the husband moving in to his wife's mother's house unless he was sufficiently powerful to establish a household of his own. Any excess of females was cared for by polygamy by chiefs or famous warriors, and the wives readily accepted this, partly from pride at association with an important man and partly to share the work of caring for him. Men married at about 25 years of age and were deemed to be elders after 40. The council of elders met regularly to decide the tribe's activities. Each hut, with its complement of often inter-related families, was governed by a chief, as was the tribe itself. Chiefs earned their status from prowess in battle, from affluence derived from having many relatives or children, from magical powers or from oratorical gifts. But chiefs wielded little power in the egalitarian tribal society: the sixteenth-century philosopher Michel de Montaigne wrote that a chief who ruled over several villages told him that his only privilege was to lead his men into battle.

Tupi tribes, like most others in the Amazon basin, were controlled by councils of male elders, who met almost daily and were only loosely directed by their chiefs. The entire tribe was, however, strictly bound to conform to accepted practice. Such rigid conservatism is probably necessary in small hunting communities in a hostile environment. It meant in practice, and still does mean, that any eccentric or noncon-formist would be condemned by the shamans as an evil spirit and killed by the rest of the community. The first foreign explorers drew almost subversive conclusions from the absence of strong rulers. 'Each man is able to provide for himself... They have no property and do not try to acquire it as other men do... They have no class distinctions or notions of dignity or ceremonial. And they do not need them. For all are equal in every respect, and so in harmony with their surroundings that they all live justly and in conformity with the laws of nature.'[7] It became a commonplace among proponents of the noble savage theory to say that Indians had 'no faith, or king, or law'. This revolutionary idea was based on faulty observation. Although Indians had no kings or class hierarchy, they did have chiefs and even paramount chiefs respected by a large number of villages. They had law, not codified of course, but in the form of complete conformity to accepted rules of behaviour. They also had faith.

[7] Gandavo, *Histories of Brazil*, 92.

The supernatural world was very real to the Tupi, even if they did not have an organized religion. They felt themselves to be surrounded by spirits or demons, some protective but most malevolent. Tribal life was enveloped in a web of legend, myth, ceremony and spiritual belief. Almost every celebration, whether related to the agricultural calendar, hunting, warfare, or the life-cycle, was steeped in spiritual meaning. Every tribe had shamans to interpret the supernatural world and to heal through the patient's faith in their special powers. Tribal elders loved to narrate the legends of their ancestors. Decisions were reached by interpreting portents or by divination. Hans Staden saved his life by successfully predicting the outcome of an illness and of an attack on another village: he, like many another European in a native village, rapidly acquired the status and aura of a shaman, hero, or oracle, so that the tribe who had once planned to kill and eat him glorified him and tried desperately to prevent his departure. Each individual Indian was also obsessed by superstition, alternately buoyed up or terrified by the spirits infesting the forest, the night, the burial places of ancestors, or malignant animals.

Sixteenth-century chroniclers recorded many complex and often lyrical legends and heroic epics. To judge by modern experience of newly contacted tribes, there were doubtless many more legends that went unrecorded. One heroic ancestor of the Guanabara Tupinamba was Monan, of whom Thevet wrote: 'They say that he is without end or beginning, being of all time, and that it was he who created the sky, the earth and the birds and animals that are in them.'[8] In one legend, Monan caused fire and flood to destroy the world before re-peopling it with the stock of a hero called Irin-Magé. Thunder was identified as the roar of a demon called Tupan – and the Jesuits, rather surprisingly, adopted Tupan as the Tupi translation of God. Of the many malevolent spirits, the one that the missionaries adopted to correspond to their Devil was Anhan (also known as Jurupari among the northern Tupi). Thevet wrote that 'This miserable people is often afflicted by fantastic illusions and persecuted by the malignant spirit, which they perceive in various forms. It appears to them and chastises them beyond measure...We sometimes heard them cry out most terribly during the night, calling on us for help, saying in their language: "Can't you see...Anhan who is beating and tormenting me? Defend me, if you wish me to serve you!"'[9]

[8] Thevet, *Cosmographie*, 38.   [9] *Ibid.*, 77.

Shamans (*pagés* in Tupi) were intermediaries between the community and the supernatural world. They were tribal elders, men or women, who had demonstrated unusual powers of healing or prophecy. Pagés led tribal dances and ceremonies, rhythmically shaking *maracá* gourd rattles and with bands of *ahouai* nuts on their legs to shake as they stamped. Predictions or converse with the spirit world were surrounded by elaborate ritual. Healing was performed in a cloud of tobacco smoke and consisted of sucking evil spirits from the afflicted person or pretending to spit out some object that had caused the illness. It was a classic healer's ritual, one performed in different ways by tribal medicine-men all over Amazonia. Successful pagés were greatly revered and obeyed; but a series of wrong predictions or unsuccessful cures could cost a shaman his reputation and probably his life.

The coastal Tupi were engrossed in deadly inter-tribal feuds and seem to have been far more belligerent than Indians elsewhere in Brazil. Warfare occupied a central position in the social and religious life of the tribe. A man's prestige was a direct result of the number of enemies he had killed or captured. The purpose of inter-tribal battles was to capture prisoners rather than to occupy land or win booty. Attacks were therefore made when omens predicted victory and were preferably by surprise or ambush – although some chroniclers reported watching large set-piece battles, on land or between flotillas of war canoes. The main weapon was the bow and arrow, which Indians fired with amazing speed and accuracy, but battles soon degenerated into fierce hand-to-hand combats with heavy wooden clubs or stone battleaxes. Jean de Léry watched one such battle.

One could scarcely believe how cruel and terrible the combat was...If any of them was hit, as several were, they tore the arrows from their bodies with marvellous courage...This did not prevent them returning, all wounded, to the combat...When they were finally in a mêlée with their great wooden swords and clubs, they charged one another with mighty two-handed blows. If they struck an enemy's head they did not just knock him to the ground, but slaughtered him as one of our butchers fells an ox...These Americans are so furious in their wars that they fight on without stopping as long as they can move arms and legs, never retreating or turning tail.[10]

Battles between groups of Tupi, sharing identical languages and societies, were fought to capture prisoners for ritual execution. Battles between tribes of different stock could be more savage. Anthony

[10] Jean de Léry, *Le Voyage au Brésil de Jean de Léry* [La Rochelle, 1578], ed. Charly Clerc (Paris, 1927), 192.

Knivet took part in campaigns of extermination, in which hundreds of enemy were killed in surprise attacks and they 'took many old men and women, which as we took them we killed'.[11] One Jesuit wrote that 'there are so many of them and the land is so great and they are increasing so much that if they were not continuously at war and eating one another it could not contain them'.[12] Another Jesuit saw warfare as 'the ordinary drain of such a multitude, without which they would not have fitted into that land'.[13]

Prisoners were taken back to be taunted by the women of the victorious village. They were expected to behave with complete composure, proudly threatening retaliation by their own kin. Valiant prisoners were kept for weeks or months, fattened by the host tribe and given a woman for intercourse, before being despatched in an elaborate ceremony. The victim was executed painlessly by a blow from behind, and was then cooked and flayed. Each member of the tribe ate a piece of his flesh, to gain his spiritual strength and to perpetuate the vendetta.

Various chroniclers attempted a geographical classification of the tribes of the Atlantic coast from the mouth of the Amazon to the savannahs of Rio Grande do Sul. There is some confusion in nomenclature, for words such as Tupinamba may have been generic terms covering portions of the Tupi, each tribe of which had a distinct name. Portuguese and French colonists sometimes had different names for the same tribe. In the study of American Indians there has always been the difficulty that, while some tribes had no names for themselves, they did have names – often pejorative ones – for their enemies: so that in the course of colonial conquest the latter name became wrongly attached to a tribe before its contact or pacification.

With these caveats, and adopting only the most common of many variations in spelling found in the chronicles, the coastal tribes were, from north to south, as follows. In the early seventeenth century most of the land from Pará to the Parnaíba was occupied by peoples known as Tupinamba. This included 27 villages with some 12,000 inhabitants on the small island of Maranhão. Tapuitapera and the coast north-west

---

[11] Anthony Knivet, *The Admirable Adventures and Strange Fortunes of Master Antonie Knivet...* [1591], in Samuel Purchas, *Hakluytus Posthumus or Purchas his pilgrimes* [1625], pt 2, bk 6, ch. 7, Hakluyt Society, 20 vols (Glasgow, 1906), XVI, 223.

[12] Afonso Braz, letter from Espírito Santo, 1551, in *Revista do Instituto Histórico e Geográphico Brasileiro*, 6 (1845), 442.

[13] Cristóbal de Acuña, *Nuevo descubrimiento del río de las Amazonas* [1641] (São Paulo, 1941), 199.

of the island was occupied by Tupinamaba groups called Caeté ('large forest' in Tupi); on the coast to the south-east there were remnants of more primitive tribes called Tremembé, possibly Gê-speakers being displaced by the Tupi; and Tobajara (possibly simply a generic name for 'inland-dwelling' Tupinamba) lived on the Ibiapaba hills and the lower courses of the Mearim, Gurupi and other rivers debouching near Maranhão island. Most, or even all, of these Maranhão Tupi had migrated there *after* the invasion of their original homes further south by the Portuguese. Careful analysis of the various written sources points to the place of origin being Pernambuco, possibly the lower São Francisco, and conceivably Cabo Frio and Guanabara. Despite this, it seems likely that some Tupi were occupying this northern area before 1500.

The stretch of 'east-west' coast between the Parnaíba and Paraíba rivers was occupied by a large and united tribe called Potiguar (meaning 'shrimp-eating people', or, possibly, Petin-guara meaning 'tobacco people' from the practice of carrying wads of tobacco in their mouths). Observers described the Potiguar as being the most advanced of any Tupi, with broad plantations supporting a large population in substantial, harmonious villages. Soares de Sousa grudgingly admired them as 'great farmers of crops, with which they are always very well provided. They are good hunters and an arrow shot by them never misses... They are great line fishermen, both at sea and in fresh-water rivers.' They were notably aggressive, capable of mobilizing armies estimated at 20,000 warriors, adept at building defences and traps and, to Soares de Sousa, 'very bellicose, warlike and treacherous'.[14] The Potiguar presented a formidable challenge to Portuguese expansion towards the Amazon, and one Jesuit complained that 'these heathen have the fault of being the largest and most united of any in Brazil'.[15]

The dominant tribe of Pernambuco and the north-eastern tip of Brazil was called Tobajara – a name that also recurs in Maranhão, among the first Tupi of Bahia, in Espírito Santo and further south in São Vicente. Whatever the uncertainties about names of the divisions of the coastal Tupi, there was no doubt about the reality of inter-tribal enmity – an enmity that the Europeans tried to exploit, just as the Indians sought

[14] Gabriel Soares de Sousa, *Tratado descriptivo do Brasil em 1587*, ch. 13, ed. Francisco Adolfo Varnhagen, Brasiliana, cxvII (São Paulo, 1938), 23–4.
[15] Anon. Jesuit, *Sumário das armadas que se fizeram e guerras que se deram na conquista do rio Paraíba* [*c.* 1587], in *Revista do Instituto Historico e Geografico Brasiliero*, 36/1 (1873), 63.

to gain from hostility between the French and Portuguese. The Tobajara were normally at war with the Potiguar to their north-west and with the Caeté to their south. Caeté lived in large numbers around Cape Santo Agostinho, between the mouths of the Paraíba and São Francisco. Tupi-speaking tribes called by the chroniclers Tupina and Amoipira are mentioned as living along the Rio São Francisco inland of the coastal tribes. South of the São Francisco, Caeté and Tupinamba mingled, but Tupinamba were in control of the rich land around Bahia, up the Paraguaçu and south to Camamú. There was hostility and fighting between villages of these Bahia Tupinamba.

Tupi-speaking tribes occupied only a thin coastal strip of the long north–south coast between Camamú and the southern Paraíba. There were Tupinikin in Ilhéus (the southern coast of the state of Bahia) and the north of modern Espírito Santo; and Temiminó on the southern coast of Espírito Santo. But the coastal plain is narrow or nonexistent in this part of Brazil, and the forested hills inland were controlled by nomadic and belligerent Gê-speaking tribes known collectively to the Portuguese as Aimoré and Botocudo. The marshes and lagoons at the mouth of the southern Paraíba were occupied by another non-Tupi tribe called Waitacá, whose difficult habitat preserved their isolation until the end of the sixteenth century. The Waitacá, in turn, traded with other non-Tupi tribes of the lower Paraíba, tribes that presumably spoke Gê-related languages.

We know much about the stretch of coast from Cabo Frio to Guanabara and on to Santos/São Vicente, because this was the location of the first Portuguese colony, at São Vicente, of the French colony at Rio de Janeiro, of the struggles between French and Portuguese, the adventures of Hans Staden and Anthony Knivet, and the early activities of the Jesuits, Nóbrega and Anchieta. The coastal region of this area was densely populated by Tamoio Tupinamba. This was the tribe who became firm allies of the French and for that reason provided the ethnographical information recorded by Thevet and Léry. The Tamoio were at war with the Temimino, who lived to the north beyond the Paraíba and also at the inner end of Guanabara bay. There was also hostility between the Tamoio and Tupi called Tobajara or Tupinikin living in the modern state of São Paulo, both on the coast near São Vicente and on the plateau of Piratininga.

The steep, forested coasts south of São Vicente were the home of large, docile tribes known in the sixteenth century as the Carijó. These were the Guaraní, who spoke a language variant of Tupi: a well-regimented people, fine agriculturists and deeply spiritual. They spread across the rich lands of the modern state of Paraná and eastern Paraguay. The character and inclination of the Guaraní–Carijó made them perfect disciples for Jesuit missionaries. They responded better than any other people of South America to the Jesuit formula of large 'reductions' supported by extensive plantations and spiritually nourished on a regime of constant prayer and devotion. A southern branch of the Guaraní called the Tape lived on the grasslands between the Uruguay river and the Lagoon of Patos. At the time the Portuguese arrived there were still large pockets of tribes speaking Gê-related languages in the forests of the upper Uruguay and what is the modern state of Santa Catarina. These were the ancestors of surviving tribes now called Caingang and Xokleng. As early as 1503–4 a French sea captain called Paumier de Gonneville spent some months among the southern Carijó, and these same tribes were very hospitable to early Spanish sailors bound for the Río de la Plata or Patagonia. The same docility that endeared them to the Jesuits made them easy prey for Portuguese slavers from São Paulo.

The heart of Brazil is the vast plateau of the Brazilian shield. Geologically very ancient, this flat, eroded land was covered before the conquest either in *mato* (low, dry woods), *campo* (semi-savannah of sandy soil, gnarled trees and bushes, palms near streams, tough grasses and numerous termite hills), or *campo cerrado* (a denser variety of *campo*, with thick dry undergrowth). This relatively open country was the home of the Gê-speaking tribes. Because they were in poorer country and further from the Atlantic, the Gê tribes escaped the initial impact of the conquest. The Gê tended to be more scattered than the coastal Tupi, more elusive in battle and hence less vulnerable to set-piece defeat by European cavalry and gunfire. They were poor agriculturists compared to the Tupi and hence were less sought-after as slaves. Even the missionaries, who learned only Tupi–Guaraní, and who were reluctant to venture far inland, ignored the Gê until recent times. The Gê are more conservative, less adaptable than the Tupi, and the result is that many of their tribes have survived to the present with their cultures intact. Most Gê tribes are non-aquatic, being often unable to swim and unfamiliar with canoes. This lack of mobility and their innate conservatism has meant that, although there have been slow shifts by tribes such as the Chavante, there have been no dramatic migrations, with the result that there are no isolated groups of Gê on rivers far from their homeland. Thus, we can obtain a reasonably accurate picture of pre-conquest Gê habitats by looking at surviving tribes and noting locations of those that have vanished.

Early literature on the Gê is easily summarized. The first chroniclers reported skirmishes with – and inordinate fear of – the Aimoré of Ilhéus and fleeting contacts with the Botocudo and Puri of the southern Paraíba and Doce valleys. In those early times, all non-Tupi speaking tribes were dismissed as 'Tapuia' and were held to be dangerously savage. The first ethnographic accounts of 'Tapuia' did not come until the 1630s when the Dutch conquered the north-east bulge of Brazil and made alliances with the Tarariu of chief Jandui in the Río Grande–Ceará hinterland. The descriptions of the Dutch envoys Jacob Rabe and, later, Roulox Baro, showed that these Gê were almost identical to the modern Canela or Krahó. They were hunter–gatherers, magnificent runners capable of pursuing and clubbing game on the savannahs they inhabited. They shunned water and slept on ground mats rather than in hammocks. Their running prowess was maintained by regular log races between the two moieties of each tribe. Identical races are still one of the most important social functions among many Gê-speaking tribes. The two teams race in relays, often starting some kilometres from the village but always ending with a run around its circular perimeter. They carry heavy lengths of palm log on their shoulders, and one runner rolls his team's log onto the shoulder of the next in the relay. Marriage is invariably into the other half of the tribal society, with the husband moving into his wife's family house. It is also clear that these Gê have changed very little in physical appearance. Their skin colour is a pale creamy brown; the women are attractive by European standards and are markedly shorter than their men; and both sexes still wear the same curious hair style, with hair hanging loose behind, but with a horizontal parting around the head above the ears so that, in Elias Herckman's words, the top looked like a bonnet. Another useful early work is by a French Franciscan missionary, Martin de Nantes, who lived among the Cariri in the middle Rio São Francisco and Bahia *sertão* (wilderness) in the mid-seventeenth century.

The ignorant adventurers who marched deep into the Brazilian interior in the seventeenth and eighteenth centuries brought back no information about the tribes they encountered. Nor did the military and civil commanders who fought fierce wars against the Gê of the north-eastern interior during the half-century between 1670 and 1720. The most heroic of all Indian revolts in Brazil was that of the mission-trained Mandu Ladino, between 1712 and 1720, when for a brief moment the Tupi and Gê of Ceará and Rio Grande do Norte buried their traditional enmity and united against the colonial invader. But these campaigns lacked any chronicler. Wars of extermination were waged against the forest-dwelling southern Caiapó during the 1740s. These tribes occupied the vast expanses of mato and campo of southern Goiás and middle Mato Grosso. The Portuguese produced no ethnographic or historical information about these Caiapó; but brief descriptions of their ambush attacks, black genipap body dye and shifting forest villages tally with the practices of northern Caiapó who have survived into the twentieth century. There is no reason to suppose that the northern Caiapó have changed markedly since 1500 in either location or society. They continue to occupy the watersheds between the middle Rios Araguaia, Xingu and Iriri, a country of rainforest near the rivers that changes abruptly to campo or cerrado when the water-table is lowered, the Caiapó tend to prefer the more open country of the hill tops. Modern anthropological studies of groups such as the Xikrin, Gorotire, Kubén-Kran-Kegn or Txukarramae would presumably give a good picture of the Caiapó at the time of the first European arrivals.

Many tribes of Maranhão and the interiors of Piauí, Ceará, Pernambuco and Bahia have disappeared since their first mention. Most were presumably Gê-speaking, with customs broadly similar to the Timbira or Chavante who survive. Some non-Tupi tribes from the eastern slopes of the Ibiapaba hills and the lower Itapicurú and Mearim may have been linguistically and socially isolated: the great anthropologist, Curt Nimuendajú, studied the speech of the last surviving Gamella and found it to be only distantly related to Gê. Further inland, however, on the plateau between the headwaters of the Rios Mearim–Corda and Grajaú and the lower Tocantins, the Timbira of Maranhão and Pará are relatively thriving by modern standards, although doubtless much reduced in numbers. Here again, there is no lack of modern ethnographic studies of the Canela (Ramco–Camecra), Krahó, Apinagé (Caracati) and Gavião (western or forest Timbira).

The broad dry plains between the São Francisco and the middle Tocantins and Araguaia were the home of warrior tribes of Gê: the Shicriabá and Acroa (Guenguen), now extinct; and the Chavante

(Shavante in English spelling) and Cherente, known collectively as Akwen. The latter have survived with their cultures and tribal spirit reasonably intact, and their societies have been explored and documented in recent times. Both tribes have moved westwards, away from the colonial frontier. The Cherente cross the Rio Tocantins to the inter-fluvial lands lying between it and the Araguaia. The Chavante, after briefly tasting subjection in government-run *aldeias* (village settlements) near Goiás in the late eighteenth century, decided to migrate south-westwards across both Tocantins and Araguaia, to occupy the north bank of the Mortes and valiantly resisted incursions by settlers or Indian Service officials until the 1940s.

Far to the south, beyond the lands once occupied by the southern Caiapó, there were Gê-speaking tribes in the forested plateau that sloped westward toward the Paraná. Being relatively near São Paulo, these tribes were known to the early chroniclers and many of them later fell victim to Paulista slavers. Tribes known in the sixteenth century as Guaianá (Goianá) or Bilreiro (wooden discs) and later as Coroado ('crowned' because of their tufted hair style) were ancestors of the present Caingang. These peoples retreated to the forests when much of their territory was occupied by Jesuit missions for the Guaraní; but the missions were destroyed in mid-sixteenth century and the Caingang ranged across the western State of Paraná, resisting settler expansion until the early twentieth century. The Gê-speaking Xokleng (sometimes given the distasteful epithet Bugre) had broadly similar experiences further south in what is now Santa Catarina.

There were, of course, some exceptions to the picture of Gê dominance of the central Brazilian plateau. On Bananal in the Araguaia, one of the world's largest riverine islands, the Karajá and related tribes had evolved a distinct culture with original social and spiritual practices, which was based on a complete mastery of their riverine environment. The Karajá language, once thought to be related to Gê, is now considered as isolated. Some Tupi groups survive to this day, far up the Rios Araguaia, Xingu or Tapajós: for instance, the Tapirapé, Kamayurá or Kayabí; but it is not clear whether they were established in their present territories before the start of European conquest. The central plateau extends to the south-west, forming the watershed between the Amazon and Rios Paraguay–Paraná, and then on into modern Rondônia. West of the southern Caiapó and south of the Chavante were numerous tribes of Bororo, implacable enemies of the

Gê and enlisted by the Portuguese to help destroy the Caiapó. Bororo language, which is also isolated, and society have been most intensively studied in this century by missionaries and anthropologists, so that we have a very clear picture of the nature of the Bororo tribes five centuries ago. Moving westwards along this high ground, the Parecis were a numerous and well-ordered Aruak-speaking people who impressed eighteenth-century travellers with the beauty of their stone artefacts and the efficiency of their agriculture. The Parecis' reward for their relatively advanced society was to be carted off in droves by Paulista slavers.

The forests of the Guaporé and sandy, arid plateau of Rondônia have been peopled, apparently for many centuries, by tribes now known as Nambikuara. Contact with the Nambikuara came only in this century. They immediately made a deep impression on anthropologists and gave rise to exotic theories by distinguished authorities. The Nambikuara language is entirely isolated from that of other Amazon tribes, and their physical characteristics, skin colour and skeletal frame seem distinct. Their way of life was primitive, with rudimentary shelters, almost no body ornament or artistic expression, simple social structures, no hammocks or sleeping furniture, and a diet based on gathering and limited hunting with bow and arrow. Some observers were reminded of Australian aborigines and there has been speculation that the Nambikuara were the product of some migration across the South Pacific. Cave shelters on the Galera river in Nambikuara territory are covered in symbols of female genitals; although evidently belonging to an earlier society, these symbols have given rise to talk of Amazon or matriarchal societies, and similar reports in the sixteenth century led Ulrich Schmidel and others to seek Amazon women in this part of Brazil. One eminent historian of the Inca has located Paititi, the refuge of fugitive neo-Inca tribes, in this area.

The first European penetration of the upper Amazon was also a response to an exotic theory: the quest for the kingdom of El Dorado, the gilded ruler. The legend apparently took root among Spanish *conquistadores* in Quito in 1540, and the first expeditions all searched for the rich kingdom in the deeply-forested Andean foothills east of Quito. Our first glimpse of the tribes of the Napo, Caquetá and possibly also the Uaupés and Putumayo rivers thus comes from accounts of the expeditions in search of El Dorado in the 1540s led by Gonzalo Pizarro (and Francisco de Orellana), Hernán Pérez de Quesada and Philip von Hutten. The picture that emerges is of occasional riparian villages, sometimes with rudimentary fortifications and capable of mobilizing large flotillas of canoes, but widely separated from one another. The impression from these and later penetration of the headwaters of these north-western tributaries is that there has been little change in either style of life or density of population during the subsequent four centuries. Our only primary descriptions of the tribes of the main course of the Amazon also result from searches for El Dorado: they are Gaspar de Carvajal's account of Orellana's descent in 1542 and various reports of Lope de Aguirre's descent in 1561. After these there was a long literary silence about the Amazon, until Cristóbal de Acuña's descent in 1639 and the arrival of António Vieira's Jesuits on the lower river in the 1650s. But by that time the original native societies had been irredeemably dispersed and destroyed.

The overriding impression left by Carvajal's chronicle was of the dense native populations along the banks of the main Amazon river. He reported 'numerous and very large settlements...and the further we went the more thickly populated and the better did we find the land'.[16] Some villages stretched for miles along the river's edge, with frequent landing stages crowded with warriors. When the expedition debouched from the Rio Napo onto the main Amazon, it passed through the territory of the Machiparo, a well-disciplined tribe, well-fed from the produce of the fertile *várzea* (floodplain). This tribe and the even richer Omagua, who lived downstream roughly between the mouths of the Javari and Putumayo-Içá, had developed the farming of turtles. They released the creatures to lay their eggs in river sandbanks and towed young turtles back to their villages to be reared in thousands in pens alongside their huts. The tribe's farming techniques were geared to the annual rise and fall of the river. Its pottery was also sophisticated, ranging in size from huge storage jars to delicate polychrome pieces that the *conquistadores* compared to Chinese porcelain. One of these riverine peoples – possibly the Yurimagua who lived downstream of the Omagua – wore long cotton shifts in the manner of the Campa of the upper Rios Ucayali–Urubamba who were also having their first contact with Spaniards in the middle sixteenth century.

Some gold objects were found among the tribes of the Rio Solimões

---

[16] Gaspar de Carvajal, *Descubrimiento del río de las Amazonas* [1542], trans. Bertram T. Lee, as *The discovery of the Amazon* (New York, 1934), 200, 202.

(Amazon) and it is clear from later chronicles that these originated among the Muisca (Chibcha) or other peoples of the northern Andes and were brought to the Rio Negro and thence to the Amazon, by the Manaus of the middle Negro, a great trading tribe. Orellana's men named the Negro river because of its black waters, but there are no narratives of the Negro or Branco basins until the eighteenth century. Seventeenth-century references to the Negro describe the establishment of missions along the banks of the lower river and systematic slaving attacks on its Aruak-speaking peoples. The main stream of the Negro was thus denuded of natives as thoroughly as the Amazon itself. By the late seventeenth century travellers moved for days on end along the river without seeing any sign of life. Both the Tarumá, who lived near modern Manaus at the junction of the Negro and Amazon, and the Manaus of the middle Negro are now extinct. Aruak-speaking tribes of the upper Negro – notably the Baré, Baniwa, Yavitero and Tukano of the Uaupés – and Carib tribes of the upper Orinoco – the Makiritare and related tribes – suffered less from European invasion. We can, there-fore, assume that, although now depleted by disease, their disposition in 1500 was similar to that encountered by Humboldt and other natura-lists of the early nineteenth century; and that on the Uaupés, Içana and other western tributaries, tribes still surviving have presumably changed little during the past five centuries – unless their numbers have been swollen by refugee groups fleeing from more exposed territories.

This same assumption can be made with even greater assurance about the Yanomami (Waika) and other Shirianá-speaking peoples of the forested hills that form the watershed between the headwaters of the Orinoco and the Negro–Branco basins. The Yanomami is the largest surviving forest tribe in South America, contacted only in recent decades and intensively studied in recent years. Small groups of nomadic Maku doubtless roamed the forests between the middle Rios Negro and Solimões in 1500 as they do now; and Carvajal refers to primitive forest tribes (Catukina, Catawisí?) who harassed the Omagua from the interior south of the Amazon. Beyond, in the rainforests of the Ríos Ucayali, Javari and upper Juruá were the Panoan tribes – notably the Amahuaca, Shipibo and Conibo – who were in contact with the Incas' forest frontier. Many groups of Aruak-speaking Campa actually paid allegiance to the post-conquest Incas of Vilcabamba.

The first descent of the Madeira was made in about 1653 by the aged *bandeirante*, António Rapôso Tavares. He reported to Jesuits at Belém do Pará that his men had found the river to be densely populated:

Fifteen days after embarking on the river [from near its source] they began to see settlements and from then on there was not a day on which they did not see some; they generally saw many every day. They saw towns in which [they counted] 300 huts...in each of which many families lived...They reckoned that one village contained 150,000 souls.[17]

At one stage they travelled for eight days through the lands of a tribe, perhaps the Parintintin, whose villages were almost contiguous on the river banks. Sixty years later, the Jesuit Bartolomeu Rodrigues was still able to list 81 tribes known to him on or near the lower Madeira.[18]

We do not know the relative importance in 1500 of the tribes who later dominated, one after another, the Rio Madeira: Tora, Mura, Maué and Mundurucú. One suspects that the Mura (whose language is curiously akin to Muisca) and the Mundurucú expanded from obscurity to fill territorial gaps created by the destruction of earlier tribes. A group of fierce Tupinamba occupied the island of Tupinambaranas, but they may have arrived there after the Portuguese conquest of the coast. The Tapajós tribe, however, was certainly powerfully established at the mouth of the river that bears its name. Dutch and other foreigners had contact with the Tapajós in the early seventeenth century, and it was some time before Portuguese slavers dared to molest this strong people. North European explorers – including English and Irish – also contacted tribes of the left bank of the lower Amazon and commanded large armies of them before being driven out by the Portuguese in the 1620s. It is not clear, however, whether the tribes occupying the left bank then or in Orellana's day were Aruak- or Carib-speaking. Some of these tribes gave Orellana's men the impression that they were led by women warriors, and thus gave rise to the legend of Amazons on the world's largest river. Carib tribes certainly dominated the upper Paru and Jari rivers and most of the Guiana highlands.

The peoples living at the mouth of the Amazon, lower Tocantins, and Pará rivers were so thoroughly destroyed in the first half of the seventeenth century that it is almost impossible to reconstruct

---

[17] Antonio Vieira, letter of Jan. 1654, in Alfred do Vale Cabral (ed.), *Cartas Jesuíticas*, 3 vols (Rio de Janeiro, 1931), I, 413.

[18] Bartholomeu Rodrigues, letter to Provincial from Tupinambaranas *aldeia*, 2 May 1714, in Alexandre J. de Mello Moraes, *Corografia histórica, cronográfica, genealógica, nobiliária e política do Império do Brasil*, 4 vols (Rio de Janeiro, 1872), IV, 365–6.

their native populations before the colonial era. We know that the Juruna were near the mouth of the Xingu, and one remnant of this tribe has survived, hundreds of miles upstream in the Xingu Indian Park. The Pacajá, living on the river of that name south-west of Marajó, fielded 500 war canoes and fought to the death. Many other tribes near Belém do Pará were briefly recorded before being lost to disease, destruction or detribalization in the confusion of mission *aldeias*.

A NOTE ON THE NATIVE
AMERICAN POPULATION ON THE EVE
OF THE EUROPEAN INVASIONS

There has been for some decades, and there continues to be, a lively debate among demographic historians about the size of the native American population on the eve of the European invasions.

For Central Mexico, the area lying between the Isthmus of Tehuantepec and the frontier with the Chichimecas, the Berkeley School (Lesley Bird Simpson, Sherburne F. Cook and Woodrow Borah) first proposed a population of 11 million and later, in the light of new sources and a more sophisticated methodology, raised their estimate to 25 million. See, in particular, S. F. Cook and W. Borah, *The aboriginal population of Central Mexico on the eve of the Spanish Conquest* (Berkeley, 1963) and *Essays in population history: Mexico and the Caribbean*, 2 vols. (Berkeley, 1971–4). Angel Rosenblat has consistently argued in favour of a lower figure (as low as 4.5 million): for example, *La población indígena de América desde 1492 hasta la actualidad* (Buenos Aires, 1945) and, especially, *La población de América en 1492: viejos e nuevos cálculos* (Mexico, 1967). For a recent critique of the Berkeley School, see William T. Sanders, 'The population of the Central Mexican symbiotic region, the Basin of Mexico and the Teotihuacán valley in the sixteenth century', in William M. Denevan (ed.), *The native population of the Americas in 1492* (Madison, 1976), 85–150. Sanders seeks to reduce the higher Cook and Borah estimate for Central Mexico by 50–60 per cent to 11–12 million.

Even more difficult to estimate, and therefore even more controversial, is the population of the Antilles and the circum-Caribbean in 1492. Figures for the island of Hispaniola, for example, range from 50,000–60,000 (Charles Verlinden) and 100,000 (Rosenblat) to perhaps 8 million (Cook and Borah). The higher figure has not found ready acceptance: see, for example, Angel Rosenblat, 'The population of Hispaniola at the time of Columbus', in Denevan (ed.), *op. cit.*, 43–66 and David Henige, 'On the contact population of Hispaniola: history as higher mathematics', *HAHR*, 58 (1978), 217–37. Recent work on the Indian population of what is now Colombia – with a figure of three million proposed – is summarized in Germán Colmenares, *Historia económica y social de Colombia, 1537–1719* (Bogotá, 1973). Estimates for Peru have ranged from two to three million to 12–15 million (and even higher). A recent statement in support of the lower figures is Daniel E. Shea, 'A defense of small population estimates for the Central Andes in 1520', in Denevan (ed.), *op. cit.*, 157–80. The most recent work, which suggests a figure of 9 million for Peru, is David Noble Cook, *Demographic collapse. Indian Peru, 1520–1620* (Cambridge, 1981). For estimates of the size of the various Indian peoples who inhabited southern South America – with the exception of the Araucanians (one million) numbering tens rather than hundreds of thousands – see *CHLA*, 1 chapter 4 by Jorge Hidalgo, *passim*.

The population of the Indian tribes who inhabited what is now Brazil at the time of the arrival of the Europeans in 1500 is particularly difficult to estimate. John Hemming, *Red Gold. The conquest of the Brazilian Indians* (London, 1978), appendix, 487–501 discusses the various estimates and the methodologies on which they are based and himself arrives at a figure of 2.4 million. However, many recent estimates tend to be higher. William M. Denevan, 'The aboriginal population of Amazonia', in Denevan (ed.), *op. cit.*, 205–34 increases his own earlier estimates for greater Amazonia (the entire tropical lowland area of South America east of the Andes except for the Gran Chaco region) to 6.8 million and for the Amazon Basin itself to five million (although in an addendum he allows a possible 25 per cent reduction to take account of uninhabited 'buffer zones' between tribes).

Part Two

EUROPE AND AMERICA

6

THE SPANISH CONQUEST AND SETTLEMENT OF AMERICA

'Without settlement there is no good conquest, and if the land is not conquered, the people will not be converted. Therefore the maxim of the conqueror must be to settle.' The words are those of one of the first historians of the Indies, Francisco López de Gómara.[1] The philosophy behind them is that of his patron, the greatest of the *conquistadores*, Hernán Cortés. It was this philosophy which came to inform Spain's overseas enterprise of the sixteenth century and did much to make Spanish America what it eventually became. But its success was not inevitable, nor was it attained without a struggle. There are several ways in which an aggressive society can expand the boundaries of its influence, and there were precedents for all of them in medieval Spain.

The *reconquista* – that great southwards movement of the Christian kingdoms of the Iberian peninsula into the regions held by the Moors – illustrated something of the wide range of possibilities from which precedents could be drawn. Fought along the border dividing Christendom from Islam, the reconquista was a war that extended the boundaries of the faith. It was also a war for territorial expansion, conducted and regulated, if not always controlled, by the crown and by the great military-religious orders, which acquired vassals in the process along with vast areas of land. It was a typical frontier-war of hit-and-run raids in pursuit of easy plunder, offering opportunities for ransom and barter, and for more intangible prizes, like honour and fame. It was a migration of people and livestock in search of new homes and new pastures. It was a process of controlled settlement and colonization, based on the establishment of towns which were granted extensive territorial jurisdiction under royal charter.

[1] Francisco López de Gómara, *Historia general de las Indias* (Madrid, 1852), 181.

149

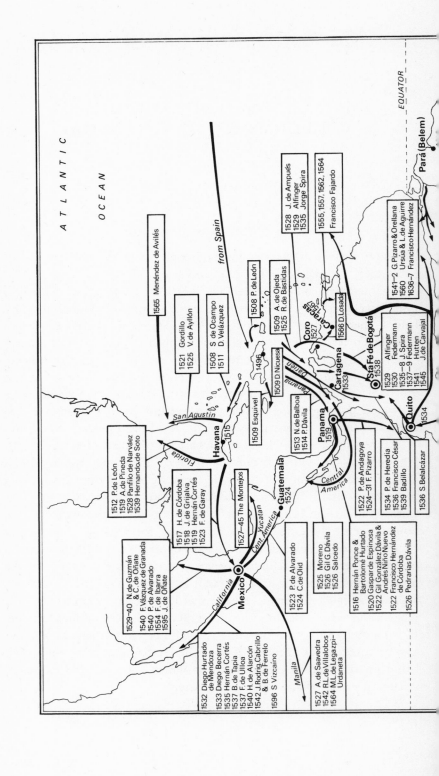

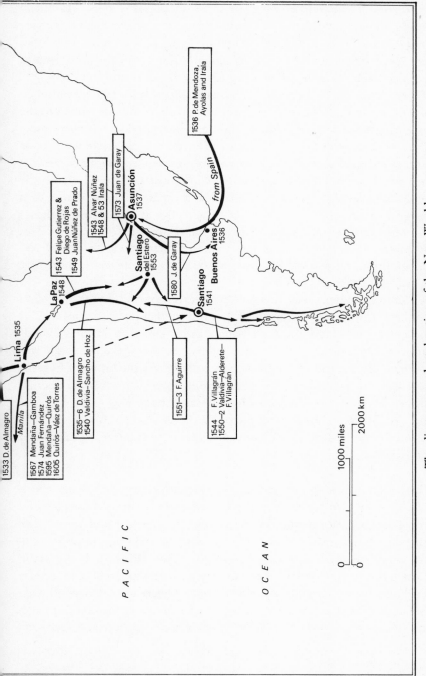

The discovery and exploration of the New World

Source: Francisco Morales Padrón, *Historia general de América* (2nd edn, Madrid, 1975), 336–7.

To conquer, therefore, might mean to settle, but it might also mean to raid, plunder and move on. Conquest in the first sense gave primacy to the occupation and exploitation of land. In the second sense it conceived power and wealth in a much less static form – in terms of the possession of portable objects, like gold, booty and livestock, and of lordship over vassals rather than ownership of land. Mobility implied adventure, and adventure in a military society enormously enhanced the opportunities to improve one's standing in the eyes of one's fellow men. The desire to 'win honour' and to be 'worth more' (*valer más*) was a central ambition in the status-bound and honour-conscious society of medieval Castile. Honour and worth were most rapidly won with the sword and deserved to be formalized in a grant of higher status by a grateful sovereign. It was in keeping with this tradition that Baltasar Dorantes de Carranza could write of the conquerors of Mexico that, although there were some *hidalgos* among them, they were now 'by presumption' all *hidalgos*, 'because all *hidalguía* originates by its nature in acts of service to the king'.[2]

The reconquista was halted but not terminated by the gradual attainment of its natural limits within the Iberian peninsula itself. The enclave of the kingdom of Granada would remain in Moorish hands until 1492, but otherwise the Christian reconquest of the peninsula was complete by the end of the thirteenth century. As the limits of internal expansion were reached, so the dynamic forces in medieval Iberian society began to look to new frontiers across the seas – the Catalans and Aragonese primarily to Sicily, Sardinia, North Africa and the eastern Mediterranean, the Castilians, like the Portuguese, to Africa and the Atlantic islands.

This expansionist movement of the fifteenth-century Iberians was a reflection both of specifically Iberian aspirations and of more general European aspirations in the later Middle Ages. Fifteenth-century Europe was a society still suffering from the economic and social dislocations caused by the ravages of the Black Death. Labour was in short supply; aristocratic incomes had fallen; monarchs and nobles competed for power and resources. It was a society, too, which felt itself threatened along its eastern frontiers by the menacing presence of Islam and the advance of the Ottoman Turk. It was a restless and relatively

[2] Baltasar Dorantes de Carranza, *Sumaria Relación de las Cosas de la Nueva España* [1604] (2nd edn, Mexico, 1970), 12.

mobile society, at once inquisitive and acquisitive – inquisitive about the world that lay beyond its immediate horizons and acquisitive in its desire for exotic luxuries and foodstuffs, and for gold which would enable it to buy these articles from the East with which it had a permanently unfavourable balance of trade.

The Iberian peninsula, with its proximity to Africa and its long Atlantic seaboard, was geographically well placed to take the lead in a movement of westwards expansion at a time when Europe was being hemmed in along its eastern boundaries. An Iberian maritime tradition had developed, both in the Mediterranean and the Atlantic, where Basque and Cantabrian fishermen had been building up a rich store of experience for the future navigation of uncharted seas. The conquest of Seville in 1248 and the advance of the reconquista to the straits of Gibraltar had given the crown of Castile–León a new Atlantic littoral, whose ports were settled by seamen from Portugal, Galicia and the Cantabrian coast.

Along this seaboard the combination of northern and Mediterranean skills created a race of sailors capable of promoting and taking advantage of advances in ship-construction and navigational techniques. The first Portuguese voyages were made in whatever reasonably suitable craft were available, but by the later fifteenth century the combination of the North European square rig with the Mediterranean lateen sail had produced in the caravel an impressive ocean-going ship, the culmination of a long period of evolution and experiment. Just as the new requirements of Atlantic voyaging helped perfect the caravel, so too they helped to improve the techniques of navigation. Once ships were travelling unknown waters out of sight of land, the old practices of dead-reckoning were no longer adequate, and the Portuguese turned to celestial observation to measure distances and determine latitude, making use of instruments long used by land-based astronomers, the astrolabe and quadrant. These instruments in turn were modified and refined to meet the needs of Atlantic voyagers. The magnetic compass, developed for use in the Mediterranean over the later Middle Ages, made it easier for navigators to take their bearings and plot direction on a chart. Here again Mediterranean experience was harnessed to Atlantic needs, for the Mediterranean region produced the first maritime charts; and the cartographical skills developed in late medieval Italy and transferred to the Iberian peninsula would make it possible to map an expanding world.

With its rich hinterland and its links to the Andalusian port-complex, Seville itself became the maritime and commercial, as well as the agrarian, capital of southern Spain. It served as a magnet to settlers from the interior of the peninsula – those predecessors of the later emigrants to the Indies – and to Mediterranean merchants, especially the Genoese. During the course of the fifteenth century the Genoese settled in growing numbers in Lisbon and Seville, where they glimpsed new possibilities for enterprise and capital at a time when their activities in the Levant were being constricted by the advance of the Turk. In the west they hoped to develop alternative sources of supply for valuable commodities – silks, dyestuffs, and above all, sugar – which were becoming less accessible to them in the east; and they were eager for access to Sahara gold.

It is no surprise, then, to find Genoese capital and skills playing an important, and at times decisive, part in Iberian overseas enterprises of the fifteenth century. The Genoese were well represented in the expeditions to the African coast for slaves and gold, and they actively supported the movement to annex and exploit the islands of the eastern Atlantic – the Canaries, Madeira and the Azores – where they hoped to establish new sugar-plantations.

But the Genoese were no more than one element, although a significant one, in the Iberian overseas movement of the later Middle Ages. Portugal in particular had a strong native mercantile community, which helped place the House of Avis on the throne in the revolution of 1383–5. The new dynasty maintained close ties with prominent merchants and was responsive to their concern for the acquisition of new markets, and of new sources of supply for dyestuffs, gold, sugar and slaves. But Portugal's overseas ventures of the fifteenth century were also guided by other, and sometimes contradictory, interests. The nobility, hit by devaluations of the coinage which reduced the value of their fixed rents and incomes, looked overseas for new lands and new sources of wealth. The princes of the new royal house combined in varying degrees acquisitive instinct with crusading fervour, a thirst for geographical information and a desire to perpetuate their names.

Under the vigorous direction of the royal house, these various motivations combined to produce among the Portuguese an intensive movement towards overseas expansion at a time when Castile had still to take anything more than a first faltering step. The Castilian crown had assumed nominal possession of the Canary islands following the first serious attempt at an expedition of conquest in 1402. But in the face of resistance by the Guanche inhabitants, the conquest lagged; and for much of the fifteenth century domestic troubles and the unfinished business of the reconquista prevented Castile from following in any systematic way the Portuguese example.

By the time of the death of Prince Henry the Navigator in 1460 the Portuguese had penetrated some 1,500 miles down the West African coast, and had pushed outwards into the Atlantic, establishing their presence on Madeira, the Azores and the Cape Verde Islands. Africa was a potential source of slave labour for the sugar-plantations that sprang up in these newly annexed Atlantic islands. Medieval Mediterranean society had devised institutional forms and techniques for trading, enslaving, planting and conquering, and the participation of the Genoese in fifteenth-century Iberian expansion helped ensure the reappearance of these same forms and techniques in the advance down the West African coast and in the island-stepping movement across the Atlantic.

The most characteristic feature of the Portuguese style of expansion was the *feitoria* (factory), the fortified trading-post of the kind established at Arguin or São Jorge de Mina on the African coast. The use of the feitoria made it possible to dispense with large-scale conquest and settlement and enabled the fifteenth- and sixteenth-century Portuguese to establish their presence over large stretches of the globe without the necessity for deep penetration into continental hinterlands. It was a style of settlement which Columbus, with his Genoese background and his Portuguese experience, had come to know well, and which would provide him with an obvious model when he reached the Caribbean islands.

Overseas expansion, however, could mean more than the establishment of trading-posts, as indeed it did for the Portuguese in the Atlantic islands and, later, in Brazil. To establish sugar-plantations, as in the Azores, it was necessary to colonize. Here the cheapest method from the point of view of the crown was to devolve responsibility for settling and developing the territory on a private individual, who would be rewarded with extensive privileges. This system, by which the *donatário*, or lord proprietor, was also the captain and commander, nicely blended the capitalist and military-seigneurial elements of medieval Mediterranean society. It was used by the Portuguese crown in the fifteenth century to develop both Madeira and the Azores, and in 1534 would be extended to the New World when João III divided the Brazilian coastline into twelve hereditary captaincies.

The Castilians, then, could draw upon Portuguese precedents as well as their own experiences in the reconquista, when at the end of the fifteenth century they turned their attention to new worlds overseas. There lay before them a variety of options. They could trade or they could raid; they could settle or move on. The option they chose would be determined in part by local conditions – the ease of occupation, the nature of the resources to be exploited – and in part by the particular combination of individuals and interests which underwrote and controlled the expeditions of conquest.

Much depended, inevitably, on the character of the leader and on the kind of backing which he was able to obtain. The *conquistador*, although highly individualistic, was never alone. He was one of a group under a *caudillo*, a leader, whose capacity for survival would be tested in the first instance by his skill in mobilizing men and resources, and then by his success in leading his men to victory. Cortés' cousin, Alonso de Monroy, master of the order of Alcántara, who distinguished himself in the peninsular conflicts of the fifteenth century, was known as 'supremely fortunate in war' and as one who 'compelled fortune to follow him'.[3] This was the reputation to which Cortés himself aspired, along with every New World caudillo.

The caudillo had at one and the same time to meet the requirements of his backers, and to satisfy the demands of the no less individualistic body of men who had placed themselves temporarily under his command. Tension was therefore built into every conquering expedition – tension about aims and objectives and about the distribution of the spoils. The discipline, such as it was, came on the one hand from the capacity of the leader to impose himself on his men and, on the other, from the collective sense of commitment to a common enterprise.

The long centuries of frontier warfare in Castile helped create that special blend of individualism and sense of community which could one day make possible the conquest of America. The personal pronoun which runs through Hernán Cortés' *Letters* from Mexico is counterbalanced by the confident 'we' of the rank and file who speak through one of their number, Bernal Díaz del Castillo, in his *True Account of the Conquest of New Spain*. But the great expansionist movement which

---

[3] Alonso Maldonado, *Hechos del Maestre de Alcántara Don Alonso de Monroy*, ed. A. R. Rodríguez Moñino (Madrid, 1935), 24.

carried the Spanish presence across the Atlantic was something more than the massive effort of private enterprise temporarily assuming collectivist forms. For alongside the individual and the collective unit there were two other participants which placed an indelible stamp on the whole undertaking – the church and the crown.

Even when the frontier war against the Moors was carried on largely by autonomous warrior bands, it continued to be conducted under the auspices of church and state. The church provided that moral sanction which elevated a plundering expedition into a crusade, while the state's approval was required to legitimate the acquisition of lordship and land. The land, and the sub-soil, were among the *regalías* belonging to the Castilian crown, and consequently any land acquired through conquest by a private individual became his not of right, but through royal grace and favour. It was for the king, as the supreme lord (the *señor natural*) to control the *repartimiento*, or distribution of lands either won, or to be won, and to authorize colonies of settlement in conquered territory. When the spoils of war came to be divided up, a royal fifth (the *quinto real*) always had to be set aside. Although the *adelantados*, or military governors of the frontier regions, possessed a large degree of autonomy, they were governors for the king.

In these and many other ways the royal presence made itself felt as the *reconquista* proceeded on its southward advance. Inevitably the effective authority of the crown fluctuated from generation to generation, but kingship itself was central to the whole organization of medieval Castilian society and was accorded an exalted position in that great compilation of Castile's legal tradition, the thirteenth-century *Siete Partidas* of Alfonso X. The vision of a harmonious society enshrined in the *Siete Partidas* is one in which the king, as God's vicar on earth, exercises a constant and active supervision within the framework of the law. It was for the monarch, as the natural lord of this society, to provide good government and justice, in the sense of ensuring that each vassal received the rights and fulfilled the obligations that were his by virtue of his station. A contractual relationship between king and vassals is implicit in this theory: kingship degenerates into tyranny if the king, or his appointed agents, disregard the common weal. The good king, as distinct from the tyrant, sees to it that the evil are punished and the just rewarded. As the dispenser of patronage he recompenses the services of deserving vassals with offices and honours in consonance with a carefully calibrated system by which, at least in theory, every *servicio* by a vassal finds its due compensation in a *merced*, or favour, from the king.

It was this patrimonial society, built around the conception of mutual obligation symbolized by the words servicio and merced, which fell into disrepair in the later Middle Ages, was reconstituted in Castile during the joint reign of Ferdinand and Isabella (1474–1504) and was then carried across the ocean to be implanted in the islands and mainland of America. Ferdinand and Isabella, the Catholic Kings, were the rulers of what was essentially a renovated medieval society. But the nature of their own kingship, although traditional in its theoretical formulations, possessed in practice elements of novelty which made their power more formidable than that of any of their medieval forbears.

Above all, they were the first authentic sovereigns of *Spain* – a Spain consisting of the union, in their own persons, of the crowns of Castile and Aragon. Even though the two crowns remained institutionally distinct, their nominal union represented a striking enhancement of royal power. As kings of Spain, the Catholic Kings had at their disposal, at least potentially, financial and military resources far greater than those which could be mustered by any rebellious faction among their subjects. They could call on deep reserves of instinctive loyalty among subjects weary of interminable civil war. They possessed, in the growing class of *letrados* (university-trained officials) a reservoir of professionally qualified servants whose own interests were best served by maintaining and extending the authority of the crown. Renaissance humanism and a reviving religion with strong eschatological overtones provided ideas and symbols which could be exploited to project new images of the monarchy, as the natural leader in a great collective enterprise – a divinely appointed mission to overthrow the last remnants of Moorish domination and to purify the peninsula of any contaminating elements as a prelude to carrying the gospel to the farthest ends of the earth.

Ferdinand and Isabella possessed the shrewdness and the skill to make the most of these various weapons in their armoury. As a result, the last two decades of the fifteenth century in Castile – where the institutional barriers against the exercise of royal authority were much less strong than those in the crown of Aragon – saw an impressive reassertion and extension of the royal power.

The presence of an intrusive state was to be critical to the whole development of Castile's overseas enterprise. Royal intervention might be actively sought by some and bitterly resented by others, but in both instances the authority of the crown was to be an automatic point of reference for all those engaged in the exploration, conquest and settlement of new lands.

There were already clear indications of this in Castile's first essay in Atlantic conquest and colonization – the occupation of the Canary Islands in the 1480s and 1490s. The Canaries were still only a nominal possession of the Castilian crown when they became an object of dispute between Portugal and Castile in the war of succession that broke out in 1475. Potentially rich in itself, the Canary archipelago was also an obvious base both for raids on the African coast and for Atlantic voyages of exploration of the type being undertaken by the Portuguese. The crown of Castile, engaged in a sharp rivalry with Portugal, therefore had a clear interest in enforcing its claims, and an expedition was sent out from Seville in 1478 to occupy the Grand Canary. This was followed by a new and more successful expedition under the command of Alfonso Fernández de Lugo in 1482; but, although the Portuguese abandoned their claims in the peace treaty of 1479, the resistance of the islanders prevented an easy occupation, and Palma was not subjugated until 1492 and Tenerife a year later. Conquest, as in the Portuguese Azores, was followed by exploitation. The Genoese helped introduce sugar production, and by 1526 there were twelve sugar-plantations on Grand Canary island alone.

The occupation of the Canaries, a natural staging-post on the route to the Indies, illustrated that conjunction of public and private interest which had characterized the reconquista and was also to characterize the enterprise of America. The lordship of the islands belonged to the crown, which therefore had to authorize all expeditions of conquest. The crown on this occasion also participated in the financing of the enterprise, but Fernández de Lugo, named by the crown as adelantado of Las Palmas, made his own private contract with a company of Sevillan merchants. Before an expedition set out, a formal contract, or *capitulación*, was signed between the crown and the commander, along the lines of similar contracts made in the course of the reconquista. By these capitulaciones the crown would reserve for itself certain rights in the territories to be conquered, while guaranteeing specified privileges and rewards to the commander and those who enlisted in his company.

When that obsessive Genoese visionary, Christopher Columbus, finally persuaded Ferdinand and Isabella in 1491 to patronize and support his projected voyage into the Ocean Sea, he therefore found himself caught up in a well-established tradition constituting the relationship between the crown and the leaders of expeditions. To this relationship he brought his own ideas, based on the Portuguese model of charters of donation for those who discovered lands west of the Azores. In the capitulaciones agreed with the Catholic Kings at Santa Fe, outside Granada, in April 1492 he was authorized, following a traditional formula, to 'discover and acquire islands and mainlands in the Ocean Sea' – in fact to 'conquer', in the sense of searching out and occupying desirable land. The crown was willing on this occasion to make a relatively small financial contribution and to provide Columbus with his ships. He was named hereditary viceroy and governor of any new found lands, 'viceroy' being the title conferred by the rulers of medieval Aragon on a deputy appointed to govern territories which the king himself was unable to administer in person. Columbus was also, at his special insistence, created hereditary Admiral of the Ocean Sea. Among the rewards promised him in the event of success was the right to appoint judicial (but not administrative) officials in the area of his jurisdiction, along with 10 per cent of the profits of barter and trade.

On 3 August 1492, when Columbus set sail from the Andalusian port of Palos, it was obviously anticipated that, if he reached the 'Indies', he would establish a Portuguese-style entrepot trade for the benefit of the crown of Castile, based on small garrison settlements. But the news which he brought back on his return to Spain in March 1493 suggested, at least to the crown, the desirability of certain modifications to the original scheme. There was some scepticism as to whether Columbus had indeed reached the East, as he himself insisted. The revelation of what appeared to be new islands and new peoples raised important questions about titles to the land and the treatment of the islanders. Who was to exercise lordship over them, and who was to undertake the salvation of their souls?

The Catholic Kings turned to the papacy, following the precedent set by the Portuguese, who had secured a formal papal donation of rights of sovereignty 'from Cape Bojador towards Guinea and beyond'. From a compliant Spanish pope, Alexander VI, they obtained what they wanted: similar rights in 'all islands and mainlands whatever, found or to be found' in the area beyond a national line of demarcation that was to be formally agreed between the crowns of Portugal and Spain in the treaty of Tordesillas of 1494. Alexander VI's bulls of 1493 might have been regarded as unnecessary in view of the Roman Law principle laid down in the *Siete Partidas* that possession belonged to the first occupiers of the land. But papal authorization gave an extra degree of security to Castilian claims against any attempted challenge by the Portuguese, and raised the enterprise of the Indies to the level of a holy undertaking by linking Castile's exclusive rights to an equally exclusive obligation to win the heathen to the Faith. This missionary enterprise, solemnly entrusted to the crown of Castile, provided it with a moral justification for conquest and colonization which at once reinforced and transcended claims deriving in one form or another from the fact of first discovery.

The crown, having moved to ensure its primacy in the international arena, also moved to ensure its primacy in Columbus's enterprise. The fitting out of the fleet for his return voyage to Hispaniola – a fleet, this time, of seventeen instead of only three ships – was entrusted to the formidable Juan Rodríguez de Fonseca, archdeacon of Seville, and a member of the council of Castile. For the next 23 years, until the death of Ferdinand the Catholic in 1516, Fonseca was to be in effect the supreme director and co-ordinator of Castile's American enterprise, charged with the almost impossible task of ensuring that, at every stage of discovery, colonization and conquest, the interests and authority of the crown were properly upheld. The inclusion on Columbus's second voyage of a deputy of the *contadores mayores* of Castile – the principal financial ministers of the crown – along with a *receptor* to collect all royal dues, and a *veedor*, or inspector of accounts, laid down the precedent for supervision and control by royal officials that was to be followed in future expeditions. Fonseca's men would follow hard on the heels of every future explorer and discoverer, and no captain in the Indies would be able to evade for long the oppressive shadow of the crown.

The 1493 expedition differed also in other important respects from its predecessor. There had been no priest on the first voyage, but this time special emphasis was laid on the conversion of the islanders, and a group of friars, specially selected by Ferdinand and Isabella and led by a Catalan Benedictine, Bernardo Boil, was given responsibility for a missionary enterprise to be undertaken at the crown's expense. Conversion, moreover, implied permanency of occupation, and the whole expedition was geared to the establishment in the Antilles of a long-term Spanish presence. This time, instead of a mere 87 men, Columbus was accompanied by 1,200, including not only soldiers and sailors and gentlemen adventurers but also artisans and agricultural labourers. The emphasis at this stage was on settlement, although *rescate* (barter with the Indian) remained central to the enterprise. A model colony, in fact, was being shipped wholesale from Seville – model except in one critical respect. It included no women.

Already by 1493, then, new elements were coming into play to modify or transform the original enterprise of the Indies as envisaged by Columbus. Trading and exploring remained powerful components of the enterprise; and the establishment of a permanent settlement in the Antilles was closely in line with the Portuguese–Genoese style of overseas activity, as already practised in Madeira and along the West African coast. But the old Castilian reconquista traditions were also tending to assert themselves, encouraged in part by the fact that the newly discovered world of the Antilles appeared heavily settled with a non-Christian population, and one which possessed objects of gold. Amidst the variety of options available to it, Castile was moving towards the one which implied full-scale conquest in the medieval peninsular tradition – the assertion of sovereignty, the establishment of the faith, immigration and settlement, and an extensive domination of land and people. But, as the first Spanish colony in the New World was launched on its precarious career, it was far from certain whether conquest and settlement, or conquest and movement, was the form of conquest that would prevail.

THE PATTERN OF THE ISLANDS

The problem that faced the crown and its agents in Hispaniola prefigured in miniature the problem that underlay the whole Spanish enterprise in America: how to impose stability in a world where almost everything was immediately in flux. Intruding into the new-found Caribbean paradise with their own aspirations, their values, and – not least – their diseases, Columbus and his men were soon on the way to transforming it into a wilderness.

The Spaniards had returned to the Antilles with clear-cut ideas. Above all, they wanted gold. While Columbus himself continued his search for India and the empire of the Great Khan, the bulk of his party established itself in Hispaniola, where it discovered that the first settlement had been wiped out in his absence. A new one, Isabela, was therefore founded on what proved to be an insalubrious site on the northern shore. The settlers, it was assumed, would build a town, plant their crops, establish their livestock and set up a chain of well-defended warehouses, in which the Indians – now subjected to the uplifting influence of Christianity – would meekly deposit large quantities of gold.

This dream was soon shattered. The quantity of gold forthcoming from barter with the Indians proved to be very disappointing, and Columbus, anxious to justify their investment to his sovereigns, tried to supplement the deficiency with another desirable commodity, the Indians themselves. By shipping Caribbean Indians back to Spain for sale as slaves, Columbus posed in acute form a question that was to dominate the history of Spain in America for the next 50 years: the status to be accorded to the indigenous population.

'Barbarians' might, according to the provisions of Roman Law, be legitimately enslaved, and 'barbarian' had come to be interpreted by medieval Christendom as 'infidel'. But although the crown appeared willing to apply this interpretation to the first consignment of Tainos which reached Andalusia, the influence of the theologians led to second thoughts. An infidel was a man who had rejected the true faith, but these new peoples had apparently, if inexplicably, lived in total ignorance of it. They should therefore be classed as pagans and not as infidels, unless, after the gospel was preached to them, they still rejected it. Isabella, counselled by her confessor, Jiménez de Cisneros, suspended the trade. These people were her subjects; and in 1500 the crown declared the Indians 'free and not subject to servitude'. This ruling, apparently decisive, was in fact far from comprehensive. It was still permissible to enslave Indians taken in a 'just war' – a term that proved eminently adaptable as employed in the Caribbean, and, later, on the mainland, embracing as it did anything from 'rebellious' Indians to cannibalistic Caribs. The immediate consequence of the crown's decision was to encourage slave-raiding expeditions against islands of the Antilles still uninhabited by Spaniards, in order to supply the market with 'legitimate' slaves. As the abuses multiplied, so did the revulsion against them, but it was not until the New Laws of 1542, which operated retrospectively as well as for the future, that the enslavement of Indians was definitively, if not universally, abolished.

The rejection, at least in principle, of Indian slavery removed one of the options open to the settlers of Hispaniola, and in consequence exacerbated the problems of survival that were already becoming acute. Disease among the colonists had forced them to move to the southern side of the island, where their new settlement, Santo Domingo, founded by Bartolomé Colón in 1498, was to become the nerve-centre of the Spanish Indies for a generation or more. But the survival of Santo Domingo as a viable settlement depended on the establishment of some equilibrium between colonists who, like all colonists, arrived with exaggerated expectations, and resources which were not only limited but rapidly diminishing.

The Columbus family, enjoying jurisdiction over the islands, proved unequal to the task. As Genoese upstarts they began at a natural disadvantage, and by temperament neither the admiral nor his brothers were equipped to deal with the endemic indiscipline of a bunch of Spaniards whose only thought was for easy wealth. The Columbus era in the West Indies ended definitively with the final return of Diego Colón to Spain in 1524, but already from the mid-1490s the crown was carefully curbing and clipping the family's jurisdiction. The real founder of Hispaniola and, through it, of the Spanish Indies, was Fray Nicolás de Ovando, appointed governor in 1501. An Extremaduran whose political skill and administrative abilities had been displayed in the reform of the military order of Alcántara, he was appointed to bring stability to an island where the settler community was torn by faction and threatened with extinction by shortage of food and of labour.

In the eight years of his government Ovando succeeded in laying the foundations for economic survival and effective centralized control. He began by refounding the city of Santo Domingo itself, destroyed by a cyclone shortly after his arrival in the spring of 1502. Rebuilt on a slightly different site, Santo Domingo became the first real city of the Spanish New World – the one that would first greet the eyes of a whole generation of new arrivals in the Indies, and which would provide the prototype for the towns that would arise in mainland America. In his *Summary of the Natural History of the Indies* (1526), that proud chronicler of Hispaniola, Gonzalo Fernández de Oviedo, would describe it as superior even to Barcelona and all the other Old World cities that he had seen: 'for as it was founded in our times... it was laid out with rule and compass, and all the streets planned on regular lines'.[4] The grid-iron plan, following models already established in Europe – not least the encampment of the Catholic Kings at Santa Fe in Granada – had safely made the transatlantic crossing.

Many of the practices and institutions that were later to be transported to the mainland of America were the direct product of the Ovando

---

[4] Gonzalo Fernández de Oviedo, *Sumario de la natural historia de las Indias*, ed. José Miranda (Mexico, 1950), 88–9.

regime in Hispaniola, which in turn drew on the experiences of the reconquista in Spain and of the conquest of the Canaries. The Spaniards, if they were to be induced to remain, must be given a stake in the island's resources, both natural and human. Hopes of a gold-barter economy had foundered on the shortage of gold, although more might be obtained from the rivers and from mines. This in turn required labour, and Columbus had already introduced a system of forced Indian labour which would help produce tribute for the king and profit for the colonists. Attempts to replace this by voluntary wage-labour proved abortive, as was bound to happen in a society to which the European concept of 'work' was totally alien. The crown, on Ovando's recommendation, therefore approved in 1503 a forced labour system, by which the governor would be free to allocate Indian labour in the mines or the fields, wages being paid by those who received the allocation.

In giving Ovando the power to allocate native labour at his own discretion, the crown had given him the means to shape the island's life to its own requirements. The repartimiento, or distribution of the Indians, was an act of favour by the crown and, therefore, carried with it certain obligations to be fulfilled by the concessionaries. The Indians had to be cared for and instructed in the faith, which meant that they were in effect temporarily 'deposited' or entrusted to individual Spaniards. It was a system which recalled the assignment, or *encomienda*, of Moorish villages to members of the military orders in medieval Spain, and the word encomienda would in due course reappear in this new, American environment, although it would now carry a very different meaning.[5] The New World encomienda included no allocation of land or of rents. It was simply a state assignment of compulsory labour, tied to specific responsibilities towards his Indian charges by the depositary or *encomendero*.

Such responsibilities could not, in theory, be lightly assigned. They must go to those most fitted to exercise them, to the meritorious and the established – and the established man in the Hispanic world was the man of property with an urban residence. His control of the labour supply therefore enabled Ovando to encourage the settlement of the Spaniards in small urban communities, each with its *cabildo*, or town council, on the Spanish model. Indian labour was to be allocated only to *vecinos*, full citizens.

To facilitate the process of allocation, the Indians were also resettled,

[5] For further discussion of the *encomienda* system, see Elliott, *CHLA*, I, ch. 9 and MacLeod, ch. 10; also Gibson, *CHLA*, II, ch. 11.

and their *caciques*, or chiefs, made responsible for the supplying of labour to the Spaniards. While some of the labour force consisted of encomienda Indians, other Indians, known as *naborías*, took up service in Spanish households as personal servants. These naborías straddled the dividing line of the harmonious society as planned by Ovando – a society in which Indian and Spanish communities co-existed under the close supervision of the royal governor, with the Indians being introduced to the benefits of Christian civilization and providing in return the labour which was all they had to offer. At the same time Ovando encouraged establishment of cattle-raising and sugar-cultivation, hoping to free Hispaniola society from excessive dependence on that elusive commodity, gold, and to tie the settlers to the land.

Under Ovando, therefore, Hispaniola made the transition from entrepot to colony, but his scheme contained within it the seeds of its own destruction. The formal establishment of forced labour for the Indian population only precipitated a process that was already becoming catastrophic – its total extinction. Within twenty years of the landing of Columbus the population of this once densely-populated island had been all but wiped out by war, disease, maltreatment and the trauma produced by the efforts of the intruders to force it into ways of life and behaviour totally unrelated to its previous experience.

In a desperate attempt to maintain the labour supply, the settlers took to massive raiding of the Bahamas and the deportation of its Lucayo population to Hispaniola. But as more batches of immigrants arrived from Spain in search of a quick fortune, the importation of forced labour from the neighbouring islands could serve as no more than a palliative. The stability sought by Ovando was proving impossibly elusive, and the attempt to impose it by autocratic means provoked fierce resentments against the governor. Setting a pattern that was to be followed time after time in the government of the Indies, local dissidents were able to mobilize influential supporters at court. Ovando was relieved of his office in 1509, the victim of Fonseca and his officials in Hispaniola. Diego Colón, who succeeded him as governor, fared no better. The pretensions of the Columbus family made him a suspect figure to the crown; and in 1511 it moved to curb his powers by establishing a permanent legal tribunal, the *audiencia* of Santo Domingo. The audiencia, modelled on the chancelleries of Valladolid and Granada, was itself to serve as a model for further such tribunals as the Spanish crown extended its control over the mainland of America. The agents of royal government were in future to be held in constant check by the agents of royal justice.

The continuing decline of Hispaniola's indigenous and imported non-white population elicited two distinctive responses, each with major consequences for the future of Spanish America. It provoked, in the first place, a powerful movement of moral indignation, both in the island itself and in metropolitan Spain. The movement was led by Dominicans horrified by the conditions they found on the island on their arrival in 1510. Its first major exponent was Antonio de Montesinos who, in a sermon preached in Santo Domingo on the Sunday before Christmas 1511, denounced the maltreatment of the Indians and refused communion to the encomenderos he held most responsible. Its greatest convert was Bartolomé de las Casas, who in 1514 renounced his encomienda and his commercial interests on the island and devoted the remaining 52 years of a turbulent life to a passionate defence of the Indian subjects of the Spanish crown.

The repercussions of this movement were soon felt at the court of Ferdinand the Catholic, where cynicism about the exploitation of the wealth of the Indies was tempered by an awareness of the obligations imposed upon the crown by a succession of papal bulls culminating in that of 28 July 1508, which gave it a universal *patronato*, or right of presentation to New World benefices, in return for the onerous duties involved in the evangelization of the indigenous population. A new code of legislation was clearly required to protect the Indians from the abuses described in such horrifying detail by Montesinos and his colleagues. The Laws of Burgos of 1512 were an attempt, however ingenuous, to provide this protection, carefully regulating the functioning of the encomienda, an institution not held to be incompatible – in view of the weaknesses and deficiencies of the majority of the Indians – with the principle of Indian liberty which the Laws also proclaimed.

The Laws of Burgos fell dead from the pens of the legislators: there was no authority on the island willing or able to ensure their enforcement. But in 1516, on the death of Ferdinand, the regent Cardinal Cisneros, under the influence of Las Casas, made a fresh attempt to tackle the problem by sending a commission of three Jeronymites to govern the island. The two years' rule of the Jeronymites vividly illustrated the difficulties inherent in pursuing good intentions in the face of unpalatable facts. It was difficult to eradicate abuses and the decline of the native population could not be halted.

Reluctantly conceding that the island economy was unable to survive without forced labour, the Jeronymites concluded that the only solution was to import it from outside, in the form of negro slaves. The institution of black slavery was well known to late medieval Mediterranean society. Portuguese traders had been importing blacks into Portugal from the Barbary coast since the mid-thirteenth century, and the number of black slaves in the Iberian peninsula increased sharply in the fifteenth century as Portuguese penetration down the Guinea coast created new sources of supply. Enjoying an effective monopoly of the trade, Portuguese dealers were extensively supplying the Spanish market from the 1460s. While Lisbon was the city with the largest black population in the peninsula, there were soon substantial numbers of slaves – some of them moors rather than negroes – in many of the major Spanish towns, where they were used in particular for domestic service. Seville, with a total population of around 100,000 in the 1560s, had at that time a slave population of 6,000, the majority of them black.

It is not therefore surprising that black slave labour should have seemed to the Spaniards to offer a natural answer to the problems of Hispaniola. The first shipment of *ladino* (Spanish-speaking) blacks reached the island in 1505 and further consignments followed, until Cisneros banned all shipment on the grounds that the presence of growing numbers of *ladinos* was a cause of serious unrest. But in 1518, after his death and with the blessing of the Jeronymites, shipments began again under the aegis of the crown, with Charles V granting a licence to a member of his Burgundian household to despatch 4,000 slaves to the Indies over the course of eight years. He promptly sold his licence to the Genoese. A new and lucrative transatlantic trade was in the making, as the Old World of Africa was brought in to redress the demographic balance of the New.

The demographic catastrophe that had overtaken the indigenous inhabitants of Hispaniola had another and more immediately potent effect. The island's excess population of Spanish settlers, driven to import labour to ensure its own survival, was also driven for similar reasons to export itself. The urge to wander was in any event instinctive to most of these men, so that necessity and inclination travelled hand in hand. The third and fourth voyages of Columbus in 1498 and 1502–4 had revealed much of the contours of the Caribbean and traced the coastline of Central America and part of Tierra Firme (Venezuela). The admiral's discoveries, like the rich pearl fisheries off the coast of

Venezuela, encouraged others to follow in his tracks. In 1499 Alonso de Hojeda charted the Venezuelan coast as far as the gulf of Maracaibo; in 1504 Juan de la Cosa explored the coast of Darien; and as the radius of explored space around Santo Domingo widened, so the pressures to conquer and migrate increased.

From 1508 the restless colonists of Santo Domingo were reaching out greedily towards the nearby islands. The settlement of Puerto Rico was begun in 1508 and that of Jamaica in 1509. Two years later Diego Velázquez, as the deputy of Diego Colón, embarked on the conquest of what was to be a major prize, the island of Fernandina, or Cuba. This would become a base for voyages of exploration and conquest to mainland America, and its port of Havana, relocated to a sheltered site on the northern coast in 1519, would replace Santo Domingo as the gateway to the Indies.

Disregarding the claims of the Columbus family, the crown was now issuing licences for the discovery and conquest of the rapidly-emerging landmass which appeared to be blocking the route to the East. Juan Ponce de León, the conqueror of Puerto Rico, discovered Florida in 1513, but did not take advantage of the authorization to settle it. More glittering prizes seemed to beckon elsewhere. Along the shores of the Gulf of Darien, barter settlements had been springing up for the *rescate* of gold from the local Indians. In 1513 Vasco Núñez de Balboa, cutting his way across the isthmus, sighted the Pacific Ocean from Darien. Three months before the sighting, orders had already been given in Spain for the despatch of an expedition from the peninsula under the command of Pedrarias Dávila, for the conquest of these mainland regions, now christened Castilla del Oro, the golden land. In the brutal search for gold Pedrarias plundered and terrorized; and in the inevitable clash with Balboa he emerged the victor. Under the direction of Pedrarias, expeditions of discovery fanned out through Central America, most of them making for the Pacific coast, where Pedrarias founded the city of Panama in 1519. In that same year Cortés landed in Mexico, and Magellan sailed on the voyage of circumnavigation that would give Spain, too late, its western sea-route to the East.

With each new forward movement by the Spanish intruders, the radius of devastation was enlarged. As one area after another of Spanish penetration lost its aboriginal population before the steady onward march of disruption, demoralization and disease, so the invaders made frantic efforts to replenish the dwindling native labour force by

mounting slave-raiding expeditions to the surrounding region. Raids
on the Bahamas and the lesser Caribbean islands to restock the
aboriginal population of Hispaniola were followed by raids on Florida
and the Gulf of Honduras to restock that of Cuba. Well before Cortés
set sail from Cuba, slave-raiders had also been active on the coast of
Yucatán. But it was in the period following the occupation of the
isthmus of Panama and the discovery and conquest of Peru that
slave-raiding became a regular and highly-organized way of life. The
disappearance of the Indian inhabitants of the Panama isthmus meant
that the Spaniards were left without a labour force to grow the crops,
pan the gold and carry the heavy freight that had to be transported
across the isthmus for shipment to Peru. To meet their needs, the
colonists turned not only to the traditional slave-producing areas of the
Caribbean, but also to the densely settled population of lacustrine
Nicaragua, where slave-raiding reached a new level of intensity. But
everywhere the hope of re-creating a lost Indian population proved
illusory. The imported slaves succumbed as rapidly as the local
population they had been brought in to replace, and the denuding of
one region was not accompanied, as the Spaniards had hoped, by the
restocking of another.

The lucrative business of the slave trade did, however, add sub-
stantially to geographical knowledge, as raiders explored the coast of
Tierra Firme, Panama, Honduras and Florida, and mapped the Bahamas
and the Lesser Antilles. It also promoted local trade within the
Caribbean and encouraged the first attempts at local ship construction
to meet the needs of men who were both raiders and traders. The 'island
period' of discovery, conquest and colonization, covering the years 1492
to 1519, culminated, therefore, in a period of intense and accelerating
activity, stimulated at once by the initial failure of Santo Domingo to
maintain its restless immigrants and by the rapidly expanding prospects
for plunder, trade and profit as the landmass of the mainland began to
be revealed.

At such a time, and with a frontier in such constant movement, the
hopes of persuading natural frontiersmen to strike roots were bound
to be defrauded. It was true that Hispaniola, with its growing black
labour force, eventually struggled through its difficulties to achieve a
modest economic viability, based on the export of sugar and hides. Yet
Santo Domingo could never have hoped to retain the pre-eminent
position accorded it by Gonzalo Fernández de Oviedo as the capital of

Spain's empire of the Indies. Once the mainland was conquered and settled, it was doomed to find itself on the margin of events. But the whole experience of Hispaniola, its peoples destroyed and its resources squandered in the pursuit of instant gain, stood as a grim warning of the effects of a *conquistador* mentality unrestrained by moral scruple or institutional control. The same process was again being repeated in Pedrarias Dávila's isthmus of Panama. Unless settlement could be more successfully linked to conquest than in the first years of the Spanish Caribbean, then the expeditions now heading for the American mainland would be conquering only to strip bare.

THE ORGANIZATION AND ADVANCE OF CONQUEST

The mainland of Spanish America may be said to have been 'conquered' between 1519 and 1540, in the sense that those 21 years saw the establishment of a Spanish presence throughout large areas of the continent, and an assertion of Spanish sovereignty, more effective in some regions than in others, over those of its peoples who did not fall within the area of jurisdiction allotted to Portugal by the treaty of Tordesillas – an area found to include the recently discovered Brazil. The Iberian peninsula, excluding Portugal, has a surface area of just under 500,000 square kilometres. The surface area of the Americas that fell to Spain in those two decades was two million square kilometres. The crown had some six million subjects in Castile and another million in Aragon; it now acquired – if only fleetingly, before death and destruction took their terrible toll – perhaps 50 million new subjects in the Americas.

Two great arcs of conquest moving outwards from the Antilles accomplished the subjugation of mainland America. One, organized from Cuba between 1516 and 1518, swept through Mexico between 1519 and 1522, destroying the Aztec confederation, and then radiated north and south from the central Mexican plateau. By 1524 the southward movement had extended through present-day Guatemala and El Salvador, but it was another twenty years before the major Mayan centres in Yucatán were brought under some sort of Spanish rule. The northwards advance from central Mexico proved to be an even slower process. Between 1529 and 1536 Nuño de Guzmán, ravaging the Mexican north and the west, carved out the vast kingdom of New Galicia. Exploration continued, with Hernando de Soto setting out in

1539 to explore the North American south-east and Francisco Vázquez Coronado searching in vain for the seven cities of Cíbola in the prairies west of the Mississippi between 1540 and 1542. But the failure of these two expeditions marked the extreme limits of the Spanish advance. The borderlands to the north of New Galicia were left to the slow forward movement of missionary, ranching and mining enterprise; and it was not until 1562–75 that another great region of the Mexican north-west, Nueva Vizcaya, was brought under Spanish rule by Francisco de Ibarra.

The other arc of conquest, starting in Panama, moved briefly upwards in 1523–4 to Nicaragua, and then, after a short pause, took the Pacific route southwards for the conquest of the Inca empire in 1531–3. From Peru the *conquistadores* moved northwards to Quito (1534) and Bogotá (1536), where they met other groups coming down from the coast of Venezuela and Colombia. While an expedition led by Gonzalo Pizarro set out from Quito in 1541 to explore the Amazon basin, other *conquistadores* moved south into Chile, where Santiago was founded by Pedro de Valdivia in 1542. The Chilean conquest petered out in a war of attrition with the Araucanian Indians. On the other side of the continent an expedition from Europe, under Pedro de Mendoza, tried but failed to occupy the Río de la Plata region in 1535–6, and ended by leaving a remote outpost of settlement in Paraguay. Buenos Aires, first founded in 1536 and destroyed in 1541, was refounded in 1580, this time not from Europe but from Asunción.

Even if the marginal areas, whether in northern Mexico or in southern South America, proved refractory, it remains true that the regions with the largest and most settled indigenous populations were brought under Spanish rule within a single generation. How is the extraordinary swiftness of this process of 'conquest' to be explained?

It is in the nature of conquest itself that the voices of the victors resound more loudly than those of the vanquished.[6] This is especially true of the Americas, where a world conquered was so soon to be a world destroyed. It was, in any event, a world of infinite variety, ranging as it did from the densely-settled populations of Mesoamerica and the Andes, through the partially sedentary peoples on the periphery of these regions, to bands of hunters and food-gatherers like those who roamed northern Mexico and the Argentine plains. Among some of these

---

[6] For a fuller treatment of the Indian and the Spanish conquest, see Hidalgo, *CHLA*, I, ch. 4 and Wachtel, *CHLA*, I, ch. 6.

peoples, oral traditions and folklore kept alive the story of conquest. Among others, the collective memory was extinguished along with the people themselves. And among a few – most notably the Aztecs and the Mayas, who had evolved systems of writing – the episodes of conquest, kept fresh in song and poetry, were either retailed to friars who wrote them down, or else were recorded in writing by those who, if they had not experienced the conquest itself, had learnt of it from members of their parents' generation.

Given the variety of the peoples, the relative paucity of the sources and the nature of the circumstances in which they were produced, it would be too much to say that the surviving records give us the 'Indian' view of the conquest. But they do provide a series of poignant recollections, filtered through the lens of defeat, of the impact made on certain regions by the sudden eruption of alien intruders whose appearance and behaviour were so remote from normal expectation. The *Relación de Michoacán*, for instance, compiled by a Spanish Franciscan around 1540 on the basis of material gathered earlier from native Tarascan informants, records as follows the Tarascans' impressions of the Spaniards:

When the Indians first saw the Spaniards, they marveled at such strange people who did not eat the same kind of food or get drunk as the Indians did. They called the Spanish Tucupacha, which means gods, and Teparacha, which means big men and is also used to mean gods, and Acacecha, meaning people who wear caps and hats. As time passed they began to call them Christians and to believe that they had come from heaven. They were sure that the Spaniards' clothes were the skins of men such as the Indians themselves used on feast occasions. Some called the horses deer, others *tuycen*, which were something like horses which the Indians made from pigweed bread for use in the feast of *Cuingo* and to which they fastened manes of false hair. The Indians who first saw the horses told the Cazonci that the horses talked, that when the Spaniards were on horseback they told the horses where they were to go as they pulled on the reins.[7]

The shock of surprise created by the appearance of the Spaniards and their horses gave the invaders an important initial advantage. But the doom-laden records of the vanquished, produced under the over-whelming impact of defeat, do not of themselves provide an adequate basis for understanding the Spanish success. By their nature, these narratives move inexorably towards catastrophe, which from the first

[7] *The Chronicles of Michoacán*, trans. and ed. Eugene R. Craine and Reginald C. Reindorp (Norman, Oklahoma, 1970), 87.

is foreshadowed by mysterious portents, like the unexplained burning
of temples or the appearance of a strange bird with a mirror in its head.
The sense of inevitability adds immeasurably to the poignancy of the
tale told by the vanquished, but it remains a tale more likely to reflect
the post-conquest perception of an event too vast to be fully
comprehended and absorbed, than to provide a reliable assessment of
the chances of the Spaniards at the moment of their arrival.

The overwhelming numerical superiority of the indigenous populations would seem at first sight to have offered little chance to small bands
of Spaniards linked by only the most precarious of supply lines to their
distant bases. But in the early stages of the conquest the complex
diversity of those populations worked to the Spanish advantage, even
if at a later stage it would pose serious difficulties. Nomadic or
semi-sedentary tribes in thinly-populated regions found it difficult to
prevent the passage of resolute and heavily-armed Europeans, although
the poisoned arrow used in some parts of the Americas took its toll of
the invaders. The more immediate problem for the Spaniards was how
to conquer and then to hold the areas of greatest interest to them – the
areas with large sedentary populations in Mesoamerica and the Andes,
where prospects of mineral wealth and a disciplined labour force made
conquest worth the effort.

But the very size and character of these Mesoamerican and Andean
populations eventually proved to be more of an asset than a liability
to the Spaniards. In both the Aztec and the Inca 'empires', a multiplicity
of competing tribes had been brought under a form of central control
which was more or less resented. This allowed the Spaniards to play
off one tribal grouping against another and to turn subjugated peoples
against their hated masters. It also meant that, once the central power
had been overthrown, the Spaniards in turn found themselves the
masters of populations already accustomed to some degree of sub-
servience. The peoples on the periphery of these 'empires', however,
and those scattered through the thinly-settled dry lands of the Mexican
north or the forest regions of southern South America, proved
incomparably more difficult to dominate, especially when they had got
the measure of the Spanish style of warfare and mastered the use of gun
and horse. Widely dispersed, semi-nomadic, and unused to externally-
imposed discipline, they revealed an exasperating capacity to elude or
resist whenever the Spaniards attempted to introduce some form of
domination. One solution was to leave them to their own devices, and

indeed this is what often occurred. But it was not always possible to ignore them, for some tribes, like those of northern Mexico, were found to be inhabiting lands rich in mineral deposits, and others threatened the tenuous supply routes to Spanish outposts of settlement, or created a permanent sense of insecurity on the borders of regions that were lightly occupied.

The characteristics of the host societies in the regions most coveted by the Spaniards provide one major explanation for the success of the conquest and the subsequent occupation. But although the settled nature of the population in these regions, and the degree of central control to which it was already subjected, proved to be assets which the Spaniards were able to turn to account, the fact remains that at many points the invaders were met with heavy military resistance by forces which vastly outnumbered their own.

The horse gave the Spaniards a major advantage, in terms both of initial surprise and of mobility; but Cortés had only sixteen horses with him on his march into the Mexican interior. The invaders also profited immeasurably from belonging to a society with a decisive technological superiority over the societies of the Indies. When a world of iron and gunpowder comes into violent collision with a world of stone, it would seem that the defeat of the latter is foreordained. But the impact of this technical superiority was not quite as clear-cut and unqualified as might appear at first sight. This was partly because the invaders were poorly equipped by the standards of sixteenth-century Europe. Most of Cortés' men were armed with nothing more sophisticated than swords, pikes and knives; and the firearms at his disposal consisted of a mere thirteen muskets, along with ten bronze cannon and four light cannon. Only with the greatest difficulty were these cannon dragged through forests and up mountains; powder was dampened in river-crossings and by torrential rains; and even when it was dry, the rate of fire of muskets could not compare with that of native bows.

Both in Mesoamerica and in the Andes the Spaniards encountered societies accustomed to large-scale warfare, although it was a style of warfare with a different rhythm and ritual to that of the Europeans. Weapons of stone and wood were no match for Spanish steel, and that otherwise lethal weapon, the obsidian-tipped club of the Mexica, known as the *macuahuitl*, would shatter against the helmet and armour of a Spaniard. In a pitched battle on open ground, therefore, the forces of the Aztecs and the Incas, in spite of their vast numerical superiority, had little hope of overwhelming a combined Spanish force of cavalry and infantry of as few as 50 men, unless they could succeed in reducing them to exhaustion. The best hope was to catch small parties of Spaniards off their guard, or attack them in places where they had no room for redeployment and manoeuvre.

The Indians had the great advantage of operating in a familiar environment, to which the Spaniards had still to become acclimatized. Superior technology served for little when, as so often happened, the Spaniards were combating the effects of heat and altitude, and the sickness produced by unfamiliar food and drink. Moreover, heavy armour proved a liability in these climes, and the Spaniards, in turning to the quilted cotton armour of the Mexica as a substitute, paid unwitting tribute to the way in which environmental circumstance could cancel out technological advantage. Yet the fact remains that the invaders had at their disposal a vastly superior store of technical expertise on which to draw in emergencies. This was particularly apparent in their use of the ship. The ability of the conquerors of Mexico and Peru to reinforce themselves by sea, and Cortés' domination of Lake Texcoco by deployment of specially constructed brigantines, suggest something of the reserves of strength which lay to hand as Europe embarked on the conquest of America.

Both the character of the societies which faced them and their own technological superiority created glittering opportunities for European invaders. But those opportunities still had to be seized, and it is here that the capacity for organization and improvization of sixteenth-century Europeans was put to the test. The fact that they failed lamentably against some of their opponents, like the Araucanian Indians of Chile, indicates that success of itself was not automatic. Different regions posed different problems and demanded different responses, and every expedition or attempt at colonization possessed its own peculiarities.

But while, especially in the early years, there was no uniform procedure of conquest and colonization, certain patterns tended to establish themselves, simply because military expeditions required organization and supplies, and trading expeditions soon found that they could not dispense with military support. In central Venezuela, which Charles V's bankers, the Welsers, attempted to colonize between 1528 and 1541, there was, as might have been expected, a strongly commercial element in the approach to colonization. In spite of this, however, trading expeditions quickly degenerated into slave-raids closely resembling those in the Antilles and Panama.

Yet just as commercial interests found it necessary to resort to military methods, so the *bandas*, the organized warrior bands, could not for long dispense with the services of the merchants. The nearest they came to doing so was in the isthmus region in the years after 1509, when the absence of capital – and of a need for capital so long as short overland expeditions were the norm – made possible the formation of warrior bands, or *compañas*, of a strongly egalitarian character. These warrior companies, based on a prior agreement for equal distribution of the plunder, were well suited to the kind of raiding warfare pursued in the Caribbean, the isthmus of Panama and frontier zones like Venezuela. Indeed they were very much the product of frontier conditions, and it is not surprising that they should have reappeared in a very similar form in Portuguese Brazil in the *bandeiras* which flourished in the late sixteenth and seventeenth centuries. Small, cohesive bodies of men, they possessed, thanks to their horses, the supreme advantage of mobility. Their expenses, apart from the cost of horses, were slight. Firearms, which were costly, and which anyhow rapidly corroded in the humid jungle, were hardly needed against the kind of opposition they were likely to meet. Armed with steel swords, and accompanied by powerful mastiffs, they hunted down the terrified Indians, killing, enslaving and seizing all the gold they could find.

As soon as there was a question, however, of more distant expeditions, especially ones which required ships, more sophisticated forms of organization became necessary. The leaders of potential expeditions then had to resort to merchants or officials with large funds at their disposal, like the *licenciado* Gaspar de Espinosa, the *alcalde mayor* of Castilla del Oro under Pedrarias Dávila, who was a dominant figure in the financing of expeditions from Panama in the early years of the conquest of the mainland.

In the circumstances it was natural that partnerships should be formed – partnerships between the captains themselves and between the captains and investors. In Panama, for instance, Francisco Pizarro and Diego de Almagro formed a profitable partnership in association with Hernando de Luque, whose clerical status did not inhibit his entrepreneurial ventures. Partners would tend to divide their functions, as in the Pizarro–Almagro relationship, where Pizarro provided the military leadership while Almagro recruited followers and arranged for the shipment of men and supplies to fixed points along the route.

Investors demanded as security for their investment the share of the spoils accruing to men who had obtained horses or equipment on credit. Many of the rank and file, therefore, unless they struck exceptionally rich booty, were liable to find themselves permanent debtors either to absentee entrepreneurs or to their own captains. The conquest of America was in fact made possible by a network of credit, which ran by way of local agents and entrepreneurs back to royal officials and rich encomenderos in the Antilles, and still further back across the Atlantic to Seville and the great banking houses of Genoa and Augsburg. But the men who formed the warrior bands were not entirely defenceless. Many of them, pooling such resources as they had, formed their own partnerships within the band, clubbing together to buy a horse and holding together for many years on the basis of mutual trust and an agreed division of the booty.

These private partnerships among the rank and file provided one element of cohesion in the naturally fluid groupings which made up the warrior bands. Regional affiliations, too, helped to provide cohesion, although they could also, on occasions, be a source of sharp divisiveness, as when a new expeditionary force under Pánfilo de Narváez landed on the Mexican coast in May 1520 to challenge Cortés for supremacy. Bernal Díaz observed tartly of the new arrivals: 'as our emperor has many kingdoms and lordships there is a great diversity of people among them, some very brave, and some braver still. We come from Old Castile and are called Castilians, and that captain…and his men come from another province, called Vizcaya. They are called *vizcaínos*, and they speak like Otomi Indians'.[8]

While the regional rivalries in the peninsula were inevitably reflected among the *conquistadores*, it was also true that the predominance of one region in a warrior band could provide a central core of loyalties, linking man to man and the men to their leader. The Extremaduran connection was to be a source of enormous strength both to Cortés and Pizarro. Coming often from a single town or a cluster of towns, the friends, relatives and followers of these two captains formed a unit within the unit, a tightly-knit group based on a shared background,

[8] Bernal Díaz del Castillo, *Historia Verdadera de la Conquista de la Nueva España*, ed. Joaquín Ramírez Cabañas (Mexico, 1944), II, 27.

shared attitudes and a set of close family and personal relationships. To his fellow-Extremadurans, the taciturn and close-fisted Francisco Pizarro was, if not a sympathetic, at least a comprehensible being.

The leaders needed this kind of support if they were to carry their expeditions through to success. From the standpoint of the captains, the conquest of America was something a good deal more complex than the triumph over a demoralized indigenous population of small but determined bands of soldiers, enjoying a decisive technical superiority over their adversaries and impelled by a common dedication to gold, glory and the gospel. Any leader of an expedition knew that the Indians were not his only, nor necessarily his most formidable, opponents. He had enemies, too, in his rear, from the royal officials who were determined to prevent the establishment of independent fiefs or kingdoms in these still unconquered regions to local rivals with an interest in foiling his success. When Hernán Cortés sailed from Cuba in 1519 he did so in defiance of the governor of Cuba, Diego Velázquez, who resorted to every conceivable device to bring about his downfall. Above all, he had enemies in his own camp, from the captains who wanted to step into his shoes to the disgruntled foot-soldiers who planned treachery because their true loyalties lay elsewhere or because they were dissatisfied with the distribution of the spoils.

Leadership, therefore, demanded political as well as military skills of a high order if an expedition were to avoid disintegration from within as well as defeat from without. But the presence of hostile Indians, generally in overwhelming numbers, did force a kind of comradeship even on the uncomradely. In the face of danger and misfortune it was preferable to fight side by side than to die singly; and the prospect of a horrifying death at the hands of heathen enemies proved sufficient to impel a closing of the ranks among men who, for all their personal feuds and grievances, were at least at one in being both Christians and Spaniards. A skilled leader like Cortés knew how to play on the remembrance of shared perils and shared successes to maintain the cohesion and morale of his followers. 'Saint James and Spain' was a battle-cry which could sink all differences in a common cause.

It was a battle-cry at once of defiance and of triumph – the cry of men firmly convinced that they would be the victors. This confidence in their own superiority over enemies who vastly outnumbered them was based, in part at least, on an actual superiority of techniques, organization and equipment. But behind any material factors there lay a set of attitudes and responses which gave the Spaniards an edge in many of the situations in which they found themselves: an instinctive belief in the natural superiority of Christians over mere 'barbarians'; a sense of the providential nature of their enterprise, which made every success against apparently overwhelming odds a further proof of God's favour; and a feeling that the ultimate reward made up for every sacrifice along the route. The prospect of gold made every hardship tolerable. 'I and my companions', said Cortés, 'suffer from a disease of the heart which can be cured only with gold.'[9] They sensed, too, that they were engaged in a historical adventure and that victory would mean the inscribing of their names on a roll-call of the immortals, alongside the heroes of classical antiquity.

The confidence that came from this sense of moral superiority and divine favour was most valuable where it was most needed: in the struggle against their apparently most formidable adversaries, the 'empires' of the Aztecs and the Incas. In the conquest by Cortés of central Mexico between 1519 and 1521, and of Peru by Pizarro between 1531 and 1533, the Spaniards displayed an almost uncanny ability to exploit the weaknesses of their opponents – an ability that itself testified to their own underlying strength.

When Cortés sailed from Cuba in February 1519 with eleven ships carrying 508 soldiers and 110 sailors, he did so with the firm intention of conquering. The two previous expeditions which had reconnoitred the coasts of Mexico and Yucatán, those of 1517 and 1518 under Francisco Hernández de Córdoba and Juan de Grijalva, had been planned only with an eye to exploration and barter. Cortés intended something incomparably more ambitious. Within a few days of his landing on 22 April 1519, he knew that there lived somewhere in the interior a powerful ruler, Montezuma (as he was called by the Spaniards), whose dominion included the peoples of the coastal plain. To a Spanish mind this piece of information suggested a natural strategy: a ruler who himself had dominion over many peoples must himself be brought, by force or by trickery, to acknowledge a yet higher lordship, that of the king of Spain. The supreme objective must therefore be to reach Montezuma – an objective achieved with the hazardous march into the interior and the encounter between Spanish captain and Aztec ruler at Tenochtitlan on 12 November 1519.

[9] Francisco López de Gómara, *Cortés*, trans. and ed. L. B. Simpson (Berkeley, 1964), 58.

Welcomed into the city as guests, the Spaniards were in a position to follow through the strategy of Cortés to its logical conclusion by taking Montezuma into custody and extracting from their unwilling host, turned involuntary guest, a recognition of the sovereignty of the king of Spain.

The alleged *translatio imperii* by Montezuma to Charles V, as described by Cortés in the ingenious tissue of fact and fabrication with which he regaled the emperor in his famous letters, marked the beginning, not the end, of the conquest of Mexico. But it showed decisively where the initiative lay. Cortés had managed to get so far, so fast, because of his extraordinary capacity to size up a situation and turn it to account. To all appearances the Aztec confederation, with a supreme ruler and an organized state structure, represented an incomparably more formidable adversary than any society so far encountered by the Spaniards either in the Caribbean or on the isthmus. But the very degree of organization and of central control from Tenochtitlan created opportunities which Cortés was exceptionally quick to exploit. Mexica domination over the other peoples of central Mexico – a domination which demanded heavy tribute and a constant supply of sacrificial victims – had bred a hatred and resentment which enabled Cortés on his march inland to represent himself as a liberator to the subjugated tribes. This, together with the alliance with Tlaxcala, which the Mexica had never succeeded in subjugating, enabled him to follow a route to Tenochtitlan through relatively friendly territory. It also furnished him with a supporting army from the indigenous population eager for revenge against Montezuma and the Mexica elite.

Montezuma's reasons for allowing Cortés to enter Tenochtitlan will always remain a mystery. He was understandably uncertain about the origin of the intruders and the purpose of their mission, but it is open to question whether, as later came to be suggested by Spanish chroniclers using Indian informants, his reactions were dictated by a conviction that Cortés was none other than the legendary Toltec chieftain, Quetzalcoatl, come out of the east to reclaim his land. It is more probable that he was following towards Cortés and his men the normal behaviour of the Mexica to ambassadors, who traditionally enjoyed immunity, although he may also have believed that by luring Cortés into the interior he would more easily destroy him if this should prove to be necessary. There is no doubt, however, that the cosmological system of the Aztecs, with its fatalistic insistence on the need to propitiate implacable gods by means of human sacrifice, was no match for the confident Christianity of their Spanish opponents. It was a cosmology more likely to inspire its followers with a heroic resignation to death than with a fierce determination to survive; a cosmology, too, which had created a ritualized style of warfare designed to capture the enemy rather than kill him, in order to provide a constant supply of sacrificial victims. Defeat in this highly ceremonial style of war could only discredit the god of war, Huitzilopochtli, the Mexicas' titulary deity, of whom Montezuma was a priest.

By seizing Montezuma, therefore, Cortés had delivered a devastating blow to the political and the religious system of the Aztecs. But this made it more difficult to pursue successfully the next stage of his policy, which was to preserve the administrative and fiscal structure that he had found, keeping Montezuma as a puppet, but effectively replacing his authority with that of the Spaniards. The priestly caste had formed an integral part of the Aztec system, and the Spanish assault on the Aztec deities inevitably constituted a direct challenge to this caste. At the same time, the insatiable Spanish demand for gold created widespread unrest which culminated, after the massacre of the nobility by the future conqueror of Guatemala, Pedro de Alvarado, in a massive popular uprising. Hopelessly outnumbered, the Spaniards successfully fought their way out of Tenochtitlan on the *noche triste*, the night of 30 June 1520, although with heavy casualties. It would take them another fourteen months to recapture the city they left in disarray that night.

The surrender of the last elements of resistance amidst the ruins of Tenochtitlan on 13 August 1521 was as much a triumph for Spanish disease as for Spanish arms. The smallpox carried by a black slave among Cortés' retainers ravaged the defenders of the city and revealed once again what had already become clear from the Antilles: that the inhabitants of the New World would have to pay a heavy price for their centuries of isolation. The conquest of America was a conquest by microbes as well as by men, sometimes running ahead of the main Spanish contingents, at others following in their wake. Especially in densely-populated regions like central Mexico, the part played by epidemics in sapping both the ability and the will to resist goes a long way towards explaining the suddenness and the completeness of the Spanish success.

Yet the collapse of a Mexica empire of some 25 million people in the face of an assault by some few hundred Spaniards cannot be explained purely in terms of external agencies, however destructive. It derived, too, from geological faults within the structure of that empire itself and, in particular, from the repressive nature of Mexica domination over the peoples of central Mexico. Cortés' conquest was as much a revolt by a subjugated population against its overlords as an externally imposed solution. What remains unclear is whether this empire, which was still young and in process of evolution, would, if left to itself, have succeeded in containing and resolving its own internal contradictions. It certainly showed signs of an inner resilience and capacity for adaptation which seem to have been lacking in the Andean civilization that confronted Pizarro, the empire of the Incas.

Pizarro, like Cortés, was able to exploit inner weaknesses and dissensions which happened to be at their worst just at the moment of his arrival. The first firm news of a rich and powerful state to the south had been brought back to Panama in 1523. This encouraged Pizarro and Almagro to organize probing expeditions down the Pacific coast, which provided further evidence of a new kingdom to be conquered. Pizarro himself was in Spain from 1528 to 1530, capitulating with the crown for the governorship of the lands he hoped to conquer and recruiting followers in his Extremaduran homeland. With 180 men and some 30 horses he left Panama in January 1531 on his expedition of conquest. By the time he actually set sail many of his Spanish recruits were dead, struck down by the tropical diseases which carried off such a large proportion of all the new arrivals to the Indies. Only a handful of his followers, therefore, had European military experience. On the other hand, many of them were veterans in the Indies themselves – probably a more useful form of experience in the circumstances. Of these only one or two had been in Mexico. The majority had gained their experience, both of the climate and the Indians, in the Antilles and central America.

The empire that faced him was more tightly organized than that of the Mexica, but the very tightness of its organization served to multiply its internal strains. The Inca state structure, with its insistent and meticulously regulated demand for labour, pressed heavily on the *ayllus*, the village clan communities, creating a subject population that, while docile, was also resentful, especially in the Quito region where Inca rule was relatively recent. As the area of Inca conquest widened, so the problems of central control from Cuzco increased, for all the carefully sited garrisons and the elaborate communications network. This rigid system of uniform control maintained by an Inca ruling caste could only function effectively as long as that caste itself maintained its internal cohesion and unity. But the death of Huayna Capac in 1527 had led to a succession struggle between his sons, Huascar and Atahualpa. The latter was on the way to victory but had not yet consolidated his success at the time of Pizarro's arrival.

Pizarro, like Cortés in Mexico, and like an earlier generation of Spaniards which had sought to profit from the internal feuds of the Nasrid kingdom of Granada, was adept at using these dissensions to further his own purposes. He also used the method employed by Cortés in Mexico and by the *conquistadores* in Central America of making an immediate bid to seize the *cacique* (chief) – in this instance the Inca emperor, Atahualpa.

The emperor, established at Cajamarca in northern Peru, responded to the news of strange invaders in the coastal region in a way that was perfectly natural to a man whose vision of the world had been shaped by the experience of the highlands of the Andes. Those who commanded the mountains effectively commanded the coasts, and beyond the coast lay an impassable sea. As long as the Spaniards remained in the coastal region their presence was not a matter of acute concern to him, because as soon as they moved into the mountain regions they would surely deliver themselves into his hands. Atahualpa therefore made no attempt to molest Pizarro's men as they began their arduous ascent, and the Spaniards still enjoyed the supreme advantage of surprise when they turned on Atahualpa and his retainers on the high plain of Cajamarca on 16 November 1532.

The capture of Atahualpa, like that of Montezuma, was designed to transfer the supreme authority into Spanish hands with a single decisive blow. Then, as in Mexico, the intention was to use the existing administrative structure to channel the profits of dominion to the Spaniards. Although tribute in the Inca empire, unlike that of the Aztecs, consisted entirely of labour, the old imperial system still functioned sufficiently well to produce for the Spaniards as a ransom for Atahualpa the enormous sum in gold and silver of 1.5 million pesos – a treasure far larger than any yet known in the Indies and the equivalent of half a century of European production. Atahualpa's reward, however, was not to be liberty, but judicial murder.

On 15 November 1533 the *conquistadores* captured Cuzco, the heart of the shattered Inca empire. That Pizarro still felt the need for a nominal Inca head of the administrative and military machine which had fallen into his hands is indicated by his selection of Atahualpa's half-brother, Manco Inca, to succeed him. But the smooth transition from Inca to Spanish domination of Peru, which the appointment of a puppet emperor was designed to assist, was made more difficult by a shift in the location of the country's power-centre. Cortés, in deciding to build his new capital of Mexico City on the site of the ruins of Tenochtitlan, succeeded in preserving an important element of continuity between Aztec and Spanish rule. Cuzco, on the other hand, was too high up in the mountains and too remote from the coast to be a satisfactory capital for a Spanish Peru which, unlike its predecessor, would instinctively face towards the sea. In 1535 Pizarro founded his new capital, Lima, on the coast, and by so doing gravely weakened his chances of maintaining control over the Andean highlands.

He weakened them, too, by his failure to keep control over his own subordinates. The growing dissension among the victors over the distribution of the spoils encouraged Manco Inca to rally the remaining Inca forces in a desperate bid to overthrow the Spaniards. The revolt of 1536–7 temporarily jolted but did not halt the process of Spanish conquest. During the year-long siege of the Spaniards in Cuzco, the Indians showed that they had learned something but not enough of the methods of their adversaries. The ceremonial approach to warfare, which had similarly hampered the Aztecs in their opposition to the Spaniards, was so deeply embedded in their mentality that they habitually chose to launch their attacks by the light of the full moon. If the conquest still remained uncompleted once Manco's revolt was suppressed, this was largely because the partisans of Pizarro and Diego de Almagro had diverted their energies to fighting each other. But the impossible geography of the high Andes allowed the continuation of a resistance movement that would have been out of the question in central Mexico. It was not until 1572 that the Inca fastness of Vilcabamba fell to the Spaniards, and isolated pockets of resistance would continue to disturb the sad tranquillity of colonial Peru.

It was precisely because they were centrally organized societies, heavily dependent on the authority of a single ruler, that the empires of Montezuma and of Atahualpa fell with relative ease into Spanish hands. Such vast areas of territory could never have been conquered so speedily if they had not already been dominated by a central power with an elaborate machinery for maintaining control of outlying regions. Both in central Mexico and in Peru the invaders unwittingly found themselves heirs to a process of imperial expansion which did not cease with their arrival. The continuing spread in the post-conquest era of Nahuatl and Quechua, the languages of the Mexica and the Incas, suggests the existence of an inner dynamic within those regions towards a greater degree of unification, which can only have worked to the conquerors' advantage. The *translatio imperii* might be a convenient legal fiction, but it had its justification, in ways of which the Spaniards themselves were only dimly aware, in pre-existing facts.

The very absence in other parts of mainland America of the conditions prevailing in the civilizations of the Andes and central Mexico goes a long way towards explaining the difficulties encountered by the movement of conquest in other areas of the continent. In the Mayan world of Yucatán the Spaniards encountered another sophisticated civilization, but one which lacked the political unity of the Aztec and Inca empires. On the one hand this gave them an opportunity to play the game at which they excelled – that of playing off one community against another. But on the other it slowed down the process of establishing Spanish control because there was no single centre from which to dominate. Francisco de Montejo set out on the conquest of Yucatán in 1527, but in the 1540s the Spaniards still had only a tenuous hold of the region, and the interior was effectively unconquered even after the passage of another century.

No doubt if Yucatán had possessed greater reserves of wealth, the Spaniards would have made more consistently vigorous attempts at conquest. The peripheral regions of America beyond the limits of the great pre-conquest empires all too often proved disappointing in terms of the kind of resources of interest to the Spaniards, as Diego de Almagro discovered to his cost on his abortive Chilean expedition of 1535–7. This did not, however, prevent the despatch of a fresh expedition under Pedro de Valdivia in 1540–1, composed of the disappointed and the unemployed among the conquerors of Peru.

Of the 150 members of Valdivia's party, 132 became encomenderos. Their rewards, however, were disappointing in terms of the expectations generated. They lived among an impoverished Indian population which they used for labour services, in particular gold-washing; but by 1560 there was little gold left, and the native population was dwindling. Rescue came in the form of the growing Peruvian market for agricultural produce. Increasingly the Chilean settlers took to farming and ranching, creating for themselves modestly prosperous farming communities in the fertile valleys north of the river Bío-Bío. They suffered, however, from a shortage of native labour and from the proximity of the Araucanian Indians – warrior tribes whose very lack of centralized authority made them dangerously elusive adversaries.

The Araucanians, 'unsophisticated' peoples in relation to those of the settled societies of Mexico and Peru, revealed a much greater degree of sophistication in adapting their fighting techniques to those of the Spaniards. As early as 1553 they inflicted a crushing defeat on the Spaniards at Tucapel, where Valdivia was killed; and by the end of the 1560s they had turned themselves into horsemen and had begun to master the use of the arquebus. The 'Araucanian wars' of the later sixteenth and seventeenth centuries, although they provided the settlers with a supply of labour in the form of enslaved prisoners of war, also imposed a heavy drain on the Chilean economy. From the early 1570s money was having to be sent to Chile from Peru to help with the costs of defence. In these distant regions horses were in short supply and the costs of war material were high; but the abandonment of this remote outpost of empire seemed an impossible option, not least because of its strategic position controlling the straits of Magellan. Madrid was therefore forced to accept the inevitable, establishing from 1603 a standing army of some 2,000 men and making a regular budgetary provision for it. A miniature war of Flanders was in the making – a prolonged and costly frontier war, in which neither Indian nor Spaniard could achieve decisive mastery.

Just as Araucanian resistance checked the southward movement of Spanish conquest and colonization from Peru, so Chichimeca resistance checked its northward advance from central Mexico. The presence of such unsubdued or half-subdued tribes on the fringes of the Aztec and Inca empires created problems for the Spaniards which evaded straightforward solution, but which they could not afford to ignore. The Mixtón rebellion of 1540–1, originating among the still largely unpacified tribes of New Galicia and rapidly spreading southward, illustrated all too alarmingly the constant threat posed by restless frontier regions to the more settled areas of conquest. It also illustrated the limitations of conquest itself, as conceived in purely military terms. By the middle of the sixteenth century the Spaniards had established their presence over vast areas of central and southern America through their military skill and resourcefulness; but the real conquest of America had hardly begun.

THE CONSOLIDATION OF CONQUEST

In view of the extreme contrasts to be found in the levels of 'civility' attained by the different peoples of pre-conquest America, there were bound to be wide variations in the character of conquest from one region to another and in the requirements for the subsequent control of the conquered population. Once the Aztec and Inca empires had been overthrown, it was possible for the Spaniards to consolidate their new regime over vast areas of territory in central Mexico and Peru with remarkable speed. Their task was made easier by the survival of a substantial part of the fiscal and administrative machinery of the pre-conquest area and by the docility of the bulk of the population, much of it relieved to see its former masters overthrown. It was symptomatic of the success of the Spaniards in establishing their control over the former territories of the Aztecs and Incas that special military measures soon proved to be unnecessary. 'Pacification' – a euphemism employed by Hernán Cortés and adopted as official terminology under Philip II – took longer in Peru, but primarily because the conquerors fell out among themselves. After the Inca rebellion of 1536–7 and the Mixtón war of 1540–1, there was no major Indian uprising in either New Spain or Peru during the Habsburg period, and the Spaniards were so sure of their safety that they never bothered to fortify their cities against possible native revolts.

While the Spaniards were to have considerable success with at least the nominal integration into their new colonial societies of Indians who lived within the boundaries of the pre-conquest empires, they were faced by more intractable problems in other parts of America. Here they often had to deal with tribes and peoples whose way of life seemed primitive by European standards. While some lived in compact villages or in more dispersed settlements, others were simply hunting and food-gathering bands, who had first to be subdued and congregated into fixed settlements before the work of hispanicization could begin.

Some of these peoples, especially the Chichimecas of northern Mexico and the Araucanian Indians of Chile, proved themselves formidable adversaries once they had adapted to Spanish methods of war. Similarly, the Apache Indians of the American plains responded to the approach of the Spaniards by transforming themselves into consummate horsemen and adopting warfare as a way of life.

Spanish success or failure in pacifying these frontier regions would depend both on the habits and culture-patterns of the various tribes with which they came into contact and on the way in which Spaniards themselves approached their task. The missionary would often succeed where the soldier failed; and mission communities, using the weapons of example, persuasion and discipline, scored notable successes with certain tribes – especially those which were neither too nomadic, nor too tightly organized into compact village communities, to be unreceptive to the material advantages and the cultural and spiritual offerings which the mission could provide.

The conquest of America, therefore, proved to be a highly complex process, in which men at arms did not always call the tune. If at least initially it was a military conquest, it also possessed from its earliest stages certain other characteristics which began to predominate as soon as the soldiers had achieved what they could. It was accompanied by a movement aimed at spiritual conquest, by means of the evangelization of the Indians. It was followed by a massive migration from Spain, which culminated in the demographic conquest of the Indies. Subsequently, as more Spaniards settled, the effective conquest of land and labour got under way. But the benefits of this went only in part to the settlers, for hard on their heels came the bureaucrats, determined to conquer or reconquer the New World for the crown. All of these movements produced a conquering society which recalled but failed to reproduce exactly that of metropolitan Spain.

The military conquest of America was achieved by a group of men which was far from consisting entirely of professional soldiers. A comprehensive survey of the background and earlier careers of the *conquistadores* still remains to be undertaken; but an analysis of a list drawn up in 1519 of the encomenderos of the new city of Panama shows that – of the 93 names for which details are available in this select group of 96 *conquistadores* – only half that number were soldiers and sailors by occupation. No less than 34 of the group had originally been peasants or artisans and another ten came from the middling and professional classes in the towns.[10]

There is no reason to think that the Panama group is unrepresentative

[10] See Mario Góngora, *Los grupos de Conquistadores en Tierra Firme, 1509–1530* (Santiago de Chile, 1962), ch. 3.

of the men who conquered America, and it suggests something of the complexity of the transatlantic migratory movement, even in the very first years after the discovery when most of the New World still remained to be won. The *conquista* was from the start something more than a bid for fame and plunder by a military caste looking for new lands to conquer after the overthrow of the Moorish kingdom of Granada. Naturally the military–aristocratic element in peninsular society was well represented in the conquest of America, although the great nobles of Castile and Andalusia were conspicuous by their absence. This is partly to be explained by the determination of the crown to prevent the establishment in the new lands of a magnate-dominated society on the peninsular model. But men with some claim to gentle birth – men from the lesser gentry or *hidalgo* class – were present in substantial numbers throughout the conquest, as was only to be expected. It was not easy for a poor man with pretensions to nobility to survive in the status-conscious world of Castile or Extremadura, as Cortés and Pizarro could testify.

Yet even if the hidalgos formed a minority element, the attitudes and aspirations of this group tended to infuse the whole movement of military conquest. An hidalgo or an artisan prepared to hazard everything to cross the Atlantic obviously did so in the expectation of being able to better himself. In the first years after the discovery the quickest way to self-betterment was participation in expeditions of conquest, which needed the services of men with professional skills – carpenters, blacksmiths, tailors – as long as they would also be prepared to wield a sword when the occasion arose. For these young men, most of them in their twenties and early thirties, the sight of gold and silver brought back from a successful foray opened up visions of a way of life beyond anything they had ever known. The model for this way of life was that provided by the great Castilian or Andalusian magnate, a man who lived to spend. 'All the Spaniards', wrote the Franciscan, Fray Gerónimo de Mendieta, 'even the most miserable and unfortunate, want to be *señores* and live for themselves, not as servants of anyone, but with servants of their own.'[11]

The men, whether professional soldiers or not, who had lived and fought side by side and achieved heroic feats, naturally felt themselves entitled to special consideration by a grateful monarch. *Servicios*, as

[11] Quoted by José Durand, *La transformación social del Conquistador* (Mexico, 1953), II, 45.

always, deserved *mercedes*, and what greater servicio could any man render his king than win for him new territories? To have been the first to advance into unconquered regions was a special cause for pride – the 607 men who first accompanied Cortés jealously guarded their pre-eminence against the 534 who only joined him later. But they banded together in a common front against all later arrivals and finally, in 1543, extracted from a reluctant Charles V a statement declaring that the first 'discoverers' (*descubridores*) of New Spain – he avoided the word *conquistadores* – were those who 'first entered that province on its discovery and those who were there for the winning and conquering of the city of Mexico'.

This rather grudging recognition of primacy was as far as the crown was prepared to go. It had set itself against the re-creation of a feudal society in America; and although some *conquistadores* received grants of *hidalguía*, very few, apart from Cortés and Pizarro, received titles of nobility. How, then, were the survivors among the 10,000 or so men who actually conquered America to be rewarded for their sacrifice? The problem was a difficult one, not least because no *conquistador* ever thought his rewards commensurate with his services. From the beginning, therefore, the *conquistadores* were a class with a grievance, although some with a good deal more justification than others.

The struggle for the spoils of conquest inevitably led to sharp inequalities of distribution. When Cortés, for instance, made the first allocation of Mexican Indians to his followers in 1521, the men associated with his enemy, the governor of Cuba, were liable to find themselves excluded. Similarly in Peru there was much bitterness over the distribution of Atahualpa's treasure, with the lion's share going to the men of Trujillo, the followers of Pizarro, while the soldiers who had arrived from Panama with Diego de Almagro in April 1533 found themselves left out in the cold. The Peruvian civil wars, in the course of which Almagro himself was executed in 1538 and Francisco Pizarro assassinated by the Almagrists in 1541, were a direct outcome of the disappointments and rivalries stemming from the distribution of the spoils of conquest, although these in turn were at least partly provoked by personal and regional tensions before the treasure was ever acquired.

Among the recipients of the booty there was also a natural inequality of shares, based on social standing and assumed variations in the value of service. The man on horseback normally received two shares to the infantryman's one, although Hernando Pizarro pronounced revolutionary words on this subject, presumably to encourage his foot-soldiers on the eve of battle with Almagro. He had been informed, he said, that those soldiers who had no horses were slighted when it came to the distribution of land. But he gave them his word that such a thought had never entered his head 'because good soldiers are not to be judged by their horses but by their personal valour... Therefore each one would be rewarded according to his service, because the lack of a horse was a matter of fortune, and not a disparagement of a man's person.'[12] As a general rule, however, the horseman retained the advantage, although even the ordinary foot-soldier could do very well in a major distribution of booty, like Atahualpa's treasure.

The actual rewards of conquest, in the form of spoils, encomiendas, distribution of land, municipal offices, and – not least – prestige, were in fact often very considerable, even if official recognition of service by the crown was grudging or non-existent. Fortunes were made, although they were often as rapidly lost by men who were natural gamblers; and while some of the conquistadores – especially, it seems, those from the better families – decided to return home with their winnings, others hoped to better themselves still further by remaining a little longer in the Indies and never succeeded in leaving them.

It was difficult for these men to settle down. Yet, as Cortés saw very quickly, unless they could be induced to do so, Mexico would be stripped bare and destroyed as the Antilles had been before it. One obvious device, already employed in Hispaniola and Cuba, was to turn soldiers into citizens. This was, in the first instance, a purely legal act. After their landing on the Mexican coast Cortés' men were formally constituted members of what was still a notional corporation, the municipality of Veracruz. Municipal officials were duly chosen from among the captains, and a *cabildo* or town council instituted. Only later did the Villa Rica de Veracruz come to acquire the physical characteristics of a town.

Although the immediate purpose in founding Veracruz was to provide Cortés with a legalistic device for freeing himself from the authority of the governor of Cuba and placing the mainland territories under the direct control of the crown at the request of the soldier-citizens, it provided the pattern for a similar process of municipal incorporation which was followed as the conquering soldiers moved through Mexico.

12 Quoted by Alberto Mario Salas, *Las armas de la Conquista* (Buenos Aires, 1950), 140–1.

New towns were created, sometimes, as with Mexico City itself, on the site of indigenous towns or villages, and at other times in areas where there were no large congregations of Indians. These new cities and towns were intended for Spaniards, although some of them from the beginning had *barrios* or quarters reserved for the Indians, and most of the others would later acquire them. Based on the model of the Spanish town with its central plaza – the principal church on one side and the town hall (the *ayuntamiento*) on the other – and laid out, wherever possible, on the gridiron plan of intersecting streets used in the construction of Santo Domingo, the New World town provided the expatriate with a familiar setting for daily life in an alien environment.

The soldier turned householder would, it was hoped, put down roots. Each *vecino* would have his plot of land; and land, both in the suburbs and outside the cities, was liberally distributed among the conquerors. But for men who brought from their home country strict views about the demeaning character of manual labour, for those aspiring to seigneurial status, land itself was of little value without a labour force to work it. Although Cortés was initially hostile to the idea of introducing in Mexico the encomienda system, which he and many others held largely responsible for the destruction of the Antilles, he was compelled to change his mind when he saw that his followers could never be induced to settle unless they could obtain labour services from the Indians. In his third letter to Charles V, dated 15 May 1522, he explained how he had been compelled to 'deposit' Indians in the hands of Spaniards. The crown, although reluctant to accept a policy which appeared to threaten the status of the Indians as free men, finally bowed to the inevitable, as Cortés had already done. The encomienda was to join the city as the basis of the Spanish settlement of Mexico and then, in due course, of Peru.

It was, however, to be a new-style encomienda, reformed and improved in the light of Spain's Caribbean experience. Cortés was by nature a builder, not a destroyer, and he was determined to construct in Mexico a 'New Spain' on foundations which would endure. He cherished the vision of a settled society in which crown, conqueror and Indian were linked together in a chain of reciprocal obligation. The crown was to reward his men with Indian labour in perpetuity, in the form of hereditary encomiendas. The encomenderos, for their part, would have a dual obligation: to defend the country, thus saving the crown the expense of maintaining a standing army, and to care for the spiritual and material wellbeing of their Indians. The Indians themselves would perform their labour services in their own *pueblos* (villages), under the control of their own *caciques* (chiefs), while the encomenderos lived in the cities, of which they and their families would become the principal citizens. The type and amount of work performed by the Indians was to be carefully regulated to prevent the kind of exploitation which had wiped them out in the Antilles; but the underlying assumption of Cortés' scheme was that the self-interest of encomenderos anxious to transmit their encomiendas to their descendants would also work to the interest of their Indian charges by preventing callous exploitation for purely short-term ends.

The encomienda was therefore envisaged by Cortés as a device for giving both the conquerors and the conquered a stake in the future of New Spain. The ruling caste of encomenderos would be a responsible ruling caste, to the benefit of the crown, which would derive substantial revenues from a prosperous country. But the encomienda would also work to the benefit of the Indians, who would be carefully inducted into a Christian civility.

As encomiendas were granted through New Spain, Central America and Peru, so this potential ruling caste began to constitute itself. It was drawn from an elite group among the soldiers of the conquest, and its numbers were inevitably small in relation to those of the Spanish population of the Indies as a whole: around 600 encomenderos in New Spain in the 1540s and around 500 in Peru. Living off the revenues produced by the labour of their Indians, the encomenderos saw themselves as the natural lords of the land. But there were in fact profound differences between their situation and that of the nobles of metropolitan Spain. The encomienda was not an estate and carried with it no entitlement to land or to jurisdiction. It therefore failed to become a fief in embryo. Nor, for all their efforts, did the encomenderos succeed in transforming themselves into a European-style hereditary nobility. The crown consistently baulked at the formal perpetuation of encomiendas through inheritance, and in the New Laws of 1542 decreed that they should revert to the crown on the death of the current holder. In the prevailing circumstances this decree was quite unrealistic. In New Spain the viceroy prudently disregarded it. In Peru, where Blasco Núñez Vela attempted to enforce it in 1544, it provoked an encomendero revolt, led by Francisco Pizarro's youngest brother, Gonzalo, who for four years was the master of Peru. In 1548 he was defeated and executed for treason by the *licenciado* Pedro de La Gasca, who arrived armed with a fresh decree revoking the offending clauses in the recent legislation.

Although the crown had retreated, its retreat was largely tactical. It continued to treat the perpetuation of an encomienda in one and the same family as a matter of privilege rather than right, thus depriving the encomenderos of that certainty of succession which was an essential characteristic of European aristocracy. It was able to act in this way with a large measure of success because social forces in the Indies themselves were working in favour of its policy. The encomenderos were a small minority in a growing Spanish population. Even if they gave hospitality and employment to many of the new immigrants, there were many more who felt themselves excluded from the charmed circle of privilege. The deprived and the excluded – many of them building up their own sources of wealth as they acquired lands, and taking to farming and other entrepreneurial activities – naturally looked jealously on the encomiendas and their captive Indian labour. The defeat of Gonzalo Pizarro enabled La Gasca to embark on a large-scale reassignment of encomiendas; and the ability to reassign encomiendas, whether forfeited by rebellion or vacated by death, became a decisive political instrument in the hands of succeeding viceroys. On the one hand it could be used to satisfy the aspirations of non-encomenderos, and on the other it served as a means of curbing and restricting the encomienda itself, since every encomendero knew that, if he antagonized the crown and its representatives, there were a hundred men waiting to step into his shoes.

At the same time as the crown was struggling against the hereditary principle in the transmission of encomiendas, it was working to reduce the degree of control exercised by encomenderos over their Indians. Here its most decisive move was to abolish in 1549 the obligation of the Indians to perform compulsory personal service. In future the Indians would only be liable to payment of tribute, the rate of which was set at a figure lower than that which they had previously paid to their lords. Inevitably the law of 1549 was more easily decreed than enforced. The transformation of the encomienda based on personal service into an encomienda based on tribute was a slow process, accomplished more easily in some regions than in others. In general the older style of encomienda, with the encomendero as the dominant local figure, drawing heavily on labour or tribute or both, was more liable to survive in the marginal regions, like Yucatán or southern Mexico, the Andean highlands, or Chile. Elsewhere, the encomienda was being transformed during the middle decades of the century, under the pressure both of royal officials and of changing economic and social conditions. Encomenderos with only poor villages in their encomiendas found themselves in serious straits as tributes dwindled along with the indigenous population. The wealthier encomenderos, reading the signs aright, began to use their wealth to diversify and hastened to acquire land and to build up agricultural estates before it was too late. There was money to be made from the export of local products, like cacao in Central America, and from the production of grain and meat to feed the growing cities.

While the crown remained deeply suspicious of the encomenderos as a class, the encomienda as an institution had its supporters, and ironically their numbers and influence tended to increase as the encomenderos were gradually stripped of their coercive powers and became little more than privileged crown pensioners. When the New Laws attempted to abolish the encomienda, the Dominicans of New Spain, traditionally less well disposed to the institution than the Franciscans, declared themselves in its favour. The crown was technically correct in stating in a decree of 1544 that 'the purpose and origin of the encomiendas was the spiritual and temporal well-being of the Indians'; and by this time there was a strong conviction among many of the missionaries in the New World that the lot of the Indians would be even worse than it already was without the fragile protection still afforded them by the encomienda.

This conviction reflected a deep disillusionment with the results of an enterprise which had begun amidst such high hopes a generation earlier. By the middle years of the sixteenth century the movement for the spiritual conquest of America had begun to falter, as a result of deep divisions over strategy and discouragement over failures. The discouragement was so great partly because the original expectations of the first missionaries to mainland America had been pitched so high, for reasons which had less to do with New World realities than with Old World preconceptions.[13]

The evangelization of America was conducted in its opening stages by members of the regular orders, as distinct from the secular clergy. The first missionaries to reach Mexico were Franciscans, the 'twelve

---

[13] For further discussion of the evangelization of Spanish America, see Barnadas, *CHLA*, I, ch. 14.

apostles' under the leadership of Fray Martín de Valencia, who arrived in 1524. They were followed two years later by the Dominicans, and then by the Augustinians in 1533. By the middle years of the century there were some 800 friars in Mexico and another 350 in Peru. The mendicants also gave Mexico its first bishop and archbishop (1528–48), the Franciscan Fray Juan de Zumárraga, a distinguished representative of Spain's Christian humanist tradition.

Among the first generation of mendicant missionaries in the New World were many who had felt the influence both of Christian humanism and of the apocalyptic and millenarian Christianity which was such a vital element in the religious life of late fifteenth- and early sixteenth-century Europe. Fray Martín de Valencia, for one, seems to have been influenced by the twelfth-century mystic, Joachim of Flora, with his prophecies of the coming of a third age of the Spirit. Those who set out from Spain to convert the Indians saw themselves as entrusted with a mission of special importance in the divine scheme of history, for the conversion of the world was a necessary prelude to its ending and to the second coming of Christ. They also believed that, among these innocent peoples of America still uncontaminated by the vices of Europe, they would be able to build a church approximating that of Christ and the early apostles. The early stages of the American mission with the mass baptism of hundreds of thousands of Indians, seemed to promise the triumph of that movement for a return to primitive Christianity which had so repeatedly been frustrated in Europe.

Very soon, however, the doubts which had always been entertained by some of the missionaries began to rise insistently to the surface. At first it looked as though the Mexican Indians possessed a natural aptitude for Christianity, partly, perhaps, because the discrediting of their own gods by defeat in war had created a spiritual and ceremonial vacuum which predisposed them to accept the leadership of the friars as the holy men of a conquering race. The simple instruction in the rudiments of Christianity given by the missionaries, their use of music and pictures to explain their message, and their mobilization of large groups of Indians to construct the great fortress-like convents and churches which changed the architectural landscape of central Mexico in the immediate post-conquest decades, all helped to fill the void left by the disappearance of the native priesthood and by the collapse of the routine of ceremonial labour governed by the Aztec calendar.

But although the rate of conversion was spectacular, its quality left much to be desired. There were alarming indications that Indians who had adopted the new faith with apparent enthusiasm still venerated their old idols in secret. The missionaries also came up against walls of resistance at those points where their attempts to inculcate the moral teachings of Christianity conflicted with long-established patterns of behaviour. The virtues of monogamy, for instance, were not easily conveyed to a society which saw women in the role of servants and the accumulation of women as a source of wealth.

To some of the missionaries, especially those of the first generation, these setbacks served as an incentive to probe more deeply into the customs and beliefs of their charges. Where the first instinct had been to obliterate all vestiges of a pagan civilization, an attempt now began to examine, record and inquire. The Dominican Fray Diego Durán argued that 'a great mistake was made by those who, at the beginning with great zeal but little wisdom, burnt and destroyed all their ancient paintings, for we are now left so unenlightened that they can practise idolatry before our very eyes.'[14] It was in accordance with this line of reasoning that the great Franciscan, Fray Bernardino de Sahagún, devoted his life to the recording and understanding of a native culture that was being rapidly swept away. Many of his colleagues struggled with success to master the Indian languages and to compile grammars and dictionaries. The realization that true conversion required a profound understanding of the evils to be extirpated provided an impetus, therefore, to important linguistic studies, and to ethnographical inquiry which often, as with Sahagún, showed a high degree of sophistication in its controlled use of native informants.

This was truer, however, of Mexico than Peru, where the unsettled conditions of the post-conquest period delayed the work of evangelization, which in some areas was not systematically undertaken until the seventeenth century. Already by the middle of the sixteenth, at a time when the first missions were establishing themselves in Peru, the humanist generation of mendicants was passing into history. In the succeeding generation there was less curiosity about the culture of conquered peoples and a corresponding tendency to condemn instead of seeking to understand. This was encouraged by some spectacular failures which helped to cast doubt on the original assumptions about

[14] Diego Durán, *Historia de las Indias de Nueva España y islas de Tierra Firma*, ed. José F. Ramirez, 2 vols. (Mexico, 1867–80), II, 71.

the Indian aptitude for Christianity. The Franciscan college of Santa Cruz de Tlatelolco, founded in 1536 to educate the children of the Mexican aristocracy, was a natural object of suspicion to all those Spaniards, whether lay or cleric, who were hostile to any attempt to place the Mexican on the educational level of the European, or to train him for the priesthood. Any backsliding by a student of the college, like Don Carlos of Texcoco, who was denounced in 1539 and burnt at the stake as a dogmatizer, therefore served as a convenient pretext for undermining a movement which took as its axiom that the Indian was as rational a being as the Spaniard.

Inevitably the prophecies of disaster proved to be self-fulfilling. The Indians, forbidden to train as priests, naturally tended to look on Christianity as an alien faith imposed on them by their conquerors. They took from it those elements which suited their own spiritual and ritualistic needs and blended them with elements of their ancestral faith to produce beneath a simulated Christianity an often vital syncretic religion. This in turn merely served to confirm the belief of those who argued that they must be kept in permanent tutelage because they were unready to take their place in a European civility.

The often exaggerated ideas about the spiritual and intellectual capacity of the Indians held by the first generation of missionaries therefore tended to give way by the middle decades of the century to a no less exaggerated sense of their incapacity. The easiest response was to regard them as lovable but wayward children, in need of special care. This response came all the more naturally to the friars as they saw their monopoly over the Indians endangered by the advent of the secular clergy. It was encouraged, too, by a genuine fear for the fate of their Indian charges in the rapidly changing conditions of the mid-sixteenth century. As the humanist vision of the first missionary generation faded, and it seemed increasingly improbable that the New World would become the setting for the New Jerusalem, the friars struggled to preserve what still remained by congregating their flocks in village communities where they could be better shielded from the corrupting influences of the world.

It was a less heroic dream than that of the first missionary generation and no less inexorably doomed to failure. For profound changes were occurring in the demographic composition of Spanish America as the number of immigrants multiplied, while that of the indigenous population diminished.

By the middle of the sixteenth century there were probably around 100,000 whites in Spanish America. The news of the opportunities for a better life in the New World encouraged a growing number of Spaniards to take ship from Seville to America, with or without official licence to emigrate. In a letter home characteristic of those written by the emigrants to the Indies, Juan de Robles wrote to his brother in Valladolid in 1592: 'Don't hesitate. God will help us. This land is as good as ours, for God has given us more here than there, and we shall be better off.'[15]

Although the Indies were officially the exclusive possession of the crown of Castile, no sixteenth-century law is known which prohibited inhabitants of the crown of Aragon emigrating to them, although Aragonese, Catalans and Valencians do seem to have been excluded in law, if not always in practice, from holding posts and benefices in Castile's overseas possessions. Emigrants from Navarre, which was officially incorporated with the crown of Castile in 1515, were in a stronger legal position. But the overwhelming number of emigrants came from Andalusia, Extremadura and the two Castiles, with the number of Basques increasing as the century progressed.

Some of these emigrants went to join relatives who had already emigrated, others to escape from conditions which, for one reason or another, had come to seem intolerable at home. Several of those on the losing side in 1521, when the revolt of the Comuneros was crushed, made their way surreptitiously to the New World; and the same was true of those whose Jewish ancestry prejudiced their chances of success at home, although there were stringent regulations to prevent the emigration of Jews and *conversos*. It is hard to believe that the emigration of all seven brothers of St Teresa of Avila was entirely unconnected with the fact that their family was of *converso* origin.

In the early years, as might have been expected, the movement of emigration was overwhelmingly masculine. But, in order to encourage settlement, the crown insisted that all *conquistadores* and *encomenderos* should be married, and this produced a growing number of female emigrants. If women represented 5 or 6 per cent of the total number

---

[15] Enrique Otte, 'Cartas privadas de Puebla del siglo XVI', *Jahrbuch für Geschichte von Staat, Wirtschaft und Gesellschaft Lateinamerikas*, 3 (1966), 78. For a selection of these letters in translation see James Lockhart and Enrique Otte, *Letters and people of the Spanish Indies. The sixteenth century* (Cambridge, 1976).

of emigrants in the period 1509–39, they were up to 28 per cent in the 1560s and 1570s. But the shortage of Spanish women in the first years of conquest naturally encouraged mixed marriages. Baltasar Dorantes de Carranza, writing of the *conquistadores* of Mexico, explains that 'because in those fifteen years when the land was won Spanish women did not come to it in any quantity', some of the *conquistadores* did not marry at all, while others married Indians.[16] This was especially true of Indian women of royal or noble blood, with the sons of these unions, known as *mestizos*, succeeding to their fathers' estates. But the rapid growth of *mestizaje* in the Indies was less the result of formal marriage than of concubinage and rape. During the sixteenth century, at least, the mestizo offspring of these unions tended to be assimilated without excessive difficulty into the world of one or other of the parents. Although the crown was soon expressing concern about their way of life, it was only in the seventeenth century, as their numbers multiplied, that they began to constitute something of a distinctive caste on their own.

It was not only the whites, however, who were transforming the ethnic composition of the population of the Indies. There was also a strong current of African immigration, as black slaves were imported to swell the labour force. Coming to outnumber the whites in the Antilles, they also constituted a significant minority group in Mexico and Peru. The offspring of their unions with whites and Indians – known as *mulattos* and *zambos* respectively – helped to swell the numbers of those who, whether white or hybrid, increasingly preoccupied the authorities by their obvious rootlessness. The Indies were on the way to producing their own population of the voluntary and involuntary idle, of wastrels, vagabonds and outcasts, which seemed so threatening to the ordered and hierarchical society constituting the sixteenth-century European ideal.

The presence of this shiftless population could only add to the forces already bringing about the disintegration of the so-called *república de los indios*. In spite of the strenuous efforts of many of the friars to segregate the Indian communities, only in the remoter regions, where the Spaniards were sparsely settled, was it possible to keep the outer world at bay. The proximity of cities established by the conquerors; the labour demands of encomenderos and the tribute demands of the crown; the encroachment of Spaniards on Indian lands; the infiltration of whites

---

[16] Dorantes de Carranza, *Sumaria Relación*, 11.

and mestizos; all these elements helped to undermine the Indian community and what remained of its pre-conquest social organization.

At the same time as it was being subjected to these powerful pressures from without, the *república de los indios* was also succumbing to a demographic catastrophe. The smallpox epidemic during the course of the conquest was only the first of a succession of European epidemics which ravaged the indigenous population of mainland America in the succeeding decades. The incidence of these epidemics was uneven. Peru, with a more sparsely settled population, seems to have escaped more lightly than Mexico, which was particularly hard hit in 1545–7. All through America the coastal regions proved especially vulnerable and here, as in the Antilles, Africans tended to replace an Indian population which had succumbed almost in its entirety.

European diseases struck a population which was disorientated and demoralized by the experiences of the conquest. Old patterns of life had been disrupted, the precarious balance of food production had been upset by the introduction of European crops and livestock, and European demands for labour services had pressed the Indian population into unaccustomed work, often under intolerably harsh conditions. Although there were some signs of successful adaptation, particularly by the Indians in the region of Mexico City in the period immediately following the conquest, it is not surprising that many Indians should have found the shock of change too great and have lost the will to live. The survivors appear in contemporary accounts as a passive and listless people, seeking escape from their woes in narcotics and intoxicants – pulque-drinking in Mexico and coca-chewing in the Andes.

If the pre-conquest population of central Mexico fell from 25 million in 1519 to 2.65 million in 1568, and that of Peru fell from nine million in 1532 to 1.3 million in 1570, the demographic impact of European conquest was shattering both in its scale and its speed.[17] No preconceived plans, either for the salvation or for the exploitation of the Indians, could hope to withstand intact the effects of such a drastic transformation. By the middle of the sixteenth century Spanish America was a very different world from the one that had been envisaged in the immediate aftermath of conquest.

The assumptions about the wealth to be derived from the conquest of the Indies had taken for granted the existence of a ·large and docile

[17] For further discussion of the demographic collapse, see Sánchez-Albornoz, *CHLA*, II, ch. 1.

indigenous population producing labour services and tribute for the conquerors. Inevitably, the totally unexpected decline of this population forced sharp readjustments both of policy and behaviour. From the mid-sixteenth century, the struggle intensified between settler and settler and crown and settler for a larger share of a shrinking labour supply. The discovery of rich silver deposits in the 1540s in both Mexico and Peru and the beginning of large-scale mining operations meant that priority was bound to be given in the distribution of Indian labour to mining and ancillary activities. The abolition of the encomienda of personal service following the decree of 1549 deprived encomenderos of their Indian workforce, which could then be mobilized for necessary public services by means of repartimientos organized by royal officials.

At the same time as less Indian labour was becoming available for private individuals, large areas of land were being left unoccupied as a result of the extinction of its Indian owners. This coincided with a rapidly growing need for land among the settler community to satisfy the dietary requirements of an expanding Hispanic population congregated in the cities, which remained addicted to its traditional habits and tastes. It wanted meat and wine, and it preferred white bread to maize. Encomenderos and other influential and wealthy settlers therefore petitioned the crown with success for grants of land (*mercedes de tierras*) on which they could grow wheat (more costly to produce than maize and requiring a greater acreage to provide a comparable yield) and raise European livestock (cattle and sheep). While Hispanic America was to remain an essentially urban civilization, there were already strong indications from the middle of the sixteenth century that the basis of this civilization was likely to be dominion of the countryside by a handful of great proprietors.

By the end of the first generation of the conquest it was already clear that new and distinctive societies were coming into being in the new world of the Spanish Indies. The conquerors, having moved in, had taken control of the land and the people; and if they had destroyed on a massive scale, they were also beginning to create. They brought with them a belief which was gradually gaining ground in sixteenth-century Europe: that it was within the capacity of man to change and improve the world around him. 'We found no sugar mills when we arrived in these Indies', wrote Fernández de Oviedo, 'and all these we have built with our own hands and industry in so short a time.'[18] Hernán Cortés, exploiting the vast estates that he had acquired for himself in the valley

---

[18] Fernández de Oviedo, *Historia general y natural de las Indias* (Madrid, 1959), I, 110.

of Oaxaca, showed that the conqueror also had the ambitions of the entrepreneur.

The kind of society which the conquerors and immigrants instinctively set out to create was one that would approximate as nearly as possible to the society they left behind in Europe. As a result, the fate of the subjugated peoples was itself pre-ordained. They would be transformed, in so far as this could be achieved, into Spanish-style peasants and vassals. They would be made to conform to European notions about work and incorporated into a wage-economy. They would be Christianized and 'civilized', to the extent which their own weak natures allowed. It was not for nothing that Cortés christened Mexico New Spain.

One of the most striking characteristics of Spain itself, however, was the increasingly powerful presence of the state. For a time, after the death of Isabella in 1504, it had seemed that the work of the Catholic Kings in strengthening the royal authority in Castile would be undone. The revival of aristocratic factionalism threatened more than once to plunge Castile back into the disorders of the fifteenth century. But Ferdinand of Aragon, who survived his wife by twelve years, manoeuvred skilfully to preserve the authority of the crown. Cardinal Jiménez de Cisneros, who acted as regent after the death of Ferdinand in 1516, displayed similarly effective gifts of command, and Charles of Ghent, Isabella's young grandson, inherited in 1517 a country at peace.

But the peace was precarious, and the initial events of the new reign did nothing to make it more secure. Charles' election as Holy Roman Emperor in June 1519, two months after the landing of Cortés in Mexico, and his subsequent departure for Germany, served to precipitate a revolt in the cities of Castile against the government of an alien and absentee king. The revolt of the Comuneros (1520–1) drew deeply on the constitutionalist traditions of medieval Castile and, if it had triumphed, would have imposed institutional restraints on the development of Castilian kingship. But the defeat of the rebels on the battlefield at Villalar in April 1521 left Charles and his advisers free to re-establish and extend the royal authority without serious impediment. Under Charles, and still more under Philip II, his son and successor (1556–98), an authoritarian and increasingly bureaucratic government was to make its presence felt at innumerable points in the life of Castile.

It was inevitable that this growing assertiveness of the state would also have its impact on Castile's overseas possessions. The aspirations to state intervention had been there from the beginning, as the *capitulaciones* between the crown and would-be conqueror bore witness. But the process of conquest itself could all too easily slip out of royal control. Time and distance played into the *conquistadores'* hands, and, if Cortés showed more deference than many in his behaviour towards the crown, this was because he had the vision to realize that he needed powerful supporters in Spain and the wit to appreciate that it could pay to explain, so long as one acted first.

But the Emperor Charles V, like Ferdinand and Isabella before him, had no intention of allowing his newly-acquired realms to slip from his control. In New Spain Cortés saw himself systematically displaced by royal officials. An audiencia, on the model of that of Santo Domingo (1511), was established in Mexico in 1527, under what proved to be the disastrously self-seeking presidency of Nuño de Guzmán. This first attempt at royal control created more evils than it cured, but the period of government from 1530–5 by the second audiencia, composed of men of far higher calibre than the first, made it clear that there would be no place for its conqueror in the New Spain of the bureaucrats.

Cortés went relatively gracefully, but in Peru the establishment of royal control was not achieved without a bitter struggle. The pretext for the revolt of the Pizarrists from 1544–8 was the attempt to enforce the New Laws; but behind it lay the unwillingness of men of the sword to accept the control of men of the pen. It was symbolic that the rebellion was crushed, not by a soldier but by one of those officials trained in the law who were the prime object of *conquistador* hostility. The *licenciado* Pedro de La Gasca triumphed over the Pizarrists because he was above all a politician, with the skill to exploit the divisions within the *conquistador* community between the encomenderos and the foot-soldiers who coveted their possessions.

In New Spain from the 1530s, in Peru from the 1550s, the day of the *conquistador* was over. A new, administrative conquest of the Indies was getting under way, led by the audiencias and the viceroys. New Spain acquired its first viceroy in 1535, in the person of Antonio de Mendoza who served until 1550; and Peru, where an audiencia was established in 1543, began to settle down under the viceregal government of another Mendoza, the marquis of Cañete (1556–60). Gradually under the rule of the first viceroys, the controlling apparatus of royal authority was clamped down on the new societies that the *conquistadores*, the friars and the settlers were in process of creating. The Indies were beginning to take their place within the capacious institutional framework of a world-wide Spanish monarchy.

7

THE INDIAN AND THE SPANISH CONQUEST*

America, isolated from the rest of the world for thousands of years, had a distinctive history, free of external influences. It was, therefore, a complex interplay of internal factors which had by the beginning of the sixteenth century bestowed upon the various indigenous societies many different forms: highly structured states, more or less stable chiefdoms, nomadic or semi-nomadic tribes and groups. And it was this hitherto completely self-contained world which suddenly experienced a brutal and unprecedented shock: the invasion of white men from Europe, the clash with a profoundly different world.

The reaction of the native Americans to the Spanish invasion varied considerably: from offers of alliance to more or less forced collaboration, from passive resistance to unremitting hostility. Everywhere, however, the arrival of these unknown beings caused the same amazement, no less intense than that experienced by the *conquistadores* themselves: both sides were discovering a new race of man whose existence they had not even suspected. This chapter examines the effects of the Spanish invasion on the Aztec and Inca empires during the first stage of colonial rule (to the 1570s) with particular emphasis on the case of the Andes; it also looks briefly at the 'peripheral' areas, north of the central Mexican plateau, south and south-east of the central Andes, in order to present the broadest possible picture of the 'vision of the vanquished'.

THE TRAUMA OF CONQUEST

In both Mexico and Peru native documents depict an atmosphere of religious terror immediately before the arrival of the Spaniards. Even

* Translated from the French by Mr Julian Jackson; translation revised by Ms Olivia Harris, Goldsmiths' College London, and the Editor.

if these were retrospective interpretations, such descriptions testify to the trauma experienced by the native Americans: prophecies and portents had foretold the end of time; then suddenly there appeared four-legged monsters surmounted by white creatures of human apearance.

In Tenochtitlan, for a whole year each night was lit up by a column of fire which appeared in the east and seemed to rise from the earth to the sky. A mysterious fire destroyed the temple of Huitzilopochtli; then that of Xiuhtecuhtli was struck by lightning. A strange grey bird, bearing a sort of mirror in the top of its head, was captured; when Moctezuma examined the mirror 'he caught sight of something in the distance: it seemed to be a procession moving at speed, in which imposing figures jostled and fought each other; they were mounted on a species of stag'.[1] Among the Mayas, the *Chilam Balam* foretold (perhaps after the event) the dawning of a new era: 'When they raise their signal on high, when they raise it with the tree of life, all will be suddenly changed. And the successor of the first tree of life will appear, and for all people the change will be clear.'[2] In Peru the last years of Huayna Capac were disturbed by a series of unusually violent earthquakes. Lightning struck the Inca's palace, and comets appeared in the sky. One day, during the celebrations of the festival of the Sun, a condor was chased by a falcon and collapsed in the middle of the main square of Cuzco: the bird was nursed, but it died. Finally, one bright night the moon seemed to be ringed by a triple halo, the first the colour of blood, the second a greenish-black, the third like smoke: according to the soothsayers the blood indicated that a cruel war would tear apart the children of Huayna Capac; the black foretold the destruction of the Inca Empire; and the last halo that everything would disappear into smoke.[3]

Widespread throughout America was the myth of the civilizing god who, after his benevolent reign, disappears mysteriously, promising men that one day he will return. In Mexico there was Quetzalcóatl who departed towards the east, and in the Andes Viracocha who disappeared in the western Sea. Quetzalcóatl was supposed to return in a *ce-acatl* (one-reed) year, based on a 52-year cycle, while the Inca state was

[1] Miguel León-Portilla, *Visión de los vencidos. Relaciones indigenas de la Conquista* (Mexico, 1959), 2–5; idem., *El reverso de la Conquista. Relaciones aztecas, mayas, e incas* (Mexico, 1964).
[2] *Chilam Balam de Chumayel*, ed. and trans. Benjamin Péret (Paris, 1955), 217.
[3] Garcilaso de La Vega, *Comentarios reales de los Incas* [1609], ed. *Obras completas* (Madrid, 1960), II, 52, 352–4.

supposed to end during the reign of the twelfth emperor. In Mexico the Spaniards came from the east, and 1519 was indeed a *ce-acatl* year; in Peru they came from the west, and Atahuallpa was indeed the twelfth Inca. Accordingly the Indians' shock assumed a specific form: they perceived events through the framework of myth, and, in certain circumstances at least, conceived the arrival of the Spaniards as a return of the gods.

It is striking that, from Mexico to Peru, the native descriptions pick on the same characteristics to demonstrate the strangeness and power of the invaders: their white skin, their beards, their horses, their writing and their firearms. Hence the following account which Moctezuma was given by his messengers:

Their bodies are completely muffled up; only their faces are to be seen and they are white as chalk. They have yellow hair, although in some cases it is black. Their beards are long; their moustaches are also yellow... They are mounted on their 'Stags'. Perched in this way they ride at the level of the rooftops... If the shot [of a cannon] touches a hill, it seems to split it, to crack it open, and if it strikes a tree it shatters it and crushes it, as if by a miracle, as if someone had destroyed it by blowing from the inside.[4]

The scene in which Moctezuma received the Spaniards (in spite of some of the doubts of his advisers) as if they were gods has remained famous: he went to meet the invaders and offered them necklaces of flowers and gold as a sign of welcome; then he delivered to Cortés the astonishing speech which has been preserved for us by the informants of Sahagun:

My lord... at last thou hast reached thy home: Mexico City. Thou hast come to take thy place on thy throne, beneath thy royal canopy...
No, this is not a dream, I am not awakening from a dream, my senses still dulled by sleep... I have already seen thee, I have already set eyes on thy countenance! Such was indeed the legacy and message of our kings, of those who ruled, of those who governed thy city: according to their words thou wouldst be installed on thy seat, on thy royal throne of majesty thou wouldst reach these places.[5]

These Mexican accounts recall those of Andean chroniclers like Titu Cusi: on their arrival the Spaniards were considered to be the Viracochas, sons of the divine creator:

They said that they had seen the appearance in their country of creatures very different from us, as much in their customs as their clothes: they resembled the Viracochas, the name by which we referred, in times past, to the Creator

---

[4] León-Portilla, *Visión de los vencidos*, 34–5.   [5] *Ibid.*, 79–80.

of all things. They saw them mounted on huge animals with feet of silver: this caused by the glint of their shoes in the sun. And they also called them Viracochas because they saw that they were able to talk to each other without difficulty by means of pieces of white Cloth: this because of their reading of books and letters.[6]

It is true that beliefs in the divinity of the Spanish were soon destroyed: their strange conduct, their frenzy at the sight of gold, their brutality, quickly shattered these beliefs. And not all Americans began with such illusions. The intrusion of the Europeans was for the indigenous societies an unprecedented event which interrupted the normal course of existence. Confronted with this incursion of the unknown, the Indians' view of the world implied at least the possibility that the white men were gods. But the answer to the question could be positive or negative according to the place and the circumstances. Evidence of this is shown by a remarkable incident. Approaching Cuzco, Pizarro's soldiers captured messengers sent by Callcuchima to Quizquiz; they were bearing important news about the nature of the invaders: 'Callcuchima had sent them to inform Quizquiz that they [the Spaniards] were mortal.'[7]

How could empires as powerful as those of the Aztecs or the Incas be destroyed so rapidly by a few hundred Spaniards? Undoubtedly the invaders benefited from superior arms: steel swords against lances of obsidian, metal armour against tunics padded with cotton, arquebuses against bows and arrows, cavalry against infantry. But this technical superiority seems to have been of limited importance: the Spanish possessed few fire-arms at the time of the conquest, and these were slow to fire; their impact at the beginning was, like that of the horses, primarily psychological.

The Spanish victory was certainly helped by the political and ethnic divisions of the Indian world: the Aztec and Inca empires had themselves been built up by successive conquests. Certain groups saw the arrival of the invaders as an opportunity to free themselves of oppressive domination: thus it was the Indians themselves who provided Cortés and Pizarro with the bulk of their conquering armies, which were as large as the Aztec and Inka armies against which they

[6] Titu Cusi Yupangui Inca, *Relación de la Conquista del Perú y hechos del Inca Manco*, II [1570], Coleccion de libros y documentos referentes a la Historia del Peru, 1st series, II (Lima, 1916), 8–9.
[7] Historical Archives of Cuzco, 'Genealogia de la casa y familia de Sayri Tupac', libro 1, indice 1, fo. 147v, and libro 4, indice 6, fo. 38r.

fought. In Mexico the recently conquered Totonacs revolted against Moctezuma and allied themselves with the Spaniards, who subsequently received decisive support from the Tlaxcalans. In Peru, the Huascar faction rallied to Pizarro, and he also secured the assistance of groups such as the Cañaris or the Huancas who refused to accept the rule of the Incas.

The outcome of the conflict did not depend only on the strength of the opposing forces: from the perspective of the defeated, the European invasion also contained a religious, even cosmic, dimension. Looting, massacres, fires: the Indians were living through the end of a world; defeat meant that the traditional gods had lost their supernatural power. The Aztecs believed themselves to be the chosen people of Huitzilopochtli, the Sun god of war; their mission was to bring under his rule the peoples surrounding Tenochtitlan on all four sides. Thus the fall of the city meant infinitely more than just a military rout. It also ended the reign of the Sun god. Earthly life had henceforth lost all meaning, and since the gods were dead it remained only for the Indians also to die:

> Let us die, then,
> Let us die, then
> For our gods are already dead.[8]

In the society of the Andes, the Inca, as son of the Sun, mediated between gods and men and was himself worshipped as a god. He represented in a sense the bodily centre of the universe whose harmony he guaranteed. The death of the Inca represented the disappearance of the living reference point of the universe, the brutal destruction of its order. It is for this reason that the whole natural world participated in the drama of defeat:

> The sun turns yellow,
> and night falls
> mysteriously;
> ...The death of the Inca reduces
> time to the batting of an eyelid;
> ...The earth refuses to bury
> its Lord,
> ...And the rocky cliffs tremble for their master
> chanting dirges.[9]

---

[8] *Libros de los Coloquios de los Doce*, in Walter Lehmann, *Sterbende Götter und Christliche Heilsbotschaft* (Stuttgart, 1949), 102; similarly in León-Portilla, *El reverso de la Conquista*, 25.

[9] *Apu Inca Atawallpaman*, in León-Portilla, *El reverso de la Conquista*, 182–3. See also, Elliott, *CHLA*, 1, ch. 6.

DESTRUCTURATION

The trauma of the conquest was not limited to the psychological impact of the arrival of white men and the defeat of the ancient gods. Spanish rule, while making use of native institutions, at the same time brought about their disintegration, leaving only partial structures which survived outside the relatively coherent context which had given them meaning. The destructive consequences of the conquest affected the native societies at every level: demographic, economic, social and ideological.

After its first contact with the Europeans, the Amerindian population everywhere underwent a demographic collapse of historically exceptional proportions. For the central Mexican plateau Sherburne F. Cook and Woodrow Borah have proposed the (perhaps excessive) figure of 25 million inhabitants before the arrival of the Spaniards. For the Andes various estimates have been made; but a population of about ten million for the whole of the Inca empire seems a reasonable assessment.[10]

But in the 30 years following the invasion the population fell at a vertiginous rate. The Indians of the island of Hispaniola, for example, were wiped out completely, while on the Mexican plateau the population fell by more than 90 per cent according to Cook and Borah:

1519: 25.0 million
1532: 16.8 million
1548: 6.3 million
1568: 2.65 million
1580: 1.9 million

The rate of the population fall seems to have been less steep in the Andes: the Indians from the cold areas, notably those of the *altiplano*, survived the catastrophe better than elsewhere. Thus the population of the Lupaca, on the west bank of Lake Titicaca, diminished by only 20–25 per cent in 30 years. On the other hand, population decline in the northern Andes, on the coast or in the warm valleys, reached levels comparable to that of Mesoamerica. So far as the fragmentary sources allow us to judge, the overall fall was, as in Mexico, very steep up to the 1560s, and then became more gradual:

1530: 10.0 million
c. 1560: 2.5 million
c. 1590: 1.5 million[11]

---

[10] See Note on the native American population on the eve of the European invasion, *CHLA* I.

[11] For a discussion of the collapse of the Indian population following the European invasions, see Sánchez-Albornoz, *CHLA*, II, ch. 1. On the Andes in particular, see Nathan Wachtel, *La*

What were the reasons for this catastrophe? The main cause was disease. The Europeans brought with them new diseases (smallpox, measles, 'influenza', 'plague') against which the American Indians, isolated for thousands of years from the rest of humanity, had no defence. As early as 1519 Aztec resistance had been weakened by the smallpox epidemic which broke out during the siege of Tenochtitlan. The epidemic then spread throughout Central America and perhaps even as far as the Andes: in 1524, even before Pizarro's first expedition, a strange disease, characterized as a sort of smallpox or measles, caused thousands of deaths (including that of the Inca Huayna Capac) in the Inca empire. In the years 1529–34 measles again affected first the Caribbean, then Mexico and Central America. The notorious *matlazahuatl* devastated New Spain in 1545 and New Granada and Peru during the following year. In 1557 an 'influenza' epidemic which came directly from Europe, hit Central America; in 1558–9 smallpox again spread to Peru. Matlazahuatl re-emerged in 1576 in Mexico. And during the years 1586–9 a triple epidemic of smallpox, plague and 'influenza', emanating from Quito, Cuzco and Potosí, ravaged the whole of the Andes.[12]

Even if it is accepted that these epidemics were the main cause of the demographic decline, it cannot be denied that the Spanish conquest was itself a period of murderous oppression. The first population censuses of the native population show an excessively high male mortality rate, most probably owing to war and the exactions of the tribute.[13] Other documents refer to individual or collective suicides and practices of abortion, at the same time betraying a mood of despair and serving as a form of protest. The age pyramids which can be constructed for the second half of the sixteenth century suggest a fall in the birth rate which can be interpreted as another consequence of the trauma of the conquest.

It is clear that a population collapse of this magnitude completely

Vision des vaincus. Les Indiens du Pérou devant la conquête espagnole 1530–1570 (Paris, 1971), 135–40, 318–21, and Noble David Cook, *Demographic collapse. Indian Peru, 1520–1620* (Cambridge, 1981).

[12] Felipe Guaman Poma de Ayala, *Nueva corónica y buen gobierno* [1614] (Paris, 1936), 114; Pedro Cieza de León, *Primera parte de la Cronica del Peru* [1550] (Madrid, 1941), 71; Fernando de Montesinos, *Memorias antiguas historiales y politicas del Peru* [1644] (Madrid, 1906), I, 254; Bernabé Cobo, *Historia del Nuevo Mundo* [1653] (Madrid, 1965), II, 447; Henry F. Dobyns, 'An outline of Andean epidemic history to 1720', *Bulletin of the History of Medicine* (1963), 493–515; Wachtel, *La Vision des vaincus*, 147–9.

[13] This phenomenon is clearly seen in the *visitas* of Iñigo Ortiz de Zúñiga, *Visita de la provincia de León de Huánuco en 1562*, I and II (Huánuco, 1967–9), and of Garci Diez de San Miguel, *Visita hecha a la Provincia de Chucuito en el año 1567* (Lima, 1964). For adults between ages 21 and 50, the former reveals the figure of 56 men for every 100 women, the latter 82 men for every 100 women.

disorganized the traditional structures of the native societies. The answers to a questionnaire which formed the basis of the *Relaciones geográficas de Indias* [1582–6] informs us how the Indians themselves viewed their own demographic situation. The investigators asked their informants whether the number of Indians had increased or declined since the period before the conquest, whether they enjoyed better or worse health, and to explain the causes of any changes that had taken place. The answers mostly point in the same direction: the Indians felt that they lived less long and were in less good health. The causes of the decline were given in order of importance as war, epidemics, migrations of population and overwork. These causes seem to be plausible and also to tally with each other. But the seemingly absurd and implausible nature of some of the answers makes them all the more revealing. In some cases the Indians attributed the fall in their numbers or their shorter life span to the fact that they had less work to do, that they were freer and better fed:

...And they lived longer in the old days than now, and they attribute this to the fact that they ate and drank less then.
...And because they indulge in more vices than before and have more freedom, they live less healthy lives...
...They lived longer because before, they say, they led more orderly lives than they do now, and because there was not such an abundance of things, nor did they have the opportunities which they now have to eat and drink and indulge in other vices, and with all the work they had to do when the Inka reigned, there was not even any wine, which generally shortens life.[14]

Can such answers be explained by a desire to please or by fear? If so, it is surprising that those answering the questionnaire did not hesitate at other times to complain about their lot. It is more likely that the apparently inexplicable feeling of too much freedom actually corresponded to the void left by the disappearance of the former structures of the state and the collapse of the traditional rules of conduct. It is striking that the last quotation also mentions the ravages of alcoholism (a theme to which we will return later) as one of the causes of depopulation. In other words, what these answers demonstrate is the disintegration of those economic, social and religious systems which had previously given a meaning to the tasks of daily life. In short, the demographic changes reflected the destructuration of the native world.

---

[14] *Relaciones geográficas de Indias* [1582–6], ed. M. Jimenez de la Espada (Madrid, 1881–98, 4 vols.; re-ed. 1965, 3 vols.), I, 88–9, 120, 222, 330.

To understand the processes of destructuration it is necessary first to outline the distinctive features of the pre-Columbian civilizations. However, since these have been discussed in an earlier section of this volume, only one example – the central and southern Andes – will be the subject of closer examination here.[15]

Before the rise of Tahuantinsuyu (the Inca state), this vast area was populated by tens of different groups of widely varying size: thus, the Chupachos of the Huánuco region consisted of a small chieftaincy of about 10,000 people, while the Lupacas on the west bank of Lake Titicaca made up a powerful kingdom of over 100,000 inhabitants. The Incas of the Cuzco region represented, at the beginning, an ethnic group of only relatively minor importance, which stood out from the others only because of its unique place in history.

The basic unit of the different ethnic groups was the *ayllu* (analogous to the Mexican *calpulli*) which formed an endogamous nucleus, uniting a certain number of kinship groups who possessed collectively a specific (but often disconnected) territory. Grouped together, these basic units fitted together to form moieties, and then larger units still, until they comprised the entire ethnic group. This same term ayllu can be applied to all the various levels superimposed in this way on each other, each more inclusive than the one before. The Inca state was in a sense the pinnacle of this immense structure of interlocking units. It imposed a political and military apparatus on all of these ethnic groups while continuing to rely on the hierarchy of local lords, or *curacas*. Within the ayllu in the strict sense of the term, grazing land was held in common and arable land was allocated to domestic family units in proportion to their size; so this distribution in theory took place periodically. In accordance with the ideal of self-subsistence which was a feature of Andean society, a family unit could claim a parcel of land in each ecological sector, so as to combine complementary products from land at different altitudes (maize, potatoes, *quinoa*, grazing for llamas, etc.). This claim was not restricted to the means of production (such as land or livestock), it also extended to the workforce: each head of family had the right to ask his relations, allies or neighbours to come and help him cultivate his plot of land; in exchange he was bound to offer them food and *chicha*, and to help them when they asked him to. This mutual

---

[15] See also Murra, *CHLA*, I, ch. 3.

aid was the ideological and material foundation of all social relations, and it governed the whole process of production.

This system of exchanges spread to all levels of social organization: between members of the ayllu at the base; within the moieties and the ethnic group in the service of a curaca; and at the level of the empire in the service of the Inca. There was, however, from one level to the next a gradual transition from reciprocity based on symmetry and equality to an increasingly hierarchical and unequal reciprocity. The services of the subjects of Tahuantinsuyu were an extension of those which they provided to the local gods and to the curacas. Collectively they worked the lands of the Inca and of the Sun, in a spirit of religious ritual, and in return they received food – chicha and coca; or they made cloth and clothes, using the Inca's flocks; and finally, they periodically performed the service of the *mita*, public works or war service. But while at the level of the ayllu (and even at that of the ethnic group) kinship continued to regulate the organization of labour, the distribution of land and the consumption of what was produced, within the framework of the empire the services provided by the Inca's subjects allowed the development of an infrastructure (granaries, fortresses, roads, etc.) of a different nature. In other words, the imperial Inca mode of production was based on the ancient communal mode of production which it left in place, while exploiting the principle of reciprocity to legitimate its rule.

The extension of the *mitmaq* system, already applied within the framework of the ethnic group, constituted one of the most remarkable achievements of the Inca Empire. We know that the nuclear settlements on the highlands – devoted to the rearing of animals and production of tubers – realized their ideal of self-sufficiency by sending 'colonists' (*mitmaq*) to settlements at lower altitudes, in order to have access to the produce of the warm valleys (maize, cotton, coca, etc.). In these complementary 'colonies' members of widely separated highland groups found themselves living alongside each other in the lowlands, so that the population of their little 'islands' became intermingled; but the centres from which they originated did not exercise political control over the territories lying in between, and in this way they formed 'vertical archipelagos' of varying size.[16] The Inca state took up this method of organization for its own purposes, in order to carve out vast

---

[16] See John V. Murra, *Formaciones económicas y políticas del mundo andino* (Lima, 1975) and *La organización económica del estado inca* (Mexico, 1978). See also Murra, *CHLA*, I, ch. 3.

areas of cultivation, whether of coca (as in the Songo Valley), or, above all, of maize (for example in the Abancay, Yucay, or Cochabamba valleys).[17]

Recent research makes it possible, in the case of Cochabamba, to analyse this process of colonization in detail: Huayna Capac, the last Inka but one, expelled almost all the indigenous populations (the Cotas and the Chuis) from the valley, and settled them at Pocona, further east, to protect the 'frontier' against the Chiriguanos; and he seized their lands for the state. To cultivate this land he transferred into the valley 14,000 workers 'of all nations', mostly from the altiplano, but sometimes from even further afield, from the Cuzco region, and even from Chile. Some were supposed to live permanently (*perpetuos*) near the fields and granaries of Cochabamba (these were mitmaq in the proper sense of the term) while others made the journey every year, as mita. Each 'nation' or ethnic group was given responsibility for a certain number of plots, or *suyus*. All the maize grown was earmarked essentially for the army. But a certain number of plots were set aside for the subsistence of the workers, and others were accorded to different curacas who could redistribute the products among their subjects. The Indians who were transplanted to the Cochabamba Valley thus acquired new land at the expense of the old inhabitants.[18]

This process was repeated in numerous regions of Tahuantinsuyu: although the model of the 'vertical archipelago' was already deeply embedded in Andean society, the Inca state extended it to a hitherto unprecedented extent, and despatched mitmaq throughout the empire. This policy was developed further by increasing the number of *yana*, personal dependants who had been cut off from any family ties, employed by the Inca at various levels within the area under his control. But did the logic of the state system not conflict with the principle of reciprocity which continued to prevail in the ayllu? It was precisely this contradiction which was brought into the open by the Spanish invasion.

---

[17] On the Abancay valley, see Waldemar Espinoza Soriano, 'Colonias de mitmas múltiples en Abancay, siglos XV y XVI. Una información inédita de 1575 para la etnohistoria andina', *Revista del Museo Nacional*, 31 (1973), 225–99; on the Yucay valley, see Horacio Villanueva Urteaga, 'Documentos sobre Yucay en el siglo XVI', *Revista del Archivo Histórico del Cuzco*, (1970), 1–184; Maria Rostworowski de Diez Canseco, 'El repartimiento de doña Beatriz Coya en el valle de Yucay', *Historia y Cultura*, (1970), 153–267; Wachtel, *La Vision des vaincus*, 168–76 and 202–6. The documents on the Songo valley (in the Archivo General de Indias at Seville) are still unpublished.

[18] Nathan Wachtel, 'Les *mitimaes* de la vallée de Cochabamba. La Politique de colonisation de Huayna Capac', *Journal de la Société des Américanistes*, 67 (1980–1), 297–324.

After the capture and death of Atahuallpa, the structures of the state collapsed; regional and, above all, local institutions survived, but divorced from the overall framework which had given them meaning. Numerous mitmaq returned to their places of origin, and the 'archipelagos' which the Inca had organized (such as those of Songo, Abancay or Cochabamba) disappeared. But the model of self-sufficiency and 'vertical complementarity' continued to be applied at the level of the ethnic groups: thus the society of the Andes embarked on a long process of fragmentation. This breaking up of economic and social activity was hastened by the Spaniards when they parcelled out the *encomiendas*: chiefdoms which had hitherto formed coherent political, social and economic units were often divided between several beneficiaries, so that far-outlying settlements found themselves detached from the authority of their legitimate lords.

Thus, the ancient kingdom of the Lupacas became a *repartimiento* of the crown, while its Pacific Coast 'colonies' were granted to a certain Juan de San Juan; it required the intervention of Polo de Ondegardo to restore the people to their settlements of origin. But this was an exceptional case: in this example the famous chronicler had been defending the interests of the crown. It should be noted that this same Polo acted in the opposite way when his personal interest was at stake. He had received part of the valley of Cochabamba as an encomienda which included the mitmaq who had been previously settled there by the Inca and were now claimed by the curacas of the altiplano, successors of their former Caranga, Sora, Quillaca and Charca chieftains. This led to prolonged litigation during which Polo argued that the mitmaq should be detached from the authority of their highland chieftains because the Carangas (like the Lupacas) had lost access to their settlements once situated on the Pacific Coast:

After His Majesty instituted the repartimiento system in this kingdom, he divided up all the mitimaes, lands and plots in the place where they happened to be, and the lands concerned were allocated to the said Indians and their encomenderos, and this was general throughout all this kingdom, and so the Carangas were left without any lands or mitimaes on the coast, and the same happened to those of Chucuito.[19]

The Carangas, indeed, lost their coastal 'colonies', but (as the *Memorial de Charcas*, drawn up in 1583, testifies) they retained some of

[19] Archivo Historico de Cochabamba, AR 1540, fos. 353r–353v.

the suyos which they had been granted by the Inka in the Cochabamba Valley, as did also the Soras, the Quillacas and the Charcas.[20] The Andean model of the archipelago thus came into conflict with the Spanish conception which linked the Indians to the place where they lived; the Andean model did survive, but only by being restricted to ever-diminishing areas.

Phenomena whose existence had hitherto been unknown transformed the pre-Columbian world: the most important elements of this process of destructuration seem to have been the new forms of tribute, the introduction of money and the market economy.

The upheavals were certainly more profound in Peru than in Mexico, since the subjects of the Inca (in contrast to the *macehuales* of the Aztec empire) only owed the state labour services and not payments in kind. During the early colonial period until the middle of the sixteenth century, in both Mexico and Peru, the level of the tribute levied by the encomenderos was not fixed by any official measure. The first tax assessments which were drawn up in the 1550s, besides including labour services (which, in the Andes, took up the ancient tradition of the mita), consisted of numerous and disparate payments: maize, wheat, potatoes, sheep, pigs, poultry, eggs, fish, fruit, coca, salt, cloth and various manufactured articles. Often, when they did not produce one of these items, the Indians had to obtain it by barter, which forced them to travel long distances. Silver tribute also dated from this period, but was limited in quantity compared to the overall payments. Soon the assessments were simplified: items of secondary importance disappeared, while silver increased, and became the major form of tribute from the 1570s.

How did the Spanish tribute compare with the pre-Columbian? We lack exact figures, but there is no doubt that at first the encomenderos imposed their decisions arbitrarily and without restraint and that later they did not always respect the letter of the tax laws. There were many examples of abuse. The method of taxation was also unfair. In each repartimiento liabilities were assessed according to the number of tributaries, and the Indians were collectively responsible for payment. However, as a result of demographic collapse, a discrepancy quickly developed between the original assessments and the declining population,

[20] Waldemar Espinoza Soriano, *El memorial de Charcas* (*Crónica inédita de 1582*) Lima, 1969).

as is revealed by the frequent cases of litigation between the encomendero and the native communities, especially soon after an epidemic. The Indians would appeal to the authorities to carry out a *revisita* to adjust the assessment to the actual number of those liable to pay. But even when a revaluation was carried out, the burden of the colonial system still had to be supported by a smaller number of Indians.

At the same time, although in a sense continuing the obligations which had in the past been owed to the pre-Columbian state, the Spanish tribute broke up the system of which they had formed a logical part. Thus, according to the investigation of Ortiz de Zúñiga in 1562, the Chupachos owed a textile tribute, as in the time of Tahuantinsuyu. But the Inca had provided them with raw materials – in this case wool – and they had made him clothes of *cumbi*. Now the encomendero demanded cotton clothes, and the transaction was entirely one-way since the Indians themselves provided the cotton, having grown it in their own fields: '...And they give them cloth not of *cumbi* but of cotton, which they grow and harvest, and the Inca used to give them wool for *cumbi* cloth.' '...And they wanted their encomendero to give them cotton to make cloth.'

The Spaniards (whether encomenderos or not), aided by the decline in population, which meant an increase in fallow land, were not slow to usurp some of the land hitherto worked by the Indians. But, since the new rulers clearly took the lands with the best soil, their appropriations drove the Indians onto marginal land. Throughout Peru the lands of the Inca, of the Sun and of the *huacas* were deemed to be the property of the crown, whose subjects benefited from this in the form of *mercedes*. Thus, the burden of the tribute was shifted onto the Indians' communal lands:

...and the lands on which they used to grow maize and foodstuffs for the Inka were in this valley, including where this village now stands, and the district round it. This land was distributed to the Spanish inhabitants when the village was founded, but now the Indians have marked out some of their own land to grow maize, wheat and potatoes for tribute.

Thus it is hardly surprising that the Spanish tribute seemed heavier than that of the Inca. One of Ortiz de Zúñiga's questions was directed precisely to finding out how much time the Chupachos now devoted to work in order to make these payments. The answer was hardly ever other than between seven and eight months. The Indians complained of having insufficient time to cultivate their own fields, to the extent of actually protesting to Lima:

And at present they feel more exhausted than ever in the past for everybody works, married men and women, old men and women, youths and girls and children, and there is nobody left, which is why they went to the court in Lima to ask for justice and the lightening of their burdens.[21]

Above all the change was a qualitative one. The ideology upon which the Inca system was based lay in ruins. In the new society dominated by the Spaniards, all idea of reciprocity and redistribution had lost its meaning. To be more precise, the Spanish system did make use of fragments of the old system, reciprocity did continue to play a part in the relations between the ayllus and the curacas, and the curacas did still provide a link between the Indians and the new rulers; but while in Tahuantinsuyu reciprocity had given rise to a rotation of wealth (even if it was theoretical and unequal) between the ayllus, the curacas and the Inca, Spanish rule resulted in a one-way transfer without reciprocity. In short, if the Spaniards had inherited the Inca's centralizing role, they failed to ensure the redistribution of wealth for the benefit of all. While the system of payments (whether real or symbolic) in the Inca empire functioned within a balanced and circular structure, the Spanish tribute was unbalanced and unilateral.

The development of the silver tribute from the 1550s forced the Indians to take up new activities in order to obtain the necessary precious metal. The mines of Mexico, especially Zacatecas from 1545, experienced an influx of free workers (*naborios*). The Potosí mines became the main pole of attraction in the central and southern Andes. From 1553 the Indians of the Chucuito province (the former Lupaca kingdom) dispatched *mitayos* to the mines, enabling their lords to gather the 2,000 pesos needed for the tribute. A new tax assessment in 1559 raised it to 18,000 pesos and stipulated that 500 mitayos should be sent. Other Indians hired themselves out to Spanish merchants as transporters of goods (by convoy of llamas) or went into the towns to work as building labourers. In this way a market economy developed in certain sectors, to the detriment of the traditional economy. Already the curacas were complaining that many of their subjects travelled far afield, and no longer came back.[22]

But at Potosí the Indians were able to impose their own working conditions on the Spaniards. For almost 30 years, from 1545 until about 1574, they controlled both the technical process of mining the ore and

[21] Ortiz de Zúñiga, *Visita*, fos. 22r, 18r, 23r, 33r.
[22] Diez de San Miguel, *Visita*, fos. 87v, 48v, 107v.

its transformation into silver. The only method used during these years was, therefore, that of the *huayra*, the traditional native foundry, usually placed in the hills to make use of the wind.[23] On the other hand, during this same period the mitayos still accounted for only a small proportion of the workforce which consisted mainly of Indians detached from their own communities, and considered as *yanaconas*. They formed teams of workers who made what were, in effect, contracts with the *mineros*: they provided their own tools, agreed to deliver a fixed quantity of ore, and were allowed to keep the surplus for themselves. Thus, the Indians, having ore at their own disposal, transformed it themselves in their own *huayras*, and produced silver directly. The *mineros* had to resort again to native labour to transform their part of the ore, and this was a further source of earnings for the Indians. During the period in which the huayra was used, the Spaniards made numerous attempts to free themselves of the Indian technological monopoly; but, as Garcilaso de la Vega describes, all such attempts failed:

The mine owners, seeing that in this way of smelting with natural wind their riches were dissipated through many hands, and as many were those who shared in them, they tried to remedy the situation in order to enjoy the metal and the proceeds themselves. They therefore began to pay the miners on a daily basis, and built their own smelters instead of using those of the Indians, for up until then, it had been the Indians who had extracted the silver, the arrangement being that the owners had a right to a certain amount of silver for every quintal extracted. In their greed, they made huge bellows, which could blow the furnaces from afar, like natural wind. But they did not even use this artifice, but made machines and wheels with sails, like those on windmills, but drawn by horses. However, they found these of no use, and no longer trusting their inventions, they stuck to what the Indians had invented.[24]

It was not until the amalgamation process was introduced under viceroy Toledo in 1574 that the Spaniards were able to break the Indian control of silver production. This was the beginning of a new era of colonial history. But it is true that, even during the huayra stage, all the silver produced by the Indians went back into circulation in the colonial system. Those who went to work at Potosí in order to pay the tribute delivered it to their encomenderos or to the crown. And as the Spaniards, on their side, dominated the rest of the market (especially

---

[23] On this so-called *huayra* period in Postosí, see Carlos Sempat Assadourian, 'La producción de la mercancia dinero en la formación del mercado interno colonial. El caso del espacio peruano, siglo XVI', in *Ensayos sobre el desarollo económico de Mexico y America Latina*, ed. Enrique Florescano (Mexico, 1979), 223–92.

[24] Garcilaso de la Vega, *Comentarios reales*, quoted by Carlos Sempat Assadourian, *op. cit.*, 246.

that of coca and maize), they recovered the silver remaining in the possession of the free workers through trade. The introduction of money, therefore, ultimately integrated the Indians into the economic system as a labour reserve.

The changes in the economic system were accompanied, both in Peru and Mexico, by the dismantling of the social structure, but the process took different forms in each area. It is not known to what extent the ayllu and the calpulli were affected by the consequences of the European invasion, but it does seem that they both continued to function as the basic cells of Indian society. The nature of the upheaval emerges more clearly at the two extremes of the social scale: those Indians, an increasingly large proportion of the population, who were no longer part of the communal sector of the economy, and those lords who lost many of their traditional powers.

In the two viceroyalties a pattern of migration developed, which the collectors of tribute soon began to bemoan. In Peru, besides the population shifts caused by the conquest itself, the civil wars between the partisans of Pizarro and Amalgro, which raged until 1548, helped to uproot the population. Many Indians, recruited into the opposing armies and taken far from their home villages, either ended up swelling the ranks of vagrants or remained as yanaconas in the service of the Spaniards. It will be recalled that in Tahuantinsuyu the term *yana* designated those Indians free of family ties and personally dependent on the curaca or the Inca. But, whereas before the arrival of the Spaniards, they had still only comprised a small proportion of the population, their numbers now began to multiply. Their status, however, continued to vary considerably: if the yanaconas of Potosí seem to have been free of personal dependence, this was not the case for those who went to work on the emerging haciendas or those employed by the Spaniards as domestic servants. Apart from such differences, the bulk of the Andean population was divided into two categories: the *hatunruna* (or Indians of the communities who were subject to the tribute and the mita); and the yanaconas, considered to be of lower social status, but in practice free from the obligations owed by the other Indians.

Out of this distinction there developed a crucial difference between the two viceroyalties in later centuries. In Peru, the expansion in the number of yanaconas (and then of *forasteros*) created a problem whose seriousness, although not evident in the sixteenth century, came into the open during the seventeenth century and was to last throughout the colonial period: it contained the embryo of the struggle between, on one side, the *hacendados* (who kept hold over part of the workforce) and, on the other, the *mineros* (deprived of mitayos) and the crown (deprived of tribute): the problem of subjecting the yanaconas and forasteros to the obligations which weighed on the rest of the Indians was to dominate the future history of the central and southern Andes.

It is true that the interests of the hacendados, the mineros and the crown also diverged in Mexico. But the pre-Columbian class of *mayeques*, in a sense comparable to the yanaconas of the Andes except that they formed a larger proportion of the population, suffered an entirely different fate. Before the arrival of the Spaniards, the mayeques owed payments not to the representatives of the *tlatoani* of Tenochtitlan but to the local native lords. Because the Spanish tribute was modelled on the Aztec system, these Indians, like the yanaconas of the Andes, at first escaped the payments that the *macehuales* of the communities owed to their encomenderos. But after 1560 the mayeques were in their turn registered as tributaries, and this blurred the distinctions of the pre-Columbian world: in this respect the native population of Mexico became increasingly undifferentiated.

At the other end of the social scale, the members of the native nobility were henceforth forced to act as intermediaries between the Spaniards and the Indians owing tribute. The descendants of the old ruling castes lost the essence of their power, although they continued to play an important role: they retained a position of privilege only because they agreed to collaborate with the Spaniards. The heirs of Moctezuma (Diego Huanintzin, Diego Tehuetzqui, Cristobal de Guzman Cecepatic, Luis de Santa Maria Cipac) held the office of *tlatoani* and *gobernador* of Tenochtitlan until 1565. Then the 'legitimate' dynasty ceased to hold any important administrative position:

No more were the natives of Mexico to be *gobernadores* or to rule the *altepetl* of Mexico Tenochtitlan. No more were there to be descendants of the great tlatoque or the *tlaçotlatocapipiltin*. There were to be only people from other places, some pipiltin, some not pipiltin, and others mestizos, whose Spanish ancestry is not known, nor do we know if they were pipiltin or maceguales.[25]

---

[25] Alvarado Tezozomoc, *Crónica mexicayotl*, quoted in Charles Gibson, *The Aztecs under Spanish rule. A history of the Indians of the valley of Mexico, 1519–1810* (Stanford, 1964), 169.

In Peru, the three sons of Huayna Capac – Tupac Huallpa (who was soon poisoned), Manco (before his revolt in 1536) and, above all, Paullu – agreed to play the role of puppet Inca, according to the designs of Pizarro or Amalgro. When Manco's son, Sayri Tupac, surrendered, he was confirmed in his ownership of the encomienda of Yucay, among other possessions; his daughter, Princess Beatriz, married Martin Garcia de Loyola (nephew of St Ignatius), and his descendants became rapidly hispanicized.

The lords of Chucuito, Martin Cari and Martin Cusi, who were respondents in the survey of Garci Diez in 1567, did not belong to the Inca nobility but to the leading dynasties of the two moieties of the former Lupaca kingdom. Their ancestors were overlords of the lands cultivated not only by their tributaries from Chucuito but also by the tributaries of six other *pueblos* of the province. But, at the time of Garci Diez's *visita*, the area of these cultivated lands had greatly diminished through lack of upkeep: Martin Cari and Martin Cusi now received payments only from the Indians of Chucuito, while the tributaries of the other pueblos no longer provided them with their traditional services: 'And in the villages of Juli, Pomata and Zepita they were obliged to plant another twenty plots in each village, and they have not done so even though there is land enough for it.' The Indians of Juli, interrogated in their turn, explained that the curacas of Chucuito had not requested them to sow the lands. Now traditionally this 'request' had of course been to a certain extent part of the framework of the bonds of reciprocity which united curaca and ayllu: it was these bonds which were now being loosened. It is revealing that, although Martin Cari still had cultivated land at his disposal at Acora, in the neighbouring Chucuito pueblo, it was no longer worked by the Indians of the community; the curaca had adopted an entirely different solution, developing a trend which had started at the end of the Inka era, and been speeded up by colonial rule: he had the fields cultivated by yanas, that is to say outside the bonds of reciprocity linking curaca and ayllu.

But, at the level of the respective moieties of other Lupaca villages, at Acora, Ilave, Juli, Pomata, Yunguyo and Zepita, the local curacas (theoretically of a lower rank than Cari or Cusi) maintained their authority over their subjects and continued to receive payments from them (as Cari and Cusi did in Chucuito). The Indians placed a certain number of mitayos at their disposal for regular service; and collectively they cultivated the fields of the lords, who provided them with the seed and rewarded them by gifts of food, coca and clothing. Thus, in the upper *Hanan* moiety of Juli:

For each of the two said caciques 30 plots of land are sown with potatoes, quinoa and cañagua, and the caciques provide the seeds, and for the planting all the Indian men, women and young men gather together to carry out the work, and they give them good meals of potatoes, chuño and meat, with coca and chicha during the days they are working, and they give Don Baltazar fourteen Indians and Don Francisco ten to serve them.[26]

At the intermediate level of the moiety lords, then, the bonds of reciprocity survived the process of destructuration intact.

On the other hand, at the lowest level, that of the ayllu lords, there was a total collapse. The former Lupaca kingdom had consisted of about 150 ayllu, that is, at least equal in number to the curacas. But for the entire province of Chucuito, Garci Diez counted only 36 lords exempt from the tribute: thus, most of the ayllu lords had lost their privileges and were subject to the same obligations as the other Indians. Their fate was comparable to that of the Chupachu lords who ruled over a much smaller ethnic group, and complained to Ortiz de Zúñiga of having to make payments to their encomenderos: 'And at present the said caciques and leading men are not held in such esteem as under the Inka, for all have to contribute whether they be caciques, leading men, or commoners.'[27]

These examples illustrate a twofold development – a fragmentation and a concentration of power: the fragmentation was a result of the lower status of the senior curacas, and the concentration benefited the intermediate level of the curacas of the moieties, at the expense of the ayllu lords.

In colonial Peru the moieties usually made up the units for the payment of tribute (just as did in Mexico the areas under the jurisdiction of the *tlatoque* which formed the *cabeceras*). The middle-ranking lords, responsible for levying the tribute for the encomenderos or the crown, thus occupied a strategic position, and formed a linchpin of colonial organization. And they frequently exploited this position of authority to make their subjects perform services which were outside the framework of the traditional bonds of reciprocity. In Chucuito, for example, Spanish merchants ordered the Indians to make them clothes:

[26] Diez de San Miguel, *Visita*, fo. 39r, fo. 45r, fo. 57v.
[27] Ortiz de Zúñiga, *Visita*, i, fo. 12r.

they gave the orders to the leading curacas, Cari and Cusi, who then distributed the work throughout the province; but it was the moiety lords (including Cari and Cusi) who received and pocketed the wages. Similarly the curacas concluded what were effectively contracts (sometimes in front of a lawyer) by which they agreed to engage a certain number of their subjects to carry out transportation work. And the Spaniards themselves admitted that they could have achieved nothing except by working through the native lords, otherwise the Indians would have refused to act.[28] At the same time, the curacas, by abusing their authority and collaborating with the new rulers, undermined their own prestige.

But the history of the chieftains of the Andes and those of Mexico differed in one fundamental respect: in spite of all the upheavals, the former enjoyed a certain element of continuity, while the latter were more radically affected by the hispanicization of the political and administrative structures. From the middle of the sixteenth century the Spaniards introduced native *cabildos* into Mexico, made up of *gobernadores*, of *alcaldes* and of *regidores* elected for one or several years. The function of these cabildos was to supervise the levying of tribute, to administer the finances of the community and to mete out justice in minor cases. The history of Mexico was characterized by a rapid differentiation between the offices of *gobernador* and *tlatoani*: different people held the two posts, so that newcomers, who were often merely descendants of *macehuales*, joined the cabildos and thus brought fresh blood into the ruling groups. But, in the viceroyalty of Peru, the curacas usually continued to combine their office with that of *gobernador*, so that the replenishment of the ruling groups was less important. Leading families (such as the Guarachi among the Pacajes, the Ayaviri among the Charcas, the Choqueticlla among the Quillacas) continued to play a significant role until the end of the colonial era, while at the same time increasingly adopting the Spanish way of life.

These new forms of labour tribute, hitherto completely unknown to the pre-Columbian world, introduced ideas alien to the traditional norms which had integrated economic and social activity in a coherent complex of concepts, rituals and religious beliefs. On the other hand, the Spaniards justified their hegemony by the fact that they were bringing the true faith to the Indians: in the eyes of the missionaries,

[28] *Ibid.*, fo. 44r.

the practices and beliefs of the natives were the work of the devil, and the 'spiritual conquest' required that they should be stamped out.

The official religion, linked to the structures of the state, disappeared rapidly in both Mexico and Peru. Local worship continued more or less illicitly (as we shall see later), but the Indians had to give up their important festivals and the practices which seemed most shocking to the Spaniards, above all, human sacrifice. Temples were systematically destroyed, codices and khipu burnt, native priests persecuted. As a result, the very course of daily life was drastically transformed. One has only to think of the effects of imposing Christian rules of marriage (the definition of new sexual taboos, the banning of polygamy) or the burial of the dead.[29]

Among the native nobility the education of children in the Christian religion gave rise to a clash of generations (at least in the immediate aftermath of the conquest). Thus, in 1524, the former priests of Tlaxcala were astonished that one of their number should be put to death by children who had been educated by the Franciscans: 'All those who believed in and worshipped the idols were horrified at the insolence of the boys.'[30] These children, going around in bands, knocked over idols and denounced pagan practices. The condemnation of these old customs and the reluctance of the older generation to adopt new norms of behaviour resulted in a condition of anomie.

One of the most dramatic symptoms of the break up of native culture and the anguish to which it gave rise, was alcoholism: a phenomenon noted by all the chroniclers.[31] In pre-Columbian society strict rules governed the use of *pulque* (in Mexico) and *chicha* (in the Andes): they could only be consumed collectively during religious ceremonies in honour of the gods, for drunkness put one in communion with the sacred. Apart from these limited circumstances, consumption of alcohol was strictly forbidden. In his first address to his subjects the ruler of Mexico would declare: 'Above all, I exhort you to leave the ways of drunkenness and not to drink *octli*.' He also put them on their guard against sexual excess: 'Observe that the ways of the flesh are ugly, and you should all turn your back on them.'[32] Solitary and profane

[29] Cf. Pablo José de Arriaga, *Extirpación de la idolatria del Piru* [1621] (Madrid, 1968), 216.

[30] Fray Toribio de Benavente ('Motolinía'), *Memoriales o Libro de las Cosas de Nueva España y de los Naturales de ella* [1541], ed. Edmundo O'Gorman (Mexico, 1971), 249–50.

[31] Serge Gruzinski, 'La mère dévorante: alcoolisme, sexualité, et déculturation chez les Mexicas (1500–1550)', *Cahiers des Amériques Latines* (1979), 22–6.

[32] Bernardino de Sahagún, *Historia general de las cosas de Nueva España* [1570] (Mexico, 1975), Libro VI, 332, 334.

drunkenness might possibly be tolerated in the old, but was strictly punished in all other cases: the culprit was publicly humiliated (by shaving of the head) and risked the death penalty. (The same was true for sexual deviance, such as incest, adultery or homosexuality. Adulterers, for instance, were burnt, stoned, hanged or clubbed to death, or had their heads crushed under the weight of a large stone.)[33]

Immediately after the conquest, alcoholism affected men and women at all levels of society. Numerous texts mention the disappearance of the old prohibitions: 'It was common practice everywhere that at the end of the afternoon the Indians started to drink, and fairly rapidly during the course of the evening they collapsed blind drunk; there was general licentiousness, devoid of all measure or restraint'. The nobles, who had once set a good example, now led the other Indians on to drunkenness: 'the *maceguales* dare to get drunk, because if the nobles did not do so, they would fear the nobles, and not dare to get drunk themselves.'[34] Intoxication as a part of religious ritual had obviously not disappeared, but was no longer distinguished from the consumption of alcohol for secular reasons or as a result of addiction.

Confronted with this spread of alcoholism, the Spaniards adopted a highly ambiguous attitude. On one hand, they condemned it for moral reasons (although their punishments, such as whipping, were incomparably milder than those of the pre-Columbian era); on the other hand, they encouraged it for obvious economic reasons: they sold wine to the Indians. Wine, more alcoholic than the traditional drinks, had even more harmful effects. Thus, in Spanish accounts, alcoholism became a typical feature of native society. But it merely mirrored the helplessness of the Indians who attempted to use alcohol to escape from a world which for them had become absurd and tragic.

The spread of the use of coca leaf in the Andes was evidence of a similar phenomenon though with less harmful consequences. Coca leaf was a plant which, like *chicha*, had been used mainly in religious ceremonies: 'In the time of the Inca kings, commoners were not allowed to take coca without permission from the Inca or his governor.'[35] After the conquest the production of coca increased considerably. The Spaniards themselves extended the acreage of the

---

[33] Toribio de Benavente, *Memoriales*, 362, 321–2, 356, 357.

[34] Toribio de Benevente, *Memoriales*, 361; Procesos de indios idolatras y hechiceros, Mexico, Archivo General de la Nación, 1912, 164, quoted by Gruzinski, 'La Mère dévorante', 22.

[35] José de Acosta, *Historia natural y moral de las Indias* [1590] (Madrid, 1954), 117; similarly Juan de Matienzo, *Gobierno del Peru* [1567] (Paris–Lima, 1967), 163.

coca plantations, sometimes at the expense of food crops; and the consumption of coca leaf became widespread throughout the population (although the plant also retained its religious significance): 'They began to grow addicted to it after the Spaniards had entered this country.'[36] Coca was particularly indispensable for the Indians working in the mines since it enabled them to work almost without eating. According to Acosta, 'in Potosí alone the trade in coca amounts to over half a million pesos a year, for 95,000 baskets of it are consumed'.[37] The Spanish merchants controlled the trade in coca leaf, but only the mass of the Indian population consumed it.

In the 40 years after the conquest, therefore, native society underwent a process of destructuration at every level: demographic, economic, social and spiritual. Certain structures did survive, but fragmented and isolated from their original context and transposed into the colonial world. These partial continuities nevertheless ensured that native traditions – somewhat modified – were passed on, while at the same time supporting Spanish hegemony.

TRADITION AND ACCULTURATION

Under colonial rule native traditions were confronted by newly introduced European practices. To what extent were these accepted or rejected? Did the phenomenon of acculturation help to re-integrate society?

Rapid economic acculturation took place, though limited to the use of a certain number of European products which extended the range of resources available to the natives without actually replacing those already in use: in both Mexico and Peru the staple foods remained the same as in the pre-Columbian era. Some fruits and vegetables (oranges, apples, figs, cabbages, turnips, etc.) spread quickly where climatic conditions were favourable, but it seems that European livestock was more readily adopted in Mexico or in the northern Andes than in the central and southern Andes where the raising of llamas was already one of the main activities. So when, from the end of the sixteenth century, the consumption of meat became a general practice in Ecuador, this signified an important evolution of dietary habit.[38] Wheat-growing was

---

[36] Hernando de Santillan, *Relación del origen, descendencia, política y gobierno de los Incas*...[1564](Lima, 1927), 107.   [37] Acosta, *Historia natural y moral*, 116.
[38] *Relaciones geográficas de Indias*, I, 171, 234; II, 22, 237.

introduced at the instigation of the Spaniards exclusively for the payment of tribute and not for consumption by the Indians. Overall economic acculturation occurred through the selection of items imported by the Spaniards which were simply juxtaposed with those already in use without otherwise modifying the context of native life. Traditional techniques survived, although some lords already possessed ploughs by the end of the sixteenth century.

There was a contrast between the rapid social acculturation of numerous lords and the persistence of tradition among the commoners. The lords soon learnt to speak and write Spanish while continuing to use the native languages. Linguistic acculturation seems to have occurred still faster in Mexico than in Peru. The famous college of Tlatelolco, intended for the children of lords, was founded by the Franciscans in the 1530s, while in the Andes similar schools (in Huancayo, and above all in Cuzco) were not set up until the 1570s. The explicit aim was to hispanicize a favoured group in order to mould a ruling class which would be obedient to the Spaniards. In accordance with this policy, certain members of the native nobility (depending on their status) adopted European clothes and some prestige symbols of the dominant culture – riding a horse, carrying a sword, or using an arquebus. But such privileges were only granted to lords of high rank: thus, at Chucuito, Garci Diez proposed that they should be restricted solely to Martin Cari and Martin Cusi. Moreover, since the colonial administration prohibited many traditional privileges (such as travelling in a litter or hammock), prestige symbols became exclusively Spanish. In this way the ruling group strengthened its function as a model to be imitated by the Indians.

Conversely, the Indians of the communities displayed their fidelity to the ancient customs. They continued to speak the native languages and usually wore traditional dress, sometimes combined with the Spanish sombrero. And, while the colonial economic system had introduced money, we have seen that the native sector remained geared towards subsistence production, supplemented by barter. It is true that forced migrations of population (*congregaciones* in Mexico from the 1560s, *reducciones* in Peru from the 1570s) radically disrupted settlement patterns and attempted to force the Indians to live in villages on the Spanish model, in which the streets were laid out in a grid pattern, and the plaza was surrounded by the church, the residence of the cabildo, the prison and the gallows. But, despite all these changes, the old communal system of organization (which had the ayllu or the calpulli as its core) persisted or was reconstructed on the foundation of those bonds of kinship and mutual aid by which its members were united. After the population resettlements, the villages and their lands continued to be organized on a dual model, thus ensuring the continuation of religious beliefs grounded in the Indians' association between their land and their ancestors.

In the religious sphere, the Indians' fidelity to their traditions expressed their rejection of colonial rule, although, again, there were differences. Whereas in Mexico during the first decades of the colonial era (until the 1570s), the Indians seemed to show real enthusiasm for Christianity, this was not the case in Peru. But in both cases the Indians held tenaciously to their own beliefs and rituals. This continuity was accompanied by a process of fragmentation corresponding to that of the institutions. If official worship of the Sun and of the Inca disappeared in the Andes immediately after the conquest, popular worship linked to the *huacas* (local gods) survived. The Indians continued to work in common the fields dedicated to their worship, and they disinterred their dead from the cemeteries and transported them to their ancient burial places (near to sites that they had had to abandon because of the *reducciones*). While they did indeed conform to the externals of Christian worship, they were able to conceal their traditional rites. The Spaniards fostered this ambiguity by raising crosses and churches on the old religious sites, while, conversely, the Indians camouflaged their idols and their rituals in a Christian disguise:

We discovered that at the church door they were keeping a large *huaca*, called Camasca, and another inside the church called Huacrapampa; and behind the main altar, at the door of the sacristy, there was yet another *huaca* called Pichacianac.[39]

While the Spaniards considered the local gods to be manifestations of the devil, the Indians interpreted Christianity as a form of idolatry. Rather than being fused together in a synthesis, however, the two religions remained juxtaposed. If the Indians admitted the existence of a Christian god they considered his sphere of influence to be limited to the Spanish world, and looked themselves for protection to their own gods. The confession manual of Diego de Torres, composed around

---

[39] 'Idolatrias de los Indios Huachos y Yauyos', *Revista Historica* (Lima), (1918), 190; cf. also Arriaga, *Extirpación de la idolatria*, 223.

1584, condemned this dichotomy as one of the 'errors against the Catholic faith':

They sometimes say of God that he is not a good god, and that he does not protect the poor, and that the Indians obey him in vain...and that as the Christians have images that they worship, in the same way one can worship the *huacas*.[40]

The religious sphere thus reflected the split between the European and the Indian world. It is striking that anthropologists still find today the idea among certain Indians (for instance, those of Puquio) that Jesus Christ remains 'separate' (*separawmi*); they are protected not by him but by the mountains, the *wamani*.[41] At the start of the seventeenth century, Arriaga described a similar conception:

They say that all that the priests say and preach is for the Viracochas and Spaniards, and that they have their *huacas* and their *malquis* and their festivals and everything else that their ancestors taught them and that their elders and priests teach them...[42]

One can see why, in a letter addressed to Philip II in 1579, Antonio de Zúñiga deplored the fact that the Indians did no more than pretend to participate in Catholic ceremonies: they were in reality no more Christian than at the time of the conquest. And Garci Diez at Chucuito made the same point: 'the majority of the Indians are not Christians'.[43]

The results of acculturation remained, therefore, on the whole, limited, both in Mexico and Peru, and the mass of the native population refused to accept most of the practices imported by the Spaniards. In the resulting interplay of continuity and change, tradition prevailed over acculturation. In general, when the Indians borrowed elements of foreign culture they merely added them to elements of their own culture or used them as a sort of camouflage. Even in the cases of the most hispanicized lords one notices how traditional ways of thinking persisted. If they did adopt certain European customs, they inserted them into the framework of Indian culture. Thus, according to a document dated 1567, when a large number of rebel Indians from

[40] Diego de Torres, *Confessionario para los curas de Indios* [1584] (Seville, 1603), 5.
[41] José Maria Arguedas and Alejandro Ortiz Rescaniere, 'La posesion de la tierra. Los mitos posthispánicos y la visión del universo en la población monolingüe quechua', in *Les Problèmes agraires des Amériques Latines* (Paris, 1967), 309–15.
[42] Arriaga, *Extirpación de la idolatria*, 224.
[43] 'Carta de Fray Antonio de Zúñiga al rey don Felipe II', in *Colección de documentos inéditos para la Historia de España*, xxvi (Madrid, 1855), 90; Diez de San Miguel, *Visita*, fo. 115r.

Vilcabamba went to pay a visit to Princess Maria Manrique, widow of Sayri Tupac, at her residence in Cuzco, they presented her with gifts of feathers and 'other items of little value', in recognition of her sovereignty. In exchange the princess offered them food and drink, llamas, nose jewellery, bracelets and gold earrings – that is, presents of a traditional nature; but in addition she offered them 'objects from Castile which she had bought in the shops'. If she had not done this, she declared, 'she would not have been acting as was expected of princesses of this kingdom'.[44] In other words, these Spanish purchases were integrated into the system of gifts and counter-gifts on the old principle of reciprocity.

There was, then, continuity of tradition, as well as synthesis by adaptation. The case of Guaman Poma de Ayala, one of the most remarkable Peruvian writers, aptly illustrates this process. Western elements were absorbed into the native system of thought which, by adapting itself, succeeded in preserving its original structure. Although Poma wrote in Spanish (albeit incorrectly) and practised Christianity, he continued to see the colonial world through the spatial and temporal categories which had shaped the organization of the Inca empire. Thus, he drew a map of the Indies which, in its lay-out, resembled a Spanish map, intersected by lines of longitude and latitude.[45] But these lines in fact corresponded to nothing at all. Poma's Peru was co-ordinated around two diagonals which demarcated the former quarters of the Inca empire, Chinchaysuyu to the west, Antisuyu to the north, Collasuyu to the east, Cuntisuyu to the south. These were explicitly marked on the map. Poma drew their four governors, the *apos*, accompanied by their consorts; above the figure representing the governor of Chinchaysuyu is the name of Capac Apo Guamanchara, Poma's paternal grandfather. There is one remarkable feature. The two diagonals intersect at Cuzco, and the old capital is placed at the exact centre of the map, surrounded by the four quarters. Lima had for a long time been the capital of the viceroyalty, but, for Poma, Cuzco remained the centre of the universe. Above his representation of the town he drew the tenth emperor, Topa. The picture is surrounded by two coats of arms, those of the pope and the king of Spain (see Fig. 1).

44 Archivo Historico del Cuzco, 'Genealogia de Sayri Tupac', libro 4, indice 6, fo. 64r, fo. 80r, fo. 61r.
45 Guaman Poma de Ayala, *Nueva Corónica*, fo. 993–4. On this development, see Wachtel, 'Pensée sauvage et acculturation. L'Éspace et le temps chez Felipe Guaman Poma de Ayala et l'Inca Garcilaso de la Vega', *AESC* (May–August, 1971), 793–840.

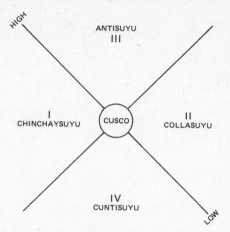

Fig. 1. Guaman Poma de Ayala's map of the Indies

We know that in the Inca empire these four quarters formed part of a system of classification, and were ordered hierarchically into two successive dualities. The first gave rise to an upper (Hanan) division – formed by Chinchaysuyu and Antisuyu – and a lower (Hurin) division – formed by Collasuyu and Cuntisuyu. The second division intersected the first: each of the halves was split in two, to form the four quarters, in which Chinchaysuyu was above Antisuyu, and Collasuyu above Cuntisuyu. The centre of the world, Cuzco, was defined by the intersection of these two dualities; in this way the quadripartite organization ended up divided into five separate parts.

But in spite of these survivals and continuities, Indian thought could not escape the upheavals caused by colonial rule. How did Poma picture to himself the world as it was after the Spanish conquest, and where did he place the other countries of America, Europe, Africa and Asia? It is remarkable that he continued to see not only the Indies but the whole universe in the same kind of system of an upper and a lower half divided into a four-part model around a central core. To construct his model of the universe he had to fit it into a duplicate of the first model, but in doing so the position of the lesser part (the Indies) was inverted within the structure of the larger part (the universe) to take account of the effects of the conquest and the internal logic of the system itself. Around the kingdom of Castile, now in the central position hitherto occupied by Cuzco and the Inca, were ranged four other kingdoms: Rome and Turkey in the upper section formerly occupied by Chinchaysuyu and Antisuyu, and the Indies and Guinea in the lower section

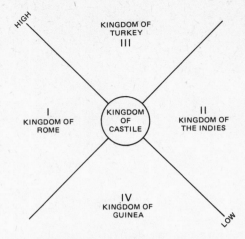

Fig. 2. Guaman Poma de Ayala's map of the universe

in place of Collasuyu and Cuntisuyu. The Indies ought to have been in the upper division and Castile in the lower division, but the colonial relationship demanded that, just as the Inca had been subsumed into the person of the king of Spain, the general ordering of the universe had to be reversed while the configuration of the system as a whole was kept intact (see Fig. 2).

Poma also applied the same pattern to his representation of time. He took up the native tradition of the five ages (Huari Viracocha, Huari, Purun, Auca, Inca), and, by following a similar procedure to that which he had employed in the case of space, he projected this five-part division onto the western time system. Thus, biblical history was broken down into five ages (Adam, Noah, Abraham, David, Jesus Christ) parallel with the five ages of Indian time.

Poma, therefore, fitted the contributions of western culture into the pre-existing spatio-temporal framework of the Indians, that is, a synthesis rigorously organized according to the logic of Andean thought. But if this synthesis imposed certain rules, it also provided the basis for re-interpretation and creation. Poma resorted to the traditional categories, but by being restructured in the context of the colonial system, they were given a new significance – that of resisting Spanish hegemony. Indeed, the chronicler associated the concept of *pachacuti* (overturning, revolution, both of the world and of time) with the end of the Inca empire: the relationship produced by the European invasion relegated the Indies to the level of Collasuyu in the lower division, whereas they ought to have been in the upper division. 'The world is upside down because there is neither God nor King',[46] and it was to inform him about the 'sickness of the world' that Poma addressed his thousand-page 'letter' to the king of Spain. With an almost messianic hope, he expected a final upheaval (another *pachacuti*) by which the king of Spain – guarantor, like the Inka, of universal order – would set the world to rights again.

RESISTANCE AND REVOLT

The Spaniards established their two main centres of colonization in Mexico and Peru, where powerful states already existed; but on the extensive 'frontiers' situated on the peripheries of these states they came up against fierce resistance, which in some cases lasted into the early years of the twentieth century. What caused this contrast? It was the result of the very nature of the different native American societies. In Mexico and Peru the European invaders came into contact with a large and dense population which was under the control of centralized institutions and long accustomed to produce an economic surplus for the profit of the ruling group. But in northern Mexico, to the south and south-east of the Charcas, or in Chile, Spanish colonization failed when confronted with mainly nomadic Indians who produced no accessible surplus, and who, owing to their mobility, eluded control.

Even in Mexico and Peru the relative ease of the conquest did not mean that hostilities suddenly ceased immediately after the invasion. The most tenacious resistance was shown in the Andes where the driving force behind the first important revolt against the Spaniards was none other than Manco Inca, one of the sons of Huayna Capac. Before the arrival of the Spaniards, he had participated in an expedition launched in the east of the empire against the *montaña* Indians, and especially against the Chiriguanos. Manco Inca began by collaborating with the Spaniards, but he rapidly became disillusioned.

I believed that they were kind people sent, as they claimed, by *Tecsi Viracochan* – that is to say, God – but it seems to me that events took the opposite course from that which I imagined; for you should know, my brothers, that from the

---

[46] Guaman Poma de Ayala, *Nueva Coronica*, fo. 1146; cf. similarly fo. 409, 448, 530, 762.

proofs they have given me since they invaded my lands, they are not sons of Viracocha but rather of the devil.[47]

Manco beseiged Cuzco for a year (March 1536–April 1537), but finally had to relax his stranglehold. He then took refuge in the inaccessible mountains of Vilcabamba to the north of the ancient capital and in the warm valleys of the Antisuyu (the base from which he had begun his previous campaigns). This region was chosen not only for strategic, but also for political and religious reasons. It was no coincidence that it included the sacred mountain-top site of Machu Picchu, the inviolate sanctuary of the native priests and the *Mamacona* of the Sun, which remained unknown to the Europeans until the beginning of the twentieth century.

In the immense territory under his control Manco continued the ancient imperial traditions and, in effect, restored a 'neo-Inca' state. In his *Relación*, Titu Cusi ascribed to his father a speech which expressed resistance to any kind of acculturation. Manco urged the Indians to renounce the false religion which the Spaniards were attempting to impose; the Christian god, he said, was only a painted cloth which was unable to speak, whereas the huacas could make themselves heard, and the Sun and the Moon were gods whose existence was visible to all.[48] After the death of Manco Inca, his son, Sayri Tupac, continued his resistance for ten years or so, and then surrendered in exchange for the rich encomienda of Yucay (the 'sacred valley' which had been the personal property of Huayna Capac). Another of Manco's sons, Titu Cusi, succeeded him as leader of the resistance, and the neo-Inca state continued to challenge Spanish hegemony.

In the 1560s the viceroyalty underwent a profound crisis. It seems that Titu Cusi had prepared a general uprising to coincide with the spread of the *Taqui Ongo* movement. This was a millenarian movement originating in the central Andes (particularly in the Huamanga region), but, according to Cristobal de Molina, the 'heresy' was started by sorcerers from Vilcabamba. The preachers announced the end of Spanish domination; the native gods who had been defeated and killed at the time of Pizarro's arrival were to come to life again, and do battle against the Christian god who would, in turn, be conquered. Then the Spaniards would be driven from the country:

They believed that all the huacas of the kingdom, all those that the Christians had burnt and destroyed, had come to life again...that they were all preparing

---

[47] Titu Cusi, *Relación de la Conquista del Perú*, 32.   [48] *Ibid.*, 78.

in the heavens to do battle against God and to conquer him...*now the world was completing its cycle*, God and the Spaniards would this time be conquered and all the Spaniards killed, their towns swallowed up, and the sea would swell up to submerge them and wipe out their memory.[49]

So Taqui Ongo predicted a cosmic event, a deluge, the end of the world. This prophecy was based on a cyclical representation of time implied in Molina's use of the term *vuelta* (turn, cycle). According to other witnesses, the Christian god was completing its mita, its 'turn to rule'; the huacas would re-create another world and other men. We have to remember that, according to tradition, the Inca empire had been preceded by four suns and four races of men. Each of these eras had lasted a thousand years, and the end of each of them had been marked by immense catastrophes. Now, in a version reported by Sarmiento de Gamboa, the Inca empire had been founded at a date which corresponded to the year 565 of the Christian era. It, too, had foundered in a veritable cataclysm after the arrival of strange, white and bearded creatures, and, as the culmination of Taqui Ongo occurred in 1565, a thousand years after the foundation of the empire, it was hardly a coincidence that it was in this same year that Titu Cusi prepared a general uprising of the Indians.

The plan of revolt, therefore, fitted into a traditional framework of ideas which was interpreted in a new way in response to the colonial situation. Since the conquest the huacas were no longer receiving the ritual sacrifices, and, instead, they wandered, abandoned, 'parched and dying of hunger'. To revenge themselves they sent sickness and death to all Indians who had accepted baptism; then they too would wander head down and feet in the air or be turned into llamas or vicuñas.[50] Only Indians faithful to the worship of the huacas would be admitted into the promised empire. The huacas forbade them to enter churches or bear Christian names; they were not allowed to eat or dress like the Spaniards. The followers of the movement thus showed their reconversion by rituals of penitence and purification. But Taqui Ongo as such did not take the form of a military enterprise. The Indians expected liberation to come less from violent action against the Spaniards than from a victory of the huacas over the Christian god. The preachers travelled from village to village restoring worship in the sacred places by rituals of 'resurrection'. The movement was accompanied by terrifying rumours. Epidemics of fear spread. Word went round that

[49] Cristobal de Molina, *Relación de las fábulas y ritos de los Incas* [1575] (Lima, 1916), 97–8.
[50] Archivo General de Indias, Audiencia Lima, Legajo 316, notebook of 1577, fo. 8r.

the white people had come to Peru to put the Indians to death in search of human fat, which they used as a medicine against certain diseases.[51] In terror, the Indians fled from all contact with the Spaniards.

The Church denounced Taqui Ongo as a sect of heretics and apostates. The 'visit' of Cristobal de Albornoz to the regions of Huamanga, Arequipa and Cuzco made it possible to uncover the main ring-leaders of the movement. According to their rank or degree of guilt, they were whipped or had their heads shaved. By the 1570s all traces of Taqui Ongo had disappeared. Besides the effects of ecclesiastical repression, they undoubtedly suffered the repercussions of the capture and death of Tupac Amaru, the last Inca of Vilcabamba.

Tupac Amaru had assumed the leadership of the neo-Inca state after the death of his half-brother, Titu Cusi, in 1571, but his reign was short-lived. The viceroy, Francisco de Toledo, determined to subdue Peru once and for all, organized one last successful expedition, commanded by Martin Garcia de Loyola (nephew of St Ignatius). The beheading of Tupac Amaru in 1572 in the public square of Cuzco, in the presence of an enormous and dismayed crowd, carried echoes of the execution of Atahuallpa. In the eyes of the mass of the Indian population the 'second death' of the Inca did truly signify the end of a world.

Near the heart of the Andes, the 'cordillera' of the Chiriguanos formed a frontier which resisted Spanish colonization for three centuries. During the second half of the sixteenth century, even Potosí and La Plata, the nerve centres of the viceroyalty, were several times threatened.[52]

Here we confront an exceptional phenomenon: the meeting of two conquering forces. Before the arrival of the Spaniards, large numbers of Guarani Indians had migrated towards the Inca empire. They had departed from the quadrilateral situated between the Paraguay–Paraná rivers and the Atlantic coast. Were they in search of *Candire*, the 'land without evil' proclaimed by their prophets? Or of 'the mountain of silver'? These migrations had moved along an arc running between the Guaporé–Mamoré and the Pilcomayo and, after an epic journey, had

[51] Molina, *Relación*, 97, 99.
[52] The following pages are based on the first chapter ('La Rencontre') of a work in preparation by Thierry Saignes on the ethnohistory of the Chiriguanos. The author wishes to thank Dr Saignes for permission to consult and quote from it.

ended up in the *montaña* to the east and south-east of the Charcas. Some of the Guarani tribes came to settle in this large zone, after having subdued the local inhabitants of Arawak origin (the Chane); they were henceforth known – and feared – under the name Chiriguanos.

It will be recalled that, at the time of the colonization of the Cochabamba Valley, Huayna Capac had removed the 'native' Chuis and Cotas and installed them in fortresses at Mizque, Pocona, Pojo and Montepuco to defend the empire against the invasions of the Chiriguanos. Later, probably during the 1520s, the same Huayna Capac sent one of his relatives, Guacane, to conquer the territory lying to the south-east of Cochabamba, towards the Guapay plain. From Mizque, Guacane explored the region, founded another fortress at Samaipata, and forced an 'alliance' on the local chief, Grigota. He then imported new *mitmaq*, began to work the gold mines and established a final fortress in the plain at Guanacopampa. At this point, 8,000 Guarani warriors from Paraguay launched an assault on these territories recently conquered by the 'son of the Sun'. They surprised the Inca troops, killed Guacane and destroyed the Inka fortresses; reinforcements from Cuzco were also put to flight. Huayna Capac, deeply affected by this disaster, had to send Yasca, one of his best captains, at the head of a large force of troops raised in the north of the empire and then reinforced in the south by Lupaca warriors. But the outcome of the struggle was uncertain, and only with great difficulty did Yasca succeed in rebuilding the destroyed fortresses.

The first Spaniards to be seen by the Chiriguanos were those who had landed on the Atlantic coast. At the beginning the two invading groups did not directly confront each other. On the contrary, after the first foundation of Asunción in 1536, the Chiriguanos several times attempted to lure Governor Irala into launching an expedition into the Andes: the Inca state had by now disappeared, but the Chiriguanos continued their slow progression into territories which were now, in principle, under Spanish jurisdiction. Their expansion took place at the expense of the 'native' population of the highlands of the Andes, especially the mitmaq previously settled there by the Inca. Thus, around 1540, the Muyu Muyus, inhabiting the last of the mountain ranges above Chaco, underwent a fierce assault during which they lost their chieftain. They departed towards the south-west to take refuge in the Inca forts of the Tarija region. But several years later the Chiriguanos drove them out again. Having appealed to the Spaniards for protection, the Muyu

Muyus were settled in the valleys near the recently founded La Plata (Chuquisaca) (thus causing numerous disputes between various encomenderos attempting to appropriate them for themselves). Further north, while Nuflo de Chaves was crossing the warm valleys beyond Mizque in 1548, he came across the Chiriguanos of Samaipata who were setting off to war against the Chuis Indians who had fallen back on Pojo.

The Spaniards therefore inherited a 'frontier infected by Guarani expansion',[53] and their position was made worse during the 1560s by an extraordinary reversal of alliances. Although hitherto fierce enemies, the Andean Indians and the Chiriguanos from Paraguay seem to have buried their differences so as to defend themselves against the white invaders. Was this a result of the diplomacy of Titu Cusi, the Inca of Vilcabamba, at a moment when, as we have seen, Taqui Ongo threatened the very heart of the Spanish possessions? The anti-Hispanic 'confederation' also included, in the south, Don Juan Calchaqui, leader of the Diaguita, who sent messengers to the Charcas curacas to encourage them to rebel. Did the authorities at La Plata exaggerate the danger? The Cuzco sources mention similar plans for collaboration between the rebel Incas and the Chiriguanos.[54] It seems that the Indian world, stunned by European invasion, was able to overcome its traditional rivalries to construct a vast alliance uniting areas as different as the Andes and the plains of the Atlantic basin.

The Chiriguanos redoubled their assaults along the whole length of the frontier. In 1564 they destroyed two forts recently founded by the Spaniards, Barranca on the river Guapay (by Nuflo de Chaves) and Nueva Rioja on the Paripiti (by Andres Manso who was killed in this attack). Further south they devastated the estancias of Juan Ortiz de Zarate, who was a rich mining entrepreneur from Potosí and encomendero of the Chicha Indians. In 1567 they pillaged other Chicha villages twelve leagues from Potosí, captured the Indians in domestic service and killed and ate the Spaniards. And, for the next ten years at least, all the area between Tarija, Potosí, La Plata, Mizque, Santa Cruz and the Chiriguano cordillera went through a period of complete insecurity.

After the pacification of Vilcabamba and the execution of Tupac Amaru, the viceroy Francisco de Toledo decided to settle the problem of the Guaranis. In 1573 he went to La Plata where he received Chiriguano ambassadors who had come to pay him homage. They

---

[53] The phrase comes from Thierry Saignes in the work cited above.
[54] Archivo Historico del Cuzco, libro 5 of the Cabildo, fo. 41r–47r.

talked of a miracle performed by Santiago, foretelling peace, and asked for missionaries to be sent. Toledo ordered an enquiry; the interval enabled the Chiriguano chiefs to flee from La Plata; and Toledo discovered that he had been duped. The Indians had simply been trying either to avoid reprisals or to gain time. In June 1574 the viceroy, at the head of a large army divided into three units, marched into the Cordillera. But the expedition wore itself out attempting to clear a way as far as the Pilcomayo, while the enemy harassed it from the safety of the highlands. Hunger and fever decimated the army, and Toledo himself fell gravely ill. Finally, the Spaniards were forced to retreat, having achieved nothing. The viceroy contented himself with founding two *villas* to protect the frontier: Tomina in the south-east and Tarija in the south.

Encouraged by Toledo's failure, the Chiriguanos continued their attacks and threatened these two newly founded establishments. 'They roam all along the frontier of this province, going as far as to appear within eight leagues of this city of La Plata', lamented the president of the audiencia. 'They ravage small towns and fields and capture Spaniards, Indian servants and black slaves.'[55] The former mitmaq, forced back on Tarabuco and Presto, found themselves directly exposed to these attacks. 'They are already at our gates', wrote their lords in 1583, 'and they keep us so hemmed in and frightened that we dare not go out of our houses to work our fields.'[56] The Chuis of the Mizque Valley, for their part, prepared an uprising with the help of the Chiriguanos of the Guapay and got ready to flee into the *yungas*. In 1584 the fort of San Miguel de la Laguna, lying between the Ríos Guapay and Pilcomayo, was attacked and destroyed. The Spaniards then organized a three-pronged expedition from Santa Cruz, Tomina and Tarija. The results were no more successful than previously. It was the last expedition led by the three cities together, and each sector subsequently looked after its own defence.

Between 1585 and 1600 the reconstruction or the foundation of La Laguna, Villar, Pomabamba, Paspaya, Cinti and San Lorenzo removed any danger from the area immediately surrounding the Charcas. A gradual policy of populating the area steadily drove the Chiriguanos

---

[55] Robert Levillier, *La Audiencia de Charcas. Correspondencia de Presidentes y Oidores* (Madrid, 1916–22), II, 37.

[56] Quoted in Richard Mujia, *Bolivia-Paraguay: exposición de los títulos que consagran el direcho territorial de Bolivia, sobre la zona comprendida entre los ríos Pilcomayo y Paraguay* (La Paz, 1972), II, 500.

back into their hide-out in the cordillera, from whence they resisted the Spaniards for another three centuries.

In Chile, at the southern extremity of the American continent, the Araucanian Indians resisted the Spaniards as fiercely as did the Chiriguanos. One feature stands out during the course of these wars: the permanence of the frontier provided by the Bio-Bio river. The tribes north of the river had come under the influence of the Inca empire: as a result the Indians of northern Chile enjoyed the advantages of better agricultural techniques; they bred livestock and also knew how to work metal. The Inca had sent his representatives among them, especially military garrisons which they had to supply. As a result, their customs and habits of thought had been remodelled: they had become accustomed to foreign domination, that is, to producing an economic surplus collected either in the form of labour service or tribute. On the other hand, the nomadic and semi-nomadic Indians to the south of the Bio-Bio had escaped Inca influence and were only familiar with rudimentary agricultural techniques, complemented by hunting and gathering; their political organization did not go beyond the traditional bonds of kinship. It was therefore no coincidence that the Spanish were able to maintain their domination to the north of the Bio-Bio, while they failed to do so to the south: the southern boundaries of central Chile ultimately coincided with those of the Inca empire.[57]

Spanish colonization was at first stimulated, as elsewhere, by the search for precious metals. But the production of gold soon began to decline, so that by the end of the sixteenth century agriculture and stock-farming were the main economic resources (in the Santiago, Osorno and Valdivia regions). The demographic collapse did not spare Chile, and this led to a shortage of labour, a problem the Spanish solved in the war against the rebel Araucanians when the captured Indians were turned into slaves and set to work either in the mines or on the farms. Many of them were sent to Peru where they were re-sold. In their expeditions against the Araucanians, the Spanish obtained the help of Indian auxiliaries familiar with the terrain and skilled at tracking down the human prey. For each 'head' captured they received a payment considerably inferior to its real value; so their catch constituted a kind of tribute.

[57] For further discussion of the Araucanians, see Hidalgo, *CHLA*, 1, ch. 4.

However, the resistance of the rebel Indians was helped by a distinctive form of acculturation. The Araucanians transformed their fighting methods to adapt them to the struggle against the Spanish. Their traditional arms consisted of bows and arrows, fire-hardened spears, clubs, slings and pikes, their armour included shields and leather jerkins. To resist the Spanish cavalry charges, the Araucanian warriors extended the length of their pikes by up to six metres and they armed the tip with sharp blades, using for this the swords, daggers or knives captured from the enemy, and they arranged themselves in two rows, the longest pikes at the rear and the shortest in the front. Most significantly, the Araucanians imitated the Spanish by using horses: by the end of the 1560s native cavalry rivalled that of the Spanish. The Indians even introduced certain innovations. They lightened the Spanish saddles and instead of stirrups they used simple wooden rings into which they put only their big toe. This highly mobile cavalry was accompanied by a system of horse-borne infantry, each horseman having an archer mounted behind him.[58]

The acculturation of the Araucanians was not limited to techniques of war. They spontaneously replaced (and this was an exceptional phenomenon) the cultivation of maize by that of the more quickly ripening wheat and barley, in order to preserve the harvest from the expeditions which the Spaniards launched during the summer. Politically, the tribes gradually came to accept that they had to abandon their dispersed mode of living and to group themselves together into larger formations during military operations. Finally, it seems that their beliefs and religious practices were also modified, by the growth of shamanism, and worship of the horse. The whole of Araucanian society was therefore restructured, in a way, however, which remained faithful to its traditional base.

In this context we can understand why European expansion in Chile failed. There was a particularly striking setback in 1598 when a general insurrection forced the Spaniards to evacuate all the territory to the south of the river Bio-Bio. The epilogue to this story is symbolic: Governor Martin Garcia de Loyola, husband of Princess Beatriz and former conqueror of Tupac Amaru, was put to death, and his head was paraded on the tip of an Araucanian pike.

---

[58] Alonso Gonzalez de Najera, *Desengaño y reparo de la guerra del Reino de Chile* [1614] (Santiago, 1889), 174–5.

In northern Mexico, as in southern Peru, the war continued and the conquest lost its momentum. In the frontier zone of the Chichimecas Spanish expansion came up against resistance as intense as that of the Chiriguanos or the Araucanians. If this area had been to some extent brought under Spanish control by the end of the sixteenth century, further north the war still went on against the Pueblos and the Apaches.

The preliminary episode of the 'Mixton war' (1541–2) was very like the uprisings in the Andes: it took place in an area far from the centre (like the revolt of Vilcabamba) and was millenarian in character (like Taqui Ongo). The revolt broke out in New Galicia, in the zone of Tlatenango and Suchipila, among the Cascan tribes. Viceroy Mendoza blamed its outbreak on the prophecies of sorcerers sent by the Chichimeca tribes living in the Zacatecas mountains, outside the territory at that time controlled by the Spaniards. Preachers announced the return of 'Tlatol', accompanied by all the resurrected ancestors, and the dawning of a golden age. For this it was necessary, as in the case of Taqui Ongo, to repudiate Christianity: the faithful had to perform rituals of penitence and purification, such as bathing the head to wash away the soiling by baptism. But, unlike Taqui Ongo of the Andes, Mexican millenarianism advocated a direct recourse to violence: at Tlatenango the Indians burnt the church and the cross; at Tequila and Ezatlan they killed the missionaries.

Like Taqui Ongo, this movement was only suppressed with difficulty: three successive expeditions, commanded by Miguel de Ibarra, Cristobal de Oñate and Juan de Alvarado, failed one after the other (and Alvarado, the famous *adelantado*, commander of the frontier region, died in battle). To put down the uprising once and for all, Viceroy Mendoza was forced to go to New Galicia in person, at the head of a large force.

But the war was only pushed further north. After the discovery of the Zacatecas silver mines in 1546 a new zone of colonization was opened up, growing gradually as more and more deposits began to be mined. The 'silver frontier' comprised the plateau area which lay to the north of the line running roughly through Guadalajara, Río Lerma, Queretaro and Mestitlan. This region, known as Gran Chichimeca, was populated by mainly nomadic Indians, living by hunting and gathering, who had remained outside the political organization of the Aztecs. Indeed, the very name Chichimeca that the Aztecs gave to these Indians meant 'barbarians'.

The war was prolonged by a process of acculturation like that undergone by the Chilean Indians. Imitating the Spaniards, the Chichimecas greatly increased their mobility by using horses. To obtain them they began by attacking Spanish settlements and convoys, but soon the animals multiplied to such an extent that herds of them wandered freely all over the country. Around 1579 Juan Suarez Peralta noted that horses were 'so numerous that they roam the country in a wild state, without owners: they are called *cimarrones*'.[59] The Chichimecas even began to practise a form of horse-breeding, since they owned ranches (corrals) where they gathered the animals together.

In order to protect their communications with the mining towns the Spanish established at strategic points on the frontier a certain number of defence posts (*presidios*) which contained a small garrison responsible for pacifying the area. The captured Chichimecas were turned into slaves and provided a labour force which was highly esteemed in the silver mines, and also in the estancias of the north and the central plateau. Like the Araucanian frontier, the Chichimeca frontier thus became a zone devoted to the hunting of slaves: that is, the war was made to pay for itself.

Chichimeca resistance was overcome by a new and original policy based on the idea of acculturation: at the end of the century, Viceroys Villamanrique and, later, Velasco introduced new methods intended to induce the Indians to give up their nomadic existence. The Spanish founded 'missions' where the Indians were regrouped and converted to Christianity; they also called on the assistance of their allies in central Mexico (especially from Tlaxcala and Cholula) and encouraged them to establish colonies which would provide the Chichimecas with the example of a Christian way of life. But, in fact, as a result of Spanish expansion, the war moved again further north into the territories which were later to form New Mexico. The settled Pueblos of the Río Grande valley were partially subdued, but the Apaches, nomads of the plains and plateaus, resisted successfully and preserved their independence.

The example of the Indians of the frontiers (the Chiriguanos, the Araucanians, the Chichimecas) confirms, albeit in a negative way, the importance of the pre-existing structures of the Aztec and Inca states

---

[59] Juan Suarez de Peralta, 'Libro de alveyteria', libro II, capitulo 6, published by François Chevalier, 'Noticia inédita sobre los caballos en Nueva España', *Revista de Indias*, (1944), 324.

as the foundation of Spanish colonization. In Mesoamerica and the Andes the colonial system was successfully imposed by making new use of pre-existing institutions; the latter survived in only fragmentary form, isolated from their previous context which was definitively destroyed. But since the traditional conceptual and religious framework persisted, a contrast developed between, on the one hand, the survival of a world view which constituted a meaningful whole, and on the other, the partial continuity of institutions detached from the cosmology which had given them significance. It was this divergence between the continuities and the changes which defined the crisis of destructuration in the Indian world immediately after the European invasion.

We have to accept that, after the initial shock of conquest, the history of colonial society, both in New Spain and Peru, was that of a long process of re-integration at all levels: economic, social, political, ideological. Depending on the pre-Columbian inheritance and on the strength of the opposing parties, the process assumed very different forms: syncretism, resistance, interbreeding, hispanicization. But between the dominant Spanish culture – which tried to impose its values and customs – and the dominated native culture – which insisted on preserving its own values and customs – the conflict goes on to this day.

8

THE PORTUGUESE SETTLEMENT OF BRAZIL, 1500–80

Late medieval Europe had long been linked with Asia via tenuous land routes, as had Asia with America across the Pacific, but it was not until the Portuguese thrust into the Atlantic early in the fifteenth century that the last great oceanic hiatus in global intercommunication came to be closed. Paradoxically, this first stirring of what was to become modern European imperialism emerged from a society in contraction. Portugal, like the rest of Europe, had suffered a severe population decline in the middle years of the fourteenth century; the ensuing abandonment of marginal land along with the depopulation of towns and villages had created a classic 'feudal crisis' with the upper strata of society economically squeezed by the loss of much of their customary revenue. Elsewhere in Europe this pinch had the effect of sending forth members of the nobility on marauding expeditions in search of booty and new sources of income; the Portuguese conquest of the Moroccan seaport of Ceuta in 1415 (the same year as Henry V's victory at Agincourt) may well be viewed in this light. But Ceuta and the accompanying vision of a North African empire that it suggested turned out to be a dead end. It proved impossible to renew the peninsular reconquest in Morocco: the Berber population was too resistant, too deeply attached to its Islamic beliefs; Portugal's population was too small, its military resources too few.

Instead, the Portuguese thrust was deflected westward, onto the sea and down the coast of Africa. Here resistance was minimal. For centuries boats from the fishing villages along the southern coast of Portugal (the Algarve) had been drawn to the Moroccan coast by the natural action of the winds and currents in that part of the Atlantic, and there they found a variety of rich fishing grounds. Now, with internal pressures for outward expansion growing, these voyagers were stimulated to investigate the opportunities for trade and plunder that beckoned from the adjacent shores.

The traditional approach to this exploration has been to attribute it (at least before 1460) almost exclusively to the inspiration of Prince Henry 'the Navigator' (1394–1460) whose deeds in directing these discoveries were promptly preserved in chronicles which gave him quasi-heroic status. But these discoveries, though certainly stimulated by Henry's desire to create an overseas *appanage* for himself, involved other members of the royal family as well, in addition to numerous followers from their households. Equally important was the participation of members of the Italian merchant community in Lisbon (whether naturalized or not) who brought to the process their Mediterranean expertise and connections. Indeed, they may well have been the decisive factor in transforming these early forays for fishing and plunder along the African coast into organized expeditions for trade.

The Portuguese thrust outward, however, was not limited to pushing down the west coast of Africa, important though that finally proved to be. These sailings inevitably brought them into contact with the islands of the Atlantic – nearby Madeira and the Canaries to begin with, the Azores and the Cape Verdes later. It was the Portuguese experience here, even more than in Africa, that created the patterns later employed in the colonization of Brazil. Taken together, these islands, including the Canaries which gradually fell into the Spanish sphere, formed a kind of 'Atlantic Mediterranean' – a collection of lands whose economy was linked together by the sea.

Madeira was known to exist as early as the fourteenth century, but it was not exploited until the fifteenth. It was the French/Spanish occupation of the nearby Canaries in 1402 that stimulated the Portuguese to initiate serious exploration leading to settlement and agriculture. This began in the years 1418–26 under the leadership of two squires from the entourage of Prince Henry and an Italian nobleman from the household of his brother, Dom João. Development of the Azores lagged behind Madeira by several years. Discovered, or rediscovered in 1427, the Azores began to be settled only in 1439. Finally, much later, the Cape Verdes were explored in the years between 1456 and 1462, but their development and settlement progressed more slowly.

As these various islands or island groups were found, they were progressively incorporated into an economic system centred in Lisbon that was controlled jointly by the Portuguese court and the rich merchants (some of Italian origin) of the capital. This process of incorporation passed through at least three rather well-defined stages which prefigure certain aspects of the economic development of Brazil in the following century.

Since the islands were uninhabited when they were found, the first stage in their exploitation was of necessity extensive. In the earliest years, when there were few or no settlers, animals were put ashore to proliferate rapidly in the new surroundings. They could then be periodically rounded up for slaughter and the products taken back to Portugal for sale. The development of Madeira began with this stage and the first inhabitants brought with them sheep, pigs and cows, if indeed these had not, as it seems, already been put ashore to propagate by themselves. Likewise sheep and goats were set ashore in the Azores in 1431, four years after their initial discovery, to multiply at will. The first settlers arrived only later, in 1439, and for several years devoted themselves to tending the already existing herds before moving on to the next stage of development about 1442. The same pattern was repeated in the Cape Verdes where, before settlement began, goats especially were set ashore to multiply freely.

Since the Portuguese population, like that of most of Europe, was at a low ebb in the first half of the fifteenth century, it took some time before these island frontiers could attract enough people for settled agriculture. But whenever the influx had created a sufficient population density, a shift took place from the initial stage of extensive exploitation via cattle raising to the second stage of more intensive exploitation through the cultivation of cereals. In Madeira, this second stage followed only a few years after the first, due largely to an unexpected migration of disillusioned settlers who had abandoned the Moroccan outpost of Ceuta. The island (as its name 'wood' implies) was covered by immense forests and as these were burned to open areas for wheat, the enriched soil gave enormous yields: up to 50 times the seeding, or so the sources, with some probable exaggeration, claim. As the population expanded, however, the richness of the soil declined with successive harvests, the costs of wheat production rose, its market advantage shrank, and investment shifted to other more remunerative products.

In the Azores, the second or cereal stage began about 1442, some fifteen years after the discovery of the archipelago, and as the wheat exports of Madeira declined those of the Azores rose in compensation. Here, early in the wheat cycle, yields approximating to those of Madeira – 40 to 60 times the seeding – were reported. Unlike Madeira and the Azores, the Cape Verdes did not pass from a cattle stage into one of cereals. Rather the subsequent stage here was one of rice, cotton and fruit and sugar – clear evidence that these islands really lay outside the 'Atlantic Mediterranean' and formed, instead, a transitional region between the ecology of Madeira and the tropical ecology of the African coast.

Finally, a third stage of capitalistic agriculture appeared, but only in Madeira. As the grain yields fell off, capital tended to shift to the more lucrative crops of sugar and fine wine. From about 1450 onward, vineyards and cane-fields began to spread. Pre-Madeiran sugar production had centred in the Near East, Sicily and Spain; it was almost certainly from Sicily that it was introduced into the island. The Azores, however, never reached this stage due to climatological conditions. After Madeira, the next great area for sugar was to be Brazil. The spread of sugar cultivation thence, however, came belatedly, only after an initial generation during which the land was exploited in a manner that resembled, not the first or cattle stage of the Atlantic islands, but rather the factory system that the Portuguese had meanwhile developed along the coast of West Africa during the period after 1449.

Along this coast the Portuguese had avoided, as a rule, any attempt at significant settlement: the native populations were too dense to be easily subdued, the area was ecologically unattractive. Instead they chose to exploit the coast after a pattern adopted from the Italian trading cities of the late medieval Mediterranean. Here the key institution was the factory (*feitoria*), or fortified trading post. This was defended by the castle garrison headed by a knight and operated by a factor (*feitor*) or commercial agent who undertook to make purchases from the native merchants or chiefs. The merchandise he secured was stored in the factory and then sold to the Portuguese captains of the trading fleets that periodically visited the factory. These, however, were often attacked by foreign pirates who seized ships and cargoes when they did not make direct attempts to breach Portugal's fragile monopoly of trade with the natives. In practice the Portuguese crown responded with coast guard patrols to drive off unlicensed ships while juridically it sought and received recognition of its monopoly rights in a series of papal bulls

(1437–81) that formed the models for the later assignment of exclusive rights in America to Spain and Portugal.[1]

By 1500, then, the Portuguese had elaborated two basic patterns for empire in the South Atlantic, a repertoire to be applied as needed to the problems they encountered: (1) the uninhabited islands they regarded juridically as extensions of the mainland kingdom, to be granted to seigneurial lords by royal gifts (*doações*) similar to those made to lords on the mainland, and to be populated by Portuguese immigrants using a settlement system whose forms were borrowed from the medieval Reconquest; (2) along the African coast, where they did encounter native peoples, they opted, instead, for trade without settlement based on the factory system of the late medieval Mediterranean.

Upon finally reaching India (Vasco da Gama, 1498), it was the 'African' system the Portuguese imposed. Finding an age-old culture difficult to penetrate or conquer, they resorted to setting up an 'empire' based on factories, defended by sea patrols to control unlicensed shipping in their area. Brazil, 'discovered' in the course of the second voyage to India, presented a more ambiguous image. Geographically it resembled the Atlantic islands, but, like the African coast, it was populated by savages whom the first Portuguese often called 'negroes'. Only with further exploration did Brazil's real nature gradually come into focus. Treated in the same fashion as the African coast during the first 30 years, it later came to be settled after the pattern of the Atlantic islands.

DISCOVERY AND EARLY EXPLORATION

Upon his return from India in 1499, Vasco da Gama, we are told, pleaded fatigue and recommended that the follow-up expedition of 1500 be entrusted instead to Pedro Álvares Cabral, a *fidalgo* and member of the king's household. Cabral's fleet of thirteen ships followed da Gama's route from Lisbon via the Canaries to Cape Verde, but after crossing the doldrums it was pulled westward by the winds and currents of the South Atlantic and came within sight of the Brazilian coast near present-day Porto Seguro on 22 April 1500. The eight days that the fleet spent refreshing itself in Brazil provided a first brief encounter between

[1] Charles-Mártial de Witte, *Les Bulles pontificales et l'expansion portugaise au XVe siècle* (Louvain, 1958), *passim*.

two civilizations, one recently embarked upon aggressive imperialism, the other a stone-age culture, virtually outside of time, living in the innocence apparently of Eden. The details of these first contacts were carefully related by the fleet scribe, Pero Vaz da Caminha, in a long letter to King Manuel of Portugal (the 'birth certificate' of Brazil, in the happy phrase of Capistrano de Abreu) that remains our principal source of information about the discovery. On 1 May, Cabral's fleet weighed anchor for its final destination, India, but the supply ship under the command of Gaspar de Lemos was detached to carry immediate news of the 'miraculous' discovery back to the Portuguese court. King Manuel I (1495–1521) promptly notified his Castilian relatives, Ferdinand and Isabella, of the discovery, emphasizing its strategic value to Portugal as a way-station for the India fleets, and organized another expedition the next year for further exploration of Caminha's 'Island of the True Cross'.[2]

This second fleet of three caravels left Lisbon in May of 1501 under the command of Gonçalo Coelho with Amerigo Vespucci aboard as chronicler. Our basic knowledge of this, as well as of the later voyage of 1503–4, comes from Vespucci's vain, if not mendacious, pen which has given birth to intricate and endless historiographical questions. Suffice it to say that the expedition of 1501–2 explored and named many points along some 500 leagues (*c.* 2,000 miles) of the Brazilian coast, from Cape São Roque in the north to near Cananéia in the south; these were soon incorporated into the Cantino map of 1502. Though Vespucci's mercantile sensibilities were not excited by what he saw, '...one can say that we found nothing of profit there except an infinity of dyewood trees, canafistula...and other natural marvels that would be tedious to describe...',[3] this second expedition brought back to Lisbon the first American samples of the brazilwood (*caesalpina echinata*) that was not only to provide the 'Island of the True Cross' with its permanent name (Brasil), but also the only compelling reason for its further exploration.

This second voyage also served to establish the sailing route between Portugal and Brazil for the remainder of the colonial period. Ships leaving Portuguese ports usually made for the Canary Islands (where

---

[2] On the seemingly endless debate regarding the 'intentionality' of Cabral's landfall, see the expert judgement of the late Samuel Eliot Morison, *The European discovery of America: the southern voyages, 1492–1616* (New York, 1974), 224.

[3] Carlos Malheiro Días, 'A Expedição de 1501–02', in *História da colonização Portuguêsa no Brasil*, ed. C. Malheiro Días (Porto, 1924), II, 202.

they often tarried to fish) and then headed for the Cape Verdes to take on fresh water and food; normally this leg of the voyage could last anywhere from fifteen to twenty days, depending upon weather conditions. From the Cape Verdes, ships steered south by southwest to cross the doldrums, a tiresome and tricky task that could easily fail, leaving the fleet to be swept up by the southern equatorial current into the Caribbean, as happened to Governor Luís de Vasconcelos on his outward voyage in 1571. Once safely across the doldrums, ships would veer westward, drawn naturally (like Cabral) in that direction by the winds and currents, until they touched Brazil somewhere between Cape São Roque and Cape Santo Agostinho, whence they could follow the coast all the way down to the Río de la Plata. A voyage, say, from Lisbon to Bahia required about a month and a half, if all went smoothly. If it did not (as with Padre Cardim in 1583), the outward voyage could take all of two months or more, even if the Cape Verdes were bypassed. Ships returning to Portugal steered north from Cape São Roque until they found the Azores whence they could ride the westerlies into Lisbon. This usually took longer than the outward voyage, often two and a half months or more.

THE FACTORY PERIOD

Once the initial phase (1500–2) of discovery and reconnaissance had been completed the Portuguese crown faced the problem of devising a system to exploit the new-found land. In the context of Portugal's prior Atlantic experience, the nature of Brazil was ambiguous. In most respects, it appeared to be simply another Atlantic island, but unlike Madeira or the Azores, it was populated by savage though comely natives. The island pattern of putting cattle ashore to multiply before the first colonists arrived was thus impossible in Brazil where the animals would rapidly fall prey to the Indians. Instead, the Portuguese felt obliged to treat Brazil like the coast of Africa and to exploit it via a system of trading factories.

To develop the few tradable commodities that were found (dyewood, monkeys, slaves and parrots) the crown opted to lease out Brazil to a consortium of Lisbon merchants headed by Fernão de Noronha, who was already important in the African and Indian trades. Unfortunately, the contract itself has not survived, but indirect evidence suggests that it resembled that by which the Guinea trade in Africa had been leased in 1469 to the merchant Fernão Gomes for a five-year period. The group, we are told, was granted a trade monopoly for three years with no payment to the crown the first year, a sixth of the profits the second, and a quarter the third. In return, the group agreed to send out six ships each year to explore 300 leagues (*c.* 1,200 miles) of coastline and to construct a fortified trading post or factory there.

We know of two fleets which the consortium sent out. Details of the first are sketchy: sailing under an unknown captain, it left Lisbon in August of 1502, made Brazil near Cape São Roque, visited the area of Porto Seguro and returned to Lisbon in April of the next year, bringing back a cargo of brazilwood and Indian slaves. The second voyage is better known, thanks to Vespucci who was in command of one of the five ships. He has left us an account of the voyage (his third and last) in his *Letters*. Departing Lisbon on 10 June 1503, the expedition ran into bad weather near the island of Fernando Noronha (named after the principal merchant of the consortium). Here Vespucci's ship, along with that of another captain, lost the fleet. The two went on together to Cabo Frio in Brazil where they stayed five months to erect the factory called for in the contract which they garrisoned with 24 men.[4] In June of 1504 the two ships returned to Lisbon with a cargo of brazilwood. It is likely that the consortium sent out a third voyage in 1504-5, but no evidence of it has survived.[5]

The profitability of these voyages is unknown, but, when the group's contract expired in 1505, indirect evidence suggests that the crown resumed direct control of the Brazil trade just as it did with regard to the India trade at the same time.[6] Thus re-established in 1506, direct crown control of Brazil was to last until 1534 when the land was again leased out, not, as earlier, to merchants for trade, but rather to territorial lords for purposes of settlement.

During the intervening years (1506-34) of royal exploitation, the Portuguese crown continued to adhere to the patterns worked out in Africa during the fifteenth century, i.e., it maintained royal factories at a number of strategic points along the coast (Pernambuco, Bahia?, Porto Seguro?, Cabo Frio, São Vicente?), but licensed private vessels to trade with the natives under its auspices. No yearly statistics for this trade

[4] The point of departure for Hythlodaeus in More's *Utopia*.
[5] Max Justo Guedes, 'As primeiras expedições portuguesas e o reconhecimento da costa brasileira', *Revista Portuguesa de História*, 12/2 (1968), 247-67.
[6] Rolando A. Laguarda Trías, 'Christóvão Jaques e as armadas Guarda-Costa', in *História Naval Brasileira*, ed. M. J. Guedes (Rio de Janeiro, 1975), 1/1, 275.

have survived, nor have we any record for most of these voyages. Good luck, however, has preserved for us a relatively detailed account of one expedition, that of the *Bretoa* in 1511, which reveals the essential nature of the system. The ship was financed by a group that again included Noronha, now in association with Bartolomeu Marchione, an important Florentine merchant settled in Lisbon who was already active in the Madeiran sugar trade. Carrying a complement of five officers and 31 crew, the *Bretoa* left Lisbon in February and arrived at Bahia in April where it remained about a month. In May it proceeded south to load dyewood at the factory established in 1504 near Cabo Frio. The factory had been sited on an offshore island (for safety against Indian attack) and contact between the crew and the natives was strictly forbidden, factory personnel being the sole go-betweens. Some 5,000 logs were cut and transported to the factory by Tupi Indians who were paid for their labour with gifts of trinkets and small tools. Members of the crew were also allowed to trade for their own account; thus, in addition to the main cargo of dyewood, 35 Tupi Indian slaves and numerous exotic animals were brought back. Sailing late in July the ship made Lisbon at the end of October. The overall profitability of the Brazil trade cannot be sensibly calculated from this one voyage, but it was evidently lucrative enough to attract at least occasional investors, especially those who were already involved in imperial trade or who had Antwerp outlets, as did Noronha.

Interest in Brazil was not exclusively economic, however. It also presented a geopolitical problem for the Iberian powers. If, as many still thought, it was really a large (but relatively poor) island, could it be rounded and a westward passage found to the much more lucrative spice islands of the East Indies? Though almost everyone agreed that the Brazilian bulge fell within the Portuguese sphere as defined by the Treaty of Tordesillas (1494), did the mouth of the Amazon and the Río de la Plata (the most likely routes around Brazil) fall on the Portuguese or Spanish side of the line? The search for answers centred largely on La Plata during most of the second decade of the century. A Portuguese expedition (the Fróis-Lisboa, financed by the Castilian-born Christóvão de Haro among others) had first discovered the Río de la Plata in 1511–12; Castile responded with the Solís expedition of 1515. This in turn helped trigger the Portuguese coastguard patrols probably begun in 1516 by Christóvão Jacques.[7] These, however, did not prevent Spain

---

[7] Or 'Jaques' as Laguarda Trías would prefer, *op. cit.*

from sending Magellan to Brazil on the first leg of his search for a westward passage in 1519. His subsequent discovery of the way around 'Brazil' to the Spiceries, though a spectacular feat of navigation, was largely useless to Castile. The route proved too long to be practical; and in the meantime Cortés had distracted the Spanish with his discovery of the riches of the Aztecs. After years of desultory negotiations, Spain pawned her claim to the Spice Islands given her by Magellan to Portugal for 350,000 ducats (Treaty of Zaragoza, 1529) and Spanish pressure on Brazil came largely to an end.

More important in the long run than Spanish probing around the fringes of Brazil was French poaching on the dyewood trade. Evidence for this is haphazard: a ship seizure here, a protest there, but it was growing, led by merchants operating out of northern French ports in Normandy and Brittany. A French ship intent upon breaking into the India trade had, like Cabral, drifted off course onto the coast of Brazil in 1504, where it remained to load dyewood instead and then returned to Honfleur. Appetites whetted, French merchants from other ports (Dieppe, Rouen, Fécamp) began to seek dyewood in Brazil. They made no attempt to establish factories after the Portuguese pattern, but traded directly from their ships, sending agents to live among the Indians, with whom good relations were developed. Not only did French competition deprive the Portuguese crown of revenue, but it lowered the price of brazilwood by increasing supplies on the Antwerp market. In addition, French seizures of Portuguese ships drove up costs to such a point that fewer and fewer merchants were willing to risk involvement in the trade.

The initial Portuguese response was to apply the tactics that had worked so well in the Indian Ocean: to dispatch a fleet to police the seas with instructions to seize or destroy unlicensed foreign ships. The expedition of Christóvão Jacques, sent to the Brazilian coast in 1516, was the first direct royal reaction in defence of Brazil. We have little information on Jacques' activities during the three years his fleet patrolled the coast (1516–19) but we know that he established a royal factory at Pernambuco[8] and may also have attempted a limited settlement there for growing sugar cane (if one can trust a document – since disappeared – cited by Varnhagen). This first coastguard expedition cannot be considered a complete success, however, for after 1520 there was a noticeable increase in French piracy which was no

---

[8] According to Laguarda Trías, he simply moved the factory Vespucci had established at Cabo Frio (or Rio de Janeiro) to Pernambuco.

longer confined to Brazil. French privateers lay in wait about strategic rendezvous points such as the Azores and the straits of Gibraltar to seize Spanish and Portuguese ships. A recent rough calculation of Portuguese vessels seized by the French works out to an average of twenty per year for the decade 1520–30. There is some evidence that the Portuguese persisted in their attempt to contain this threat with coastguard patrols (in 1521–2 probably; in 1523–5 perhaps). In any case, Jacques was sent back to Brazil in 1527 at the head of a fleet of six ships with orders to eliminate the interlopers at all costs. Running into some French loading dyewood at Bahia, he seized their (three) ships, either hanged or buried alive numerous members of their crews and then proceeded to sweep the coast down to Cabo Frio. Ensuing protests from the French court brought issues to a head.

In contrast to the Castilians who accepted the juridical bases of the Portuguese claim and argued only over boundaries, the French presented a fundamental challenge to Portugal's exclusive rights to Brazil. These rested, as in Africa, on papal bulls that embodied the medieval canonistic tradition of universal papal jurisdiction over the world, a concept classically formulated by Hostiensis and Augustinus Triumphus in the thirteenth century. This gave the pope legitimate authority to assign monopoly rights over newly-discovered seas and lands to rulers who would undertake to evangelize them. But this thirteenth-century concept soon came under attack from Thomistic critics whose ideas had recently been reinforced by the Renaissance revival of Roman law, especially of the Code of Justinian. Indeed, the papal position was no longer accepted by progressive scholars even in Iberia (e.g. Francisco de Vitória). Armed, then, with a more 'modern' concept of empire based on the secular law of nations (*ex iure gentium*), the French court insisted upon its right to trade freely and declined to respect any title not backed up by effective occupation. The French considered their ships and merchants free to traffic with any area of Brazil not actually occupied by Portuguese – which meant, in fact, virtually the entire coast.

Under constant pressure during the 1520s, the Portuguese crown retreated on nearly all fronts. It found it impossible to drive out the French with sea patrols – the open coast was too long and royal resources too few. Juridically the papal bulls and the Treaty of Tordesillas were recognized only by Castile; and the intellectual acumen of the French lawyers made the Portuguese king uneasy. Unable to persuade the French king of his legal rights (he even argued, with a tinge of desperation, that he and his predecessors had 'purchased' Brazil through the Portuguese lives and money expended in the early expeditions), João III (1521–57) temporarily resorted to bribing Chabot, the admiral of France, in his attempt to control French piracy and poaching (1529–31).

This afforded a short respite and Portuguese policy now evolved rapidly. By 1530 João III and his advisers concluded that some kind of permanent colony would have to be planted in Brazil. This is one of the meanings of the expedition of Martim Afonso de Sousa (1530–3). His fleet of five ships carrying some 400 settlers really had three discernible aims, and in its variety of orientations looks both back to the earlier policy of royal coastguards as well as forward to the coming solution of settlement. Sousa's first charge – to patrol the coast – reveals that the crown had still not completely abandoned the view that the defence of its Brazilian interest was largely a question of clearing the seas of unlicensed ships, while his second charge – to establish a royal colony (São Vicente, 1532) through revocable (not hereditary) landgrants to settlers – adumbrates the emergence of a new policy in Brazil; lastly, in preparation for settlement, the expedition was instructed to explore the mouths of the Amazon and La Plata rivers to determine, among other things, their proximity to the meridian of Tordesillas.

The ambiguities in Portuguese policy were resolved while Sousa was still in Brazil. Prompted by Diego de Gouveia, the Portuguese principal of the college of Sainte Barbe in Paris, a fundamental shift in policy occurred which, in effect, moved the Portuguese line of defence from the sea to the land. Instead of attempting to keep French ships from reaching the Brazilian coast, the Portuguese would instead establish a number of settlements to prevent the Indian population from direct trading with the French. At the same time these settlements would answer the French juridical challenge: Portugal could now claim 'effective possession' of Brazil. Direct royal control would cease; instead of a single royal colony at São Vicente, a plurality of private settlements would blanket the coast from the Amazon to the Río de la Plata. Growing strains on crown income at this time made it useful to shift the costs of such extensive colonization to private investors, several of whom had already expressed interest in taking up New World lordships with the aim of growing sugar cane. Demand for sugar was booming in these years, and production had recently been greatly expanded on the island of São Tomé. The first tentative experiments with sugar in Brazil (Pernambuco, 1516, and São Vicente, 1532) had demonstrated the climatic and topographical suitability of large stretches of the Brazilian coast.

THE PERIOD OF PROPRIETARY SETTLEMENT

Grants were made to a group of twelve proprietary captains ranging from soldiers of fortune who had proven themselves in the Orient (Duarte Coelho, Francisco Coutinho) to a number of bureaucrats including a humanist historian of high intellectual distinction (João de Barros). What all of them had in common was court connections, especially with António de Ataíde, the Overseer of the Treasury (*Vedor da Fazenda*), who, in directing and co-ordinating Portugal's colonial enterprise, played a role similar to that of Bishop Fonseca in Castile until the death of Ferdinand in 1516. The fact that none of them came from the high nobility is hardly cause for surprise (as some historians have implied). João III was the heir of the New Monarchy created by João II and Manuel I and preferred to entrust power and bestow rewards on the university educated (*letrados*) and upwardly mobile servants of the crown whatever their birth.

The twelve grantees received fourteen captaincies in fifteen lots (one captaincy had two sections and two grantees got two captaincies each) by royal 'gift' (*doação*) – hence the terms 'donatary captain' and 'donatary captaincy'. The institution derived, slightly modified by circumstance, from the typical royal grant of lordship in late medieval Portugal. In essence it was the hereditary grant of a large portion of royal jurisdiction over a specified territory and its inhabitants to a lord who thereafter acted as the king's *locum tenens* to the extent spelled out in the gift. In a constitutional sense, land under the direct control of the crown (*reguengo*) was converted into a lordship (*senhorio*) in which royal rights were now restricted to certain attributes of 'greater lordship'. All twelve grants were similar in essentials; that made to Duarte Coelho will serve to illustrate them all.

Coelho received his captaincy of Pernambuco as an hereditary possession of which he and his successors were to be 'captains and governors'. Inheritance was more liberal than in the peninsula: the exclusion there of bastards and transverse or collateral relatives (the *Lei Mental*) was specifically disavowed. Coelho had the right to appoint all notaries, scribes and other subordinate officials in his captaincy, and he or his officials were granted most civil and criminal jurisdiction except for certain cases and persons reserved to the crown as evidence of its 'greater lordship'. He was also given the right to establish towns and to supervise the elections of their officials. In addition to these jurisdictional powers, Coelho was made a territorial lord by the gift of ten leagues of coast (in several parcels) of which he was direct owner. To attract settlers, the rest of the land was to be subgranted by him to colonists, in full ownership, obligated only to pay the tithe to the Order of Christ. Finally, as captain, he had the right to license all important capital improvements such as mills for grinding cane; these were the 'banal rights' commonly possessed by lords throughout medieval Europe.

As for the captain's rents, they were largely made up of taxes that would normally have gone to the king: a tenth of the tithe, a half of the tenth levied on fish caught by the colonists, a tenth of all royal revenues in the captaincy and a twentieth of the profits from the brazilwood cut; the latter was usually kept from the *donatário* and directly controlled by the king. Structurally these donations were indistinguishable from similar grants of royal authority made in Portugal as well as in the Atlantic islands in the late medieval period, and should be seen as adaptations of these. Attempts which have been made to force the institution into ideological categories (feudal or capitalistic) simply confuse its understanding.[9]

The letter of donation to the captain was complemented by a kind of mini-constitution (*foral*) for his lordship. This spelled out in some detail the relations between the settlers and the captain as well as the rights of the crown. In medieval Portugal the foral had usually been issued to his settlers by the lord himself, but the New Monarchy early in the sixteenth century had recovered this right from the donataries and royalized it, as it were. Coelho's foral exempted the inhabitants from the *sisa* and other royal taxes, but the crown retained its previous monopoly of the dyewood trade as well as its right to a tenth of the fish caught, a fifth of the minerals mined and a tenth on commerce in and out of the captaincy. Trade with the captaincies was open to both Portuguese and to foreigners, but only the captain and the Portuguese

[9] See H. B. Johnson, 'The donatary captaincy in historical perspective: Portuguese backgrounds to the settlement of Brazil', *HAHR*, 52 (1972), 203–14.

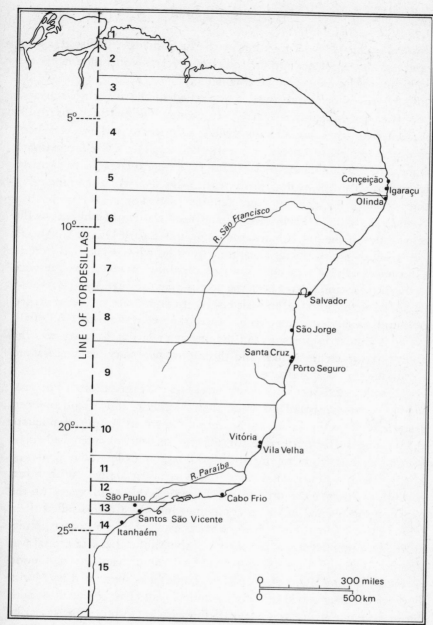

5°

10°

LINE OF TORDESILLAS

20°

25°

1

2

3

4

5 — Conçeição • Igaraçu
Olinda

6 — R. São Francisco

7

Salvador

8 — São Jorge

Santa Cruz
9 — Pôrto Seguro

10 — Vitória
Vila Velha

11 — R. Paraíba

12 — São Paulo — Cabo Frio
13 — Santos São Vicente
14 — Itanhaém

15

0   300 miles
0   500 km

Key to Captaincies

1. João de Barros e Aires da Cunha (Pará), 2nd Part   2. Fernão Alvares de Andrade (Maranhão)   3. Antônio Cardoso de Barros (Piauí)   4. João de Barros e Aires da Cunha, 1st Part   5. Pero Lopes de Sousa (Itamaracá), 3rd Part   6. Duarte Coelho (Pernambuco) 7. Francisco Pereira Coutinho (Bahia)   8. Jorge Figueiredo Correia (Ilhéus)   9. Pero do Campo Tourinho (Pôrto Seguro)   10. Vasco Fernandes Coutinho (Espírito Santo)   11. Pero de Goís (São Tomé)   12. Martim Afonso de Sousa (Rio de Janeiro), 2nd Part   13. Pero Lopes de Sousa (Santo Amaro), 1st Part   14. Martim Afonso de Sousa (São Vicente), 1st Part   15. Pero Lopes de Sousa (Sant'Ana), 2nd Part

Captaincies of Brazil in the sixteenth century

residents were allowed to trade with the Indians. Finally, the king reserved the right to appoint officials directly concerned with the collection of his rents in the captaincy.

Only ten of the captaincies were settled in the sixteenth century; two (Ceará and Santana) were left abandoned by their lords. Of the ten that were settled only two (São Vicente and Pernambuco) could be termed genuinely successful before 1550. Of the remaining eight, five were moderately successful, for a time at least (Santo Amaro, Itamaracá, Espírito Santo, Porto Seguro, Ilhéus), while the remaining three rapidly became complete failures (São Tomé, Maranhão–Rio Grande and Bahia). Their various fates can be attributed in part to the capabilities of the individual captains; in this regard Duarte Coelho in Pernambuco stood out as exceptionally able, while Francisco Pereira Coutinho in Bahia was not. Still, the capability or even the presence of the captain cannot have been the decisive factor, since Martim Afonso de Sousa never bothered to visit his grant of São Vicente, yet it turned out, under able lieutenants, to be one of the two most successful of all. Evidently more important than the character of the donatary was the ability to attract the settlers and the capital necessary for success and to subdue the local Indians.

Obtaining sufficient settlers was not easy; the population of Portugal in the 1530s numbered no more than a million and a half at most, scattered over some 34,200 square miles of territory (*c.* 40–4 per square mile). With so little pressure for emigration, settlers often had to be sought instead from among the *degredados*, or exiles, who could be anyone from a political offender to a common criminal. With a few exceptions, they were on the whole undesirable, and many of the captains complained of them, sometimes bitterly. Coelho called them 'this poison' and tried instead, with considerable success, to attract sturdy peasants from his own region of the Minho. Lack of capital was another difficulty that could prove fatal. Some captains had good financial backing. Pero de Góis (São Tomé) was supported by Martin Ferreira, a businessman of Lisbon, while Coelho had connections with Florentine merchants, and Jorge de Figueiredo Correia (Ilhéus), scribe of the Treasury, could call upon the Giraldi, a family of Italian merchants settled in Lisbon. When Correia and Giraldi had problems getting the Indians to help set up sugar plantations in Ilhéus, they could afford to import 400 wage labourers and Guinea slaves during the years

1545–9 to defend the settlements and till the fields.[10] Reserves such as this often spelled the difference between success and failure. Others, on the other hand, like Pero de Campo Tourinho, could scarcely put together the amount needed to set off and had nothing to fall back on when circumstances turned adverse. The greatest challenge of all, however, came not from the problems of Europeans adjusting to a virgin land but rather from the hostility of the coastal Tupi-speaking and, to a lesser extent, Gê-speaking Indian population.

During the 'factory period' (1502–34), Portuguese relations with the Indians had been generally amicable. They furnished the Indians with technological artefacts that immensely increased the levels of productivity in their traditional economy, while in return the grateful Indians provided the labour necessary to fell and transport the brazilwood for loading on Portuguese ships, as well as the food required by the personnel of the factory. French incursions into this trade network may have been annoying to the Portuguese, but they did not seriously disturb their relations with the Indians.

Settlement, however, created a different situation. Given the intention of most captains to set up sugar plantations, Indian land rights were of necessity infringed. Though the migratory tendencies of Indian society blinded the Portuguese to it, the Indians did have a general sense of territoriality which the Portuguese plantations violated.[11] More importantly, sugar planting and sugar mills required a large and growing labour force that the settlers could not supply even had they been willing to do so, which they were not. The only recourse, therefore, was to Indian labour. But since work of the sort necessary to run a sugar plantation was unfamiliar to Indian culture, and (because of the often rigid schedule involved) antithetical to it, the two cultures – with their contrasting visions of the world – came into direct conflict. Tupi men were attuned to felling trees and had no difficulty satisfying Portuguese needs during the 'brazilwood' period, but field work was the traditional preserve of Indian women; Indian men refused to do it. They were profoundly unmaterialistic and unambitious, and in any case the settlers had little to offer which might make labour on plantations worthwhile. Given the recalcitrance of the labour force, the Portuguese settlers were soon driven to enslaving Indians for work on the growing

[10] *As Gavetas da Torre do Tombo* (Lisbon, 1962), II, 583.
[11] *As Gavetas da Torre do Tombo* (Lisbon, 1969), VIII, 512.

number of plantations and mills (*engenhos*). Slavery, of course, was an institution already known to Tupi culture, but largely in relation to ritual cannibalism. Enslaved Indians from neighbouring tribes were eventually sacrificed which usually led to a declaration of war by the kin of the enslaved. In this cultural context it is not difficult to understand how the growth of sugar planting and the slavery it entailed led to a state of constant conflict with the native population of the coastal area.

The Indians were always at a disadvantage in their struggle with the Portuguese. While the invaders had at their disposal arquebuses, swords and sometimes cannon, the Indians had to fight back with bows and arrows (though in their hands these were formidable weapons), wooden axes, as well as whatever guile and surprise they could add to the attack. Before disease had taken its toll, the Indians' main strength, however, lay in their numbers. At times they could simply overwhelm the Portuguese, who often had to take refuge in the fortified towers which formed the centre of most of their colonial settlements; they could then sometimes be worn down through starvation. On the other hand, if the Portuguese managed to hold out long enough (as they often did) the Indians usually became frustrated and went away. Another Portuguese tactic was terror: using the advantage of their technology they often frightened the Indians into submission, as did Jerónimo de Albuquerque in Pernambuco:

...after determining which [Indians] were the killers of the whites, he ordered some of them put into the mouths of cannon which he then had fired in front of the rest so that the culprits were blown to bits....[12]

Another weapon was fire which could be devastating against the palm thatch of the Indian *malocas*, as Mem de Sá demonstrated when he pacified the Indians around Bahia soon after his arrival by burning 60 of their villages. Finally, in addition to fire and gunpowder, the Portuguese had the weapon of bribery: defeated Indians who submitted could be rewarded with European artefacts such as fish hooks, scythes and metal axes.

Given the immense extent of the Brazilian coast that the Portuguese attempted to settle, from Cabo Santo Agostinho in the north to Cananéia in the south, these struggles were always local. The Indians' inability to overcome inter-tribal rivalries made it easy for the Portuguese

[12] Frei Vicente do Salvador, *História do Brasil, 1500–1627* (6th edn, São Paulo, 1975), 121.

to divide and rule; to make an alliance with one tribe against a second, and then to turn on their erstwhile allies at a later date was a standard Portuguese tactic.

During the first ten years after their arrival, the Portuguese settlers usually had either the co-operation of the Indians or the upper hand in the struggle with them; but in areas where settlement had failed to sink deep enough roots and was still fragile, native resistance, like the wave that swept the coast in the mid-40s (Bahia, 1545; São Tomé, 1546; Espírito Santo, c. 1546; Porto Seguro, 1546), could prove disastrous. It effectively wiped out the colonies of Bahia and São Tomé and severely crippled those of Espírito Santo and Porto Seguro. Only São Vicente, Ilhéus and Pernambuco/Itamaracá emerged intact, though the latter was seriously threatened in 1547–8. By 1548, the damage was clear; and the disappearance of effective Portuguese control in important centres such as Bahia and elsewhere increasingly exposed Brazil to the ever-present threat of French incursions and settlements. As Luís de Góis, brother of the donatary of São Tomé, summarized the situation in a letter to the king (1548): 'If Your Highness does not shortly aid these captaincies and coast of Brazil... You will lose the land.' Emphasizing the renewed threat of French invasion, he continued: 'But as long as these captaincies are standing with their inhabitants and Your Highness's aid and favour, the sea and coast will be rid of them.'[13] João III took Góis' advice and promptly decided to extend that 'aid and favour'.

THE ESTABLISHMENT OF ROYAL GOVERNMENT

The crown's decision to send a royal governor to Brazil was not intended to abrogate the donatarial grants. Most of these lasted through the next century and some of them into the eighteenth. Rather the king intended to resume, as it were, some of the authority that he had so generously given out at a time when royal resources were strained and rapid development had been sought. The Brazilian historian, Sérgio Buarque de Holanda, has related the establishment of the royal governorship to the Spanish discovery of silver at Potosí (1545); others, like Frédéric Mauro, have seen it as a decision to substitute Brazilian sugar for the waning spice trade of the Estado da India. On the other hand, one should not forget that the eventual resumption of royal control was a normal practice of *ancien régime* monarchies and the leasing

[13] As quoted in Serafim Leite, *Nóvas páginas de história do Brasil* (São Paulo, 1965), 261.

out of royal rights often a temporary expedient. This had been the case with the dyewood trade, farmed out between 1502–5 and royalized in 1506; it was now repeated with regard to the settlements that had been created between 1535–48. After private initiative had paved the way, the royal bureaucracy stepped in to appropriate a functioning enterprise. A glance at the Spanish parallels is instructive: only fourteen years passed in Mexico between Cortés' conquest and the arrival of the first viceroy; in Peru, the period between private conquest and the creation of a royal administration was no more than twelve years. If the donatarial captaincies are viewed as the phase of 'private conquest' in Brazil, then the arrival of a royal governor fourteen years later conforms perfectly to the general Iberian pattern. In a broader cultural sense one might view the royalization of both empires as a New World expression of the various 'closures' taking place in Catholic Europe about the middle of the sixteenth century: the definitive form given to dogma at Trent; the general retreat from Erasmian toleration; more specifically for Portugal, the final establishment of the Inquisition in 1547. In other words, it could be seen as part of a reaction against the ambiguity, openness and experimentation of the first half of the century, a move towards rigidity and codification, an exclusion of alternatives, demonstrating a new atmosphere of definite decisions having been finally made.

Whatever general interpretation may be preferred, immediate royal motivations are clearly revealed in the standing instructions (*regimento*) that accompanied the new governor, Tomé de Sousa (1549–53), another close relative of António de Ataíde, the Overseer of the Treasury. In the first place, he was charged to defend the weaker captaincies from possible attack and to revitalize those that had failed. These failures in every instance had been the result of Indian attack, not French conquest; yet, as Luís de Góis had written, the French threat was still alive, and captaincies weakened by Indian attacks were prime targets for possible French settlement. Secondly, the crown obviously wanted to increase the royal revenues from Brazil; not only was the king being cheated of what was due him, but the unsuccessful captaincies failed to provide him with the income he had expected from their development.

To deal with these problems João III chose three important officials: first, a governor to defend and bolster up the unsuccessful captains and to set general policy for dealing with the Indians; second, a *provedor-mor* of the Treasury to oversee the collection of crown revenues; and third, a captain-major of the coast to set up the policing of the littoral. Bahia was selected as the governor's seat; it was a central site with a potentially rich hinterland. And, due to the late donatary failing to deal with the Indians, it was possible to repurchase the captaincy from his heirs and re-incorporate it into the *reguengo* (land under the direct control of the crown). Tomé de Sousa (the first governor) was given detailed instructions for building a city of stone and mortar, centred on an impregnable fort, a worthy reflection of the royal determination to remain in Brazil. The sugar mills, satellite centres of Portuguese control, were also to be armed and fortified against possible attack. Once the governor's position in Bahia had been made strong, he was to visit the other captaincies to assess their needs and provide them with military assistance.

If increased military strength was one part of the solution of the Indian question, the other aspect was the elaboration of a workable Indian policy. Ultimately this would have to issue, as in the Spanish empire, from certain fundamental juridical decisions made by the crown. Brazil had been incorporated into the crown by the will of Manuel I,[14] but the native Indians (*gentio*) did not automatically, even by implication, become crown subjects. In contrast to the Spanish situation where Charles I simply succeeded to the thrones vacated by the Aztec and Inca emperors, the Portuguese could not discover any civilized structures in Tupi society – it appeared to lack identifiable laws and religious institutions. Indeed, the very innocence that had led Pero Vaz de Caminha in the beginning to see it as ripe for domination and conversion, was now revealed to be a frustrating obstacle. Tupi social organization did not fit any of the categories the Portuguese could comprehend; hence the crown's confused hesitation in defining the status of the Indians. In vain one searches contemporary documents for an unequivocal statement that the *gentio* are royal subjects. In short, the status of the Brazilian Indians within Portuguese colonial society was still to be worked out.

As early as the voyage of the *Bretoa* (1511), the crown placed the Indians under its legal protection, and the *regimento* given Tomé de Sousa emphasized that no harm should be done them as long as they were peaceful. Good treatment was essential if they were to be evangelized. That was the juridical justification for the whole enterprise,

---

[14] *As Gavetas da Torre do Tombo* (Lisbon, 1967), VI, 122.

whether derived from the papal bulls or Vitória's law of nations. On the other hand, rebellious Indians who resisted Christianity were equated with the Muslims of Africa and could thus be enslaved. So there gradually evolved in Brazil, as in the Spanish empire, the crucial distinction between peaceful Indians, minors to be protected by the crown while gradually being acculturated into full citizenship as Christians, and bellicose Indians against whom 'just wars' could be waged, who could be resettled by force if necessary and ultimately enslaved for use by the colonists. The crux of the matter, of course, was economic. Indiscriminate enslavements (*saltos*) were among the prime causes of Indian resistance, and this in turn made development of the economy impossible. Nevertheless, Indian labour for the developing sugar industry was essential and only enslavement could supply the workers required. The resolution of this contradiction was one of the principal tasks of the new generation of administrators.

As his special agents for converting and pacifying the Indians, the king chose the Jesuits, the missionary order founded only nine years before (1540) and brought to his attention by Diego de Gouveia in Paris. The first group of six (including Father Manuel de Nóbrega) came out with Tomé de Sousa; reinforcements arrived on subsequent voyages. But their total number was small; only 128 for the period up to 1598. The numerous diffuse letters they sent back to Europe reveal (as well as conceal) their work in Brazil. Up to 1580 Jesuit activity can be divided into five general stages: an initial period of experimentation (1550–3); an interlude of stagnation (1553–7); the full flowering of their settlement or *aldeia* system (1557–61); the crisis of the Caeté war and the ensuing waves of disease and famine (1562–3); and a final period of adjustment to the resultant decline of the Indian population (1564–74).

The initial period closely coincided with the term of the first royal governor; these were years of evaluation and experimentation. The Jesuits' aim was conversion, pacification and acculturation: the Indians' response, after some initial curiosity and acceptance, evasion, hostility and backsliding. Jesuit attitudes towards their task – the transformation of stone-age savages into quasi-European peasants living in settled villages practising the religion of an agrarian society – varied from dogged optimism to pessimistic self-pity. In contrast to Las Casas, few of them had much love or respect for their charges. Nóbrega compared the Tupi to dogs and pigs, and Anchieta described them as more like animals than men. Yet, in contrast to the colonists, they *did* believe in the possibility of changing Indian society. The Jesuits' reputation was at stake, and they applied themselves to their goal with a military determination.

At first they followed the methods of the Franciscans who always preferred to catechize Indians *in situ*, however slow the task might be. The Jesuits soon discovered, however, that the Indians they thought they had converted during their first visit to the village had gone native by the time they returned. To hasten the process and preserve their gains, they decided to remove Indians from their native villages and resettle them in aldeias whose large size was dictated by the scarcity of Jesuits to serve as supervisors. Here the Tupi could undergo intensive indoctrination. Nóbrega enunciated the plan of aldeias in 1550 and the first one was tried out near Bahia in 1552. They were not conspicuously successful; Indians often ran away: like minnows they wriggled through the net of Jesuit acculturation. Still, the determined fathers would have persisted but for political obstacles.

The settlers had never fully supported the Jesuit aldeias which removed so many Indians from the pool of potential slaves, and they soon found a powerful ally in the first bishop of Brazil, Dom Pedro Fernandes Sardinha. The crown's decision to create a royal governor was followed shortly after (1551) by the erection of a diocese for Brazil, located in Bahia, the extension to the *conquistas* of the metropolitan union of throne and altar. The king's choice of bishop, however, did not prove as happy as his choice of governor. Sardinha came with excellent credentials: trained as a humanist at the Sorbonne (where he had taught Loyola in the Portuguese-dominated college of St Barbe) his previous service as vicar general in Goa had been highly satisfactory. The Jesuits themselves had recommended him to the king. But once in Brazil contact with the savage Tupi seems to have stirred up his rigid moralistic tendencies. Not unreasonably, he did not share the Jesuit belief in the convertibility of the Indians; he insisted upon their full acculturation before baptism. Nor did he approve of the syncretic tendencies of Jesuit evangelization, the mere painting of a Christian patina over an obdurate Indian culture: e.g., tolerance of Indian nudity in Church, Indian songs and dances blended into the liturgy. As long as the Indians were cultural minors, they were not to participate in organized Christian life. In short, he envisaged in Brazil a dual society of the sort he had known in India, with a small 'republic' of Portuguese ruling over an alien world of mainly heathen natives.

His indifference towards the Indians was compensated by his fixation on the mores of the settlers. Their general adoption of Indian ways, a kind of ironic reverse acculturation that produced the proverbial squaw men such as João Ramalho in São Vicente and Caramurú in Bahia, drove him into a puritanical fury. Still, the settlers found his attitude towards the Indians and his non-support of the Jesuits congenial to their interests. The conflict between the bishop and the Jesuits gave them an opportunity to continue slaving and made it virtually impossible for the second governor, Duarte da Costa (1553–7), to exercise effective authority during his term of office. Because their work of evangelization was impeded by Sardinha's hostility and was not effectively supported by the harried governor, the Jesuits soon moved the centre of their activity to the southern captaincy of São Vicente where the Tupinikin Indians proved more receptive and malleable. Here they expanded on the aldeia system first conceived around Bahia, and established in 1554 an important Indian congregation (aldeia) at São Paulo de Piratininga. This site at the edge of the inland plateau commanded the basin of the Tieté river and formed the original nucleus for the future city of São Paulo.

Word of the conflict between the governor and the bishop in Bahia prompted the crown to recall the latter to Lisbon (1556) but his ship was wrecked along the coast of Brazil where, ironically, he suffered martyrdom, being killed and eaten by the Caeté Indians he so heartily disdained. Duarte da Costa's term of office ended the next year (1557) and with a new governor, Mem de Sá (1557–72), and a new bishop, Dom Pedro Leitão, royal consolidation of Portuguese Brazil entered a new phase.

Sá was, above all, a willing and enthusiastic collaborator of the Jesuits, who now returned to focus their activities around the royal city of Bahia. With the governor's military arm at their disposal, they made significant inroads into Indian paganism by sharpening the distinction, already adumbrated, between rebellious Indians, who might be enslaved, and peaceful, acculturating Indians, who were encouraged to accept the protection of the aldeias. Thus, the early period of Sá's long rule was the golden age of the aldeias. These now expanded from two or three to no less than eleven by 1561, with a total population of 34,000 at the beginning of 1562.[15]

Two developments brought this expansion to a halt. First, in 1562

[15] Alexander Marchant, *From barter to slavery* (Baltimore, 1942), 108.

Mem de Sá declared a 'just war' against the Caeté who had martyred bishop Sardinha six years before, declaring open season on that entire Indian nation. As retribution for the bishop's death this came a bit late; more likely this Caeté 'law' was conceived to placate colonists angered by the growth of the Jesuit aldeias which removed so many Indians from the slave pool. Unfortunately, the Caeté war overflowed even the lax conditions imposed by Sá; Caetés were not only seized *in situ*, but also in the Jesuit aldeias which they had earlier entered confident of Jesuit promises of protection. The effect on the aldeias was disastrous and Sá quickly revoked his 'law', but it was too late; the damage had been done.

On the heels of this uncontrollable war came another crisis to flagellate the colony: disease. It arrived in two waves: the first came in 1562 and struck the Indians in the area around Bahia; the second, in 1563, was more widespread. Together they may have carried off from one-third to one-half of the Indian population which, of course, lacked all immunity to European diseases, such as tuberculosis, influenza, smallpox and measles, brought by the Portuguese and others. The resulting decline in the Indian population not only reduced the number of aldeias from eleven to five, but significantly intensified the settlers' competition for the labour of those who survived.

One consequence was the transfer of physical control over the remaining aldeias to 'lay captains' for the next few years (*c.* 1564–*c.* 1572). This change was favoured by the General of the Jesuit Order in Rome who had never cared for the deep Jesuit involvement in the day-to-day administration of the aldeias. In practical terms, the result was to create a type of *repartimiento* of Indian labour (earlier rejected by Nóbrega) in order to ration their services among Portuguese claimants. At the same time the famine that followed the plague prompted many Indians to sell themselves or their relatives to the settlers for food or maintenance. These developments forced the crown and the Jesuits to focus their attention on fundamental questions about the Indian population in colonial Brazil. Many ambiguous questions left unanswered for years now came to the fore: under exactly what condition could Indians be 'justly' enslaved, if they could be enslaved at all? How were runaway Indians (both from aldeias as well as from sugar mills) to be treated? Could Indians legally sell themselves or their relatives into slavery?

The debate may be said to have begun in 1566 with the Junta charged by the king to make recommendations about Indian policy in Brazil. Mem de Sá, bishop Leitão, the Jesuits Grã and Azevedo as well as the crown judges (*ouvidores mores*) participated.[16] On the basis of recommendations hammered out by this Junta, King Sebastião (1554–78) enacted a law in 1570 on the status of the Indians. Born free, they could, nonetheless, be enslaved in two situations: (1) in the course of a 'just war' declared by the king or his governor; (2) if caught practising cannibalism. The system of *resgate* – the early practise of rescuing or ransoming Indians taken as captives in inter-tribal wars and about to be killed and forcing upon them in return a lifetime of servitude to the ransomer – was declared illegal. It had been widely abused: tribes were incited to fight one another for captives and soon any Indian seized and enslaved by the Portuguese was nominally 'ransomed'. Though King Sebastião's law could be, and was, interpreted very liberally, the settlers still sent violent protests to Lisbon, as the Peruvians had done after the New Laws of 1542. The law of 1570 was therefore revoked and replaced in 1574 by a modified code of Indian enslavement. Resgates were again permitted, but all Indians so enslaved had to be registered with the *alfândega* (custom house).

However, the final achievement of a *modus vivendi* with the Indian population came not so much from laws issued in Lisbon as from changes and developments in colonial society itself. Of these the most important was the increasing number of black slaves imported from Africa. When the first African slaves arrived in Brazil is unknown; a few were probably brought over by settlers in the early donatarial period. By the early 1540s it is clear that there were sizeable groups of them. In 1570 an early historian of Brazil, Magalhães de Gândavo, estimated that there were between 2,000 and 3,000 blacks in Brazil; seventeen years later, José de Anchieta put their number at 14,000. Though, on certain estates, Indian slaves still outnumbered Africans at the end of the century, the growing reliance on black slaves – about whom there were few if any moral qualms and no royal legislation – defused to a large degree the issue of Indian slavery. On the other hand, the years of attack on Tupi society by the Jesuits, the governors and the settlers had left their mark; traditional Indian culture was disintegrating in the settled areas of the coast. The remnants either blended into a new proletariat of *mameluco* half-breeds or else fled to

---

[16] Nóbrega would have participated, but was then in São Vicente. He later expressed his written opinion in an *Apontamento*: Leite, *Nóvas páginas*, 120.

the interior, the only place in which they might hope to preserve their cultural identity. Distance did not, however, provide absolute security. By the end of the century, the earlier occasional *entradas* into the interior gradually took on the character of the organized slaving expeditions (*bandeiras*) that were to develop into one of the dominant themes of Brazilian history in the next century. With increasing frequency governors declared 'just wars' on Indians of the *sertão*, or backlands, and issued licences for resgates, as Father Vicente do Salvador graphically describes in his account of the governorship of Luís de Brito (1572–8):

...the governor gave the settlers the licences they requested to send *mamelucos* to the interior (*sertão*) to bring back Indians. [The slavers] did not go so confident of their eloquence that they neglected to take along many white and friendly Indian soldiers, with bows and arrows, whom they used to bring back the Indians by force if they did not come willingly and peaceably. But in most cases the word of the *mamelucos* who told them of the abundance of fish and shellfish that they lacked in the interior, and the freedom they would enjoy if they did not resist, was sufficient. With these tricks and some gifts of clothes and tools to the chiefs (*principais*) or articles of barter (*resgates*) that they gave to those who held Indians enslaved and about to be eaten, they wiped out whole villages. When they got within sight of the coast, they separated sons from fathers, brothers from sisters and even, at times, wives from husbands, some going to the *mameluco* captains, some to the outfitters, others to those who sought the licences, or to those who granted them, and all made use of them on their plantations, or else sold them, with the declaration, however, that they were Indians 'of conscience' and that they were only selling their services. But the purchasers branded them on the face for the first fault committed or attempted escape, saying that they had bought them and they were their captives. Preachers banged their pulpits over the matter, but they were preaching in the desert.[17]

In short, epidemic disease, enslavement and religious proselytization by the well-meaning Jesuits effectively shattered the defeated Indian culture and societies, leaving the survivors to be re-integrated into a colonial society structured on Portuguese terms.

The French, the other threat to Portuguese permanence in Brazil, presented none of the religious and moral complications associated with the Indians. Though French attacks on Portuguese shipping continued after 1535 (as the creation of a captain-major for the coast in 1548 indicates) the donatary captaincies did effectively prevent French

[17] Salvador, *História do Brasil*, 180–1.

attempts at colonization in areas settled by the Portuguese. Nevertheless, the French had not abandoned the idea of founding a colony, and their attention was increasingly drawn to one extraordinarily attractive site (long important in the dyewood trade) at the northern edge of the captaincy of São Vicente that had never been occupied by the Portuguese: Rio de Janeiro.

It was here that Nicolas Durand, chevalier de Villegagnon, decided to locate his colony of *France Antarctique*. Growing religious strife in France had by 1550 produced groups (as later in England) who saw the New World as the perfect location for a new commonwealth, based on 'right' religion and free from the corrupt entanglements of European society. For an ambitious entrepreneur like Villegagnon, born to a bourgeois family but risen to be vice-admiral of Brittany, these religious dissenters formed a heaven-sent nucleus of willing immigrants for his purpose. He presented his plan to Admiral Coligny, a member of the high nobility who had gone over to the Reformed Church, and the latter in turn solicited the support of the king, Henry II. With additional backing from Norman and Breton merchants who had long been trading in Brazilian dyewood, Villegagnon and company set off in 1555 on three ships carrying some 600 persons for *la France Antarctique*. Though Villegagnon gave the impression of having Protestant leanings while attempting to recruit his colonists, he was compelled to accept Catholics as well as Huguenots to complete his expedition and some ex-convicts as well. After a difficult voyage, the little group reached Guanabara Bay where it finally built a fort and small settlement on Serigipe Island. The local Indians proved friendly, due to the Frenchmen's indulgent treatment and lack of demands, but Villegagnon's strict rule created discontent among the colonists, many of whom deserted to the mainland where they founded Henryville on the site of present-day Rio de Janeiro. His position precarious and in danger of Portuguese attack, Villegagnon solicited a second levy of immigrants from Calvin in Geneva, among them Jean de Léry who has left us one of the best accounts of the colony as well as of Tupi culture in general. These new arrivals were the seeds of the settlement's final destruction. Straight from Geneva, dogmatic, rigid and imbued with Calvin's steely will, they soon propelled the group into theological disputes that came to focus on the nature of the Eucharist: for Léry and his co-religionists, the Catholics' adherence to transubstantiation in the midst of a society of savage cannibals was too much to swallow. Angered by the disruptive activities of the Calvinists whose resistance he was unable to break,

Villegagnon suddenly reverted to an orthodox Catholicism, abandoned the colony and sailed back to France in 1559, where he finished his days as a member of the ultra-Catholic party of the Guises.

Antarctic France presented Portuguese Brazil with a serious threat, a base from which the French could support Indian opponents, expand their control down to the Río de la Plata and possibly raid Portuguese shipping lanes to India. To counter this threat governor Mem de Sá, as soon as he had re-established order around Bahia, turned his attention to Rio. Receiving naval aid from Portugal he gathered together a force of Indian allies and departed for Guanabara Bay early in 1560. The island fortress was taken by assault and the surviving French forced to flee for shelter to the Indian villages about the bay. But Sá lacked the personnel and material necessary to rebuild and occupy the fort, so it was abandoned, much to the concern of Nóbrega who sensed the importance of a permanent Portuguese presence there. As he feared, once the Portuguese left, the French survivors re-established themselves on various islands in the bay and a second expedition was required to dislodge them.

This second attack was led by Estácio de Sá, Mem de Sá's nephew, who arrived in Bahia in 1563 at the head of another fleet sent out from Portugal. Gathering together local reinforcements from Espírito Santo as well as São Vicente, Estácio sailed to Rio in 1565 where he first established a military base – the germ of the future city of Rio de Janeiro – at the foot of Sugarloaf Mountain. His position was strong enough to repel French attempts to dislodge him, but insufficient to take the offensive until additional reinforcements from Lisbon arrived under the command of Christóvão de Barros, the son of António Cardoso de Barros, donatary of the abandoned captaincy of Piauí and subsequently first *provedor-mor* of the crown in Brazil. As soon as Barros arrived, Estácio attacked the French on the west side of the bay (now Praia do Flamengo) with complete success. Sá was wounded in battle and died a few days later, but his uncle Mem de Sá now took the time to establish a permanent Portuguese settlement on the site of present-day Rio. Town officials were appointed, the bay and surrounding region separated from São Vicente and the area converted into the second royal captaincy in Brazil. With the appointment of Salvador Corréia de Sá, another nephew of Mem de Sá, as royal governor, there began the long and intimate association between Rio and the Sá family that was to last throughout most of the colonial period.

SOCIETY AND ECONOMY C. 1580

The end of Mem de Sá's heroic governorship (1572) brought Brazil's years of uncertainty to a close. Having survived two challenges to its continued existence – internally from native Indian resistance and externally from the threat of French conquest – Portugal's American 'conquest' had emerged intact from its precarious infancy. While neither problem completely disappeared (the French still attempted from time to time to establish colonies in sparsely settled areas and Indian resistance merely shifted to the interior), still, after 1580, neither was ever again strong enough to call into question the existence of a Portuguese Brazil.

Freed from these preoccupations the colony entered its first major economic 'cycle', based on the expanding sugar industry with its attendant population growth as well as social and administrative development. This shift from a concern with survival to concentration on consolidation and growth is clearly reflected in the historical sources. The first 70 years of Brazilian history provide little data that can be interpreted statistically. Rather, the story depends on a precise narration of events, descriptions of the institutions created and inferences regarding royal policy. But from 1570 on, our knowledge of the colony is greatly enriched by the appearance of a series of descriptive treatises written principally to excite interest in settling the new land. Used with caution and a tolerance for the inexactitude with which they were composed, they not only offer us our best information on the vicissitudes of the early settlements but also provide significant statistical information: i.e., rough estimates, captaincy by captaincy, of the Portuguese population plus occasional, less exact, estimates of Indians and Africans; and approximate figures for the number of *engenhos* (sugar mills) in each captaincy (see Table 1).[18] A rapid glance at the population figures indicates that of the eight settled captaincies, three – Pernambuco, Bahia and Rio de Janeiro – were growing, while the rest were in various stages of decline – Porto Seguro, Itamaracá and São Vicente rather rapidly; Ilhéus and Espírito Santo more gradually. The remaining captaincies had effectively been abandoned. How had these varying fortunes come about?

[18] Whilst, strictly speaking, the word *engenho* referred only to the mill for grinding the sugar cane, the term came to be applied to the whole economic unit: the mill itself, the associated buildings, the cane fields, pastures, slave quarters, estate house, etc. The term 'plantation' was never used by the Portuguese or Spaniards of this period.

Table 1 *Colonial Brazil: White Population and Engenhos, 1570 and c. 1585*

Captaincy (main towns)	1570 white population*	engenhos	c. 1585 white population*	engenhos
Itamaracá (Conceição)	600 (2.9%)	1 (1.7%)	300 (1.0%)	3 (2.5%)
Pernambuco (Olinda, Igaraçú)	6,000 (28.9%)	23 (38.3%)	12,000 (41.0%)	66 (55.0%)
Bahia (Salvador, Vila Velha)	6,600 (31.8%)	18 (30.0%)	12,000 (41.0%)	36 (30.0%)
Ilhéus (São Jorge)	1,200 (5.8%)	8 (13.3%)	900 (3.0%)	3 (2.5%)
Porto Seguro (P. Seguro, Santa Cruz, Santo Amaro)	1,320 (6.4%)	5 (8.3%)	600 (2.0%)	1 (1.0%)
Espírito Santo (Vitória, Vila Velha)	1,200 (5.8%)	1 (1.7%)	900 (3.0%)	5 (4.0%)
Rio de Janeiro (São Sebastião)	840 (4.0%)	0 —	900 (3.0%)	3 (2.5%)
São Vicente (São Vicente, Santos, Santo Amaro, Itanháem, São Paulo)	3,000 (14.4%)	4 (6.7%)	1,800 (6.0%)	3 (2.5%)
Totals	20,760 (100)	60 (100)	29,400 (100)	120 (100)

Sources: Pero de Magalhães Gândova, *Tratado da terra do Brasil e história da província de Santo Cruz* (*c.* 1570); Fernão Cardim, *Informação da província do Brasil para nosso padre* (1583); Fernão Cardim, *Narrativa Epistolar* (1583); José de Anchieta, *Informação do Brasil e de suas capitanias* (1584); Gabriel Soares de Sousa, *Tratado descriptivo do Brasil em 1587*.
* Calculated on the basis of six persons per household (*fogo*).

Espírito Santo, granted to Vasco Fernandes Coutinho, an old India hand and comrade of Duarte Coelho, had prospered in the beginning and some four sugar mills were in operation by 1540. But at this point, for reasons not entirely clear, the donatary decided to return to Portugal, leaving his colony in charge of subordinates who proved unable to hold out against the wave of Indian attacks that struck in the mid-1540s (native Tupi allied to the fierce Tapuia Goiticazes who had already wiped out São Tomé). When he finally managed to return, Coutinho found little more than one small surviving settlement in a state of constant siege. Old, ill and now impoverished, he was incapable of remedying the situation. The colony led a bare existence until 1560 when Mem de Sá, the new governor, decided to send his son, Fernão, with six ships and 200 men to subdue the Indians and incorporate the captaincy into the crown. Fernão lost his life in the struggle, but his cousin, Baltasar de Sá, continued the campaign and pacified the region. Although the colony never seemed able to attract many settlers (indeed its population declined some 25 per cent between 1570 and 1585), its sugar industry was expanding rapidly and by the 1580s the settlers who remained enjoyed one of the highest per capita incomes in Brazil.

Immediately to the north, the captaincy of Porto Seguro, granted to Pero do Campo Tourinho, an accomplished seamen from Viana do Castelo, had begun in a promising fashion. Nonetheless, it too succumbed to the general crisis of the 1540s which took the form here of a 'palace coup' over the question of the donatary's orthodoxy. Unpopular among the settlers, Tourinho was accused of heresy and blasphemy by a cabal of clerics and was soon hustled off to Lisbon (1546) to stand trial before the Inquisition. Though absolved, he never returned to Brazil. His colony was thenceforth administered by royal agents. After his death in 1556, it passed to his son Fernão, and then to his daughter, Leonor. She was granted a royal licence to sell it to the first duke of Aveiro who already had a sugar mill there; he converted it into an entail for the second sons of his house. In the process of further developing the sugar industry, however, Aveiro's agents exterminated or drove out most of the native Tupi, thus exposing the area to the incursions of the far more fearsome Tapuia Aimorés. They so terrorized the colony that only one mill was left standing by 1585 and two (Santo Amaro and Santa Cruz) of the three towns that had been established were virtually emptied of settlers.

Located between Porto Seguro and Bahia, Ilhéus also had an auspicious beginning, though the donatary, Jorge de Figueiredo Correia, secretary of the Treasury (*escrivão da fazenda*) never bothered to visit his grant in person. Rather he ran it through a Castilian agent, Francisco Romero. Although not above criticism, Romero did establish effective relations with the Tupi and even secured their aid in the construction of a number of sugar mills. After Correia's death in 1552, his heirs sold the captaincy (1561) to a merchant capitalist of Lisbon, Lucas Giraldi, who already possessed a land grant (*sesmaria*) in the colony. In spite of a sequence of events similar to that of neighbouring Porto Seguro (destruction of the Tupi tribes opening the way to attacks by the Aimoré who drove out many of the settlers), the sugar industry managed to survive on the offshore islands of Tinharé and Boipeba at the northern edge of the colony. Thus, in 1587 Gabriel Soares de Sousa could still call it a land 'rich in sugar'.

At the southern extremity of effective Portuguese settlement (the captaincy of Santana having gone unoccupied), São Vicente, along with its enclave of Santo Amaro, rode out the crisis of the mid 1540s virtually unscathed. Though it was never revisited by its captain, Martim Afonso de Sousa, after his epoch-making expedition of 1530–3, the colony made good progress under the administration of a sequence of capable lieutenants, including Brás Cubas, the founder of Santos (1543). In 1548 Luís de Góis was able to describe it to the king with pride, mentioning a population of 600 Portuguese, some 3,000 slaves and six sugar mills. From then on, however, expansion slowed down. São Vicente was farthest of all the settlements from Europe and was located in a harsher climate less suited to sugar cultivation. As a result its economy came to be increasingly oriented towards the interior settlement of São Paulo, the centre of a territory of wheat, barley and vineyards that soon became the principal base for slaving expeditions into the interior. The resulting decline in the export sector and contraction of the economy, plus a tendency towards quasi-subsistence agriculture produced an accompanying decline in both population and wealth. Beginning to be overshadowed by Pernambuco as well as the revitalized Bahia, its earlier success was still apparent in 1570. Fifteen years later, however, its population had dropped almost by half and its revenue value to the crown was no more than that of the fledgling colony of Rio de Janeiro, which after the expulsion of the French in 1565, blossomed under royal solicitude and a series of capable royal captains from the Sá family.

In contrast to these areas of settlement which, apart from Rio de Janeiro, were either declining or barely holding their own, the last quarter of the century was for Bahia and Pernambuco a period of unqualified success: these captaincies were to become the focal points of Brazil in the next century.

Bahia was settled in 1535 by Francisco Pereira Coutinho, an old warrior from the Orient where he had served as captain of Goa. The Bay of All Saints was already the home of Caramurú, a Portuguese castaway who, along with several others, had found a ready welcome among the uxorilocal Tupi of the coast. Thus Coutinho had expert assistance, at least in the beginning, in establishing good relations with the Indians of the region. The next year (1536) he was at work constructing his capital of Vila Pereira and by 1545 had managed to build two sugar mills (*engenhos*). Nonetheless, his northern neighbour, Duarte Coelho, described him as too old and ill to maintain the discipline necessary for an effective colony. And when the crisis of the mid 1540s struck Bahia, the colony succumbed; many of the settlers fled to Ilhéus in 1545. Coutinho joined them, only to be lured back to Bahia by the Indians and treacherously killed in 1547. The collapse of Bahia, exposing an important anchorage to French attack, was one of the most important reasons why it was decided to establish a royal administration there. And after 1549, Bahia's history becomes, in effect, that of the royal administration in Brazil. With royal support and organization, Bahia was rebuilt; by 1585 it had sufficient population (12,000 whites) to support nine parishes and 36 sugar mills.

Even more impressive than the resurrected Bahia was Pernambuco. Along with its satellite colony of Itamaracá, it marked the northern limit of effective Portuguese settlement before 1580. (Paraíba was not occupied until the 1580s, Río Grande do Norte in the 1590s: the northern coast remained to be conquered early in the seventeenth century.) Arriving in Pernambuco in person in March of 1535 with a host of followers, Duarte Coelho optimistically dubbed his grant 'New Lusitania' and built his first settlement near the site of the earlier royal factory. Subsequently Coelho scouted his territory for a more central location which he found at Olinda in 1537. There he constructed a tower for defence in case of siege, along with other essential buildings, and then made a tour (almost a royal 'progress') through his captaincy to expel any French interlopers he might find and to pacify the Caeté Indians of the area. His policy towards the Indians was a firm one, and he controlled them, as Vicente do Salvador put it, echoing Machiavelli, 'more through fear than good will'. What made this policy work, one suspects, was his equally firm control of the Portuguese colonists, the other facet of his outstandingly successful policy. The crisis of the mid-1540s did not damage Pernambuco, and this was crucial for its survival and prosperity. By 1546 five sugar mills had been built (compared to two in Bahia and six in São Vicente by that time) and more were under construction. When Coelho died in 1554, he bequeathed his two sons the best established colony in Brazil – so well established, in fact, that it was exempted from interference by the royal governor who had recently arrived in Bahia. In 1570 Pernambuco rivalled Bahia as the leading settlement; by 1585 it had clearly moved ahead, at least economically, with a per capita income almost double that of the governor's seat. Indeed the opulence of Pernambuco society was legend: when the lords of the sugar mills (*senhores do engenho*) came to town they were surrounded by a multitude of retainers, both Indian and African. They dined on foodstuffs imported from Portugal (wheat bread, olive oil and wine) instead of the native diet of manioc flour, palm oil and rum that was the lot of the ordinary settler, and they prided themselves on the conspicuous consumption, not to mention gaudy dress, of their women. It was, in fact, the possibility (or at least the belief in the possibility) of attaining a like opulence that constituted one of the main attractions for most of the immigrants who arrived during the last quarter of the century.

The majority of those immigrants were naturally Portuguese, but other Europeans, mainly Italian, could also be found in Brazil. And in contrast to the fifteenth century, when the Atlantic islands seem to have drawn the bulk of their population from the southern province of the Algarve, the majority of Portuguese emigrants to Brazil in the sixteenth century came from the populous northern province of the Minho as well as from the hinterland of Lisbon, which had by now supplanted the Algarve as the hub of the empire.[19] These immigrants joined some sixteen or seventeen fledgling settlements scattered along the vast eastern coast of Brazil (São Paulo alone was situated inland). Each captaincy had at least one main town and some also included several satellite communities, though in the declining captaincies these were shrinking (e.g., Santa Cruz and Santo Amaro in Porto Seguro). Most of these towns had been set up by the first donatary, as provided in his charter. He granted town lots to each settler with land to cultivate (*sesmarias*) in the surrounding territory (*termino*) – a replica of the system used to populate the reconquered areas of southern Portugal in the later Middle Ages. The captain usually had the power to nominate the members of the town council, at least in the beginning. Thereafter, according to the royal Ordinances, the councillors (in form at least) were

[19] Orlando Ribeiro, *Aspectos e problemas da expansão Portuguesa* (Lisbon, 1955), 24–7.

to be elected by the propertied citizenry (*vizinhos*), though the captain's right to supervise the process probably meant that his influence still predominated. In the crown captaincies (Bahia, Rio de Janeiro) municipal officers were almost always direct royal appointments.

Each colonial town drew most of its food as well as domestic labour from the surrounding pacified and (at least superficially) Christianized Indian villages (*aldeias*) whose existence was carefully noted by most of the writers as one of the captaincy's main forms of wealth. Colonists who did not live permanently in the towns were to be found on the sugar estates, small communities in themselves, where the lord (*senhor*) of the 'mill' (*engenho*) was surrounded by and ruled over his workers, free and slave, Indians and blacks who were being imported in increasing numbers from Africa. As the productive centres of the colony these estates were more significant than the towns and tended to overshadow them. It is revealing for example that clerics attached to the chapel of an estate were invariably better paid than those serving the town churches. Indeed, the growth in the number of sugar estates in a captaincy is probably a better indication of its 'success' than a growing population in the towns, for without the engenhos there would be little reason for the settlers to come or stay.

From 1570 to 1585 the white population grew from approximately 20,760 to some 29,400 (see Table 1), or at a rate of roughly 2.7 per cent a year. During the same period the number of engenhos doubled, from 60 to 120, thus increasing at a rate of 6.6 per cent per year.

Thus began the late sixteenth-century sugar boom and the rapid growth in per capita income of whites in Brazil. The principal source of revenue to the crown, the royal tithes, a 10 per cent levy on whatever the land produced – sugar, manioc, bananas, potatoes, sheep, goats, pigs, chickens, etc. – and theoretically (but not always in practice) intended for the support of the church, enables us (1) to estimate the gross product (minus services) of the Christianized (or colonial) economy, in addition to (2) the per capital income of the colonial population, captaincy by captaincy, as well as (3) of Brazil as a whole. Table 2, based on the royal tithe of 1593, indicates the gross product captaincy by captaincy, and Table 3 the average (white) per capita income (in milreis) by captaincy (except for Itamaracá, for which the data is inadequate).

These figures confirm all contemporary accounts of the colony which describe Pernambuco as by far the richest of the captaincies while

Table 2 *Colonial Brazil: Gross Product, 1593**
(in milréis)

Itamaracá	10,600$000	5%
Pernambuco	116,000$000	56%
Bahia	56,000$000	27%
Illhéus	6,670$000	3.2%
Porto Seguro	1,800$000	<1%
Espírito Santo	6,000$000	2.9%
Rio de Janeiro	5,000$000	2.4%
São Vicente	5,000$000	2.4%
Paraiba	1,400$000	<1%
Total	208,470$000	100

* Calculated on the basis of royal tithes from the production (services omitted) of the
'Christian' sector of the economy.
Source: Francisco Carneiro, 'Relação de todas as rendas da coroa deste reyno de Portugal
que nelle se arracadão de que procedem, modo, e lugar em que se pagão', ed. Francisco
Mendes da Luz, *Boletim da Biblioteca da Universidade de Coimbra* (1949), 101–2.

Table 3 *Colonial Brazil: Average (white) per capita income in 1593*
(in milréis)

1. Pernambuco	9$660
2. Ilhéus	7$410
3. Espírito Santo	6$660
4. Rio de Janeiro	5$550
5. Bahia	4$660
6. Porto Seguro	3$000
7. São Vicente	2$770
Average	6$750

Source: see Table 2.

putting São Vicente logically last due to the low average income of the
population in the inland settlement of São Paulo. At the top end of the
scale, Mem de Sá's yearly salary as governor from 1557–72 was 600$000
and Fernão Cardim reported that 'more than 100' sugar-mill owners
in Pernambuco had incomes of some 2,000$000 per year.

In contrast to the rapid growth in real income experienced by many
of the settlers in the last quarter of the sixteenth century, the Portuguese
crown seems to have shared far less in Brazil's development. Using data

on royal income assembled by the historian Vitorino Magalhães Godinho, it is possible to estimate that Brazil, as a whole, provided some 1 per cent of the crown's income near the beginning of the century (1506), compared to some 27 per cent coming from India at the same time. Eighty-two years later, in 1588, Brazil still accounted for no more than 2.35–2.5 per cent of the crown revenues, while India was still furnishing about 26 per cent.[20] If the cost of maintaining control over the Brazilian coast, as well as the expenditures necessary to reduce the Indians to submission and drive out the French, are taken into account, there must have been a deficit for long periods of time.

Thus, it is difficult to accept purely economic explanations either for the crown's tenacious commitment to Brazil during the sixteenth century or for its progression through four stages of ever-increasing involvement: from leasing out the land (1502–5), to exploiting it directly through royal trading factories (1506–34), to granting it out to proprietary lords for settlement (1534), finally culminating in the creation of a fully-fledged royal administration (1549). Instead, these stages are more convincingly seen as so many necessary responses to perceived threats of territorial loss. Once Brazil had been incorporated into the Portuguese crown, it was not easily abandoned, however great the burden. The royal attitude was well summed up by João de Barros, historian of empire and donatary of Maranhão, in his *Decadas*,

...for a prince who prides himself on leaving a reputation of having done glorious deeds, nothing, not even increasing the revenues of his kingdom nor constructing great and magnificent buildings, can be compared to augmenting the Crown of his kingdom or adding some new title to his Estate.[21]

Fundamentally seigneurial in its attitudes, the Portuguese crown found its Brazilian rewards, at least in the sixteenth century, not in the economic realm but rather in that of status and prestige. Indeed, considering Portugal's record over the entire period, what strikes the historian is not any 'neglect' of Brazil with which it has so often been charged, but rather the tenacity with which this small European country held on to its possession in the New World whose ultimate value was so largely unknown, when its main colonial effort was being made in India and the Far East.

[20] V. M. Godinho, *Ensáios II* (Lisbon, 1958), 57, 65–7. In 1593, Francisco Carneiro calculated that Brazil contributed some 3.3 per cent of crown revenue (F. Carneiro, 'Relação de todas as rendas da coroa deste reyno de Portugal que nelle se arracadão de que procedem, modo, e lugar em que se pagão', ed. F. Mendes da Luz, *Boletim da Biblioteca da Universida de Coimbra* (1949), 53, 101.

[21] João de Barros, *Asia, primeira decada*, ed. António Baião (Coimbra, 1932), 216.

9

SPAIN AND AMERICA IN THE SIXTEENTH AND SEVENTEENTH CENTURIES

The Emperor Charles V adopted as his emblematic device the pillars of Hercules decorated with scrolls bearing the motto: *Plus Ultra*. When the device was first invented in 1516 it was essentially a humanist conceit designed to suggest that there would be no limits to the power and dominions of the young Charles of Ghent; but increasingly, as more and more of the New World was discovered and subjected to his rule, the device acquired a special kind of geographical appropriateness as the symbol of global empire.

Spain's conquest of America created the possibility of the first genuinely world-wide empire in human history, as Hernán Cortés was characteristically quick to perceive when he wrote to Charles from Mexico that it now lay within his power to become 'monarch of the world'. Indeed, for Cortés, impressed by the might of Montezuma, Mexico constituted an empire in itself: 'one might call oneself emperor of this kingdom with no less glory than that of Germany, which, by the Grace of God, Your Sacred Majesty already possesses'.[1] For Charles V and his advisers, however, there could be only one empire in the world, the Holy Roman Empire; and even after Spain and the Empire were separated on the abdication of Charles in 1556, Philip II respected this convention by retaining the style of 'king of Spain and the Indies'. Yet it became increasingly obvious that America had added a new, imperial dimension to the power of the king of Spain. Philip II and his successors might officially be no more than kings of the Indies, but that great chronicler of the New World, Gonzalo Fernández de Oviedo, had

---

[1] 'Hernán Cortés, *Letters from Mexico*, ed. A. R. Pagden (Oxford, 1972), 48 (second letter, 1520).

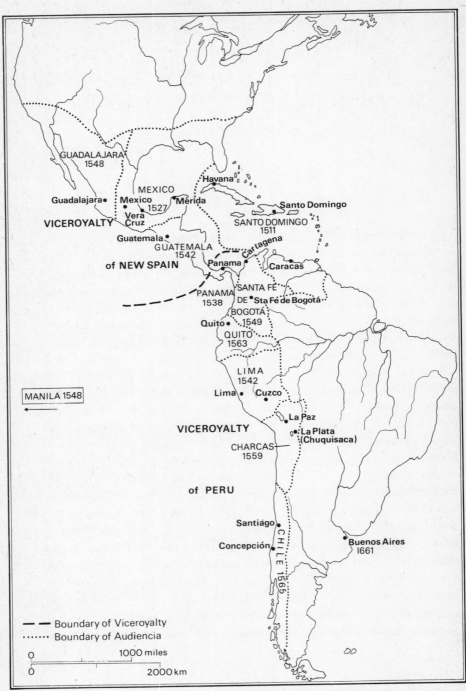

Viceroyalties and audiencias in the sixteenth and seventeenth centuries

Source: Francisco Morales Padrón, *Historia general de América* (2nd edn, Madrid, 1975), 391.

written of 'this occidental empire of these Indies' as early as 1527,[2] and the recurrent appearance, especially in the seventeenth century, of the phrase *imperio de las Indias*, and even of *emperador de las Indias*, testified to an underlying consciousness of American empire.

If the phrase *imperio de las Indias* had difficulty in acquiring wide general acceptance before the coming of the Bourbons, this was partly because the Indies were conceived as forming part of a wider grouping which was known as the Spanish monarchy, the *monarquía española*. In this agglomeration of territories, acquired either by inheritance or by conquest and owing allegiance to a single ruler, most states were equal, but some were more equal than others. Castile came to enjoy an effective predominance in the monarchy, and from the beginning the Indies stood in a special relationship to Castile. Alexander VI's *Inter Caetera* of 1493 vested the government and jurisdiction of the newly found lands, not in the kings of Spain but in the kings of Castile and León. Consequently, the Indies were to be regarded as the possession of Castile and to be governed, where appropriate, in accordance with the laws and institutions of Castile. This implied that the benefits of conquest were to be reserved for Castilians – a convention flouted, when it suited his purposes, by Ferdinand of Aragon, but which gave sixteenth-century Castile an effective monopoly of New World offices and trade. It also meant that the parliamentary and representative institutions which were central to the political life of the crown of Aragon would not be allowed to reproduce themselves in the new American territories.

The intimate association of Castile and the Indies was reflected in the crown's employment of Juan Rodríguez de Fonseca, of the council of Castile, to handle Indies affairs in the first years of discovery and conquest. The rapidly increasing volume of business, however, meant that what originally began as the work of one highly efficient administrator and a small group of assistants would soon have to acquire an institutional form. The pressure was felt first in the organization of the fleets to Hispaniola, and in 1503 the *Casa de la Contratación* – a trading-house comparable to the *Casa da India* in Lisbon – was established in Seville. It was soon responsible for organizing and controlling the passage of men, ships and merchandise between Spain and America. The sweeping regulatory powers conferred by the crown on the officials of the Casa during the next few years established a pattern

[2] *Sumario de la natural historia de las Indias*, ed. José Miranda (Mexico, 1950), 272.

of trade and navigation that was to last for a century and a half, and convert Seville into the commercial centre of the Atlantic world.

By channelling all the American trade into Seville, the crown was seeking to ensure a maximum degree of control over what was expected to be a highly lucrative enterprise, to the benefit of its own finances and of a Castile which claimed monopolistic rights over the newly discovered lands. It was only by the exercise of rigorous control over sailings that undesirable elements could be kept out of America, and the American trade – or so it was hoped – be kept in native hands. Time would show, however, that a controlled trade had a way of producing its own form of uncontrolled infiltration, and that the undoubted organizational advantages of monopoly had to be set against the no less undoubted disadvantages of putting enormous power in the hands of a small group of strategically placed officials.

These officials were concerned essentially with the mechanics of the Indies trade – with the equipping of fleets, the licensing of passengers and the registration of silver. Policy towards the Indies was formulated at a higher level; and here again the growing pressure of business forced institutional developments which replaced the informality of the Fonseca regime with a formal bureaucratic apparatus. In the early years the monarchs would turn for advice on Indies affairs to Fonseca or to a handful of members of the council of Castile; but in 1523 a new council came into being, independent of the council of Castile – the council of the Indies. Given the peculiar structure of the Spanish monarchy this was a logical development. A conciliar organization, with distinctive councils responsible for the distinctive states and provinces of the monarchy, was the best means of combining plural interests with unified central control. Taking its place alongside the councils of Castile and Aragon, the council of the Indies provided the formal machinery for ensuring that the affairs of the Indies were regularly brought to the attention of the monarch, and that the monarch's wishes, embodied in laws, decrees and institutions, were duly transmitted to his American possessions.

Royal government in America was therefore royal government by consultation, in the sense that the king's decisions were reached on the basis of *consultas* – the written records of conciliar debate, issuing in a series of recommendations – which would be sent up to him by his council of the Indies. The councils were nominally attendant on the person of the king and only in 1561 found their permanent home in the royal palace in Madrid, which from that year became the seat of the court and the capital of the Monarchy. Of all the councils, that of the Indies was the one furthest removed in time and space from the area of its jurisdiction, although even this was not far enough for some. According to Sir Francis Bacon, 'Mendoza, that was viceroy of Peru, was wont to say: That the government of Peru was the best place that the King of Spain gave, save that it was somewhat too near Madrid.'[3] Royal officials in the Indies, theoretically at large in the great open spaces of a great New World, in practice found themselves bound by chains of paper to the central government in Spain. Pen, ink and paper were the instruments with which the Spanish crown responded to the unprecedented challenges of distance implicit in the possession of a world-wide empire.

Inevitably this style of government by paper brought forth its own breed of bureaucrat. Of the 249 councillors of the Indies from the time of its foundation until 1700, all but a handful – and these in the seventeenth century rather than the sixteenth – were *letrados*, men trained in the law at the universities, although members of the nobility were strongly represented among the 25 presidents of the council over the same period. Very few of the letrado members of the council seem to have had any American experience – only seven in the best part of 200 years occupied posts in one of the American *audiencias* before promotion to the council.[4] Most of them had spent their careers in judicial or fiscal posts in the peninsula itself, and inevitably they tended to see the problems of the Indies through the prism of their peninsular experience. Their formation and outlook was legalistic; they thought in terms of precedents, of rights and of status; and they saw themselves as the exalted guardians of the king's authority. This made for careful rather than imaginative government, more inclined to regulate than to innovate, although now and again an outstanding president like Juan de Ovando (1571–5) would inject life into a naturally slow-moving system and reveal gifts of creative organization which had an impact thousands of miles away.

Once the objectives of government in the Indies were determined, however, and its structure settled – and this was largely achieved by the middle of the sixteenth century – the sheer problems of distance tended to ensure that routine would prevail. Routine has its own

---

[3] *The works of Francis Bacon*, ed. J. Spedding (London, 1859), VII, 130–1.
[4] See J. L. Phelan, *The kingdom of Quito in the seventeenth century* (Madison, 1967), 135.

defects, but judged by the criterion of its ability to maintain a fair degree of public order and a decent respect for the authority of the crown, Spanish government in sixteenth- and seventeenth-century America must be accounted a remarkable success. After the collapse of the Pizarrist rebellion in the 1540s and a conspiratorial flutter in Mexico City in 1566 around the person of Don Martín Cortés, the son of the conqueror, there would be no further direct challenge to the royal authority by a settler community often bitterly resentful of the mandates of Madrid. This high degree of quiescence is in part a reflection of the sense of deference to the crown inculcated from one generation to the next; but it is primarily to be attributed to the character of a system which was all too successful in its almost obsessive determination to prevent the excessive concentration of power at any single point. There was no need to challenge the royal power directly when an indirect challenge could be successfully mounted by playing on the weaknesses of a system in which power was so carefully dispersed.

The diffusion of authority was based on a distribution of duties which reflected the distinctive manifestations of royal power in the Indies: administrative, military, judicial, financial and religious. But often the lines of demarcation were not clearly drawn: different branches of government would overlap, a single official might combine different types of function, and there were endless possibilities for friction and conflict which was likely to be resolved, if at all, only by the lengthy process of reference to the council of the Indies in Madrid. But these apparent sources of weakness might in some respects be regarded as the best guarantee of the survival of rule from Madrid, since each agent of delegated authority tended to impose a check on the others, while at the same time the king's subjects in the Indies, by playing off one authority against another, were left with adequate room for manoeuvre in the interstices of power.

In the first years of the conquest the principal representatives of the crown in the Indies were the *gobernadores*. The title of governor, usually combined with that of captain-general, was given to a number of the early *conquistadores*, like Vasco Núñez de Balboa, appointed governor of Darien in 1510. The *gobernador*, like the *donatário* in Portugal's overseas territories, was given the right to dispose of Indians and land – clearly a major inducement to undertake further expeditions of conquest. The governorship was therefore an ideal institution for extending Spanish rule through the Indies, particularly in remote and poor regions like Chile, where the rewards of conquest were otherwise exiguous. Since the crown had firmly set itself, however, against the creation of a race of feudal lords in the Indies, the days of the governorship seemed to be numbered. Appointments were made short-term – from three to eight years – and came to be non-hereditary. This principle was firmly established once Columbus' grandson, Luis Colón, was finally induced in 1536 after long and complicated legal proceedings to renounce the family claim to a hereditary governorship, retaining only the purely honorific hereditary title of Admiral.

Governorships, however, did not disappear from the Indies once the conquest was completed. They had proved their usefulness as an institution for administering and defending outlying regions. Instead of being abolished, therefore, they were permitted to survive; but, like other institutions which succeeded in surviving the transitional stage of conquest, they were gradually bureaucratized. The new breed of governors of the post-conquest period were administrators, not *conquistadores*, and they had judicial as well as administrative and military functions. Thirty-five provincial governorships existed at one time or another in the sixteenth and seventeenth centuries – the number was not constant because of mergers and boundary changes. They included among their number Guatemala, Costa Rica, Honduras and Nicaragua in Central America; Cartagena, Antioquia and the New Kingdom of Granada, which was governed from 1604 by the presidents of the audiencia of Santa Fe; Popayan, Chile, Paraguay, from which Río de la Plata was separated in 1617 to form a new governorship; and in New Spain, Yucatán, Nueva Vizcaya and Nuevo León. Hernando de Soto, who died on the banks of the Mississippi in 1542, was joint governor of Cuba and Florida, as also was Pedro Menéndez de Avilés from 1567 to 1573; thereafter Florida became a separate governorship. The Philippine Islands, whose conquest was begun in 1564 by their first governor, Miguel López de Legazpi, also constituted an American governorship, dependent on New Spain.

In spite of the survival of the governorships, the most important administrative unit in the Indies was to be not the governorship but the viceroyalty. Columbus had held the title of viceroy, as had his son Diego Colón; but with Diego it became purely honorific and was lost to the family on the death of his widow. It was in 1535 that the viceroyalty was revived as an effective institution, when New Spain was created a viceroyalty and Don Antonio de Mendoza was appointed its

first viceroy. In 1543 Blasco Núñez Vela was named viceroy of a second
viceroyalty, that of Peru. New Spain and Peru, with their capitals in
Mexico City and Lima, were to be the only American viceroyalties under
the Habsburgs. The Bourbons added two more: the viceroyalty of New
Granada in 1717, with its capital in Santa Fe de Bogotá, and that of
Río de la Plata, with Buenos Aires as its capital, in 1776.

The New Laws of 1542 institutionalized the new viceregal system of
government: 'the kingdoms of Peru and New Spain are to be ruled and
governed by viceroys who represent our royal person'. The viceroy,
therefore, was the king's *alter ego*, holding court in his viceregal palace,
and carrying with him something of the ceremonial aura of kingship.
He combined in his person the attributes of governor and captain-
general, and he was also, in his role as president of the audiencia,
regarded as the principal judicial representative of the crown. The
immense prestige of the post, and the lucrative possibilities that it
appeared to offer, naturally made it highly attractive to the noble houses
of Castile. In practice the crown, always suspicious of the ambitions of
the grandees, tended to reserve it for cadet members of the great families
or for titled nobles of middling rank. Don Antonio de Mendoza, the
first viceroy of New Spain (1535–49) and one of its greatest, was the
sixth of the eight children of the marquis of Mondéjar by his second
marriage and had served at court and on a diplomatic mission to
Hungary before being raised to his New World eminence at the age of
40.

The length of Mendoza's service was exceptional – once the system
was established, a viceroy could reasonably expect a six-year term of
office. But this might not prove to be the end of his viceregal functions
in the Indies. Of the 25 men sent out from Spain to serve as viceroys
of Mexico between 1535 and 1700, nine went on to become viceroys
of Peru. The experience gained by these viceroys in the government
of the Indies should have made their voices immensely valuable in the
highest councils of the monarchy on their return to Spain; but
surprisingly it was not until 1621 that a former viceroy of the Indies,
the marquis of Montesclaros (viceroy of New Spain 1603–6 and of Peru
1606–14) was given a seat in the highest of all councils, the council of
state.

The American viceroyalties, for all their apparent attractiveness, all
too often turned out to be a source of disappointment to their
occupants, ruining their health, or their reputation, or both. The count

of Monterrey, so far from making a fortune, died in office in Peru in 1606 and had to be buried at the king's expense. Don Martín Enríquez de Almansa, viceroy of New Spain from 1568 to 1580, explained for the benefit of his successor that:

although they imagine in Spain that the post of viceroy here is a very easy one, and that there cannot be much to do in these new lands, my own experience and the work I have had to undertake have disabused me of this. You will discover the same, for the viceroy here is responsible for all those duties which are shared out at home among several different people.[5]

One of Enríquez's predecessors, Don Luis de Velasco (1550–64), described his working week. On Mondays and Thursdays the mornings were devoted to receiving delegations of Indians accompanied by their interpreters and to drawing up a list of points to be discussed with the audiencia, which he attended in the afternoon. In the evening, from eight to ten, he despatched government business with his secretary. On Tuesdays and Fridays he attended the discussion of suits in the audiencia in the morning and from one o'clock until three despatched religious business and gave audiences to Spaniards – something he had to be ready to do at any time in the week. He then went on to discuss financial business with the treasury officials. Wednesday mornings were also set aside for hearing Indians and Wednesday evenings to the business of Mexico City.

And all the rest of time is taken up with reading letters from prelates, friars, *alcaldes mayores*, *corregidores*, and other individuals who are in a position to provide information. This is an immense labour, and when ships arrive or leave the work is trebled. And the hardest work of all is to fill the *corregimientos* and *alcaldías mayores*, and to search for the right people for offices, and to put up with the *conquistadores* and their children with all their documents and their demands that they must be saved from starving. There are two hundred posts and two thousand people who want them.[6]

The woes of a viceroy, however, did not finish here. His hands were tied from the beginning by the instructions which he received from the king on appointment, and he was always receiving new orders from Madrid, many of them totally inapplicable to the situation in which he found himself. Don Antonio de Mendoza wrote in despair that in his fifteen years as viceroy of New Spain there had been three major changes in the system of government, and that the members of the council of

[5] *Los virreyes españoles en América durante el gobierno de la Casa de Austria*, ed. Lewis Hanke (Biblioteca de Autores Españoles, CCLXXIII, Madrid, 1976), I, 203. [6] *Ibid.*, 128–9.

the Indies were like doctors who assumed that they were not curing the patient unless they were always bleeding and purging him.[7]

Mendoza and his successors found themselves hemmed in at every point by the vast and growing body of laws and decrees relating to the Indies. These came in varying types and possessed varying degrees of solemnity. The weightiest of all orders from the crown was the *provisión*, which bore the king's name and titles, and was sealed with the chancellery seal. The provisión was in effect a general law relating to matters of justice or government – the New Laws, containing 54 articles relating to the organization of government and to the treatment of the Indians, were in fact provisiones. The document more commonly used was the *real cédula*, starting with the simple words *El Rey* followed by the name of the recipient. It communicated in the form of an order a royal decision based on a recommendation of the council of the Indies, and was signed *Yo el Rey*. In addition to the provisión and the cédula, there was also the *auto*, not directed to any recipient, but embodying the decisions of the council of the Indies or the audiencias.

Already by the late sixteenth century there was an enormous corpus of laws and provisions relating to the Indies. In 1596 Diego de Encinas published a compilation of some 3,500 of them, but the need for a proper codification was becoming increasingly obvious. Juan de Solórzano Pereira, a distinguished jurist on the council of the Indies, did the fundamental work in the 1630s, but it was not until 1681 that the great four-volume *Recopilación de las Leyes de Indias* finally appeared in print. The laws printed in these tomes were more reliable as a guide to the intentions of the crown in Madrid than as an indication of what actually happened in America; but the very fact of their existence was bound to enter the calculations of the governors and the governed alike as they went about their daily life in the Indies. Every viceroy knew that his enemies would seek to use non-compliance with some law or royal order as a charge against him. He knew, too, that his every action was scrutinized by the official guardians of the law, the *oidores*, or judges, of the audiencia.

During the sixteenth century ten audiencias were set up in the New World. In the Viceroyalty of New Spain: Santo Domingo (1511); Mexico (1527); Guatemala (1543); Guadalajara (1548). In the Viceroyalty of Peru: Panama (1538); Lima (1543); Santa Fe de Bogotá (1548); Charcas (1559); Quito (1563); Chile (1563–73; refounded 1606).

[7] *Ibid.*, 58.

Between them, these audiencias accounted for some 90 posts at the level of president, *oidor* and *fiscal*. The thousand men who occupied them during the two centuries of Habsburg rule constituted the elite of Spain's American bureaucracy. Viceroys came and went, while there was no fixed limit on the tenure of the oidores, who consequently provided an important element of administrative as well as judicial continuity. While the audiencias were intended to be the supreme judicial tribunals in the New World, seeing to the proper observance of the laws of the Indies, they also acquired certain attributes of government, especially by virtue of the New Laws. In particular, the audiencias of Mexico and Lima assumed the functions of government in the interim between the departure of one viceroy and the arrival of the next, while the presidents of lesser audiencias might act as governors and captains-general of the area of their audiencia's jurisdiction. Their governmental duties, either in a direct or an advisory capacity, gave the audiencias of the New World an extra degree of influence which was not enjoyed by their originals in the Iberian peninsula, where the chancelleries were confined to purely judicial functions. Enjoying direct communication with the council of the Indies, where they could count on a sympathetic hearing from their fellow-letrados, the oidores were well placed to bring viceroyal irregularities to the attention of the king.

The oidores, however, like the viceroys, were carefully held in check by a crown congenitally suspicious of its own appointed officials. There were strict regulations governing their style of life, and everything possible was done to preserve them from contamination by their environment. They were not supposed to marry a woman from the area of jurisdiction of their audiencia, nor to acquire landed property or engage in trade. This attempt to turn them into Platonic guardians, judging and governing without the distraction of local ties and pressures, was inevitably doomed to failure, not least because their salaries were so often inadequate. But the crown, if it set an impossibly high ideal, showed no serious expectation that the ideal would be realized. On the contrary, it acted on the assumption that human failing was endemic and legislated against this unfortunate state of affairs by ensuring that the activities of the oidores, like those of all its officials, should be subjected to careful scrutiny. Independent judges were sent out to conduct *visitas*, or visitations of inquiry, into given areas or into the activities of a given set of officials, while every official was subject to a *residencia* at the end of his term of office, which would allow aggrieved parties to bring charges and state their case before the presiding judge.

Viceroys, governors and audiencias formed the upper level of secular administration in the Indies. The areas of jurisdiction over which they ruled were subdivided into smaller units, which went under different names. In New Spain they were known either as *alcaldías mayores* or *corregimientos*, and in the rest of the Indies as *corregimientos*. Some of the more important *alcaldes mayores* and *corregidores* were appointed by the crown, the lesser ones by the viceroys. They were appointed for a limited term of office, and the more important ones at least were not supposed to be local landowners or *encomenderos*. Their area of jurisdiction was based on a city or town, but extended – as it did in Castile itself – into the surrounding countryside, so that corregimientos were essentially large districts with an urban centre.

The emphasis of local government on the town was characteristic of life in the Indies as a whole. From the standpoint of the law, even those Spanish settlers in the Indies who lived in the countryside existed only in relation to their urban community. They were *vecinos* (citizens) of the nearest urban settlement, and it was the town which defined their relationship to the state. This was very much in line with the traditions of the Mediterranean world; and, in spite of the growing importance of the large estate in Spanish America, rural settlements never quite attained the importance they enjoyed in Brazil, although here too the cities enjoyed the preponderant influence.

Each town had its town council, or *cabildo*, a corporation which regulated the life of the inhabitants and exercised supervision over the properties in public ownership – the communal lands, woods and pastures and the street colonnades with their market stalls – from which much of its income derived. There were great variations in the composition and powers of the cabildos through the cities and towns of Spanish America, and the institution of the cabildo itself changed over the course of the centuries in response to changing social conditions and to the growing financial distress of the crown. Essentially, however, it was composed of judicial officials (*alcaldes*, who were lay judges, and presided over the cabildo, whenever the corregidor was not present) and *regidores*, town councillors, who were responsible for municipal provisioning and administration and represented the municipality in all those ceremonial functions which occupied such a substantial part of urban life.

The cabildos, as might have been expected from the pattern of municipal government in metropolitan Spain, were, or soon became, self-perpetuating oligarchies of the most substantial citizens. In the early years of the conquest, governors and captains would nominate alcaldes and regidores, some of them for life. Where elections occurred, the right of election tended to be confined to the more prominent citizens; and, as from the days of Philip II the crown increasingly resorted to the sale of public office, so the balance between elected and hereditary office-holders tilted towards the latter, reducing still further any 'popular' element which had originally existed in municipal life. Sometimes a *cabildo abierto* – an open cabildo – was held, which allowed for a wider representation of citizens to discuss matters of urgent concern, but by and large city governments were closed corporations which, by their character, were more representative of the interests of the urban patriciate than of the generality of the citizens.

The desirability of a seat in the cabildo varied greatly, according to the wealth of the town, the powers of its officers and the perquisites to be expected. There must have been many towns like Popayán, one of the most typically 'colonial' towns in present-day Colombia, where for long periods the elective positions were left unfilled. With the governor of Popayán responsible for the principal functions of government, the duties of the cabildo were largely confined to choosing minor municipal officials. The financial benefits of office were limited, and the obligations – largely honorific – could be time-consuming.[8]

A cabildo, however, was not only an institution of local self-government and a corporation in which the rivalries of the principal local families were played out. It also formed part of that larger structure of authority which reached upwards to audiencias, governors and viceroys, and thence to the council of the Indies in Madrid. It was only by operating within this structure and resorting to lobbying and petitioning that the urban patriciates could hope to exercise any influence over governmental action and decree, for no other constitutional outlets were available to them. In 1528 Mexico City unsuccessfully petitioned Charles V for a vote in the Cortes of Castile. Periodic suggestions were made thereafter either for representation of the cities of the Indies in the Castilian Cortes, or for regional meetings in the Indies themselves of representatives of the leading towns. But the

---

[8] See Peter Marzahl, 'Creoles and government: the cabildo of Popayán', *Hispanic American Historical Review*, 54 (1974), 636–56.

sixteenth-century Castilian crown set its face firmly against such dangerous constitutionalist tendencies. America had been conquered and colonized at a time when the thrust in metropolitan Spain was towards the theoretical and practical enhancement of royal sovereignty, and the Indies, as virgin territory, provided opportunities for the assertion of the presence of the state to a degree that was not possible even in Castile, where constitutionalism, however mortally wounded, had not yet expired.

The power of the state was all the greater in the Indies because of the extraordinary concentration of ecclesiastical power in the hands of the crown. This derived originally from precedents already established in the church of Granada, along with the rights accruing to the Castilian crown under the papal bulls conferring upon it the responsibility for the evangelization of the newly discovered lands. By a bull of 1486 the papacy had given the crown the *patronato*, or right to present to all bishoprics and ecclesiastical benefices in the Moorish kingdom of Granada, which was then on the point of reconquest. Although nothing was said in the bulls of 1493 about presentation, the Catholic Kings took Granada as their model; and in 1508 the position was regularized when Ferdinand secured for the rulers of Castile in perpetuity the right to organize the church and present to benefices in their overseas territories. A bull of 1501, amplified by further bulls in 1510 and 1511, had already vested in the crown the tithes collected in the Indies, so that the newly established church was also assured of permanent endowment, raised and managed in conformity with the wishes of the crown.

The effect of the patronato was to give the monarchs of Castile in their government of the Indies a degree of ecclesiastical power for which there was no European precedent outside the kingdom of Granada. It allowed the king to represent himself as the 'vicar of Christ', and to dispose of ecclesiastical affairs in the Indies on his own initiative, without interference from Rome. Indeed, no papal nuncio was allowed to set foot in the Indies or have any direct communication with it; and all documents passing in either direction between Rome and the New World needed the prior approval of the council of the Indies before being allowed to proceed to their destination. The crown's ecclesiastical power in the Indies was, in effect, absolute, with theoretical rights buttressed by a total control of patronage.

The church in the Indies was by nature and origin a missionary or teaching church – a fact which made it natural that the religious orders should take the lead in the work of evangelization. But, as the first pioneering work was accomplished, the mendicants, powerful as they were, found their ascendancy challenged by a secular clergy based in the towns and operating within the framework of a now well-established institutional church. In the later sixteenth century other religious orders were allowed to join the original three orders of Augustinians, Franciscans and Dominicans; and the Jesuits, who founded their Province of Paraguay in 1607, were to play an especially important part in missionary work in the remoter areas and the frontier regions. The frontier mission indeed became one of Spain's most effective colonial institutions along the fringes of empire, whether in Paraguay, the eastern fringe of the Andes, or northern Mexico. But by 1574, when the crown's *ordenanza del patronazgo* set a firm limit on the work of the regular clergy and brought them under episcopal control, it was clear that, at least in the urbanized areas, the heroic missionary age was officially at an end.

The agents used by the crown to bring the missionary church to heel were the bishops, a considerable proportion of whom, especially in the first decades, were themselves drawn from among the regular clergy. The first New World diocese, that of Santo Domingo, was founded in 1504; the first mainland diocese, Sant María de la Antigua of Darien (later transferred to Panama) in 1513. By 1536 there were fourteen dioceses; in 1546 Santo Domingo, Mexico City and Lima were raised to archbishoprics; and by 1620 the total number of archbishoprics and bishoprics in Spanish America was 34. The occupants of these sees were in effect royal functionaries who, in addition to their spiritual duties, exercised an important influence, both direct and indirect, on civil life. The dividing line between church and state in Spanish America was never sharply defined, and clashes between bishops and viceroys were a constant feature of colonial life. It was symptomatic that Juan Pérez de la Serna, archbishop of Mexico from 1613–24, came into conflict first with the marquis of Guadalcázar and then with his successor, the marquis of Gelves – two viceroys who could hardly have been more dissimilar in their temperaments and policies.

The bishops, like the letrados who staffed the audiencias, were metropolitan rather than local in their affiliations, although Philip III (1598–1621) recognized local aspirations to the extent of appointing 31 creoles to American bishoprics. In selecting from among the religious orders he also showed a preference for Augustinians over Franciscans and Dominicans. The latter in particular had been very strongly represented in the sixteenth century – of the 159 occupants of bishoprics in the Indies between 1504 and 1620, 52 were Dominicans.[9] This high proportion of Dominicans, many of them friends or followers of Las Casas, suggests a determination on the part of the sixteenth-century crown to enforce its pro-Indian policies as far as possible against the pressures exercised by encomenderos and settlers. For a time, indeed, the crown appointed bishops as official *protectores* of the Indians – an experiment that proved unsatisfactory because, as Juan de Zumárraga, the first bishop of Mexico, unhappily discovered, the duties of the post were ill-defined and led to endless conflicts of jurisdiction with the civil authorities. But, if it was found necessary to transfer these duties to civil functionaries, the crown remained heavily dependent on the episcopate for supervising both the material wellbeing and the spiritual progress of the Indian community.

In the early years of Spanish rule the bishops had in their hands an important instrument of control, over settlers and Indians alike, in the inquisitorial powers that were vested in them. A number of unfortunate cases, however, raised the whole question of whether the Inquisition, as a device for preventing Judaizing and heresy, was an appropriate means of ensuring the orthodoxy of the Indians; and in 1571 these were finally removed from all inquisitorial jurisdiction and placed under the direct control of the bishops where matters of faith and morals were concerned. At the same time, the Holy Office began establishing its tribunals in the New World – in Lima (1570), Mexico City (1571) and a third in Cartagena in 1610 – to guard the faith and morals of the settler community, whether against corruption by sexual delinquents, or against contamination by the numerous *conversos* who had managed to slip into America and by foreigners peddling their dangerous Lutheran heresies. In due course this New World Inquisition, secretive, arrogant and ruthless, like its Old World original, came into conflict not only with the secular and regular clergy, but also with the episcopate. Here, as elsewhere with the church in America, there were too many competing organizations and interests for it ever to become a monolithic institution.

It is this fragmented character of authority, both in church and state, which is one of the most striking characteristics of Spanish colonial

---

[9] See Enrique Dussel, *Les Evêques hispano-americains* (Wiesbaden, 1970), for a statistical survey of the American bishops in the sixteenth and early seventeenth centuries.

America. Superficially the crown's power was absolute, both in church and state. A stream of orders issued from the council of the Indies in Madrid, and a massive bureaucracy, both secular and clerical, was expected to put them into effect. But in practice there was so much jockeying for power between different interest groups – between viceroys and audiencias, viceroys and bishops, secular clergy and regular clergy, and between the governors and the governed – that unwelcome laws, while deferentially regarded because of the source from which they emanated, were not obeyed, while authority itself was filtered, mediated and dispersed.

The presence of the state, therefore, while all-pervasive, was not all-commanding. The certainties of Madrid were dissolved in the ambiguities of an America where to 'observe but not obey' was an accepted and legitimate device for disregarding the wishes of a supposedly ill-informed crown. In fact the crown was extraordinarily well informed, in the sense that a vast quantity of written information flowed in from across the Atlantic – information that was often, no doubt, a year or more out of date, but which reflected the widest possible range of views, from those of the viceroy's inner circle to the humblest Indian community. A system under which 49,555 sheets of paper could be used in the course of a visita into the activities of a single viceroy of Peru is not one that can be described as suffering from a dearth of facts.[10]

Well-informed administration of its overseas territories became, indeed, almost an end in itself for the crown, especially in the reign of Philip II with his inclinations towards planned and orderly government. Juan de Ovando, one of the officials who most closely reflected the spirit of Philip II's regime, concluded after conducting a visitation of the council of the Indies in 1569–70 that it still lacked sufficient information about the lands it governed, and during his relatively brief tenure of the presidency of the council in the early 1570s he set out to remedy this deficiency. Detailed questionnaires were sent out to officials in the Indies about the region and peoples subjected to their charge (a device that was also employed in Castile), and the responses, as they came in, were carefully ordered and summarized. In 1571 the post of *cronista de las Indias* (official chronicler and historiographer of the Indies) was established, and the first holder of the post, Juan López de Velasco,

[10] See Lewis Hanke, 'El visitador licenciado Alonso Fernandez de Bonilla y el virrey del Perú, el conde del Villar', in *Memoria del II Congreso Venezolano de Historia* (Caracas, 1975), II, 28.

produced on the basis of the *relaciones* sent in by the officials a *General Description of the Indies* which represents the first comprehensive statistical survey of Spain's American possessions.

Professionalism for its own sake is always liable to be a feature of government when the bureaucrats take control. But all imperialists need an ideology, whether they recognize the need or not. Sixteenth-century Castilians, imbued with a deep sense of the need to relate their enterprises to a higher moral end, had to articulate for themselves a justification for their government of the New World which would set their actions firmly in the context of a divinely ordained purpose. The silver of the Indies, which it was the crown's object to exploit to the maximum in order to enhance its revenues, was itself seen as a gift of God which would enable the kings of Castile to fulfil their world-wide obligations to uphold and propagate the Faith. Empire, therefore, was sanctioned by purpose; and empire in the Indies was regarded as a sacred trust, the character of which was summarized by the great seventeenth-century jurist, Juan de Solórzano y Pereyra in his *Política Indiana* [1648]. The Indians, he wrote, 'because they are so barbarous...needed somebody who, by assuming the duties of governing, defending and teaching them, would reduce them to a human, civil, social and political life, so that they should acquire the capacity to receive the Faith and the Christian religion'.[11]

But by what right could Spaniards wage war on Indians, subject them to their rule and reduce them to a 'human, civil, social and political life'? Although the juridical question of Castile's right to subjugate the Indies might seem to have been largely resolved by the papal bulls of donation, the confrontation between Europeans and the numerous and very diverse peoples of the Indies raised a host of problems, moral as well as juridical, which were at once so new and so complex that they were incapable of being summarily disposed of by a stroke of the papal pen. In principle, the doctrine of *compelle eos intrare* – 'Go into the highways and hedges, and compel them to come in' (Luke xiv. 23) – might seem justification enough for a forcible reduction of a pagan people to Christianity. But it did not need a high degree of moral sensitivity to appreciate that there was something ludicrously inadequate about confronting the Indians, before engaging them in battle, with a reading of the *requerimiento*, the document drafted in 1513 by the jurist, Palacios

[11] Book I, chap. IX, 119.

Rubios, which briefly expounded the history of the world since Adam and called on uncomprehending hearers who knew not a word of Spanish to submit to the authority of the church and the kings of Castile.

Uneasiness over the requerimiento merged with the more generalized concern over the ill-treatment of the Indians once they submitted or were conquered, to provoke an intensive and wide-ranging debate throughout the first half of the sixteenth century on the question of Spanish titles and Indian subjection. It was conducted in the convents and universities of Castile, but its repercussions were felt both at court and in the Indies, ruled as they were by legislation which would be shaped by the arguments of the victorious party.

In view of the vitality of Aristotelian and Thomist thought in the intellectual life of sixteenth-century Spain, it was inevitable that all claims to government in the Indies should be subjected to critical scholastic scrutiny. Already in 1510 the Scottish Dominican, John Major, had argued on Aristotelian grounds that infidelity was insufficient cause to deprive pagan communities of the right to property and jurisdiction, which belonged to them by natural law. This Aristotelian doctrine was at the heart of the great series of lectures, the *Relectio de Indis*, delivered by the Spanish Dominican, Francisco de Vitoria, at Salamanca university in 1539. If civil authority was inherent in all communities by virtue of reason and natural law, neither pope nor emperor could justifiably claim world-wide temporal dominion over-ruling and annulling the legitimate rights of non-Christian communities. By a daring stroke, therefore, Vitoria had undermined the justification for Spanish rule in the Indies on the basis of papal donation. Equally, he rejected titles based on alleged rights of discovery and on the unwillingness of Indians to accept the Faith.

In the circumstances it is not surprising that a stern rebuke was issued in November 1539 against 'those theologians who have called in question, through sermons or lectures, our right to the Indies...' Vitoria's arguments could only be a grave embarrassment to the emperor at a time when other European states were challenging Castilian claims to exclusive American dominion. He did not, however, go so far as to leave his sovereign without a fig-leaf to cover his nakedness. He was prepared to concede that the pope, by virtue of a 'regulating' authority, could charge a Christian prince with the mission of evangelization and that this charge was binding on his Christian colleagues. But it was not binding on the Indians themselves, and it carried with it no entitlement for war or conquest. How then could Spanish domination of the Indies, which was after all a *fait accompli*, be justified? Vitoria's answers, although impressively reasoned, were not entirely comfortable. If, as he argued, there was a law of nations, a *jus gentium*, embracing all mankind, the Spaniards had the right to trade with and preach the gospel to the Indians, and the Indians were bound to receive them peaceably. If they refused to do so, then the Spaniards had just cause for war. While this doctrine might perhaps be adequate justification for Spaniards in their relations with the Indians, it was less useful to them in their relations with other European powers. If there was indeed a world community in which all peoples had freedom of movement and trade, it was not immediately apparent why Europeans other than Spaniards should be rigorously prevented from setting foot in the Indies. It is not, therefore, surprising that later Spanish apologists of empire should have preferred to fall back on the argument of prior discovery, buttressed by claims of a Christianizing and civilizing mission formally entrusted to Castile.

Vitoria's arguments, as he himself ruefully accepted, had long since been overtaken by facts, and they remained at a level of theoretical abstraction which inevitably reduced the impact of their radical message. But they illustrate the difficulty inherent in the formulation of any coherent theory of empire, and suggest why the Spanish crown tended to fall back on a set of attitudes and responses rather than purveying any clear-cut 'imperialist' ideology. As long as Spain's dominion over the Indies was to all intents and purposes unchallengeable by its European rivals, facts in any event spoke louder than words, although this did not preclude considerable defensiveness in the face of international public opinion – a defensiveness suggested by the official replacement in 1573 of the word 'conquest' by 'pacification'.

There were, however, in Vitoria's rather hesitant justification of Castile's title to the Indies, a number of arguments which might be put to use by the crown. In particular he hinted at the idea of a possible right of tutelage over the Indians if they were demonstrated to be irrational beings in need of guidance. But what kind of tutelary control should be exercised over them, and, above all, who should exercise it?

For Bartolomé de Las Casas, waging his bitter campaign against the maltreatment and exploitation of the Indians by the Spanish settlers, there could be only one answer. The crown, and the crown alone, had jurisdiction over the Indians, by virtue of the bulls of 1493. This jurisdiction, which was tied to the missionary enterprise, could not be delegated to other Spaniards or transferred by means of encomiendas to private individuals. Las Casas, in fact, was advocating a form of tutelary kingship, which would provide the necessary conditions for the conversion of the Indians but would not deprive them of the rights of property and of government by their own rulers that belonged to them by virtue of natural law.[12]

In the circumstances of the late 1530s and the 1540s such arguments were well calculated to appeal to the crown. If the emperor was concerned on one front with the international challenge to his government of the Indies, he was still more concerned by the internal challenge represented by the encomenderos as a potential feudal aristocracy owning Indian serfs. The settlers threatened both his own authority and, by their scandalous treatment of the Indians, the evangelizing mission that was the *raison d'être* of Spanish rule. That the Indians were being cruelly abused was clear not only from the violent denunciations of Las Casas himself, but also from letter after letter that arrived from the Indies – from Archbishop Zumárraga, from Viceroy Mendoza, and from the licenciado, Vasco de Quiroga, that New World admirer of Sir Thomas More, whose *Utopia* provided a model for the Indian communities that he would establish in the Valley of Mexico and beside Lake Pátzcuaro in his diocese of Michoacán.

The agitation about the wellbeing of the Indians was reaching a climax at the time when Charles V returned to Spain after two years' absence in 1541. Along with reports of the factional struggles between Pizarrists and Almagrists in Peru it helped create a climate in which a radical re-thinking of royal policy in the Indies became a matter of urgency. The councillors of the Indies, suspected of being in the pay of the encomenderos, were not to be trusted, and the emperor, therefore, turned to a special *junta* to advise him on the encomienda question. It was this junta which produced the New Laws of 20 November 1542 – laws which, if implemented, would have realized Las Casas' ideals by abolishing all forms of personal service and transforming encomienda Indians into direct vassals of the crown.

The explosive reaction of the New World settlers forced the emperor to retreat. But the campaign against the New Laws was waged not only in the Indies themselves, but also at court, where the settlers' lobby

[12] For Las Casas and his writings about the treatment of Indians, see Elliott, *CHLA*, 1, ch. 6.

worked hard to bribe and influence the royal councillors, and where Cortés and his friends organized a formidable opposition to the Las Casas group. They needed an effective publicist, however, and they found one in the great Aristotelian scholar, Juan Ginés de Sepúlveda, whose *Democrates Alter*, written in 1554–5, was circulated in manuscript around the councils, although it failed to secure a licence for publication. In his treatise Sepúlveda raised a question that was fundamental to the whole problem of government in America: that of the rational capacity of the Indians. John Major had argued in 1510 that they lived like beasts and that consequently, in accordance with Aristotelian principles, their natural inferiority condemned them to servitude. It was this line of reasoning which Sepúlveda pursued, although with greater difficulty than Major, because the discovery of the Mexican and Andean civilizations had revealed the existence of peoples with a capacity for political and social organization impressive even to European eyes. Sepúlveda, however, from the safe distance of Castile, did his best to remain unimpressed. The Indians, it was clear, were a people naturally inferior to the Spaniards, and as such were properly subject to Spanish rule.

Sepúlveda was arguing not for the enslavement of the Indians, but for a form of strict paternalistic control in their own best interests. This was an argument for tutelage, exercised, however, by the encomenderos and not by the crown. The *Democrates Alter* was, in fact, advocating government by a natural aristocracy drawn from the settler community and, as such, was bound to be anathema to the royal authorities. Equally it was anathema to Las Casas, who had hurried back to Spain from his Mexican diocese of Chiapas in 1547 in a desperate bid to shore up the anti-encomendero policy which he saw collapsing in ruins around him. In April 1550 the crown responded to the storm of protest unleashed by Las Casas and his fellow-Dominicans by ordering a temporary suspension of all further expeditions of conquest in the New World, and by summoning a special meeting of theologians and councillors to consider the whole question of the conquest and conversion of the Indians. In the great debate staged at Valladolid in August 1550 between Las Casas and Sepúlveda, the 76-year-old bishop of Chiapas launched into a five-day public reading of his new treatise *In Defence of the Indians*, in the course of which he challenged Sepúlveda's theory of Spain's civilizing mission.[13]

[13] Bartolomé de Las Casas, *In defense of the Indians*, trans. Stafford Poole (DeKalb, Illinois, 1974), 171.

Although the Sepúlveda–Las Casas debate was superficially concerned with the justice of military conquest, it really reflected two fundamentally opposed views of the native peoples of America. Within the Aristotelian framework in which the debate was conducted, proof of 'bestiality' or 'barbarism' would serve as justification for the subordination of Indian to Spaniard. It was this which made it so important for Las Casas to prove that the Indians were neither beasts nor barbarians. But, for all the violence of the disagreement, there was a certain unreality about it in the sense that Las Casas, even as he questioned the benefits conferred on Indians by Spaniards, did not really doubt Spain's mission in the Indies. Where he differed from Sepúlveda was in wanting that mission pursued by peaceful means rather than coercion, and by the crown and the missionaries rather than the settlers.

The members of the junta, not surprisingly, were divided in their reactions, with the jurists apparently supporting Sepúlveda and the theologians leaning towards Las Casas. The latter may be said to have 'won' in the sense that the ban on the publication of the *Democrates Alter* was upheld. The stringent new conditions laid down in Philip II's new ordinances of 1573 for the procedures to be followed in future conquests in the Indies may also be seen as an expression of the crown's determination to prevent a repetition of the atrocities against which the bishop of Chiapas had fulminated year in and year out. But the age of conquest, even under the euphemism of 'pacification', was largely at an end by the time the ordinances were issued; and Las Casas lost the battle he most wanted to win – the battle to rescue the Indians from the clutches of the Spaniards.

He did, however, win another and more dubious victory, this time in the court of international public opinion. The 'black legend' of Spanish brutality pre-dated Las Casas, as it also pre-dated, at least in some form, any major European preoccupation with news from America. But Las Casas' devastating denunciation of the behaviour of his compatriots in his *Brief Account of the Destruction of the Indies*, first published in Spain in 1552, was to provide, along with Girolamo Benzoni's *History of the New World* (Venice, 1565), a repository of horror stories which Spain's European enemies would plunder to advantage. French and Dutch translations appeared in 1579 and the first English edition in 1583, as the antagonism between the Spain of Philip II and the northern Protestants mounted to its climax. The lurid engravings of Theodore de Bry reinforced the written word with a visual image of Spanish atrocities against innocent Indians which was to impress a crude stereotype of Spanish imperial rule on the minds of generations of Europeans.

Inevitably, the assault on Spain's record in the Indies provoked an apologetic literature in response and helped create that sense of Spain as a beleaguered fortress defending Christian values which itself became an important element in the Castilian national consciousness. Measured by the legislation which emerged from the discussions of the council of the Indies, the record of sixteenth-century Spain in America was in many respects remarkably enlightened. Strenuous efforts were made to protect the Indians from the grosser forms of exploitation, and there was a genuine if misconceived attempt on the part of crown and church to introduce the inhabitants of the Indies to what was automatically assumed to be a higher way of life. But the gulf between intention and practice was all too often hopelessly wide. Metropolitan aspirations, deriving as they did from different interest groups, all too often tended to be mutually incompatible; and over and over again the best of intentions foundered on the rock of colonial realities.

COLONIAL REALITIES

When the first viceroy of Mexico, Don Antonio de Mendoza, handed over the government to his successor, Don Luis de Velasco, in 1550, he made clear the existence of a fundamental incompatibility between the crown's desire to protect the Indians, and its desire to increase its revenues from the Indies. The crown was genuinely concerned to preserve the so-called *república de los indios*, threatened as it was by the depredations of unscrupulous settlers who took advantage of the 'innocence' of the Indians and their ignorance of European ways. On the other hand, the crown's perennial shortage of money naturally drove it to maximize its revenues from the Indies by every means at its command. The bulk of these revenues derived directly from the Indies in the form of tribute, or indirectly in the form of labour producing goods and services yielding a dividend to the crown. At a time when the size of the Indian population was shrinking catastrophically, the attempt even to preserve tribute rates at the levels set in the immediate post-conquest period was likely to be a source of growing hardship to Indian communities, while there was also a diminishing amount of labour available for distribution. Any attempt, therefore, to augment the Indian contribution could only disrupt still further a república de los indios which increasingly appeared doomed to destruction as a result of the impact of conquest and population decline.

The payment of tribute, in specie or in kind, or in a combination of the two, was obligatory on the Indians under Spanish rule almost from the conquest until its abolition during the wars of independence at the beginning of the nineteenth century. Paid either to the crown or to the encomenderos, tribute occupied a central place in Indian life as an inescapable imposition, harshly discriminatory in that only Indians were liable. In New Spain in the 1550s the tribute had to be reassessed in the light of the patent inability of dwindling Indian communities to pay their allotted share, and the same process occurred in Peru during the viceroyalty of Don Francisco de Toledo (1568–80), that austere servant of an austere royal master. All nobles other than caciques (chiefs) and their eldest sons now lost their tax exemption, and the same occurred for other groups lower down the social scale which, for one reason or another, had until now escaped tribute. The inevitable result of this was to accelerate the levelling process already at work in the Indian communities and to undermine still further their already weakened structure.[14]

The organization of tribute collection was placed in the hands of a new breed of officials, the *corregidores de indios*, who were making their appearance all over the more densely-settled areas of Spanish America from the 1560s. These corregidores de indios, who held appointment for only two or three years, were designed as the crown's answer to the encomenderos. Either Spanish-born Spaniards, perhaps drawn from the entourage which each viceroy brought with him from home, or else creoles (Spaniards born in the Indies) without land or encomiendas of their own, they would, it was hoped, prove reliable agents of the crown, in a way that the encomenderos, with a direct interest in the Indians under their charge, could never be. The new *corregimientos*, however, tended to have many of the defects of the old encomiendas, together with new ones of their own. The duties of the corregidor de indios included not only tribute collection but also the administration of justice and the organization of the labour supply for public and private works. Dependent on a small salary drawn from Indian tribute he naturally used his brief tenure to make the most of the enormous power with which he suddenly found himself vested. There was little to prevent him from

[14] For a further discussion of Indian tribute, see Gibson, *CHLA*, II, ch. 11.

making his own private extortions as he organized the tribute and directed part of the work-force into enterprises of benefit to himself. Where the encomendero had tended to rely on the traditional indigenous authorities to get his wishes obeyed, the corregidor, living like a lord among the Indians, had his own little army of officials, whose activities undercut those of the caciques, and so reduced still further their influence among their own people.

The very officials, therefore, who were intended to watch over the interests of the traditional república de los indios were themselves among its most dangerous enemies. But it is the operation of the labour system under the supervision of the corregidores de indios which most vividly reveals the inherent contradictions in the crown's Indian policies. In theory the Indians were supposed to lead segregated lives. Spaniards, other than royal officials, were not allowed to live among them, and they in turn were not allowed to live in Spanish cities, unless in specially reserved *barrios*. But, while strenuous attempts were being made to confine them to a world of their own, they were also being inexorably drawn into a European labour and money economy. This was a natural consequence of the abolition of personal labour services for the encomenderos in 1549. With slavery forbidden, and the service-encomienda tending to be replaced by the tribute-encomienda, alternative methods had to be devised for mobilizing Indian labour. The viceroys of the second half of the sixteenth century encouraged a wage-labour system to the best of their ability, but with the Indian population diminishing rapidly they also found it necessary to resort to coercion in order to save the fragile economic life of the Indies from collapse. There was nothing new about forced labour in either Mexico or Peru. It had existed before the conquest as well as after it, but it was reorganized in the 1570s on a systematic basis, although with regional variations inspired by earlier regional practices. Conscripted Indian labourers were ruthlessly wrenched from their communities and drafted to the fields, to public works, to the *obrajes*, or textile workshops, for the production of wool and cotton cloths and, above all, to the mines. Efforts were made by the crown in the early seventeenth century to legislate against the worst abuses of the labour system, but without much success. In so far as the deployment of labour was at least more tightly controlled, this was facilitated by the vast reorganization of the declining Indian population which had taken place in both New Spain and Peru during the second half of the sixteenth and the first decade of the seventeenth centuries. Under the so-called policy of *congregaciones* and *reducciones*, Indians scattered through the countryside had been congregated into larger settlements where they could be more easily governed and Christianized.

By the beginning of the seventeenth century the old-style república de los indios, based on structures inherited from the pre-conquest period, was in a state of advanced disintegration and the assumption which had governed the crown's policy towards the Indians in the first post-conquest decades – that the old Indian polity could be preserved without major changes – had lost all validity. The pressures to incorporate the Indians into the life and the economy of the new colonial society – even while still attempting to keep them at arm's length from the vigorous new world of settlers, mestizos (half Indian-half Spanish) and mulattos (half African-half Spanish) – were simply too powerful to be resisted. Those Indians who moved to the cities to become servants and employees of the Spaniards, were gradually assimilated and Hispanicized. Outside the Spanish cities, however, a new world was in process of formation. Paradoxically the establishment of the new corregimiento de indios and of the reducciones gave a new lease of life to the república de los indios, although it was now a república of a very different style from that of the immediate post-conquest period. The Indians congregated into settlements did in fact assimilate certain elements of Christianity; they appropriated for their own use European techniques, plants and animals and entered the monetary economy of the surrounding world. At the same time they preserved many of their indigenous characteristics, so that they remained genuinely Indian communities, conducting their own lives under the supervision of royal officials but through their own largely autonomous municipal institutions. The more successful of these Indian municipalities developed their own forms of resistance against encroachments from outside. Their *cajas de comunidad*, or community chests, allowed them to build up financial reserves to meet their tribute and other obligations. They learnt how to secure their lands with legal titles and how to engage in the petitioning and lobbying techniques which were essential for political survival in the Hispanic world. As a result, these indigenous communities, consolidating themselves during the seventeenth century, came to act as breakwaters against the engulfing tide of the large estate, or hacienda, which swept around them without ever quite submerging them.

The separate development of the *república de los indios*, ministering to the needs of the *república de los españoles* without forming a part of it, implied the development of Spanish America itself as two worlds, indigenous and European, linked to each other at numerous points but preserving their distinctive identities. Between them, belonging wholly neither to one nor the other, were the mestizos, rapidly increasing in numbers and acquiring during the course of the seventeenth century some of the characteristics of a caste. But, inevitably, in this tripartite society now in process of constitution it was the república de los españoles which dominated.

Within the Hispanic community, although the crown had triumphed over the encomenderos, it was incapable of preventing the establishment of what was in practice, although not in name, a New World nobility. This nobility differed in important ways from that of metropolitan Spain. Whereas Castilian society was divided between taxpayers (*pecheros*) and those who, by virtue of their noble status, were exempt from taxes, all the Hispanic population of the Indies was tax-exempt, and therefore stood in an aristocratic relationship to the tribute-paying Indian population. Consequently the elite among the creoles (*criollos*)[15] – those of Spanish blood who were native to the Indies – was not distinguished by any special fiscal privileges. Nor, unlike its metropolitan equivalent, did it possess any rights of jurisdiction over vassals, since its attempt to transform encomiendas into fiefs had failed. It lacked, too, any substantial titular differentiation. The crown was extremely sparing of titles for creoles; and in 1575 it withdrew from the encomenderos certain honorific privileges associated with the status of *hidalgo* in Castile, although in 1630, under the pressure of its financial needs, it changed its policy and authorized the viceroys to put privileges of *hidalguía* up for sale in the Indies. Similarly, that other perquisite of many Spanish nobles and hidalgos, membership in one of the great military orders of Santiago, Calatrava and Alcántara, was largely unavailable to

[15] Although the term 'creole' is commonly used in modern historical writing to describe the sixteenth- and seventeenth-century colonists, *criollo* does not seem to have been in common use at that time. The Indies-born settlers spoke of themselves as 'Spaniards' and were referred to as such in official documents. It is, however, noticeable that the renegade English Dominican, Thomas Gage, who travelled extensively in Mexico and Guatemala between 1625 and 1637, refers on a number of occasions to 'Creoles' or the 'Creole faction'. See *Thomas Gage's Travels in the New World*, ed. J. Eric S. Thompson (Norman, Oklahoma, 1958), 105, 127. On this question, see Lockhart, *CHLA*, II, ch. 8.

the conquerors and first-generation settlers. Only sixteen of them became members of these orders in the sixteenth century. Here again, however, there was a major change in the seventeenth century, during the course of which 420 creoles were granted membership.

The greater inclination of the crown in the seventeenth century than in the sixteenth to respond to the creoles' eager demand for honours was an obvious reflection of its pressing financial problems, which in one area after another would make it sacrifice what had once been tenaciously held policies for the sake of immediate fiscal advantage. But it also reflected social changes in the New World itself, as a creole elite consolidated itself in spite of the unwillingness of the crown to concede it formal recognition.

By the end of the sixteenth century this elite was a composite one, based on old settlement, new wealth and influential connections. The *conquistadores* – the natural aristocracy of the Indies – seem to have been strikingly unsuccessful in meeting the first challenge confronting all aristocracies, the establishment of a dynastic succession. In 1604 Baltasar Dorantes de Carranza said that there were only 934 living descendants of the 1326 conquerors of Mexico; and, even if several names were omitted, it is clear that the conquerors, at least as far as legitimate children were concerned, had been a demographically unfortunate group of men. Of those who surmounted the demographic hazard, many fell at the next fence. It was only a very small group among the conquerors – a group drawn largely from among the captains and the men on horseback – which acquired wealth and substantial encomiendas. These would live in major cities, like Mexico City or Puebla, while their former comrades, many of them fallen on bad times, would settle down to relatively obscure lives in small settlements remote from the main urban centres.

This small group of successful *conquistadores* was joined by a number of the early settlers who, for one reason or another, prospered in the new environment. It was a particular advantage, for instance, to have influential relatives at court, as did the Ruiz de la Mota, the Altamirano and the Cervantes Casaus families in New Spain, and so to have access to sources of patronage. Royal officials, and especially treasury officials like Alonso de Estrada, Rodrigo de Albornoz and Juan Alonso de Sosa, with large sums of money at least temporarily at their disposal, married their families into those of the leading settlers of New Spain. So, too, did members of each new viceregal entourage and the judges of the audiencias, in spite of the crown's attempts to keep them segregated. The outgoing viceroy of New Spain in 1590, for example, reported to his successor that the *fiscal* of the audiencia of Guadalajara had married his daughter without receiving a royal licence, and that the audiencia had sprung to his defence when an effort was made to deprive him of his office.[16]

As the century proceeded, this nucleus of leading families assimilated further elements, especially from among those who had made their fortunes in mining. Carefully planned matrimonial alliances, in which the rich widows of encomenderos played a decisive part, produced a network of interlocking families, which resorted to the Castilian system of *mayorazgos*, or entails, to prevent a dispersal of family wealth.

Inevitably, the consolidation of local oligarchies proved easier in some areas of the Indies than in others. Much depended on the biological chance of family survival and on the degree of wealth locally available. In a provincial backwater like Popayán, encomiendas were poor, local landowning families failed to establish entails, and there was a rapid turnover in the urban patriciate – apparently only one of its twenty principal families at the end of the seventeenth century went back in the male line to the first generation of settlers. Elsewhere, however, and especially in the viceroyalties of New Spain and Peru, a number of leading families, benefiting from their close associations both with the viceregal administration and with influential figures in metropolitan Spain, built up for themselves a formidable power base in their local regions.

The process by which this was done still has to be charted in detail; but as far as New Spain is concerned, the viceroyalties of the two Don Luis de Velasco, father and son, seem to have been the critical periods. The second Don Luis himself had a creole upbringing, living in Mexico as a boy and young man during his father's tenure of the viceroyalty from 1550–64. In due course he became viceroy himself, from 1590–5, and again from 1607–11, and then returned to Spain, where, with the title of count of Salinas, he was president of the council of the Indies until 1617, the year of his death. This long and close Velasco connection with the creole elite appears to have given it wide opportunities to secure lucrative privileges and consolidate its hold over major offices not reserved for Spaniards. Links with well-placed officials, for instance, could sway decisions in major lawsuits, and especially lawsuits for the

[16] *Los virreyes*, I, 281.

control of that most precious commodity in a dry country, the water supply. Possessing irrigated lands in well-chosen areas, members of the elite monopolized the grain-provisioning of the cities, where they and their relatives occupied *regimientos* and *alcaldías* and used their influence to control the world of local politics.

Inevitably the ties of kinship and interest which linked this increasingly entrenched creole oligarchy to sectors of the viceregal administration and also to nobles and high officials in metropolitan Spain, made it potentially difficult for Madrid to pursue with any consistency policies which tended to conflict with the oligarchy's wishes. The strengthening of the New World oligarchies, too, coincided with a weakening of the central government in Madrid following the death of Philip II in 1598; and this weakening in turn gave new impetus to the consolidation of oligarchical power that was already occurring as a result of local conditions. For the Indies, as for Spain itself, the reign of Philip III (1598–1621) was a period in which the late king's vision of a just society governed by an upright monarch in the interests of the community as a whole, was tarnished by the success of special interest groups in securing the commanding positions of power. In this respect the Mexican viceroyalty of the marquis of Guadalcázar (1612–21) was characteristic of the reign. Government was lax, corruption rampant and collusion between royal officials and a handful of leading families led to the further enrichment of a privileged few.

Once the oligarchies were established in the Indies, it proved virtually impossible to loosen their hold. There was one abortive attempt to do so in New Spain at the beginning of the reign of Philip IV in 1621, by a zealous viceroy, the marquis of Gelves, who was sent out from Spain with a specific mission to reform the system. Within a short period of his arrival in Mexico City in the autumn of 1621 Gelves had managed to alienate almost every influential section of the viceregal community. This was partly the result of his own political ineptitude, but it also reflected the strength of the vested interests which felt themselves threatened by his reforming projects. During the interim between the departure of Guadalcázar and the arrival of Gelves, government had been exercised by the audiencia under the presidency of Dr Vergara Gaviria. The judges, having acquired a taste for power, were reluctant to surrender it. They were also deeply involved with the local landowners who controlled Mexico City's grain supply and who had forced up the price of maize and wheat to artificial levels. In attempting to lower prices and bring the racketeers to book, Gelves inevitably arrayed against him some of the most powerful figures in the viceroyalty, including the audiencia of Vergara Gaviria. Simultaneously he rode roughshod into a world where angels feared to tread – that of the Mexican ecclesiastical establishment – and alienated one party after another, including Juan Pérez de la Serna, the archbishop of Mexico. He also antagonized the mercantile community and the *consulado* of merchants of Mexico City by attempting to put a stop to the contraband trade and raising a forced loan. There was always an acute shortage of liquid capital in the viceroyalty, whose economy depended on the smooth functioning of an extremely elaborate system of credit. By defying the merchants and by insisting that royal officials should pay tribute money directly into the royal treasury, instead of retaining it for a time in their own hands and using it for interesting entrepreneurial operations, he undermined the credit system on which Mexico's mining economy depended and plunged the viceroyalty into an economic crisis.[17]

It is not, therefore, surprising that the personal clash between viceroy and archbishop should have escalated into a full-scale confrontation between Gelves on the one hand and on the other an alliance of royal officials, high clerics and local oligarchs, whose own sectional rivalries were suddenly and dramatically swallowed up in their common fury at the activities of an over-zealous reformer. On 15 January 1624, after days of mounting tension in Mexico City, crowds manipulated by the anti-*gelvistas* attacked the viceregal palace, and forced the unhappy Gelves to flee for refuge to a Franciscan priory. The audiencia took over the government; Madrid sent out a new viceroy; and although, in order to save face, Gelves was ceremoniously restored to office for a day after his successor's arrival, nothing could alter the fact that a viceroy had been driven from office by a powerful combination of local forces determined to thwart the policies which he had been instructed by Madrid to implement.

Although there was to be another uprising in Mexico City in 1692, provoked by temporary shortages of wheat and maize, the Mexican 'tumults' of 1624 represented a more dramatic challenge to the authority of the crown in the Indies than any other it had to face in the seventeenth century. But, if at other times and in other parts the drama was less spectacular, the same underlying forces were at work.

[17] For a further discussion of mining in Mexico and Peru, see Bakewell, *CHLA*, II, ch. 4.

Oligarchies were in process of establishing themselves through the Indies, in the more developed areas and the frontier regions alike, and were evolving effective forms of resistance to the commands of a distant royal government. The growing power and self-confidence of these oligarchies was one of the major if least easily documented elements of change in what was in reality a continually changing situation. For the relationship between Spain and the Indies was never a static one, from the original moment of conquest to the extinction of the Spanish Habsburgs on the death of Charles II in 1700. Each party to the relationship had its own internal dynamic, which at once affected, and was affected by, developments in the other. Nor did the relationship exist in a vacuum. Instead, it existed within a wider framework of international interests and rivalries, from which neither the aspirations of the metropolis nor the realities of life in the New World could for any length of time be detached.

THE CHANGING RELATIONSHIP BETWEEN SPAIN AND THE INDIES

Charles V, having renounced his earthly titles, died in his Spanish retreat of Yuste in 1558. In dividing his inheritance between his brother, Ferdinand, who succeeded him in the imperial title and the German lands of the Habsburgs, and his son, Philip, to whom he left Spain, Spanish Italy, the Netherlands and the Indies, he was in effect recognizing the failure of the great imperial experiment which had dominated the history of Europe during the first half of the century. In the end he had been defeated by the multiplicity of challenges which faced him – the rise of Lutheranism in Germany, the rivalry of France, the perennial threat from the Turks in central Europe and the Mediterranean – and by the sheer scale of the enterprise on which he had embarked. Distances were too large, revenues never large enough; and when the Spanish crown defaulted on its obligations to the bankers in 1557, the 'bankruptcy' was that of a whole imperial system which had hopelessly overdrawn its credit.

Philip II's inheritance was, at least in theory, more manageable than that of his father, although the Netherlands were already assuming the appearance of an exposed outpost in a northern Europe increasingly attracted by the doctrines of Luther and Calvin. At the start of Philip's reign the most pressing need was for a period of retrenchment in Spain, where Castile was showing the strain of its heavy contributions to the emperor's finances. In leaving the Netherlands for Spain in 1559, Philip II was acknowledging the realities of the day – that Spain was to be the heart of his dominions, as was, within Spain, Castile.

In a reign of some 40 years, Philip succeeded in imposing the stamp of his own character on the government of the Spanish monarchy. A deep concern with the preservation of order and the maintenance of justice; an austere approach to the duties of kingship, which he looked upon as a form of slavery; a profound mistrust of his own ministers and officials, whom he suspected, usually with good reason, of placing their own interests above those of the crown; a determination to be fully informed on every conceivable topic, and a corresponding tendency to lose himself in minutiae; and a congenital indecisiveness which imposed still further delays on a naturally slow-moving administrative machine – these were to be the hallmarks of the regime of Philip II. He gave his dominions firm government, although the effectiveness of the royal orders and decrees pouring forth from Madrid and the Escorial was inevitably diminished by distance and blunted by the opposition of competing local interests. He succeeded, too, in saving his dominions from heresy, with the exception of the Netherlands, where revolt broke out in 1566. To the world at large his power and authority seemed overwhelming, especially after he had completed the unification of the Iberian peninsula in 1580 by securing his own succession to the throne of Portugal. But against these achievements must be set the strains imposed on the monarchy, and especially on Castile, by almost unremitting war.

The hopes of peace which accompanied Philip's return to the peninsula in 1559 were dashed by the revival of the Mediterranean conflict with the Turks. The 1560s proved a difficult and dangerous decade, as Spain concentrated its resources on the Mediterranean front, only to find itself embroiled simultaneously in northern Europe with the revolt of the Netherlands. After the great naval victory of Spain and its allies at Lepanto in 1571, the war with Islam moved towards a stalemate; but a new battlefront was developing in northern Europe as Spain found itself challenged by the forces of international Protestantism. During the 1580s the struggle of the northern provinces of the Netherlands to retain their freedom from Spain broadened out into a vast international conflict, in which Spain, as the self-proclaimed defender of the Catholic cause, attempted to contain and defeat the

Protestants of the north – the Dutch, the Huguenots and the Elizabethan English.

It was inevitable that this northern struggle should extend into the waters of the Atlantic, for it was here that Spain seemed most vulnerable to its enemies and here that the greatest prizes stood to be won. While the empire of Charles V had been a universal empire, at least in the eyes of its apologists, it had always been in essence a European empire, although with an increasingly important American extension. The *monarquía española* inherited by his son was, in contrast, to develop the characteristics of a genuinely transatlantic empire, in the sense that the power and fortunes of the Spain of Philip II were directly related to the interplay between the metropolis and its transatlantic possessions. During the second half of the sixteenth century the possession of overseas empire became a critical determinant of power relationships within Europe itself, and was seen as such by the enemies of Philip II as they pondered on what seemed to them the unique advantages accruing to him from his dominion of the Indies. As the interdependence of Spain and the Indies became more marked, so the determination of the north Europeans to challenge the Iberian monopoly of the New World increased; and their challenge in turn had its own consequences for the character of the Spanish-American connection.

It was as a silver empire that Spain and Europe saw the Indies. Before the discovery of Mexico, specie exports from the Indies consisted entirely of gold, but in the 1520s silver made its first appearance. American silver production for the next two decades was still small in relation to the European output: the silver mines in the Habsburg hereditary lands produced nearly four times as much silver as the Indies between 1521 and 1544. In the later 1540s and 1550s, however, these proportions were reversed as a result of the discovery and early exploitation of the rich silver deposits of Mexico and Peru. The great silver mountain of Potosí in Peru was discovered in 1545. In the following year large deposits were found in Zacatecas in northern Mexico and then further large deposits to the south at Guanajuato. After the introduction into Mexico in the mid-1550s and into Peru around 1570 of the amalgamation process for refining silver with mercury, massive increases in production led to a dramatic increase in silver exports to Europe.

The economic and financial life of Spain and, through it, of Europe, was heavily dependent on the regular arrival of the fleets from the Indies, with their new consignments of silver. Once the silver arrived in Seville and was registered at the *Casa de la Contratación*, it was released for a variety of purposes. The king's share – probably some two-fifths of the total consignment – deriving from the *quinto*, or fifth part of all production, and from the yield of any taxes collected in the Indies, was used to meet his domestic and international commitments, for which he was perennially in arrears.

The contribution of the Indies to the royal exchequer was at first sight less spectacular than contemporary obsessions might suggest. An English member of parliament in the 1620s was only repeating a commonplace of the age when he referred to the king of Spain's 'mines in the West Indies, which minister fuel to feed his vast ambitious desire of universal monarchy'.[18] In reality, the crown's American revenues, although four times as large in the 1590s as in the 1560s, represented only about 20 per cent of its total income at the end of Philip II's reign. But this 20 per cent was, in fact, crucial for the great enterprises of Philip's later years – the struggle to suppress the revolt of the Netherlands, the naval war against the England of Elizabeth and the intervention in France. It was precisely because it consisted of liquid capital in the form of silver, and was therefore in keen demand by the bankers, that it formed such an attractive part of the revenues. It was on the strength of the silver remittances from America that the king could negotiate with his German and Genoese bankers those large *asientos*, or contracts, which kept his armies in pay and tided over the difficult period before a new round of taxes replenished the royal coffers.

The remainder of the silver reaching Seville belonged to private individuals. Some of it consisted of remittances from colonists to friends and family at home. Some of it was brought back by returning *indianos* – those who had made their fortunes in the Indies and came back to lead a life of suitable ostentation at home. But a large proportion took the form of payments for commodities that had been shipped in earlier fleets sailing to the major American entrepots, Veracruz, Cartagena and Nombre de Dios. In so far as these commodities were of Spanish origin, the payments had a Spanish destination. But as Spain itself proved increasingly incapable of meeting the needs of a developing American market, so the non-Spanish share in the Seville trade grew, and much

---

[18] L. F. Stock, *Proceedings and Debates of the British Parliaments respecting North America* (Washington, D.C., 1924), I, 62.

of the silver automatically passed into the hands of foreign merchants and producers. Both through foreign participation in the transatlantic trade and through the mechanism of the asientos, 'Spanish' silver was dispersed throughout Europe, so that any marked fluctuation in the New World remittances had widespread international repercussions. Times of *largueza*, or easy money, in Seville were times of international business confidence, but when the Sevillans sneezed, western Europe shivered.

The second half of the sixteenth century, although it began with a recession (1555–9) and was punctuated by years of misfortune, was in general a long period of expansion in the Indies trade. From the early 1590s to the early 1620s, the trade, while no longer expanding, remained at a high level of activity, but from the 1620s both the volume and the value of the trade began moving sharply downwards. By 1650 the great age of the Sevillan Atlantic was over, and as Cadiz began to replace Seville as Europe's gateway to America, and more and more foreign vessels forced an entry into Spanish American waters, new patterns of transatlantic trade began to form themselves.

Within the fluctuating boundaries of this transatlantic trade, Spain's economic relationship with its American possessions underwent important changes. In the first half of the sixteenth century the economies of Castile and of the settler communities springing up in the New World were reasonably complementary. Castile and Andalusia were able to provide the settlers with the agricultural products – oil, wine and grain – which they required in bulk, and simultaneously the growing demand in the Indies also served as a stimulus to a number of Castilian industries, especially the cloth industry. By the 1540s, however, problems were already arising. There was increasing complaint in Castile about the high price of domestic manufactures, particularly of textiles, and a tendency to blame this on exports to the Indies. In 1548 and again in 1552 the Castilian Cortes urged the crown to prohibit the export of home-made cloths to America. The crown successfully resisted the pressure from the Cortes to exclude Castile's textiles from its own overseas markets, but it is clear that the American connection, while initially acting as an encouragement to certain sectors of Castilian industry, was also creating problems to which the relatively unsophisticated Castilian economy had difficulty in responding.

It was not only a question of the ability of Castilian industry to increase supply to meet a growing American demand, but also one of how to produce, for both the domestic and the American markets, at internationally competitive prices. The high prices which were a source of such vociferous complaint among Castilian consumers in the mid-sixteenth century were high not only in relation to prices in Castile at the beginning of the century, but also in relation to those of foreign imports. There is no single explanation of the inability of Castilian manufacturers to remain internationally competitive, but a central place must be accorded to the influx of precious metals from America into an economy starved of specie – an influx whose effects were felt first in Castile and Andalusia before extending over Europe in a kind of ripple effect. It was, appropriately, a Spaniard, Martín de Azpilcueta Navarro, who first, in 1556, clearly related the high cost of living to the inflow of bullion from the Indies: 'We see by experience that in France, where money is scarcer than in Spain, bread, wine, cloth, and labour are worth much less. And even in Spain, in times when money was scarcer, saleable goods and labour were given for very much less than after the discovery of the Indies, which flooded the country with gold and silver.'[19]

The inflation of prices which undercut Spain's international competitiveness was a disturbing counterbalance to the visible assets of empire – to the manifest prosperity of the fast-growing city of Seville and to the rising revenues of the crown. The assets of empire, however, were for a long time more easily perceived than its disadvantages, and the veneer of prosperity helped to conceal the detrimental consequences to Castile of major changes that were occurring in the pattern of transatlantic trade during the second half of the sixteenth century. Until the period 1570–80 the agricultural products supplied by Castile and Andalusia constituted the dominant exports from Seville; but as the Indies began to develop their livestock production and to grow more and more of their own wheat, the demand for Spanish produce began to decline. Its place in the cargoes was taken by manufactured goods, which found a ready outlet. Some of the manufactures originated in Spain, but from around the 1580s foreign articles appear to have taken the lead over Castilian goods in the shipments – a clear indication of the inability of Castilian industry to adapt itself to the new and more sophisticated market requirements of the Indies. There was a growing demand among the settlers for European luxury articles of a type that Spain failed to produce; a demand, too, as the Indies developed their

[19] Marjorie Grice-Hutchinson, *The School of Salamanca* (Oxford, 1952), 95.

own production of cheaper lines in textiles, for high quality silks and cloths.

In the years after 1567, when trading links were first established between Mexico and the Philippines, the merchants of Peru and New Spain found it increasingly advantageous to look to the Far East rather than to metropolitan Spain for the supply of these high quality textiles. The rapid growth of the oriental trade – of textiles, porcelain and other luxuries from China – entailed a trans-Pacific diversion by way of Acapulco and Manila of large quantities of American silver which would otherwise have had a transatlantic destination. In 1597, for instance, the volume of the silver sent from Mexico to the Philippines exceeded the value of Mexican transatlantic trade for that year. The attempts of the crown to restrict the Philippines trade to one Manila galleon a year, and to prevent the re-export of Chinese goods from Mexico to Peru by prohibiting in 1631 all trade between the two viceroyalties, resulted in large-scale contraband: the Indies could not be indefinitely confined within an exclusively Hispanic system designed primarily to meet the wishes of the merchants of Seville.

If, then, the economies of Castile–Andalusia and the Indies complemented each other reasonably well until around the 1570s, there was thereafter a divergence which no amount of Spanish protectionist legislation could entirely prevent. The Indies simply had less economic need than they once had of metropolitan Spain; but Spain, on the other hand, had a great and growing need of the Indies. Like an addict, it had become dangerously dependent on regular injections of American silver to maintain the expansive style of life to which it had grown accustomed.

When the silver could not be obtained in the form of payment for Castilian products, it had to be raised by other means: through the manipulation of customs dues, the introduction of some form of taxation and the resort to a variety of fiscal expedients. The white population of the Indies was not subjected to direct taxation; but the Castilian sales-tax, the *alcabala*, was introduced in New Spain in 1574 at a rate of 2 per cent, and in Peru in 1591. From the last decades of the sixteenth century the crown also attempted to raise its American revenues by selling land, or else the titles to land already illegally settled (a form of sale known as *composición de tierras*). It collected cash from the legitimization of mestizos, from 'voluntary' donations and from monopolies. It also had recourse to a practice which was to have important social and administrative repercussions – the sale of offices, which yielded an annual revenue of 38,000 ducats (the annual salary of a viceroy of Mexico was 20,000 ducats, and of a viceroy of Peru, 30,000). As long as these were minor administrative or notarial offices this practice in itself did no great harm, although this was less true of the sale of regimientos in the cities, which accelerated the process whereby municipal power was concentrated in the hands of closed oligarchies. But it also involved the unnecessary multiplication of offices, with large numbers of new posts being created, especially in the seventeenth century, in response to the needs of the government rather than the governed. The result was the creation of a large and parasitic bureaucracy, looking on its offices as an investment ripe for exploitation. The presence of yet another layer of intermediaries with its own interests to protect, only served to hamper still further the implementation of orders from Madrid.

The combination of rising output in the mines with these new devices for extracting money from the settler population brought a large increase in the crown's American revenues in the later years of Philip II. If the crown was receiving an average of a million ducats a year from the Indies in the 1570s, the figure stood at two and a half million in the 1590s. The increase, however, failed to save the crown – which had already defaulted on its debts in 1575 – from another 'bankruptcy' in 1596. Expenditure consistently outran income as Philip II committed himself to the enormous military and naval enterprises of the last years of his reign.

For these enterprises more and more silver was required from the Indies. But Philip II's involvement in northern Europe also had the paradoxical effect of keeping silver *in* the Indies – silver with which to pay for their defence against raids by his northern enemies. Both contraband and piracy had been a fact of transatlantic life ever since regular sailings were established between Spain and the Indies; and the seizure by a French corsair off the Azores in 1523 of part of the Mexican booty sent home by Cortés was no more than an unusually spectacular example of the dangers to which the *carrera de Indias* was increasingly exposed.[20] Ships from Seville began sailing in convoys from the 1520s, and from the 1560s a regular convoy system was definitively established. This system, although expensive, justified the outlay. Over a century and a half, the

[20] For a full description of the *carrera de Indias*, see MacLeod, *CHLA*, 1, ch. 10.

treasure fleets fell victim to enemy attack on only three occasions – in 1628 when the Dutch admiral, Piet Heyn, captured the fleet in the Bay of Matanzas off the coast of Cuba, and in 1656 and 1657 when Admiral Blake attacked it once in Spanish waters and once off the Canaries.

The defence of the fleets, however, proved more feasible than the defence of the Indies themselves. The area to be defended was simply too large and too sparsely inhabited by Spaniards. As Spain's European enemies came to identify the source of Spanish power as the silver of the Indies, so their ambition grew to cut Spain's transatlantic lifelines and to establish their own settlements in the Caribbean and on the American mainland. One possible response by the Spaniards was to found new settlements of their own in regions vulnerable to attack. It was the attempt by the Huguenots in 1562 to found a colony in Florida which prompted Spain to establish its own permanent settlement of San Agustín in 1565. But this was a policy that could not be uniformly adopted: every new outpost posed its own problems of supply and defence, and its isolated defenders were all too likely to be driven by the sheer necessities of survival into contraband trade with the same foreign interlopers whose incursions they were supposed to prevent.

The fiasco that overtook John Hawkins at San Juan de Ulúa in 1568 showed that, as the possessing power, Spain enjoyed very considerable advantages in American waters against expeditions mounted by its European rivals. But as the Protestant offensive developed, and first the English and then, in the seventeenth century, the Dutch turned their attention to the Indies, so an over-extended Spanish empire became increasingly conscious of its vulnerability. It was Drake's Caribbean raid of 1585–6 which first compelled the Spaniards to plan the defence of the Indies on a systematic basis. In 1586 Philip II sent out the Italian engineer, Juan Bautista Antoneli, to review the defences of the Caribbean. In the light of his report, elaborate fortifications were constructed for the protection of the principal ports – Havana, San Juan de Ulúa, Puerto Rico, Portobelo and Cartagena. The effectiveness of the new defence system was demonstrated by the discomfiture of the Hawkins–Drake expedition of 1595, but the cost of building and maintaining fortifications inevitably entailed a heavy burden on royal revenues in the Indies.

Philip II's accession to the throne of Portugal in 1580 represented initially an accretion of Spanish strength. It gave him an additional fleet; a new Atlantic seaboard, with a first-class port in Lisbon; and, in Brazil, a vast new dominion. But it was followed by the incursion of the Dutch into South American waters for the first time, acting as carriers for the Portuguese; and from the end of the sixteenth century Dutch shippers were showing an unhealthy interest both in the Brazil trade and in the Caribbean, to which they turned in search of salt. The twelve-year truce of 1609–21 between Spain and the United Provinces had little effect on the new-found interest of the Dutch in the possibilities of America. Their infiltration of the Brazil trade continued; and in 1615 a Dutch expedition, following Drake's route through Magellan's Strait, moved up the Pacific coast on its way to the Moluccas. The appearance of the Dutch in Spain's Pacific waters showed that a vast unguarded coastline was henceforth no longer immune from attack. Fortifications had to be constructed at Acapulco, and the prince of Esquilache, viceroy of Peru from 1614 to 1621, embarked on a costly programme of coastal defence – too costly at a time when Spain was becoming seriously preoccupied by the deteriorating position of the Habsburgs in Central Europe.

In 1617 and 1618 the Spanish council of finance was complaining bitterly about the decline in the crown's share of the silver remittances from the Indies and blamed this decline on the retention of large sums by the viceroys of Mexico and Peru. Much of this money was being used to improve defences against corsair attacks, and Peru also bore the additional burden of subsidizing to the tune of 212,000 ducats a year the interminable war against the Araucanian Indians of Chile. The figures for remittances to Seville bear out the ministers' complaints. Where Philip II was receiving two and a half million ducats a year in the 1590s, the figures in the later years of Philip III barely reached a million, and in 1620 they dropped to a mere 800,000 ducats.[21]

The costs of imperial defence, therefore, were soaring at a time when the crown's receipts from the Indies were dwindling, and when the Seville trade itself, in which Spain was playing a diminishing part, was beginning to show signs of stagnation. Consequently, the early seventeenth century appears as a critical period in the relationship between Spain and the Indies. The balmy days of easy silver appeared to be drawing to a close, and there was a growing awareness in Castile of the costs of empire rather than its benefits. As the Castilians of the reign of Philip III embarked on a great debate about what they were beginning to perceive as the decline of their country, it is therefore not

[21] J. H. Elliott, *The revolt of the Catalans* (Cambridge, 1963), 189–90.

surprising that the role of the Indies should have been brought into the discussion. What benefits, after all, had the Indies conferred on Castile? For Martín González de Cellorigo, writing in 1600, the psychological consequences of empire had been disastrous for his countrymen, creating false illusions of prosperity and persuading them to abandon pursuits which would have made them richer than all the treasures of the Indies.[22]

At a time when the wealth of states was increasingly being measured by the number of their inhabitants, there was also a growing pre-occupation with the demographic consequences for Castile of emigration to the Indies. The Mexican-born Rodrigo de Vivero y Velasco, writing in the early 1630s with firsthand knowledge of conditions on both sides of the Atlantic, was one of the many seventeenth-century Spaniards to lament the high rate of emigration to the Indies: 'at the present rate Spain will be denuded of people and the Indies run the risk of being lost, because they are receiving many more people than they can conveniently take'.[23] He described the large number of passengers making the crossing without a licence, buying their passages from ships' captains in San Lúcar, Cadiz or Seville for twenty or 25 ducats with as much ease as if they were buying bread or meat. This stream of emigrants, perhaps on average 4,000 a year over the course of the seventeenth century, helped to create in the Indies themselves a floating population of unemployed, who constituted a constant source of worry to the authorities. But from the Spanish side of the Atlantic the problem seemed even more serious, for the Indies, instead of yielding up their treasures for Castile, were draining it of its lifeblood.

The sense of disillusionment about the value of the Indies stood in sharp contrast to the sixteenth-century assumption that the conquest of America was a special signal of God's favour for Castile. The degree to which attitudes had changed can be gauged by the fact that in 1631 the principal minister of the crown, the count-duke of Olivares (whose family estates in Andalusia exported wine to the Indies), wondered aloud at a meeting of the council of state whether its great conquests had not 'reduced this monarchy to such a miserable state that it might fairly be said that it would have been more powerful without the New World'.[24] A statement like this, even if made in a passing moment of

[22] *Memorial de la política necesaria y útil restauración a la república de España* (Valladolid, 1600), 15v.
[23] *Du Japon et du bon gouvernement de l'Espagne et des Indes*, trans. and ed. Juliette Monbeig (Paris, 1972), 93.
[24] Archivo General de Simancas, Estado, legajo 2332, *consulta* of 7 September 1631.

exasperation, suggests a kind of emotional distancing which may itself have played a part in changing the relationship between Spain and the Indies in the seventeenth century. On both sides of the Atlantic there was a gradual drawing apart, a first weakening of the ties of natural affinity between the metropolis and its overseas dominions.

Yet Castile never needed the Indies more than it needed them after the accession of Philip IV in 1621, when the truce with the Netherlands expired, and Spain found itself once again saddled with enormously heavy European commitments. Spain's new involvement in a conflict that threatened to extend over Europe was bound to increase its dependence on its American possessions. Threatened by the collapse of the Castilian economy under the fiscal pressures of war, the regime of the count-duke of Olivares (1621–43) set out to exploit and mobilize the resources of the various states and provinces of the Spanish monarchy, including the American viceroyalties. The disastrous Gelves government in Mexico constituted a first attempt to reverse the trend of declining revenues. Comparable efforts were also made to increase the crown's income in Peru. In 1626 Olivares launched an elaborate scheme for sharing the burdens of defence. By this scheme, known as the Union of Arms, each part of the monarchy was to guarantee to contribute a stipulated number of paid men over a fifteen-year period. It was agreed in Madrid that it was not practicable to demand soldiers from the Indies. Instead, the council of the Indies proposed in 1627 that Peru should make an annual contribution of 350,000 ducats and New Spain 250,000, the money to be devoted to the fitting out of a naval squadron for the protection of Atlantic shipping.

It proved almost as difficult to introduce the Union of Arms in the Indies as it did in metropolitan Spain, where Portugal and the states of the crown of Aragon showed themselves more conscious of the costs than the benefits of the scheme. The count of Chinchón, appointed viceroy of Peru in 1627 with the assignment of introducing the Union, found good reasons to prevaricate, and it was only in 1636 that the project began to get under way with a doubling of the alcabalas from 2 per cent to 4 per cent and comparable increases in the customs dues. In New Spain the alcabalas were also raised to 4 per cent for the same purpose in 1632, and then again to 6 per cent in 1639, this time to finance a project which had long been under discussion in Spain and the Indies – the creation of a special fleet, the *armada de barlovento*, to police the sealanes of the Caribbean.

The 1620s and 1630s, therefore, may be seen as a period of new and intensified fiscalism in the Indies, just as in Spain itself and in Spain's European territories. Increased taxes, forced gifts and loans, and the sale of rights, privileges and offices – these were the hallmark of the Olivares years on both sides of the Atlantic, as the government in Madrid struggled to sustain its gigantic military effort and to save Castile from collapse. The Indies were being called upon to bear the costs of their own defence, while simultaneously they were also expected to contribute more to the central exchequer.

But how far were Spain's American territories capable in these years of responding to Madrid's intensified demands? At least for New Spain there are clear indications that the 1620s were a time of economic difficulties. In part this was the result of Gelves' heavy-handed attempts at reform, with their disastrous impact on confidence and credit. But this was also a decade of unusually bad climatic conditions, reflected in a run of poor harvests, heavy mortality among livestock, and, in 1629, disastrous flooding in Mexico City caused by the overflow of the waters of Lake Texcoco. Mine-owners, too, were reporting increasing production problems, with labour in short supply and once-rich veins being worked out. On the other hand, the Zacatecas mines, which may have been responsible for as much as a third of the total Mexican production at this period, continued to produce at high rates until the mid-1630s, when they moved into a period of decline that lasted 30 years. In the Potosí silver mines of Peru, production, although it never reached the peaks it had attained in the late sixteenth century, kept up reasonably well until the 1650s, aided in part by Madrid's willingness to give Peru priority over New Spain in the allocation of mercury exports from Europe which helped to supplement the faltering native supplies from the mines of Huancavelica.

To keep the mines producing, however, was an increasingly costly business. This was partly because labour was scarce in many mining regions, and because easily accessible deposits which had produced such a rich yield in the sixteenth century were now nearing exhaustion. But it also reflected the declining value of silver itself in Europe, where its abundance had lowered the value of a silver *peso* relative to gold. In Spain the legal gold–silver ratio, which had stood at 10.11 to 1 in the early sixteenth century had moved to 15.45 to 1 by the mid-seventeenth.[25] The mining economies of the New World, therefore, were less

[25] Earl J. Hamilton, *American treasure and the price revolution in Spain, 1501–1650* (Cambridge, Mass., 1934), 71.

remunerative to the producers than in earlier years; and while the economic life of both Peru and New Spain was being diversified in the seventeenth century by the development of local agriculture and industry, the transitional phase through which the economies of both viceroyalties were passing left them highly vulnerable to the kind of arbitrary fiscalism to which they found themselves subjected during the Olivares years.

In demanding large *donativos*, or in appropriating, as in Peru in 1629, one million *pesos* from the mercantile community, the crown was fatally undermining confidence, removing specie from circulation in regions where it was generally in short supply, and playing havoc with the credit system by which local and transatlantic transactions were conducted. In the circumstances, it is not surprising that merchants in the New World, finding their silver subject to appropriation by the crown either at home or on its arrival in Seville, showed a growing unwillingness to subject it to the hazards of the Atlantic crossing. As a result, the delicate mechanism of the *carrera de Indias*, the sea link between Spain and the New World, began to approach breakdown in the 1630s. If substantial sums were still arriving in Seville for the crown, private individuals were now holding back, and consequently there was less money available in Seville for investment in the next outgoing fleet. In 1640 – that fatal year for Spain itself as both Catalonia and Portugal rebelled against the government in Madrid – no treasure-fleet put in at Seville. The crown's excessive fiscal demands had brought the transatlantic system to the point of collapse.

During those middle decades of the century, from the 1630s to the 1650s, it seemed indeed as if the Spanish monarchy as a whole was on the verge of disintegration. The monarchy was so extended, its lines of communication so fragile, its limited resources under such intense pressure from the strain of a war being fought simultaneously on several fronts, that there was reason to fear that one part after another would break off, or succumb to enemy attack. Although, under Philip II, the international conflict had extended into the waters of the Atlantic, the New World of America had remained on the margin of the struggle. Under his grandson, however, European rivalries took on a global dimension, in which the Americas found themselves in the front line of attack. The English settlements in North America in the years following the Anglo-Spanish peace of 1604 had already shown that hopes of maintaining an Iberian monopoly of America were illusory; but it was the aggressiveness of the Dutch in the years following the expiry of the twelve-years' truce in 1621 which revealed the true scale of the problem of defence that now confronted Madrid.

In 1624 an expedition organized by the newly founded Dutch West India Company seized Bahia in Brazil. A joint Spanish–Portuguese expedition dislodged the Dutch in the following year, but it represented a major effort for the Spanish war machine, difficult to repeat at a time when resources were heavily committed in Europe. In 1630 the Dutch launched their second invasion of Brazil, and this time, although Olivares planned a counter-attack, it had to be postponed from one year to the next. During the 1630s, therefore, the Dutch were able to consolidate their hold over the sugar-producing regions of north-eastern Brazil, and the new armada, finally dispatched from Lisbon in 1638, accomplished nothing of note before dispersing after an inconclusive encounter with a Dutch fleet in Brazilian waters in January 1640.

The inability of the Spanish crown to save Pernambuco from the Dutch had major repercussions in the Iberian peninsula. The union of the Spanish and Portuguese crowns in 1580 had never been popular in Portugal, but one of the arguments in its favour was that it enabled the Portuguese to draw on all the resources of Spain for the defence of their own overseas dominions. This argument, already disproved in the East Indies in the earlier years of the century, was now disproved also for what had become Portugal's most lucrative overseas territory, Brazil. Simultaneously, Portuguese merchants, who had profited from the union of the crowns to move into Spanish America and especially into the viceroyalty of Peru, found themselves subject in the 1630s to mounting hostility and discrimination from Spaniards and creoles. By 1640, therefore, it was becoming obvious to the Portuguese mercantile community that the union of the crowns was no longer offering the advantages that had once made it relatively acceptable; and this in turn predisposed many of them to accept the *fait accompli* of 1 December 1640, when the duke of Braganza was declared king of an independent Portugal.

The secession of Portugal was another crippling blow to the *carrera de Indias*, undermining still further the confidence of Seville, and depriving it of investments from Lisbon which it could ill afford to lose. Moreover, at the same time as Brazil was being lost to the monarchy, it was also suffering further losses in the Caribbean. Here once again it was the Dutch who gave the lead. Dutch fleets in Caribbean waters in the later 1620s provided a cover behind which the English and French could move in to occupy the unpopulated or sparsely populated islands of the Lesser Antilles. In 1634 the Dutch established themselves permanently in Curaçao, and by the early 1640s – with Tortuga, Martinique and Guadalupe overrun by the French, with the English in Barbados, St Christopher and Antigua, and Dutch trading posts established in the islands off the Venezuelan coast – the Caribbean was becoming a European lake.

The Spaniards responded as best they could. The *armada de barlovento* at last went into operation in 1640, but was not as effective as its advocates had hoped, partly because it frequently had to be diverted to escort the transatlantic convoys. The colonists themselves succeeded in repulsing a number of attacks, and the mainland and the principal islands were successfully defended with the assistance of strengthened and reconstructed fortifications. But the capture of Jamaica by the English in 1655 was symptomatic of the major change that had occurred in the Caribbean during the previous half-century. Direct links between Spain and Jamaica had virtually ended twenty years earlier, in 1634. In effect, then, Spain was now concentrating its diminishing resources and abandoning remote outposts which it had become prohibitively expensive to maintain. This policy worked, in the sense that Spain emerged from its mid-century troubles with its 'empire of the Indies' still very largely intact. What had gone for all time, however, was its New World monopoly. This fact was tacitly recognized in the peace settlement of Münster in 1648 ending Spain's 80 years' war with the Dutch – a settlement which allowed the Dutch to remain in possession of such territories as they actually occupied, although forbidding them to trade with the Spanish Indies. In 1670 it was recognized on a more significant scale in the Anglo–Spanish treaty of Madrid, by which Spain effectively accepted the English argument that it was not prior discovery but genuine occupation and settlement which gave title of possession.

The relationship between Spain and the Indies, then, underwent a decisive change as a result of the international conflict of the 1620s to 1650s. Spain itself was disastrously weakened; the Caribbean was internationalized and turned into a base from which illicit trade could be conducted on a large scale with mainland America; and the colonial societies of the Indies found themselves thrown back on their own resources, not least in the area of military organization.

The task of defending the Indies from enemy attack had traditionally devolved upon the encomenderos, who were expected to take to arms if a hostile fleet were sighted. But, as the encomienda itself lost its institutional effectiveness, so the encomenderos ceased to constitute a satisfactory defence force, and by the seventeenth century the crown found it more advantageous to appropriate a proportion of the revenues of their encomiendas for the upkeep of paid men. Although professional soldiers were imported from Spain to serve in the viceregal guards and to man the coastal fortifications, the growing irregularity and inadequacy of these troop reinforcements meant that garrisons tended to be dangerously undermanned, and the colonists became aware that there was little hope of salvation unless they saved themselves. Urban militias and voluntary levies therefore played an increasingly important part in the defence of the Indies as the seventeenth century progressed. The viceroyalty of Peru, for instance, responded to Captain Morgan's attack on the isthmus of Panama in 1668–70 with a general mobilization. The failure of Olivares' scheme for a Union of Arms throughout the monarchy had driven the settler population of the Indies to develop the art of self-defence.

Militarily, then, as well as economically, the ties between the Indies and metropolitan Spain were at least temporarily loosened by the dramatic weakening of Spain itself during the middle decades of the century. Yet at the same time the Indies were being subjected to intensified fiscal pressures and to the whole top-heavy weight of Spanish bureaucratic control. This seventeenth-century combination of neglect with exploitation could not fail to have a profound influence on the development of the New World societies. It created opportunities for the local oligarchies, profiting from the crown's weakness, to consolidate still further their domination of life in their communities by acquiring through purchase, blackmail or encroachment extensive areas of land. If for New Spain, and, to a lesser extent, for Peru, the seventeenth century was the century of the formation of the *latifundia*, the great landed estate, this was not unrelated to the temporary weakening of royal control in the Indies. Nor, for that matter, was the development of what was to be another permanent phenomenon of life in Latin America, rural *caciquismo*. In the political and administrative context of the seventeenth century there were innumerable opportunities for the local magistrate to transform himself into the local boss.

Latifundismo and *caciquismo* were both to some extent the products of metropolitan neglect. A third long-term product of the age was the growth of *criollismo* – the sense of a separate creole identity – which reflected that other facet of seventeenth-century life in the Indies, metropolitan exploitation. Relations between creoles and new-comers from Spain, the so-called *gachupines*, had never run entirely smooth. There was resentment on one side, contempt on the other. The resentment came from those innumerable pinpricks which new arrivals from the homeland inevitably administer to colonials with ambivalent feelings about the mother country. It came, too, from the frustrations of a mercantile community chafing beneath the constraints of Seville's exercise of its monopoly. Most of all it came from the fact that so many of the offices, and almost all the best offices, in church and state, were reserved for Spaniards.

The religious orders in particular were bitterly divided by peninsular–creole rivalries. It was in order to dampen these rivalries that the system of the *alternativa* came increasingly to be adopted in the seventeenth century. Under this system the provincial government of the religious orders alternated between native-born Spaniards and creoles. But the alternativa itself could be a cause of bitterness, as it was among the Peruvian Franciscans in the 1660s when the Spaniards, now heavily outnumbered by the creoles, secured a papal decree imposing the system in a bid to safeguard their own position. The truth was that each new creole generation felt itself one step further removed from metropolitan Spain, and therefore increasingly reluctant to accept the kind of tutelage implicit in the relationship between the mother country and its colonies.

But the ties of kinship, interest and culture linking the metropolis to the settlers of the Indies were all-pervasive and not easily broken. The developing urban culture of the Indies was, and remained, heavily dependent on that of Spain. Although Mexico City acquired a printing press in 1535, and other presses were established in the sixteenth and seventeenth centuries in Lima, La Paz, Puebla and Guatemala, most of the local production was reserved for books used for the evangelization of the Indians. For their culture the settlers depended on the printing presses of Spain; and it is an indication of the closeness of the ties and the remarkable speed of transmission to even the most distant outposts of the monarchy that in 1607, three years after the publication of the first part of *Don Quixote*, the knight of La Mancha and his squire made their first American appearance in a *fiesta* held at Pausa in Peru.[26]

While Spanish books and plays kept the settlers in touch with the latest intellectual trends in Madrid, the Dominican and Jesuit colleges that sprang up through the New World provided a traditional Hispanic education. In 1538 the Dominican college of Santo Domingo was raised to the status of a university, modelled on that of Alcalá de Henares. Mexico City and Lima acquired their own universities in 1551. Their statutes, privileges and curricula were borrowed from Salamanca, as Francisco Cervantes de Salazar, professor of rhetoric in Mexico, proudly pointed out in an imaginary dialogue of 1554 in which a visitor was shown the principal sights of the city.[27] The metropolitan-style scholastic education which the sons and grandsons of the first *conquistadores* and encomenderos received in their native universities was at once a symbol of social standing and an indication of their participation in a wider cultural tradition which knew no Atlantic frontier.

Yet, even as Hispanic culture sought to reproduce itself overseas, it was subjected to subtle changes. These occurred first in the vocabulary of the settlers, which soon included words of Indian origin – *cacique*, *canoa*, *chocolate*. New kinds of sensibility struggled to express themselves through traditional artistic and literary forms; and there was a growing sense of territorial attachment among the Spaniards of the Indies to their own New World – an attachment which began to find literary expression in works like the *Grandeza Mexicana*, the long poem of Bernardo de Balbuena, published in 1604.

During the seventeenth century the indications multiply that the creoles had embarked on the long search to establish their own identity. The growing popularity of the cult of the Virgin of Guadalupe in New Spain, for example, was a means of proclaiming that Mexico was a distinct and separate entity, without yet going so far as to break the links of loyalty to the crown and the Spanish homeland. If any one symbol can be found to illustrate the new-found sense of a distinctive historical community in New Spain it is the triumphal arch erected in Mexico City in 1680 for the entry of the new viceroy, the marquis of La Laguna. For the first time on a triumphal arch of this kind the gods and emperors of the Aztecs were displayed. Once the pre-Hispanic past

[26] See F. Rodríguez Marín, *Estudios Cervantinos* (Madrid, 1947), 573–96.
[27] *México en 1554 y Túmulo Imperial*, ed. Edmundo O'Gorman (Mexico City, 1963), 22 (diálogo primero).

could be used by descendants of the *conquistadores* as a means of self-identification before a metropolitan Spaniard, it is clear that at least one part of colonial society had crossed a major psychological divide.

By 1700, therefore, when the Habsburg dynasty which had ruled Spain and the Indies for the best part of two centuries was finally extinguished, the Bourbons found themselves entrusted with a legacy which did not lend itself to easy management. During the sixteenth century the crown, for all its failures, had succeeded in keeping a surprisingly tight control over the new, post-conquest society that was developing in the Indies. As in metropolitan Spain itself, however, by the end of the reign of Philip II the strains were beginning to tell. The crown's financial necessities, brought about by its heavy expenditures in the pursuit of an immensely ambitious foreign policy, were everywhere forcing it into compromises with local communities and privileged social groups. The Indies were no exception. Here, as in Castile or Andalusia, offices were put up for sale, tacit bargains struck with local elites, and the state, even if still intrusive, was visibly in retreat.

During the seventeenth century the crisis in metropolitan Spain deepened; and if this entailed fresh attempts at a crude exploitation of the Indies for the benefit of the metropolis, it also meant expanded opportunities for the increasingly confident and assertive oligarchies of America to turn to their own advantage the desperate needs of the state. The constraints within which those oligarchies operated remained the same as they had been in the sixteenth century. Everything still had to be officially resolved by reference to Madrid. But within those constraints there was a growing latitude for independent manoeuvre. A swollen bureaucracy in the Indies afforded endless opportunities for bending the rules to suit local needs; a remote and bankrupt crown could generally be bought off when it interfered too officiously in the details of the relationship that was developing between the settler elite and the Indian population. In the Indies, just as in the other parts of Spain's global monarchy, the seventeenth century was pre-eminently the age of aristocracy.

The system which the eighteenth-century Bourbons found established in Spain's American possessions was, then, a system which might best be described as self-rule at the king's command. The oligarchies of the Indies had achieved a kind of autonomy within the wider framework of a centralized government run from Madrid. It was a system which fell far short of the aspirations of Charles V and Philip II, but one which also left the Indies still heavily dependent on the Spanish crown. Reflecting a tacit balance between metropolis and the settler communities, it provided stability rather than movement; and its principal victims, inevitably, were the Indians themselves. It enabled Spanish America to survive the calamities of the seventeenth century and even moderately to prosper; and, in spite of foreign depredations, Spain's American empire was still largely intact when the century drew to a close. It remained to be seen whether so comfortably flexible a system could survive a new kind of rigour – the rigour of eighteenth-century reform.

10

SPAIN AND AMERICA: THE ATLANTIC
TRADE, 1492–1720

Spain and its American empire, Old World and New, were linked by the Atlantic Ocean. Wooden sailing ships, tiny by modern standards, lumbered to America and back year after year for more than three centuries along routes of impressive consistency and regularity. These ships, the ports from and to which they sailed, the courses and time they took, and the people who worked or bought passage on them form a fascinating chapter in the history of the sea. The *carrera de Indias*, as the Spanish-American sea link was often called, and the trade which it carried, was also, of course, an economic and, ultimately, a social and cultural factor of great importance. The fleets brought to Europe maize, potatoes, sugar, tobacco, as well as gold and silver. In return Europe sent, as well as people and manufactured goods, wheat, pigs, sheep and cattle which had sweeping effects on American diets and landscapes. It is this Atlantic trade during the sixteenth and seventeenth centuries that will be explored in the following pages. The carrera itself went through a series of cycles, short and long, which both reflected and affected socio-economic conditions in the mother country and the colonies. Moreover, as European imperial rivalries increased, especially in the Caribbean, the carrera was threatened, directly by pirates and privateers and indirectly by the efforts of northern European smugglers to replace it as supplier to and buyer from the Spanish-American empire.

Spain's, or to be more precise, Castile's colonial enterprise in the Atlantic followed nearly a century of Portuguese exploration of the coasts of the eastern Atlantic. Portugal had also pioneered the settlement of the islands on the European and African continental shelf. That Castile arrived in the New World before Portugal was accidental: it was due to Columbus' decision to leave Lisbon and the court of João II and

341

to look for support from Ferdinand and Isabella. Spain's discovery and settlement of America was thus part of a Portuguese-led, fifteenth- and sixteenth-century Iberian expansion into and across the Atlantic.[1]

Spain and Portugal enjoyed a great advantage among the nations of western Europe in their possession of the coast and its estuaries between Lisbon and the Río Guadalquivir. There the Mediterranean and the Atlantic met, and so too did their sea-faring traditions and navigational techniques. There were many fine ports in Galicia, Asturias and the Basque country, and some of them built and supplied ships to the carrera, including Columbus' first ship, throughout the centuries of the Indies trade; but the prevailing winds in northern Spain were, for most of the year, from the south-west. From the very beginning Seville and the ports on or near the mouth of the Río Guadalquivir in south-western Andalusia were Spain's main connection with the Indies. The prevailing winds in the favoured south-west of the peninsula, especially in the summer months, were northerly. The advantages for a sailing ship trying to leave the Iberian coast to travel south or west, more usually south and then west, are obvious. Moreover, the ocean south and west offered several groups of stepping-stone islands suitable for refitting and restocking, whether the destination were to be the African coast and India or the Caribbean. The Canaries became the obvious and preferred stop on the way to the Spanish Indies, and the Cape Verdes the stop used while sailing the coast of Africa or going to the East. The Azores, and to a lesser extent Madeira, were more suitable for returning fleets from America, and Spanish ships used them when they had to and when the Portuguese would permit it. The Canaries became something of a laboratory for the conquest and settlement of Spanish America. Many of the techniques and institutions of conquest and settlement, and some of the new crops and industries, were tested, refined and established in the Canaries. Their role, and that of some of the other stepping-stone islands, lasted throughout the colonial centuries and beyond, not only as way stations and laboratories but also as trading partners and suppliers of immigrants to the Indies.

Columbus' first voyage, the famous 1492 expedition with its three caravels and 87 men, followed a more northerly route to the Caribbean than those taken later. The three ships dropped south-south-west from the Spanish coast with the wind behind them until they reached the

---

[1] The story of Spain's conquest and settlement of America is told in Elliott, *CHLA*, 1, ch. 6 and the story of Portugal's settlement of Brazil in Johnson, *CHLA*, 1, ch. 8.

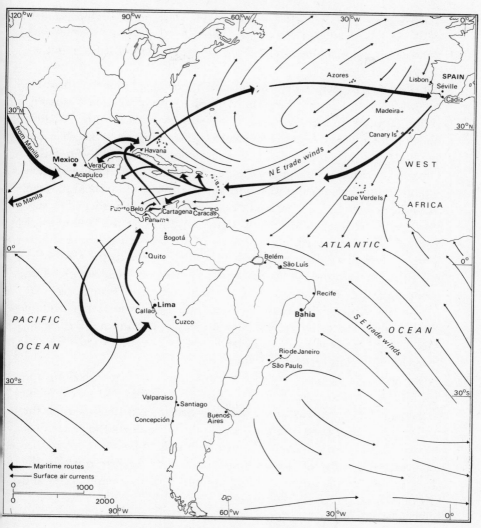

Spain and America: maritime routes

Canaries, but then the little fleet turned due west, with very little south until the last third of the voyage. Thus the three ships reached the Bahamas, in colonial times more often the exit from the Caribbean rather than the entrance.

Columbus, in fact, stayed too far north, but in spite of this, because of good luck and better seamanship, his first voyage was a fast crossing and, indeed, his fourth was one of the fastest ever made in the Atlantic under sail. However, later fleets usually followed a more southerly route as winds and tides dictated. They would copy Columbus as far as the Canaries, picking up provisions, exports and migrants there, but then would continue south and west with the north-east trades behind them until they could pick up the south-east trades – if they managed to stay north of the dreaded doldrums. With the south-east trades behind them and helped by the north equatorial and Caribbean currents, the ships were pushed through one of the southern entrances to the Caribbean which run among the islands between Trinidad and Guadeloupe, often stopping at this second group of stepping stones for restocking, care of the sick and repairs. Between 1536 and 1650 over 75 per cent of Spanish ships entering the Caribbean stopped at Dominica, Martinique, Guadeloupe, and the two small islands of Désirade and Marie Galante, a remarkably close pattern for any age of sail.

Return voyages normally took a more northerly route, leaving the Caribbean by the straits between Cuba and Florida and skirting the Bahamas. The hope was to use the Gulf Stream and then to catch the westerlies of the north Atlantic. Columbus' voyages set the pattern for returns too. These routes, to be further examined below, were factors of great weight for the growth and location of Spanish ports in the Indies, and for the stimulation or inhibition of economic zones and products in the Spanish possessions.

The basic ship of the early days of Atlantic exploration was the caravel. It was small even for the times, perhaps averaging about 100 tons, but fast and seaworthy. As voyages became longer and trade volume grew it was joined by a larger merchant ship, the square rigged *nao*. By 1550 or so the galleon had developed and soon replaced the caravel. It was larger, around 400 tons perhaps, much more heavily armed, and had greater cargo space. Its hull resembled that of the Mediterranean galley. Although first used by the Spanish and Portuguese the versatile galleon was soon adopted by their northern rivals the Dutch and the English. Generally speaking, before 1700 the Spanish fleets retained heavier ships, more unwieldy and with more castles, than their northern rivals. As the *nao* and the galleon became more important the pioneer caravel was relegated to coastal trading between Spain and the Canaries, and to longshore work in the Caribbean.

Little research has been done on the average lifespan of sixteenth-century ships. Much depended on care and maintenance, which involved laborious careening at regular intervals. Wooden ships soon rotted in damp, tropical climates, and the bottoms were attacked by toredo worms and the host of marine pests known to the Spanish as *barva*. Wrecks on poorly charted coasts, storms in the Atlantic and hurricanes in the Caribbean, pirates and overloading, all shortened the lives of these vessels. *Nuestra Señora del Pilar*, a galleon of 640 tons, was built in Havana in 1610 and made eighteen Atlantic crossings in the next thirteen years, following almost exactly the inward and outward routes described above. She was finally broken up at Veracruz in 1623 for her timbers and metal fittings. Her life may be typical, or just a little longer than average.

Ships were built where the necessary materials were available. The complex of Andalusian ports lacked supplies of large hardwoods and ships' stores such as pitch and cordage. Many of the early ships were built in the northern ports, but as Spain's decline set in this area supplied few or none, and Holland and the Indies took over. By 1650 Spain built less than a third of its Indies fleets, while Holland and the West Indies supplied more than a third each. The lowest period for Spanish shipbuilding was the 1650s and 1660s. Shipbuilding in the Caribbean was especially depressed in the 1670s and 1680s. After that Spanish and Caribbean shipbuilding revived slowly and recovered a larger share of the ships in the carrera.

In the Spanish-American colonies shipbuilding began early, with the Pacific coast leading the way. Guatulco in New Spain and Realejo in Nicaragua had access to stands of hard pine, pitch for caulking, also from the pines, and cotton, *cayuga*, *pita* and cactus for sails, cordage and caulking. Later Guayaquil, near forests of hardwoods and its own pitch lake, became important and remained so throughout the period. The Caribbean was slower to develop shipbuilding yards, but, by the late sixteenth century, Havana, Maracaibo and Campeche had recognized yards, with smaller establishments in Puerto Rico, Santo Domingo, Jamaica and in the little ports on the north coast of Tierra Firme. By 1500 cannons cast in bronze, which could be dragged along with the army, were mounted on ships. Like Portugal, Spain imported cannons from Flanders and North Germany and copper from Antwerp. As her interest in the Atlantic grew, Spain made strenuous attempts to lessen her dependence on foreign suppliers. Gun foundries were established at Medina del Campo, Málaga, Barcelona and, belatedly in 1611, at Seville. In spite of this attempted import substitution Spain's foundries never came close to supplying her needs and northern European imports were always required.

Guns on board ships were first carried on the upper deck or on the castles. Caravels were too small and light to carry many. Portuguese ships on the African coast in the fifteenth century usually carried some fifteen small cannons. In the early sixteenth century the cutting of cannon portholes in the hulls of ships, plus the growing use of the galleon and the nao, changed all this. Rows of cannons on each deck became common on ocean-going warships after 1550. These numbers of light cannons served two purposes. They provided armaments for sea warfare or bombardment and could be dragged off ships for landward expeditions in unknown territory. Cortés' cannons on his march to Tenochtitlán would have been considered as antiquated and second rate by the leading gun manufacturers of northern Europe, but they served their purpose. All of them had been removed from ships and then set on wheeled platforms. Such cannons, stripped from ships, were dragged along by mules or men. Sailors pulled those of the Cortés expedition until Indian auxiliaries took over.

The most hackneyed word to describe the ships' crews of the sixteenth and seventeenth centuries is motley, but this tells us little, and in fact sailors of the period, as a class, have been little studied. It is obvious that most of the ordinary seamen belonged to the poorer classes. Much has been made of the minor criminals among them, men escaping the latest brush with the law by taking to the sea. Men were also pressganged, when either intoxicated or in debt, and found themselves at sea before they knew where they were. Others were slaves or condemned criminals, forced to become sailors against their will. Many of the early mariners in the Atlantic carrera were probably unemployed men from the waterfronts of Seville, Cadiz, Palos and the smaller ports of that coast. One can guess that the level of enthusiasm and professionalism among such seamen would be low.

The life at sea (described below in more detail), was hardly attractive; it was dirty, dangerous and very unhealthy. Food and living conditions were abominable, so that on the longer voyages overdue ships resembled nothing more than charnel houses when they docked. Scurvy, the result of vitamin deficiencies and inadequate diet, appeared almost inevitably after two or three weeks at sea. Although the efficacy of citrus fruit was not entirely unknown by the late seventeenth century, its general use to ward off the ravages of scurvy came much later. The basic diet of weevilly ship's biscuit, salt pork fatback and brackish, lukewarm water caused remarkably little grumbling at that early stage, as far as we can gather from a scanty record, but discipline for minor offences was harsh. Capital punishment was common and added to the very high deathrates on board ships sailing the Atlantic.

Research will probably modify somewhat the unsavoury picture presented above. We know, for example, that some of the Andalusian and Portuguese seamen of the early sixteenth century, and possibly some of those in the seventeenth century too, came from seafaring families from the small ports along the favoured coast. These men were knowledgeable, hardy and enthusiastic. Their experience usually placed them in the upper ranks of the crew. We find them as pilots, boatswains and mates. The Pinzón brothers who sailed with Columbus are the best-known representatives of these maritime families. Ships needed skilled artisans. Carpenters, coopers for wine and water casks, blacksmiths, sailmakers and gunners (Greeks were prominent as gunners in the Spanish fleet) were all to be found on most large ships.

There seems to have been a constant shortage of sailors during the sixteenth and seventeenth centuries. Presumably the life did not attract many who had any choice in the matter. Experienced, skilled sailors and artisans were even scarcer and, of course, more essential. As ship size grew the number of ordinary seamen and professionals required per ton declined. (A 600-ton ship carried a larger crew than a 100-ton ship, but not much larger.) But demand did not slacken to any great extent. Shipowners and masters who were determined to get to the Caribbean, and possibly back again to Spain, had to make sure that a full complement sailed from Seville. In fact the more prudent probably signed up a larger number than was initially needed. Deaths at sea were numerous and seemingly inevitable, and employers allowed for these losses. To fall below the minimum essential complement needed to run the ship was the nightmare of owners and sailors alike. The unmanageable vessel would then drift and yaw about the Atlantic until, in the worst case, the crew died of thirst and disease. To carry too large a crew was a disaster of another kind. Sailors occupied space and consumed supplies which might have been occupied and eaten by paying passengers. Worse still, they and their food hampers and trunks took away precious cargo space in small ships with limited room. All these harsh realities had far-reaching effects on the Atlantic carrera and, indeed, on the Spanish New World.

Officers and distinguished passengers lived above deck, sleeping in the castles or other small structures on the top deck. Just forward of the main mast was the *fogón*, a charcoal brazier standing on a metal floor, where men crowded around once a day to receive warm food when the weather permitted cooking. The men slept on mats or *petates* between decks (hammocks were a later introduction) as best they could, surrounded by officers' and passengers' trunks, their own meagre bundles and hampers, gun carriages and coils of ropes. Ships pitched and rolled constantly, and in stormy weather the crew slept quite literally in the scuppers as seas broke over the ship and drained away between decks. Men and their clothing were often wet for days on end. Below the men were the hated pumps, which on wooden ships had to be worked for a greater or less time, depending on the conditions of the caulking and seams. The cargo hold was amidships. Often it was closed and out of bounds to the crew.

We have a few first-person accounts of voyages, but it is, of course, hard to tell how typical any of them are. One of the most entertaining is by the Dominican friar, Tomás de la Torre, who travelled from Salamanca to Ciudad Real in Chiapas between 1544 and 1545, accompanying Bishop Bartolomé de las Casas and other friars to his new diocese. His journey to Seville took exactly a month, a tiring preliminary to the ocean voyage for many another migrant. From Seville the friars made their way downriver to San Lúcar de Barrameda, but they were forced to wait some five months for the fleet from New Spain, an expensive and futile interlude which was all too common. The fleet that year consisted of 25 naos and caravels, and one galleon. Among the distinguished migrants was the viceroy's wife, bound for Mexico.

On 10 July the ships crossed the bar of San Lúcar with some difficulty. Torre complains of the extreme heat of these summer days, stuck on the bar at the mouth of the river, and of the seasickness which afflicted many during the first few days on the high seas. French corsairs were seen on the horizon but did not approach. At once Torre complains of the thirst caused by the heat, the ships' biscuits and the salted food. He also grumbles about the filthy and uncomfortable living and sleeping conditions. On 19 July the ships sighted Tenerife in the Canaries, and the following day they landed on La Gómera for ten days of replenishing and rest. Sailing again on 30 July, many fell sick in the rough seas, and complaints of thirst and poor food soon resumed. By 20 August the ship was becalmed and for another seven hot, sultry days made little progress. Shortly thereafter they sighted Désirade and Marie Galante, but did not land for fear of Caribs. Heat, thirst and desultory winds continued until 3 September when they landed at San Juan, Puerto Rico. There the fleet split up; some ships dropped out because there had been too many deaths on board, and one because it leaked too much. Twelve naos and a caravel continued for Veracruz.

They made a stop at Santo Domingo on 9 September, exactly 40 days after leaving the Canaries. There they abandoned the main fleet and on 14 December took a lone ship bound for the coast of Campeche. The crew and passengers were now much afraid of French pirates because the ship lacked armaments and was alone. They ran into their first great storm from 16 to 21 December and talked of abandoning ship. Finally, on 9 January 1545 they landed at the small *villa* of Campeche. But even then their sufferings were not at an end. While travelling along the inland waters between Campeche and Tabasco a canoe overturned and nine of the friars were drowned in the Laguna de Términos. Once ashore the survivors found the going equally difficult. They had to cross the hot, unhealthy lowlands of Tabasco, then face the brutal ascent from Tabasco to the highlands of Chiapas. They arrived in Ciudad Real on 12 March 1545.

The journey, including some lengthy stops in Andalusia and the islands, had taken one year and two months, yet it seems to have been fairly normal and, the Atlantic part of it at least, relatively tranquil. What appears astonishing today is that such a long, difficult and unpleasant voyage was a common experience and formed the link between the colonies and the mother country.

The regularity of these voyages and the accuracy of the navigation still remain something of a mystery. In the course of the sixteenth century many *derroteros* or *rutters* were written down and some were published. In them seafarers or literati tried to assemble a mixture of fact, lore and legend for the next generation of navigators. Perhaps the

most famous of these rutters was Pedro de Medina's *Arte de navegar*
which was translated into English and French before the end of the
sixteenth century. It seems to have been quite widely used.

Pilots, however, seldom made heavy use of such manuals. Indeed
some openly scorned them. In spite of a rudimentary education at the
Casa de Contratación (House of Trade) in Seville, or in Lisbon, many
experienced pilots, a notoriously rough and ready lot, would have little
to do with written or technological aids, and, like Columbus, relied
mainly on dead-reckoning. We may well ask how this was done when
tiny errors could be magnified over the length of an ocean crossing.
In fact pilots of the time were seldom out by more than 50 miles unless
storm driven. 'No such dead-reckoning navigators exist today,' writes
Admiral Morison, 'no man alive, limited to the instruments and means
at Columbus' disposal, could obtain anything near the accuracy of his
results.'[2] And so these early mariners of the Atlantic run keep their
secrets.

Among the Andalusian ports on or near the lower Guadalquivir, Seville
early became predominant and remained so until replaced by Cadiz in
the eighteenth century. At first sight this is puzzling. Cadiz was a busy
port before the discovery of America, had a good harbour and was on
the sea. Columbus himself sailed from Palos on his first voyage, and
Huelva, Moguer and San Lúcar, although small, all had adequate
harbours, fishing fleets and longshore caravels. In fact, most of the early
voyages sailed from these ports. Seville's position at the centre of the
Atlantic economy dates from 1503 when the Casa de Contratación was
established there. In its early days the Casa was little more than a royal
warehouse for storing the proceeds of the royal *quinto*, or fifth, from
the islands and any other royal goods or taxes collected in the New
World. Gradually, however, as bureaucratic agencies will, the Casa
moved into regulation, standardization and centralization. Sailings to
the Indies had to leave from Seville, and all fleets had to return there
after no more than a stop at Cadiz or San Lúcar. Licences for people
and goods for the Indies were obtained at the Casa, import and export
taxes were paid there, and ships gathered, were inspected and approved
for the crossing. Still later the Casa took on more functions. It became
a navy yard for the Spanish Atlantic, careening ships, stockpiling ship's

---

[2] Samuel Eliot Morison, *The European discovery of America: the southern voyages, 1492–1616* (New
York, 1974), 176–7.

stores, and training pilots, shipfitters and cartographers. It was, to a limited extent, a university of the sea, a repository for rutters, maps and retired veterans of previous crossings. All of this activity was centred on Seville as the crown took control of the Spanish Atlantic.

At first sight Seville was a poor choice. It was an inland town, many miles up a sluggish, winding river. The Guadalquivir's course was marked by shifting sandbars and mudflats, not least the final one near San Lúcar at the mouth of the river. However, Seville did, in the early days of the Indies trade, enjoy some major advantages. To lie 70 miles upstream, for instance, was an advantage. It was protected not only from the Atlantic storms which battered the exposed Cadiz promontory, but also from the depredations of Berber and English pirates and navies. Moreover, as ships, especially caravels, were still quite small in the sixteenth century, the shallow river was not yet a major problem. But, above all, Seville was a major market which Cadiz and the small seaports were not. Seville had a well-established merchant class, a sizeable consumer population and a rich agricultural hinterland for feeding sailors, stocking ships and supplying the early settlers in the Caribbean islands, with their scorn for the native cassava, beans and maize, and their yearnings for Andalusian wheat, wine and oil. Seville had an old mercantile tradition and the financial institutions to back it. Northern Italian merchants from Genoa, Bologna and Pisa had established themselves in Seville shortly after it was retaken from the Moors, and the opening up of the New World quickly attracted them. The Genoese were omnipresent. 'Of the twenty-eight noble Genoese houses established by the law of 1528, twenty-one were represented in Seville during the sixteenth century.'[3] Dutch and English merchants were also present in the city before 1520. Seville also had a powerful *consulado*, or guild of merchants, who enjoyed favour with the crown. In fact, there was little debate until the second half of the seventeenth century about which ports should lead the Indies trade. Within Spain the ports of the south-west Atlantic corner chose themselves because of winds, history and geography, and among them Seville quickly and naturally predominated. Any doubts as to its primacy as the port for the Indies were quickly resolved by the centralizing and regulatory tendencies of the Casa de Contratación. In 1668 a sort of compromise between Seville and Cadiz led to loading and unloading at San Lúcar. In 1679, that is

[3] Ruth Pike, *Enterprise and adventure: the Genoese in Seville and the opening of the New World* (Ithaca, New York, 1966), 2.

for the last 40 years of the period under discussion, Cadiz became the principal port for the Indies trade.

Two sets of similar circumstances determined the location of Spain's colonial Caribbean ports. At the time of the European discovery the demographic, agricultural and mineral wealth of what was to become Spanish America was concentrated in two areas, Mexico and the central Andes. As a result these two areas, with their capitals at Mexico City and Lima, became the centres of the Spanish colonial empire. Obviously it was of paramount importance to connect them both securely and expeditiously to Seville. Both, then, required a Caribbean port. Mexico City, the former Tenochtitlán, was connected to Spain by Veracruz and its harbour at San Juan de Ulúa, near the spot where Cortés and his band had landed. It was simply the most convenient place with a harbour near Mexico City. Lima and its port of Callao were connected to the Caribbean and Seville by the isthmus of Panama. Various attempts by interest groups in Nicaragua, Guatemala and Tehuantepec to win away the isthmian trade, or *trajín*, came to nothing despite long campaigns. The narrow isthmus at Panama was the most logical spot for trade via the Caribbean from and to the Pacific coast of South America.

Nevertheless, the Panama link did cause many problems. The nature of the terrain and the proximity of the two seas made it impossible to hide the principal city far inland, as in the case of Mexico City and Bogotá. The narrowness of the isthmus made towns there easy prey for pirates, unlike Lima and Santiago de Chile tucked away far down the Pacific coast. Therefore, the towns of Panama, a vital link in the Spanish colonial system, were hard to defend, often attacked, and caused the imperial government great concern. Panama's Caribbean coast also lacked good harbours. Nombre de Dios, never more than a collection of shacks on an open beach, was abandoned in 1598 and a new port founded nearby in Portobelo. The harbour was somewhat better but far from adequate and eventually just as unhealthy as Nombre de Dios.

These two ports, and indeed all the other ports of the Caribbean mainland not cooled by the trade winds, were tropical pest-holes during the colonial period. This inhibited their growth and gave them a unique seasonal life, created by and totally dependent on the carrera. The somnolent inhabitants of groups of squalid huts such as Portobelo would suddenly rouse themselves when the great fleets arrived from Spain. As the fair began, tent cities of merchants would spring up along the beach, rents for cabins and food prices would soar to extraordinary levels, the population would double or treble, and royal officials would quickly appear like flies to the honeypot to collect taxes, control or participate in the brawling and gambling, issue permits and inspect the loading and unloading of the ships. Once the ships had sailed all who could afford to quickly abandoned the hot, sickly, shanty towns.

Other ports served secondary areas. Cartagena was the main port of the north coast of Tierra Firme and of the interior of New Granada. It was of considerable importance during the heyday of the sixteenth-century carrera, and became the base and refuelling point for the Panama run. By 1620, however, it had fallen back to a secondary position. Various unsatisfactory little harbours, almost empty for most of the year, were tried in the Gulf of Honduras and served the highlands of the audiencia of Guatemala.

The carrera itself, and the characteristics of its route, created some of the island ports. Santo Domingo, the first city of the Spanish Indies, was to some extent a case apart, although it owed much of its early vitality to trade with Spain. Havana, in spite of its exchanges with the interior of Cuba and with other parts of the Caribbean, lived and died by the carrera in the years before its sugar industry developed. It existed as a last refuelling stop, with its tiny outlier of Saint Augustine in Florida, before the long voyage back to Seville. The fleets from San Juan de Ulúa and Portobelo reunited there. Havana's role was in many ways to serve as the Canary Islands of the Caribbean. Its importance in the link was recognized by the crown which subsidized its existence by means of various subventions from Mexico and by other favours. It was heavily fortified since, like Panama, its importance and exposed position attracted the attention of pirates and hostile foreign powers.

Far more important than the geographical distance between ports was the distance in time. Wind-blown ships were slow, and they could not maintain constant speeds over long distances. The average voyage from the Andalusian ports to Trinidad in the sixteenth and early seventeenth centuries took about 32 days. What is today easily forgotten, however, is the fact that if a ship's ultimate destination were Veracruz or Nombre de Dios/Portobelo, then by the time it reached Trinidad not even half of the voyage was over. An average voyage to Veracruz lasted 75 days and one to the isthmus of Panama a day or two longer. Because of the southerly route imposed by winds and currents, the geography of the

Caribbean for a ship coming from Spain was somewhat distorted. Trinidad, Puerto Rico, Hispaniola, and even Cartagena, were relatively near to Spain. Havana was at a middle distance, Veracruz and Nombre de Dios/Portobelo were the ports of the far Atlantic, and Florida, quite close to Spain in geographical distance, and certainly closer than Cartagena and Veracruz, was the most distant destination of all for ships coming from Spain and bound for the Caribbean.

Ships leaving the Caribbean for Andalusia, however, had to face a different geography of time. Florida was now part of the near Atlantic, indeed was the nearest part of the Caribbean to Spain. In the islands, because of the northerly return routes and prevailing winds, Havana was closer to Spain than was Hispaniola, which, in turn, was closer than Puerto Rico. Cartagena, which took just over 50 days from Spain, compared to 65 for Havana, was much further away for return voyages. From Cartagena, ships took about 115 days to reach a Spanish port, while from Havana, now nearer Spain, they took only 65. Veracruz and Nombre de Dios/Portobelo remained the chief ports of the far Atlantic, both going and coming, but whereas the isthmian ports were only a day or two further away from Veracruz for ships coming from Spain, they were over ten days more distant for ships going back to Spain.

In general, therefore, voyages to America were more rapid than voyages to Spain. Or, in the minds of the people of the times, America was nearer to Spain than Spain was to America.

If, then, Mexico and Panama were the far Atlantic, what of Peru? That area should perhaps be called the remote Atlantic. As for Manila, that distant administrative outlier of and appendage to New Spain, journeys to and fro had to cross two oceans and a continent. Measured in time, the Philippines were much more remote than the moon is today.

We have seen how shipowners worried over the size of the ships' crews. In view of the constraints of ship size and above all speed, they were far more worried about the weight, bulk, perishability, and therefore profitability of the goods they carried. Wine and olive oil from Seville, still marketable in Cartagena or Santo Domingo after 50 days or so, might well have turned to vinegar or to a rancid loss by the time the flagons had spent another two weeks baking in a hot damp hold crossing the Caribbean to Panama or Veracruz. Spanish wine and oil, both needed not only for day-to-day living (the water was usually undrinkable and most people knew it), but also by the Church for sacramental purposes, could not hope to reach Lima or Santiago de

Chile, far less Manila, in a usable condition. Small wonder, then, that the Peruvian and Chilean wine and oil industries started up so quickly and met such slight opposition among the agriculturists and monopolistic consulados of Andalusia. Compare this with their prohibition of vineyards and olive groves in New Spain and the islands, a prohibition which lasted until the wars of independence in the early nineteenth century.

Weight and bulk were even more important than perishability in determining where in the colonies commodities were likely to be produced. Sugar cane, a bulky product requiring elaborate processing and handling by the standards of the period, might, if grown in Cuba for instance, still show a profit in Seville after a voyage of 70 days, whereas if grown in the Mexican lowlands around Veracruz, after a voyage of 130 days from Seville, it was far less likely to be profitable. In fact, the further from Spain in time were the goods produced, the smaller in bulk and, to a lesser extent, the lower in weight they had to be in order to show a profit. Thus, the near Atlantic had an advantage over the far Atlantic, and what was profitable when sent to Europe from Mexico in the far Atlantic was less so when sent from Guayaquil or Callao on the Pacific coast. Last, and most remote in this time continuum, was Manila, whence only the lightest and most expensive products, such as quality Chinese silks, rare spices and precious stones, could be sent to Spain with any hope of profit.

Of course other forces were also at work. Silver became the chief export of Mexico and Peru, not only because it packed great value into small bulk, and thus could show a profit when sent from the far, or even remote, Atlantic but because the major deposits and the labour to work them were in Mexico and Peru and not in the islands or Venezuela. Furthermore, much depended on the health of the carrera and of Spain. When the carrera and the Spanish economy were flourishing, other lesser plantation crops could thrive – cochineal in Oaxaca or indigo in San Salvador – on the margins of the export trade in silver. In more difficult days, however, when fewer ships were reaching Veracruz, and when they were carrying fewer items from a declining Spain, bullion and gems became all-important and marginal products were squeezed out. From Peru such marginal agricultural exports were nearly always impossible. They could not reach Spain and still show a profit even in the heyday of the carrera.

One important factor complicating the rather simple relationship between time, weight, bulk and profitability was, of course, price. As some Spanish American goods, such as chocolate, sugar, or chinchona bark for medicinal purposes, became more fashionable or necessary and thus commanded a higher price, they could be sent from a greater distance and still show a profit.

Another factor was the value of the goods going to America. If high profits were made on the outer leg, then lower ones, or even minor losses, might be tolerated on the journey back to Europe. Even logwood could be carried back to London as little better than ballast if the products of England's early industrial revolution had sold well on the beach during the annual fairs at Veracruz or Portobelo. Then, of course, as ship size and speed grew, the balance of the equation tipped. Ships could carry more, get to market quicker, and so freight rates went down and profitability rose.

The difficulty in judging profitability was further complicated by the difficulty of assessing supply and demand. In the early and middle sixteenth century this was not too hard. The colonies had not yet created many import substitutes of their own and Spain's European rivals had not yet begun to compete seriously with Seville as suppliers. But once trade between colonies began to develop, and once Dutch and English smugglers began to intrude from entrepots and gigantic warehouses, such as Curaçao and Jamaica, then Spanish merchants, having heard, for example, that pots and pans were much in demand in Veracruz, might rush to transport a cargo there six to eight months later only to find the market glutted by some quicker colonial or foreign entrepreneur.

All these complicating factors, however, developed slowly, and did not become important until the late sixteenth, and, in many cases, the late seventeenth century.

During the first phase of the carrera de Indias – from Columbus' initial voyage to the end of the mainland conquests (that is to say, the first 40 years) – people formed the main cargoes out from Europe. At least 200,000 people, possibly as many as 300,000, went to the New World before 1600, and perhaps one-third, nearly all Spaniards, migrated during the first two decades. Some 450,000 followed during the seventeenth century. The early migrants were broadly representative of Spanish society – with some significant exceptions. Both the highest and the lowest extremes of the social ladder were under-represented; the very rich and the high nobility, presumably, because they did not have any compelling reasons to leave, and the peasantry because they could not afford to travel or were prevented from doing so. The lesser nobility, the *hidalgos*, personified later by Don Quijote, a class of limited financial means but old martial traditions and high expectations, may well have been over-represented, at least in the early years of the Antilles and conquests. The very old and the very young are also missing from the early passenger lists. Unsettled circumstances and long voyages kept them at home. As permanent towns and a more settled life emerged, parents and children were sent for more often. Women made up, it can be assumed, some 50 per cent or more of the peninsular population, but only about 6 per cent of New World arrivals to the Antilles in the early days. As conditions became more secure more wives and daughters arrived. By the 1540s some 20 per cent of migrants were women and this percentage slowly increased throughout the century. As one would expect, the south-western corner of Spain supplied a disproportionately large share of the migrants. Western Andalusia and southern and central Extremadura, and especially the major cities there, such as Badajoz, Cáceres, Huelva, Córdoba and, above all, Seville, sent large contingents. Seville alone probably provided about 40 per cent of all the urban migrants in the sixteenth century.

In the early years many returned to Spain. It was 28 years, after all, before news of the discovery of Tenochtitlán began to change the crown's mind about the importance of its New World possessions. The islands were a great disappointment, and even after the decisive mainland conquests began many people returned home. The first generation of conquerors in New Spain and Peru does not seem to have had a settler mentality. In general the aim was to accumulate sufficient wealth, either by looting or extracting surplus capital from the Indians, to return to Spain to a life of ease, or, perhaps, to move up the social ladder by buying land, houses, *mayorazgos*, or even, the apex of all ambitions, a title or a small government position. Many conquerors died in the attempt, others never made quite enough to go home in style and resigned themselves, like Bernal Díaz del Castillo, to a life of moderate comfort and considerable prestige in some quiet corner of the newly conquered lands. But some of the conquerors succeeded in transferring their wealth to Spain and returning there. A few of them, often leaders like Cortés and Alvarado, crossed and recrossed the ocean many times. Later generations of migrants contained more permanent settlers.

Once the age of conquest had passed and officialdom took over from the campaign leaders, migration to the Indies became, to some degree, less spontaneous. Large sponsored groups went out to the colonies together. A very typical case would be a move to the Indies of newly appointed civil or ecclesiastical high officials. Such men would bring with them not only their own immediate households of family members, servants and slaves, but also a swarm, sometimes numbering a hundred or more, of distant relatives, subordinate business associates, hangers-on and friends. All these under-employed but ambitious and well-connected people had to be placed by the office-holder as quickly as possible once he was installed in the Indies, and this had a serious impact on the economy and social structure of the colony.

The main return cargo during the early history of the carrera was gold. Typically, when a new area was invaded, previous accumulations of the metal were seized as booty from the aboriginal inhabitants, especially the elites. This set the Spaniards to looking for local sources of supply. Gold panning in nearby rivers would begin, gradually intensifying as news of the best rivers spread about. Indian slaves usually provided the labour, although a few rivers in New Spain produced so much, even if only briefly, that black slaves were imported on the profits realized. Such gold panning would peak in a few years, then die away to little or nothing. Seldom did these fleeting booms along any river last more than ten years. Thus gold production in the half-century or so of discovery and conquest goes through a series of intersecting minor cycles, each one slightly larger than the one before because of the cumulative addition of new territory, elite treasures and fresh rivers. As Santo Domingo begins to peak about 1510, Puerto Rico, Panama and Cuba start to produce. As their production slackens about 1520, or slightly later, Mexico and Central America enter the scene and, as they peak, Peru begins. Gold production for the Spanish colonial period probably reaches its highest level a year or two before 1550.

We know little of production levels. Not much of the precious metal was retained in the New World, at least compared to the percentages of silver which were later kept back, but the new imperial bureaucracy being set up in Spain had not yet established a regular system yielding annual statistics. Pierre Chaunu estimated that 25–30 tons of gold went to Spain from the islands during the first cycle. Mexico produced twenty tons before 1540, and Peru perhaps about the same before the cycle ended. Although these quantities are far from impressive, such was the value and prestige of gold that it had considerable impact on the Atlantic trade. Chaunu and others have noticed a brief depression in Atlantic trade in the 1550s and in Spain between 1550 and 1562. Perhaps a pause in a long period of otherwise steady growth gives a better perspective. This pause of the fifties is too close to the end of the gold cycle to be ignored. It may be explained as simply the hiatus between the waning of the Age of Gold and the rise to dominance of the Age of Silver. It was more, perhaps, the pause between the Age of Booty, of removing previously accumulated surpluses and surface wealth, and the next overlapping cycles of tribute, *encomienda* and silver mining, all undertakings requiring much more organization, investment and commitment of time and energy.

If the end of the gold cycle caused a massive readjustment in the economies of the Indies, the high value of gold also had its effect in Spain. Although the amounts sent to Andalusia seem small, nevertheless they slowly and haltingly increased all through the first half-century after 1492. This gradually drew the attention of merchants, shipowners and, above all, the crown, to the Indies, an area which under Columbus and his immediate successors had seemed a poor and secondary discovery. At first the crown had been almost confiscatory over gold, collecting as much as two-thirds of the amount arriving in Spain. By 1504 it realized that the gold industry might have a future and set about stimulating it. In 1504 the royal tax was fixed at one-fifth, the famous *quinto real*. (In time reductions to stimulate production reduced the quinto to one-tenth almost everywhere and last of all in Peru and Alto Peru in 1736.)

Gold was also the chief stimulus for the creation of the early pre-Mexican carrera. Its prestige set the crown to establishing an administered and regular trade. Its value compared to compactness and density allowed it to show a large profit in Seville even in the days of unscheduled, intermittent sailings and tiny caravels poorly designed for shipping cargo.

Before 1550 gold also played a major role in the price revolution which swept through Spain and then most of the rest of Europe. Pierre Vilar and others have pointed out that the economic expansion in

Europe antedated the influx of American gold and was based largely on endogenous factors such as demographic and economic expansion. Among European imports spices may have had more of an impact on late fifteenth and early sixteenth-century growth than did gold. Nevertheless, although American gold became a factor late in this expansionist phase, it was closely linked to the rapid price rise of the first half of the sixteenth century, and this rise, in turn, further stimulated the volume of circulating currency, business and exchanges.

Gold's chief companion on the journeys back to Spain was hides. Within twenty years of 1492 hides were being shipped back to Spain, and the quantities involved rose steadily for almost a century. Hides and leather were a principal trade of the sixteenth century, their uses far more numerous than they are today. Although Spain had been one of Europe's leading producers for many years, the commodity was always in short supply in western Europe. In many parts men and their agriculture competed with domesticated animals for space, thus reducing the number of cattle which produced the hides needed for leather.

In the New World cattle and horses ranged over vast areas, multiplied rapidly, met few natural enemies and little competition. Often they were able to graze the formerly cultivated, fertilized fields of dead or departed agriculturists. To some extent semi-feral cattle filled the demographic vacuum left behind by the Indians. In the early sixteenth century there was very little demand for their meat. Spaniards and Africans were few in number and the Indians were not yet accustomed to beef. As a result there was little systematic butchering of the best of the vast wild herds which appeared on the larger islands and in Mexico and Central America soon after they were conquered. Instead these animals were rounded up, killed and skinned where and when needed. No capital had been invested in care or feeding, except perhaps by previous generations of Indians. Little was expended on transportation to the ports on the islands. So hides, often only partly cured or tanned, could pay the freight to Europe and still show a small but tidy profit there.

Cattle, too, went through a seemingly ineluctable demographic cycle in the New World. The reasons are not all clear, but late in the sixteenth century colonists complained that the cattle population was falling. Perhaps too many had been wastefully slaughtered for their hides. In some areas the roaming herds may have put Malthusian pressures on the land and on their own numbers by overgrazing. Moreover, as the

Spanish cities grew and the remaining Indian populations became converted to the taste of beef, so an organized meat supply, the mass production of jerky and salted beef and more careful management of butchering came into existence. The result was a decline in the trade in hides.

The early years of discovery and conquest also saw the transfer of exotica to the Old World. Strange beasts and birds, plants both useful and curious, were sent to Spain. So, too, were some of the vestiges of the great Amerindian civilizations which, it was hoped, would be of interest to crowned heads or other patrons. Feathered headdresses, breastplates and shields, gold, jade and silver ornaments which had escaped the melting cauldrons of the *conquistadores*, were sent home and ended up in the royal collections and museums of western and central Europe. Codices which were not destroyed or burned as idolatrous were also sent, although some of them crossed the ocean much later. The exotica with which the conquerors proved their exploits and showed off the new lands were to prove invaluable to modern generations of ethnohistorians, anthropologists and art historians. Finally, pearls from Margarita and some of the other small islands were of some importance in the early years, and continued to move to Spain intermittently throughout the colonial period.

The great age of the Spanish fleets followed the conquest of the two densely populated mainland nuclei, and the commencement of large-scale silver mining. It reached its greatest heights in the twenty or so years after mid-century, somewhat earlier in Mexico, later in Peru, and was beginning its slow decline by the 1590s, certainly by the 1620s.

Spaniards on the mainland lived off surplus capital extracted from Indian society. This was done by two important institutions, encomienda and tribute. Encomienda, in theory at least, a contractual arrangement whereby Indians were entrusted to the temporal and to some extent the spiritual care of a Spaniard in return for their labour and some of their surplus goods, gradually weakened as an economic force as the crown in Mexico and Peru was able to remove the labour element.[4] Only in more peripheral regions, such as Paraguay, Tucumán, or Caracas before cacao and sugar, did the encomienda continue to be a means for compelling Indians to perform work. The tribute or Indian head tax

[4] For a detailed explanation and discussion of the *encomienda* system, see MacLeod, *CHLA*, II, ch. 7 and Gibson, *CHLA*, II, ch. 11.

was closely related to the encomienda. Paid because of their vassalage and subjugation, the tribute was collected and turned over to *encomenderos* or to the crown. After the labour obligation was removed, the tribute became the main relationship between Indians and encomenderos. Indians who were not subject to private encomiendas, those who were, in the parlance of the times, 'in the crown', paid their tributes directly to royal or local officials.

Such a system worked well in an era when large numbers of Indians provided capital to a small number of conquerors, but it began to weaken when the Indian population fell, royal legislation increased and the Spanish and *casta*, or mixed blood, population grew. One of the problems involved in both the encomienda and the tribute was how to hispanicize it. At first Cortés and his men preferred to continue Moctezuma's system. This included some items, such as feathers, obsidian, or wild animal skins, which were of limited use to Spaniards. These were soon eliminated. But nearly all pre-conquest tribute had been collected in produce. What was to be done, for example, with the huge quantities of maize delivered up in the early days, together with all the cloth and beans? Some of it could be eaten or worn, but even then there were problems of distribution. Not even a majority of Spaniards were encomenderos, clergy, or royal officials. Then again, neither the crown nor creditors in Spain could be expected to receive payment in heaps of mouldy maize on the docks of Seville. Somehow the crown's share and the other portions of the tribute destined for Spain by private individuals had to be transformed into transportable goods, preferably silver or coinage, before being sent to the fleets. The final difficulty was that maize was an Indian staple, consumed by Spaniards only when wheat was unavailable or too expensive. This gave rise to two problems: how to return some of the extracted tributary maize to Indian society, and how to oblige Indian society to pay at least some small portion of its tribute in a European agricultural product such as wheat.

Spaniards used many devices to hispanicize and to partly monetize the tribute, to redistribute it and to prepare part of it for the carrera for the use of the crown and Spain. Two of these devices in particular stand out. Very early, encomenderos and royal officials set up a system of auctions whereby some of the bulk products of the tribute such as maize, beans and cotton cloth were sold off to those who needed them in return for cash, silver or, once in a while, other products or services which were more compact or necessary. This device served several purposes. It distributed maize and other staples to Spaniards, mestizos and castas who were not encomenderos, clergy or royal officials, and it returned some of these staples, often via one or two middlemen, to Indian society. There were, however, some inherent problems, one of which was hoarding. Encomenderos tended to keep back their maize until just before the next harvest season, hoping thus to obtain higher prices. Another problem was that royal officials dominated most auctions so that the coinage produced went first to royal coffers and was syphoned off to Spain too rapidly for the good of the colony, thus demonetizing the system of exchange all over again and returning it to barter. This problem could be remedied while the silver mines were expanding but became a serious impediment to exchanges and commerce in general when silver production began to decline.

The second device was through encomenderos and officials experimenting with the tribute itself. In the first half of the sixteenth century the amounts collected in goods were gradually reduced and the amounts collected in coinage increased. At one stage this went too far, and the tribute became almost entirely a tax in money. However, the government backed away from this position and by the late sixteenth century the tribute had settled down as a mixed tax, roughly half in staples and half in coinage.

There were several reasons for these adjustments. Obviously, if coinage could be extracted directly from Indian society, then the extent and size of tributary auctions could be correspondingly reduced, and money could go directly to the royal coffers or to the purses of the encomenderos. At the same time, if less maize and other staples were taken out of Indian society then less would have to be returned there after the auction process. But a balance between coinage and goods was necessary. If the tribute were paid entirely in coinage Indians might be tempted to crowd into the Spanish- and *casta*-dominated marketplaces as merchants, and cheap foodstuffs from Indian agriculture would not enter the Spanish cities in sufficient quantities. If the tribute were paid entirely in staples the new rulers would find it difficult to force the Indians to sell their goods or labour, or to travel to distant workplaces. As a result of these various experiments, encomienda and tribute became standardized. This helped to revive Indian petty trade, constituted a compromise between the needs of the carrera and the crown and the needs of the new colonial elites, and provided much of the early capital which allowed some of the more prescient of the early encomenderos to diversify away from their dependence on a shrinking Indian population base. For our purposes here it played a principal role in collecting the silver and other coinage which went into private savings and royal coffers, and from there to the galleons for Spain.

The famous silver mines of New Spain and Peru were, of course, the great source of silver for the ships bound for Spain. Gold had been a feature of the islands and lowlands, of the early days and the conquests. Silver came from highland mines, and in its beginnings it was tied to large Indian populations and, to a lesser extent, to the encomienda. Later, the silver mines, especially those of Potosí in Upper Peru, would be closely related to Indian rotational labour drafts (*repartimientos* or *mitas*). Mexico came to depend more on free labour.

Mines were a large source of taxes and other income for the crown. Zacatecas and Guanajuato were opened in 1548 and 1558, and Potosí, somewhat slower to develop at first, in 1545. Amounts from these areas combined gradually increased throughout the sixteenth century and reached enormous quantities. From the 1570s until the third decade of the seventeenty century Potosí was probably the richest mine in the world.

The use of mercury as an amalgam for separating the silver from the other ores opened up a subsidiary industry. The murderous mine at Huancavelica in Peru supplied the mines of that area with mercury and sent some to Mexico via coastal Pacific shipping. Mexico's other supplier was Almadén in western Andalusia, and mercury formed a large part of the westbound cargoes of the carrera to Veracruz in the late sixteenth century.

The whole output of silver did not flow to Spain as was the case with gold. The growing Spanish colonial bureaucracy and local economies needed more silver to pay salaries, finance exchange and provide a currency. Silver was also in demand for intercolonial trade. Barter could not keep pace with an increasingly complex trade, and silver and coinage, intended in part for the fleets and for Spain, entered the commerce between Mexico and Peru, Mexico and Guatemala, Mexico and Venezuela and Peru and Chile. When the link between Acapulco and Manila was established after 1567, there was an even greater drain on the silver intended for Spain. Many of the oriental imports to Mexico and Peru were paid for by silver from the mines of Zacatecas,

Guanajuato and Potosí. The crown was unable to halt these colonial exchanges, although its prohibitions doubtless slowed down their growth.

Such was the increase in silver output, and such was the flood of silver going to Seville, that this drain on the total shipped did not cause great concern in the sixteenth century. Potosí increased its output until the 1590s, producing by that date half, or more, of all Spanish silver. Until 1630 its decline was quite slow. Mexico's totals also increased for most of the century, and serious decline did not begin until the 1630s.

By the decade of the 1530s silver had passed gold in weight as a cargo. Some 86 tons were shipped during that decade compared to just over fourteen tons of gold. Between 1560 and 1570, with the introduction to Mexico of the patio process of amalgamation, silver pushed far ahead of gold in weight and value. Mexican production led until about 1575 and was then surpassed by the two Perus, now using mercury from Huancavelica. The crown's income from the Indies, composed of the royal fifth, some of the Indian tribute, sales and excise taxes, part of the ecclesiastical tithe and several minor imposts and monopolies, grew throughout the century, and in the years of the last decade was four times greater than it had been in the 1560s. Royal silver may have made up about a quarter of the total imported. In the sixteenth century most of it went to pay first German then later Genoese bankers. In total, up to 1600, the fleets had probably carried to Spain some 25,000 tons of silver, a staggering quantity to be introduced into a previously silver-starved western Europe in so short a time. The flood of bullion caused severe strains and dislocations in the Spanish-American, Spanish and European economies.

In Mexico and Peru the rapid growth of the money supply before 1580 caused price inflation. While the cost of basic commodities still seemed low to recent arrivals from the peninsula, people long established in the New World felt the impact and complained about it. The rise in prices coincided with the fall in Indian rural population, two facts which were not unconnected, and the result was food shortages and higher prices for staples in the growing Spanish cities. Many citizens moved to the countryside to escape this inflation and to provide for their own basic needs outside the urban marketplace. This was only one of the factors which caused a vast readjustment in the Spanish colonies between the 1580s and 1620s.

The flood of silver into Spain, reaching its first peak somewhere in the 1590s at about 11 million pesos annually, had an even greater impact on its destination. While American bullion formed only one part of crown revenues – perhaps about a fifth in the late sixteenth century – yet its manner of arrival and its nature caused it to have a great political and psychological impact. It arrived in Seville to the blare of trumpets, as it were, all in one shining and spendable lump. It did not dribble in and dribble out as did Castillian taxation. The crown was provided with the means for spectacular projects and large payments in coin, thus attracting the attention of many people and the jealousy of rival powers. Interests ranging all the way from idle mercenaries to shrewd German and Genoese bankers were impressed by these enormous, and regular, windfalls, and the psychological impact of the annual arrival of silver at Seville thus meant more soldiers for the crown's campaigns in an era before regular standing armies and more eager creditors to provide the loans which financed the monarchy's most grandiose plans. In the European economy, silver was the basis of a coinage which, at this early stage, was not yet backed by paper money or a very complete system of credit. Issuing coins, mostly silver or copper, was the main way of expanding the circulating medium, so American silver was far more important than the mere quantity shipped to Spain might suggest.

It is worth noting that the large remittances of American bullion by and to private individuals also played their part. Private remittances were two-and-a-half or three times as large as those to the crown in the late sixteenth century, and some of them reached the crown's coffers via domestic taxes, especially in the case of Castile. Then, too, on rare occasions the crown confiscated all bullion on arrival, promising to pay it back later with interest. Not that any of this was neatly managed, even by standards of the time. Expenditure far exceeded income, and at an increasing pace, all through the reigns of Charles V and Philip II. Royal finances were in crisis by 1575 and bankrupt when the second suspension of payments was announced in 1596.

Silver also contributed to the continuing price rise, which slowed down somewhat after 1550 while still distorting the Spanish economy. The price rise began in Andalusia, as was to be expected: there the bullion arrived, there much of it was coined and put into circulation. Throughout the sixteenth century Andalusia led Spain in price inflation, and Spain as a whole led France and England. The influx of silver affected even the European periphery, where the now plentiful coinage pushed out barter and ushered in a money exchange.

The importation of all this bullion was balanced by a growing Spanish export trade. The biggest fleet and cargo of all was dispatched to the Caribbean in 1608. Spain was an agricultural country and the bulk of its exports to the colonies was composed of grains, wine and oil of Castile and Andalusia, staples most sought after by the colonists. But it is noticeable that there was still a fair balance, compared to later days, between home-grown raw materials and home-made manufactured goods. To be sure, even in the sixteenth century, too many of the manufactured goods exported from Seville were re-exports which originated in France and the Low Countries, and too many of the merchants of the Seville consulado were already little more than *testaferros*, or straw-men, for Genoese or Dutch bankers and merchant houses. Nevertheless, for much of the sixteenth century Spain sent large quantities of home-produced manufactures to America, including furniture, iron wares, coarse and finished cloth both plain and elaborate, and regional food and craft specialties. Spain was producing almost enough to pay for the influx of silver at mid-century and even later.

The growth of the fleet system in the second half of the sixteenth century reinforced belief in mercantile monopoly. Spain and its great guilds or consulados of merchants in Seville, Cadiz, Veracruz and Lima came to rely on a trade and convoy system based on exclusion of rivals, rigid scheduling, bottlenecks where trade could be supervised – Seville and Panama being the two most notable – and subordination of the colonies to Spanish priorities. Foreigners and foreign products were not all they tried to exclude. Lesser Spanish and American ports, such as those of Galicia and the Río de la Plata, were rigidly, if unsuccessfully, prohibited from playing a part in the Indies trade.

The capacity and dependability of the fleets also stimulated new industries, trades, and routes in America itself. Cochineal, a fast red dye, came from several areas in Mesoamerica, above all from Oaxaca. Its production and shipment depended on several features which did not affect mining, such as hailstorms, winds, or diseases among the dye-producing beetles and cactus. As a result harvests, and therefore totals shipped, fluctuated quite widely from year to year. The largest shipment made before the late eighteenth century was in 1587, and a noticeable deterioration set in after 1595. The value of shipments is a different story, of course, because cochineal prices inflated rapidly after 1604. The cargo of 25,200 *arrobas* in 1587 was worth only 381,150,000 *maravedís*, while that of 1619, only 8,306 arrobas, was almost equal in value at 373,370,000 maravedís.

Indigo, a blue vegetable dye, was never quite as valuable as cochineal. Vegetable blues were to be found in Europe, the manufacturing process was simple compared to that of cochineal, and indigo had long been imported from the Far East by the Portuguese and others. Much larger quantities were sent, however, both from Veracruz and the Bay of Honduras. The dye was produced in many parts of New Spain, Central America, Venezuela and the islands, but the biggest source was the Pacific coast of Guatemala and San Salvador. Indigo's production cycle began more slowly but held up better than that of cochineal, at least so far as shipments to Seville were concerned. In 1614, the best year, 280,950 lb arrived in Spain. Prices fluctuated wildly depending on quality, demand and supplies from rival areas outside Spanish America. The large cargo of 1614, for example, had a value of 168,379,900 maravedís, while a much smaller shipment of two years before was worth 236,625,000 maravedís.

Other American products which accompanied sixteenth-century silver to Andalusia included dyewoods, many of them from Campeche, Isla de Términos and Tabasco, brazilwood from the larger Antilles, sugar, mostly from Santo Domingo before the 1590s, pearls and hides. In 1589, 143,734 hides arrived in Spain, a total never again approached until the eighteenth century.

Late in the century some new trade items began to appear in the manifests. Chinese silks and damasks, via the Philippines and New Spain, were shipped in small but very valuable quantities in the 1580s and reached impressive totals in the second decade of the seventeenth century. Then they too fell away. Cotton, largely for sail making, and *pita* thread for caulking seams, were imported from time to time. Salsaparilla, a medicinal root thought to be a specific for a multitude of ailments, was shipped in fairly sizeable quantities from Veracruz, Campeche and the Bay of Honduras in the last 30 years of the sixteenth and the first twenty years of the seventeenth centuries. There are also fleeting mentions of consignments of such items as ginger, amber, tobacco, which was to reach such importance in the eighteenth century, and balsam. Chocolate and its accompanying spice vanilla hardly appear yet. They had to wait for seventeenth-century European changes in taste and were popular only in the New World.

Silver and the fleets also stimulated the growth of a shipping industry on the Pacific coast and in the Caribbean. In general, New Spain's economy diversified more rapidly than that of Peru, and from the days of Cortés a small fleet of ships took Mesoamerican products such as Indian slaves, pitch, dyes and cotton to Guayaquil and Callao. Mexico also trans-shipped unknown but probably considerable quantities of Chinese silks in the late sixteenth century. In return Peru sent silver, some of it for the fleets for Spain, some to pay the Mexican and Manila merchants. Peruvian silver always had a poor reputation, although disrespect for it was, of course, relative. When minted there the coinage was often underweight, debased with alloys, restamped and shaved. But the silver was sufficiently valuable to create a minor fleet system of its own. Once a year it was carried by a protected fleet from Callao to Panama, there to be transported across the isthmus by *recuas* of mules to Nombre de Dios, and later Portobelo, to meet the fleets from Seville.

Well before the end of the century Peru was also sending wine, olives and olive oil to Panama and New Spain, much to the disgust of merchants and royal officials in the mother country who made strenuous efforts to control this trade. Unable to do so they banned the importation of Peruvian wine and oil into Panama in 1614 and into New Spain in 1620. All trade between Mexico and Peru was forbidden in 1631, not to be revived officially until the eighteenth century. The bans were unsuccessful but may have played some role in the decline of the size and frequency of shipments in mid-seventeenth century.

Shorter inshore routes also flourished along the Pacific coast after mid century. Guayaquil sent wood and pitch to Callao. Chile sent wheat. Guatemala exchanged its cacao, almost a staple to Mexican Indians, for Mexican cloth and silver.

The silver shipments also stimulated Caribbean trade. Apart from the traffic in groceries which developed in places such as Caracas and Costa Rica, some of it specifically traded to provision the carrera, there was also a considerable volume of business between Veracruz and Havana. Havana, an important garrison and carrera port, was supplied with cereals, cloth, armaments and a money subsidy from Mexico. There was also a sizeable trade in sugar between the islands and the highlands of the Mesoamerican interior.

Many of these products, however, were mere adjuncts to the silver trade. The carrera, with its two main spurs running to and from Veracruz and the isthmus of Panama, lived and died by silver and the Spanish and European goods sent back to pay for it.

Official silver *remesas*, or remittances, to Spain, seem to have peaked in 1595. They held up fairly well at a lower level until 1619, then fell off steadily, despite an occasional good fleet, usually an accumulation of the mine production of several years, until the trade became small and intermittent in the 1640s and 50s. Apart from a small revival in the 1670s, the downward slide in official imports continued until the end of the century. Unofficial bullion was, of course, another story. The year 1595 was also one of the best years for the value of total goods sent to Spain, although it must be remembered that value held up longer than volume because as silver grew scarcer it inflated rapidly in price. (Gold and silver reached their highest prices of the century between 1660 and 1680.) The most valuable shipment of the sixteenth and seventeenth centuries arrived on the fleet of 1624, although the amount of bullion sent was less than half of 1595.

The volume and value of the other goods sent to Spain peaked somewhat later than silver, probably around 1618 or 1619, but when decay came the lesser cargoes fell away at a faster pace than silver. In fact, the needy crown seems to have reserved space for silver and excluded the other items when fleets were small and intermittent. Thus cargoes such as cochineal, indigo and sugar were squeezed out.

Exports from the Seville ports complex to America, most of which were paid for in silver, were in a rough correspondence to treasure imports, so it is no surprise to find that the official export of Spanish and European goods peaks about the same time. The biggest year for legal Spanish exports before the eighteenth century, both in volume and variety, was 1608. Thereafter, although in general they held up better than imports from America, the size of the fleets, the regularity of the sailings and the value of the goods sent fell away rapidly.

Thus the Atlantic trade reached a series of high points in the years between 1580 and 1620. Obviously these were decades of change and readjustment in Spain and her colonies. Half a century of growth came to a halt, paused at a lower level for a few years, before sliding downwards to the mid-century trough. There were many different but interrelated factors at work.

The 1570s were a crucial decade for the Indian population of New Spain which had in any case been falling since the time of first contact. Now, in the 1570s, a terrible series of epidemics swept through the land reducing numbers to a fraction of what they had been at the time of the conquest. Production and trade was affected in a variety of ways: labour services and tribute payments declined; prices rose; more silver had to be retained in the New World to pay the higher prices; thus less went to Spain. The effects of the fall in the labour supply on the plantation economies, on sugar, cochineal and indigo, are, however, unclear. Sugar in the islands had already come to depend on black slaves. Presumably the other two products also felt the impact, although they were never as labour intensive as sugar. Certainly both declined precipitously in production after the 1620s, and probably well before that. Silver mining does not seem to have been affected in any immediate way. The labour draft, or *mita*, supplied Potosí adequately, and in Mexico an increasing use of free labour and slaves filled the gap.

The silver mines, however, were beset by a crisis of their own. Production began to fall off: in Potosí after 1592, a decline which lasted for much more than a century, and in New Spain after about 1630 until late in the century. One of the causes was difficulty in finding ready supplies of mercury. The mines of Huancavelica started to decline about 1595. Mercury from Almadén in Spain fell off when the fleet system faltered in the early 1630s. In northern New Spain some of the larger silver veins began to be worked out at about the same time. Moreover, as Indian populations disappeared food prices escalated and feeding the miners cost more. And the decline in the numbers of Indians forced the non-Indian population to retain more bullion in the New World to pay higher prices at the very moment when mining production was diminishing.

At the same time that the colonies began to send less to Spain they also came to need less in return, and the mother country proved increasingly incapable of sending the goods which the colonists wished to buy. The amount of import substitution in the colonies during these crucial decades has probably been overstated, but Mexico, Peru and Chile did become self-sufficient in grains, and, to a certain extent, in wine, oil, ironware, woodcrafts and furniture. Spaniards could no longer count on the Indian population for basic supplies, and Spanish farms and haciendas began to pick up the slack. This reduced dependency on Spain coincided with the decline in the mother country. As her industry decayed her exports fell away, and these, such as they were, consisted more and more of raw materials and primary products, and less and less of manufactured goods. And it was precisely raw materials and food products which were most perishable on the long Atlantic run, and least needed in the colonies.

Spain's decline in the late sixteenth and seventeenth centuries has been discussed at great length. Weak leadership relinquished none of its extravagant ambitions, taxation increased steadily in Castile, industry and agriculture decayed in the face of vigorous foreign competition, and by the 1620s, or even before, the fleets and cargoes leaving Seville were controlled by foreign merchants and shipped foreign goods. To compound her misery seventeenth-century Spain was battered by a new series of virulent plagues, failed harvests and prolonged famines. Her political cohesion was shaken by revolts on the periphery, and a run of defeats at sea and on the battlefields of Europe impaired her prestige and bargaining power. Bullion from the Indies, reduced in quantity and sporadic in arrival, quickly drained away to the advancing economies of north-western Europe. Small wonder, then, that the fleet system, so prosperous and regular up to the 1620s, fell apart so quickly. By mid-century it was a shell of its former self, sailing late in the season, unable to sail for years at a time, composed of ageing and unsafe ships, many of them built abroad, and often postponed simply because the cargoes were insufficient or of low value, and thus not worth sending to America. At the other end the great fairs of Portobelo and Jalapa declined, and many tropical ports in the Indies became ghost towns.

In all this the crown and its Casa de Contratación had played a pernicious role. Especially harmful were confiscations of cargoes. These intrusions began early in the sixteenth century when, on several occasions, Charles V seized private treasure from America as a desperate measure to pay armies or creditors. In most cases these confiscations had been paid in *juros* or guaranteed annual payments against the royal fisc. After 1600 these seizures became commonplace and were not limited to bullion. In some years all the cargo arriving in Seville was seized, and repayment was now promised in patently worthless *juros* from an obviously bankrupt treasury.

No doubt such governmental disruptions harmed commerce and productivity. One can imagine how discouraging the expectation of confiscation would be to merchants in the colonies. Many of them, either reluctantly or willingly, turned away from reinvestment or development of their productive resources and concentrated on becoming royal pensioners or landowners. Others, still trying to advance financially in spite of adverse times, turned to local Spanish American trade or to dealing with foreign smugglers.

Much has been made of a growing Spanish-American independence and self-sufficiency in the middle of the seventeenth century. Obviously there had been some import substitution, especially in the case of basic foodstuffs. But these self-sufficiencies must have been very local in scope, regional autarchies of some sort, because there is little evidence of an increase in Spanish-American inter-regional trade after the third decade of the seventeenth century.

In fact, wherever one looks one finds evidence of a decline in such trades until the last decade or two of the century. Peruvian shipping to Panama, Realejo and Acapulco fell off considerably after the silver of Potosí became less plentiful. Much of it was illegal and this imposed extra costs on the smugglers. For several years around mid-century there is little evidence of any merchant shipping at all between Mexico and Peru. (It should be noted that some scholars discern an increase in local Peruvian longshoring.) The Philippine trade declined too, as the sailings of the Manila galleons became more sporadic, and, if mid-century commentators are to be believed, less profitable. Shipping between the Caribbean islands also suffered. Havana, which had traded heavily with Cartagena, Honduras, Santo Domingo, Yucatan and Veracruz in the early years of the century, practically lost touch with all but Veracruz in the 1650s and 1660s. All had become self-sufficient in basic foodstuffs, even sugar, and had little to exchange. Even the memory of these once vigorous trades disappeared. When they recommenced late in the century the participants thought of them as new routes and exchanges.

There were, of course, exceptions, but even where we find flourishing new trades they tend to reinforce the impression of a near stoppage of exchanges in the third quarter of the seventeenth century. Cacao is a good example. As Central America's Indians and cacao bushes died off, the still sizeable chocolate-consuming Indian populations of central Mexico were forced to look elsewhere, and much further away, for their supplies. Guayaquil began shipping cacao beans to Mexico in the late sixteenth century, but by 1615 this was banned by a jealous crown and Seville consulado as being a subterfuge, which it sometimes was, for the introduction of Peruvian wine and oil. This was not the end of the matter. Guayaquil cacao was smuggled into Realejo and Sonsonate in Central America, re-labelled as a local product and sent on to Puebla and Mexico City. But, for reasons not yet understood, Guayaquil cacao went into a slump of its own in mid-seventeenth century and did not begin to recover until the late 1680s.

Caracas benefited from the difficulties in Central America and Guayaquil. Forced by the decline of the fleet system to turn away from its role as a supplier of wheat to the fleets in Cartagena and Portobelo, the region began in the 1620s to send wild cacao to Veracruz. The trade grew steadily until about 1660, then fell off dramatically until 1670, not reaching former levels until 1680. After that date exports picked up again, and increased rapidly until well after 1700.

Two other facts stifled inter-regional trade in the colonies after about 1630. One was piracy. The Chaunus have made a good case to prove that it had surprisingly little effect on the workings of the carrera. Except for the famous but rare years when the Dutch or the English seized the whole treasure fleet – as Admiral Piet Heyn did at Matanzas Bay near Havana in 1628 – the carrera, they say, was large enough and well enough armed to fight off, or even ignore, all but the best navies. Other scholars now claim that the Chaunus have underestimated these losses, but, of course, the effect of piracy on longshore shipping was much more severe. Single pirate ships, or small fleets of two or three, which avoided the galleons and the fortified major towns, played havoc with small unarmed canoes, pinnaces and caravels and frequently burned minor towns such as Trujillo, Campeche or Río de la Hacha. There is scarcely an account of a local Caribbean sea voyage after 1630 until nearly the end of the seventeenth century which does not tell of at least a chase by a pirate ship. The *armada de barlovento*, a fleet of warships which was supposed to protect the Spanish Caribbean, proved worse than useless. It could not cover such a vast area and was undermanned, made up of aged hulks and never around when needed. While pirates were never as great a threat in the Pacific, their presence there inhibited Spanish coastal trade all the way from Valparaiso to Acapulco throughout the seventeenth century.

Pirates drove trade from the holds of ships onto the backs of mules. Before mechanization and metalled roads, land transport was obviously slower and costlier. On the Spanish-American mainland overland routes faced additional problems. If the mule-train followed the mountain tracks, breakages, time and length of journeys and, consequently, freight costs increased. If the *recuas* followed lowland routes then, with a few exceptions such as coastal Peru or the area around Buenos Aires, they were in the wet tropics, so that passage was possible only in the dry season, which in some places like Tabasco hardly existed. It would seem that inter-regional trade must have dropped off, slowed down and been reduced to the shorter inland routes. That is certainly what the people of the time said.

The other factor stifling inter-regional trade at mid-century was lack of currency. The colonies were suffering a severe shortage of coinage with serious results. Local trades were too small to develop elaborate mechanisms of exchange or credit. Trade was, in fact, backed by a generally accepted silver coinage, and without such a backing trade inevitably declined because it had to use bulky substitutes such as cacao beans or flagons of wine, or even to revert to straightforward barter, which was difficult to sustain over any distance.

We cannot be quite sure of the whereabouts of the silver produced in Mexico and Peru between 1640 and 1680. Although the carrera had declined, the crown collected its share and its taxes with surprising efficiency, given the conditions of the time, and it may well be that a higher proportion of overall silver production than we think was draining off to Spain. In the early part of the century large quantities of silver were retained in the New World. Yet these stocks of coinage had disappeared by 1650, except perhaps in central Mexico. It seems unlikely that much more than before was going to the Philippines: probably less. Smuggling with interlopers had not yet fully developed as we shall see. Local sea trade, apart from the Caracas–Veracruz run, and perhaps longshoring on the coasts between Guayaquil and Santiago de Chile, was in eclipse.

Part of the problem lies in the long history of forgery and falsification in Peru. Peruvian coinage had been suspect since the conquest and, as silver supplies from the south fell, it became more and more debased. This angered the crown, which needed the silver and, through its local colonial authorities, was foolish enough to resort to a series of restampings, revaluations, devaluations, withdrawals and finally a reissue of suspect *macacas* and *moneda recortada*, which in the 1650s shattered merchant confidence in the coinage. Mexican money remained relatively well supervised and minted, and this led to the ineluctable workings of Gresham's Law. Mexicans hoarded good coinage, sent it to Spain, or kept it for only the most lucrative trades. Local markets were opened to the debased, shaved Peruvian coins trusted by nobody.

Creole merchants, then, faced some intractable problems after 1630. The carrera was unreliable and in decline for at least 30 or 40 years. When it did sail its arrival in Seville might attract a predatory, bankrupt crown, which would confiscate the cargoes and repay years of effort in almost worthless *juros*. Many other trades were either moribund, harassed by pirates, or restricted to very short range. Local self-sufficiency was in many cases a kind of autarchy of basic foodstuffs and cloth. This left little to be traded between autarchic regions.

For the landowner who was still interested in commercial agriculture and for the merchant who still dreamt of long-distance trade the solution was the foreigner. Before this solution could present itself, however, the eager creole had to wait for events and developments to catch up with his ambitions. Contraband on a large scale did not fully develop until the latecomer nations in the Caribbean had gone through a series of experiments and transitions of their own. Smuggling as a basic means of trade took nearly a century to develop in the Caribbean and on the River Plate. Several obstacles stood in the way. The main one was war and piracy. Smuggling and piracy are usually mutually exclusive, for even smugglers have to work up some minimal trust with their counterparts on shore.

The period between 1620 and the 1680s was the great age of Caribbean piracy, of European naval attacks on Spain's possessions, of 'no peace beyond the line'. Foreign powers had not left Spain to the exclusive enjoyment of its new empire. As early as 1521 corsairs among the Canaries had begun to pick off stragglers among the ships coming from America and, as rumours grew of the wealth arriving in Seville, privateers and pirates from western Europe became more numerous. The sporadic but destructive and daring exploits of the early French privateers and then of the Elizabethan heroes, Hawkins, Drake and Raleigh, caused great concern to the Spanish crown, but it responded, given the times, quickly and effectively. Philip II's naval expert and *adelantado*, Pedro Menéndez de Avilés, was responsible for the organization in 1575 of two small fleets in the Caribbean, one at Cartagena to protect the isthmus and one at Santo Domingo to watch over the safety of the eastbound fleets for Spain. These subsidiary squadrons performed well until the carrera went into decline. They were far more effective than the wandering, defensive fleet of the seventeenth century, the inept *armada de barlovento*. At this time Spain also began the construction of major fortifications in the Indies. Between 1580 and 1620, under the direction of the Italian military engineers, Juan Bautista Antoneli father and son, massive defences were gradually constructed at several major ports, such as Havana, San Juan and Veracruz. The costs of these fleets and forts were certainly debilitating, and the unprotected, smaller and less strategic towns complained that they were now receiving even greater and more malevolent attention from the frustrated pirates, but until the 1620s, and even somewhat later, Spain's defence of its fleets and major possessions was reasonably successful.

The first challengers of any great consequence were the Dutch. In the late sixteenth century they were the only European nation with sufficient seapower to challenge Spain and Portugal in the New World and in the East Indies. The Dutch fleet was the largest in Europe, twice the size of England's in 1560. The long-drawn-out Dutch war of independence against Spain (1568–1648) gave them an extra incentive for their attacks. After 1590, when strains first began to appear in the carrera, Dutch ships entered the Caribbean in considerable numbers. Piracy on the seas and attacks on Spanish colonial towns took place, but this kind of activity was not the main Dutch reason for being there. They hoped to seize the fleet, and, although this second purpose was in direct contradiction to the first, to trade for hides, sugar, chocolate and dyes. For several years they had fair success, trading surreptitiously with Venezuela and the islands of the Main. They were also attracted to the great salt flats of the coast of Tierra Firme. The salt extracted, combined with the Newfoundland fisheries, enabled them to dominate the European trade in salt codfish and herring, both staples of the everyday diet.

Some of this activity ended with the sixteenth century. During the twelve-year truce in the Dutch–Spanish war, between 1609 and 1621, the Dutch withdrew most of their ships from the Caribbean. The English, not nearly so numerous, also signed a cease-fire with Spain. As soon as the truces ended hostilities in the Caribbean were renewed, and the Dutch West Indies Company (founded in 1621), an alliance which allowed private and powerful mercantile interests to band together with the enthusiastic support and military backing of the state, was a new and threatening departure. It enjoyed a great coup in 1628 thanks to Admiral Piet Heyn, and sent large numbers of ships, as many as 80 in one year, to harass Spanish shipping, raid small ports and trade here and there, if it were possible.

However, it was becoming apparent to some in Holland and England that it would be impossible to crack the Spanish empire, decadent though it now was, by piracy, privateering and attacks on the carrera. Sir Francis Drake, in a confused kind of way, was the model for an alternative strategy: that of seizing and holding strategic ports and thus strangling the Spanish commercial system. For years a great hater of Spain, he had realized that the Spanish monopolistic trade system in the Indies depended on a few strategic bottle-necks, and that two of them, at least, the isthmus of Panama and Havana, were quite vulnerable to attack from the sea. But without the full backing of an ambivalent Elizabeth, and with an inferior organization and no local base, he accomplished little more than lucrative surprise attacks and temporary occupations. Thus, he raided Panama in 1572 but left with only half the gold he came for; took Santo Domingo in 1585 and again left with a disappointing sum; abandoned his occupation of Cartagena the following year before the ransom was collected because of fever among his crew; and had to return to England after bypassing the isthmus and Havana and burning little St Augustine in Florida in a fit of exasperation, because of lack of supplies and deaths among the crew. In 1596 he died off the coast of Panama, almost within sight of Portobelo, still unable to accomplish his dream of throttling the Spanish commercial system by seizing and holding its bottle-necks. Sir Francis had the imagination but not the means. Half a century later Oliver Cromwell, no less a hater of Spain, revived Drake's plan. A huge expedition for that time, with 2,500 men on board ship, set off in 1655 to seize Santo Domingo and, then, if possible, Havana. It was defeated twice outside the walls of Santo Domingo, and, in trying to avoid disgrace and to come home with a consolation prize, occupied the lesser island of Jamaica, the base of a small handful of Spaniards and slaves. Almost as an afterthought, England, like Holland and France, had seized small pieces of territory in the Caribbean that Spain had not seen fit to occupy effectively. During the 1630s and 1640s the Dutch had occupied Curaçao and established trading posts on the islands off Venezuela. The French had occupied Guadeloupe, Martinique and harbours on the north-west coast of Hispaniola. And now the English occupied Barbados and Jamaica as well as Antigua. Not that piracy came to an end. A long and acrimonious struggle was waged on Jamaica, for example, between a pirate's party, supported by some of the early governors and planters who wished to grow sugar and indigo on the island and wanted no mainland competition, and a trader's party, who wanted to establish a contraband connection with the Spanish towns of Cuba, New Spain and Central America. For some 30 years after the English occupation of 1655, the heyday of Port Royal and the likes of Henry Morgan, the pirate and planter camp held the ascendancy, and Spanish local merchants in the lands near Jamaica, eager to trade with the English, had to wait for better days.

There were a whole series of logistical and geo-political reasons which explain why more of Spain's empire was not picked off by her imperial rivals in the seventeenth century and why piracy and raiding remained preferable to contraband trade.

The latecomers' first obstacle was the human and epidemiological geography of the Caribbean. The Spaniards had settled there first and had dug themselves in, and this was no small matter. The major towns, such as Mexico City, Puebla and Bogotá, were tucked away inland, practically inaccessible to the size of armies which Europeans could send across the Atlantic in the small ships of the period. Above all, the colonial populations of the Americas lived for the most part outside the zones of virulent tropical diseases, visiting seaports such as Veracruz, Portobelo or La Guaira only when they had to. Europeans foolish enough to live in the tropics died in large numbers, especially recent arrivals from Europe. In fact, the lore of the times expected the new arrivals to fall ill, to go through an acclimatizing process in the first few months. Only if the immigrant survived his first, seemingly inevitable bouts of ague (malaria), flux (dysentery) or 'yellow jack', could he expect to thrive in the Caribbean. Spanish tacticians knew this and made use of it. Drake evacuated Cartagena rather than wait for all of his ransom demands because the longer he stayed the more his unseasoned English sailors died of the ague and the flux. Penn and Venables, the leaders of Cromwell's 1655 expedition, failed to take Santo Domingo partly because of their own incompetence, but also because they were naive enough to settle down for a long siege of the city in the swamps around it, all much to the delight of the Spanish defenders who knew what would befall them if they lingered there. Within little more than a week, dysentery and fever began to cut down the attackers and the survivors were forced to leave. Many more members of the same expedition were to die after the occupation of Jamaica before their acclimatization was over.

There were other factors which prevented the development of extensive contraband trade with Spain's empire. The Dutch, and to a lesser extent the English, were able to undercut many Spanish prices from the late sixteenth century almost to the wars of independence, but they faced severe, mutually-reinforcing problems of supply and demand, warehousing and stockpiling, and movement of bulky goods. If the Casa de Contratación in Seville had difficulty forecasting the needs of the Veracruz, Portobelo and Lima markets six months into the future, then what of the merchants of Amsterdam, legally barred from colonial business information and often relying on surreptitious gossip picked up on dark beaches by pirates, smugglers or Spanish renegades? Nor could the interlopers hope to establish a New World stockpile while they waited for demand and prices to swing in their favour. They had no warehouses in the islands before the 1630s and did not come round to the idea of using captured islands for this purpose until much later, when the struggle between pirates and traders had ended. Nor could the latecomers mass produce and supply in quantity, which would have lowered costs and reduced potential losses. They faced the same restraints of slow ships with little cargo space as did the Spaniards, although the Dutch, especially, did have better ships, and their exports were from a Europe which was just beginning to reorganize for the first stages of the industrial revolution. Mass production and fast delivery to the market were still some way off. It was usually much easier to receive goods from the New World and to send northern products back there, via Seville, where the bankruptcy of Spain and the collapse of its agriculture, industry and commerce had allowed the foreigner to capture and dominate all business and trade.

Above all, piracy, wrecked ports and captured islands reflected the thinking of the times. Chartered companies such as the Dutch West Indies Company and Colbert's *Compagnie de commerce* had been a beginning, and Dutch contraband cacao was sent from Venezuela to Amsterdam in quantities, but 'no peace beyond the line' had lasted too long to disappear quickly. One did not trade with the enemy if one had enough force to seize his goods and wreck his fleets and towns. 'War and trade were still the closest of neighbors', wrote Professor

A. P. Thornton, 'and those who saw them as natural enemies were thinking too radically for their own times.'[5]

In the late 1680s, however, several significant shifts prepared the way for the change to the age of contraband or informal imperialism. In Jamaica, the merchant class won its long struggle with the pirates and their patrons, the more protectionist planters. Governor Lynch, a convert to the trade party, replaced the notorious Henry Morgan as governor of Jamaica in 1681. The Duke of Albemarle, who governed briefly, 1687–8, represented some return to former policy and was more favourably disposed to protectionist planters and their piratical allies. But, with Albemarle's death, the English government quickly ordered a return to the encouragement of peaceful trading and the supplying of African slaves. Mutual trust was not built up overnight, but by 1690 it was clear that the great age of piracy had passed. As Spanish creole merchants became more convinced that the foreign rulers of the islands were sincere in their efforts to capture and hang the remaining pirates, their confidence increased and so did their eagerness to trade with the enemies of Spain.

Thus, Barbados, Curaçao, St Kitts, Jamaica – and, finally (1685), Saint-Domingue (the western third of Hispaniola) – all seized as consolation prizes that were not much missed by Spain, and all used for many years as plantations and pirate nests and only incidentally as slave pens and entrepots, became, somewhat to the surprise of their colonists and home governments, part of the solution to the problems which had delayed the development of a vigorous contraband: problems of supply and demand, weight, volume of goods, distance and profitability. Jamaica and Curaçao, especially, became warehouses and emporia, places where goods and slaves could be stored until prices and demand were strong in the Spanish colonies. They were close to the market and could get fairly accurate news from it. Small ships, so much restricted by time and cargo space on the long Atlantic run, could deliver goods from Jamaica to Veracruz, or from Curaçao to Cartagena, at no great additional cost.

Spain's imperial rivals penetrated another part of the American trade in the seventeenth century: this was the trade in African slaves, which

[5] A. P. Thornton, 'Spanish slave-ships in the English West Indies, 1660–85', *HAHR*, 35/3 (1955), 384–55.

were needed primarily as a substitute population in the islands and on the tropical coasts where the Indian population had been destroyed. Spain had handled its own slave trade, more or less, in the sixteenth century. She had no depots, factories or colonies on the slave coast of Africa, but she was able to contract with private agencies who purchased from Portuguese and Dutch sources. Supply seemed adequate for the limited demand, although some regions complained of shortages from time to time, and the annexation of Portugal by Philip II helped to assure ready access to the sources. Until the Portuguese revolt of 1640 Portuguese concessionaries supplied most of the slaves needed in the colonies, but after 1640 they could be used as suppliers no longer. Demand, however, was now low and the stagnant colonies, short of coinage, could afford few purchases. The *asiento*, or contractual leasing system, was allowed to lapse for over twenty years, another sign of Spain's weakness and the decline in production.

In 1663 the asiento system was revived. At first it progressed very slowly in the hands of inexperienced creditors of the crown, the Genoese bankers and merchants Grillo and Lomelín. The period of the Grillo asiento lasted until 1678. Their main source of supply seems to have been Curaçao, where the price of slaves was lower than in the English islands, and their favourite destinations were Portobelo, Veracruz and Havana. Between 1685 and 1689, after a few more years of trying to do without an asiento, the Spanish crown reluctantly awarded it to the Dutch firm of Coymans. The origins of this firm are not clear, but it may well have been a front for a group of larger interests. In any case, for a while Coymans remained the thin end of the wedge, and the Spanish crown had nowhere else to go if it wanted a supply. These Dutch slave ships from Curaçao carried a multitude of forbidden goods, and, as in so much else, were the pioneers of the new age of contraband.

The French laid less emphasis on smuggling, although they too participated via privateers, and before 1702 and the formal Franco-Spanish alliance they concentrated more on dominating the legal trade out of Cadiz and Seville. Our information seems to show that French goods and capital provided well over half the needs of the carrera in the late seventeenth century – when it sailed. This left the English as the main rivals of the Dutch and out in the cold. Having disposed of their pirates they envied the Dutch their *entrée* to the Spanish colonial market. They could see that several regions were suffering from labour shortages and seemed willing to pay the price for slaves: perhaps the growing need for slaves could be used as a way in. Governor Lynch, ever astute, certainly wished to use the slave gambit and issued a proclamation in 1683 inviting Spanish ships to come to Jamaica, guaranteeing them full protection and a cordial reception. His invitation, to his chagrin, was premature. There was still too much suspicion of pirates and too few slaves. Shortly thereafter the Coymans asiento began.

By the 1690s much of this had changed, and English slave ships were arriving in larger numbers from the coast of Africa. Jamaica itself was absorbing more slaves, and the French were beginning their heavy importations to Saint-Domingue which was to become the greatest sugar colony of them all. Some of this new supply of Africans was passed surreptitiously to the Spanish mainland and to the major islands, accompanied, we must suppose, by some of the products of English industry. Although pretences had to be kept up, Spanish records from places such as the small ports of the Bay of Honduras show that they were very perfunctory and thin. Spanish officials at every level became involved.

After the death of the last pathetic Spanish Habsburg, the French Bourbons came to the Spanish throne and the Franco-Spanish alliance began. The asiento was granted to the French Guinea Company in 1702, and for about eleven years France not only dominated the legal carrera, even providing the warships to protect it, but pushed into the slave trade and took over much of the contraband in the Pacific and the Caribbean.

When the War of Spanish Succession ended in 1713 the English too extracted concessions. By the peace treaty they obtained a limited right to trade legally in slaves. An annual ship owned by the South Sea Company was allowed to sell slaves at the annual fairs which were held when the *flotas* arrived from Spain. These rights, which all involved knew were a way of getting a foot in the door, were further expanded in 1716 when it was agreed that the annual ship could go to Cartagena and Portobelo even in years when there was no fleet and no fair, which turned out to be most years. The English, arguing that the slaves had to be cared for before sale, soon built a compound in Portobelo, which, almost at once, became a warehouse. Contraband could now enter freely, and the English scarcely bothered to hide it. And not only at the designated ports. At Buenos Aires, where Portuguese, Dutch and French merchants had pioneered a back-door contraband trade with

Potosí and Lima, the South Sea Company built a large factory or trading post, although there was hardly any slave trade there at that time.

Jamaica and Curaçao as warehouses and slave pens, the African slave as an unwilling *entrée* to the Spanish colonial market – together these innovations had provided the basis for a solution to the problems of direct trading between the Spanish colonies and north-western Europe. Changes there, however, and especially in England, may have played an equally important role.

Between 1660 and 1689 English shipping grew rapidly in quantity and tonnage. Much of its growth was in large ocean-going ships rather than in small coastal vessels. The growth in numbers and tonnage going to the West Indies and America is especially notable. It doubled between 1663 and 1686. Although this growth slowed somewhat thereafter the reorientation of English trade continued. The country was quite rapidly moving away from an emphasis on trade with the European continent to an oceanic trade with the Orient, the Arctic and the Americas. Notable too was the growth of England's re-export business. She was taking over Holland's earlier role as the middleman of Europe and the supplier to the colonial world.

As volume and tonnage increased and efficiencies of scale accumulated, freight rates on the long voyages declined. English goods which could not pay the freight to Jamaica in the 1660s were able to do so by 1700. Of course they were cheaper and more numerous when loaded onto the ships too. Part of the problem of balancing weight, bulk, cargo space and time against profitability had been solved. The merchants of the Spanish colonial cities were now able to reinvest in export agriculture and mining and sell their wares to the growing nations of northern Europe.

The years between 1680 and 1720 in Spanish America have been little studied and present several puzzles and paradoxes. In Spain Charles II's reign was bleak, but recent studies show convincingly that the worst of the depression took place in the early and middle years of the century. After that the peripheral regions began a slow but significant recovery. The centre and south, that is the two Castiles, Andalusia and Extremadura, the parts of Spain most closely tied to the colonies, were slower to recover because of the epidemics of 1676–85 and a rapid inflation which lasted until about 1686. Thereafter, the core areas achieved a slow expansion until the end of the century.

The history of the carrera for these years is complex. We know that the decline in the number and tonnage of ships involved, by this time sailing for the most part to and from Cadiz, continued. Official bullion also continued to decline, apart from a very minor recovery in the 1670s, until well into the eighteenth century. The remittances of illegal bullion, however, seem to have increased slowly after 1670, slumped briefly in the early 1680s, then accelerated again until the end of the century. Large *indultos* and other bribes were paid to the indigent crown by the consulados, and the crown in turn obliged by failing to inspect incoming vessels and by neglecting to prosecute merchants who were obviously guilty of fraud and contraband. Much of the information comes from foreign consuls residing in the south of Spain, a very different source of information from that used in studies of the preceding years, and this creates a problem of comparability. Nevertheless, the increase in the amount of American bullion sent to Spain seems to be generally accepted and needs further examination and explanation. Obviously the fleets, still declining, were placing heavy emphasis on precious metals, to the exclusion, no doubt, of other cargoes. The revival in silver and mercury mining in the New World in the late seventeenth century must have played a part too.

The recovery was most noticeable in the 1690s, but legal trade slumped badly again between 1700 and 1720, years dominated by the War of Spanish Succession, before resuming growth as a different and freer system of licensed ships for most of the century. Such was the debility during the war that the fleets from Cadiz had to sail under French protection. Not one fair was held in Portobelo between 1708 and 1722 and the sporadic flotas to New Spain were smaller than the ones of the 1690s. In the old centres of the empire, moreover, this twenty-year period saw many signs of strain. Revolts, a new shortage of currency, crop failures and famines dominate the scene in southern Mexico and Central America.

Yet it is obvious that a new period of expansion had also begun. Spain was making strenuous efforts, some of them pragmatic, most illusory, to reform its navy and maritime trades and to revive shipbuilding. Cadiz, a deep-water port, definitely replaced Seville. *Avisos*, or news ships began to sail more frequently thus bringing supply and demand closer together.

Foreign merchants appeared in small colonial cities where such individuals had not been seen for about a century. Silver production in New Spain was growing again and would soon revive in Peru. Venezuela's cacao exports to New Spain, Spain and Curaçao reached new heights. Trade grew between Mexico and Peru, Mexico and the Philippines, and Peru and Buenos Aires. Havana established routes to many Caribbean ports. New regions rose to importance. Cuba, Puerto Rico and Santo Domingo, now better supplied with slaves, became plantation islands trading sugar with foreigners and with the mother country. Contraband was the main trade vehicle almost everywhere, although illegal trade with Spain was also reaching new heights.

By 1720 the stage was set for a new period of expansion, although much of it had come about because of illegal exchanges with the mother country or because of trade with Spain's rivals. Spanish America had emerged from over half a century of near isolation and had reorientated its products and markets, especially in formerly peripheral areas such as Cuba, Venezuela and Buenos Aires. Spain's attempt to shake off its backwardness and lethargy and recapture her colonial trade from the foreign interlopers would form a large part of the history of the eighteenth century.

The Atlantic link between Spain and its American colonies was at once a major result of the expansion of Europe and a reinforcement of it. It was also both a result and a reinforcement of monopolistic mercantilism. Colonies existed as bases for the extraction of desired goods, and other rival extractors were to be excluded if at all possible. These policies led to a dependent, monocultural, export-orientated Spanish America, characteristics which have lasted from the greatest days of the Seville trade to the present. Temporary escapes from this dependence were, and are, caused by factors extraneous to Spanish America. The carrera was the basis of this export dependence during the first two centuries of Spanish rule, and its needs imposed a structure of communication on Spanish America whereby all major routes led from the cities, plantations and mine-heads to the seaport. Productive areas within each colonial landmass did not need to be interconnected. In fact this was discouraged. There was only limited inter-regional trade, mono-cultural producers of only raw materials have little to exchange with one another, and many Latin American nations today still enjoy better communications with Europe and North America than they do with their immediate or nearby neighbours.

The carrera had a profound impact on the European economy. American gold and silver caused at least part of the European price revolution. The creation of an American market helped to stimulate Genoese, German and Dutch banking, mines in Idria, the textile industry in Flanders, and the movement of a French migrant labour force southwards across the Pyrenees. This new market, unlike the markets of the East, mainly demanded European consumer goods, and contributed in this way to the mobilization of traditional forces of production within Europe. After the pause, crisis, or readjustment of the seventeenth century, bullion exports from America to Europe, especially after Potosí revived, helped to regenerate European trade. In this phase, moreover, Europe invested heavily in the intensive plantation, its overseas capitalist creation *par excellence*. Studies of individual sugar plantations show us that nearly everything on them was ordered from the Old World, the labour force, the machinery, the management, even some of the food. The whole enterprise, to a much greater degree than the hacienda or even the silver mine, was dominated from the European centre.

One major question provoked by the influx of American bullion is: what was its role in the creation of a European 'world system'? Many writers have believed that American silver, itself a result of Europe's early expansion, later provided the sinews or the lubricant for the transmission of a European-imposed capitalist structure to a large part of the world. What we still have to explain satisfactorily is exactly how it was done. Silver arrived in Seville or Cadiz from America and passed to western Europe. In the seventeenth century Spain, in Wallerstein's words, was acting as little more than a 'conveyor belt'. By that time, too, much of the bullion was going to Amsterdam, and played a large part in paying for Dutch expansion in the East. In general, then, American bullion helped to finance the European penetration of the Eastern world. Certainly American bullion ended up there in large quantities. It was, in Braudel's phrase, the 'necropolis' of American silver. Not all of it went there via the carrera and the western European markets. Some went directly via the Manila galleon. Still other quantities, exact totals will never be known, flowed into Brazil via Portuguese merchants in Lima and the smuggling base at Colònia do Sacramento, thence round the Cape of Good Hope to India. But much of it left through Europe to pay for Eastern spices, Eastern armies and bribes to people from the East. The fine details of how Europe used bullion extracted from its Far West to open new areas in the East are still to be revealed, but the *carrera de Indias* in a more general sense was very much part of the complex of factors which brought about the rise of capitalism, the Industrial Revolution and the hegemony of Europe throughout the world.

11

BOURBON SPAIN AND ITS AMERICAN EMPIRE

THE BOURBON STATE

If the decadence of Spain was to provide students of politics from Montesquieu to Macaulay with manifold occasion for the display of liberal irony, the practical consequences of that decline still haunted the Bourbon statesmen who laboured to rebuild the ramshackle patrimony bequeathed by the last Habsburgs. As to the sheer prostration of the country at the end of the seventeenth century, there can be little doubt. The reign of Charles II, *el hechizado* (1664–1700), proved an unmitigated disaster, a bleak chronicle of military defeat, royal bankruptcy, intellectual regression and widespread famine. By 1700 the very population had fallen by at least a million below its level under Philip II. About the only qualification to this image of pervasive decay offered by recent research is that the nadir of the crisis occurred during the 1680s. It was during that decade, when a series of bad harvests brought famine to Castile, that the first steps were taken to resolve the financial problems of the monarchy, through the partial repudiation of the heavy burden of debt inherited from previous reigns. At the same time the progressive inflation caused by repeated debasement of the currency was halted by a return to gold and silver as the standard of value. Then again, there is evidence to suggest that Catalonia and Valencia exhibited signs of economic revival well before the advent of the new dynasty. None of which, however, should in any way obscure the fact that Spain had lost her industries and was reduced to exporting agricultural produce in return for foreign manufactures. In colonial trade, Cadiz acted as a mere entrepot for the exchange of American bullion for European merchandise.

No matter how desperate the condition of the economy might appear, it was the enfeeblement of the crown which threatened the survival of the country. Defeated by France in the struggle for mastery in Europe, the Habsburg state then fell prey to internal foes. With the accession of Charles II, a near imbecile, the territorial aristocracy extended their seigneurial jurisdiction over entire districts and towns, and dominated the central councils of the monarchy. The famous *tercios*, once the finest troops in Europe, declined into local militia raised and commanded by the nobility. Then again, the talented elite of lawyers, on whom the Catholic kings and immediate successors relied to manage the kingdom, had degenerated into a mere *noblesse de robe* recruited from six *colegiales mayores*. The Estate Assemblies of the kingdom of Aragon had successfully resisted the imposition of taxes on the scale that had proved so ruinous for Castile. Throughout the peninsula both tax-collection and the supply of arms and victuals to the army were farmed out to private contractors, prominent among whom were several foreign merchants. In short, whereas elsewhere in continental Europe dynastic absolutism had come to base its newfound power on a standing army and a fiscal commissariat, in Spain the monarchy had suffered a progressive loss in authority.

The eventual price of an enfeebled crown was civil war, foreign invasion and partition of the dynastic patrimony. For the long-awaited death of Charles II in 1700 precipitated a general European war in which the succession to the Spanish throne figured as the chief prize. The court's choice of Philip of Anjou, grandson of Louis XIV, enjoyed widespread support in Castile, where his French troops were welcomed. But the Habsburg contender, Archduke Charles of Austria, was backed by Great Britain, Holland, Portugal, the provinces of Catalonia and Valencia and a considerable part of the Castilian aristocracy who feared that the new dynasty would strip them of their power. In the ensuing civil conflict the peninsula served as a battlefield, with Madrid taken and re-taken by the opposing forces before French troops ensured the final Bourbon victory.

The relatively passive role played by Spain in the war which decided its fate became fully apparent at the Peace Treaty signed in 1713 at Utrecht. For, in compensation for his renunciation of the Spanish throne, the Austrian emperor received the Low Countries, Milan, Sardinia and Naples. The king of Savoy was awarded Sicily. Worse yet, Great Britain retained Gibraltar and Minorca, and obtained the *asiento* for a period of 30 years. Under this clause Britain enjoyed a monopoly right to introduce African slaves throughout the Spanish empire and, in addition, secured the right to despatch an annual ship with 500 tons of merchandise to trade with Spain's colonies in the New World. Finally, Sacramento, a settlement on the east bank of the Río de la Plata, ideally located for contraband, was ceded to Portugal, Britain's faithful ally. If the treaty stripped Spain of its European possessions which had embroiled the monarchy in constant warfare, the breach in its monopoly of colonial trade was to prove a potent source of future conflict.

The accession of Philip V under challenge of civil war and foreign invasion enabled his French advisors to lay the foundations of an absolutist state with remarkable rapidity. The uprisings in Catalonia and Valencia allowed the revocation of their privileges. Henceforth, with the exception of Navarre and the Basque provinces, all Spain was subject to much the same range of taxes and laws. Equally important, Philip followed the example of his grandfather and excluded the aristocracy from the high councils of state. Although the grandees were eventually confirmed in possession of their lands and private jurisdiction, they no longer influenced the direction of crown policy. Similarly, the creation of Secretariats of State reduced the traditional *Consejos* to advisory and judicial functions. Then again, as early as 1704 the old system of *tercios* armed with pikes was replaced by French-style regiments equipped with muskets and bayonets. A corps of royal guards for service in Madrid, separate units of artillery and engineers, together with the formation of a class of career officers – all these reforms marked the beginnings of a new army. To finance this force, fiscal experts drafted in from abroad succeeded in doubling revenue from a mere five million pesos to 11½ million by 1711, a feat largely accomplished by close scrutiny of accounts, a reduction in official places, a repudiation of previous debts, and the incorporation of the kingdom of Aragon into a common fiscal system. With the arrival in 1714 of Elizabeth Farnese of Parma as Philip's second wife, the pace of reform noticeably slackened. Moreover, Elizabeth squandered the hard won resources of the new monarchy in mere dynastic adventures conquering Italian fiefdoms for her two sons. As a result of the Family Pacts with the French Bourbons, signed in 1733 and 1743, the Peace of Utrecht was partially overturned. The price paid by Spain in these wars has yet to be assessed. As late as 1737 the English ambassador, Sir Benjamin Keene, described the country as 'destitute of foreign friends and alliances, deranged in its finances, whose army is in a bad condition, its navy in a worse, if possible, and without any minister of heat.'[1] The accession of Ferdinand VI (1746–59) marked the abandonment of dynastic ambition in favour of a policy of peace abroad and retrenchment at home. The termination of the British *asiento* in 1748 followed by a Treaty of Limits with Portugal (1750), which fixed the frontiers of the viceroyalties of Peru and Brazil, removed potential sources of international friction. However, it was only with the advent of Charles III (1759–88) that Spain at last acquired a monarch actively committed to an entire programme of reform. Although Charles III's renewal of the Family Pact in 1761 brought defeat to Spain in the last stages of the Seven Years War, the rest of his reign was marked by a remarkable increase in prosperity both in the peninsula and the colonies, and for a brief period Spain once more figured as a European power.

If the ambitions and personalities of the Bourbon monarchs undoubtedly influenced the direction of policy, nevertheless, it was the ministerial elite who introduced what amounted to an administrative revolution. Indeed, it remains an open question as to whether the history of these years should be written in terms of kings or of ministers. In particular, the record of José de Patiño (1727–36) and the marquis de la Ensenada (1743–54) as Secretaries of State, has yet to be clearly assessed. The count of Floridablanca (1776–92) and the other ministers of Charles III, built upon the work of these men. As yet we lack any rounded characterization of this administrative elite. Although some aristocrats still attained high office – the count of Aranda is an example – the majority of ministers were impoverished gentry or commoners. It is striking that in the reign of Charles III most ministers appointed after 1766 were *manteistas*, lawyers who had failed to enter the socially prestigious *colegios mayores* at Valladolid, Salamanca and Alcalá. In contrast with contemporary England, or with Habsburg Spain, the Bourbons relied on a service nobility, bestowing titles on its trusted servants, both as reward and to strengthen their authority.

Although it is customary to view the Spanish *Ilustración* as part of the European Enlightenment, it must be remembered that most of its leading figures were public servants, actively engaged in the governance of their country. Small wonder that Jean Sarrailh defined its approach

---

[1] Quoted in Jean O. Maclachlan, *Trade and peace with old Spain, 1667–1750* (Cambridge, 1940), 101.

as '*dirigiste et utilitaire*'. Haunted by the past glory and recent decline of Spain, distressed by the glaring contrast between the growing prosperity and power of France and England and the weakness and impoverishment of the peninsula, alarmed by the inertia of Spanish society – these men all looked to the crown for remedy. The absolutist state was the essential instrument of reform. As a result provincial interests or corporate privileges were regarded with deep suspicion. Whereas under the Habsburgs, Mariana could debate the justice of tyrannicide and Suárez insist on the contractual basis of government, in the Age of Enlightenment their works were banned as subversive. By contrast, the theory of the Divine Right of Kings became virtual orthodoxy in official circles. In short, the servants of enlightened despotism did not forget the source of their power.

If, with the new emphasis on royal authority, the aristocracy were simply excluded from the councils of state, by contrast the church came under severe attack. The regalist tradition in canon law, with its insistence on the rights of the national church against the claims of the papal monarchy, and its assertion of the ecclesiastical role of the king as vicar of Christ, won a signal victory at the concordat of 1753 in which the papacy ceded to the crown the right of appointment to all clerical benefices in Spain. Equally important, the Erasmian tradition, once so influential, flowered anew among the party in the church known as Jansenists. In 1767 the Jesuit Order, the chief bastion of the Counter-Reformation and the sworn defenders of the papacy, were expelled from Spanish dominions. In general, the religious orders were seen as more of a burden on society than as spiritual fortresses. Behind this entire approach was to be found the influence of France, an uneasy blend of seventeenth-century Gallicanism and Jansenism.

The main concern of the administrative elite, however, was the great problem of economic progress. How was Spain to recover its former prosperity? A favourite answer lay in the promotion of science and useful knowledge. The government launched a national census which compiled a vast array of statistics dealing with all aspects of economic life. More to the point, canals and highways were constructed to open up new routes for trade. And, just as in the seventeenth century France and England, confronted by the commercial hegemony of Holland, had brought in protective measures to defend and encourage their shipping, industry and trade, now the ministers of the Bourbon dynasty in Spain consciously attempted to apply much the same set of policies to liberate the peninsula from its dependence on the manufactures of northern Europe.

The starting point for any interpretation of eighteenth-century Spanish mercantilism is *Theórica y práctica de comercio y de marina*, a lengthy tract first circulated in 1724 and then published with official sanction in 1742 and again in 1757. Its author, Jerónimo de Ustariz, a ministerial protégé of Patiño, accepted 'the decadence and annihilation of this monarchy' quite simply as 'a punishment for our negligence and blindness in the organization of trade'. It was ill-considered tariffs and excise duties which had destroyed domestic industry and rendered the peninsula dependent on manufactures imported from abroad. Remedy could only come from a close study and application of 'the new maxim of State', or, as he elsewhere put it, '*la nueva política*' of France, England and Holland, countries whose trade had increased at the expense of Spain. Although obviously conversant with the *arbitristas*, the Spanish advocates of reform in the previous century, Ustariz sought practical guidance in Huet's *Commerce d'Hollande* (he had secured a Spanish translation), the French tariffs of 1664–7, and the English Navigation Laws. In particular, he praised Colbert as 'the most zealous and skilful minister concerned with the advance of trade and shipping that Europe has ever known'. His actual recommendations were simple: he insisted that tariff rates must always distinguish between primary produce and elaborated goods; that imported merchandise should always pay higher duties than exports of native manufactures; and that where possible internal excise should be eliminated. The premise behind these recommendations was that wise regulation of tariffs would release the productive energy of Spanish industry. More positively, he advocated an active procurement policy in respect of equipment, munitions and uniforms for the armed forces, so that all these supplies should come from Spanish workshops and foundries. The main goal here was the creation of a strong navy, its ships built, armed and outfitted in royal arsenals. Thus, if 'the establishment of manufactures in Spain (is) the chief measure on which the restoration of the monarchy is to be based', an essential prerequisite was an expansion in the armed might of the crown.[2]

[2] Gerónimo de Ustariz, *Theórica y práctica de comercio y de marina* (3rd edn, Madrid, 1757); quotations taken from pages 4, 46, 96, 238.

The failure of government either to change the methods of agricultural production or to develop manufacturing industry has become the subject of lively debate. The great achievement of the new dynasty was, however, the creation of a bureaucratic, absolutist state, dedicated to the principle of territorial aggrandizement. The revival in the authority and resources of the monarchy clearly preceded the awakening of the economy. Indeed, there are grounds to suggest that much of the economic renewal, at least in its first stage, derived from the necessities of the armed forces and the court. The furnishing of uniforms and munitions for the army, the construction of warships in naval arsenals, the reliance on domestic iron foundries for canon, the provision of luxury textiles and tapestries for the court, and the sheer concentration of consumption in Madrid attendant on the increase in revenue – the most summary catalogue attests to the all-pervasive impact of government expenditure. As yet, however, little is known about the administrative revolution which lay behind the new-found vitality of the state. But if colonial practice be any guide, the chief innovation lay in the reliance on career officials, both military and civilian, subject to regular appraisal and promotion, who lived off fixed salaries instead of gratuities or the fees of office.

At the head of the new regime stood the ministries, the Secretariats of State, Exchequer, Justice, War, Navy and the Indies, which replaced the old Habsburg councils as the chief source of executive action. In the first years several of these offices were grouped together under one powerful minister, so that it is not clear when each secretariat acquired a permanent body of officials. At the provincial level the intendant was the key figure, the symbol of the new order. Employed at the start for specific tasks, it was only in 1749 that these officials were appointed throughout Spain, charged with responsibility for the collection of taxes, the commissariat of the army, the promotion of public works and the general encouragement of the economy. In its reliance on a salaried fiscal bureaucracy the Spanish monarchy in certain measure advanced well beyond the practice of contemporary France where sale of office and tax farmers continued to dominate the financial system until the Revolution. The new type of official certainly proved his worth, since public revenue rose steadily from a mere five million pesos in 1700 to about 18 million in the 1750s, only then to climb to an average 36 million pesos in the years 1785–90. It is in these figures that we find the secret of Spain's political revival.

As in any dynastic state the first call on the budget was the royal family and the court. If estimates as to the construction cost of the three new palaces at Madrid, Aranjuez and La Granja are not available, in 1787 the overall expenditure of the 'royal house' came to five million pesos, a sum equal to 15 per cent of all revenue. By contrast, the much vaunted programme of public works obtained only one-and-a-quarter million pesos. The major item in the budget was the armed forces, which absorbed some 60 per cent of all public revenue, a figure which, if war expenses were included, would undoubtedly rise yet further.

Although the formation, expansion and maintenance of a standing army and a permanent navy were objects of prime concern for the Bourbon state, remarkably little information is as yet available about the organization and operation of these forces. By all accounts it was José de Patiño, first as intendant at Cadiz and later as secretary of state, who was chiefly responsible for the building of warships in royal arsenals. Then, the War of Jenkins' Ear (1739–48) drove the marquis de la Ensenada to extend the programme, so that in the years 1741–61 Spain launched no less than 54 ships of the line, armed with 3,688 cannon. By the close of the reign of Charles III, the navy boasted a fleet of 66 ships of the line supported by the usual assortment of frigates and packet boats.

If the concentration on naval power sprang from the strategic necessities of empire, the scale of the land forces reflected the overseas ambitions of the dynasty. By 1761 the regular army numbered nearly 60,000 men, divided into 50,445 infantry, 5,244 cavalry, 1,329 artillery-men and 2,758 troops stationed in the North African garrisons. Recruitment was by levy, a system which avoided the reliance on foreign mercenaries found in other armies of the day. Moreover, at least a third of the officers were commoners, in many cases promoted from the ranks, so that only the regiments of royal guards had much pretence to social prestige. Nevertheless, it was the formation of this officer corps, men of some education, accustomed to discipline and dependent on royal service for their livelihood, which provided the dynastic state with indispensable agents of government. Foreign travellers commented that the highest provincial authority was vested in the captains general, the commanders of the regional brigades, to whom intendants and other civilian magistrates were subject.

If Frederick the Great of Prussia once assessed Spain as a European power of the second rank, comparable with Austria and Prussia, in part it was because the Italian wars of Philip V had demonstrated that the armed might of the monarchy was sufficiently restored to allow it to carry forward the territorial aggrandizement which that enlightened king defined as the guiding principle of the absolutist state. Stripped of its European possessions by the Treaty of Utrecht, Spain, however, now depended on its vast American empire to ensure it a place in the Concert of Europe. In the New World the Bourbon state proved remarkably successful both in safeguarding its frontiers and in the exploitation of colonial resources. The revival of Spanish power during the reign of Charles III in large measure derived from the efflorescence in trade with the Indies, and from the increased revenue which it yielded.

THE REVOLUTION IN GOVERNMENT

Although both Alberoni and Patiño are credited with the view that the key to Spain's revival was to be found in the New World, the Italian adventures of Elizabeth Farnese prevented these statesmen from effecting much change in the American empire. Similarly, if José del Campillo y Cossío, Secretary of the Treasury, Navy and Indies (1741–3), drew up a comprehensive programme of reform designed to overhaul the entire system of imperial trade and government, his term of office was dominated by the demands of war in both Europe and the Indies. Only in 1754, with the appointment of Julián de Arriaga as Secretary of the Navy and Indies, was the empire at last governed by a minister with American experience (he had served as Governor of Caracas) who had few other administrative tasks to distract his attention. Until then all the emphasis in ministerial circles had been on Europe: the creation of a new system of government and the provisioning of the Italian wars had absorbed virtually all the energy of the administrative elite.

Yet this preoccupation with the Old World had led to a remarkable erosion of imperial power in America. Indeed, during the first decades of the eighteenth century Spain did little more than rebuff foreign incursions into its territory and consolidate its possession over threatened frontiers. To understand the magnitude of the task it is necessary to return to the bleak years of the 1680s. For it was in that decade that the Portuguese established the colony of Sacramento on the estuary of La Plata and the French pushed southwards from Canada to found New Orleans. At much the same time English and French buccaneers burnt

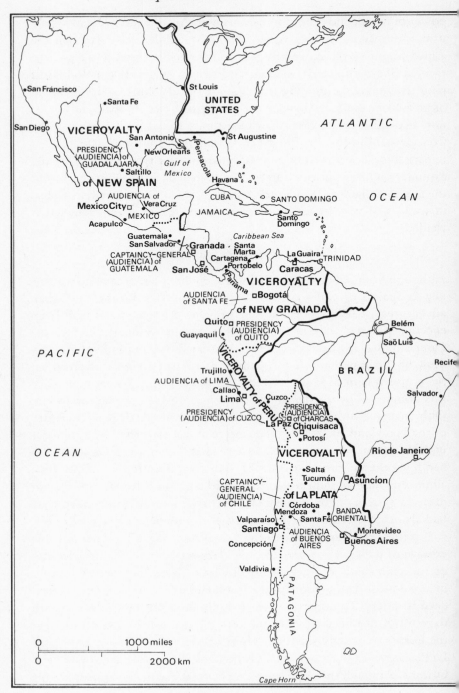

San Francisco

Santa Fe

St Louis

UNITED STATES

ATLANTIC

San Diego

VICEROYALTY

San Antonio

St Augustine

PRESIDENCY
(AUDIENCIA) of
GUADALAJARA

New Orleans

Pensacola

Gulf of
Mexico

Saltillo

of NEW SPAIN

Havana

OCEAN

AUDIENCIA of

CUBA

SANTO DOMINGO

Mexico City □

Vera Cruz

MEXICO

JAMAICA

Santo
Domingo

Acapulco

Guatemala

San Salvador

Granada

Santa
Marta

Caribbean Sea

La Guaira

TRINIDAD

CAPTAINCY–GENERAL
(AUDIENCIA) of
GUATEMALA

Cartagena

Portobelo

Caracas

San José

Panamá

VICEROYALTY

AUDIENCIA
of SANTA FE

□ Bogotá

of NEW GRANADA

Quito □

PRESIDENCY
(AUDIENCIA)
of QUITO

Belém

Guayaquil

Saõ Luis

PACIFIC

BRAZIL

Recife

VICEROYALTY of PERU

Trujillo

AUDIENCIA of LIMA

Cuzco

Salvador

Callao

Lima

PRESIDENCY
(AUDIENCIA) of CUZCO

PRESIDENCY
(AUDIENCIA)
of CHARCAS

La Paz

□ Chiquisaca

Potosí

OCEAN

Rio de Janeiro □

VICEROYALTY

Salta

CAPTAINCY–
GENERAL
(AUDIENCIA)
of CHILE

Tucumán

□ Asunción

of LA PLATA

Córdoba

Mendoza

Santa Fé

BANDA
ORIENTAL

Valparaíso

Santiago □

AUDIENCIA
of BUENOS
AIRES

Montevideo

Buenos Aires

Concepción

Valdivia

PATAGONIA

0   1000 miles

0   2000 km

Cape Horn

Spanish America *c.* 1790

and ravaged their way across the isthmus to raid the shores of the Pacific. Panama City, Cartagena, Veracruz and Guayaquil were all eventually captured and sacked by these freebooters. In New Mexico the Pueblo Indians rose in rebellion and expelled both settlers and missionaries from a province under effective occupation for almost a century. So weak had Spain become that during the War of Succession it was necessary to beg the protection of French warships to escort the treasure fleet home from Veracruz.

Equally important, in each province of the empire, government had come to be dominated by a small colonial establishment, composed of the creole elite – lawyers, great landlords and churchmen – a few long-serving officials from the peninsula and the great import merchants. At all levels of the administration sale of office was prevalent. The management of the mint, the collection of *alcabalas* (the excise duties) and the very maintenance of the *alcaldes mayores* and *corregidores* (the district magistrates) were all farmed out to merchants of the viceregal and provincial capitals who controlled the import trade and the issue of credit. It was the clergy, both secular and religious, rather than the formal delegates of the crown, who exercised true authority within society, acting as the intellectual and spiritual leaders of the elite and as the counsellors and guardians of the masses. As in the last decades of Habsburg rule in Spain, the crown's power to tap the resources of society was limited by the absence of effective military sanctions. If the new dynasty was to profit from its vast overseas possessions, it had first to recapture control over colonial administration and then to create new institutions of government. Only then could it introduce the economic reforms.

The catalyst of change was war with Great Britain. Spain's tardy entrance into the Seven Years War (1756–63) brought immediate defeat with the British capture of Manila and Havana. Moreover, if at the subsequent peace treaty, these ports were returned, Spain had to cede Florida to Britain and once more hand back Colónia do Sacramento to Portugal. The acquisition of Louisiana from France was but poor compensation for the loss of that ally's support on the mainland. It was at this point that the ministers of Charles turned to the reform programme elaborated in Campillo y Cossío's *Nuevo sistema de gobierno económico para la América* (1743), a manuscript in circulation since 1743 and published in 1762 as the second part of Bernardo Ward's *Proyecto económico*. There they found advocacy for a return to the Habsburg practice of a general visitation, to be followed by the introduction of permanent intendancies. The text also contained warnings about the excessive power and wealth of the church. If his proposals in the political sphere often consisted of the application in America of reforms already introduced in Spain, their implementation proved more drastic in its effects. For the administrative revolution in the empire was inaugurated by soldiers and officials despatched from the peninsula. Small wonder that it has been called the Reconquest of the Americas.

The first step in this programme was the provision of adequate military force, as a safeguard both against foreign attack and internal uprisings. The fall of Havana and Manila in 1761 and the virtual elimination of French power from the mainland signalized the magnitude of the threat from abroad. Once peace was declared, Alejandro O'Reilly, Spain's leading general, was despatched to Cuba to inspect the defences and to organize a local militia. The following year, an inspector-general, Juan de Villalba, arrived in New Spain, at the head of two regiments sent from Europe, charged with a similar task of raising a reserve army of militia. In 1768 a regiment of regular troops was stationed for permanent duty at Caracas. As a result of this activity, an official report of 1771 estimated there were 42,995 soldiers of different categories stationed across Spanish America, with 4,851 men in Cuba, 2,884 in Puerto Rico and 4,628 at Buenos Aires. Not all provinces were so blessed. In New Granada the *comunero* rebellion in 1781 surprised the viceregal authorities with only 75 regular soldiers outside the port garrison at Cartagena. Then again, it was only after the Tupac Amaru rebellion in Peru (1780–1) that the crown sent out two regiments for duty in that viceroyalty. Here is no place to describe the history of the colonial army. Suffice it to say that, by the close of the century, local recruitment and transfers meant that the overwhelming majority of the men in the ranks were native Americans and that a good proportion of the officers, from captain down, were creoles. Numbers depended on local resources. If New Spain eventually boasted an army of 9,971 men, divided into four regiments of infantry and two of dragoons, by contrast Peru managed with a force of 1,985 and Chile had but 1,249 men mainly engaged on frontier duties. It was the circle of fortresses in the Caribbean which still required soldiers from Europe, with the insalubrious port of Cartagena maintaining a garrison of 2,759.

This emphasis on military strength yielded considerable returns. In

1776 an expedition of 8,500 men crossed the Río de la Plata, took Sacramento for the third and last time, and expelled the Portuguese from the entire east bank province, a victory ratified at the Treaty of San Ildefonso (1778). Soon after, in the War of American Independence (1779–83), another force invaded Pensacola, the coastal strip adjoining Louisiana, an initiative which led to the subsequent British cession of that territory, together with Florida. Similarly, in Central America the fortress of Omoa was recaptured and the British settlements along the Mosquito coast finally eliminated. At much the same period expeditions were mounted in New Spain to ensure effective possession of the northern provinces of Sonora, Texas and California. In this drive to secure the frontiers of its American empire, the Bourbon monarchy at last displayed the expansive enterprise of a true imperial power.

Alongside the recruitment of colonial regiments maintained on a permanent footing went the organization of numerous militia units. Admittedly, at times these forces had more reality on paper than on the parade ground, but, despite criticism and occasional disbandment, they eventually proved their worth. For if the 50,000 men allegedly enrolled in the Peruvian reserve army were rarely to be found in uniform, by contrast the 22,277 troops raised in New Spain were reasonably well-armed and disciplined. Elsewhere in Buenos Aires it was the militia which successfully repelled the British invasions of 1806–7. Equally important, the distribution of military titles and legal privileges was viewed as a decisive means of arousing the loyalty of the creole elite. Indeed, a traveller observed of the upper classes in Venezuela: 'At present they seek an epaulette with as much avidity as they did formerly the tonsure.'[3] Moreover, the existence of the militia provided the colonial state with armed sanctions against popular unrest.

The monarchy asserted its power over the church in dramatic fashion when in 1767 Charles III followed the example of Portugal and decreed the expulsion of all Jesuits from his dominions. It was, of course, a measure which warned the church as to the necessity of absolute obedience. For the Jesuits were notorious for their independence of episcopal authority, their intransigence over the payment of ecclesiastical tithes, their devotion to the papacy, their extraordinary wealth and their skill in litigation with the royal bureaucracy. In Paraguay they had established a virtual state within a state, governing over 96,000 Guaraní

[3] F. Depons, *Travels in South America during the years 1801–1804*, 2 vols. (London, 1807), I, 361.

Indians protected by their own armed militia. Elsewhere, in Sonora and the Amazonian provinces of Quito, the order operated a series of mission stations. Equally important, in all the principal towns of the empire, Jesuit colleges educated the creole elite. Moreover, unlike other religious orders, they preserved relative harmony between their American and European members. All in all, the Jesuits exercised formidable influence in colonial society, an influence supported by the wealth which accrued from the efficient management of entire chains of haciendas located in every major province. When Charles III listened to his Jansenist ministers and decreed the expulsion, the loyalty of his colonial subjects was strained to the utmost, as there sailed for Italian exile over a thousand American Jesuits, the very flower of the creole elite.[4] Thereafter, in 1771, Provincial Church Councils were summoned in Lima and Mexico with the aim both of tightening clerical discipline and of emphasizing royal authority over the church. But although any number of reforms were projected, little came of this regalist activity. The religious were subjected to a general inspection. Convents of nuns were exhorted to introduce communal dining. The jurisdiction of ecclesiastical courts over probate of intestate property was terminated. Legal appeals from church courts were admitted by the audiencias with growing frequency. More important, in criminal cases, the very principle of clerical immunity from all royal jurisdiction was challenged, and a handful of priests were actually imprisoned. Then again, an attempt was made to regulate the collection of tithes. By and large, however, although these measures certainly embittered the priesthood, they achieved remarkably little in the way of real change.

More far reaching and effective was the radical reform in civil administration. In 1776 a new viceroyalty was established with its capital at Buenos Aires, covering the vast area now occupied by Argentina, Uruguay, Paraguay and Bolivia. The result was a dramatic shift in the geo-political balance of the continent. For, with its commercial monopoly already broken by the opening of the trade route via Cape Horn, Lima, the former capital of the entire empire in South America, suffered a severe loss in status. The inclusion of Upper Peru in the new viceroyalty, designed to provide Buenos Aires with the fiscal

---

[4] For a discussion of the expulsion of the Jesuits from Brazil, see Mansuy-Diniz Silva, *CHLA*, I, ch. 13, and Alden, *CHLA*, II, ch. 15.

profits of Potosí, prepared the way for the permanent political division of the Andean zone. Elsewhere, the changes were less radical in their impact. The viceroyalty of New Granada, created in 1739 to ensure the defence of Cartagena and the coast, was further buttressed by the introduction of a captain-general at Caracas, assisted by an intendant, who was responsible for the government of the Venezuelan districts. Finally, in the north of New Spain, a comandant-general was appointed to superintend the defences and administration of the entire frontier region, his freedom of action, however, limited by continued financial dependence on revenue remittances from the central Mexican treasury.

Charles III, adopting Campillo's proposal, also revived the ancient Habsburg remedy for colonial misrule, the *visita general*. Moreover, so successful was José de Gálvez as visitor general to New Spain (1765–71) that first Peru (1776) and then New Granada (1778) were subjected to a similar review of the machinery of government. Through the establishment of the tobacco monopoly and a reorganization of alcabala collection, Gálvez secured an immediate increase in revenue remittances for Madrid. Steps were also taken to raise silver production through tax exemptions and reductions in the costs of monopoly materials such as mercury and gunpowder. Gálvez superintended the expulsion of the Jesuits; brutally suppressed the popular uprisings against this measure; and then led an expedition to pacify and settle Sonora. The reward for this remarkable display of administrative energy was a seat on the Council of the Indies, followed by his life-long appointment as Secretary of the Indies (1776–87). It was Gálvez who was mainly responsible for the creation of the viceroyalty at Buenos Aires and the despatch of his protegé, Juan Antonio de Areche as visitor-general of Peru. Like his protector, the count of Floridablanca, this poor Malagueño lawyer was a *manteista*, whose services to the crown were rewarded with the title of marquis of Sonora. As imperious as he was ambitious, Gálvez drove through the revolution in colonial government with single-minded tenacity. Judged from the perspective of Madrid, the results were impressive. But the price was alienation of the creole elite. For Gálvez made no secret of his contempt for the abilities of American Spaniards. During his term of office he became renowned both for his implacable nepotism – his brother and nephew succeeded as viceroys of New Spain – and for his preference for peninsular Spaniards to the exclusion of creole candidates in all branches and levels of colonial government.

Small wonder that one high-placed critic could prophesy: 'Gálvez has destroyed more than he has built...his destructive hand is going to prepare the greatest revolution in the American Empire.'[5]

Nowhere was the impact of the new policies more evident than in the changing composition of the audiencias, the high courts of justice, whose judges counselled the viceroys on all important questions of state. For the reign of Philip V had been characterized by the perpetuation of all the worst abuses of the last Habsburg. In the years between 1687 and 1712 and again during the 1740s, places on the American audiencias were offered for sale to any qualified bidder. As a result, wealthy creole lawyers purchased judgeships on an unprecedented scale, so that by the 1760s the audiencias of Mexico, Lima and Santiago de Chile had a majority of American Spaniards, men related by descent or through marriage to the landowning elite of these capitals. It was during the 1740s that this policy reached a climax when of a total 66 judicial appointments, 39 places were sold, with some two-thirds of the 36 creoles obtaining office through purchase.[6] True, once Arriaga became minister a virtual ban on all further creole appointments was enforced, but it was left to Gálvez to reverse this unforeseen legacy of past abuse. In 1776–7, he moved decisively to enlarge the membership of most audiencias, and then, through a determined policy of transfer, promotion and retirement, to break the creole predominance. Of the 34 appointments made in these two years, only two went to American Spaniards. By the end of his term as Secretary of the Indies creoles comprised between a third and a quarter of the judges in American audiencias, a proportion which was maintained until 1810.

Along with this renewal of peninsular control, there went a revived insistence on promotion between and within audiencias, a system which had been interrupted by sale of office. Once again, it became the rule for judges to start as *alcaldes del crimen* or as *oidores* in lesser courts, such as Guadalajara or Santiago, and then to transfer to the viceregal courts of Lima or Mexico. In 1785–6 new audiencias were created at Caracas, Buenos Aires and Cuzco. The legal advisors of both intendants and viceroys were now also included within the scale of promotion. Equally important, Gálvez created a new judicial post of *regente* to replace the

[5] Quoted in D. A. Brading, *Miners and merchants in Bourbon Mexico, 1763–1810* (Cambridge, 1971), 39.
[6] Mark S. Burkholder and D. S. Chandler, *From impotence to authority: the Spanish crown and the American audiencias 1687–1808* (Colombia, Miss., 1977), 104–8, 157, 170, 196.

viceroys as presidents of the audiencias. The system was completed by the transfer of regents and some senior oidores to the Council of the Indies, which for the first time in its long history now came to include a large proportion of members with official experience in the American empire. Here, then, we observe the formation of a true judicial bureaucracy, its autonomy from colonial society based on recruitment in Spain.

The centre-piece of the revolution in government was the introduction of intendants, officials who embodied all the executive, interventionist ambitions of the Bourbon state. To assess the importance of this measure, it has to be remembered that in the sphere of local government the practice of the early Bourbons marked a deterioration rather than an improvement over the past. Since 1678 the district magistracies – alcaldes mayores and corregidores – had been up for sale in Madrid. Although these officials were still charged with the collection of Indian tributes, the new dynasty had curtailed their salaries, or, in the case of New Spain, made no further payment. In consequence, since the fruits of justice and other fees did not provide a subsistence, many magistrates engaged in trade, distributing merchandise and livestock on credit and issuing cash in advance for produce such as cochineal, indigo and cotton. Illegal in the first instance, in 1751 these *repartimientos de comercio* were finally recognized by the crown on condition that the viceregal authorities compile a tariff of prices and values of goods for distribution. In operation for the most part in zones of Indian settlement, where magistrates often enjoyed a virtual monopoly in trade, the repartimientos often provoked great popular unrest. For most corregidores had but five years in which to recoup the cost of their office and repay the great import houses of Lima and Mexico who supplied them with cash and merchandise. In effect, therefore, the judicial authority of the crown was both purchased and employed for the safeguard and furtherance of mercantile profit.

Once more, it was José de Gálvez who was responsible for radical improvement in this ill-conceived system of government. In 1768, with the collaboration of Viceroy Croix of New Spain, he presented proposals for the outright abolition of both alcaldes mayores and repartimientos and their replacement by intendants. The district magistrates, so he argued, both oppressed the Indians and defrauded the crown of tribute monies. The premise behind his paper, elaborated in subsequent debate, was that if the Indians were liberated from the coercive monopoly of the alcaldes mayores and corregidores, they would freely enter the market as producers and as labourers. His opponents, however, asserted that without repartimientos de comercio the Indians would retreat into a subsistence economy or simply renege on all obligations of credit. In any case, the overseas provinces of the empire were too backward to warrant the intervention of intendants, who would prove both costly and ineffective. Despite the introduction of one intendant in Cuba in 1763, it was not until Gálvez became Secretary of the Indies that any further progress was achieved. The floodtime of reform came in the 1780s, starting in 1782 with the appointment of eight intendants in the viceroyalty of La Plata, followed two years later by another eight in Peru and crowned by the establishment in 1786 of twelve intendancies in New Spain. Elsewhere, Central America was allotted five of these officials, Cuba three, Chile two and Caracas one, with New Granada and Quito left exempt.

Recruited from a combination of military men and fiscal officials, with the overwhelming majority peninsular Spaniards, the intendants met with but qualified success and in no sense fulfilled the expectations of the reformers. For the introduction of a range of provincial governors did not correct the deficiencies in local government. At the district level the alcaldes mayores and corregidores were replaced by subdelegates, who were expected to subsist on 5 per cent of tributes and the fruits of justice. As a result, these officials were either selected from the local elite or else were obliged to engage in trade, even if the great import houses no longer offered financial support. It was in the provincial capitals that the reform made its greatest impact. For here the intendants were at their most active, paving streets, building bridges and prisons and suppressing popular disorders. Assisted by a legal advisor and treasury officials, the intendant was living proof of the new executive vigour of the monarchy. Liberated from its former dependence on mercantile credit, colonial administration was immeasurably strengthened by the appointment of career bureaucrats, who by reason of their peninsula background, preserved their independence from the society they governed.

In the capitals of Lima, Buenos Aires and Mexico, Gálvez installed *superintendentes subdelegados de real hacienda*, officials who relieved the viceroys of all responsibility in exchequer matters. In addition, a central finance committee was set up to supervise the activity of the intendants and to review all questions arising from the collection of revenue. It should be emphasized that the appointment of superintendents was designed to reduce the powers of the viceroys, which Gálvez thought far too extensive. His idea was to establish a troika system, with regents heading the judiciary, superintendents the exchequer and intendants, and the viceroys retaining civil administration and the military. In the event, a series of disputes over questions of revenue led to the abolition of the office of superintendent in 1787 after the death of Gálvez. The prestige of the viceroys was too great to be so easily diminished. Moreover, the extraordinary expansion in all branches of government, when taken with the new reliance on the army, all served to augment the effective authority of the king's alter ego. That most viceroys after the accession of Ferdinand VI were career officers in the armed forces further illustrates the nature of the new colonial state.

If the intendants were less effective than anticipated, in part it was because the system of revenue had been largely reformed before their arrival. The key innovations were the appointment of a salaried fiscal bureaucracy and the establishment of new crown monopolies. Hitherto, the collection of excise duties, the *alcabalas*, had been farmed out (for an annual contracted sum) to the *consulados*, the merchant guilds and their provincial delegates. The treasuries, situated at ports or in mining camps, only administered the customs duties and the tithe levied on silver production. But in 1754 the alcabalas of Mexico City were entrusted to salaried officials and in 1776 the same system of direct administration was applied throughout the colony. Henceforth all the leading towns were blessed with a local director and accountant of excise, assisted by a band of guards. The same system was introduced into Peru during the *visita* of Areche and thereafter extended across the empire. The other great innovation occurred in 1768 with the creation of the tobacco monopoly in New Spain. The area of planting was severely restricted and all growers were obliged to sell their produce to the monopoly, which both manufactured the cigars in its factories and distributed them via a network of salesmen and their assistants in the chief towns. At its peak the tobacco monopoly in New Spain had a turnover of nearly eight million pesos, employed a workforce of over 17,000 and yielded net profits of nearly four million pesos. Moreover, if in other provinces of the empire receipts never attained such heights – in Peru the monopoly only sold tobacco – it certainly formed a major source of additional revenue. It was only, therefore, in the more rigorous scrutiny and collection of Indian tributes, where increase in returns easily exceeded any expansion in population, that the intendants and their subdelegates played any perceptible role.

In effect, the appointment of a salaried bureaucracy, supported by an extensive army of guards, enabled the Spanish monarchy to reap an extraordinary fiscal harvest from the expansion in economic activity effected by its reforms in commerce and its encouragement of colonial exports. Once more, it was New Spain which was pacemaker, with treasury receipts rising in the course of the century from three to 20 million pesos, the increase largely concentrated in the years 1765–82, when the gross budget leapt from six to $19\frac{1}{2}$ million pesos. It is significant that Indian tributes only contributed about a million pesos to this grand total, compared with the $4\frac{1}{2}$ million provided by the silver tithe, mint charges and mercury monopoly, and the four million profits accruing from the tobacco monopoly. In all, once fixed charges and monopoly costs had been deducted, there remained about 14 million pesos of which four million were retained for the maintenance of government and the military costs of the northern frontier. The remaining ten million pesos were shipped abroad, either to finance the fortresses and garrisons of the Caribbean, the Philippines and North America, or else remitted directly to Madrid. No other colony was as profitable to its metropolis as New Spain. By 1789 gross receipts in Peru amounted to no more than $4\frac{1}{2}$ million pesos, with the 1.2 million pesos supplied by the silver mining industry closely matched by the 920,000 pesos of Indian tributes. By contrast, in New Granada customs duties of 1.3 million were the largest item in a total budget of 4.7 million, with the tobacco monopoly accounting for 953,000 pesos and Indian tributes a derisory 166,000 pesos. Similarly, despite the still numerous Indian population of Upper Peru, the bulk of fiscal receipts in the viceroyalty of La Plata – a total $3\frac{1}{2}$ million – derived from the mining industry and customs duties. Clearly, in most areas of the empire, it was the export economy which yielded the highest returns to the crown.

In these estimates of revenue are to be found the true significance of the changes in colonial government. In effect, the administrative revolution created a new absolutist state, based, as in Europe, on a standing army and a professional bureaucracy. This state was dedicated, as much as its counterparts in the Old World, to the principle of territorial aggrandizement, albeit chiefly at the expense of the Portuguese in South America and of roaming Indian tribes in North America. But it differed from its European exemplars in that it failed to form any true alliance, founded on common interest, with the leading sectors of colonial society. The influence of the church, hitherto the chief bulwark of the crown, was attacked. The economic power of the great import houses was undermined. But if the standing armies provided armed sanctions against popular unrest, the titles and provileges offered by the militia were a poor substitute for any real share of profits or power. In short, the price of reform was the alienation of the creole elite. Nevertheless, judged from the perspective of Madrid, its rewards were considerable. If, as we shall see, the economic revival of the peninsula in no way matched the opportunities presented by growth in colonial trade, the administrative revolution allowed the crown to reap a remarkable fiscal profit. Once again, it is New Spain which offers the best measure of change. Whereas in the years 1766–78 only 3.94 million pesos of the total 11.93 million pesos legally exported from New Spain were on the king's account, in the period 1779–91 no less than 8.3 million pesos of the total 17.2 million consisted of revenue remitted to the Caribbean colonies or Madrid. By this time, up to 15 per cent of the royal budget derived from the colonies, leaving to one side the monies raised from customs duties at Cadiz. It is in these figures, rather than in the dubious claims for peninsula industry and exports, that we encounter the true basis of the revival of the monarchy. In the last resort, the fiscal profit of empire and the commercial monopoly were more important to the Spanish state than were the commercial returns to the Spanish economy.

EXPANSION OF COLONIAL TRADE

The revival of the colonial economy, as much as that in the peninsula, derived from the application of mercantilist policies. The authoritative text here was Campillo's *Nuevo sistema de gobierno económico para la América* (1743). For the starting point of his analysis was a direct comparison of the high profits which accrued to Great Britain and France from their Caribbean sugar islands with the derisory returns of Spain's vast mainland empire. To remedy this sorry state of affairs he advocated the introduction of *gobierno económico*, by which term he clearly meant the doctrines and measures associated with Colbertian mercantilism. In particular, he called for the termination of the Cadiz commercial monopoly and the system of periodic fleets. In America land was to be distributed to the Indians and both silver mining and agriculture encouraged. Above all else, Campillo viewed the colonies as a great untapped market for Spanish industry: its population, especially the Indians, were the monarchy's treasure. But, to increase colonial demand for Spanish manufactures, it was necessary to incorporate the Indians into society by the removal of malign monopolies and to reform the prevailing system of government. It was also necessary to destroy colonial industry. Throughout his text, Campillo was at pains to assert the supremacy of public interest over private profit, a distinction embodied in the contrast he drew between 'political' trade and 'mercantile' trade.

If reform came but slowly it was because the War of Succession and the subsequent Peace of Utrecht threw open the empire to foreign shipping and contraband. In effect, throughout the first half of the eighteenth century, Spain was engaged in a desperate battle to regain control over colonial commerce. Contraband was rife. Yet the great import houses of Mexico and Lima still sought to restrict the flow of merchandise from the peninsula in order to safeguard their monopoly profits. If Spain was to benefit from its American possessions, it was thus necessary first to oust foreign manufactures and contraband from their dominant role in the Atlantic trade and then to dislodge the mercantile confederacy from its commanding position within the colonies.

At the outset the commercial performance of Spain was lamentable. In 1689 it was estimated that of 27,000 *toneladas* of merchandise legally despatched to Spanish America, only 1,500 originated in the peninsula. The bulk of exports from Cadiz consisted of manufactured goods shipped in from France, England and Holland. Even the fiscal yield from customs duties was undercut by the high incidence of contraband trade in the Caribbean and from Sacramento. Indeed, with the War of Succession the last of the barriers against interlopers crumbled, for in 1704 ambassador Amelot obtained permission for French merchant ships to enter the Pacific and trade freely with Peru and Chile. In the period 1701–24 at least 153 French trading vessels visited these coasts and in 1716 alone some 16 ships brought such an abundance of European merchandise that the markets remained glutted for years to come.

Faced with this open challenge to Spanish commercial monopoly, the authorities in Madrid desperately tried to restore the old system of periodic fleets sailing from Cadiz, with the trade fairs at Portobelo and Veracruz serving as the only legal points of entry for imported merchandise. For South America this decision implied the continued closure of the route via Cape Horn and severe restriction on landings at Buenos Aires. For New Spain the old system had never entirely broken down, since in the crucial years 1699–1713 at least five convoys had reached Veracruz. Moreover, the transfer of the fair in 1720 to Jalapa meant that transactions could now be conducted in a pleasant hill town just above the port. By contrast, only one fleet set out for Tierra Firme and the subsequent fair at Portobelo proved quite disastrous for the Lima merchants who purchased goods, owing to the influx of cheap French goods.

If diplomatic pressure eventually secured the exclusion of French ships from colonial ports, there was no way of escape from English traders. For the South Sea Company enjoyed the legal right, conceded at the Treaty of Utrecht, to despatch an annual merchantman to Spanish America (see above, p. 391). Since the goods it carried avoided both customs duties at Cadiz and the internment charges attendant on the delayed departures of the official convoys, the Company could easily undercut the high prices of the Spanish monopolists. In consequence, the English ship effectively ambushed the trade fairs held at Portobelo in 1722 and 1731 and at Jalapa in 1723 and 1732. Indeed, in the last fair at Portobelo about half the nine million pesos sent from Lima went directly into the coffers of the South Seas Company. The Cadiz shippers who had accompanied the fleet were either ruined or else obliged to linger in the colonies for years to come, awaiting purchasers for their costly goods. It was precisely this commercial disaster which led to the suppression of the Tierra Firme fleet. In addition, the volume of merchandise sold at Jalapa in 1736 was decidedly below previous levels.[7] It was no chance matter, therefore, that hostilities arose from Spanish attempts to prevent English contraband.

The War of Jenkins' Ear (1739–48) marked a watershed in the development of colonial trade. For Vernon's destruction of Portobelo put an end to any further hopes of reviving the Tierra Firme fleet. Henceforth all legal trade with the Caribbean islands and South America was by *registros*, individual ships sailing under licence from Cadiz. Equally important, the Cape Horn route was opened and more ships

[7] Geoffrey J. Walker, *Spanish politics and imperial trade 1707–1789* (London, 1979, *passim*).

were allowed to disembark at Buenos Aires. With the marked fall in prices, the European commerce of the entire Peruvian viceroyalty increased, bringing Chile and the zone of the Río de la Plata into direct trade with Spain. Indeed, since the British fleet was none too successful in its blockade, the very years of war witnessed a certain expansion. The other great benefit brought by war was the end of licensed interloping. At the peace treaty of 1750 the South Seas Company renounced both the asiento and the right to an annual trader in return for payment of £100,000. At last, after four decades, Spain had regained unrestricted exercise of its commercial monopoly over the American empire.

An important element in the revival of Spanish trade during the middle decades of the century was supplied by the Royal Guipuzcoa Company of Caracas which Patiño had established in 1728 with exclusive rights of trade between San Sebastian and Venezuela. Authorized to maintain coast boats to put down contraband, in 1729 the company outfitted no less than eight warships and raised a small army after the outbreak of hostilities with Great Britain. Thereafter, the curve of exports rose markedly, with shipments of cacao increasing more than threefold in the years 1711–20 and the 1760s. Moreover, whereas in the first period most cacao went to New Spain, in the latter decade the peninsula took 68 per cent of all shipments. Although the monopoly exercised by the company grew steadily more irksome to the Venezuelan population, it was not until 1780 that the crown first opened the colony to other traders, and then five years later dissolved the company. The success of this Basque venture led ministers to sponsor a series of other companies, of which the most important were the Habana Company (1740) created to handle the export of tobacco from Cuba and the Barcelona Company (1755) to trade with the other remaining Caribbean islands. But as none of these bodies were granted a monopoly of trade they soon foundered.

If for South America and the Caribbean the 1740s ushered in a new epoch, by contrast in New Spain the vested interests of the *consulados*, the merchant guilds of Cadiz and Mexico, prevailed on the crown to restore the fleet system. As a result, six great convoys sailed for Veracruz in the years 1757–76. But although the revived system brought security to the peninsula traders, the lion's share of profits, so critics alleged, went to the *almaceneros*, the great import merchants of Mexico City. At the Jalapa fair it was these men, often with over 100,000 pesos to spend, who dominated transactions, since the Cadiz shippers, faced with storage charges and forbidden further entrance up-colony, were clearly at a disadvantage, with more reason to sell than the *almaceneros* had to buy. Whatever the balance of profit, the system obviously worked to the detriment of both Spanish producers and Mexican consumers, since the volume of merchandise was limited in the interest of high prices. This revival of the fleet system for New Spain – by far the most prosperous of the colonies – demonstrates the nature and power of the vested interests against which the administrative elite had to battle. If foreign interlopers had at last been expelled from colonial ports, the further expansion of Spanish commerce now depended on a direct challenge to the great merchant houses of Mexico and the shippers of Cadiz.

The catalyst of change, once more, was war with Great Britain when Spain's tardy entrance into the Seven Years War led to the capture of Manila and Havana. Equally important, the British occupation of Havana promoted a remarkable increase in Cuban exports. The necessity to reform, both administrative and commercial, was only too evident. In consequence, in 1765 the Caribbean islands were thrown open for trade with the nine leading ports of the peninsula. At the same time the absurd practice of assessment of customs duties by cubic volume of merchandise, known as *palmeo*, was replaced by a 6 per cent *ad valorem* duty on all exported goods. The success of these measures made possible the promulgation in 1778 of the famous decree of *comercio libre*, which finally abolished the Cadiz staple and the fleet system. Henceforth trade between the chief ports of the empire and the peninsula was conducted by individual merchant vessels. The few restrictions which applied in New Spain were removed in 1789 and the Caracas company monopoly abolished in 1780. At the same time customs duties at Cadiz were lowered and preference given to Spanish manufactures.

The period from the declaration of comercio libre to the opening of the British naval blockade in 1796 turned out to be a brief golden age for colonial commerce. Within a decade registered exports tripled. Once the War of American Independence (1779–83) was concluded, unheard of quantities of European merchandise inundated colonial ports. In the one year of 1786 no less than sixteen ships entered Callao bringing goods worth 22 million pesos, at a time when the annual purchase of Peru was little more than five million pesos. The short-term result of this influx was, of course, a commercial crisis. Throughout the empire prices tumbled and profits dwindled as markets were saturated with imports. Many merchants went bankrupt and others cut their losses by withdrawing from transatlantic trade, preferring to invest their capital in agriculture and mining. Bullion drained out of local circulation as great sums were shipped abroad to finance the rising tide of European imports. Small wonder that consulados from Chile to Mexico clamoured for the crown to limit the influx of merchandise by a return to the old system of restricted entry. Ruin threatened their members. But the viceroys who investigated the matter, in particular Teodore de Croix in Peru and the count of Revillagigedo in New Spain, rejected these pleas out of hand. Echoing Campillo, they insisted that public interest should not be confused with the private profits of a handful of merchants. The expansion in trade, they said, had brought great benefits both to the colonial consumer and to Spanish industrialists. Moreover, in the case of Mexico, if the old almaceneros had now invested their capital in mining and the purchase of estates, this was all to the good, the more especially since their trading role had been taken up by a new breed of merchant, men content with a relatively small profit on a more rapid turnover of goods. More generally, statistics were assembled to demonstrate that the increase in the import bill was more than matched by the rising curve in silver production. That these years did in fact witness an extraordinary efflorescence of colonial exports, there can be little doubt. The rapid growth of Buenos Aires is testimony of the efficacy of the new policy.

Few things impress posterity more than the conviction of success and the servants of Charles III were not slow to boast of their achievements. In the course of a standard memorandum on the export of flour from Mexico to Cuba, the treasury *fiscal*, Ramón de Posada, after referring to Spain's former splendour and subsequent decadence, exclaimed: 'It was reserved for the superior wisdom and august protection of Charles III to initiate the splendid enterprise of recovering that former happiness.' But if the unhappy experience of the Hispanic world in the early nineteenth century led historians of that epoch to accept these claims at face value, recent research has greatly modified the traditional image. Above all, it is the role of the peninsula within the commercial system which has been brought into question. In his remarkable survey of registered trade between Cadiz and America for the years 1717–78, Antonio García-Baquero González has found that whereas the royal navy was constructed in Spanish arsenals, by contrast the merchant fleet sailing from Cadiz was mainly composed of vessels purchased from abroad. Although locally owned, only 22 per cent of the ships were built in Spain, with another 4.2 per cent coming from colonial yards. Equally important, it appears that most of the merchants at Cadiz were little more than commission agents for foreign traders resident in the city. The census of 1751 compiled on the instruction of the marquis de la Ensenada listed 162 merchants from abroad as against 218 native traders. Yet the Spaniards only accounted for 18 per cent of the declared income of the trading community, the French clearly being the leaders with 42 per cent of the total. Moreover, whereas over a fifth of the foreign merchants enjoyed incomes ranging from 7,000 to 42,000 pesos a year, only two Spaniards figured in this bracket. Further confirmation of the limited range of their financial operations can be found in their investments, which largely consisted of houses and property in the city of Cadiz.

If the monopolists of Cadiz turn out to be mere intermediaries working for a commission, it should come as no surprise to learn that in the same period the contribution of Spanish industry to colonial exports was derisory. True, measured by volume, peninsula produce occupied 45 per cent of cargoes bound for America, but it consisted of wine, brandy, oil and other agricultural commodities. Measured by value, the metropolitan share drops dramatically. On the most generous calculation, Spanish goods shipped by the 1757 fleet to New Spain accounted for 16 per cent of the total cargo value. In short, in colonial trade, Spain figured as a primary producer with little in the way of elaborated goods for export.[8] Elsewhere, we learn that for the years 1749–51 the royal factories of Guadalajara and San Fernando, which produced quality woollen cloth, exported no more than twelve *toneladas* out of an estimated output of over 10,000.

But what of the years after 1778? Certainly statistics were published which showed that about 45 per cent of exports to the colonies emanated from within the peninsula. The nascent cotton textile industry of Catalonia, its machinery bought in England, competed effectively in American markets. Here indeed was an industry whose growth in large measure derived from colonial trade. The projects of Ustariz and Campillo here yielded a rich harvest. But it must be emphasized that

[8] Antonio García-Baquero González, *Cádiz y el Atlántico 1717–1778*, 2 vols. (Seville, 1976), I, 235–7, 309, 319, 326–30, 489–95.

as late as 1788 Cadiz still accounted for 72 per cent of all shipments to the American empire, and if Barcelona had raised the value of its exports from a mere 430,000 pesos before comercio libre to 2.79 million pesos in 1792, nevertheless it still only supplied 16 per cent of all colonial exports. Not that the importance of the American markets should be minimized, since in Barcelona, as elsewhere in Spain, trade with Europe depended on wine and other agricultural produce. The problem is that if Catalan cotton goods were shipped direct from Barcelona to the colonies, how was it possible for Cadiz to register some 45 per cent of its exports, measured by value, as Spanish produce? In fact, there is evidence of widespread contraband and simple re-labelling.[9] Insofar as the bulk of registered exports, measured by value, consisted of textiles, it follows from what we know of Spanish industry that the overwhelming proportion of these goods came from abroad. Indeed, even Catalan cottons and Valencia silks were not exempt from the charge of being French goods bearing a Spanish stamp.

On the other side of the Atlantic the stress on export-led growth stands in less need of revision. Here evidence is certainly partial and clusters about the last years of the century; nevertheless, there can be little doubt that the eighteenth century witnesses a remarkable expansion in overseas trade with Europe. Provinces such as Chile and Venezuela, hitherto neglected and isolated, were now brought into direct contact with Spain through the opening of new trade routes. At the same time, the mining industries situated along the cordilleras of the Sierra Madre and the Andes experienced a dramatic revival in their fortunes. The traditional basis of the expansion in transatlantic trade requires emphasis. In the years 1717–78 bullion still accounted for 77.6 per cent of the assessed value of all shipments from the New World registered at Cadiz, the remainder of the cargoes consisting of tobacco, cacao, sugar, indigo and cochineal. With the promulgation of comercio libre the pace of economic activity gathered momentum, with the coasts and islands of the Caribbean yielding an ever greater harvest of tropical produce. Yet, in the 1790s, bullion shipments still supplied over 60 per cent of the value of colonial exports to the peninsula, a calculation which does not include the monies despatched on the king's account.

By this period the leading province within the American empire was New Spain, with registered exports averaging over 11 million pesos in

---

[9] Barbara H. Stein and Stanley J. Stein, 'Concepts and realities of Spanish economic growth 1759–1789', *Historia Ibérica* (1973), 103–20.

the years 1796–1820. Silver accounted for 75.4 per cent of value and cochineal 12.4 per cent, with sugar providing what remained. The Andean zone was characterized by a similar reliance on bullion to finance its overseas trade, with an overall production of over nine million pesos flowing directly out of the ports of Lima and Buenos Aires. For if the latter port, raised to the condition of a viceregal capital, could boast of exports worth five million pesos in 1796, only one-fifth was supplied from the pampa estancias in the form of hides, jerked beef and horns; the remainder consisted of coin sent down from the Potosí mint. In Chile the story was much the same, with gold and silver supplying 856,000 pesos of total exports worth a million, as against 120,000 pesos brought in by copper. Further north in Colombia, gold comprised 90 per cent of the exports valued at two million. In Central America, however, indigo shipments from Guatemala brought in 1.2 million pesos, a sum close to the 1.4 million pesos earned by Mexican cochineal and far in excess of the 250,000 pesos which was the estimated annual produce of the silver mines of Honduras. Dyestuffs apart, it was the growth in sugar, cacao and tobacco which challenged the predominance of bullion in Spain's Atlantic commerce. By the 1790s the value of exports from Venezuela had mounted to over three million pesos, distributed between cacao, indigo and coffee. But the great success story of these last years of the century was Cuba, where alongside the traditional cultivation of tobacco, sugar production expanded dramatically after the revolution in Saint-Domingue (1789–92). If at the start of the 1790s exports were valued at over three million pesos, by the years 1815–19 they averaged about 11 million, a total equal to the silver exports of New Spain.

One last comment is necessary. In the middle of the eighteenth century, Campillo had pointed to the Caribbean sugar islands as the yardstick by which to measure the commercial performance of the Spanish empire. As yet we lack any general survey of colonial trade, a task rendered all the more difficult by the frequent wartime blockades which interrupted the regular flow of shipping. By way of international comparison, it is perhaps helpful to recall that in the years 1783–7 Great Britain imported from her West Indian islands produce worth £3,471.673 a year, a sum equivalent to 17.3 million pesos. Similarly, by 1789 exports of sugar, cotton and coffee from Saint-Domingue were valued at 27 million pesos and another source estimated the total value of produce shipped from the French West Indian islands at $30\frac{1}{2}$ million

Table 1 *The Spanish Balance of Trade in 1792*
(millions of pesos)

(i) *The Peninsula*					
Exports	19.84	Imports	35.74	Deficit	15.9
(ii) *Trade with Colonies*					
Exports		Imports		Deficit	
National goods	11.15	Bullion	21.01		
Foreign goods	10.32	Produce	15.91		
Total	21.47	Total	36.92	15.45	

Source: José Canga Argüelles, *Diccionario de Hacienda*, 2 vols. (Madrid, 1833), 1, 639–45.

pesos. These figures provide a perspective on the Bourbon achievement. For, if the available statistics for all the provinces of the Spanish empire in the New World are put together, the grand total for exports in the early 1790s does not exceed 34 million pesos. Corroboration for this figure can be found in a contemporary balance of trade for 1792 described as the best known year for Spanish commerce (see Table 1).

To generalize from one year's trade at a time of violent fluctuation could easily mislead. Moreover, the table fails to elucidate the relation between peninsula and colonial trade, although the presumption must be that the great proportion of Spanish imports were re-shipped to the colonies and that the peninsula's deficit on the external trading account was met by the despatch of American bullion. But the degree to which colonial trade actually subsidized Spain's commercial balance of payments is not made clear. At the same time, the table omits any entry of the shipments of bullion arriving from the New World on the king's account, which is to say that it fails to take into consideration the fiscal profits of empire. Measured by past performance, the Bourbon revival was decidedly respectable, but, if judged on an international scale, the commercial expansion appears far less impressive.

THE EXPORT ECONOMIES

Whereas the peninsula derived but modest benefit from the revival in Atlantic trade, many of the American colonies were born anew. To sharpen our perspectives on Bourbon achievement, it is necessary to turn to the past. Viewed for the purpose of comparison, the Habsburg monarchy in the New World appears as a successor state raised on foundations built by the Aztec confederacy and the Inca empire. That it was the free labour and tribute of the Indians which allowed the encomenderos and missionaries to create an overseas equivalent of Spanish society within little more than a generation goes without dispute. What requires emphasis is that the pre-hispanic political experience continued to determine the organization of colonial society well into the seventeenth century. The Inca reliance on labour levies as against the Aztec preference for tributes decisively influenced viceregal policy. If Potosí came to act as a magnet for the entire imperial economy, it was largely because Viceroy Toledo summoned a vast annual migration of over 13,000 Indians to work in the mines of the great peak. The failure of the Mexican mining industry to emulate its Andean rival demonstrates that no matter what the importance of Spanish technology, the decisive agent in the rapid expansion of production was the massive input of labour provided by the *mita*. In short, Inca precedent allowed Toledo to mobilize the peasantry in the service of the export economy. By contrast, in New Spain labour drafts were recruited in the immediate locality of each mine, with the result that much of the industry came to rely on free workers and African slaves. The mainspring of the Habsburg trading system was the revival of a command economy in the Andean highlands.

By the eighteenth century, however, the regional balance of commercial activity had shifted away from the Mesoamerican and Andean cultural heartlands out towards frontier zones once inhabited by roving tribes or down to the tropical coasts and islands of the Caribbean and Pacific. The pampas of the Río de la Plata, the farmlands of Central Chile, the valleys about Caracas, the plantations of Cuba, the mines and haciendas of Mexico north of the river Lerma – these were the regions of rapid growth in both population and production. The workforce consisted either of free wage-labourers recruited from the casta (half-caste) or creole community, or, alternatively, of slaves imported from Africa. In contrast to the Habsburg period when the crown furnished the supply of labour, it was now merchants and entrepreneurs who advanced the cash necessary for the purchase of slaves or the payment of wages. The old command economy only survived in the mita at Potosí and in the infamous *repartimientos de comercio*, where royal authority was employed to coerce the Indian peasantry into either consumption or production of trade goods. Even here, it can be argued that the key element was the advance of cash by the merchant backers of the magistrates.

To stress the shift in the regional location of production for export might suggest that the removal of all legal barriers to commerce between the leading ports of the peninsula and the American empire played a decisive role in the opening of new lines of trade. But it would be false to suppose that mere arrival of merchandise from Europe could stimulate local agriculture or mining. As the British experience after American Independence clearly demonstrated, the greater availability of manufactures in American ports did not of itself evoke a matching supply of exports. Although Bourbon statesmen were swift to hail the expansion in Atlantic trade after comercio libre as the result of crown policy, the bureaucracy here, as elsewhere, simply took credit for other men's toil and ingenuity. The decisive agent behind the economic growth of the Bourbon epoch was an entrepreneurial elite composed of merchants, planters and miners. It was a relatively small group of colonial businessmen, in part peninsula immigrants, in part creoles, who seized the opportunities afforded by the opening of new trade routes and the fiscal inducements offered by the crown. These men readily adopted new technology where it proved feasible and did not hesitate to invest large sums of capital in ventures which at times needed years to yield a profit. The emergence of this elite is all the more extraordinary if we pause to consider that in the peninsula the merchant community were mainly content to act as intermediaries for foreign traders and offered small challenge to the hegemony of the territorial aristocracy. By contrast, in the New World merchants actively backed the development of both mines and plantations and at times invested their capital in production for export.

The showpiece of the Bourbon age was undoubtedly the Mexican silver-mining industry.[10] As early as the 1690s the mid-seventeenth century depression was overcome as mintage attained its former peak of over five million pesos. Thereafter, output rose steadily to reach 24 million pesos by 1798, with the 1770s registering the most rapid increase owing to new discoveries and fiscal incentives. Through this quadrupling of production in the course of a century the Mexican

[10] For a further discussion of mining in Spanish America in the eighteenth century, see Bakewell, *CHLA*, II, ch. 4.

industry came to account for 67 per cent of all American output of silver and Guanajuato, the leading centre, equalled the production of the entire viceroyalty of either Peru or La Plata.

The Spanish crown played a central role in promoting this dramatic resurgence. The dependence of the Mexican refining mills on the royal mine at Almadén for mercury to purify their silver meant that without the thorough-going renovation of this ancient mine (where, in fact, output soared from a mere 2,000 cwt to over 18,000 cwt) the industry would have remained hamstrung. Equally significant, the visitor-general, José de Gálvez, halved the price of this indispensable ingredient and increased the supply of gunpowder, another royal monopoly, cutting its price by a quarter. At the same time, he initiated the policy of granting tax exemptions and reductions for renovations or new enterprises of high risk, which required heavy capital investment. While he was minister of the Indies, Gálvez established a mining court to head a guild which exercised jurisdiction over all litigation within the industry. A new code of mining law was introduced and the court was made responsible for a central finance bank to sponsor investment and renovations. This battery of institutional reforms was rounded off in 1792 with the foundation of a mining college staffed in part by mineralogists brought in from Europe. The magnificent neo-classical palace which housed the court and its college expressed the central importance of Mexican silver mining within the Bourbon empire.

In no sense, however, do government measures offer a sufficient explanation of the eighteenth-century silver bonanza in New Spain. By this period the population of the colony was on the increase so that recruitment of a workforce through the provision of wages offered few difficulties. Indeed, Mexican mineworkers, for the most part mestizos, mulattos, poor creoles and migrant Indians, formed a free, well-paid, highly mobile, often hereditary, labour aristocracy who in most camps obtained a share of the ore in addition to their daily wage. But the decisive element in the expansion was to be found in the activity and collaboration of merchant-capitalists and miners, who displayed both skill and tenacity in ventures which on occasion required years of investment before striking rich. The industry was sustained by an elaborate chain of credit reaching from the silver banks and merchant-financiers in Mexico City to local merchants and refiners in the leading camps who in turn backed the actual miners. The tendency over the course of the century was for individual mines to become larger and in the smaller camps for an entire lode to be dominated by one great enterprise.

The scale of operations and the time expended was often extraordinary. It took over twenty years before the famous count of Regla benefited from his investments at the Veta Vizcaína in Real del Monte, owing to the necessity of driving a drainage adit 2,881 yards underneath the lode. With the enormous profits that followed Regla purchased a chain of haciendas and at the cost of nearly half a million pesos constructed the great refining mill that still stands as his monument. By far the greatest enterprise, however, was the Valenciana at Guanajuato which by the 1790s employed over 3,000 workers. With four shafts and a multitude of work tunnels reaching out across the lode, the Valenciana resembled an underground city. The octagonal central shaft with a circumference of 32 yards and a depth of over 600 yards, was a stone-lined construction, serviced by eight mule-drawn whims, which cost over a million pesos to cut and face. In the scale of its workforce and investment, there can have been few enterprises in Europe equal to the Valenciana.

That Government incentives were not sufficient to revive an ailing industry was demonstrated by the example of Peru. For in the Andean highlands the revival of mining was slow and limited. It was not until the 1730s that the industry began to recover from the depression of the previous century. But from a low point of about three million pesos, production only edged forward to just over ten million pesos in the 1790s, a figure only briefly sustained, and which included both viceroyalties of Peru and La Plata. The basis of this revival was the emergence of new camps, such as Cerro de Pasco which relied on wage labour, and the survival of Potosí, through the labour subsidy of the mita. The crown applied much the same measures as in Mexico – the mercury price was reduced, a technical mission despatched and a mining guild and court established. But certain key elements failed to materialize. The inability of the administration at Huancavelica to expand production – in fact after 1780 it declined – placed severe limits on the quantity of mercury available to the Andean industry, since New Spain always enjoyed preferential rights on all imports from Europe. Equally important, most mines remained small, employing but a handful of workers. The Andean industry lagged far behind its northern rival in the application of available technology. Behind this limited response to the new opportunities for profit created by government initiative lay a shortfall in capital for investment. The great merchants of Lima had lost their dominant position in South American trade and lacked the resources to emulate their counterparts in Mexico. Their rivals in Buenos Aires made no attempt to invest in the Andean industry. Thus, although by the end of the eighteenth century the mines of Upper and Lower Peru produced as much silver as in the reign of Philip II, recovery derived not from any new concentration of capital or labour, but rather from new discoveries and the mere survival of past endeavours. At the same time, bullion remained the only export of any consequence and the purchasing power generated by the industry still sustained a wide range of inter-regional commerce.

Apart from the tropical plantations worked by slaves, the remaining export trades relied on merchant capital, which financed a variety of producers ranging from Indian villagers and mestizo smallholders to Chilean miners and *estancieros* of the Argentine Pampas. Cochineal production in southern Mexico was promoted by repartimientos de comercio, which in this case simply meant cash disbursed by the district magistrate half a year in advance of the crop. If the great import house of Mexico City withdrew from these operations after repartimientos were prohibited by the Intendancy Code of 1786, local merchants in Oaxaca and Veracruz continued to lay out their monies in this trade. The same mercantile domination can be observed in the indigo trade of Central America, where the merchants of Guatemala City advanced credit both to smallholders and to landowners, with the result that through foreclosure merchants became directly involved in production for export. In Central America, therefore, the two dyestuffs were mainly procured through the collaboration of smallholders and merchant capital, with or without the intervention of the crown.

In the southern cone, in Chile and along the Río de la Plata, the merchants of Buenos Aires and Santiago financed the estancieros of the Pampas and the miners of the Chilean north. Both gauchos and mineworkers received a wage, even if the bulk of their clothing and drink often came from stores managed by their employers. It is difficult to ascribe any decisive cause for the growth of exports in these regions other than the simple opening of trade routes via the Río de la Plata and Cape Horn, combined with an increase of population sufficient to provide a workforce. Such expansion as occurred was important for the local economy, if as yet without much weight in the international market. The export of hides from Buenos Aires mounted rapidly from about 150,000 at mid-century to nearly a million by its close, as prices rose from six to twenty *reales* a quintal. The mining industry in Chile was largely the creation of the eighteenth century, with the overall value of its gold, silver and copper rising from an average 425,000 pesos in the 1770s to nearly a million pesos by the 1790s.

The other main lines of the export trade in Spanish America consisted of tropical produce from the Caribbean and Colombian gold. The workforce in all these areas was mainly provided by the import of slaves from Africa. In Colombia the gold placer workings in Popayán and Antioquia were operated by miners who employed relatively small gangs of slaves, their ventures financed by local merchants. Mintage at Bogotá rose from 302,000 pesos in 1701 to over a million pesos by the early 1790s, supplemented by an increase at the Popayán mint from an average 423,000 pesos in the years before 1770 to nearly a million pesos by 1800. Despite the failure of the crown to introduce intendancies in New Granada, its overseas trade equalled in value the export produce of the southern cone.[11] Yet more successful was its neighbour Venezuela, where cacao production mounted steadily across the century as annual exports rose from just under 15,000 *fanegas* in the years 1711–20 to over 80,000 *fanegas* by the 1790s. The plantations which grew cacao were owned by the great families of Caracas who formed a planter aristocracy. The workforce consisted of African slaves who by the turn of the century comprised an estimated 15 per cent of the total population. The long years of neglect prior to the establishment of the Caracas Company had permitted the development of an extensive native population, mulattos, mestizos and isleños from the Canaries. Beyond the coastal mountain valleys lay the great plains of the interior from which came the dried beef and the 30,000 mules shipped across the sea to the islands of the Caribbean.

The phoenix of the late Bourbon period was Cuba. For although the island had produced sugar and tobacco since the sixteenth century, it was only after the British occupation of Havana in 1762 that it seriously sought to emulate the pattern of production found in the French and British possessions. The crown took decisive action to promote the

[11] For these figures see A. J. Macfarlane, 'Economic and political change in the viceroyalty of New Granada with special reference to overseas trade 1739–1810' (Ph.D. dissertation, London University, 1977).

sugar industry through an increased importation of slaves, generous grants of land to planters and permission to import cheap flour from the United States. Between 1759 and 1789 the number of sugar mills rose from 89 to 277 and in much the same period production tripled. But then, with the revolution on Saint-Domingue and the subsequent destruction of its plantations, the Cuban industry entered a period of rapid expansion and technical change as both prices and profits soared. The planter aristocracy and the Havana merchants were if anything more entrepreneurial than their Mexican counterparts, alert to technical innovation, adopting steam-power for their mills and Tahitian strains of sugar for their plantations. In the last resort, however, the boom depended on the massive purchase of African slaves, whose numbers rose from nearly 86,000 in 1792 to some 286,000 in 1827, with annual arrivals after 1800 amounting to 6,670. If Cuba did not participate in the Insurgency after 1810, it was in good measure because the servile element by then comprised almost a third of the entire population. Within a generation Cuba had created an economic system and society more reminiscent of Brazil than of the remainder of Spanish America. Smallholders still dominated the cultivation of tobacco, but were increasingly at the mercy of the great planters who enjoyed the support of the colonial administration. The returns here were remarkably high. If exports were valued at about five million pesos in the 1790s, within just over another decade they had attained 11 million and hence equalled the registered overseas trade of New Spain. By then Havana had become the second city of Spanish America with over 70,000 inhabitants.

No matter how dramatic or rapid the economic transformation wrought in Spanish America by the importation of slaves or the investment in deep-shaft mining, the technological basis of that development remained thoroughly traditional. The purchase of a few steam engines did not effect an industrial revolution. Here a comparison between the two great colonial industries may prove instructive. For, despite the emergence of great capitalist enterprises, both silver-mining and sugar-growing remained trapped within a stage of production in which human muscle was the chief source of energy both for the extraction of ore and the cultivation of cane. Moreover, despite what were at times remarkable concentrations of manpower, all enterprises – mines and mills – were governed by much the same set of costs. As Professor Moreno Fraginals has argued, the great Cuban sugar mills, the *ingenios*, were simply quantitative amplifications of the previous range of small mills. Similarly, in New Spain, a great refining mill merely aggregated a larger number of crush-mills (*arrastres*) under one roof. In both cases the increase in scale of operations brought little, if any, qualitative change. Whether the organization of production became more efficient is another question. A study of the sugar plantations of Morelos found that between the sixteenth and late eighteenth century there was a fourfold increase in productivity calculated on the ratio of output as against the number of workers and draught-animals employed. Much the same sort of improvement occurred in North Atlantic shipping during this period. Without any significant change in maritime technology, a continuous improvement in organization allowed smaller crews to handle larger cargoes and spend much less time in port.[12] A similar process undoubtedly occurred in Mexican silver-mining where the unification of entire lodes under one management rendered drainage less haphazard. Improvements in refining spread from one camp to another. Nevertheless, in the last resort, both sugar-growing and silver-mining depended on a seemingly endless replication of the units of production, without any significant reduction in costs either from technical innovation or from increase in the scale of operation.

One last comment seems appropriate. By 1789 the produce shipped from the French colony of Saint-Domingue came close to equalling the value of the exports of the entire Spanish empire in the New World. This remarkable feat sprang from the deployment of a slave population of over 450,000 consisting in great part of young men imported directly from Africa. The entire colony was obviously geared for production for Europe. Clearly, if the export earnings of the $14\frac{1}{2}$ million inhabitants of Spanish America barely exceeded the output value of a single island in the Caribbean, it was because the bulk of its population found occupation and sustenance in the domestic economy.

THE DOMESTIC ECONOMY

The strategic weight and high profit of the Atlantic trade captured the attention of both contemporary statesmen and subsequent historians. By contrast, the humdrum transactions of the domestic American

---

[12] Manuel Moreno Fraginals, *The sugar mill, the socio-economic complex of sugar in Cuba 1760–1860* (New York, 1976), 40; Ward Barrett, *The sugar hacienda of the Marqueses del Valle* (Minneapolis, 1970), 66–70, 99–101; Douglass C. North, 'Sources of productivity change in ocean shipping 1660–1850', *Journal of Political Economy*, 76 (1968), 953–67.

market passed virtually unnoticed, with the result that entire cycles of economic activity, both industrial and agricultural, have sunk into oblivion. Yet all the available evidence attests to the existence of a lively circle of exchange which at the lower end consisted of barter arrangements within or between villages, at its middle reaches centred on the urban demand for foodstuffs, and in its most profitable lines involved long-distance, inter-regional dealings in manufactures, livestock and tropical cash-crops. Well before the Bourbon heyday, several frontier provinces were aroused into production by market demand exerted from the viceregal capitals within the New World. In particular, the emergence of a colonial textile industry bore witness to the strength of the internal economic revival which preceded the epoch of export-led growth. What recent research has demonstrated beyond dispute, however, is that the mainspring of this economic growth and prosperity was the increase of population. The eighteenth century witnessed a significant, though limited and uneven, recovery of the Indian population in Mesoamerica and to a lesser extent in the Andean highlands together with an explosive growth of the American-Spanish (creole) and casta (half-caste) population throughout the hemisphere but especially in formerly peripheral areas like Venezuela, New Granada, Chile, Argentina and Mexico north of the river Lerma. It has been estimated that by 1800 the American empire possessed a population of $14\frac{1}{2}$ million compared with Spain's population of $10\frac{1}{2}$ million.[13]

The bulk of this colonial population found employment and support in agriculture. In the eighteenth century many Indian villages, possibly the majority, still possessed sufficient land to support their inhabitants. Such was certainly the case in Oaxaca, Yucatán, highland Michoacán, large areas of Puebla, Huancavelica, Jauja and the region surrounding Lake Titicaca, to mention only those provinces for which data is to hand. Most Indian communities produced the bulk of their own foodstuffs and clothing. Their exchange of goods rarely extended beyond the locality and production for the market was limited, although the tendency of Indian villages to remain entrenched within their local peasant economy had been challenged and in part broken by the demands of the crown for tribute and labour service, by the invasion of community lands by the great estate and by the infamous repartimientos de comercio.

In contrast the great estates were geared from the outset to the market

---

[13] For a full discussion of the population of Spanish America at the end of the colonial period, see Sánchez Albornoz, *CHLA*, II, ch. 1.

economy and in particular to production for towns. Most plantations, it is true, catered for European demands, although in both Peru and New Spain the sugar industry also supplied domestic markets. Stock raising estancias, however, served largely domestic markets; only hides from Argentina were sent to Europe in any great quantity. Yet with the exception of the extensive sheepfarms of the Andean *puna*, they were mostly located in frontier zones several hundred miles away from their markets. Thus, each year over 40,000 mules were driven from their breeding grounds in the Argentine pampas to the trade fair at Salta and from there distributed across the Andean highlands. Similarly, the great flocks of Coahuila and Nuevo León supplied Mexico City with mutton (over 278,000 *carneros* a year by the 1790s) and wool for the mills at Querétaro. Chile despatched tallow and horns to Lima and Venezuela shipped 30,000 mules across the Caribbean. In these frontier zones, the workforce, be they called *guachos*, *llaneros* or *vaqueros*, were free workers, attracted by wages paid either in cash or kind, and, unlike African slaves on sugar plantations, themselves provided a significant market for the produce of colonial industry. The haciendas which produced cereals and other basic foodstuffs for the network of provincial capitals, mining camps and ports dealt in low-priced bulky commodities for which the market was limited by the cost of transport. In so far as the expansion of the export economy caused an increase in urban population, it also entailed an extension in the cultivation of basic foodstuffs. At the same time, the domestic sector maintained its own rhythm of production with prices fluctuating in response to seasonal and yearly variations in supply, which, in the short term at least, bore little relation to any changes in the international economy.

The tendency on haciendas was to rely on a small nucleus of resident peons and to hire seasonal labour from neighbouring villages or from the estate's own tenants. For in Mexico it has been shown that many landowners threw open a considerable part of their land to tenants in return for rents paid either by cash, in kind, or through provision of labour. By contrast, in Chile erstwhile tenants were converted into *inquilinos*, a service tenantry under obligation to supply the landlord with labour. Similarly, in Peru the *yanaconas*, or resident peons, were paid mainly by the lease of land for subsistence cultivation.[15] Only in New Spain was a balance maintained between peons, at times bound to the estate by debt, and the tenants and sharecroppers paying rent and supplying seasonal labour.

The development of the great estate was thus accompanied by the emergence of a new peasantry composed of mestizos, mulattos, poor Spaniards and acculturated Indians. The degree of subordination to the landlord varied from province to province. Certainly, in many parts of Mexico, along the Peruvian coast and on the Chilean frontier the first settlers who occupied small farms were bought out and reduced to the condition of tenants and sharecroppers. Even in these areas, however, important nuclei of smallholders survived, so that both the Valley of Putaendo in Chile and the Bajío in Mexico housed entire clusters of minifundia. Elsewhere, in Antioquia and Santander in New Granada most of the countryside was occupied by small proprietary farmers. Much the same was true in Arequipa in Peru or Costa Rica in Central America, or in the tobacco-growing districts of Cuba. This new peasantry at times competed with the great estate, at times was thrust into dependence on its operations. But across the empire it was the same social group which was largely responsible for the demographic increase and the economic growth of the frontier regions which played such an important role in the Bourbon revival.

Alongside this variegated pattern of production in the countryside there existed a considerable range of industrial activity, both rural and urban. To start with, most Indian villages were accustomed to spin and weave their own cloth, be it woollens in the Andean highlands or cottons in Mesoamerica. They also made their own pottery. Admittedly, at the other end of the social scale, the Hispanic elite paraded in finery imported from across the Atlantic, drank Spanish wines and brandy and fed off ceramic ware made in China and Europe. But there was also an extensive class of families resident in the leading towns, the mining camps and in frontier regions who relied on colonial industry to supply their apparel and other items of domestic use. As early as the sixteenth century large workshops called *obrajes* had been established in America to cater for the growing demand for cheap cloth, a domestic market which flourished by reason of the sheer cost of transatlantic shipping. In addition to these enterprises, however, there also emerged a certain range of cottage manufacture, especially for cotton cloth, which also catered for the urban market.

As yet there is insufficient evidence for any rounded survey of the structure and cycles of colonial industry and commerce during the eighteenth century. The story is decidedly complex. For it must both assess the deepening impact of the Atlantic trade and also register the decisive shifts in the balance of regional exchange within the American empire. The starting point of any analysis lies in the middle decades of the seventeenth century when the crisis in silver production and the failure of the Seville fleet system promoted the expansion of a domestic economy catering for the growing Hispanic and casta population. By all accounts the seventeenth century was the golden age of the *obrajes* of Puebla and Quito, the epoch when their fine woollen cloth commanded a wide distribution across the entire empire. Even at this stage, however, marked differences existed between the two industries, since whereas in Puebla the *obrajes* were situated within the city and operated with an assorted workforce of African slaves, sentenced criminals and apprentices retained through debt peonage, in Quito the *obrajes* were all located in the countryside, built on the great sheep-farms or in Indian villages, with a workforce recruited from the estate peons or operated by a village mita to meet tribute obligations.

The vitality of this American economy is further demonstrated by the growth of exports from Chile and Venezuela. From the 1680s the *hacendados* of central Chile started to ship considerable quantities of wheat to Lima, with the assessed volume rising from 11,556 fanegas in 1693 to 87,702 fanegas in 1734, this latter figure accounting for 72 per cent of all exports. Similarly, cacao shipments from Venezuela started in the 1660s, with annual cargoes rising from 6,758 fanegas to 14,848 fanegas in the decade 1711–20, with New Spain absorbing all but a tenth of these exports. In short, the prostration of Spain, when combined with the steady growth in colonial population, allowed the emergence of a distinctively American economy based on long-distance, inter-regional exchange of foodstuffs, bullion and manufactures, with Mexico City and Lima acting as the dominant centres within this trading network. It was at this period that the pattern was set for the eighteenth century. In South America, cloth came from Quito, brandy and sugar from the coastal valleys of central Peru, wheat and tallow from Chile, coca and sugar from the semi-tropical valleys close to Cuzco, mules from the Argentine pampas, mercury from Huancavelica, with bullion from Potosí providing the mainspring for this vast internal market. Much the same exchange prevailed in New Spain, with *tierra adentro*, the northern interior, supplying bullion, meat, hides and wool in return for cloth and tropical produce.

It must be emphasized, however, that the flow of internal trade changed dramatically during the Bourbon period. In the first half of the eighteenth century renewed competition both from Europe and other colonial centres undermined the prosperity of the textile industry of Puebla and Quito to the point where their *obrajes* ceased operation. In South America the opening of the new sea routes via Cape Horn sharply reduced the prices of imported cloth. At the same time, new *obrajes* situated in the countryside were opened in Cajamarca and Cuzco, the workforce recruited either by landlords or by corregidores as a means of collecting tribute. The success of these establishments over Quito presumably derived from their greater proximity to their markets. Much the same replacement occurred in New Spain where the industry at Puebla was destroyed by competition from Querétaro, which, by reason of its location at the edge of the Bajío, was better placed to purchase its wool from the great estancias of Coahuila and Nuevo León and to supply its market in the mining towns of the north. By 1790, Querétaro, with a population of over 30,000, had become a leading manufacturing centre, since the textile industry employed at least 3,300 workers divided between eighteen *obrajes* which produced fine woollens, ponchos and blankets and 327 workshops (*trapiches*) which mainly wove coarse cottons. The rise of these new centres drove Quito and Puebla to find alternative markets or start new lines of manufacture. By the 1780s Quito had turned from producing quality cloth for Lima to weaving coarse woollens for the market in New Granada. By contrast, Puebla succeeded in recapturing a measure of prosperity through specializing in the fine *rebozos* or shawls, cottons with a handsome silken sheen.[14] At this stage, the industry was dominated by a small group of merchants who purchased the cotton from Veracruz, put it out for manufacture by a numerous class of independent weavers, and then despatched the finished cloth for sale in Mexico City. It is estimated that in the years 1790–1805 Puebla annually supplied the capital with over one million pounds of cloth.

Shifts in the regional exchange of agricultural produce were less dramatic or pronounced than in textiles. Once again, Puebla suffered, with its outlets for flour severely reduced by reason of competition from

[14] G. P. C. Thomson, 'Economy and society in Puebla de los Angeles 1800–1850' (D.Phil. dissertation, Oxford University, 1978); Robson B. Tyrer, 'The demographic and economic history of the Audiencia of Quito: Indian population and the textile industry 1600–1800' (Ph.D. dissertation, University of California, Berkeley, 1976).

Table 2 *Value of New Spain's annual production,* c. *1810*
(millions of pesos)

Agriculture	106,285	(56)
Manufactures	55,386	(29)
Mining	28,451	(15)
Total	190,122	(100)

the Bajío in the markets of Mexico City and from the United States in Cuba. At much the same time, Venezuelan cacao was diverted from New Spain, so that by the 1790s greatly increased annual exports of over 80,000 fanegas went almost entirely to the peninsula. But this shift in the flow of trade offered an opportunity for the coastal province of Guayaquil which now captured the Mexican market, with overall production rising from 34,000 fanegas in 1765 to over 150,000 in 1809. Similarly, the concentration of tobacco growing in Veracruz provided an opening for Cuba to meet the demands of the Mexican market. In the southern cone the Atlantic trade was imposed over and above the internal pattern of exchange without much apparent distortion, since although in Chile bullion soon constituted the chief value of exports, wheat and tallow shipments to Lima still continued to expand in volume despite a falling price curve. In the Río de la Plata the remarkable increase in the export of hides in no way undercut the breeding of mules for the Andean highlands.

To strike the balance between the transatlantic and American sectors of the colonial economy is a hazardous task. The secretary of the Veracruz consulado provided estimates, recently revised, for the overall value of Mexican production, broken down by sectors.[15]

These figures must be treated with caution, since they are simple extrapolations from an assumed minimum consumption of the population and in no sense express the value of goods actually entering the market. One general point may be advanced. Whereas tropical plantations with their servile labour force generated relatively little

---

[15] José María Quirós, *Memoria de estatuto. Idea de la riqueza que daban la masa circulante de Nueva España sus naturales producciones* (Veracruz, 1817). See also Fernando Rosenzweig Hernández, 'La economía novo-hispánica al comenzar del siglo XIX', *Ciencias políticas y sociales* 9 (1963), 455–93.

demand for local produce, by contrast the mining sector provided an extensive market for both agriculture and domestic industry. To take a well-known case, in Guanajuato with about 55,000 inhabitants by the 1790s, about half the working population were employed in the mines and the refining mills. The remaining half consisted of artisans and servants. Less than two days' journey away lay the city of Querétaro, where the textile industry and the tobacco monopoly factory also provided support for an equally large number of workers and artisans. Both these cities offered a valuable market for local agriculture. Without the export of silver a great part of this exchange between town and country and between regions and cities would have disappeared, leading to a partial evacuation of urban centres in favour of agriculture. It is doubtful whether the shift to quality textiles attendant upon any decline in the transatlantic exchange of silver for European cloth could have compensated for the loss of a mass market in the cheaper lines of textiles and for foodstuffs. Clearly, the export sector generated high profits and made possible capital accumulation on a scale unimaginable in the domestic economy. Yet much of this capital was subsequently invested in the purchase and development of landed estates which survived through production for the domestic market.

Although some historians have taken up the contemporary lament that the flood of imports after comercio libre drained the continent of its circulating currency, it must be emphasized that without any increase in bullion shipments to Europe mining production inevitably would have fallen in consequence of inflation caused by an over-abundance of silver. Thus the Bourbon epoch constituted a relatively brief period of equipoise between the external and domestic sectors of the economy in which, if the rising curve of silver production certainly helped to finance the revival of the military power of the crown and allowed the colonies to import great quantities of fine cloth from Europe, it also generated a considerable range of employment which in turn created a lively market for domestic industry and agriculture. Indeed, it was the existence of this complex and variegated internal economy which allowed the emergence of an equally complex and distinctive colonial society.

THE LAST YEARS OF EMPIRE

In 1788, the count of Floridablanca, chief minister for more than a decade, had presented a general report, in which he celebrated the success of Spanish arms in the recent war against Great Britain. He hailed the threefold expansion in colonial trade and the doubling of customs revenue which followed the declaration of comercio libre. Public credit stood so high that the debts incurred during the War of American Independence had been funded by the new Bank of San Carlos through the emission of *vales*, bonds which circulated at face value. The programme of public works, in particular the construction of highways and canals, was a source of special pride. This image of a strong enlightened government actively promoting the prosperity of its subjects, both in the peninsula and America was not diminished by the accession of Charles IV (1788–1808), since, with first Floridablanca, and then the count of Aranda guiding the king, no change was evident until 1792. True, in colonial administration a certain loss in executive momentum became apparent, after the death of Gálvez, when in 1787 the ministry of Indies was first divided into two departments and then in 1792 virtually abolished, with its functions distributed among the various ministries, leaving only the Council of Indies exclusively responsible for the American empire. But at the level of colonial administration, the rule of the count of Revillagigedo as viceroy of New Spain (1789–94) and Fray Francisco Gil de Taboada y Lemos as viceroy of Peru (1790–6) marked the apogee of enlightened despotism in the American empire.

But the Bourbon revival of the Spanish monarchy always had depended on the protection afforded by the balance of power in Europe. No matter how effective they were in frontier warfare or auxiliary action, neither the Spanish fleet nor the Spanish army were any match for their chief opponents in the Old World. In 1793 the crown unwisely joined the continental coalition against the revolutionary regime in France, only to suffer outright defeat as French troops swept across the Pyrenees. By the close of 1795 Spain was forced to make peace and obliged both to renew the traditional alliance and to cede Santo Domingo. The consequences of this reversal proved incalculable, since the British fleet now imposed a rigorous naval blockade. In 1798 alone 186 ships leaving Cadiz were commandeered. Thereafter, apart from the brief but invaluable peace of Amiens (1802–4) all trade between Spain and the empire was suspended until the French invasion of 1808 lifted the siege of its ports. Confronted with the seizure of their ships or years of inactivity, many, if not most, of the leading merchant houses in Cadiz were forced into liquidation. At the same time, the commercial crisis led to a dramatic fall in revenue, so that with the budget already deranged by the high costs of the war against France, the treasury plunged headlong into debt. As the sum of *vales* in circulation grew rapidly, public credit collapsed. All hopes of any immediate recovery were brought to an end with the defeat and destruction of the Spanish fleet at Cape St Vincent (1798) and Trafalgar (1805). The loss of Trinidad to Great Britain and the cession of Louisiana to Napoleon offered further confirmation of Spain's impotence. Moreover, these years of international humiliation were accompanied by a marked deterioration in the quality of government at home. Since 1792 Manuel Godoy, an ex-guardsman and the queen's favourite, presided as chief minister over a regime mainly characterized by incompetence and corruption. Leading figures of the old administrative elite such as Floridablanca and Jovellanos were subject to confinement. Small wonder that many enlightened public servants welcomed the advent of Joseph Bonaparte as a means of achieving reform.

For the American empire the enforcement of the British blockade offered damning proof of the inability of Spain to protect the interests of its colonial subjects. In Mexico silver production plummeted as mercury stocks ran low and several mines were obliged to suspend operations. However, stocks at Almadén grew apace, so that with the peace of Amiens (1802) over 80,000 cwt of mercury were quickly shipped to Veracruz, enough to guarantee four years' production. If the impact of the blockade was less severe than might have been anticipated, it was largely because in 1797 permission was granted for neutral shipping to enter colonial ports, a freedom which was renewed in the years 1805–7. Throughout this period contraband was rife. Although French goods were effectively barred from the Atlantic, British merchandise now flooded into Spanish America, either as contraband from the West Indies or through the intervention of American traders. At the same time Cuba enjoyed the exceptional right to deal directly with the United States, exporting sugar in return for flour and other goods. Then again, the very restrictions imposed by the blockade afforded a certain measure of protection for colonial manufactures, which in some provinces enjoyed a last boom before their final eclipse.

Yet this very success of the colonies in preserving their prosperity despite the commercial rupture with the metropolis obviously brought into question the value of the imperial link. If Great Britain had now replaced France as the chief source of imports for Spanish America, why should its goods be shipped to the New World via the port of Cadiz merely to provide a fiscal profit for the crown? The estancieros of Buenos Aires and the planters of Venezuela all stood to gain from direct access to world markets.

Furthermore, it must be remembered that the revolution in government launched by Gálvez and his associates had provoked a series of popular uprisings. In New Spain the establishment of the tobacco monopoly, the formation of the militia and, more important, the expulsion of the Jesuits led to urban riots and open revolt. Only the previous arrival of veteran regiments from the peninsula allowed Gálvez to suppress the movement with unprecedented severity. In 1780–1 the application of much the same set of measures – the more efficient collection of alcabalas, the rigorous supervision of tribute payments and the restrictions on tobacco cultivation coupled with higher prices – set off widespread revolts in both New Granada and the Andean highlands. In southern Peru, José Gabriel Condorcanqui, a local cacique, took the name of Tupac Amaru, the last Inca emperor, as a means of rallying the Indian peasantry against the colonial regime. Only the vigorous defence organized by its creole bishop saved Cuzco from assault and capture. It required expeditionary forces from Lima and Buenos Aires to suppress a rebellion which stretched from Cuzco to La Paz. By contrast, in New Granada the *Comunero* uprising was defused by the skilful negotiation of the archbishop and interim viceroy, Antonio Caballero y Góngora, who cancelled the more unpopular fiscal decrees and granted amnesty to the leaders of the movement. The common theme in all these popular rebellions was resentment against the new taxes imposed by the Bourbon state. But whereas in Mexico the wealthy creoles co-operated with Gálvez to defeat the rebels, in Peru several caciques assisted Tupac Amaru in his venture and in New Granada the local dignitaries allowed themselves to be pressganged into revolt so as best to control the outcome. In short, no matter what the degree of popular mobilization, it was the involvement and leadership of the creole elite which was the decisive agent.

Traditional loyalty to the crown was eroded by the Bourbon attack on the church. For the expulsion of the Jesuits was followed by a series of measures designed to abrogate ecclesiastical jurisdiction and autonomy. The Code of Intendants contained clauses which entrusted the collection of the tithe to juntas controlled by royal officials, an innovation which met such a flurry of clerical protest that it had to be cancelled. Yet in 1795 the crown suspended the total immunity from civil courts hitherto enjoyed by the priesthood and decreed that in cases of grave crime clerics could be tried by royal magistrates. Not for nothing did the bishop of Michoacán warn the crown in 1799 that similar attacks on ecclesiastical privilege in France had so weakened the influence of the church as to allow the *philosophes* to go unchallenged in their plans to change society. Echoing Montesquieu, he declared that if the nobility and church were undermined, then the fate of the monarchy was in doubt. Undeterred and in urgent quest for revenue, in 1804 Godoy introduced the consolidation or amortization decree, by which all ecclesiastical property had to be sold and the receipts deposited in the royal treasury, which henceforth would be responsible for the payment of interest on the capital. Despite the chorus of protest from all leading institutions in New Spain, Viceroy José de Iturrigaray, a venal protégé of Godoy, hastened to implement a measure which dealt a grievous blow not merely to the church, whose income was threatened, but also to the landowning class on whose estates most ecclesiastical capital was invested in the form of annuities and chantry funds.

The campaign against ecclesiastical jurisdiction and property should not be construed simply as a mere assault on corporate institutions which had grown too wealthy or become unduly privileged. The attack on the church signalled the imminent demise of the traditional authority of the crown. For priests throughout the empire had always preached obedience to monarchy as a divine commandment. Their residence at the Escorial, which housed monastery, palace and sepulchre, had invested the Catholic Kings with a sacral aura. But the Bourbon dynasty slowly dissipated the moral and political capital bequeathed by their Habsburg predecessors. Although the Divine Right of Kings was still sedulously purveyed, the doctrine was increasingly detached from its natural background in scholastic theology and baroque sensibility. By the close of the eighteenth century the works of Suárez and Vitoria lay unread: the Hispanic world now looked to France for its inspiration, albeit as much to the France of Bossuet and Port Royal as of Montesquieu and Raynal. The cycle of baroque architecture which had dominated the towns and churches of Spanish America since the late sixteenth century was brought to an abrupt end in the 1790s with the promulgation of the neo-classic as the only acceptable style. At one stroke past glories became an antique embarrassment. The clergy themselves were as much affected by the new climate of opinion as their opponents. Whereas in the first decades of the Bourbon era devotional exercises and liturgical celebration still flourished, the emphasis later changed to practical morality, good works and education. In short, the administrative elite who served enlightened despotism undermined the institutions and the culture which had revered monarchy as a mandate from heaven.

Viewed within the context of Spain's position in the European Concert, the revolution in government and the expansion in the export economy was a desperate rearguard action hastily devised in Madrid first to avert British expropriation of Spain's overseas possessions and then to exploit their resources to strengthen the monarchy. If the measures met with apparent success, the price was the permanent alienation of the creole elite. For the ancient constitution, all the more powerful for being unwritten, which had presumed consultation over taxation and a consonance of interest between king and people was broken asunder by the new reliance on executive decree and military sanction. The vogue in Madrid for the terms metropolis and colonies brought small comfort to territories which formerly had been defined as the overseas kingdoms of a universal Christian monarchy. For many American Spaniards the economic prosperity of these years, so often engineered by peninsular bureaucrats for the benefit of *gachupín* merchants, was no consolation for exclusion from public office. At the same time the establishment of the chief institutions of absolutist monarchy in the leading provinces of the empire provided the creole elite with sufficient machinery of state to assure any future independence. When in 1807 Viceroy Iturrigaray assembled an army of over 15,000 men in the hills above Veracruz to guard against a British assault, he assembled a force recruited in New Spain, led in large part by creole officers and entirely financed by revenue raised in the colony. Similarly, it was the urban militia rather than the regular garrison which repelled the British invasion at Buenos Aires in 1806–7. The reconquest of America had alienated the colonial establishment yet fortified its economic position and provided it with an army and a bureaucracy. With traditional loyalties quite eroded, and the example of the Thirteen Colonies before it, small wonder that, when news arrived of the abdication of Charles IV, the creole elite at once sought a voice in the governance of their countries.

Far from being the natural culmination of 300 years of colonial development, the late Bourbon era was an Indian summer, a fragile equipoise, easily broken asunder by changes in the balance of power in Europe. Once more, the peninsula served as a battlefield for contending armies of British and French troops. But whereas in the War of Succession colonial society had remained somnolent and indifferent, in 1808 when French bayonets made Joseph Bonaparte king of Spain, the creole elite in most provinces of the empire demanded representative juntas to provide a legal basis for government. Events in Europe thus provided the occasion rather than the cause of political upheaval in America. Two years later, when the Cortes met at Cadiz, charged with the task of framing a constitution for the entire monarchy, the overseas provinces either called for immediate autonomy or burst into open revolt.

12

PORTUGAL AND BRAZIL: POLITICAL AND ECONOMIC STRUCTURES OF EMPIRE, 1580–1750*

Portugal in the sixteenth century was in the first place, to use João Lúcio de Azevedo's term, an 'agrarian monarchy'. Land, its major asset, was largely held in the form of the great manorial estate. The king himself was a landowner – *unus inter pares*. He could retract land grants made in the past. Moreover, lands bestowed by him could devolve only on the eldest legitimate son. These measures maintained the cohesion of the great estates and ensured the obedience to the king of their titular owners.

At the same time Portugal has also been called a 'maritime monarchy'. Endowed with a relatively long oceanic seaboard, Portugal had in the late Middle Ages made use of the sea for both coastal trading and long-distance voyages. Fishing was a significant resource and extended beyond the coastal waters as far as Newfoundland. The salt marshes of Aveiro, Lisbon and Setubal supplied not only Portuguese needs but also those of ships from the Mediterranean sailing to northern Europe and the Baltic. Thus was Portugal able to maintain a larger population than if she had merely depended on her agriculture and the export of corn. After the Great Discoveries in the fifteenth century the Atlantic island colonies – Madeira and the Azores – and the trading stations of Morocco, the Cape Verde islands and the Guinea coast brought products such as timber, sugar and wine to Portugal for re-export to Europe. Then gold from Guinea, spices from India and first brazilwood and, later, sugar from Brazil transformed the Portuguese economy.

The economic and social structure created by these developments was dominated by the merchant-king who possessed the monopoly of trade. As circumstances dictated he reserved it for himself or farmed it out,

* Translated from the French by Mrs Elizabeth Edwards; translation revised by Cynthia Postan; chapter reduced in length and partly reorganized by the Editor.

granting licences to private Portuguese or foreign merchants (*contra-tadores*) whom he was content to supervise. By the sixteenth century he was represented by agents in Antwerp and throughout his expanding maritime empire. Many foreign merchants, particularly Spaniards, Italians and Germans, were also established in Lisbon. The Spaniards were predominantly New Christians who had come to Portugal when the Jews and the Moors were expelled from Spain in 1492, a fortunate event for Portugal since for two centuries they were to form the backbone of the Portuguese trading class in Europe and overseas. The great landowners who composed the Portuguese nobility seemed more interested in colonial expansion because they needed land for their younger sons, although they did not hesitate to engage in trade. Overseas, first in the Atlantic islands, then in Brazil, the younger sons, titular incumbants of *sesmarias* (land grants) or even of *capitanias* (captaincies) became producers and exporters of agricultural products, of sugar in particular.

The social structure of Portugal was unlike any other in Europe not only because of the important part played by the king in the economy and the lack of a 'national bourgeoisie' in the accepted sense of the term but also because, as Albert Silbert has pointed out, Portugal had not experienced the feudal system. Apart from the fact that the 'property of the crown' was a much more important part of the economic power of the high and middle-ranking nobility than any patrimonial inheritance, the king had never surrendered his rights and powers (*direitos reais*) in the field of justice. Nor was the organization of military service founded on the feudal tie: it had always been both general and remunerated. The Portuguese crown also gained strength from its religious and cultural role. The king, for example, enjoyed considerable powers of patronage (*padroado real*), that is to say, the right to nominate candidates for ecclesiastical benefices, to present them, if priests, for the approbation of the bishop, or, if bishops, for the approval of the pope, at least in his overseas possessions. In addition, the king played a major part in the *Reconquista* and, after the death of King Sebastian at Alcacer Quibir in 1578, the myth of the Crusader King who had sacrificed himself for the Faith became a powerful element in the charisma attaching to the monarchy.

The financial position of the Portuguese crown was also relatively strong. The king derived his income from two sources, the traditional and the colonial, and the latter, of course, increased considerably in the fifteenth and sixteenth centuries. During the early decades of the sixteenth century receipts from colonial trade represented 65–70 per cent of the total revenues of the state. In turn, colonial trade stimulated agriculture and the economy of the towns and coastal regions of Portugal and further increased the fiscal revenue of the crown. In the early decades of its settlement Brazil made an insignificant contribution to royal income (less than 2 per cent compared with India's 26–27 per cent). But with the beginnings of the great sugar cycle in the 1570s and 1580s Brazil and especially Bahia and Pernambuco became and remained one of the keystones of the Portuguese empire.[1]

PORTUGAL AND BRAZIL, 1580–c. 1695

Any description of the administration of the world-wide Portuguese empire, including Brazil, from the late sixteenth to the late seventeenth century is complicated by the fact that Portugal was united with Spain in a dual monarchy during the first half of this period. In 1580 Philip II of Spain, nephew of João III (1521–57), became Philip I of Portugal. He was succeeded by Philip III (Philip II of Portugal) in 1598 and by Philip IV (Philip III of Portugal) in 1621. Only in 1640 did the Portuguese successfully revolt against Habsburg rule and proclaim the duke of Braganza João IV. During the union of the two monarchies, the Spanish Habsburgs on the whole respected the pledges made at Thomar in 1581 to allow considerable Portuguese autonomy and to maintain the two empires as separate entities. Public offices were reserved for Portuguese subjects at home and overseas. The king was represented at Lisbon sometimes by a 'governor' and sometimes by a viceroy. Important matters, however, were referred to Madrid, where they came before the Council of Portugal (which met in the same premises as a *Junta da Fazenda de Portugal*). And at least from 1631 one of the three Secretaries of State belonging to the Council bore the title of 'Secretary of State for India and the Conquered Territories'. Moreover, a commission of jurists set up to reform the legal system produced a new code for Portugal, the *Ordenações filipinas*, promulgated in 1603.

In Lisbon there was a Council of State without clearly defined administrative powers, and the Spanish kings maintained the system of two secretaries of state, one for the kingdom and the other for 'India',

[1] For a discussion of the early settlement of Brazil 1500–80, see Johnson, *CHLA*, I, ch. 8.

that is to say, for the colonies, despite several conflicts over jurisdiction, until the creation of the *Conselho da India* in 1604. In the same way they retained the *Mesa de Consciencia e Ordens*, which was both tribunal and council for religious affairs and was responsible for administering ecclesiastical appointments and for the property of the military orders in the colonies as well as in the mother country. Also preserved was the *Desembargo do Paço*, the supreme tribunal of the kingdom and of the empire, which on occasions advised the king on political and economic as well as judicial matters, and the court of appeal, the *Casa de Suplicação*.

Under Philip I (Philip II of Spain) in 1591 the four *Vedores da Fazenda* (overseers of the Treasury) were replaced by a *Conselho da Fazenda* composed of one Vedor da Fazenda presiding over four councillors (two of them lawyers) and four secretaries. One of the secretaries was responsible for colonial affairs, which occupied an important place in the deliberations of the council. Its meetings were frequent – every morning and twice a week in the afternoon as well. Moreover, from 1623 onwards, an additional afternoon each week was devoted solely to colonial affairs. From 1604 the newly created Conselho da India was invested with powers for all overseas affairs, apart from matters concerning Madeira, the Azores and the strongholds of Morocco. Colonial officials were appointed and their despatches handled by it. However, it was the Conselho da Fazenda which dealt with naval expeditions, the buying and selling of pepper and the collection of the royal revenues, in fact with all economic business. The Conselho da India, therefore, exercised only limited powers. As a creation of the Spanish king it was regarded with disfavour by the Portuguese and because of the jealousy of the Mesa da Consciencia disappeared in 1614.

After the Restoration, João IV preserved most of the administrative institutions which he found in existence on ascending to the throne and ratified the *Ordenações filipinas*. However, in the realm of finance, the king reverted to the former system of Vedores da Fazenda, while the Conselho da Fazenda appears to have continued only as a tribunal. A single Secretary of State was retained, but inspired by the Conselho da India (1604–14), the king created in 1642 a *Conselho Ultramarino* (Overseas Council). It was composed of a president, the *Vedor da Fazenda da repartição da India*, several councillors, a lawyer and a secretary. From November 1645 the council met on Mondays, Tuesdays and Wednesdays to discuss the business of India, on Thursdays and Fridays for Brazil and on Saturdays for the affairs of the other colonies, although Madeira and the Azores were outside its jurisdiction. There were inevitable conflicts over jurisdiction between the overseas council and the other councils.

In sixteenth-century Lisbon the major government offices, apart from the customs house (*alfandega*), primarily concerned with fiscal matters were the Casa da India and the *Casa da Guiné e da Mina*. Established on the river-bank at the western end of the present Terreiro do Paço, they occupied the ground-floor of the royal palace. Both were under the control of the same director and three treasurers, one for spices, one for the revenue from spices and the third for remaining business. Five secretaries shared the administrative work between them – three for the Casa da India and two for the Casa da Guiné. The Casas collected certain dues, ratified contracts with traders and explorers on behalf of the king, organized the fleet, supervised the loading and unloading of vessels and acted for the king in all the tasks which were necessary for the development of the colonies. A *factor* was in touch with *factores* in all the Portuguese trading-stations in the world. With them he conducted the business of the 'merchant-king' and from them he learned what merchandise the king and his subjects had at their disposal and what method of payment could be used. Lastly he kept a register of all the Portuguese ships which had set out from Lisbon and of the cargoes and passengers which they conveyed. During the union with Spain the *factor* was replaced by a *provedor* and the two Casas were fused into a single Casa da India, which from 1591 onwards came under the authority of the Conselho da Fazenda. In the seventeenth century the fiscal role of the Casa became relatively more important. Quite separate from the Casa da India, the *Armazem* (or *Armazens* – general stores or depot) *da Guiné e Indias* was in charge of all nautical matters, such as the construction and fitting of ships, the training of pilots and the issue of marine charts, master-copies of which were preserved by the depot itself. The naval dockyards came under its authority. The crews of the king's ships were appointed by the *provedor dos Armazens*, but they had to be registered with the Casa. Expenditure incurred by the Armazens, as for the purchase of materials or settlement of accounts, was defrayed by the treasurer of the Casa.

The colonial territories were lands belonging to the crown or to the crown's beneficiaries. In Brazil where royal government had been established in 1549 the first governor, Tomé de Sousa (1549–53), exercised authority over the settled areas of the country from Salvador da Bahia and was represented in each captaincy, either by a donatary captain or, if the captaincy had been redeemed by the monarchy, by a captain-general (sometimes a governor). The powers of Brazil's governor (sometimes styled governor-general) had been defined by the *regimentos* (standing instructions) of 1549. Like their Spanish counterparts, they might be subjected to an inspection (*visita*) during their tour of duty and to a final inspection (*residencia*) at the end of it. The governors-general, always drawn from the Portuguese nobility, but, at least from 1640, with some administrative experience, remained at their postings on average for six and a half years in the sixteenth century, for three and a half years in the seventeenth century and for a little less than six years in the eighteenth century. Many captains-general, the majority of whom were army officers, spent twenty or even 30 years in Brazil, changing from one post to another.

The authority of the governor-general gradually diminished as the Portuguese in the last decades of the sixteenth and the first half of the seventeenth centuries penetrated the interior of Brazil and expanded on the northern and southern extremities of the colony far beyond the line of Tordesillas, and as successive changes in the administrative structure of the colony were imposed from Lisbon.[2] The Portuguese, for example, with Spanish assistance, expanded north in the 1580s from Pernambuco into Paraíba at the expense of the French and the Indians – and later into Ceará. In 1614–15 they removed from Maranhão a French expedition under Sieur de la Ravardière which had arrived there in 1612. The Portuguese then moved to Pará and founded Belém at the mouth of the Amazon in 1616, although for more than a decade the occupation of the lower Amazon continued to be disputed by the French, the English, the Dutch and the Spanish. The captaincies of the south – Espírito Santo, Rio de Janeiro and São Vicente – were twice detached from Bahia (1572–8 and 1608–13) and administered separately. Even more significantly, in 1621 a separate *Estado do Maranhão* was formed from the recently established crown captaincies of Ceará, Maranhão and Pará and a number of small private captaincies, with its own governor-general in São Luís do Maranhão. There were sound geographical reasons for this division of Brazil: it was easier to travel from São Luís or Belém to Lisbon than to Bahia. The rest of Brazil, the crown captaincies from Rio Grande do Norte to São Vicente in the

---

[2] For a discussion of the territorial expansion of Brazil from the late sixteenth century, see Schwartz, *CHLA*, II, ch. 12 and Hemming, *CHLA*, II, ch. 13.

south and the remaining private captaincies, was now called the *Estado do Brasil*.

In 1652 the Estado do Maranhão was reunited with the Estado do Brasil, but separated once more two years later, and in 1656 Ceará was permanently transferred to the Estado do Brasil. In 1715 Piauí became a crown captaincy within the Estado do Maranhão, and in 1737 the capital was transferred from São Luís to Belém. Within the Estado do Brasil, after the recovery of Pernambuco from the Dutch in 1654 (see below) the new captain-general was concerned to assert his autonomy in relation to the governor-general in Bahia. Moreover, a conflict broke out between Salvador de Sá, who had been appointed governor and captain-general of the captaincies of the south, and the governor-general to decide which of them had authority over the captaincy of Espírito Santo. A viceroy had first been appointed in 1640–1, but the title had subsequently disappeared. The post was revived in 1663 in the person of Dom Vasco de Mascarenhas, count of Óbidos, the king's nephew. He demanded that no royal decree should be executed in any captaincy without having been first passed by himself, and he sent a *regimento* to all the captains-general which redefined their duties and reminded them that they were subordinate to Bahia and to no other authority. There was a reminder also to the governors of Pernambuco and Rio de Janeiro of the exact limits of their powers. The governor of Rio deferred, at least on paper, but the governor of Pernambuco did not. In the late seventeenth and early eighteenth centuries there was a process of regrouping captaincies: those of medium size became subordinate captaincies and their captains-general were placed under the authority of their most important colleagues, who acquired the title of 'governor and captain-general' and administered a captaincy-general (Rio 1698, São Paulo 1709, Pernambuco 1715). The office of governor-general at Bahia appears to have been raised permanently to the rank of viceroy from 1720 onwards, but, although the viceroy henceforth enjoyed a higher stipend, he lost his powers over the internal administration of the captaincies-general, whose title holders dealt directly with Lisbon. Theoretically they remained subordinate but in fact the viceroy could intervene only in his own captaincy-general.

The original donatary captains of Brazil were assisted, in matters of justice, by *ouvidores* (crown judges) and in 1549 there arrived in Bahia, with the first governor, an *ouvidor-geral*. In 1588 the Spanish regime decided to set up in Bahia a *Relação* (High Court of Appeal) similar to the *Relação do Porto*, responsible for the north of Portugal, and the *Relação da India*. The magistrates sent to establish it were, however, thrown off course by winds and currents and their ship was finally discovered at Santo Domingo. The crown was unable to implement its plans for the establishment of the court until 1609. It was then suppressed in 1626, in part as an economy measure during the Dutch War (see below, p. 449) and was not restored until 1652. For the next century it remained Brazil's only high court. (Following the adminis- trative division of Brazil into two estados in 1621, the Estado do Maranhão had remained directly responsible to the *Casa da Suplicação* in Lisbon.) *The Relação da Bahia* was presided over by the governor- general and was composed of a chancellor, three *desembargadores dos agravos* (high court judges), the *ouvidor-geral*, the *provedor-mor dos defuntos e residuos*, responsible for administering the property of deceased persons, and two *desembargadores extravagantes* (extraordinary judges). These crown judges were assisted by six secretaries, a doctor, a chap- lain, an usher and a treasurer (*guarda mor*) charged with the collection of fines. The *ouvidores* continued to function in the captaincies as judges of the first instance, and they were often also *provedores de fazenda*, responsible for financial administration and collection of crown revenue.

The municipal organization of Salvador (Bahia) may be taken as typical of urban administration in Brazil. The first municipal council was created in 1549, at the time of the foundation of the city. The *mesa de vereação* was composed of three *vereadores* (councillors), two *juizes ordinarios* (elected magistrates) and a *procurador da cidade*, elected annually on a three-year basis, as in Portugal. After the Restoration (1640), at least in Bahia, the artisans of the city were represented by two *procuradores dos mesteres* and a *juiz do povo*. In 1696 the elective system was suppressed and it was the judges of the *Relação* who were responsible for choosing the municipal officers on the triennial rolls. The presidency of the municipal council was no longer assumed by each of the *vereadores* in turn but by a professional crown magistrate, the *juiz de fora* ('the judge from outside'). The appointment of ordinary judges was abolished and henceforward the *senado da câmara* was composed of the *juiz de fora*, three *vereadores* and the *procurador*. The secretary, or *escrivão da camara*, was, in practice, present and had a voice in the consultations. Although all these officers were paid by the crown, they preserved their freedom of speech in relation to the viceroy. The juiz do povo and the two *procuradores dos mesteres*, already objects of distrust, were finally suppressed by the king at the request of the *vereadores* in 1713. The *vereadores* appear to have been recruited almost invariably from among the *senhores de engenho* (sugar mill owners). However, the holders of office were often changed – an important difference from the *regidores* of Spanish America, whose responsibilities had come to be for life and were more or less hereditary.

For long periods during the second half of the sixteenth and the whole of the seventeenth centuries much of Europe was at war. Portugal and its empire was at first relatively secure, even after the union with Spain, although its shipping came under attack from Barbary corsairs in the Lisbon–Madeira–Azores triangle from the 1570s to the 1590s and, increasingly, from Dutch, English and French pirates around the turn of the century. However, with the end of the Twelve-Year Truce (1609–21), in the long and bitter struggle between the United Provinces and Spain, the newly founded Dutch West India Company looked on the Portuguese empire as a prime target for its military and naval operations. Salvador da Bahia was captured in 1624 and in March 1625 Salvador de Sá and Piet Heyn fought a battle off Espírito Santo. Bahia was recovered the following May by a joint Spanish and Portuguese fleet and expeditionary force led by Don Fadrique of Toledo. From March to June 1627 there were raids by Piet Heyn on the Brazilian coast after the Portuguese fleet was sunk in January in the Bay of Biscay. (In 1628 the same Piet Heyn captured the Spanish silver fleet at sea in the Caribbean.) The seizure of Recife by ships of the Dutch Company in 1630 marked a new stage in the conflict. It was the prelude to the conquest and occupation for a quarter of a century of the whole of the Brazilian north-east from the São Francisco river to Maranhão, including Pernambuco, one of the two most important sugar-producing captaincies. In 1637 the Dutch also occupied São Jorge da Mina on the West African coast. In 1638 a great Portuguese fleet under the command of count da Torre left for Brazil but it was defeated by the Dutch off Itamaracá in 1640.

Portugal and Holland made peace in 1641 following the restoration of the Braganzas. But the war continued in Africa and Brazil, with the Dutch taking Luanda in August, Sergipe and Maranhão in November. In 1642 Maranhão revolted against the Dutch, and in 1644 the Dutch were obliged to withdraw. In June 1645 Pernambuco planters revolted against the Dutch, but in September a squadron under Serrão de Paiva was destroyed at Tamandaré. In 1647 van Schoppe occupied briefly the island of Itaparica at the entrance to the Bahian Recôncavo and the Dutch defeated a Portuguese expedition to Angola. The year 1648 was difficult, but eventually decisive. Two Portuguese fleets, under Villa-Pouca and Salvador de Sá, had left for Brazil in 1647. Meanwhile Spain had finally recognized the independence of the United Provinces and Witte de With's fleet reached Recife. However, in April (1648) near Recife, the first battle of the Guararapes gave the Portuguese a victory. Four months later, Salvador de Sá recovered Luanda, Benguela and São Tomé in Africa. In 1649 Francisco Barreto won another victory at the second battle of Guararapes. The Dutch increasingly lost control of the hinterland of Pernambuco and in 1654 the last Dutch strongholds fell. Brazil was once again fully under Portugal's control. Holland and Portugal made peace in 1661 and hostilities gradually subsided. In 1668 Spain also finally settled its differences with Portugal and recognized the Braganza Restoration.

Half a century of war – and more than a century of piracy – put an enormous strain on the administration and especially the defence of the Portuguese empire in Asia, Africa and America and exhausted Portuguese resources. Fortifications were built and rebuilt; the *Armada do Mar Oceano*, the fleet of the high seas, was reorganized in 1633; coastal defence fleets were created; naval squadrons and armies on several continents had to be provisioned; the navy shipyards worked at full strength; troops and naval crews were levied; even foreigners were conscripted, although certain traditionally overpopulated areas, such as the region between the Douro and the Minho, the Azores, Madeira and even Lisbon itself, supplied the majority of recruits. The war for Pernambuco alone cost 500,000 cruzados a year, and increased taxes and duties in Portugal and throughout the empire failed to provide the crown with the revenue it required. Recourse was had to other means for obtaining revenue including loans, both voluntary and forced.

Charts and log-books preserved from the sixteenth and seventeenth centuries show that most direct Atlantic routes between Europe and America had been discovered by the Portuguese at an early date. They were determined by climatic and hydrological factors, based on the trade winds in the tropics and the prevailing westerly winds in the northern and southern temperate zones. Latitude was calculated with the help of the astrolabe, the quadrant and other instruments which measured

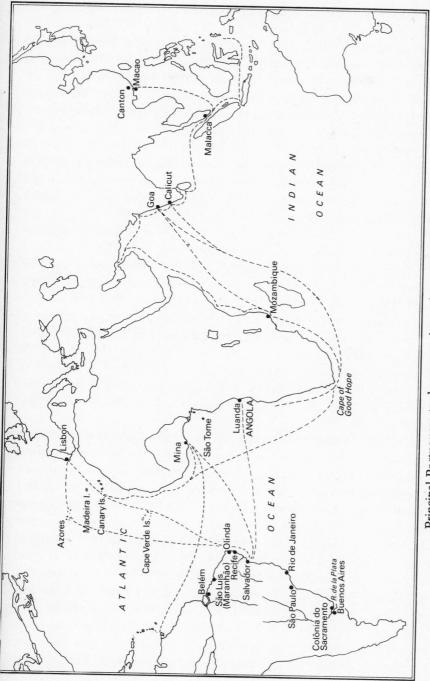

Principal Portuguese trade routes, sixteenth to eighteenth centuries

the height of the sun or of a star in relation to the horizon or to the pole, corrected according to the season of the year by tables which the cosmographers of King João II had formulated. However, navigation in the sixteenth and seventeenth centuries was far from reliable. And voyages were both long and uncertain: for example, it took from ten to fourteen weeks to sail from Lisbon to Bahia. Moreover, the voyage was uncomfortable for passengers, bundled together as they were with cargo and cannon. Food was bad and deteriorated, while storms and shipwrecks were frequent. The islands of Madeira and the Azores served as staging-posts; the former on the outward passage before the difficult stretch of the Atlantic where equatorial calms were encountered, and the latter before the last part of the voyage to Lisbon, where pirates and corsairs lay in wait.

Although the vessels carrying the Portuguese Atlantic trade were naturally ocean-going ships, they were certainly not as big as the ships reserved for the East India traffic. The caravel and the *navio*, built for heavy cargoes but slower and smaller, were the craft most commonly used. During the union with Spain, Portuguese galleons were, it appears, sometimes designed to imitate the gigantic lines of the Spanish galleons; one such was the *Padre Eterno* of 2,000 tons burden and armed with 114 pieces of cannon. It was built in Brazil – in the Bay of Guanabara (Rio de Janeiro) – and first visited Lisbon in 1665. The increase in the size of ships was a general phenomenon at this period, as Pierre and Huguette Chaunu have shown in their research on Seville's Atlantic trade.

Portugal's restriction of its colonial trade to its own nationals did not preclude the licensing and use of foreign ships nor the investment by foreigners in Portuguese colonial enterprises. Portugal never possessed a merchant fleet large enough to handle, in particular, the bulky Brazilian sugar trade. It was not possible for the *Mesa do Bem Commun dos Mercadores* (the corporation of Lisbon merchants) to maintain a strict monopoly of colonial trade. Dutch ships operating under Portuguese licence were prominent in the Brazil trade from an early date, as were English ships. Since the late Middle Ages the English had had a special relationship with Portugal, importing spices, salt, fruit and wine and exporting cloth (the balance of trade favourable to England). English merchants were already well established with special privileges in Lisbon when the development of the Portuguese colonial economy completely transformed English trade with Portugal. As early as 1595 the value of English sugar imports was already much higher than that of spice imports. After the union with Spain in 1580 which had a more 'closed' concept of empire, sporadic embargoes were imposed on Dutch and English shipping in the colonial trade (which served to increase the level of illegal trading). Licences were now granted more readily to Spanish merchants than to other nationalities. Eventually, however, the Portuguese became fearful that the Spaniards might take their trade with Brazil away from them, at a time when the Dutch had already partly appropriated the East Indian traffic and trade with northern countries was much reduced by reason of the taxes on salt. Spanish attempts to penetrate the Portuguese commercial system were thus largely rebuffed. At the same time the Portuguese themselves made good use of the loosening of political boundaries between the two empires. Contracts for the slave trade to Spanish America, in particular, opened up new markets to Portuguese merchants. In general, Portuguese merchants, often New Christians, established themselves in Lima, Potosí, Cartegena and Mexico City as well as Seville. Buenos Aires, above all, became in effect a Portuguese factory for illegal trade with Peru. The silver of Potosí became common coin in Brazil during this period. Meanwhile, Dutch interests were protected in Lisbon by the German, Conrat Rott, who acted as consul for both Germans and Flemish. During the first decade of the seventeenth century the number of Dutch ships in the Brazil trade more than doubled and it is estimated that during the Twelve-Year Truce (1609–21) one-half to two-thirds of the ships were Dutch.

The extension of hostilities between Holland and Spain to the Portuguese empire after 1621 led not only to the loss of the north-east of Brazil and its trade but also, especially after 1640 when the activities of Dutch privateers intensified, severely disrupted Portugal's trade with the rest of Brazil. Portuguese naval resources – eight galleons, part of the Portuguese-Spanish fleet, cruising off the coasts of Brazil – were totally inadequa for the protection of the sugar trade. Merchant shipping losses mounted: 108 ships were lost in 1647 and 141 in 1648, i.e. 249 ships out of a total of 300, or 83 per cent in two years. The king took a series of panic measures, such as despatching the royal fleet from the Tagus to Brazil, ordering ships in France, borrowing from New Christians to purchase ships in Holland, inviting foreigners to send vessels to Brazil, prohibiting the construction of small ships and even, in 1648, banning the transportation of sugar so long as the Dutch should continue at their existing strength at sea. Finally, at the initiative of the Jesuit Father António Vieira, the frequently-discussed idea of a monopoly trading company was revived and on 10 March 1649 the statutes of a *Companhia Geral do Comercio* were approved by the crown. Shipping between Lisbon and Brazil would for the first time be confined to a fleet (*frota*) system and provided with adequate escort vessels. The company would maintain 36 galleons for the protection of maritime trade.

The capital for the foundation of the company came from the property of New Christians condemned by the Inquisition and contributions from Lisbon merchants. The administration of the company was entrusted to a junta of deputies, elected for three years from among those merchants who had contributed at least 5,000 cruzados. The total subscribed was 1,255,000 cruzados (cruzado = 400 réis), which, when it came to the point, proved to be insufficient. The cost of a convoy (provided from the 36 galleons) was covered by the premiums paid against loss: 600 reis per case of sugar or tobacco to insure the ships and 1,400 réis per *arroba* of white sugar to insure the cargo. These premiums were to be paid to the agents of the company in the customs houses of the kingdom of Portugal when the vessels returned. The company had another source of revenue from the transport by warships of certain commodities, particularly the four over which it had a monopoly – wine, flour, oil and codfish. It also had the monopoly of brazilwood. In short, the company enjoyed a considerable number of privileges and exemptions.

Meanwhile the Anglo-Portuguese treaties of 1642 and 1654, besides re-affirming and extending the special status of the English factory in Lisbon, had conceded wide privileges to English merchants in the Portuguese colonial trade. For example, precedence was to be given to the English if additional ships were required by the company. Normal trading relations were re-established with the Dutch in 1661, the French in 1667 and the Spanish in 1668.

The company was well received and its early stages were full of promise. However, before long there was criticism that the capital of the company was Jewish, that it failed to maintain the 36 galleons stipulated in the charter and that it did not keep the Brazilians supplied with the four foodstuffs for which it held the monopoly. Between 1662 and 1664 it was gradually transformed into a state company, administered by a *Junta do Comercio*, which ultimately came under the authority of the Conselho da Fazenda. It continued, however, to pay dividends to the shareholders. As hostilities, privateering and piracy in the Atlantic all declined, the company became more effective and the frotas under escort regularly left Rio towards the end of March, picked up the sugar ships at Bahia in April and arrived safely in Lisbon in July or August. A separate trading company was established for Maranhão in 1678.

Although the Companhia Geral do Comercio was eventually abolished by King João V in 1720 the frota system was retained. In the eighteenth century there were separate fleets for each of five colonial ports, though outbound fleets often sailed together and two or more returned together. In addition, one or two supposedly swift vessels capable of eluding capture annually sailed from Lisbon to major ports as despatch boats (*naus de aviso*) or licensed priority cargo ships (*naus de licença*). São Luís and Belém were irregularly served by one or two ships a year until cacao generated more trade. The fleet system itself was abolished in 1765–6.[3]

The trade between Portugal, the rest of the Portuguese empire and Brazil was dominated east–west by slaves and west–east by sugar. Traders used two main regions of Africa as their source of slave supply. The first was West Africa, where the general term 'Sudanese' was used to describe several tribes, such as the Wolof, the Mandingo, the Songhai, the Mossi, the Hausa and the Peul. Generally speaking, men from these tribes were powerfully built, usually herdsmen, sometimes belonging to the Islamic faith; thus they tended to be independent and prone to revolt. The other region was Central and Equatorial Africa, where men from the Bantu tribes were small, more submissive, animist in religion and, for the most part, cultivators of the soil of settled habit. In the sixteenth and early seventeenth centuries most slaves were 'Sudanese'; by the eighteenth century the majority were Bantu. From the middle of the seventeenth century there were also contingents of Bantu from Mozambique in East Africa.

The slave trade was open to all Portuguese on payment of a due. The collection of dues was farmed out, by means of an *asiento* (contract), to a *contratador*, who delivered the *avencas* (agreements) to the traffickers. From being simply a contract, the asiento was to become, by the end

---

[3] For further reference to the fleet system in the eighteenth century, see Mansuy-Diniz Silva, *CHLA*, I, ch. 13, and Alden, *CHLA*, II, ch. 15. In the final revision of this section of the chapter the Editor wishes to acknowledge the help of Professor Dauril Alden.

of the seventeenth century, an agreement under international public law. Although there were asientos for supplying slaves in Spanish America, there were none in Brazil, except perhaps late in the colonial period in Maranhão. The asiento merely constituted a permit for the shipment of slaves from Africa: there are examples for Angola dated 1573 and for Cape Verde dated 1582 or 1583. The purchase was conducted by intermediaries; in Guinea these men were *tangosmaus* or *lançados* (adventurers who lived like natives) and in Angola *pombeiros* (Africans who were already the slaves of white planters and who went off into the interior to look for slaves).

Conditions in the slave ships, or *tumbeiros* (literally 'hearses'), were appalling. They were overloaded, with as many as 500 slaves being stowed away in a single caravel. The length of the voyage varied, averaging 35 days from Angola to Pernambuco, 40 days to Bahia and up to 50 days to Rio. The unfortunate Africans were herded so closely together that epidemics broke out and many – sometimes half the total number – died. On arrival in Brazil the surviving slaves were given time to recover and were cared for in order to increase their value; they were then sold by auction. Owing to the high death rate and the perils of the voyage, there was not much profit for the transporters, especially when the price of slaves was low. In 1612, for example, a male slave in good condition and under 25 years of age, could be bought for 28$000 réis in Brazil. However, he had already cost 4$000 in dues and 9$600 to transport in addition to his purchase price in Africa, not counting his share of the cost of those who died on the voyage.

The number of Africans transported to Brazil is not easily calculated, as the Portuguese bureaucracy was not so highly organized as the Spanish and the slave trade was subject to very little control. Information is widely dispersed in various archives. Not much is known about Brazil's role in the slave trade during the sixteenth century.

Originally individual senhores de engenhos (mill owners) were authorized to bring over their own slaves from Africa, and in 1559 a royal decree limited the size of each contingent to 120. There were apparently from 2,000 to 3,000 black slaves in Brazil by 1570, and from then onwards the number increased rapidly. In 1575 Angola exported 12,000 'peças', 4,000 of whom died on the voyage. Between 1580 and 1590 there were, according to Father Anchieta, 10,000 black slaves in Pernambuco and 3,000 in Bahia. However, two other contemporary observers arrived at different figures. In the opinion of Fernão Cardim there were only 2,000 black slaves in Pernambuco and 3,000–4,000 in Bahia, while according to Gabriel Soares de Sousa there were 4,000–5,000 and 4,000 respectively. It is estimated that the number of black slaves living in Brazil in about 1600 must have been 13,000–15,000 distributed over 130 engenhos, where the labour force would already have been 70 per cent black. For the first half of the seventeenth century approximately 4,000 slaves were imported per annum. Between 1650 and 1670 this figure increased to 7,000–8,000 per annum and then declined. According to Philip Curtin, the Brazilian share represented 41.8 per cent of the total number of slaves imported into America between 1601 and 1700, while, for example, Spanish America took 21.8 per cent, the English colonies 19.7 per cent and the French colonies 11.6 per cent.[4]

By the end of the sixteenth century sugar had ceased to be a 'drug' in limited supply and had become a 'food'. And for a century from 1570/80 Brazil was by far the largest producer and exporter of sugar in the world.[5] Until the crisis of the 1680s the secular trend in Brazilian sugar production was upward (which is particularly remarkable since Dutch Brazil is excluded from the account). Moreover, against the general pattern of the seventeenth-century 'depression' abundant and increasing production did not affect the movement of sugar prices which was also upward, as was the price of slaves. The crisis of the seventeenth century did not seriously affect Brazil until towards the end of the century.

The century-long Brazilian sugar cycle can be divided into a number of phases:

(a) a period of expansion from *c.* 1570 to *c.* 1600; as the number of mills increased there was a corresponding increase in production and export and it is possible to discern behind the slow rise in the price of taxed sugar a more rapid upward movement of prices on the free market;

(b) a plateau with output at a high level (15–20,000 metric tons per annum from over 200 mills in the 1620s) until *c.* 1625; prices dropped slightly in the 1610s during the Twelve-Year Truce, but

[4] Philip Curtin, *The Atlantic slave trade. A census* (Madison, 1969), table 34, p. 119; for a further discussion of the slave trade to Brazil in the colonial period see Marcilio and Alden, CHLA, II, ch. 2 and 15.

[5] For a detailed discussion of the Brazilian sugar industry from the end of the sixteenth to the end of the seventeenth centuries, see Schwartz, *CHLA*, II, ch. 12.

rose again in the 1620s as the war resumed and Dutch attacks disrupted Portuguese Atlantic shipping and higher taxes were imposed to pay for defence;

(c) a further phase of growth which lasted until shortly before 1640;

(d) a downturn in production and export *c.* 1640–60 following the Dutch occupation of Pernambuco and the subsequent reorganization and relocation of the sugar industry by the Portuguese; prices, however, continued to rise as a result of the war and the various additional taxes imposed on Brazilian products including sugar;

(e) a resumption of growth in the 1660s following the creation of the Companhia Geral do Comercio and the frota system, the ending of the war and the recovery of Pernambuco production;

(f) the beginnings of a depression *c.* 1680 as prices on the international sugar market fell during the 1670s and 1680s largely as a result of increased production in the Antilles. (Sugar prices fell from 3$800 per arroba in 1654 to 1$300 in 1685.) As in previous periods of commercial difficulty the senhores de engenho in both the northeastern captaincies and the more marginal south produced less, stopped buying slaves and directed the existing labour force to other commercial crops less vulnerable to international trade recessions, to cattle raising and to subsistence agriculture. It would appear, however, that, in spite of these vicissitudes and although the sugar producers themselves were not doing well, substantial profits were still being made by the merchants.

The sugar processed in the Brazilian engenhos was to a large extent exported to Europe, consignments being despatched in the name of the senhores de engenhos, the *lavradores* (sugar cane growers), or the merchant-exporters. Until 1640 ships transported between 200 and 600 crates each, but after that date the ships were larger and therefore the number of crates must also have increased. The call at Lisbon was often part of a round trip; ships which had come from Africa with slaves returned with sugar. The cost of transport (or *frete*) was high. During the convoy period there were also the *avaria* duties, exacted to pay for protection of the ships.

In addition to the legal trade through Lisbon by Portuguese merchants and foreigners under licence from the king, there was the lively contraband trade carried on by the English, the Spaniards (via the Canaries), the French (through La Rochelle) and finally the Dutch, who, as we have seen, had the lion's share of the illegal traffic.

Amsterdam became the entrepot for sugar and Dutch ships kept the market supplied by a combination of privateering, smuggling and licensing. The Amsterdam archives are full of sugar dealings which, like those in brazilwood, were quoted on the Bourse. Sugar arrived from all directions: the islands of the eastern Atlantic, Brazil and Central America, and, if not already refined, it was refined on the spot before being re-exported throughout northern Europe. This traffic reached its height between 1630 and 1654, when sugar from Pernambuco, under occupation by the Dutch, was transported direct to the United Provinces. By 1650 sugar-refining absorbed much of the available Dutch capital. A quarter of the customs duties collected were paid on sugar and a hundred ships were permanently engaged on its transportation. Jews, particularly Portuguese Jews, played an important part in this industry, although public opinion often favoured banning them from participating in it. By 1665 there were signs of a decline as a result of Colbert's efforts to create a French sugar industry. There were no refineries in Portugal in the seventeenth century. The mother country left sugar-refining to Brazil itself; indeed a royal mandate of 1559 had actually prohibited sugar-refining in Lisbon.

Among other commodities in the Atlantic trade, tobacco was the most important. In the first half of the seventeenth century Portuguese policy was to restrict the cultivation of tobacco at home and in the Atlantic islands in order to encourage Brazilian production. In 1674 a *Junta do Tabaco* was set up to supervise the tobacco trade and an unsuccessful attempt was made to have all taxes collected by a tax farmer appointed by the king. As the slave trade to Brazil grew, Brazilian tobacco and rum were the commodities chiefly used to barter for slaves on the coasts of Africa. On the other hand, cotton became less important during the seventeenth century. Antonil does not even mention it in his *Cultura e Opulencia do Brasil* (Lisbon, 1711). As early as the end of the sixteenth century the cost of transporting raw cotton to Lisbon equalled its production costs, probably about 2$000 milreis per arroba.

Imported into Brazil were many other goods apart from slaves and ivory from Africa. A number of ships travelling to Europe from Asia stopped at Bahia in the seventeenth and especially the eighteenth centuries, bringing silks and other luxury products. From Europe, of course, came all manufactures, including tools, materials for the engenho (particularly copper utensils), arms and textiles, for the most part made in France or England, with Lisbon serving only as an intermediary. There were also certain foodstuffs, such as salted meat which, like leather and silver, came from the Río de la Plata, salt-fish and wines, especially from Oporto and Madeira, which, it was alleged, were improved by the sea voyage. Lastly there were cereals, particularly wheat which reminded the Portuguese settlers of home. Finally, salt played a notable part in the Atlantic trade. It was not only essential for the diet of man and beast, but it was also indispensable for preserving fish and meat. Salt production was important to Portugal and other supplies were available from the Cape Verde Islands, Guinea and Angola. The Indians in Brazil used a vegetable salt and, along the São Francisco river, cattle found a briny soil which they were able to lick. The settlers created saltpans at Maranhão, between the Rio Grande and Ceará and between Paraíba and the Rio Grande, but the yield was quite insufficient and Brazil was obliged to import salt. In 1632 the supply of salt to Brazil came under state control, a monopoly which only ended in 1821. In 1665 and again in 1690–1 attempts were made to prohibit the production of salt in Brazil to prevent competition with salt imported from Portugal.

PORTUGAL AND BRAZIL, *c.* 1695–1750

The crisis in the Brazilian sugar industry in the 1680s after a century of growth and prosperity triggered off an economic crisis in Portugal. Revenue from colonial trade fell so much that Portugal was no longer able to purchase from abroad (especially England) manufactures for both the metropolis and the colonies. It is this fact which explains the economic policy of Count Ericeira, chief minister of Pedro II (1683–1706), who attempted to protect and promote Portuguese industry as a substitute for imports while also, in 1688, devaluing the currency. In order to earn Spanish silver piastres in the Spanish-American markets he created a joint stock company to carry on the slave trade on the Guinea coast. The silver piastre helped to some extent to redress the deficit in the balance of Portuguese foreign trade. Ericeira committed suicide in 1692 and his successor, the marquis of Fronteira, had little time to continue his policy before the Luso-Brazilian economy began to recover. One reason for this was increased demand and somewhat higher prices, for Brazil's agricultural products, above all sugar, but also cotton and hides as well as Portugal's own olive oil and wine. Exports of sugar from Brazil showed a temporary upward movement at the turn of the century although the long-term trend was now down. Antonil tells us that between 1688 and 1706 the price of white sugar rose first from 800 or 900 réis to 2$400 réis per arroba, declining afterwards to 1$600 réis. According to other sources, the price of white sugar is likely to have fluctuated between 1$200 and 1$400 réis between 1688 and 1743. It was, however, gold which transformed the Luso-Brazilian economy and initiated a new era. The economic crisis had stimulated the search for gold in the interior of Brazil. Expeditions of *bandeirantes* beginning with that of Fernão Dias Pais in 1674 became more numerous and determined. Finally, in 1695 at Río das Velhas between present-day Ouro Preto and Diamantina there occurred the first significant gold strike. During the next 40 years others followed in Minas Gerais, Bahia, Goiás and Mato Grosso.

Throughout the long reign of Dom João V (1706–50) production of gold in Brazil and its exportation to Portugal expanded. It increased five times between 1700 and 1720, grew steadily from 1720 to 1735, increased dramatically in the late 1730s and more modestly from 1740 until 1755 when it began to decline, although at first only slowly.[6]

The discovery of the diamond mines at Cerro Frio, north of Minas, should also be mentioned here. Their production very soon became sufficient to cause the value of diamonds to drop by 75 per cent on the international market. In all about 615 kg were extracted during the eighteenth century, and diamonds mined in Bahia, Mato Grosso and Goiás must be added to this figure. They remained an important item in Portugal's balance sheet.

Exports of gold and diamonds in such quantity allowed Portugal to cover its balance of payments in the short term. It also led to the abandonment of the early attempts to industrialize – and to modernize and diversify agriculture – with damaging long-term consequences. The reorganization of the Luso-Brazilian economy around gold in the first half of the eighteenth century also reinforced Portugal's ties with England. The Methuen treaties (1703) reaffirmed an already clearly defined commercial relationship in which the Portuguese provided wine and olive oil, the English textiles, other manufactured goods and wheat. Table 1 on p. 462 shows that wine constituted between 70 and 90 per

---

[6] For a full discussion of gold production, see Russell-Wood, *CHLA*, II, ch. 14. See in particular, Table 1 based on Virgílio Noya Pinto, *O Ouro brasileiro e o comércio anglo-português* (São Paulo, 1979), 114. For more detailed figures on gold exports, see tables in Michel Morineau, 'Or brésilien et gazettes hollandaises', *Revue d'Histoire Moderne et Contemporaine*, 25 (Jan.–Mar., 1978), 15–16, 18.

Table 1 *Patterns of Trade between Portugal and England: 1700–50*
(Annual Averages)

Years	Portuguese wines		English textiles	
	Exported to England (in thousands of £)	Percentage of Portuguese exports to England	Exported to Portugal (in thousands of £)	Percentage of English exports to Portugal
1701–05	173	71	430	71
1706–10	170	71	463	71
1711–15	217	86	488	77
1716–20	288	83	555	80
1721–25	326	84	620	76
1726–30	302	84	729	80
1731–35	287	88	744	73
1736–40	263	87	871	75
1741–45	367	86	882	79
1746–50	275	85	848	76
Total	2,668		6,630	

Source: H. E. S. Fisher, *The Portugal Trade 1700–1770* (London, 1971), Appendix I, 142–3, 'The Trade between England and Portugal, 1697–1773'.

Table 2 *Balance of Trade between Portugal and England: 1701–50*
(Average annual value in thousands of £s)

Years	Exports Portugal–England	Imports England–Portugal	Balance
1701–05	242	610	− 368
1706–10	240	652	− 412
1711–15	252	638	− 386
1716–20	349	695	− 346
1721–25	387	811	− 424
1726–30	359	914	− 555
1731–35	326	1,024	− 698
1736–40	301	1,164	− 863
1741–45	429	1,115	− 686
1746–50	324	1,114	− 790
Total	3,209	8,737	

Source: Elizabeth Boody Schumpeter, *English Overseas Trade Statistics (1697–1808)* (Oxford, 1960), pp. 17–18.

Table 3 *Slave Imports into Brazil, 1700–50*

Years	Countries of Origin		Total
	Costa da Mina	Angola	
1701–10	83,700	70,000	153,700
1711–20	83,700	55,300	139,000
1721–30	79,200	67,100	146,300
1731–40	56,800	109,300	166,100
1741–50	55,000	130,100	185,100
Total	358,400	431,800	790,200

Source: Philip Curtin, *The Atlantic Slave Trade* (Madison, 1969), p. 207.

cent of Portuguese exports to England and textiles 70–80 per cent of English exports to Portugal. Table 2 reveals a huge and growing trade imbalance in England's favour. The balance was was made up by an outflow of gold and diamonds. It is also an undeniable fact that a large proportion of the Brazilian gold which entered Europe was clandestinely imported by the English. Trade between Lisbon and the Thirteen Colonies of North America was also far from negligible. Pitch, rice, tobacco and timber were among the American products which the Portuguese needed. Lisbon also served as a revictualling port on the route from London to the British Antilles. There was a considerable trade in cod between Newfoundland and Portugal, and there was free trade between the Thirteen Colonies, Madeira and Porto Santo, since the Portuguese islands, belonging as they did to Africa, did not come within the terms of the Navigation Laws. Salt was sent to Newfoundland from the Portuguese islands of Maio and Boavista in the Cape Verde group, and in 1713 120 vessels were needed for its transportation. Almost all Portuguese merchandise exported from Portugal was carried in English ships.

The Brazilian gold cycle had an important impact on one other aspect of the Atlantic trade – the slave trade from Africa. Demand for labour in gold-producing areas maintained the level of the slave trade despite the depression in the sugar regions. Table 3 shows that the number of slaves imported into Brazil actually increased from 1720 and even more after 1730. Angola was the main supplier of slaves to Brazil, as it had been since its recovery by the Portuguese in 1648. That part of the trade in slaves paid for directly by Brazilian products (mainly tobacco and rum), and therefore outside the triangular traffic between Europe, Africa and Brazil, seems to have grown in the course of the eighteenth century. The treaty of asiento signed between England and Spain in 1713 gave the English the idea of signing another similar treaty with Portugal. The Commissioners for Trade and Plantations, however, refused, on the grounds that the participation of England in the Brazilian slave trade could only serve to increase the number of slaves entering Brazil and would, in consequence, cause a reduction in their price and in that of the sugar which they still produced. There was a risk that Brazilian sugar might become a dangerous rival to sugar from the British Antilles which together with sugar from the French colony of Saint-Domingue, now dominated the international market.

The economic crisis of the 1680s, the end of the sugar cycle and the beginning of the gold cycle gave a new impetus to the expansion of the Brazilian frontier. Brazil was ceasing to be a coastal archipelago and was on the threshold of becoming a sub-continent. The far west in particular was opened up and settled during the era of gold and this is reflected in the major reorganization of colonial administration: in 1720 Minas Gerais was separated from the captaincy-general of Rio de Janeiro to form a new captaincy; in 1744 the captaincy of Goiás and in 1748 the captaincy of Mato Grosso were created from the captaincy-general of São Paulo. In the south, Salvador de Sá, to whom the king had in 1658 entrusted the captaincies of Espírito Santo, Rio de Janeiro and São Vicente, had had the idea of creating a 'captaincy of Santa Catarina' south of São Vicente, as a means of developing southern Brazil and perhaps of reopening the clandestine route for silver coming from Potosí by way of Buenos Aires, from which, at the beginning of the seventeenth century, Portuguese trade had profited considerably. But the idea was not taken up. In 1680 the Portuguese had founded the Colônia do Sacramento on the east bank of the Río de la Plata as a depot for the contraband trade with Buenos Aires, which was now becoming one of the chief ports of Spanish America. It was a vulnerable outpost, captured twice by the Spanish before Portuguese possession was upheld in the Treaty of Utrecht (1713) and even then subject to constant attack. Situated only fifteen miles from Buenos Aires across the estuary Colônia do Sacramento was hundreds of miles from Rio and the other major Brazilian ports. In the days of sailing ships it lay at less than a day's voyage from Buenos Aires, but seven days from Santa Catarina and no less than fourteen days from Rio de Janeiro. To offset this weakness, it would have needed an adequate population as well as strong defence. However, not until 1718 were families sent there to settle. The total population of Colônia do Sacramento probably never exceeded 3,000.

However, the Portuguese had begun to occupy the vast territories which separated them from Colônia and the Río de la Plata. By the end of the seventeenth century the coast of Santa Catarina had been occupied from the sea at three points: São Francisco do Sul, in the north (1653), Laguna, in the south (1684) and Nossa Senhora do Desterro in the middle of the island of Santa Catarina, opposite the continental mainland. And in 1738 a land route from São Paulo to Laguna was opened up. In the eighteenth century the coast was to be populated by settlers who came from the Azores under contracts resembling those for 'indentured servants' in the French and English Antilles. By 1749 there was a total of 4,197 inhabitants. During the first half of the eighteenth century the Portuguese also occupied the areas south of Santa Catarina. In 1737 the city of Rio Grande was founded at the entrance to the Lagoa dos Patos. The administration of southern Brazil was then reorganized and Santa Catarina and Rio Grande de São Pedro were detached from São Paulo, to become 'sub-captaincies' under the captaincy-general of Rio de Janeiro.

The decision to pitch the Portuguese tent on the lands to the south was a direct consequence of Portuguese-Spanish conflict on the Río de la Plata which broke out again in 1723. Since 1716 relations had been strained and the governors of Buenos Aires and Colônia do Sacramento watched each other closely and attempted to create posts and settlements at other points on the left bank of the estuary, to secure their own trade in meat, leather and pitch and to contain their enemy's expansion. In 1723 António Pedro de Vasconcellos, the governor of Colônia (1721–49), backed by the governor of Rio, Aires de Saldanha de Albuquerque, prepared a small expedition of 150 men commanded by Manuel de Freitas de Fonseca and established a settlement at Montevideo downstream from Colônia, but the following year they had to abandon the port owing to lack of resources. The Spanish quickly established themselves there and founded the port city of Montevideo in 1726. Their presence made communications between Colônia and Laguna, Santos and Rio very difficult for the Portuguese. The long-term consequences were momentous since, despite the fact that the original discovery (1513) and the first permanent settlement (1680) were both Portuguese, the *Banda Oriental* was henceforth largely populated by Spaniards and, instead of a Brazilian 'Cisplatine' province, eventually became the Spanish-speaking state of Uruguay.

By 1729, however, peace between Spain and Portugal seemed to have been restored. Dom José, the hereditary prince of Portugal, had married the Infanta of Spain, Mariana Vitoria, and the Prince of the Asturias, the future Ferdinand VI of Spain, had married the Infanta of Portugal, Dona Maria Barbara de Braganza, the daughter of João V. Then, in 1735, a sordid incident concerning the servants of the Portuguese ambassador to Spain, Pedro Alvares Cabral, provoked a rupture of diplomatic relations; it was an event which had no military consequences in Europe, but provided a good pretext for disturbing the *status quo* on the Río de la Plata. The governor of Buenos Aires attacked Colônia; António Pedro de Vasconcelos held out from October 1735 to September 1737 and only an armistice signed in Paris saved the Portuguese. The two countries were by now determined to settle their differences. Nevertheless, the dispute was to continue for a further thirteen years and was not resolved until the reign of Ferdinand VI in Spain (1746–59) – and then only temporarily. To make reconciliation possible, José de Carvajal y Lencastre, president of the Council of the Indies and principal minister in Spain, renewed his government's offer to exchange an equivalent piece of territory for Colônia do Sacramento. Carvajal had good reasons for these negotiations; in his view the trading-post at Colônia was responsible for the loss to Spain of much Peruvian silver. If the economy of the Río de la Plata was to be developed, Portuguese competition had to be eliminated. It was also important to avoid conflict with Portugal, for that automatically made England an enemy of Spain.

On the Portuguese side, too, there were many who wanted peace. Alexandre de Gusmão, a royal councillor of long standing and an experienced diplomat, had been born at Santos and knew Brazil well. Although he realized all the advantages which could be derived from peace with Spain, he wanted more than merely the settlement of the problem of Colônia; he sought a definitive solution to all frontier disputes between Portugal and Spain which would take into account the *de facto* possessions of both powers in South America. Although not believing that Colônia had a future under Portugal (a view not shared by the merchants of Lisbon), he still thought capital could be made out of its surrender. In his view the future of Brazil was to be identified with the Amazon, a region still little known but generally thought, in accordance with the preconceived notions of the times, to be potentially the richest simply because it was the hottest. Unlike, for example, the 'snowy acres' of French Canada, the vast region of the Amazon was thought to contain precious metals, rare plants or fruits and exotic animals. In the south, Rio Grande de São Pedro had all the advantages and economic potential and none of the inconvenience of Colônia do Sacramento and the left bank of the Río de la Plata. Portugal's title to the territories east of the Uruguay, like her title to the territories of the upper Amazon and, for that matter, Minas Gerais, Goiás and Mato Grosso, was dubious and confirmation of title could be exchanged for Colônia do Sacramento.

To Carvajal this seemed a high price to pay. Moreover, the territory claimed by Gusmão included the prosperous Seven Missions of the Jesuits, and he knew the Society of Jesus would oppose cession of this territory to the Portuguese. Nevertheless, desire for agreement was so strong in Madrid that the Portuguese conditions, subject to a small concession in the Amazon area and complete renunciation of all claims in the Philippines, were finally accepted by Ferdinand VI.

The Treaty of Madrid (1750), signed after three years of arduous negotiations, was the most important agreement about overseas possessions to be signed by the Portuguese and the Spanish since the Treaty of Tordesillas (1494). The two countries finally abandoned the underlying principle of Tordesillas which no longer bore any relation to reality and adopted that of the *uti possidetis*, that is, 'each of the parties retains that which it has occupied'. However, four key articles constituted exceptions. Under Articles XIII and XV Portugal renounced all claims to Colônia and recognized Spanish supremacy on the Río de la Plata, and under Articles XIV and XVI Spain abandoned all territory east of the river Uruguay and promised to evacuate the Seven Missions. The boundaries of the Spanish and Portuguese possessions – subject to precise definition in both the Amazon and the south by a mixed commission – were traced on the famous 'Map of the Courts'. The Treaty of Madrid, the 'Boundaries Treaty', gave Portugal sovereignty over vast areas (over half) of South America and Brazil the shape which to a large extent it has retained to the present day.[7]

[7] For further discussion of the Treaty of Madrid, see Mansuy-Diniz Silva, *CHLA*, I, ch. 13.

The years 1580 to 1750 were decisive for the development of Brazil. First sugar and then gold, together with tobacco, cotton, livestock and diamonds, had shaped it and had finally given it pride of place in the Portuguese empire. The Portuguese imperial system, which had originally been based on Africa and the East, had come to be founded essentially on Brazil and the Atlantic. And it was Brazil which enabled Portugal to achieve a balance of payments with the outside world. It also gave Portugal the means and authority to defend itself against Spain, both in the peninsula and in South America, and reinforced the special relationship between Lisbon and London. Finally, it was increasingly Brazil which made it possible for Portugal to maintain her political – and cultural – influence in Europe, a remarkable position for a country so small, so backward and so poor.

In 1750 Dom José I came to the throne and brought to power the Marquis of Pombal, who was to play a dominant role in Portugal and its empire for more than a quarter of a century. At the same time the production of gold in Brazil, and therefore the income of the Portuguese crown, reached its peak and then began sharply to decline. It was the start of a new era for the Luso-Brazilian world.

13

PORTUGAL AND BRAZIL: IMPERIAL REORGANIZATION, 1750–1808*

Around 1738 the Portuguese ambassador to Paris, Dom Luís da Cunha, wrote that 'in order to preserve Portugal, the king needs the wealth of Brazil more than that of Portugal itself'.[1] Despite the abundance and diversity of its natural resources and manufactures, its large population and its military and naval strength, Portugal could not have survived if it had been reduced to its European territory alone. For two and a half centuries the Portuguese crown and a large part of the population had derived their main income from the commercial exploitation of the resources of their overseas territories. By the middle of the eighteenth century Brazil was by far the most important. A brief survey of the Portuguese empire will show how accurate Luís da Cunha's statement remained at the accession of Dom José I in 1750, and will help to explain the policy adopted with regard to Brazil during the second half of the eighteenth century.

To the east of the Cape of Good Hope, the *Estado da India*, which comprised all the Portuguese possessions from the east coast of Africa to Macao and Timor and which was controlled from Goa on the west coast of India, had been suffering from local rebellions and wars as well as the incursions of other European colonial powers. The Portuguese had long since lost their trading and shipping monopoly in the East and the Portuguese presence there was restricted to a few ports and trading posts. The *Estado da India* was thus weakened territorially – and also economically. It faced severe competition from England, Holland and France in importing goods from the East (spices, silks, cotton

---

* Translated from the French by Mrs Susan Burke; translation revised by Cynthia Postan; chapter reduced in length and in part reorganized by the Editor.
[1] *Instruções inéditas de D. Luís da Cunha a Marco António de Azevedo Coutinho* (ed. Pedro de Azevedo and António Baião, Academia das Sciencias de Lisboa, Coïmbra, 1930), 218.

goods, porcelain, furniture and diamonds) and it had practically abandoned imports from Mozambique (ivory, slaves, gold) to Indian traders from Surat, with the result that the Portuguese crown had for some time been earning less than it was spending on the maintenance and defence of those conquests which in this part of the world were all that remained from a glorious past.

Various Portuguese settlements along the west coast of Africa had been either repeatedly attacked by foreigners or else the scene of local riots, notably in the Cape Verde islands and in Angola. Brazil had suffered two civil wars (the War of the *Emboabas* in the gold mines of the Rio das Mortes, 1708–9, and the War of the *Mascates* at Recife, 1710–11) and two attacks by the Spanish on the outpost of Colônia do Sacramento at the mouth of the Río de la Plata (1706 and 1736). However, this western part of the empire, especially Angola and Brazil, had made, and was continuing to make, considerable territorial gains.

Moreover, on the economic side, while Angola and the territories in the Gulf of Guinea were treated more and more as reservoirs of slave labour, from Minas Gerais, Mato Grosso and Goiás came gold, and from the Serro do Frio diamonds; from Grão Pará e Maranhão came some coffee and cacao, which were added to Brazil's traditional exports of sugar, tobacco, brazilwood, timber, drugs and spices, whale oil and whalebone. Every year the *frotas* (fleets) of Bahia, Pernambuco, Rio de Janeiro and Maranhão unloaded cargoes of sugar and tobacco at Lisbon, through which all the empire's trade had to pass. Only a very small proportion of this was destined for the market of the metropolis: the rest formed the major part of Portugal's exports, along with wines from Oporto and olive oil, to the great markets of Europe, where they were exchanged for manufactured goods and grain which then returned to Brazil via Lisbon, where only essential supplies for the metropolis and for the rest of the empire were unloaded. Increasing quantities of gold from Brazil also went to centres of foreign trade, especially London, as an official means of balancing the trade deficit, but also as a result of the smuggling and fraud which was common in Brazil, the Río de la Plata and even the port of Lisbon itself. Thanks to its products and its trade, Brazil had thus become, by the middle of the eighteenth century, not only an important element in the wealth of the metropolis but also one of the chief sources of government income. This was accomplished through a complex fiscal system involving taxes on production, consumption, internal circulation, imports and exports in addition to special temporary duties. It is, however, impossible to estimate with any degree of accuracy exactly what proportion of Portugal's total income at mid-century came from Brazil.

During the second half of the eighteenth century and the early years of the nineteenth century – the reigns of Dom José I (1750–77), Dona Maria I (1777–92) and the Prince Regent Dom João (1792–1816) – Portuguese colonial policy was largely in the hands of three remarkable men: Sebastião José de Carvalho e Melo, better known as the Marquis of Pombal (1699–1782), a representative of the lesser nobility who had been envoy extraordinary in London and then Vienna (1738–49) before entering the service of Dom José I as Secretary of State for Foreign Affairs and War and later Secretary for Internal Affairs and President of the *Erário Régio* – in effect a prime minister in charge of the most important affairs of the empire from 1750 to 1777; Martinho de Mello e Castro (1716–95), son of a governor of Mozambique and grandson of the Count of Galveas, viceroy of Brazil, who was Portuguese envoy at The Hague and London (1751–70) and then Secretary of State for the Navy and the Overseas Territories (1770–95); Dom Rodrigo de Souza Coutinho (1755–1812), son of a governor of Angola and ambassador to Madrid, who was Portuguese envoy at Turin (1778–96) and then Secretary of State for the Navy and the Overseas Territories (1796–1801), president of the *Erário Régio*, the Royal Treasury (1801–3) and, finally, Secretary of State for War and Foreign Affairs (1808–12). All three were *estrangeirados*, that is to say, men who had acquired great experience in the more advanced courts of Europe, and who were fired with a burning desire to pass on to their country the benefits of their experiences abroad in order to raise it to the level of those nations which were currently the most intellectually and economically developed. All three were of noble birth, though coming from different strata of the aristocracy; they all belonged to families with past or present connections with the colonial administration; they had all received a legal training at the University of Coimbra; and their policies were based on a firm belief in the absolute power of the king, supported by an 'enlightened' government. As far as colonial policy was concerned their aims were identical: they believed that Brazil was vitally important to the very survival of the metropolis, and so they wanted to extend its territory as far as possible, to strengthen its administrative, judicial and military structures by reinforcing the absolute power of the monarchy, and to ensure that the Brazilian economy developed strictly within the framework of the colonial pact, in other words, to the exclusive benefit of the metropolis. Their intention was to preserve the internal unity of the enormous territory of Brazil and, above all, the unity of the empire as a whole, which was achieved, with the establishment of the Portuguese court at Rio de Janeiro in 1808.

TERRITORIAL CHANGES IN BRAZIL

The last great act of Dom João V's reign had been the Treaty of Madrid (1750) which, superseding all previous treaties from Tordesillas in 1494 to Utrecht in 1713, had attempted to delimit the frontiers of Spanish and Portuguese possessions in America, Africa and Asia on the basis of actual occupation. There was one exception: Portugal renounced all claim to Colônia do Sacramento, while in exchange Spain ceded an area on the east bank of the Uruguay river occupied by Jesuits and Indians grouped into *aldeias* – the so-called Territory of the Seven Missions – which Spain undertook to evacuate as soon as possible. Although agreement on frontiers had to be reached, the exchange of territories was openly criticized by many, in both Madrid and Lisbon as well as in South America. Pombal – Dom José I's Secretary of State for War and Foreign Affairs – had to implement a treaty that he had neither negotiated nor approved. He doubted whether the Territory of the Seven Missions would actually be ceded and he resolved not to hand over Colônia until the Seven Missions had been completely evacuated. In return, the Spanish had strong grounds for suspecting that the Portuguese would not in fact give up their claim to Colônia, a centre for silver smuggling and strategically important for control of the Río de la Plata. The negotiations over the implementation of the treaty, therefore, took place in an atmosphere of mutual distrust, and so did the work of two mixed commissions of engineers, mathematicians, cosmographers, cartographers and other experts which were supposed to conduct a geographical survey of the interior of Brazil to mark the frontiers. In fact, the northern commission never got off the ground. And the southern commission experienced endless delays and disputes. Meanwhile, in the Territory of the Seven Missions the Spanish Jesuits and the Guaraní Indians refused to obey the order to evacuate and in 1754 openly rebelled against His Catholic Majesty's troops. The War of the Guaranís ended in 1756 with the crushing of organized resistance, though peace did not come to the region. Mutual suspicion deepened,

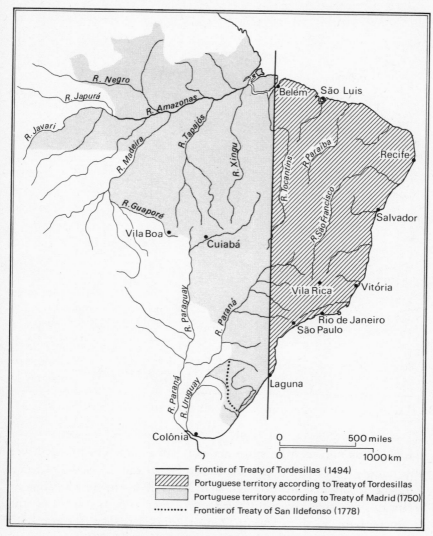

R. Negro
R. Japurá
R. Javari
R. Amazonas
R. Madeira
R. Tapajós
R. Xingu
R. Guaporé
R. Paraguay
R. Paraná
R. Paraná
R. Uruguay
R. Tocantins
R. Paraiba
R. São Francisco

Belém
São Luis
Recife
Salvador
Vila Boa
Cuiabá
Vila Rica
Vitória
Rio de Janeiro
São Paulo
Laguna
Colônia

| 0 | | 500 miles |
| 0 | | 1000 km |

——— Frontier of Treaty of Tordesillas (1494)
▨▨▨ Portuguese territory according to Treaty of Tordesillas
▨▨▨ Portuguese territory according to Treaty of Madrid (1750)
·········· Frontier of Treaty of San Ildefonso (1778)

Brazil before and after the Treaty of Madrid, 1750

the discussions became increasingly hostile and it was clear that the Treaty of Madrid was unenforceable. On 12 February 1761, in a treaty signed at the Pardo, it was nullified.

Territorial disputes between Portugal and Spain continued for a further sixteen years before a new compromise was reached. The Treaty of San Ildefonso (1 October 1777) was less favourable to Portugal than

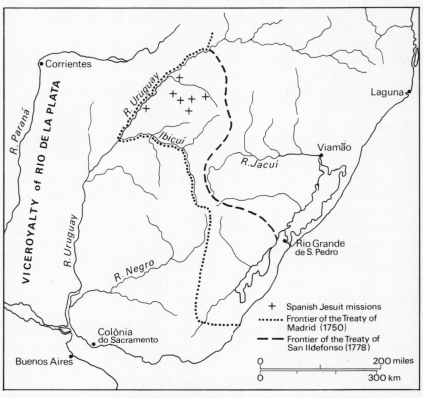

The territories exchanged: the Seven Missions and Colônia do Sacramento

the previous two treaties, since her only advantage was to retain her
sovereignty over the Rio Grande de São Pedro and the island of Santa
Catarina, losing Colônia do Sacramento as well as the Seven Missions
territory. The treaty was followed by further attempts at fixing the
frontiers, both north and south, but progress was slow because both
governments still secretly hoped to expand. The news that Portugal had
been invaded by Spain in 1801 led to another flare-up of war in southern
South America between their Catholic and Most Faithful Majesties,
when the Spaniards tried unsuccessfully to establish themselves to the
south of the Mato Grosso and the Portuguese invaded the Territory
of the Seven Missions, making a successful conquest which the silence
of the Treaty of Badajoz (1801) later confirmed.

While military operations continued in the southern part of Brazil throughout the whole of Dom José I's reign, Pombal, following the policy initiated by his predecessor, Marco António de Azevedo Coutinho, exploited Portugal's advantages in the key areas of the north and west, vast regions not yet fully explored: the Estado do Maranhão, bordering the French, Dutch and Spanish colonies to the north of the Amazon, and the captaincy of Mato Grosso, created in 1748 and considered to be 'the key and the rampart' of the interior of Brazil on the Peruvian side.[2] Before the Portuguese-Spanish mixed commissions began work on the frontiers it was clearly necessary to collect as much geographic information as possible, to encourage new discoveries, even to take possession of territories which had not yet been occupied by the other powers – in other words, the sovereignty of the Portuguese crown had to be asserted over as large an area as possible. To do so, the Portuguese strengthened their defences by adding to the network of fortresses along the Amazon river and its main tributaries and by encouraging the occupation of areas which were still deserted or where the population had been decimated by epidemics. This was done mainly by installing Portuguese settlers from areas with a surplus of labour – the famous *casais* of the Azores and Madeira. They were given material assistance and were expected to work without the help of slave labour. In this way the fortresses of Gurupá, Macapá, São José de Rio Negro, São Joaquim, São Gabriel, São José de Marabitanas, Tabatinga, Braganza and Principe da Beira were restored or created, as well as the new capital of Mato Grosso, Vila Bela, on the east bank of the Guaporé river.

However, these relatively simple measures did not provide an adequate solution to the problem of how to colonize such vast regions. This was particularly true in the Amazon basin where a small population of Portuguese extraction, mostly poor, lived amongst a large Indian population, part of which was still at liberty outside the influence of the colonizing power while the rest led a miserable existence either in the aldeias of the Jesuits and other missionaries or in slavery – in defiance of the law – in the service of individual settlers. Pombal, helped

---

[2] See the royal instructions given in 1749 to the governor of Mato Grosso, and in 1751 to the governor of the Estado do Grão Pará e Maranhão, in Marcos Carneiro de Mendonça, *A Amazônia na era pombalina*, 3 vols. (Instituto Histórico e Geográfico Brasileiro, Rio de Janeiro, 1963), I, 15–24 and 26–38.

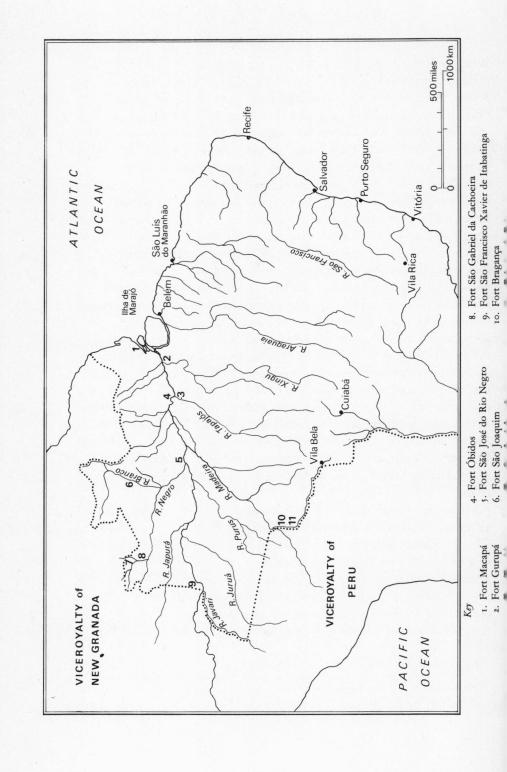

ATLANTIC OCEAN

PACIFIC OCEAN

VICEROYALTY of NEW GRANADA

VICEROYALTY of PERU

Recife

Salvador

Purto Seguro

Vitória

Vila Rica

São Luís do Maranhão

Belém

Ilha de Marajó

Cuiabá

Vila Bela

R. São Francisco

R. Araguaia

R. Xingu

R. Tapajós

R. Madeira

R. Purus

R. Juruá

R. Javari

R. Japurá

R. Negro

R. Branco

500 miles

1000 km

Key

1. Fort Macapá
2. Fort Gurupá
3.
4. Fort Óbidos
5. Fort São José do Rio Negro
6. Fort São Joaquim
7.
8. Fort São Gabriel da Cachoeira
9. Fort São Francisco Xavier de Itabatinga
10. Fort Bragança

by his half-brother, Francisco Xavier de Mendonça Furtado, governor and captain-general of the Estado do Grão Pará e Maranhão, drew up a set of measures concerning the Indians. According to Pombal, 'the only way to dominate a barbarous nation is to civilize it and establish a bond between conquered and conquerors, who will live in society under the same laws, as one people without any distinctions; if we conduct ourselves there (in Brazil) in relation to these wretched Indians as the Romans conducted themselves here (in Portugal), in no time at all in Pará there will be as many Portuguese as there are at present natives living in the forests – just as we ourselves have lived at certain periods'.[3] Mendonça Furtado himself wished to introduce *casais* from the Azores into the villages of Xingú and Tapajós Indians in order to encourage active relations between the two groups – which was forbidden under the constitution of the Jesuit missions – and he did not hesitate to suggest that marriages between white men and Indian girls, far from being regarded as shameful, should become a source of honour and privilege, since this was the only way to 'populate this vast Estado and to make the local people realize that we honour and esteem them, and most suitable to change into genuine love the hatred that they quite naturally feel for us as a result of the poor treatment and the scorn we have meted out to them, and to give us a common purpose. Without this', he concluded, 'it is not possible for this vast country to survive and prosper.'[4] The interests of the state are transparently obvious in these statements, as well as the underlying hostility of the Portuguese government towards the Jesuits and their mission to convert and educate the Indians. However, we should not doubt the sincerity of 'enlightened' men anxious to save their brothers from 'the darkness of barbarism' and to establish a new relationship with them, nor deny the significance and consistency of the legislation promulgated between 1755 and 1758 intended to give dignity to the Indians, to liberate and educate them and integrate them into Portuguese society. The aldeias were converted into parishes (*paróquias*) under the jurisdiction of the secular clergy. The largest of them were elevated to the status of *vilas*, with their own local administration and a Portuguese instead of a Tupi name: over 70 vilas were created in this way, with names like Alenquer,

---

[3] Pombal to Mendonça Furtado, Lisbon, 15 May 1753, in Carneiro de Mendonça, *A Amazônia na era pombalina*, I, 390–1.
[4] Mendonça Furtado to Pombal, Pará, 11 October 1753, in Carneiro de Mendonça, *A Amazônia na era pombalina*, I, 414.

Barcelos, Borba, Chaves, etc., reminiscent of Portuguese provincial towns.

In the southern half of the country there were similar attempts to forestall foreign invaders by means of a settlement programme, though these took different forms. The defences of Río Grande de São Pedro and the island of Santa Catarina were strengthened, and *casais* from the Azores and emigrants from other parts of Brazil were actively encouraged to settle there. In the captaincy of São Paulo Pombal sought to maintain Portuguese sovereignty over the western territories by establishing settlements every ten leagues, by civilizing the Indians and by teaching them to work – in other words, by setting up 'colonies of vilas and aldeias complete with judges, aldermen and municipal authorities (*câmaras*), modelled on those founded by Francisco Xavier de Mendonça Furtado in Pará'.[5]

Finally, Pombal completed the administrative reorganization of Brazil which had been begun during the reign of Dom João V. The aim was to provide a political and administrative structure to serve the geographical and strategic needs arising from the Treaty of Madrid and the new economic realities and problems of communications arising from the continuing exploration and settlement of the interior of Brazil. Essentially, the measures were of two kinds: first, new captaincies were carved out of territories which were too vast and too difficult to administer directly, and secondly, the last remaining small captaincies, nominally in private hands but often abandoned by their donataries, were taken back by the crown.

The vicissitudes of the Estado do Maranhão provide a good example of the kind of reorganization which took place. The Estado was made up of three crown captaincies (Pará, Maranhão and Piauí) and six small private captaincies (Cabo do Norte, Ilha Grande or Marajó, Xingú, Cametá, Caeté and Cumá on the periphery of the Amazon delta) but after 1751 its structure was radically altered when it received the title Estado do Grão Pará e Maranhão. This officially recognized the strategic importance and superior economic strength of Pará. The Estado was split into two 'governments', with a governor and captain-general residing permanently in Belém do Pará, the capital since

---

[5] Pombal to Dom Luís António de Souza, governor of São Paulo, 22 July 1766 (MS of the Arquivo Histórico Ultramarino, Lisbon, *Conselho Ultramino*, Códice 423 (São Paulo), 'Estado Político nº 7').

1737, and a 'deputy' governor living in the old capital, São Luís do Maranhão. Between 1752 and 1754 the six small captaincies were taken away from their donataries and incorporated into the Estado, while in 1755 the western part of the enormous captaincy of Pará was hived off to form a new subordinate captaincy, São José do Rio Negro, like Maranhão's subordinate captaincy of Piauí.

The Estado do Brasil was similarly reorganized, beginning in 1752. The last small private captaincies were taken back from their owners and incorporated into the nearest crown captaincies: Itamaricá into Pernambuco; Itaparica, Paraguaçu, Ilhéus and Porto Seguro into Bahia; Campos dos Goitacazes into Rio de Janeiro and Itanhaém into São Paulo. The captaincy of São Paulo, which was subordinate to that of Rio de Janeiro, was restored to its former status as a captaincy-general (1765). Finally, the seat of government was moved in 1763 from Bahia (where it had been established since 1549) to Rio de Janeiro. This was a logical consequence of the displacement of the economic, political and strategic centres of gravity in the Estado do Brasil, which had been taking place since the end of the seventeenth century, from the north-east (Bahia and Pernambuco) towards the centre (Minas Gerais, São Paulo and Rio de Janeiro) and the south (island of Santa Catarina, Rio Grande de São Pedro and Colônia do Sacramento). Lastly, the Lisbon government's desire to unify all its South American territories outweighed any consideration of the peculiarities of the immense area of the Amazon basin. The Estado do Grão Pará e Maranhão was dissolved in 1774. Its captaincies were then transformed into captaincies-general (Pará and Maranhão) and subordinate captaincies (São José do Rio Negro and Piauí) and integrated into an enlarged Estado do Brasil.

ADMINISTRATIVE REORGANIZATION

The process of simplifying the administrative divisions of Brazil was not accompanied by a parallel simplification of the administrative machinery of government either in the metropolis or in the colony. Nor were any concessions made to local autonomy. Throughout the second half of the eighteenth century, as the economic dependence of the metropolis on its richest colony grew, the administration of the empire became increasingly complex and political authority was further centralized and strengthened.

In Portugal the new government of José I, soon dominated by

Pombal, reacted against the weakening of royal authority during the last years of João V and took various measures which were intended to re-establish respect for the authority of the state and to discourage disputes which hampered the smooth functioning of government as well as to stifle criticism of the king and his ministers. Individuals, factions and institutions who were accused or merely suspected, rightly or wrongly, of criticizing the power of the state were eliminated. The *Mesa do Bem Comun dos Mercadores* (the corporation of Lisbon merchants) which dared to protest against the creation of a trading company for Grão Pará e Maranhão was abolished at a stroke in 1755; aristocratic families were accused of plots against the king and were tortured or imprisoned for life (for example, the trial of the Távoras and the Duke of Aveiro in 1759); other noblemen, higher civil servants, magistrates, priests and clergy who were suspected or accused of either plotting, criticizing, maladministration or corruption were imprisoned or exiled; and the Jesuits who were accused of betraying the principles and basic aims of their mission, accumulating excessive wealth, establishing a state within a state, obstructing the implementation of the Treaty of Madrid, disloyalty, even treason, were expelled in 1759 from Brazil and the whole of the Portuguese empire.[6]

Throughout the reigns of Dom José I, Dona Maria I and the Prince Regent Dom João there was a long campaign, not entirely successful, to strengthen and rationalize the machinery of government affecting Brazil. As early as 1736 the creation of three secretaries of state (Home Affairs; Navy and Overseas Territories; and War and Foreign Affairs) had been a move in this direction, but it was Pombal who was largely responsible for making the system work, and for giving the ministry of the Navy and Overseas Territories effective control over the other metropolitan bodies which shared responsibility for colonial affairs. This higher body, placed under the direct control of the king, nominated the principal officials of the administration in the colonies (the viceroy, the governors of the captaincies, the financial and judicial officials, and the highest ranks in the army and the church). It also supervised general policy and issued orders about the economy and the administration of justice, as well as about the affairs of the missions. However, some specialized matters continued to go through the

[6] For further discussion of the expulsion of the Jesuits from Brazil, see Alden, *CHLA*, ii, ch. 15.

traditional channels of existing councils and organizations (such as the *Conselho Ultramarino*, the *Mesa da Consciência e Ordens*, the *Conselho da Fazenda*, the *Junta do Tabaco*). Therefore the intricate web of authority and overlapping functions so characteristic of the old regime did not disappear. It was even compounded by the creation of new administrative bodies set up to resolve the various problems which, in one way or another, arose concerning colonial affairs. The following were amongst the most important of the new bodies. The *Junta do Comércio* (Board of Trade), 1755, had as its original purpose the encouragement and regulation of commerce and everything to do with trade and navigation, including the organization of fleets bound for Brazil and the prevention of smuggling (see below p. 489). This committee was essential to Pombal's policy for the industrial development of the metropolis (see below p. 491). It was a symbol of the close alliance between the great merchants involved in the tobacco monopoly and the central government, and it acquired increasingly wide powers until in 1788 it was elevated to the status of a royal tribunal under the title of *Real Junta do Comércio, Agricultura, Fábricas e Navegações destes Reino e seus Domínios* (Royal Committee for Trade, Agriculture, Factories and Navigation). The Royal Treasury (*Erário Régio*), 1761, had overall control of all the financial transactions of the metropolis and its colonies, and Pombal himself was its first president. It took over all the functions of the ancient *Casa dos Contos*, destroyed in the earthquake of 1 November 1755. The Royal Treasury broke with tradition in two ways: in its centralizing function – important from the political angle – and in the introduction of techniques not yet common in public accounting, such as double-entry book-keeping and the systematic treatment of the various kinds of income and expenditure. The Treasury was divided into four departments (*Contadorias*), each responsible for part of the empire; administration of the finances of Brazil was thus divided between two Contadorias, based on the two major judicial divisions (Bahia and Rio de Janeiro). The Council for Finance (*Conselho da Fazenda*), was reformed in 1761, when the Erário Régio was created. Its function was to deal with disputes over the collection of crown revenues, and it continued to control the *Armazéns da Guiné e India*, its associated shipyards and the *Casa da India*, whose function had been reduced to that of a customs office. In 1790 the Conselho da Fazenda was taken over by the Erário Régio. The jurisdiction of the Ministry of Financial Affairs (*Secretaria de Estado dos Negócios da Fazenda*), 1788, covered all economic aspects of the empire, and the fact that the secretary of state in charge was *de jure* president of the Erário Régio ensured that these two bodies worked closely together. The Council for the Admiralty (*Conselho do Almirantado*), 1795, was responsible for the navy, and hence for organizing convoys for the merchant fleet and a permanent squadron to protect the Brazilian coast.

Within Brazil, following the transfer of the seat of government from Bahia to Rio de Janeiro in 1763, it became customary for the governor-general (viceroy) to receive letters-patent designating him the *Vice-Rei e Capitão General do Mar e Terra do Estado do Brasil*. The holder of this office was given such wide powers that the absolute power of the sovereign, with authority over all the captaincies, appeared to be delegated to him. In practice, his only real authority, as before, was over the captaincy in which he lived – previously Bahia, now Rio de Janeiro. Only the governors of the subordinate captaincies of Rio de Janeiro were under his control: all the governors of captaincies-general were directly dependent on the Ministry for the Navy and Overseas Territories in Lisbon, to which they were answerable and from which they took their orders. Only in an emergency could the viceroy request direct military aid from them.

The municipalities represented an important sector of the Brazilian-born population and were a potential source of conflict with Lisbon. However, the system was now so highly centralized that the Câmaras in the capitals of captaincies were even deprived of one of their essential powers: in the absence of the viceroy or the governor, the town council (*Senado da Câmara*) had originally been responsible for the interim administration of public affairs, but in 1770 Pombal withdrew this prerogative in favour of a provisional government of three members: the bishop or dean; the *Chanceler* of the *Relação* (High Court of Appeal); and the highest-ranking officer in the army – the *Ouvidor* (crown judge) of the Câmara being able to replace the bishop or the *Chanceler* only if either of these were not available.

The creation of the Erário Régio in Lisbon produced an important reform affecting the powers of the *provedores da fazenda*, the principal local financial administrators. From 1767 the finances of each main captaincy were to be administered by a *Junta de Fazenda*, a collegiate body of five or six members, including the *provedor*, with the governor as its president. These juntas, which were independent from one another, were responsible for collecting and distributing royal income and they were accountable only to the inspector-general of the Erário Régio in Lisbon, as the office of *Provedor-mor da Fazenda* was abolished in 1770. The creation of these Juntas da Fazenda was thus the means by which reforms attempted in Portugal were to be extended to Brazil. The provedores also lost some of their powers through the creation of specialized bodies; for example, checking the quality of sugar and tobacco which was taken over in 1751 in Bahia, Recife, Rio de Janeiro and São Luís do Maranhão by *Mesas de Inspecção de Açúcar e Tabaco*, and the management of ammunition stores and shipyards which was handed over to a naval intendant (*Intendente da Marinha e Armazéns Reais*), in Bahia, Rio de Janeiro and Recife. A campaign to raise the standard of administration and to stamp out bribery and extortion should also be mentioned: the rights and duties of the various offices were defined and fixed salaries were introduced, thus putting an end to the traditional system of bonuses paid in cash or kind. However, as local magnates and business men were closely involved with the administration of finance, either because they were tax farmers (*contratadores*), owned certain offices, or else exercised certain functions, such as serving on a Junta da Fazenda, this reform was largely ineffective.

The first of the judicial measures taken by the new government of José I was to establish in 1751 a second *Relação* (High Court) in Rio de Janeiro, with the purpose of giving speedier justice to the people who lived in the south, far away from the Relação in Bahia. It was made up of ten *desembargadores* (high court judges), including the *ouvidor do cível* and the *ouvidor do crime* and was presided over by the governor. The Relação in Rio de Janeiro had jurisdiction over the thirteen districts (*comarcas*) covered by the captaincies of the south and the interior, and like the Relação at Bahia, it possessed both judicial and administrative powers. The attempts to speed up judicial procedures were backed up by the introduction first in Pará and Pernambuco (1758), then throughout Brazil (1765) of committees of justice (*Juntas de justiça*) composed of one or two ouvidores, the *juiz de fora* (district crown judge) and the governor of the captaincy. Pombal also introduced legislation designed to reduce corruption in the judicial system. By fixing the stipends of magistrates and officers of justice in the various comarcas of Brazil, together with those of the magistrates in the Relações of Bahia and Rio de Janeiro (1754), the oppression suffered by plaintiffs and prisoners was alleviated. Another important innovation was that

Roman law was abandoned in favour of natural and international law, and secular magistrates were no longer allowed to base their decisions on canon law. Henceforward 'in the temporal matters within their jurisdiction', they could only follow 'the laws of our country and subsidiary laws, together with praiseworthy customs and legitimately established practices' (*Lei da Boa Razão*, 1769). This modernization of judicial concepts might be compared with other decisions taken during Pombal's ministry, such as the freedom granted to the Indians in Brazil (1755 and 1759), abolition of African slavery in Portugal (1761 and 1773), abolition of discrimination between 'old Christians' and 'new Christians' (1768 and 1773), turning the Inquisition into a tribunal dependent on the government (1769), and even reforming the University of Coimbra (1772). These reforms should be regarded as an attempt to free Portugal from 'obscurantism' and to place her amongst the most 'enlightened' nations of Europe.

The Treaty of Madrid focused attention on the need to defend Brazil's frontiers and led as we have seen to the construction and repair of fortresses in the north and south. Dom José I's government was also concerned with the problems of military organization in general, starting with the recruitment of regular troops in metropolitan Portugal (*tropas de linha*, *tropas regulares*, or *tropas pagas*). Ever since the beginning of the period of overseas expansion, Portugal had, in fact, adopted the habit of sending to the colonies regiments largely composed of delinquents, vagrants and other elements deemed undesirable at home. These regiments were then made up to strength by the more or less compulsory enlistment of local personnel, often of similar quality. As a result, there were problems arising not only from the lack of discipline within the regiments but from the trouble they frequently caused in the community, which provoked numerous complaints from the governors.

   The main efforts to reform the army took place during the 1760s, as a result of serious military defeats which were sustained more or less simultaneously in various parts of the Portuguese empire. During the Seven Years' War, not only did Spanish troops invade north-west Portugal but from Buenos Aires the Spanish seized Colônia do Sacramento (October 1762) and launched a successful attack on the captaincy of Rio Grande de São Pedro (April 1763). These defeats were particularly serious because of the almost total lack of resistance by

Portuguese troops, their lack of discipline and the excessive number of desertions. To remedy this situation, Pombal called on his traditional ally, England, which immediately sent reinforcements to Portugal under the command of one of the most prestigious officers of the time, the Count of Schaumburg-Lippe. It was he, together with the English and German officers who accompanied him, who took in hand the Portuguese troops, who were poorly organized, poorly trained, poorly equipped and poorly paid. His reforms, which only affected Portugal itself, encompassed the whole organization of the army, from recruitment and equipment to tactics. This work was to be rounded off some years later when the reforms in the education system which Pombal had promoted began to bear fruit; in other words, when young Portuguese nobles educated at the Royal College of Nobles at Lisbon (inaugurated in 1766) and then at the University of Coimbra (reformed in 1772) had acquired the intellectual baggage of mathematics, physics and military arts considered indispensable for the training of officers. However, there were never enough trained Portuguese personnel, as we can see from the permanent presence of foreign officers – German, English, French and others – in the Portuguese regiments and squadrons, in the metropolis as well as in the colonies, from the reign of José I to that of João VI.

In Brazil, Pombal was most concerned with the protection of the threatened captaincies of the south and in 1767 he sent to Rio de Janeiro three of the best (and recently reformed) Portuguese regiments, as well as two military specialists, the Austrian general, J. H. Böhm (who had been the adjutant of the Count of Lippe in Portugal and to whom was given the title of inspector general of the troops of Brazil), and the Swedish general, J. Funk (who had come to Portugal from England in 1764), who had the job of reinforcing the fortifications of Rio. General Böhm, who was used to dealing with European troops in European conditions, did not take sufficient account of the social and even the climatic conditions of Brazil and his rigid methods sometimes had dire results which were severely condemned by the Marquis of Lavradio, viceroy of Brazil, under whom he served (1769–79). One of the most serious faults with which he was reproached was that of not having understood the exceptional importance of locally enlisted troops, the only ones capable of solving the Portuguese problem of defending an empire infinitely greater than herself and scattered all over the world. A force of this kind had been planned from the beginning of the first governor-generalship (*regimento* of Tomé de Souza, 1548), being divided into two types: first, the permanent militia (*tropas auxiliares* or, from 1796, *milícias*) who were recruited by unpaid conscription and with officers of the same type who were sometimes instructed by officers of the Portuguese regiments, and, secondly, reserve troops, known as *ordenanças*, who included the rest of the available male population and whose activity in peace time was restricted to occasional exercises. The milícias were frequently called upon to defend their territory whereas the corpos de ordenanças were more important in maintaining order, by supporting the action of the civil administration. Since their officers were chosen by the governors of the captaincies from lists drawn up by the Senados das Câmaras according to social hierarchy criteria, they did, in fact, reinforce this social hierarchy, based as it was on wealth and ownership of land.

Throughout the second half of the eighteenth century, the various ministers in charge of colonial policy urged the governors of the Brazilian captaincies to reduce the number of exemptions and privileges which a large section of the male population could invoke to avoid military service, as well as to organize and train the troops needed to supplement the Portuguese regiments of the *tropa paga*. In addition, the captaincies had to be ready to help one another in the event of an attack from outside, and from 1757 this was one of the essential points in Pombal's directives. These instructions, which sprang directly from the effects of the Treaty of Madrid, became incorporated into what, some years later, was to be called 'the fundamental system which today governs the political, military and civil administration of the whole of Portuguese America, adapted to each captaincy of this continent, according to its situation and circumstances' and which was constantly evoked through the last decades of the eighteenth century.[7]

REORGANIZATION OF THE ECONOMY

A balance sheet of the Portuguese economy in mid-eighteenth century reveals the disastrous situation into which, paradoxically, Brazilian gold

---

[7] See, for example, the instructions to the governors of the captaincies of Mato Grosso (13 August 1771), Goiás (1 October 1771), São Paulo (20 November 1772 and 24 January 1775), Minas Gerais (24 January 1775), quoted by Marcos Carneiro de Mendonça, 'O Pensamento da metropole portuguesa em relação ao Brasil', *Revista do Instituto Histórico e Geográfico Brasileiro*, 257 (1962), 52–5, as well as instructions to the governor of Minas Gerais (29 January 1788) (MS of the Biblioteca Nacional, Lisbon, *Coleção Pombalina*, Códice 643, f. 168).

and diamonds had led the empire during the previous 50 years. A prisoner of clauses of the famous Methuen Treaty of 1703, Portugal had gradually relinquished her developing manufactures in favour of a return to viticulture and the export of wine and olive oil. She found herself increasingly dependent on the outside world and, above all, on England, her principal trading partner and major supplier of manufactured goods, and time-honoured guarantor of her political independence. Had they been invested in a more general effort at development, Brazilian gold and diamonds could have stimulated a better exploitation of Portugal's natural resources, agriculture and mining and, even more, the manufactures needed to satisfy the increased demand in Brazil arising from population growth and greater wealth. Instead, they were used for ostentatious expenditure and, above all, as an easy method of financing a steadily worsening deficit in the balance of payments. At the same time, Brazilian gold, clandestine as well as legal, was one of the factors in England's own industrial and commercial growth. Towards the end of Dom João V's reign the easygoing climate and false euphoria of a long period of peace was already beginning to evaporate and signs of a crisis were increasingly apparent, and during the reign of José I the crisis deepened. Lisbon was destroyed by an earthquake and fire on 1 November 1755 and the rebuilding was to prove immensely costly. Two expensive wars with Spain over the southern borderlands of Brazil during the third quarter of the century put a further great strain on Portugal's resources. And at the same time, the crown's income from Brazil declined sharply from the 1750s to the 1770s, largely because of a 50 per cent drop in the yield from gold and diamond mining.[8]

Economic policy under Pombal

Pombal, who had been brought up on the ideas of English mercantilist thinkers of the first half of the eighteenth century and was impressed by the wealth and power of England which he had observed closely for several years, was without doubt the politician of his age who had most understanding of the serious imbalance in the Portuguese economy and of its causes. All Pombal's policies sprang from two main concerns: to increase crown revenue by encouraging trade, especially with Brazil,

[8] For gold and diamond mining in eighteenth-century Brazil, see Russell-Wood, *CHLA*, II, ch. 14.

and, at all costs, to reduce the deficit in the overall balance of trade, and hence to reduce Portugal's economic dependence on England. Pombal, a pragmatist, found his weapons in the traditional arsenal of mercantilist ideas and policies, but made them more wide-ranging and effective, adapting them to changes in economic conditions and trends.

Because sugar, tobacco, gold and diamonds, Brazil's main products, played a crucial role in Portugal's overall balance of trade and in crown revenue, Pombal first turned his attention to them when he attempted to stimulate the economy by introducing fiscal measures controlling production, prices and transport costs. With regard to gold, Pombal abandoned the capitation tax which had been in force since 1734 and returned to the system of taking 20 per cent of the gold dust compulsorily smelted in the *Intendências do Ouro* and the *Casas de Fundição* (*alvará* of 3 December 1750 and *regimento* of 4 March 1751). He simultaneously banned the use of gold as currency, as well as its removal from the mining zone. These measures had three aims: they were to spread the tax burden more fairly, to make the repression of smuggling more effective and to increase production to meet the obligation to provide the Royal Treasury with an annual quota (100 arrobas of gold, about 1,400 kg). As for diamonds, so many had been produced that prices had fallen on the European market and, despite severe penalties, diamond smuggling was almost out of control. Since duties were payable to the crown in the form of a capitation tax levied on each slave employed, according to a system (*contrato*) in force since 1739, the administration of the contrato was changed in 1753 in order to maintain prices and stabilize the market. Henceforth, the mining of, and trading in, diamonds were separated into two contratos under the strict control of the crown. The initial success of this new arrangement proved ephemeral and the government actually lost revenue. Therefore, in 1771 Pombal ended the contrato system by setting up a general inspectorate for diamonds. This was dependent solely on the Erário Régio and its function was to administer directly the royal monopoly for the mining and sale of diamonds.

As sugar and tobacco were taxed so heavily that they ceased to be competitive with sugar and tobacco produced in the English, French and Dutch colonies, steps were taken to lighten export duties and reduce freight charges (*regimento da Alfândega do Tabaco* of 16 January 1751 and *decreto* of 27 January 1751). Inspection offices were set up in Bahia, Recife, Rio de Janeiro and São Luís do Maranhão to control the quality and price of these two commodities (the *Mesas de Inspecção do Açúcar e Tabaco*, set up by *alvará* of 1 April 1751). Efforts were also made to develop cultivation of these products in new areas (e.g. tobacco around Rio de Janeiro and sugar in the Amazon basin). Pombal paid special attention to tobacco, a particularly valuable foreign export, as is clear from a later regulation aimed at improving the cultivation, processing and storage of tobacco (alvará of 15 July 1775).

It was obvious that if all these industries were to be stimulated there had to be more slave labour and various attempts were made to channel the slave trade towards Brazil alone: the export of African slaves outside the Portuguese colonies was totally prohibited in 1751, in 1761 slaves sent to Portugal itself were given their liberty, and these two measures were followed, logically, in 1773, by the total abolition of slavery in Portugal.

Finally, the desire to profit from all Brazil's products and to make a stand against smuggling (which had reached vast proportions during the reign of Dom João V) led to a strengthening of the fleet system in which fleets sailing between Portuguese and Brazilian ports left on fixed dates (alvarás of 28 November 1753 and 25 January 1755). The *comissários volantes*, small-scale itinerant merchants trading between Portugal and Brazil, whose activities were hard to control, were banned (alvará of 6 December 1755).

The suppression of the *comissários volantes* fitted in with Pombal's policy of creating a highly structured commercial sector, in which small middlemen were to be deliberately squeezed out to the advantage of owners of large amounts of capital, and monopoly trading companies modelled on those of England (especially the British East India Company), Holland and Spain were to be encouraged. One company had been formed in 1753 to increase trade with China and with the Indian coast. This was the *Companhia de Comércio do Oriente*, whose principal shareholder was Feliciano Velho Oldemberg, one of the most important merchants in Lisbon, and well known as a tobacco farmer and as the man who introduced emigrants from the Azores into Brazil. In 1755 the *Mesa do Bem Comun dos Mercadores* (the corporation of Lisbon merchants) was abolished (decreto of 30 September 1755) (see p. 480) and the *Junta do Comércio* (Board of Trade) set up (decreto of 30 September 1755 and statutes of 12 December 1755) (see p. 481). During the same decade several trading companies – for Brazil, for metropolitan Portugal and for Mozambique – were established.

That Pombal wanted to attract men who disposed of large amounts of capital is clear from the constitution of the great companies. Important social privileges were granted to the shareholders: nobles were offered guarantees that they would not lose their status; commoners – government officials, metropolitan and colonial merchants, colonial landowners – who applied for a certain number of shares were given access to the military orders and opportunities for ennoblement; and foreigners received an assurance that they could participate on the same terms as nationals. The new companies had much wider objectives than previous trading companies. They were to promote shipbuilding as well as navigation and to develop vast areas of Brazil by improving traditional methods of production and by introducing new crops. Pombal also hoped that, through these companies, he would be able to control all economic activity, avoid over-production, fix prices in the light of the international competition on the European markets, guarantee the quality of the products and, finally, achieve a better balance between imports of manufactures and the means to pay for them.

Three monopoly trading companies were created for Brazil: the *Companhia Geral do Comércio do Grão Pará e Maranhão* (1755–78) was set up, (a) as the means by which African slaves could be introduced into the Amazon basin to take over from the local labour force after Indian slavery was abolished (1755–8), (b) to contribute to the agricultural development of a potentially rich region through the purchase and transportation of colonial staples, traditional and new and, later (c), to control and regulate imports of manufactures from metropolitan Portugal, through a monopoly of trade and navigation. Its role was of great importance in the development of the cultivation of rice and cotton, in an increased production of timber and dyestuffs, as well as in the production of meat (cured and salted) and hides. The *Companhia Geral do Comércio de Pernambuco e Paraíba* (1759–79) was closely modelled on that for Grão Pará and Maranhão. It was to help remedy the shortage of agricultural labour by importing large numbers of African slaves and to contribute to a revival in the production and export of sugar. It was also hoped to increase exports of leather, tobacco and new commodities such as cacao. Like the Maranhão company, it was later expected to develop the colonial market for Portuguese manufactures. Finally, the *Companhia de Pesca da Baleia das Costas do Brasil* (1765–1801) took the place of the farmed-out royal monopoly. It increased the quantity and quality of whaling and of the extraction of oil and whalebone, thanks to a heavy investment of capital in slave labour and in equipment (boats and tools) for the new fishing grounds. It also encouraged sperm whale fishing hitherto untried in Brazil.

During the period 1753–65 colonial trade had been considerably reorganized: shipping controlled, capital concentrated, monopolies reinforced. The greater part of the Brazilian colonial trade in the ports of Belém do Pará, São Luís do Maranhão and Pernambuco was henceforward monopolized by the fleets of the companies of Grão Pará and Maranhão, and of Pernambuco and Paraíba. The maintenance of the *frotas* – which in practice now served only Bahia and Rio de Janeiro – was not so important. In any case, more than ten years' experience had once again made clear the inconveniences of this rigid and always controversial system: the failure to establish proper shipping schedules in Portugal and in Brazil, the deterioration of perishable goods like sugar and tobacco as a result of being kept too long, the consequent problem of disposing of them at a profit and the long delays in getting payments, extensive contraband. All efforts by the Junta do Comércio to reform the fleet system failed. So, in 1765, in a move which illustrates Pombal's pragmatism, the frotas were abolished. Licensed vessels were free to sail to and from the ports of Bahia, Rio de Janeiro and all other ports where the companies did not have exclusive rights. The following year the ban on coastal trade between the Brazilian ports was also lifted.

Historians usually date the beginnings of Pombal's 'industrial' policies to the years 1769–70, thereby giving the impression that up till then the minister had neglected manufacturing. In fact, Pombal's observations even before he joined the government of José I in 1750 reveal that he understood clearly that a large number of prosperous small-scale workshops needed to be encouraged just as much as the large-scale manufactures, such as the famous Lisbon silk manufactory (*Real Fábrica das Sedas*). Pombal's 'industrial' policy rested on two fundamental elements: (1) obtaining raw materials within Portugal itself and the colonies, and (2) maintaining and developing small manufacturing units whose output could be integrated into the working of larger concerns which undertook the finishing processes. The organization charged with promoting industrial development by recruiting foreign master craftsmen, creating workshops, factories and the larger productive units and granting privileges of manufacture and sale was the *Junta do Comércio*. Set up in 1755, it was given responsibility for the Real Fábrica das Sedas in Lisbon, then in financial difficulties. This indicates clearly the destination for which at least some of its output was intended, since, as well as representatives of the junta itself, there were on the board representatives of the Grão Pará and Maranhão company, and, some years later, of the Pernambuco and Paraíba company. During the 1760s a series of shocks – the costs of war in Europe and southern Brazil, the continuing decline of sugar exports from Brazil, the beginning of the decline in Brazilian gold production, the consequent decline in revenue from tithes, the fifth and other taxes and dues – profoundly altered the basis of the economic structure of the Portuguese empire. It now became more essential than ever to reduce the deficit in the trade balance, especially by stimulating production of Portuguese manufactured goods to compete with English and French goods in Portugal, Brazil and other colonies. The Junta do Comércio set in motion by means of loans the policy of import substitution which Pombal had planned through the creation of factories and workshops. In the years 1765–6, but continuing into the early nineteenth century, factories producing cotton, linen, wool and silk goods, hats, leather goods, hardware, glassware, tapestries, clocks and watches, buttons, metal buckles, ivory combs and many other luxury items were set up, in large part due to *private* initiative. The years 1769–70 did not, as is generally accepted, represent the point of departure for Pombal's 'industrial' policy, but saw the culmination of an *official* initiative which provided assistance to a very few large factories, either reorganized or newly formed, and imposed various protectionist measures. The Portuguese manufacturers had close ties with the Brazilian trading companies, who supplied them with the raw materials, for example for dyeing and weaving, and subsequently conveyed the finished products to Brazil.

In Brazil the great trading companies of the north and north-east helped to improve the production and export of traditional staples (cacao in Pará, sugar in Pernambuco) and to introduce new export crops (cotton in Maranhão, rice and coffee in Maranhão and Pará).[9] The authorities in the central and southern captaincies also tried with some success to stimulate traditional agriculture (sugar and tobacco). They were also encouraged by Pombal, especially after 1765, to diversify agriculture and adapt new products which were likely to find a market in the metropolis and further the policy of import substitution. And

[9] For a full discussion of the agricultural renaissance in Brazil in the second half of the eighteenth century, see Alden, *CHLA*, II, ch. 15.

the extremely energetic viceroy, the second Marquis of Lavradio (1769–79) gave his active support. Planters were provided with seeds and cuttings brought from the metropolis or selected locally, and profitable sales were guaranteed, the crown itself sometimes being the main purchaser. Though good in intention and principle, the policy did not always work out in practice because private enterprise was feeble and royal finance lacking: there were both successes and failures. Tobacco was a commercial failure. The inferior quality produced in the captaincies of Rio de Janeiro and São Paulo could only be marketed locally or in Africa. Cotton and silk were also failures, and only insignificant quantities were produced. Hemp, greatly in demand for ships' ropes and for which Portugal depended entirely on foreign imports, also failed as a crop. There were repeated attempts to cultivate it in the captaincy of Rio Grande de São Pedro, but to no avail, even though the climate appeared to be favourable. Cochineal, a dyestuff for which New Spain was the main source of supply to Europe, was partially successful in Rio Grande de São Pedro and on the island of Santa Catarina. On the other hand, there were several very significant successes. There was, for example, a great expansion in sugar production in the Campos de Goitacazes region, to the north-east of Rio de Janeiro. Between 1769 and 1778, the number of *engenhos* (mills) doubled, the production of sugar increased by 235 per cent and that of *cachaça* (rum) by 100 per cent. Wheat, already grown in the captaincy of São Paulo, was introduced without difficulty into Rio Grande de São Pedro, and early success in the decade 1770–80 was the prelude to the profitable development of this cereal. Finally, under the Marquis of Lavradio's government, rice and indigo, already since the 1750s reasonably successful in the captaincy of Rio de Janeiro, were protected to give planters and merchants an incentive to take up production. Export of these products to the metropolis then began in ever greater quantity.

There is still insufficient information from Portuguese sources to make an overall evaluation of the economic policies pursued in Pombal's time, especially as the available statistics are distorted by smuggling. But British statistics (see Table 1 on p. 494) reveal a favourable trend in Portugal's balance of trade with England.

Portugal's deficit at the start of the period appears unusually large, but we can see that 25 years later it had been reduced by about 70 per cent, exports having increased by just over 34 per cent and imports decreased by just over 44 per cent. The sharp decline in the import of

Table 1 *Portugal's Balance of Trade with England: 1751–75*
(average annual value in £1,000s)

Years	Exports Portugal–England	Imports England–Portugal	Balance
1751–55	272	1,098	−826
1756–60	257	1,301	−1,044
1761–65	312	964	−652
1766–70	356	595	−239
1771–75	365	613	−248
Total	1,562	4,571	

Source: Elizabeth Boody Schumpeter, *English Overseas Trade Statistics (1697–1808)* (Oxford, 1960), 17–18.

manufactured goods, most noticeable after 1765, illustrates the success of Portugal's joint policies of manufacturing import substitution and great colonial companies. For example, 78 per cent of manufactures imported into Brazil by the Companhia Geral do Comércio de Pernambuco e Paraíba between 1760 and 1777 were produced by the Real Fábrica das Sedas in Lisbon which administered several units producing widely differing goods (silks and various textiles, buttons, hats, combs, clocks, etc.).[10]

Economic policy after Pombal

The death of Dom José I in 1777 brought some important political changes. Dona Maria I's accession was followed immediately by the fall of Pombal (who actually resigned of his own accord), precipitated by a powerful reaction – known as the *Viradeira* – to 27 years of tyranny: political prisoners were liberated and rehabilitated, political exiles were allowed to return to Portugal – a breath of freedom swept through the country. However, most of the men who had held government office in Pombal's time remained in power. Martinho de Mello e Castro, for example, had been Secretary of State for the Navy and the Overseas Territories and remained so until his death in 1795. Economic policy followed the same broad lines. There were very few measures which

[10] Percentage calculated from Kenneth R. Maxwell, *Conflicts and conspiracies: Brazil and Portugal 1750–1808* (Cambridge, 1973), 261, table 3. On the Real Fábrica das Sedas, see J. Borges de Macedo, *Problemas de história de indústria portuguesa no século XVIII* (Lisbon, 1963), 152–3.

ran directly counter to Pombal's policies and these largely affected the two companies trading with Brazil. Ever since these had been set up they had become ever more unpopular with merchants in Portugal and Brazil and with colonial landowners who were critical of their pricing policies, especially with respect to slaves, and their limited achievements after two decades. The Companhia Geral do Comércio of Grão Pará and Maranhão was abolished in 1778 and that of Pernambuco and Paraíba in 1779. Free trade between Portugal and northern Brazil was established. In 1777 the control of factories in Portugal was transferred from the Junta do Comércio to a specially-created body, the *Junta de Administração das Fábricas do Reino*, but ten years later (1788) there was a return to Pombal's formula, with a single *Real Junta do Comércio, Agricultura, Fábricas e Navegações* (see above p. 481). Otherwise, not only was the policy of import substitution and expansion of trade pursued with remarkable continuity throughout the reign of Dona Maria I and the *de facto* regency of her son, Dom João, after 1792, but the principle of the colonial pact was also reaffirmed on several occasions, by Martinho de Mello e Castro as well as by his successor Dom Rodrigo de Souza Coutinho.

In metropolitan Portugal preference was always given to private enterprise, so new factories were set up and the management of the woollen mills at Fundão, Covilhã and Portalegre was granted to individuals (1788). The efforts of the state itself concentrated particularly on stimulating silk manufacture. Finally, new protectionist tariffs favoured the entry into the colonies of goods manufactured in the metropolis (1794 and 1797).

In Brazil the development and production of traditional and new staples continued to be encouraged, and the economic policies begun under Pombal benefited from two important geopolitical changes. The first came after 1777 when the North American War of Independence forced England to look for new sources of raw materials for her rapidly developing cotton industry, especially cotton itself and dyestuffs, and the second came after 1789, when the French Revolution and Napoleon's rise to power led to revolution in Saint-Domingue (and the destruction of the world's leading sugar industry) and war on the European continent. As a result Portugal found other profitable outlets on the international market for her colonial products like sugar (from Pernambuco, Bahia and, increasingly, Rio de Janeiro), cotton (from Maranhão but now also Pernambuco, Bahia and Rio de Janeiro), tobacco, indigo,

cochineal and cacao, and, naturally, demand pushed up prices. Moreover, rice production was expanding rapidly in Rio de Janeiro as well
as in Pará and Maranhão, and the metropolis was soon self-sufficient.
Rice, like indigo, was the object of very important protectionist
measures between 1777 and 1783. Coffee cultivation, grown largely for
local consumption, spread throughout Brazil during the eighteenth
century. Its production was now concentrated in the captaincies of Rio
de Janeiro, São Paulo, Espírito Santo and Minas Gerais, where climatic
conditions were nearly perfect, and, towards the end of the century,
exports to the metropolis and other European markets, especially from
Rio de Janeiro, became increasingly significant.

Meanwhile the various illicit forms of trade (gold smuggling inside
and outside Brazil, illegal exports of colonial products and imports of
foreign manufactures) were undermining Portugal's whole economic
policy during the difficult years of recovery, but they were not the only
problems posed by Brazil to a government more than ever anxious to
preserve its prerogatives. There was concern that small workshops
producing all kinds of luxury cloths and gold and silver embroidery
were proliferating. This local production was not only competing with
similar industries in the metropolis, but was in the long run threatening
to engender in the richest of Portugal's colonies a desire for economic
and political independence. The existence of these problems led
Martinho de Mello e Castro to publish simultaneously in 1785 two
alvarás, one of which was intended to strengthen the measures against
all forms of fraud and smuggling, while the other ordered all workshops
and factories in Brazil producing cloth other than the coarse cotton
intended as clothing for slaves or as packing material for exported goods
to close. In fact, the second of these alvarás may not have had the impact
some historians have assumed. But it is true, all the same, that the
'Pombaline' policy adopted by Mello e Castro reaffirmed Brazil's
political and economic dependence on the metropolis, in accordance
with the principles of the mercantilist colonial system. Until the court
of the Braganzas was transferred to Rio de Janeiro in 1808, the colonial
pact was never called into question by the government which, even after
the independence of the United States of America and Saint-Domingue,
or after the two attempted revolts in Brazil in 1789 and 1798, never
admitted the possibility of relaxing its hold. However, the growth of
a more liberal spirit can be detected, particularly in the attitude of Mello

e Castro's successor, Dom Rodrigo de Souza Coutinho, who put forward somewhat different arguments for maintaining the links between Portugal and Brazil. These arguments were no longer based on the authority of classic mercantilist principles, but were inspired by 'mercantilism influenced by enlightenment, enlightened mercantilism'[11] and by a new vision of the Portuguese empire.

The first attempts to reform the Portuguese education system had been undertaken at Pombal's instigation and they continued during the reign of Dona Maria I. They quickly produced a generation of men with a new philosophical, scientific or technical outlook, who joined forces with an older generation of 'enlightened' men in an attempt to introduce reform and progress into Portugal. Besides traditional institutions such as the University of Coimbra, which was reformed in 1772, various other bodies made a powerful contribution to this movement. Curiously enough, it was in Brazil that the first scientific academy in the Portuguese empire was created in 1772. This was the *Academia Científica* of Rio de Janeiro which was founded to stimulate the study of natural sciences, physics, chemistry and agriculture, and hence to develop or improve Brazil's economy. Like another institution which followed it a few years later (the *Sociedade Literária*, 1786–94), the Academia Científica did not survive for long (1772–9) but it helped promote the diffusion of new staples for export. In Lisbon, the *Academia Real das Sciencias*, founded in 1779, played an important role by arousing public interest in the study of subjects connected with the economy and industry. The first three volumes of the famous *Memorias Economicas da Academia Real das Sciencias de Lisboa para o adiantamento da Agricultura, das Artes e da Industria em Portugal e suas Conquistas* were published as a series of articles between 1789 and 1791. They included various studies relating to Brazil which illustrate the persistence of colonial mercantilism, combined with a desire for improvement. There were monographs on whaling, cotton, sugar prices, raw materials still needing to be exploited and sectors of the economy needing development. A 'physical and economic' description of the Ilhéus region of Bahia even contained a detailed development plan. The Academy of Science applied itself to the stimulation of agriculture, but as part of

[11] The expression is Fernando Novais's in *Portugal e Brasil na crise do antigo sistema colonial (1777–1808)* (São Paulo, 1979), 230

a general trend which emphasized agrarian development rather than as a result of genuine physiocratic influence.[12] However, it also took an interest in metallurgy, notably by enabling two young Brazilians trained at the University of Coimbra to make the long journey to Europe to study the most important metallurgical establishments and to inform themselves about current scientific theories. As a scientific body, the Academy could not intervene directly in economic policy, so it was at the most no more than what we would today call a pressure group. On the other hand, some of its members later held important office in the government or in the administration and had a hand in policy-making. For example, the specialists in mineralogy and metallurgy sent to Europe by the Academy rose to highly responsible and influential positions, one as inspector general of Brazil's gold and diamond mines (Manuel Ferreira da Câmara) and the other as inspector general of Portugal's mines (José Bonifácio de Andrada e Silva).

But clearly it was at government level itself that 'enlightened' men were to be found, capable of formulating overall policies, of influencing the decisions of the sovereign and of shaping the destiny of the nation. The most important of these men, especially for Brazil, was undoubtedly Martinho de Mello e Castro's successor, Dom Rodrigo de Souza Coutinho. While Secretary of State for the Navy and for the Overseas Territories (1796–1801), and later, while president of the *Erário Régio* (1801–3), Dom Rodrigo de Souza Coutinho corresponded almost daily with the prince regent. These letters, and those he wrote to the viceroys, governors and other officials in Brazil, religious and secular, offer ample evidence of the wide scope of his projects and, in particular, of his persistent efforts to consolidate Brazil's pre-eminent position in the Portuguese empire. He was tireless in seeking to promote progress in every aspect of Brazilian life, especially in the economic sector. Some of his projects were a continuation of the work of his predecessors (e.g. the attempts to introduce crops, such as hemp, and to develop others, such as cinnamon, pepper, cochineal, etc.). But some projects were extremely original; for example, he wanted to make a cadastral survey

[12] The question is a controversial one: see especially Magalhães Godinho, *Prix et monnaies*, 284, and Albert Silbert, *Le Problème agraire portugais au temps des premières Cortès libérales 1821–1823* (Paris, 1968), 22. Here I accept the conclusions of Abílio Carlos d'Ascensão Diniz Silva, 'La Formulation d'une politique de développement économique au Portugal à la fin du XVIIIe siècle', Mémoire for the diploma in Sciences Économiques, University of Paris-I, 1969, 44–5 and 56–7, whose views depend on the analysis of the *Memorias Economicas* and on the observations of Joseph A. Schumpeter, *History of economic analysis* (6th edn., London, 1967), 157–8.

of the territory; he also wished to introduce the ox-drawn plough and to popularize 'scientific' agriculture among Brazilian landowners by distributing free pamphlets on agronomy printed in Lisbon and specially written in, or translated into, Portuguese by the learned Brazilian, Frei Mariano da Conceição Veloso. Some of Dom Rodrigo de Souza Coutinho's other projects sought to extend the use of cleaning and shelling machinery for cotton and coffee and of new technology in sugar production; to protect the forests by strictly controlling felling; to encourage the search for saltpetre; to improve the productivity of the iron mines in the captaincy of São Paulo, to develop the nascent iron and steel industry there and to extend these efforts to the captaincies of Rio de Janeiro and Minas Gerais; to promote the establishment of banks offering credit and discounts to agriculture and trade, as well as insurance companies; to promote freedom of circulation of goods in the Brazilian interior; and to establish regular packet-boats sailing between metropolitan Portugal and Brazil. His most important ideas are set out in a long report on 'the improvement of His Majesty's domains in America' which he put before the government and the Council of State in 1798, two years after he had been appointed Colonial Secretary.[13]

Leaving aside for the moment the political aspects of this important document, let us consider the economic proposition based on the minister's own ideas and on the various reports from his advisers. At the risk of encroaching on a domain reserved in theory for the president of the *Erário Régio*, who had sole responsibility for the administration of finance throughout the empire, Souza Coutinho considered it part of his duty to suggest ways of remedying the lamentable state of royal finances. Not only did he propose ways of reforming their administration, but also of modifying fiscal policy itself. He suggested that in every captaincy the junta de fazenda should administer all taxes directly. In other words, the 'pernicious' system of tax farming (contratos) would be abolished, an experiment which had already been carried out successfully in Minas Gerais. Book-keeping would be improved, estimates and accounts would be drawn up annually; and a plan to replace the tithe by a land tax proportional to the net income of the land would be studied. Next, local currency and the circulation of gold dust would be abolished and replaced by paper money. Coins of the

---

[13] Published by Marcos Carneiro de Mendonça, *O Intendente Câmara, Manuel Ferreira da Camara Bethencourt e Sá, Intendente Geral das Minas e Diamantes 1764–1835* (Rio de Janeiro, 1933), 268–90.

same value as those in circulation in metropolitan Portugal, however, could continue to be used. One or two mints were to be established in the captaincies of Minas Gerais and Goiás, while those in Rio de Janeiro and Bahia would be abolished. The *districtos diamantinos* were to be opened up and their deposits freely exploited. However, the diamonds were still to be sold to authorized representatives of the crown alone. The 20 per cent tax on gold would be reduced to 10 per cent; the tax on salt would be abolished altogether; all duties on imports and exports would be reduced to 4 per cent and a preferential system would be introduced for goods from the metropolis: 2 per cent on manufactured goods and a complete exemption for iron, steel, wines and olive oil. Duties payable on black slaves would be abolished throughout Brazil, except in ports, where they would be reduced. The special import duties (*entradas*) on black slaves and on various products (iron, steel, copper, gold dust, olive oil and wines) would be abolished in the captaincy of Minas Gerais. To compensate for the loss of revenue resulting from all these changes it would be necessary to introduce a stamp duty, already in force in the metropolis, together with moderate taxes on houses in the coastal towns and on all shops, inns and drinking establishments. There would also be a reduced capitation tax on all slaves. A postal service would be introduced throughout the Brazilian interior, the profit going to the Fazenda Real; and finally, lotteries would be set up, as in the metropolis.

For Souza Coutinho, influenced as he was by Adam Smith, the wealth of nations depended on 'the products of the land, the wages of agricultural workers and craftsmen, and on the income from accumulated capital which was used either to improve the land and make it productive or to increase the work force, and only in our time had this indisputable truth been concealed by the subtleties of the sect of Economists' – in other words, the physiocrats. So it was from within the framework of a pre-liberal economy that Souza Coutinho made his first attempts to reform the fiscal system in a way which was to affect not only Brazil but the whole empire: by relieving fiscal pressure he hoped to stimulate economic activity in Brazil, certainly, but also in Portugal since any increase in production in the colonies should improve her trade. In fact, the prosperity of the whole empire was at stake, since any increase in state revenue was essentially derived from the increased income of private citizens.

As is well known, the government of the Prince Regent Dom João was never distinguished for making speedy decisions; in addition, there was considerable opposition to a daring programme which was likely to disrupt cumbersome administrative machinery and the entrenched interests of a powerful financial oligarchy. We should not, therefore, be surprised that many of the measures put forward by Dom Rodrigo de Souza Coutinho in his report of 1798 were only slowly realized, and that many more were indefinitely postponed. Nevertheless, the minister did manage to abolish the farming of the salt tax in 1801. The farm of the tax on whale fishing was partially abolished in May 1798 and dropped completely in 1801. The planned reduction in tariffs and the introduction of new taxes were modified to suit local needs and the requirements of the Treasury.

Souza Coutinho was particularly concerned about the decline in gold production. We know that the regulations governing the various stages of production and the levying of the *quinto* (fifth) had not changed since Pombal's time, in spite of the social upheaval provoked by the unfair compensatory tax (the *derrama*), notably in Minas Gerais in 1789 where the Inconfidência Mineira was an unsuccessful plot for independence.[14] At last, in 1803 efforts were made to revive this basic industry along the lines suggested by the minister and his advisers: exchange bureaux for gold dust were to be set up in each of the captaincies involved; the Rio de Janeiro mint was to be transferred to Minas Gerais and the Bahia mint to Goiás; and a junta was to be set up to administer the mines and the minting of money. This junta was to be composed mainly of mineralogists (mine-owners with experience or trained technicians), and the presence of such experts working alongside the civil servants shows that there was a new spirit, which was also reflected in the plan to set up local schools of mineralogy and metallurgy modelled on German schools. It was hoped that techno-logical progress would in this way jolt gold production out of the rut it had been in since 1765. To encourage the efforts of the mine-owners the quinto was reduced to a tax of 10 per cent. As for diamonds, the oppressive system of totally isolating areas containing diamond deposits was abandoned: the Districto Diamantino was opened up again, gold prospecting was authorized there and a new method of sharing out and working the concessions was adopted. Miners were advised to form societies or companies in order to increase their profits. The sale of diamonds, however, was still the exclusive prerogative of the crown:

[14] For the further discussion of the Inconfidência Mineira, see Alden, *CHLA*, II, ch. 15.

the stones were either inspected and bought in the main diamond centre (Arraial do Tijuco) by a junta de fazenda specially created for the purpose, or else, in areas too far from this centre, in the exchange bureaux which had been set up to deal with gold dust.

No doubt the delay in deciding to put these measures into practice often reduced their impact. The reforms came too late. However, they were necessary and helped prepare the way for the upheavals which were to shake the empire after 1808.

A fair idea of the success of the economic policy of Pombal's successors can be gained from examining Portugal's trade with England, as was done for Pombal's period, using as a basis the English data which run in a continuous series up to the year 1800. However, it is worth checking the result against Portuguese sources on the balance of trade for which we also have a continuous series from 1796.[15] This series is particularly interesting because it covers the whole of Portugal's export trade, not only with foreign countries but also with each of her colonies. The figures enable us to evaluate the internal structure of the economy of the Portuguese empire and to assess the efforts made to reorganize it. We shall, therefore, draw on English data for the period 1776–95, and on Portuguese data for the period 1796–1807.

Table 2 on p. 503 shows that between 1776 and 1795 there was the same continuous trend in Anglo-Portuguese trade already observed in Pombal's period (see above, Table 1 on p. 494).

Between 1776 and 1795, Portugal's exports to England increased by 90 per cent, while imports from England only increased by 13 per cent. During the period 1791–5 this led to the first spectacular reversal of the balance of trade in favour of Portugal: the balance which had previously been negative now showed a large surplus. Benefiting from the international trends which worked in favour of her trade, Portugal had clearly succeeded in expanding her trade by promoting her colonial products. Brazilian cotton, for example, was playing an increasingly important role in Portuguese exports: between 1781 and 1792 the total

---

[15] Pointed out and used for the first time by Adrien Balbi in his famous *Essai statistique sur le royaume de Portugal et d'Algarve*, 2 vols. (Paris, 1822), I, 401–45, these trade figures have been used more recently and partially by a number of historians, notably Magalhães Godinho, Borges de Macedo, Silbert and, above all, by Fernando Novais, *Portugal e Brasil*, 285–96 and 306–91 (graphics and figures), as well as by José Jobson de A. Arruda, *O Brasil no comércio colonial* (São Paulo, 1980).

Table 2 *Balance of Trade with England: 1776–95*
(average annual value in £1,000s)

Years	Exports Portugal–England	Imports England–Portugal	Balance
1776–80	381	525	−144
1781–85	340	622	−282
1786–90	597	622	−25
1791–95	724	594	+130
Total	2,042	2,363	

Source: Elizabeth Boody Schumpeter, *English Overseas Trade Statistics (1697–1808)*, 17–18.

weight of Brazilian cotton exported annually from Portugal to England rose from 300,000 lbs to 7,700,000 lbs, while during the same period France also imported about 1,376,000 lbs of cotton per annum.[16]

For the period 1776–95, Portuguese sources can only provide two complete sets of trade figures, one for 1776 and one for 1777 (see Table 3). These indicate that a radical change in the economic structure of the Portuguese empire was taking place, an observation which is confirmed by later data (from 1796).

Table 3 *Portugal's Balance of Trade: 1776–7*
(value in milréis)

Years	Portugal–Colonies	Portugal–Foreign Countries
1776	+1,177,159	−1,795,390
1777	+545,329	−1,492,427

Source: Fernando A. Novais, *Portugal e Brasil na crise do antigo sistema colonial (1777–1808)*, p. 289.

Table 3 shows us the beginnings of the change since the deficit in Portugal's trade with other countries was reduced by nearly 17 per cent, while the balance favouring the metropolis in its trade with its colonies decreased by nearly 54 per cent. The latter figure is particularly

---

[16] For English data, see Maxwell, *Conflicts and conspiracies*, 255, and for French data, Magalhães Godinho, *Prix et monnaies*, 361.

important as it shows clearly that the colonies were tending to improve their economic position as against the metropolis, and we shall see later that Brazil's dominant position – for which we have precise data after 1796 – was preparing the way for the colony's economic and political independence.

It is no exaggeration to say that the period 1796–1807 appears to have been a new Golden Age for Portuguese trade. In her dealings with foreign countries Portugal enjoyed a constant surplus in her balance of trade, except in 1797 and 1799. The average annual value of exports increased by nearly 4 per cent and imports by only 2.6 per cent, as Table 4 shows.

Table 4 *Portugal's Balance of Trade with all Foreign Countries: 1796–1807*
(value in milréis)

Years	Exports Portugal–Foreign Countries	Imports Foreign Countries–Portugal	Balance
1796	16,013,356	12,652,771	+ 3,360,585
1797	11,822,970	14,498,399	− 2,675,429
1798	15,053,960	14,729,238	+ 324,722
1799	17,688,107	19,755,284	− 2,067,177
1800	20,684,802	20,031,347	+ 653,455
1801	25,103,785	19,337,425	+ 5,766,360
1802	21,405,349	17,942,240	+ 3,463,109
1803	21,528,379	15,068,304	+ 6,460,075
1804	21,060,962	17,841,034	+ 3,219,928
1805	22,654,204	19,656,685	+ 2,997,519
1806	23,255,505	16,440,921	+ 6,814,584
1807	20,999,506	13,896,318	+ 7,103,188
Total	237,270,885	201,869,966	

Source: Novais, *Portugal e Brasil*, 320 and 322.

After 1798 Portugal's trade with England always showed a balance in Portugal's favour, and from 1800 there were even some significant improvements, as can be seen in Table 5 on p. 505.

If we compare Tables 4 and 5, we can see that Portugal's imports from England represented 34 per cent of the total value of her imports from all foreign countries, and that Portugal's exports to England represented 39 per cent of the total value of all her exports to foreign countries. This shows clearly that, while England remained one of

Table 5 *Portugal's Balance of Trade with England: 1796–1807*
(value in milréis)

Years	Exports Portugal–England	Imports England–Portugal	Balance
1796	4,887,076	4,951,737	−64,661
1797	3,979,976	4,627,613	−647,637
1798	6,828,261	6,661,419	+166,842
1799	9,058,217	8,835,649	+222,568
1800	6,702,836	2,911,061	+3,791,775
1801	9,651,014	4,879,357	+4,771,657
1802	8,472,170	6,693,774	+1,778,396
1803	10,514,250	5,587,493	+4,926,757
1804	7,462,492	5,764,885	+1,697,607
1805	8,865,210	5,837,705	+3,027,505
1806	6,587,150	8,201,116	+1,613,966
1807	7,971,196	5,422,272	+2,548,924
Total	92,593,814	68,760,115	

Source: Novais, *Portugal e Brasil*, 356 and 358.

Portugal's main trading partners, she was no longer the almost exclusive partner that she had been for so long. Portugal maintained regular trading relations with about fifteen countries, and the volume of business conducted annually with Hamburg, Russia, Spain and France, for example, is evidence of an interesting diversification.[17]

An analysis of Portugal's trade figures from 1796 to 1807 also yields much detailed information about the economic structure of the Portuguese empire – both within itself as well as in relation to foreign countries.

If we look at the overall picture of Portugal's trading relations with its colonies, Portugal showed a deficit in the balance of trade in most years, as we can see from Table 6 on p. 506.

Imports from the colonies, then, increased annually by an average of 10 per cent. On the other hand, the growth rate of exports from Portugal to the colonies, which had averaged over 17 per cent per annum until the end of 1799, fell after this year to just below 3 per cent per annum – an indication of the growing importance of the contraband trade in English manufactures. At the end of the period the balance of trade showed an overall surplus of 10.6 per cent in favour of the

[17] Balbi, *Essai statistique*, I, 431–42.

Table 6 *Portugal's Balance of Trade with all her Colonies: 1796–1807*
(value in milréis)

Years	Exports Portugal–Colonies	Imports Colonies–Portugal	Balance
1796	7,527,648	13,413,265	− 5,885,617
1797	9,651,734	5,519,870	+ 4,131,864
1798	12,418,654	12,802,090	− 383,436
1799	20,458,608	15,169,305	+ 5,289,303
1800	13,521,110	14,850,936	− 1,329,826
1801	13,133,542	17,527,723	− 4,394,181
1802	12,800,313	12,966,553	− 116,340
1803	12,741,308	14,193,353	− 1,452,045
1804	14,905,960	13,579,874	+ 1,326,086
1805	12,245,019	15,843,481	− 3,598,462
1806	11,313,313	16,103,966	− 4,789,653
1807	10,348,602	16,968,810	− 6,620,208
Total	151,065,811	168,939,226	

Source: Novais, *Portugal e Brasil*, 310 and 312.

colonies. This amply confirms the trend noticeable from the figures for 1776 and 1777, when the surplus in favour of the metropolis had begun to decline.

These trade figures also enable us to assess the exact place Brazil occupied in the total volume of Portugal's trade: Brazil alone accounted for over 83 per cent of the total value of goods imported by Portugal from her colonies, and for 78.5 per cent of Portugal's exports to her colonies.[18] Even more striking are the respective percentages from each part of the Portuguese empire within the total value of Portuguese exports to foreign countries (100 per cent): products from the metropolis, 27.43 per cent; products from Brazil, 60.76 per cent; products from other colonies, 2.95 per cent; re-exports, 8.86 per cent.[19]

Thus, despite a certain revival of Portuguese commerce with those of her colonies in Asia which had in earlier times been her principal source of wealth, the overwhelming preponderance of Brazil is clear,

[18] Novais, *Portugal e Brasil*, 290. See also, Alden, *CHLA*, II, ch. 15, table 11, 'Brazilian exports to Portugal 1796 and 1806', and table 13, 'Balance of Trade between Portugal and leading Brazilian captaincies, 1796–1806'.

[19] Novais, *Portugal e Brasil*, 292–3. See also Alden, *CHLA*, II, ch. 15, table 12, 'Origins of exports from Portugal to Europe, Barbary and United States, 1789, 1796, 1806'.

whether we look at the internal or the external structure of Portugal's economy. Portugal's international trade owed its positive balance to the exports of Brazilian staples.

At the end of the eighteenth century, when Britain and France's union with several of their American colonies had already been severed, the question of Brazil's dependence on Portugal was raised. In the preamble to the report 'on the improvement of His Majesty's domains in America', the economic aspects of which have been examined above, Dom Rodrigo de Souza Coutinho (in charge of colonial affairs since 1796) expounded his ideas on the political system which he considered would enable Portugal to keep its overseas empire. Assuming *a priori* that 'the happy position of Portugal' as middleman between northern and southern Europe made the union of the Portuguese colonies with the metropolis 'as natural as the union of the other colonies, which have declared their independence of the motherland, was unnatural', the minister defended 'the inviolable and sacrosanct principle of unity, the basis of the monarchy, which must be jealously maintained so that Portuguese, wherever they are born, may consider themselves uniquely Portuguese'. He then went on to state its corollary: it was important to reinforce commercial links between the metropolis and its colonies, above all Brazil, 'the chief of all the possessions that Europeans have established outside their continent, not because of what it is at present, but because of what it can become if we can develop all the advantages offered by its size, situation and fertility'. To ensure the defence of Brazil from its neighbours Dom Rodrigo recommended that it should again be divided into two great regions, each depending on a military centre, Belém do Pará in the north and Rio de Janeiro in the south, according to a geopolitical plan which would allow Portugal 'gradually and imperceptibly' to 'expand to the true natural frontier of our possessions in South America, in other words, the northern bank of the Río de la Plata' – the old expansionist dream which none of the three frontier treaties signed with Spain since 1750 had been able to dissipate.[20]

A few years later, another ancient dream was revived by certain statesmen anxious to preserve the integrity of the Portuguese empire and the independence of its rulers from increasing French pressure. This was an idea of the old diplomat, Dom Luís da Cunha, who, in 1738, had foreseen that the king of Portugal would transfer his court to Brazil

[20] Memorandum of Dom Rodrigo de Souza Coutinho, see note 13.

and assume one day the title of Emperor of the West.[21] Soon after the breakdown of the Peace of Amiens (1802), Dom Rodrigo de Souza Coutinho and other counsellors, weighing up 'the new risks and imminent dangers' which threatened the Portuguese monarchy, decided that in the last resort the prince regent must move to Brazil.[22] However, the dream did not become a reality until France invaded Portugal. On 28 November 1807, under the protection of an English squadron, the royal family and part of the court left Portugal for Brazil.

Thus, the reorganization of the empire, which had been in progress ever since 1750, was brought to its logical conclusion by pressure of outside forces. Already the most important economic unit in the world-wide Portuguese empire, Brazil became its political centre from 1808 until 1821 when the ex-prince regent, Dom João VI, king of Portugal and Brazil since 1816, returned to Lisbon.

The step taken in 1807 had been a decisive one, but not in the way Souza Coutinho had imagined it would be. Far from serving as a base for the 'complete reintegration of the monarchy' Brazil initiated the disintegration of the Portuguese empire by proclaiming its independence in 1822.

[21] *Instruções inéditas de D. Luis da Cunha a Marco António de Azevedo Coutinho*, 211.

[22] Dom Rodrigo de Souza Coutinho to the Prince Regent Dom João, 16 August 1803, in Angelo Pereira, *D. João VI Principe e Rei*, 4 vols. (Lisbon, 1953–7), 1, 127–36. Totally rejected at the time by the Portuguese government, this hypothesis was analysed in all its consequences a year later by the British Admiral Donald Campbell in an important report to the Foreign Office: see Andrée Mansuy, 'L'Impérialisme britannique et les relations coloniales entre le Portugal et le Brésil: un rapport de l'Amiral Campbell au *Foreign Office* (14 août 1804)'. *Cahiers des Amériques Latines*, 9–10 (1974), 138, 147–8, 152 and 186–9; also Maxwell, *Conflicts and conspiracies*, 233–9.

Part Three

THE CHURCH IN AMERICA

14

THE CATHOLIC CHURCH IN COLONIAL
SPANISH AMERICA

THE TRANSPLANTATION OF THE CATHOLIC CHURCH TO THE
NEW WORLD

To comprehend fully the establishment and organization of the Catholic
church in the Americas in the sixteenth century it is necessary first to
consider conditions in the Iberian peninsula at the time. In the later
Middle Ages the Iberian kingdoms had undergone a decisive experience:
the reconquest of once-Christian territory from the Islamic invader. It
is an over-simplification to identify the *Reconquista* directly with the
general model of the crusade, but there was in it the same interplay of
worldly enterprise and religious purpose. There was also the idea that
the faith could and should be propagated by military means. It is even
possible to argue, with Américo Castro, that the Castilian participants
in the *Reconquista* had absorbed some ideas and beliefs – above all,
religious messianism – from their Muslim adversaries. Within their
territories the rulers of the Hispanic kingdoms had for many centuries
practised relative tolerance towards their non-Christian subjects. However, from the early fifteenth century onwards insistence upon assimilation into the body of Christianity grew steadily. Spanish Jews had in
1492 to choose between baptism as Christians or banishment from the
realms of Ferdinand and Isabella; the Moors were faced with the same
choice in Castile in 1520, and in Aragon in 1526. Spain was by then
already far removed from the missionary attitude held in the thirteenth
century by such as Ramon Llull; the emerging modern state demanded
at least the façade of uniformity of belief. At the same time ideas
propounded by Italian jurists since the fourteenth century on the secular
justification of the polity, in which state authority had to control every

---

* Translated from the Spanish by Dr Richard Boulind; translation revised and chapter in part
reorganised by the Editor.

force in society, including the ecclesiastical, increasingly gained acceptance. Naturally, such models of society had no place for a theocracy, that is, for Augustinianism in politics, no place in particular for the view that the pope was *dominus orbis*.

In the fifteenth century, in the absence of a powerful bourgeois class, the crowns of Portugal and Castile themselves took the lead in the expansion of their dominions beyond the peninsula: the former in Madeira, the Azores and along the west coast of Africa, the latter in the Canary Islands. These were the places where the solutions to the problems which the conquest of America would later present were tested out. What was legitimate occupation? How were the conquerors to treat the conquered? What missionary duty did the sovereigns have, and what were their rights of patronage?

At the time of Columbus' first arrival in the Antilles, the papacy had for over half a century been intervening in both Portugal's and Castile's expeditions of exploration and conquest. In the bulls *Romanus Pontifex* of Pope Nicholas V (1455) and *Cum dudum affligebant* of Calixtus III (1456), for example, the papacy focused its interest on the human and religious problems of the conquered populations while at the same time it conferred legitimacy upon the conquest. In the case of the Spanish Indies, the bulls *Inter caetera* (1493) and *Eximiae devotionis* (1493 and 1501) of Alexander VI, *Universalis ecclesiae* (1508) of Julius II and *Exponi nobis* (1523) of Hadrian VI, conferred upon the Castilian crown, determined the essential framework for the work of Catholic evangelization in America.

In exchange for this legitimation of the rights they claimed in a continent still only partially conquered or explored, the Catholic monarchs were obliged to promote the conversion of the inhabitants of the newly discovered lands and to protect and maintain the church militant under the *patronato real* (royal patronage). The crown of Castile took control of the life of the church to a degree unknown in Europe (except in recently conquered Granada). Ecclesiastical policy became one more aspect of colonial policy co-ordinated after 1524 by the Council of the Indies. The crown reserved the right to present candidates for ecclesiastical appointment at all levels and undertook the obligation to pay salaries and to build and endow cathedrals, churches, monasteries and hospitals out of the tithes on agricultural and livestock production. The crown also reserved the right to authorize the passage of ecclesiastical personnel to the Indies and, in 1538, explicitly ordered that all communication between Rome and the Indies be submitted to the Council for its approbation (the *pase regio*, or *exequatur*). And while, on the one hand, Philip II proved unsuccessful in 1560 in his attempt to have two patriarchates, with sovereign powers, created for America, in 1568 Pius V failed in his attempt to despatch papal nuncios to the Indies. The church in America had a practical mission assigned to it: it was to hasten Indian submission and Europeanization and to preach loyalty to the crown of Castile. Any resistance by the church to the fulfilment of this function was viewed as a political problem and dealt with accordingly.

This arrangement was logically desirable for the state, but less clearly so for the church. Just why did the church allow itself to be bound hand and foot to the interests of the Spanish crown? There were many reasons, among them the following: the preoccupation of the worldly Renaissance popes, especially Alexander VI, the Borja pope from Valencia, with family aggrandizement, European politics and, after 1517, the rising tide of Protestantism; Rome's lack of means to organize and finance the propagation of the faith in the New World if political auxiliaries were not available; the chauvinistic zeal of many Spanish ecclesiastics who recognized that the king of Spain had in any case much more to offer them than the pope in distant Rome. Under the *patronato real* the clergy enjoyed a surprising degree of toleration, which permitted them to be heard in all the processes of government. However, in contrast with the opportunities the church authorities had in Spain and America for challenging the system under which they worked, the number of times the chance was taken was insignificant.

The first setting for the conflicts of conscience suffered by the authorities was the Antilles. In 1509 King Ferdinand had legalized *encomienda*, the system by which the Indians were shared out among the settlers who could exercise rights over them practically for life, although they were not, in fact, officially slaves. In December 1511 the Dominican friar, Antonio de Montesinos, denounced the settlers from the pulpit: 'You are all in a state of mortal sin', he said, 'and you are going to live, and to die in it, because of the cruelty and the tyranny you are inflicting on these innocent victims.' With this broadside, the lines were drawn for the first battle between the gospel and colonialism, in the struggle which was to be a lightning rod for the life of the church in America. The state's first reaction was to pass the Laws of Burgos in 1512, which inaugurated a series of attempts by the authorities to mediate between the two incompatible interests. Two years later Bartolomé de Las Casas, Dominican friar, parish priest and *encomendero* in Cuba, began his great defence of the Indians which was to last until his death in 1566. This first (Caribbean) stage of Spanish colonialism in America served to throw into relief an inherent contradiction: if the papal bulls made the conversion of the natives the justification for Spanish sovereignty, then the very persons now responsible for the missionary endeavour increasingly found themselves obliged to censure the social and economic aims of the colonial enterprise.

The two decades after 1519 represent the decisive phase in Castile's domination of America. From their base in the Antilles, the Spaniards conquered Mexico and Central America and then moved southwards from Panama and Venezuela, via the Pacific, to conquer the Inca empire. The *conquistadores* stepped into an unknown world. Territorial expansion meant the discovery of complex societies organized according to systems totally alien to those of Europe. Moreover, their religious structures were functionally rooted in the life of those societies. Only after the geographical and human horizon had opened up so overwhelmingly did the church realize the size of the task of evangelization now demanded of it in the New World. The *conquistadores* themselves were driven in part by religious fervour to perform their staggering feats. They were convinced that in subjugating populations previously unknown to Christendom they were serving equally their monarch, as vassals, their faith, as missionaries, and themselves, as men of honour. Once Spanish authority had been established, the missionary orders came on the scene to evangelize the conquered peoples. The friars in turn were always backed up by the repressive sword of authority. Thus, military and political conquest came first, then spiritual conquest followed. Both church and state stood in need of the services mutually afforded.

During the second half of the fifteenth century and the first half of the sixteenth, the Iberian peninsula was the scene of reforming movements of great intensity. The Catholic monarchs themselves were determined to reform the episcopate through a more rigorous selection of candidates and a stricter use of patronage. The men they selected as bishops were thoroughly grounded in theology and zealous in their observance of church discipline: the prototypes were Alfonso Carrillo, Hernando de

Acuña and Pedro González de Mendoza. Later, Hernando de Talavera, Diego de Deza and, above all, Francisco Jiménez de Cisneros, cardinal of Toledo and Isabella's confessor, conformed to this ideal for the Spanish episcopate. The holding of diocesan synods, such as those at Aranda de Duero in 1473 and Seville in 1478, was also intended to restore and breathe new life into Christian practice. In the sixteenth century, amidst the first signs of the Lutheran schism, we find one of the greatest figures within the reformist tradition in Spanish Catholicism: Juan de Avila, professor of theology, mystic, preacher, spiritual director and counsellor. The winds of reform and of the restoration of primitive obedience blew also into the monasteries, specially affecting the Dominican and the Franciscan orders.

Within the ambit of missionary activity in America the reforming ideas of the peninsula were already caught up in the confluence of the currents of millenarianism and utopianism. For many, the New World was the opportunity offered by Providence for establishing the true 'gospel kingdom', or 'pure Christianity': the early church restored. Marcel Bataillon has traced evidence of Joachimism (from the twelfth-century mystic Joachim of Flora) among the first Franciscans in Mexico. John Leddy Phelan has highlighted millenarian influences in the work of the Franciscan Geronimo de Mendieta, for example.[1] Such men as Fr Juan de Zumárraga, first bishop and archbishop of Mexico, Don Vasco de Quiroga, Fr Julian Garcés and Fr Bartolomé de Las Casas himself were all deeply influenced by the humanistic spirit of Erasmus and by Thomas More's *Utopia*.

The Jesuits, formed in 1540, were themselves the fruit of the reforming ideal. So, too, was their intervention in America. They travelled light, unencumbered by the baggage of the past. They sought to implant a Christianity free from the errors defacing the Faith in Europe. Their utopian impulse came to full flower in the seventeenth century, with their so-called Indian Reductions (notably in Paraguay). Their deference to Rome and their marked hierarchical structure also fitted the model of Christianity endorsed at the Council of Trent (1545–63).[2]

It has been customary to claim that the Tridentine reform had no

[1] Marcel Bataillon, 'Evangélisme et millénarisme au Nouveau Monde', in *Courants religieux et humanisme à la fin du XVe et au début du XVIe siècles* (Paris, 1959), 25–36; J. L. Phelan, *The millennial kingdom of the Franciscans in the New World* (Berkeley, 1956).

[2] See M. Bataillon, 'D'Erasme à la Compagnie de Jésus: protestation et intégration dans la Réforme catholique au XVIe siècle', *Archives de la Sociologie des Religions*, 24 (1967), 57–81.

influence in America because the church of the Indies did not take part. This is too formalistic a conclusion. Latterly, it has proved possible to point out a number of aspects of Catholicism in America in which the Council of Trent had a role which, directly or indirectly, was to prove decisive. Even though no canon adopted there can be pointed out as specifically intended for American conditions, the spirit of Trent is observable in many of the forms that were taken by the church then being organized in Spanish America.[3]

Certainly evangelism in the Indies was affected in a negative sense by the tendencies the Council ratified. Thus, the liturgy continued to be in Latin. Access by the faithful to the Word of God was restricted. The Council evinced hypersensitivity to theological orthodoxy. Ecclesiastical structures were consolidated, and the life of the church was left largely in the hands of the clergy – a situation which, in America, was aggravated by the racial superiority complex which determined the behaviour of most colonists, lay or clerical.

At the same time, reaction in the Council of Trent to the secession of the Protestants in Europe promoted or emphasized a whole series of practices that clearly differentiated the Catholic church from Protestantism. Although no Protestants then existed in America, processions, veneration of the saints, devotions observed on behalf of souls in purgatory and indulgences, for example, were prominent features of Christianity in the Indies. External and institutional features were to some extent exalted over personal experience.

The church in the New World was thus the outcome of the merging of two currents. One was the transplantation of the chracteristics of the church in the Iberian peninsula in the era of the discoveries; the other was the ratification of these characteristics by the Council of Trent. Following the guidelines established by the Council of Trent, a royal decree, the *Ordenanza del Patronazgo* (1574) reaffirmed episcopal authority. The bishop became the cornerstone of ecclesiastical life in each diocese. Not just the secular clergy but the regular clergy as well, through the parish or the *doctrina*, were gradually brought under the authority of the local bishop.

And it cannot be denied that Trent, and the reformist traditions which we have seen, preceded it in the Iberian peninsula, contributed to producing a type of bishop different from the prelacy of the Middle Ages

<hr>

[3] On this point see, for example, Juan Villegas, *Aplicación del Concilio de Trento en Hispanoamérica, 1564–1600: provincia eclesiástica del Perú* (Montevideo, 1975).

and the Renaissance. Spanish America can claim a distinguished array of men doggedly devoted to spreading the gospel in the most unpropitious circumstances. They were poor, devout, rigorous in the theological training they had received, highly conscious of their duties and little inclined to let interference from the civil power impress them. It is in no way coincidental that colonial circumstances caused most of them to stand out as defenders of the Indians: Antonio de Valdivieso in Nicaragua, Juan del Valle in Popayán, Pedro de la Pena in Quito, Alfonso Toribio de Mogrovejo in Lima and Domingo de Santo Tomás in La Plata are only some of the names from among the many that deserve to be mentioned here.[4]

Lastly, the Council of Trent must be given the credit for a conciliar and synodal tradition which grew up in America. Eleven provincial councils were celebrated there between 1551 and 1629, the majority in Lima and Mexico City, but also two in La Plata (Chuquisaca) and Santo Domingo. None was called during the next century and a half, evidence in itself that the church was now well established. The number of diocesan synods held was even greater: there is evidence that over 25 met between 1555 and 1631 alone. The importance of synods is at once both greater and less than that of councils. Less, because they were usually for the application of legislation decided at the corresponding provincial level. More, because they made decisions applying to a specific area, and because a significant portion of the clergy responsible for putting the decisions into practice took part in them.

The church as an institution in Spanish American, as in Spain, functioned through its bishoprics. Dioceses were established as a consequence of military conquest or – much further on in the colonial period – of the growth in economic importance of certain regions. The first diocese – Santo Domingo – was created in 1504; by the middle of the sixteenth century, as Table 1 shows, nearly half of the dioceses were already in existence, just as the basic occupation of all the territory effectively colonized by Spain had already taken place by that date. Not only were relatively few dioceses established after 1600, but not one constituted a major centre of ecclesiastical organization. (The sole exception, and that a relative one, was Buenos Aires, a see founded in 1620.)

[4] See E. D. Dussel, *Les Évêques hispanoaméricains, défenseurs et évangelisateurs de l'indien* (Wiesbaden, 1970).

Table 1 *Foundation of Bishoprics in Spanish America*

Sixteenth Century	{1504–1550	22}	31
	{1551–1600	9}	
Seventeenth Century			5
Eighteenth Century			6
Nineteenth Century			3

What significance did a bishopric have in colonial society? In itself, it constituted an autonomous administrative centre, taking care of consecrations, of appointments and of the judicial functioning of the church. Among other things, it was responsible for missionary work, for legislation within the diocesan synod and for the training of seminary priests. In relation to civil authority, it presented candidates for appointments, interacted with the civil administrative structure at every level and was charged with executing the laws that emanated from the political authorities – the Council of the Indies, the viceroy and the audiencia. In this respect, the multiplication of dioceses meant the proliferation of centres of ecclesiastical activity and initiative and of responsibility for Castile's colonizing enterprise. In each diocese the individual bishop worked closely with the cathedral chapter which took over the administration in the event of a prolonged vacancy; this often occurred in American sees because of the death or translation of the holder. Another central organ of the diocese was the seminary, with its potentially dual function as a college-hostel for university students in the humanities and divinity, and as a seminary for the training of the clergy.

At the local level, the keystone of church organization was the parish, an institution introduced from Europe, where it had already undergone a long evolution from its origin in ancient Rome. The Council of Trent ratified it as the basic cell in Catholic life. The parish took root in America alongside the episcopate: with the latter, it made up the church outside the walls of the religious houses (even when, as so often happened, parishes were themselves entrusted to friars). The parish had to adapt itself to American conditions: the missionaries – the immense majority members of the religious orders – set up *doctrinas* as evangelistic units, while the secular clergy founded parishes for the Spaniards. The former were mostly rural, the latter totally urban. *Doctrinas* discharged the duties of proselytizing and civilizing the natives, including teaching the doctrines of Christianity to adults and children, placing restrictions on certain of the sacraments, watching for certain idolatrous practices and repressing them, organizing the social lives of converts, and so on. Parishes took on the pastoral task of transplanting and protecting the True Faith in the Spanish community.[5]

The extraordinary importance of the religious orders in bringing Christianity to Hispanic America is generally accepted. There were very concrete reasons for this: for example, greater missionary zeal and greater 'manageability' of specific numbers of workers. By contrast, the mass of the secular clergy were morally and intellectually decadent and their work was difficult to co-ordinate. From the first decade of the sixteenth century the Catholic monarchs had a clear policy for America. They decided to dispense with monks as such: monks were medieval in nature and ill-suited to serve as pastors of congregations. They also resolved to manage without the services of the military orders, who predominated in the peninsular territories which had been reconquered from the Moors. Instead they resorted to the services of the mendicant orders, the mature product of the new urban civilization of the later Middle Ages and the Renaissance. And they preferred among the friars those who were 'reformed' or 'observant': not only were they available for the adventure of preaching the gospel but they had no seigneurial pretensions, had vowed themselves to poverty and were zealous for conversion.

To speak of the mendicants in the evangelization of America is to speak of the four great orders – the Franciscans, the first to arrive in Mexico (1524) and Peru (1534), the Dominicans, the Augustinians and the Mercedarians – which were so visibly at work within the structure of any city in colonial Spanish America. Each order quickly spun a host of links at all levels of local settler society – through Third Orders, fraternities, boards of trustees, leaseholders of estates, chantries, schools, families whose children took holy orders, public worship, festivals of saints. To these four orders the Jesuits were soon to be added (1568–72): they had only recently been founded in Europe, but they were extraordinarily mobile. Without any exaggeration, it can be said that the greater part of the burden of Christianizing America fell upon these

[5] See Constantino Bayle, *El clero secular y la evangelización de América* (Madrid, 1950); Pedro Borges, *Métodos misionales en la cristianización de América* (Madrid, 1960).

five religious orders. They formed the church's strategic reserve, providing men for missionary work in the front line whenever new areas of colonization were opened up. In the case of the Jesuits, proselytizing was matched by the importance of their contribution in the field of education.

Later to appear on the scene was another group of orders, of varying characteristics but largely devoted to caring for the sick and the destitute in the cities. Their very existence attested the new needs of an increasingly complex colonial society. The Hospital Brothers of the Order of St John of God were present in America from 1602 onwards and spread notably across both New Spain and Peru. Then there were the Hippolytans (from 1594 onwards), the Antonins (from 1628) and the Bethlehemites (from 1655) – all orders founded on American soil, in New Spain. Only the Bethlehemites spread to some extent throughout the continent.

Other orders busied themselves with similar pastoral work – the Carmelites, the Hieronymites, the Trinitarians and the Minims – although they were represented by only tiny groups in a few cities. Even so, Philip III ordered them to return to Spain because they lacked royal authorization to be in America at all. On the other hand, from the second half of the seventeenth century, the Capuchins put down strong roots in several of the missions in Venezuela – Cumaná, Llanos de Caracas, Guayana and Maracaibo. In the same era the Oratorians founded houses in Panama, Lima, Cuzco and, at the end of the eighteenth century, in Chuquisaca.[6] Because their character was so exceptional, the limited presence of Benedictines from Montserrat may be mentioned here. They were present in Lima from 1592 onwards and in Mexico City from 1602. But they confined themselves to encouraging the cult of the Black Virgin of Montserrat, to whom they owed their dedication, and to the collection of offerings for their home monastery. This was in stark contrast with what happened in Brazil, where they were to develop strong pastoral, educational and cultural work.

In the early days of Castilian colonization in America, priests made the decision to travel to the New World individually and spontaneously. As time went on, however, a procedural machinery came into being, which was, to some degree, the result of the progressive regimentation

---

[6] Constantino Bayle, 'Ordenes religiosas, no misioneras, en Indias', *Missionalia Hispanica* 1 (1944), 517–58.

of 'passage to the Indies' by the crown. To a large extent the seculars continued to act as individuals throughout the whole of the colonial period; the regulars, on the other hand, from the second half of the sixteenth century onwards, operated within an organizational structure for filling vacancies in the mission field. The American side of the endeavour to staff the missions was itself based on a 'mission' – the sending of one or more representatives of the order in America, to find brothers in religion in Europe willing to travel to, and work in, the Indies. These temporary procurators – *procuradores* – generally carried commissions to undertake other business, as well, for the Province which had entrusted them with responsibility for recruiting. They made the round of the respective order's houses in Europe on a propaganda tour, with the previous permission of the superior-general and the respective Provincials, who would issue the permit for the migration once those involved had formally agreed to go.

The European end of the recruitment system centred on the commissary-general, alias vicar-general of the order, or procurator for the Indies. In the case of the Franciscans and the Augustinians, the commissaries-general were real powers, intermediary between the orders' headquarters within the Curia in Rome and the respective Provinces in America. At the same time, they acted as the chief links between the American Provinces of their orders and the central organs of the Castilian state. The Jesuit vicars-general were, however, mere executors, or agents, of requests coming in from the Indies. In all cases one or other of these officials was the essential lever for obtaining whatever permit was required, either from the Council of the Indies or the Casa de la Contratación in Seville or Cadiz.[7]

The despatch of missionaries to America was, in the last resort, a question of imperial policy. Hence, for example, it was only when the crown acquiesced in the practice that the religious orders were allowed to enrol brothers from outside Spain – foreigners, in all the complex variety that such a term connotes. In principle, the regulars were subject to the same requirements as the secular clergy, but there were variations

[7] Luis Arroyo, 'Comisarios generales de Indias', *Archivo Ibero Americano*, 12 (1952), 129–72, 258–96, 429–73; Félix Zubillaga, 'El Procurador de la Compañía de Jesús en la corte de España (1570)', *Archivum Historicum Societatis Iesus*, 15 (1947), 1–55; *idem.*, 'El Procurador de las Indias occidentales de la Compañía de Jesús (1574); etapas históricas de su erección', *Archivum Historicum Societatis Iesu*, 22 (1953), 367–417; Q. Fernandez, 'El Vicario General de Indias: una controversia jurisdiccional entre el General Andrés de Fivizzano (1592–8) y el provincial de Castilla fray Gabriel de Goldárez (1592–6)', *Miscellanea Ordinis S. Augustini Historica*, 41 (1978), 25–63.

in practice. From the early seventeenth century onwards, for instance, the Jesuits secured more and more permits allowing them to send their priests to America from any part of the dominions associated with the crown of Castile, and even from the current and past dominions of the Holy Roman Empire. Thus, among the Jesuits going to America we find Flemings, Neapolitans, Sicilians, Milanese, Bavarians, Bohemians, Austrians and other non-Spaniards. At times, though, they managed it apparently by camouflaging their real identities with Castilianized surnames. On the other hand, in the case of the other orders working in America, it seems that the recruitment of non-Spaniards was much rarer, perhaps because their structure was more locally-orientated, or perhaps because they were inspired by a more visible nationalism.[8]

As soon as the missionaries' decision to accept the call was ratified by the relevant authorities, they travelled to Seville – or, later, to Cadiz – or to Puerto de Santa Maria, Jérez de la Frontera, or San Lúcar de Barrameda, where they waited for authorization from the Casa de la Contratación to embark. They also had to wait for the actual ship that was to transport them to the New World. This waiting-period could last for almost a year, but finally, when the crown had paid the fare for their transatlantic passage and the costs of their maintenance, the missionaries put to sea under the leadership of the procurator who had come to Europe to recruit them. Once they reached port safely – something not to be taken for granted, since either shipwreck or capture by pirates were very real hazards – they were divided among the religious houses in the particular Province. In this way, they were incorporated into the great politico-ecclesiastical machine of America: they had become new missionaries under the patronage of the crown of Castile. The gears had meshed productively.[9]

From the second half of the seventeenth century, we encounter a variation, so far as the Franciscans were concerned. Within the Iberian peninsula, mission colleges were founded, with the intention of training young men who from the beginning of their religious careers planned to work in America or Africa. One example was the celebrated college of Escornalbou, founded in 1686 by that great missionary of New Spain, Antoni Llinás.

[8] See Lázaro de Aspurz, *La aportación extranjera a las misiones del Patronato Regio* (Madrid, 1946).
[9] Pedro Borges, 'Trámites para la organización de las expediciones misioneras a América (1780)', *Archivo Ibero-Americano*, 26 (1960), 405–72.

We have no overall statistics for the frequency or size of these expeditions to recruit missionaries, but we do know that they varied according to periods, according to order and even according to the different provinces or divisions within an order. Sometimes the expedition was undertaken just for one Province on its own; at other times, led by one procurator or by several it recruited personnel for more than one Province. There were Provinces which sent a recruiting expedition every three to five years; in other cases, the search for recruits became sporadic, or even unnecessary, as the American Provinces of the orders became thoroughly creolized.

The need for a locally recruited clergy was recognized from an early date. However, although creoles increasingly joined *peninsulares*, the church remained overwhelmingly white throughout the colonial period. Some early attempts to create a native (Indian) clergy for New Spain – for example the Colegio de Santa Cruz at Tlatelolco founded in 1536 and run by the Franciscans for the education of the sons of the Indian aristocracy – produced such meagre results that they seemed to justify a defeatist assessment of the possibilities. Most missionary friars and diocesan prelates, deeply ethnocentric, adopted an absolutely negative position on the question of the suitability of Indians for the Catholic priesthood.

Indians were thus virtually excluded from Holy Orders, even though the canons made by Provincial councils and diocesan synods never amounted, thanks to the influence of the Council of Trent, to any explicit total denial of ordination for them. Mestizos (half Spanish, half Indian) were in most cases excluded from ordination anyway, by reason of the impediment that their illegitimate births represented. In 1576 Pope Gregory XIII granted mestizo candidates a dispensation from this impediment, on account, as he said 'of the great shortage of priests who know an Indian language'; nevertheless, in practice, exclusion persisted and the door the pope had opened was left unused. Neither the general policy of the Congregation for the Propagation of the Faith in Rome after 1622 nor the condemnation of the continued exclusion of Indians and mestizos by the College of Cardinals in 1631 did anything to change the situation. Only in the second half of the eighteenth century, following a series of royal directives, can we identify significant numbers of Indian or mestizo priests in many bishoprics. Some were even canons of cathedrals. More often than not, however, they constituted a sort of 'second-class' clergy, who were relegated to remote rural parishes and who were denied most prospects of promotion.[10]

The female religious orders were born, in many cases at least, on American soil and appear not as a transplantation from the metropolis but as an autonomous local product. There occurred what amounts to a re-foundation of orders, with no juridical, only spiritual, affiliation to houses in the peninsula. All the female orders in Spanish America – Franciscans, Augustinians, Carmelites – were of the monastic, contemplative life and were neither missionary nor educational. Their missionary function so far as the 'republic of the Indians' was concerned was negligible. Since they were founded in America, the personnel of the female orders was, by an overwhelming majority, creole and to a lesser extent mestizo. Convents for women played an educational and charitable role of considerable importance for the daughters of the creole sector of society. They prepared girls for married life and received as permanent members those who would not, or could not, marry. Indian women were not, however, accepted as equals within the life of the convent. Some native women were admitted to convents, but they constituted a lower stratum of sisterhood, who attended to the manual labours within the convent. Indians and mestizos were more likely to be found as *beatas*, a somewhat inferior species of religious life which first appeared in New Spain shortly after the Spanish conquest, and one which served to evangelize women and to elevate them culturally as well as to enable them to devote themselves to social work. Some young creole and mestizo women engaged in a formal religious life outside the established orders, although in some cases they belonged to the Third Order (Franciscan). They would make a house that they owned into a convent, where they would devote themselves to prayer and to more or less extreme forms of penitence; at times, also, to charitable works. Two of the American women who have achieved official canonization belong to this category – St Rose of Lima (1586–1617) and St Mariana de Jesús (1618–45). Both of them correspond to a peculiarly

[10] Werner Promper, *Priesternot in Latëinamerika* (Louvain, 1965), 107–17; Juan Alvarez Mejía, 'La cuestión del clero indígena en la época colonial', *Revista Javeriana*, 44 (1955), 224–31, 245 (1956), 57–67, 209–19; Juan B. Olaechea Labayen, 'Sacerdotes indios de América del Sur en el siglo XVIII', *Revista de Indias*, 29 (1969), 371–91; *idem.*, 'La Ilustración y el clero mestizo en América', *Missionalia Hispanica*, 33 (1976), 165–79; Guillermo Figuera, *La Formación del clero indígena en la historia eclesiástica de América, 1500–1810* (Caracas, 1965).

Iberian type of devotion which had in itself little connection with the specific problems of Christianity in colonial Spanish America.[11]

Finally, it may be useful to single out a few individuals representative of the first century of evangelization, so long as we bear in mind that they cannot represent the whole diverse spectrum of early Christianity in America. Let us concentrate on four personalities among the Spanish-American episcopate in this first, missionary, stage. Though their circumstances differed, they had one thing in common: fully conscious of what a labour it would be, each was prepared to take on the mission of establishing a Christian church in America despite the ties to colonialism with which it was burdened from the outset.

Bartolomé de Las Casas, a Dominican friar (1484–1566) was bishop of Chiapas effectively for only one year (1545–6). His achievements lay elsewhere. He had his eyes opened in 1514 to the reality of America, and thereafter devoted the remaining half-century of his life to the defence of the Indians, battling against the shape the colonial system was taking. He fought it as a secular priest, as a friar, as a bishop, as a councillor at court, as a polemicist, as a historian and as delegate for the Indians. He allied himself with the crown to get the settlers' privileges annulled; he exerted pressure on the friars' conscience to stop them giving absolution to the encomenderos; he propagated his own vision of what the Indies should be in writing; he prophesied the destruction of Spain as its punishment for the cruelties it had inflicted on innocent Indians. It is true that he acquiesced in the importation of Africans as slaves to obviate the enslavement of native Americans. Some of the statements in his pamphlets and his histories were no doubt exaggerated. His greatness, however – untouched by his detractors – lies in the way he denounced and dissociated himself from the historical process of which he was a part. Insofar as Las Casas' life's work was founded on his convictions as a Christian, a friar and a bishop, he belongs among the greater reformers and 'liberators' in the church's history.[12]

---

[11] Fidel de Lejarza, 'Expansión de las clarisas en América y Extremo Oriente', *Archivo Ibero-Americano*, 14 (1954–5), 131–90, 265–310, 393–455, and 15 (1955–6), 5–85; Josefina Muriel de la Torre, 'Conventos de monjas en Nueva Espana, Oaxaca y Guadalajara', *Arte en América y Filipinas*, 2 (1949), 91–6; Aurelio Espinosa Pólit, *Santa Mariana de Jesús, hija de la Compañía de Jesús* (Quito, 1957).

[12] On Las Casas, see also Elliott, *CHLA*, I, ch. 6 and 9.

Vasco de Quiroga (1470–1565) first arrived in America as a priest, but holding a lay office, that of *oidor* in the audiencia of Mexico, where it took him no time to gauge the degradation of the Indians in colonial urban society. In 1532 he founded the Hospital de la Santa Fe for them, in the environs of the capital, an institution combining charitable, health and welfare, educational and catechetic functions. His experience in Mexico was to repeat itself in Michoacán, of which he became bishop in 1538. Modelled upon Platonist, humanist and evangelical ideals, the hospitals revived within the context of the colonial system the fraternity of the indigenous community which that system had destroyed: the residents enjoyed, among other things, communal property, work as a collective, religious and professional instruction, equality of economic status and community administration of their productivity. To furnish workers in the mission field, he founded the Seminary of St Nicholas in the shadow of the cathedral of Pátzcuaro: over 200 priests had already graduated from it by 1576. Quiroga represents the espousal of nativist policies without oppression, intended to free the Indians from exploitation by encomenderos. He also put into practice a missionary alternative which did not depend on either economic servitude or Hispanicization.[13]

Domingo de Santo Tomás, a Dominican friar (1499–1570) was typical of mendicant theologians and missionaries. He had long experience of Peru, where he arrived in 1540. In Lima he became a professor of theology, a specialist in questions affecting the natives, and a correspondent and informant of Las Casas. It was as a delegate of the Indians that he went to Spain in 1555 and remained until 1561, during the interminable and tortuous negotiations between the colonists, the Indians and the crown about the perpetuity of encomiendas. Earlier, he had toured the mountainous part of Peru and parts of Charcas, seeking out recommendations of the Indians being allowed to 'purchase' their freedom from the encomienda and collecting the funds that would be needed for them to do so, in an atmosphere highly charged with conflict. During his period of residence in Spain he published the first grammar of the Quechua language (1560). He made a deep impression upon the court, and in 1562 he was appointed to the see of La Plata in succession to Tomás de San Martín, his brother in religion and the

---

[13] Fintan B. Warren, *Vasco de Quiroga and his Pueblo Hospitals of Santa Fe* (Washington, D.C., 1963); M. Bataillon, 'Utopia e colonizaçao', *Revista de Historia*, 100 (1974), 387–98; 'Don Vasco de Quiroga, utopien', *Moreana*, 15 (1967), 385–94.

championship of Indian rights. He attended the Second Peruvian Provincial Council in 1567.

St Toribio de Mogrovejo (1538–1606) was educated at the Universities of Valladolid and Salamanca. He worked in the Inquisition of Granada till Philip II selected him for nothing less than the archbishopric of Lima (1580). In a whole quarter-century of governing the Peruvian church he carried out an immense task of organization. Several Peruvian Provincial Councils were held under his presidency – the Third in 1582, the Fourth in 1591 and the Fifth in 1601; likewise, the ten earliest Lima diocesan synods (1582, 1584, 1585, 1586, 1588, 1590, 1592, 1594, 1602 and 1604). He carried out pastoral visitations of his enormous archdiocese in the years 1581, 1582, 1584–8, 1593, 1601 and 1605–6. Without a doubt, Mogrovejo embodied several of the chief features of the Council of Trent's vision of a model bishop. Among them was his consciousness that responsibility for what took place under his jurisdiction could not be delegated. This brought him repeatedly into confrontation with viceroys and audiencia, and even with Philip II himself, for his so-called 'crime' of informing the pope directly about the situation of the church in the Indies.[14]

CONSOLIDATION OF THE CHURCH

By the first half of the seventeenth century, the church in all its aspects, secular and regular, clerical and lay, had been transplanted from the Iberian peninsula to the American colonies. After 1620, for example, no new bishoprics were created till 1777. Stabilization and consolidation were in every sense the watchwords. The church was, in effect, now living on the income it could draw from the great investment of effort it had made in the sixteenth century.

In one specific area only can one fairly speak of growth: the founding of universities. If we bear in mind that only two state-patronized universities (Mexico City and Lima) and three privately-organized universities (Santo Domingo, Quito and Bogotá) had been established in the sixteenth century, the extension of higher education in the seventeenth century was decisive. And it was the religious orders who largely shouldered this responsibility. The Jesuits established universities at Santiago de Chile, Córdoba, La Plata, Cuzco, Quito, Bogotá

[14] Vicente Rodríguez Valencia, *Santo Toribio de Mogrovejo, organizador y apóstol de Sur-América*, 2 vols. (Madrid, 1956–7).

and Mérida (Yucatán); the Dominicans at Santiago de Chile, Quito and Guatemala; the Franciscans at Cuzco. By contrast, in the eighteenth century most universities – Santiago de Chile, Caracas, Mérida (Maracaibo), Havana, Guadalajara, León (Nicaragua) – were founded by the episcopate. Admittedly, a significant proportion of these so-called universities were really nothing more than institutions for training the clergy; most offered instruction only in philosophy and divinity; only a few of them possessed chairs in canon or civil law; even fewer had chairs of classical or Indian languages; and universities offering instruction in medicine or natural sciences were very few indeed until well into the eighteenth century. Even in a large university like that of Mexico City, jurists and theologians were still overwhelmingly preponderant: as late as 1793 the university had 172 teachers of law, 124 of theology and a mere twelve of medicine. The colonial Spanish American universities achieved little in the way of original learning and research and offered little in the way of critical appraisal of society. Like the church which supported them, their social function was to confer legitimacy on the colonial system. Nevertheless, each of these academic centres fomented some intellectual activity in its area and laid the foundation for some kind of local tradition of advanced thought.[15]

Another seventeenth-century phenomenon was the much tougher attitude adopted towards the natives' practice of religion in the central zones of colonial hegemony. Up to a certain point, it may fairly be said that in the previous century the ideal of the local church and the cultivation of a measure of inter-cultural dialogue had taken precedence over the preaching of the gospel, but in the seventeenth century it was noted with concern that pagan religions had survived and went on affecting the lives of the natives in a thousand different ways. An enormous amount of evidence exists to demonstrate what might be considered a partial failure of the methods of evangelization that had been employed. It might logically look as though the conclusion should have been to launch a new missionary campaign to frustrate this developing syncretism, but reality was quite different. The epoch of the great missionaries was allowed to become a thing of the past and was replaced by a conservative and routine pastoral regime. The decision was taken to destroy anything that might be seen as evidence condemning past failures.

[15] See Agueda María Rodríguez Cruz, *Historia de las universidades hispanoamericanas: período hispánico*, 2 vols. (Bogotá, 1973); John Tate Lanning, *Academic culture in the Spanish colonies* (New York, 1940); Francisco Esteve Barba, *Cultura Virreinal* (Barcelona, 1965).

This conception was specially evident in the several campaigns undertaken 'to extirpate idolatry' in the Andes during the first half of the seventeenth century. The apparently casual discovery that certain pagan practices had persisted there let loose a war to the death, waged by Inquisitorial methods. Preaching against idolatry would systematically take place in each village; those alleged guilty of it were denounced to the authorities, and either their 'reconciliation' followed, or they were adjudged to be 'contumacious'. The sequel was imprisonment, physical destruction of any symbol deemed to be idolatrous and harsh punishment of the so-called sorcerers. The Indians were effectively terrorized, and a schizophrenic duplicity forced upon their lives. Outwardly they became Christian, while inwardly they remained adherents of indigenous religious creeds, ever more debased and disorganized. It is difficult to overestimate the impact of this turning inwards of the missionary endeavour. It certainly seems that the Indians' alienation from the world of the settlers, so often noted as one of the main features of their attitude to whites, was reinforced by these episodes.[16]

As in Spain, the instrument for dealing with religious dissent was the Inquisition which had been established by Ferdinand and Isabella. It had been transferred to America at least by 1519 and, later on, functioned through tribunals at Lima (founded 1570), Mexico City (founded 1571) and Cartagena (founded 1610). The Inquisition, however, had strictly speaking no jurisdiction over Indians. Its main function was to suppress Judaism and Protestantism (as well as witchcraft and sexual deviancy).

When those Jews who refused to be baptized as Christians were expelled from Spain in 1492, some of them took refuge in Portugal, though even there they had no lasting security. They arrived in the colonies of Castile either directly, under the most amazing varieties of camouflage, or indirectly, via Brazil. This resulted in Spanish American colonial society coming to consider the terms 'Portuguese' and 'Jewish' to be identical in meaning. It seems that many Jews became peacefully integrated with the settlers, and never attracted attention, as is demonstrated by the fact that only a very small number of cases was ever brought against them by the Inquisition. Others persisted in a state of

[16] L. Millones, 'Introducción al estudio de las idolatrías', *Aportes*, 4 (1967), 47–82; Pierre Duviols, *La Lutte contre les religions autochthones dans le Pérou colonial: l'extirpation de l'idolâtrie* (Lima and Paris, 1971).

crypto-Judaism. Of the crypto-Jews who fell into the hands of the Inquisition, perhaps the most noteworthy were those in the group led by Luis de Carvajal of Pánuco. The *auto de fé* of 1596 dealt with 80 heretics, of whom 25 were so-called *judaizantes*. Nine of Carvajal's relatives perished at the stake; he himself had his sentence commuted to banishment from the Indies. The Inquisition's annals abound with single cases of Portuguese who were alleged to be judaisers, specially in the port cities such as Veracruz, Cartagena, Buenos Aires and Lima and in such great centres of trade as Potosí. Often, however, the clandestine exercise of the Jewish religion could not be proved against them. In periods when antagonism to *conversos* was on the rise – particularly when Portugal was recovering her independence from Castile (1640–67) – simply to be Portuguese was enough to attract suspicion. One form of discrimination suffered by the Portuguese at the hands of the colonial authorities was that they were mulcted by them of *composiciones*, repeated money payments made in order to regularize their presumably illegal residence in the colonies. The Spanish crown regularly resorted to this exaction to meet its frequent financial crises.

In view of the bloody repression inflicted by the Spanish Inquisition on anyone thought to have the slightest leaning to, or sympathy for, Lutheran or other Protestant doctrines, it is not at all surprising that there are very few indications of any substantial Protestant presence in Spain's overseas dominions. Almost all the cases in this category coming before the Inquisition concerned foreigners – English, French, Dutch, Belgian and German. It is by no means clear, even then, whether the real motive for the trial was religious, rather than political, as for instance in the trials conducted in sixteenth-century New Spain, where almost all the defendants were seamen or pirates from the ships of Gaspard de Coligny, Jean Ribault, John Hawkins, Francis Drake and their like. Apart from these cases, there were short-lived plantings of Protestantism into Venezuela under the Welsers, in 1528–46, and on the Isthmus of Panama at the time of the Scottish colony there in 1698–1700.

The Inquisition in Spanish America did interpose its authority against blacks, slave and free, punishing them as much for any 'superstitious' practices as for any inclination to revolt. From this, it may be discerned that the slaves found that practising what African religion they could recall, while hiding behind a façade of conformity to Catholicism, kept alive simultaneously both the hope of liberation and the affirmation of the identity that was being denied them in colonial society. For the clergy, evangelizing the black slaves was a marginal concern, although there were some outstanding exceptions, such as Bishops Pedro de Carranza of Buenos Aires and Julian de Cortázar y Torres of Tucumán, and the two heroes of Cartagena, that great port of arrival for new slaves, the Jesuits, Alonso de Sandoval and Peter Claver. There were numerous sodalities which were composed exclusively of blacks and these provided opportunities for forms of religious expression in which syncretic practices could have full play.

The process of consolidating colonial ecclesiastical institutions, which, it is suggested, characterized the seventeenth century, corresponded to an important material change: this was the era when the patrimonial holdings of the religious orders and the secular parishes were formed. Originally, there were two basic forms of holding: money and property. These holdings originated in bequests by the settlers, the commonest source of the church's wealth from the sixteenth century onwards. At death, a settler would bequeath a capital sum to a specific religious house in return for spiritual services from the legatee, either as a chantry in which to say Mass for the departed, as a dowry for daughters as yet unmarried, or as another endowment. If the bequest took the form of money, the beneficiary would generally invest in *censos*, then the most usual form of credit. If the bequest took the form of property, the legatee would work it directly or lease it out to a third party, as was done in the case of many haciendas, urban properties and mines. The institutional character of the religious orders explains how they amassed patrimony; it almost always increased and hardly ever diminished. In such circumstances, it is little wonder that each religious order, and even each house, should have come to wield considerable financial and economic power. The case of the Jesuits, who were expelled from the Indies in 1767 and had their 'temporalities' sequestrated by the state, is well known. Modern studies of Jesuit-owned haciendas,[17] for instance, highlight their businesslike management (which included the use of slave labour), and have contributed to the impression that the Society of Jesus was an immensely powerful institution. But in this sense it was in no way exceptional among the religious orders.

The secular church, too, enjoyed an agrarian patrimony, based on

[17] E.g., Germán Colmenares, *Haciendas de los jesuitas en el Nuevo Reino de Granada, siglo XVIII* (Bogotá, 1969); Pablo Macera, *Instrucciones para haciendas de Jesuitas en el Perú* (Lima, 1965); Herman W. Konrad, *A Jesuit hacienda in colonial Mexico: Santa Lucia 1576–1767* (Stanford, 1980).

precisely the same foundation as that of the friars. In addition, it levied tithes on whites and mestizos and even, to a certain degree, on Indians, which constituted a form of taxation for the support of those on episcopal, capitular and parochial payrolls. The sums collected in this way varied greatly from one diocese to another, according to the density of population in the region and the degree of economic prosperity. (In the decade 1620–30, for instance, the yield of the tithe could vary between 60,000 pesos and less than 10,000 pesos, depending on the bishopric.) The amount produced by the tithe became an important factor in grading episcopal sees into a hierarchy. As time passed, the collection of tithes was farmed out to laymen in return for their payment of a sum of ready money. In many places, the volume of bequests received, and of investments made, produced a situation in which bishoprics were able to function as financial institutions. They started by managing the returns from bequests of real estate for the support of works of devotion (*juzgados de capellanías*) and ended by becoming the major source of credit and investment capital in colonial Spanish America.[18]

Another indication of the stagnation into which the church had sunk in the seventeenth century is the narrowing of vision, the channelling of the energies into a multiplicity of internal, domestic disputes which have been amply chronicled in historical writings on the church. There were lawsuits over questions of jurisdiction between bishops and the civil power, ranging from the fundamental to the trivial, and others between bishops and secular clergy and religious orders. (One need only recall the litigation of Cárdenas with the Jesuits in Paraguay, or of Palafox with the Jesuits of Puebla.) Religious houses also had lawsuits with one another over supposed defamation, or in defence of their respective dependants. Within a particular religious order, creoles and peninsular Spaniards contested matters concerning the government of the order, which had to be settled from Madrid or Rome, often with directions to adopt the artificial practice of the *alternativa*: that is, alternation in office, with the groups taking it in turns to hold directive office in each jurisdiction. We have here what is probably one of the most revealing features of the Baroque religious mentality in America.[19]

[18] See, for example, Michael P. Costeloe, *Church wealth in Mexico* (Cambridge, 1967).
[19] A. Tibesar, 'The Alternativa: a study in Spanish-Creole relations in seventeenth-century Peru', *The Americas*, 11 (1955), 229–83.

Whilst in the seventeenth century the central administration of the church appeared to be dozing in the sunny uplands of pastoral conservatism, a most important extension of the missionary front was taking place, thanks to the regulars, principally the Jesuits and the Franciscans, the orders which had remained outside the vicious circle of inertia and stagnation, and which had never entirely interrupted their missionary efforts, though they often experienced ill-success, or lacked continuity. The Jesuits, the last of the great religious orders to make an appearance in the work of converting America, for that very reason enjoyed the best prospects for establishing themselves in the mission field. Thus, for example, right from the start they showed notable reluctance to take on *doctrinas* in the central zones of colonial occupation, and the few that they did in the end accept, like Juli, beside Lake Titicaca, were assumed under significant restrictions. Two sorts of problem area appealed to the Jesuits: communities handicapped by the fact that few of the religious lived outside the walls of their houses, and those where the church was excessively dependent upon patrons and intimately involved with the encomenderos.

The Jesuit Reductions, dating from the first decade of the seventeenth century, embodied a clear alternative to existing methods of pastoral evangelism and marked a break with the concepts that had prevailed since the period of missionary experimentation in the first half of the sixteenth century and a return to the world of Las Casas and Quiroga.[20] The Jesuits have the historic merit of putting into large-scale practice a model of evangelism that contrasted with the then reigning formula of preaching the gospel and at the same time colonizing and hispanicizing the converts, as though evangelists had to act as the transmission for the engine of integration. The Reductions defiantly proclaimed the need to construct a society parallel to that of the settlers, free of interference either from them or from a civil administration sensitive to their interests. Since the Reductions refused to act as reservoirs supplying the settlers with labour, they were able to set about an evangelism that was based upon concern for the convert's whole personality. Their aim was not simply to indoctrinate, but to strengthen the economic and social lives of the Indians in every respect. We can arrive at an

[20] See A. Echanove, 'Origen y evolución de la idea jesuítica de reducción', *Missionalia Hispanica*, 12 (1955), 95–144 and 13 (1956), 497–540; X. Albó, 'Jesuitas y culturas indígenas', *América indígena*, 26 (1966), 249–308, 395–445.

Table 2 *Jesuit Reductions in Spanish America*

Missionary area	Activity begun	Number of centres	Number of Indians settled in Reductions in 1767
Paraguay	1607	40	*c.* 130,000
Moxos	1682	15	18,500
Mainas	1700	32	19,200
Los Llanos and Casanare	1659	36	?
Tarahumara, Sonora and Sinaloa	1614	40	*c.* 40,000
California	1695	19	*c.* 22,000

approximate idea of the proportions of the 'sacred experiment' throughout Spanish America from Table 2.

The effectively utopian character of the Reduction system is clear from the many antagonisms it excited – from Spain's colonial competitors, from the civil authority, from the settlers (deprived of access to Indian labour) and from the diocesan church, among others. As its basic principle, evangelism through the Reduction system adopted the belief that 'one has to make men before one can make Christians'. But it has also to be recognized that the system was doomed to a less than full measure of success in that 'it required the so-called Christian world of the colonies to permit the Indian to be fully a man, and fully free, without suffering either injustice or exploitation', as Bartomeu Meliá said. Antagonism towards the Reductions was to be one factor behind the expulsion of those responsible for them in the late eighteenth century.

Elsewhere in the mission field a renewed Franciscan cycle of evangelism is also clearly visible. The order had a missionary and teaching tradition which stretched back to early days in the Antilles; in New Spain it had notable achievements to its credit, as we may reflect if we recall, for example, the work of Zumárraga, or Sahagún, or Motolinía. The order had also passed through a process of creolization, with a dimming of its evangelistic ardour. Although, of all the orders, it was the one with most missionaries at work, from the mid-seventeenth century onwards it had to return to dependence on volunteers from Spain to assist both in the old and in the new mission fields.

The revival of the Franciscan missionary impulse took on a reforming

Table 3 *Franciscan Colleges in Spanish America*

College	Year of foundation	Missions served by the College
Querétaro	1683	Zacatecas, Nayarit, Texas
Mexico City	1731	Tamaulipas, Tarahumara, California
Ocopa	1734	Huallaga, Ucayali, Urubamba, Apolobamba
Chillán	1754	Araucania, Chiloé
Tarija	1755	Chiriguanos
Moquegua	1795	Santa Ana del Cuzco, Karabaya, Apolobamba
Tarata	1795	Yuracarés, Guarayos

tinge right from the start. In 1683 the Majorcan Friar Antoni Llinás led a group of Spanish Franciscans who transformed the convent at Querétaro into the first Apostolic College for the Propagation of the Faith, the explicit purpose of which was missionary work. It was the beginning of a whole chain of similar colleges across the Americas as can be seen in Table 3.[21] Just as the Jesuits had been inspired to some degree by the Franciscans in sixteenth-century New Spain, so the Franciscans in the late seventeenth and eighteenth centuries adopted many of their missionary methods from the Jesuits. This repeatedly brought them into bitter confrontation with the settlers as, for example, in Chiriguanos. After the departure of the Jesuits in 1767, the Franciscans widened their responsibility and took over, and sometimes extended, many of the Jesuit missions, often in conjunction with other orders: California (shared with the Dominicans), Los Llanos de Orinoco (though the Dominicans took on the missions in Casanare), Chiriguanos and some of those in Paraguay (where others were assumed by the Dominicans and the Mercedarians). At any rate, at the end of the colonial period it was the Franciscans who were taking the lion's share of the church's missionary work – from the south of Chile to California, Arizona and New Mexico.

[21] Isidro Félix de Espinosa, *Crónica de los Colegios de Propaganda Fide de la Nueva España* (2nd edn, Washington, 1964); Félix Saiz Díez, *Los Colegios de Propaganda Fide en Hispano-América* (Madrid, 1969).

THE EFFECTS OF THE NEW REGALISM ON THE CHURCH IN THE LATE EIGHTEENTH CENTURY

An intense conflict of ideologies, with profound political and ecclesiastical repercussions, took place in eighteenth-century Spanish America, just as it did in contemporary Spain. We have already seen that as a result of a series of pontifical concessions the crown exercised patronage over the church in Spanish America from the sixteenth century onwards. During the seventeenth century ambitious theoretical treatises defending regalism were written by, amongst others, Juan de Solórzano Pereira, Pedro Frasso and Juan Luis López. With the advent of the French Bourbons, regalism was considerably reinforced by gallicanism. Eighteenth-century treatises by, for example, Alvarez de Alren, Rivadeneyra and Manuel Josef de Ayala, took the view that ecclesiastical patronage was an inalienable prerogative of sovereignty, a consequence of the divine right of kings. At the same time, gallicanism was reformist in tendency and enlightened in temperament, fond of critical erudition and deeply interested in education at all levels. Its programme derived from the ideas of such men as Mabillon, Bossuet, Fleury, Alexandre and van Espen, and from the eager collaboration of Feijóo, Barbadinho, Macanaz, Mayans and others, in the Iberian peninsula. In the Americas, gallicanism found its advocates in Toribio Rodríguez de Mendoza in Lima, José Pérez Calama in Mexico and Quito, Espejo y Santa Cruz also in Quito, Moreno y Escandón in Bogotá, José Antonio de San Alberto in Córdoba (Tucumán) and La Plata, and Fabián y Fuero and Manual Abad y Queipo in New Spain, to name but a few.[22]

Enlightened reformers saw the Jesuits as the decisive obstacle to the further assertion of state power over the church. The Jesuits held positions of wide power in the field of education and, more generally, in matters of conscience. 'Jesuit doctrine' came, as a term, to be virtually synonymous with suspected disloyalty to the crown and to the rights it now claimed. The Thomist doctrine concerning the popular origins of sovereignty, put forward by, for example, Francisco Suarez (1548–1619) and Juan de Mariana (1536–1624), has been alleged as a ground for such a suspicion, but the scholastic tradition was, in fact, common to the whole church. If the Jesuits became odious to the

[22] Mario Góngora, 'Estudios sobre el galicanismo y la "ilustración católica" en América española', *Revista Chilena de Historia y Geografía*, 125 (1957), 5–60. And Mario Góngora, *Studies in the colonial history of Spanish America* (Cambridge, 1975), 194–205.

governing class in the era of enlightened despotism, the reasons have to be sought elsewhere. One possible explanation was the Society's closely-knit hierarchical structure, which, from its foundation, had made it almost impervious to manipulation by Madrid. Of all the orders, the Jesuits were the most independent of episcopal authority, the most devoted to the papacy, the most resistant to royal bureaucracy. The Jesuits were at least as powerful and wealthy in Spain as they were in the colonies, so that the theme – on which their detractors continually harped – of the so-called state within a state in Paraguay was no more than a political stalking-horse. Spanish politicians did no more than fill their sails with winds already blowing in at gale force from France, Portugal and Austria. Beyond this, it has also to be observed that when the Spanish government seized its chance to dismantle the solid socio-economic patrimony the Jesuits had built up – haciendas, as well as colleges and missions – those sectors of society and the clergy whose self-interest was served did not need to ape anyone else to express their own long-felt desires.

The anti-Jesuit campaign was quite clearly under way from the middle of the eighteenth century. Every conceivable tactic was deployed against them. Finally, Charles III, listening to his Jansenist ministers, discharged the full weight of his fears and suspicions in the Pragmatic Sanction of 27 February 1767, by which, following the example of Portugal (1759), he expelled all members of the order from his dominions, both in Europe and America. The consequences could not fail to be calamitous, despite the unquestionable determination of the state and many of the bishops to fill the place left vacant by the Jesuits. Universities, colleges and missions lost staff in the persons of over 2,500 Fathers, the majority creoles, all of them cosmopolitan, well-qualified, disciplined and efficient. In effect, the defeat of the Jesuits was the defeat of the one force within the church best able to dispute the authoritarian aspirations of the new regalism. Without its Jesuits, the church lay practically defenceless before the state and had to enter the immediate pre-Independence period disarmed.

Regalism on the offensive, having rid itself of the Society of Jesus, now moved in the direction of placing the ecclesiastical apparatus under even closer state control. Charles III forbade first the teaching and then the public defence of 'Jesuit doctrine'. In 1768–9 he summoned a series of Provincial councils of the church in Spanish America 'to exterminate pernicious new doctrines, replacing them with the old, sound ones'.

Four councils, the first for over a century and a half, met in 1771–4, but the results were less than striking. Mexico's council was far from obsequious to the monarch and actually asked the pope to make all the Jesuits secular clergy. In Bogotá the proceedings were so ambiguous that the decisions were inconclusive and had to be declared void. In Lima the council busied itself with reform of the clergy but, in denouncing 'Jesuit doctrine' as it was bidden to do, failed to display the passion civil authority looked for, whereupon Madrid riposted by showing extreme lack of interest in approving or ratifying the determinations of the prelates at the council. Lastly, in La Plata the council became a battleground between the local metropolitan, who championed acceptance of the royal call, and his brother of Buenos Aires, who remained unimpressed by it. What the La Plata assembly in fact produced was one of the earliest formulations of that essential feature of democratic behaviour – recognition that the decisions of the majority were binding upon the minority.[23]

During the last decades of Spanish colonial rule the church (especially the predominantly Spanish higher clergy) was more dependent on and subordinate to the state than ever before. In the tax revolt of the Comuneros in the Provinces of El Socorro, Tunja, Sogamoso, Pamplona and Los Llanos of New Granada in March 1780 the protagonists were the creoles (although, as in other places, they used the mestizos and Indians to defend their interests). The representative of the colonial authority who had to face up to the crisis was Archbishop Caballero y Góngora of Bogotá. His strategy was a masterly piece of Machiavellianism. First, he appeared to accept the demands of the insurgents, as long as it looked as though they were carrying the protesters to victory. Later, he denounced the agreements signed, and let repression loose when authority secured the military advantage to do so.[24] At the same time Peru was convulsed by the deepest commotion that ever wracked Andean society: thousands of Indians and mestizos rebelled against colonial abuses, both old and new. August 1780 saw the central area of the Audiencia of Charcas (Upper Peru) – Chayanta, Yampara, Purqu and Aullagas – break out in open revolt; November 1780, the regions of Cuzco, Arequipa, Huamanga and Puno; and March 1781

[23] A. Soria-Vasco, 'Le Concile Provincial de Charcas de 1774 et les Déclarations des Droits de l'Homme', *L'Année Catholique*, 15 (1971), 511.
[24] The role of Archbishop Caballero y Góngora in the suppression of the comuneros of New Granada has been examined in John L. Phelan, *The people and the king. The Comunero Revolution in Colombia, 1781* (Madison, 1978).

those of La Paz, Oruro, Cochabamba and Chuquisaca. On which side did the church align itself? The few priests who fought or sympathized with the rebels did so from necessity. On the other hand, however, from the outset the whole clerical estate intuitively identified its destiny with that of the white minority and allowed itself to be used by the oppressive civil power as an instrument for the 'pacification' (that is, subjugation) of the non-whites. The sharpness of the division between the two sides furnished further evidence that the church was there to serve the colonial state rather than the Indians. There has been some speculation about the alleged Tupamarist sympathies of the creole bishop of Cuzco, Juan Manuel de Moscoso y Peralta; in fact, however, he never had any such sympathy; there was only a conspiracy between a local canon and two royal officials, Benito de la Mata Linares and Jorge de Escobedo. If such sympathies existed anywhere among the lower clergy or the missionaries, their indoctrination by the church authorities would have trained them to hide such feelings successfully.

By 1808–10 and the final crisis of the colonial system, however, the loyalty of the predominantly creole lower clergy to the crown was less certain. They increasingly resented the virtual monopoly of high ecclesiastical posts by the *peninsulares*. Many of their privileges, especially the *fuero eclesiastico* which gave them immunity from civil jurisdiction, were coming under attack. And a series of measures culminating in the consolidation or amortization decree of 26 December 1804 attempted (with only limited success, it should be said) to appropriate the landed properties and the capital belonging to religious foundations and chantries. Parish priests were dependent on the income from these endowments to supplement their low salaries. For the vast armies of clerics with no benefice under royal patronage (estimated to be four-fifths of the secular clergy in New Spain at the end of the eighteenth century), as well as for large numbers of regulars, they were the only source of income. The lower clergy played a leading role in some of the revolutions for independence, most notably the revolts of Hidalgo and Morelos in Mexico (1810–15). Although the rejection of the traditional authority of the crown throughout Spanish America during the second and third decades of the nineteenth century inevitably put in question the authority of the church, so closely linked were the two, the latter, of course, survived the wars of independence. But so did the concept of the *patronato*. The governments of the new republics were just as determined as the Spanish crown had been to control the Catholic church by claiming and exercising the right to make appointments to ecclesiastical offices and at the same time restricting its power and privileges and reducing its property. The relationship between church and state was a central political issue in most Spanish American republics throughout the nineteenth century.

15

THE CATHOLIC CHURCH IN COLONIAL BRAZIL*

The history of the church in Brazil has traditionally been open to two basic interpretations. These interpretations are irreconcilable, because they represent the views of two sectors of society which have been in permanent conflict ever since the establishment of the Christian church there. The first interpretation stems from the attitude of the original colonizer. It can best be summed up in the words of King João III addressing Tomé de Souza, the first governor-general of Brazil: 'The main reason which has lead me to colonize Brazil is to convert the people therein to our holy Catholic faith.'[1] According to this view, European settlement of Brazil was motivated above all by spiritual priorities, for it was aimed at the conversion of the Indian, the expansion of the church and the spread of the true faith to those in darkness. The second interpretation is attributable to those people who suffered the conse-quences of the labour demands of the European settlers. These were mainly Indians, Africans imported as slaves and their descendants born into slavery in Brazil. According to the chronicler, Claude d'Abbeville, an Indian elder named Momboré-uaçu told French colonizers in Maranhão in 1612: 'The Portuguese sent for their priests, who came and put up crosses and began to teach our people and baptize them. Later, the Portuguese said that neither they nor their priests could live without slaves to serve and work for them.'[2] This view equates evangelization with exploitation and slavery.

The process of evangelization in colonial Brazil, spread over three centuries, occurred in five movements, or cycles, which corresponded

---

* Translated from the Portuguese by Dr David Brookshaw; revised and reduced in length by the Editor.
[1] Quoted in E. Hoornaert, 'A evangelização e a cristandade durante o primeiro período colonial', in *História da Igreja no Brasil* (Petrópolis, 1977), 24.
[2] Claude d'Abbeville, *Histoire de la mission des Pères capucins de l'Ile de Maragnon et terres circonvoisines*

to five areas of colonization: the coastal belt (especially the north-east); its hinterland; Maranhão and Pará (the Amazon); Minas Gerais and the west; and São Paulo and the south. Missionary activity was undertaken by four religious orders – Jesuits, Franciscans, Carmelites and Benedictines – under the aegis of the *Padroado Real* (Royal Patronage) in Lisbon, and two other orders – Capuchins and Oratorians, who depended on the *Propaganda Fide* in Rome (founded in 1622 to centralize the missionary work of the Catholic church and to counteract the *Padroado* in Portugal and the *Patronato* in Spain). In the *Diálogo sobre a conversão do gentio* (1556), which was the first theological treatise to emerge from the Brazilian missionary experience, the Jesuit Manuel de Nóbrega defended the view that the conversion of the Indian was only possible after he had been subjugated. Collaboration between soldiers and missionaries was thus given an air of legitimacy. Indian religions were viewed as idolatry. The missionaries sought to exorcize all vestige of that which was seen as idolatry, ignorance, superstition and deviation from the 'Holy Catholic Faith'. Often undergoing considerable hardship, the missionaries made contact with the Indians in order to persuade them to abandon their mistaken ways. Later, the famous Jesuit, Antônio Vieira (1608–97), put forward in numerous writings his view of the colonization of Brazil, according to which the colonizing process was part of God's general design to permit all peoples of the world to know the true faith. According to Vieira, evangelization was impossible without colonization. For this reason, the 'discovery' and 'conquest' of the Indies were thought to have been the work of God Himself, and were even considered the greatest event in the history of salvation after the creation of the world and the coming of Christ.

It was during the reign of João III (1521–57) that Portugal became interested in Brazil as providing a suitable environment for the production of sugar. However, as sugar-cane could only be cultivated in the humid, tropical coastal zone, the colonial sugar boom was limited mainly to the north-eastern coastal belt between Natal and Salvador, with lesser centres in the area around Vitória, Rio de Janeiro, São Vicente and Santos in the south, and São Luís do Maranhão in the north. Sugar remained the most important cash crop throughout the history of colonial Brazil, and the demands of sugar production led to a system of labour based on slavery, first Indian, then African. The deep-seated traditions of Portuguese Catholicism permeated the whole ideology of agrarian capitalism in Brazil. Religious practices, however, were intricately linked to the patriarchal family structure of the great sugar plantations and centred on the chapel, the private oratory and devotion to the saints. They did not generally require the presence of missionary priests. The religious orders directed their activity above all at converting the Indians and, it might be said, transforming their way of life and work to fit in with the new priorities of the Portuguese colonizing state.

From the beginning the Jesuits were the most active in the coastal areas. The first six arrived at Salvador da Bahia with Governor Tomé da Sousa in 1549, less than a decade after the Society's foundation and more than two decades before they made their appearance in Mexico.[3] The experiences of Manuel de Nóbrega (1517–70) and José de Anchieta (1534–97) on the Brazilian coastal belt preceded those of Matteo Ricci (1551–1610) in Macao and of Roberto de Nóbili (1577–1656) in Goa. The growth of the Jesuit community in Brazil was rapid, and the number of Brazilian-born Jesuits steadily increased until the sudden expulsion of the order in 1759 (see Table 1).

Table 1 *Jesuits in Brazil*[4]

1549	6 Jesuits		all foreign
1574	110 ,,	14%	Brazilian
1610	165 ,,	17%	,,
1654	170 ,,	34%	,,
1698	304 ,,	37%	,,
1732	362 ,,	45%	,,
1757	474 ,,	44%	,,

The Jesuits organized their missionary activity by linking their colleges, which were situated on the coast, to Indian villages and missionary settlements (*aldeias*). The colleges trained missionaries for service in the villages, at least at an initial stage. The network of mission settlements was begun in 1553 in the area around Salvador da Bahia at the instigation of the third governor-general, Mem de Sá, but with the steep decline in the Indian population,[5] and the growth of the

---

[3] On the arrival of the Jesuits in Brazil and their activities up to 1580, see Johnson, *CHLA*, I, ch. 8.

[4] Hoornaert, 'A evangelização', 46.

[5] On the decline of the Indian population, see Marcílio, *CHLA*, II, ch. 2.

labour requirements of the sugar plantations, the Jesuits tried later to establish their missions far from the centres of colonization, in order to protect the Indians from the slave system. This was the case in the north-eastern hinterland and in the Amazon. In the coastal belt the Jesuits, like other orders, began to cater more exclusively for the white population of the towns and their black slaves.

There was never any missionary activity directed specifically at the blacks. Rather, the African slave was seen as belonging by right to a patriarchal family, at the head of which was a white master. Christian teaching was carried out in Portuguese from the very beginning and, in this sense, contrasted with the method of instruction to which the Indians were subjected and which was carried out in a type of Tupi *lingua franca* devised by the Jesuits especially for the purpose. The Jesuits themselves relied on black slavery, not only in their colleges, but also on their landed estates (*fazendas*) and in the mission settlements (*aldeamentos*). Those of them who dared to criticize this state of affairs, such as Gonçalo Leite (1545–1603) and Miguel Garcia (1550–1614), were quickly repatriated.[6]

The Franciscans also operated through a tripartite system involving coastal convents, landed estates and mission settlements in the interior. In fact, all the orders dependent on the *Padroado* possessed *fazendas*, for it was a way of obtaining a certain amount of economic independence within the Portuguese colonial system. Beginning in 1585, the Franciscan order fanned out along the coastal belt from Olinda, concentrating above all on the strip between Paraíba and Alagoas, but also with convents in Salvador, Espírito Santo and Rio de Janeiro. The activities of the Franciscans were less vigorous than those of the Jesuits, and certainly less radical, being concerned mainly with offering 'spiritual guidance' to the inhabitants of Olinda, Igaraçu, Itamaracá, Goiana, Salvador, Rio de Janeiro, São Vicente and Santos. Only rarely did the Franciscans enter the debate on 'Indian freedom'. On the contrary, they often supported 'justifiable war' against the Indians (for example during the campaign against the Caetés in 1560). Moreover, they occasionally took on the responsibility of administering settlements which the colonial administration had confiscated from the Jesuits, such as happened in Paraíba in 1585. During the second half of the eighteenth century Franciscan friars in Brazil numbered more than 1,000. But after

6 Serafim Leite, *Historia da Companhia de Jesus no Brasil*, 10 vols. (Rio de Janeiro, 1938–50), II, 227, 229.

1767 their number and importance declined, as did those of all the religious orders in Brazil.

The Carmelites, who arrived in Brazil in 1580, similarly established *fazendas* and *aldeamentos*. They also possessed a considerable number of African slaves. The order spread northwards from its base at Olinda throughout Pernambuco, Paraíba, Maranhão, Pará and the Amazon, where it administered an important network of mission settlements during the first part of the eighteenth century. Further south, the Carmelites were active in Bahia, Rio de Janeiro, Santos, Santa Catarina, São Paulo and Minas Gerais.

The Benedictines arrived in Bahia in 1581. From there they spread to Rio de Janeiro (1585), Olinda (1592), Paraíba (1596) and São Paulo (1598). In the south they reached São Vicente (1643), Santos and Sorocaba (1660) and Jundiaí (1668). The Dutch occupation of the north-east (1630–54) had a disastrous effect on the order, but in the mid-eighteenth century there were some 200 Benedictine monks in Brazil, after which numbers began to decline. The Benedictine order did not administer many mission settlements, the hub of its activity being in the monasteries and on the landed estates. In order to survive, the order depended on large numbers of slaves, who were called 'slaves of the saints'.

The hinterland behind the sugar belt was opened up in the seventeenth century along the navigable rivers, the Rio São Francisco and its tributaries, the Parnaíba and Paranaíba, not least because of the demand for Indian labour. Four religious orders – Capuchins, Oratorians, Jesuits and Franciscans – participated in the expeditions from Pernambuco and Bahia and provided missionaries for the Indians. The Capuchins – French, or more precisely Bretons, prior to 1698 and the break in diplomatic relations between Portugal and France and from 1705 Italian – were from 1646 active in the interior of Pernambuco. They gradually established Hospitals in Olinda (1649), Recife (1659) and Rio de Janeiro (1653) in order to finance their work with the Indians. The Capuchins were 'apostolic missionaries', that is, they depended directly on the *Propaganda Fide* in Rome as opposed to the 'royal missionaries', whose support came from the *Padroado* in Lisbon. And the Capuchins were popular. The Italians, in particular, used the system of ambulatory missions recommended by the Council of Trent which were well received by the people. The most outstanding missionaries of the Breton period were Martinho and Bernardo of Nantes, and of the Italian period, Apolônio de Todi, Clemente de Adorno, Carlos José de Spezia and Anibal de Genova. The opposition to Indian slavery voiced by Martinho of Nantes brought him into conflict with the great estate owners of the area. The Oratorians, who were also active in the interior of Pernambuco from 1669, were Portuguese. They took over four villages which, prior to the Dutch occupation, had been the responsibility of the Jesuits and Franciscans. The Oratorian missionary movement was, however, short-lived. From 1700, they were mainly involved in giving spiritual assistance to the white settlers and their slaves as the Indians had all but disappeared from the interior of Pernambuco. The Franciscans also operated in the interior along the valley of the Rio São Francisco. In 1657, the order was given responsibility by the king for new missions situated between Bahia and Paraíba. Finally, the Jesuits were also active in the interior. Indeed, they were the first order to penetrate inland, for during the 1650s there was already a Jesuit college on the banks of the lower São Francisco, opposite Penedo. In their settlements in the interior they had excellent missionaries, such as Jacob Roland, José Coelho, João de Barros, Antonio de Oliveira and Luís Vicêncio Mamiani, who developed plans for building villages far from the towns, plantations and sugar mills. The proximity of mission settlements to centres of colonization had been responsible for the elimination of a large proportion of the Indian population on the coastal belt. In the interior, the Indians survived better because of the abundance of unoccupied lands.

In the Estado de Maranhão which included the whole of the Amazon region, missionaries were in effect military chaplains, at least in the beginning. The city of São Luís do Maranhão was taken from the French in 1615 by an expedition which included two Carmelites. Immediately following this, military expeditions established an outpost at Belém (1616) and began to penetrate the vast river system of the Amazon, building forts at Gurupá, Pauxis (present-day Óbidos), Tapajós (present-day Santarém), São José do Rio Negro (present-day Manaus), as well as others at the head of the Rios Negro, Branco, Solimões and Madeira. Missionaries accompanied the military expeditions and attempted to herd the many Indians encountered into mission settlements, wherever possible without violence. Most of the modern municipalities in the Amazon region date from these settlements which were normally situated at the junctions of rivers, or in areas rich in herbs, spices and other natural forest products – sarsaparilla, cloves, cinnamon, cacao, indigo, rubber, different types of oil and groundnuts, all of which were known and used by the Indians.

There were three predominant religious orders in the Amazon region: the Carmelites (from 1615), Franciscans (from 1617) and Jesuits (from 1638). Here again the most active were the Jesuits. From the beginning, missionaries came into conflict with the Portuguese settlers who relied on Indian slaves, as the state of Maranhão was poorer than the state of Brazil and did not therefore have such easy access to African slave labour. The Jesuits were eventually able to enjoy considerable administrative power and influence over the regional economy which was based on the harvest of natural crops – harvested not by slave labour as such but rather through a type of forced labour peculiar to the area and known as *repartição*, which was described by the Jesuit chronicler, João Daniel. There were various periods of conflict between settlers and Jesuits over the use of Indian labour; in Maranhão one of them led to the expulsion of Antônio Vieira in 1661. Between 1667 and 1678 there was further conflict and social upheaval in Belém do Pará, followed by a period of relative calm up until the time when Portugal, during the reign of José I (1750–77), embarked upon a policy in Maranhão and Pará which brought it into conflict with the missionaries and resulted in the expulsion of 155 Jesuits from the region in 1759 (along with 474 from Brazil).

The Carmelites played an important role in their missions along the banks of the Rios Negro and Solimões during the first half of the eighteenth century. Certain aspects of their activities require further research: for example, their role in the frontier disputes between Portugal and Spain, their supposed participation in the 'War of Ajuricaba' (1723–7) and their attitude towards Indian forced labour. Three different branches of the Portuguese Franciscans were summoned by the king to work in the Amazon region: the Piety (Piedade) in 1683; Our Lady of the Conception (Conceição) in 1706; and Saint Anthony (Santo Antônio) in 1717. The Brothers of Mercy (Mercedários), of Spanish origin, also participated in missionary activity in the Amazon from their massive convent at Belém. The king spent vast sums of money to establish these missions, which were distributed after 1693 in the following manner: Jesuits along the northern bank of the Amazon; Franciscans and Brothers of Mercy along the south bank;

Carmelites in the upper Amazon region above the settlement of São José do Rio Negro (present-day Manaus).

Northern Brazil was the great field for missionary activity. By the second half of the eighteenth century some 50,000 Indians were settled in *aldeias*, most of them under the control of the Jesuits and the Franciscans. In the 1750s, however, not only were the Jesuits expelled, but under Pombal's legislation (1755–8), first applied to Maranhão and Pará and then to the rest of Brazil, the aldeias were transformed into parishes, parish priests substituted for missionaries, Tupi replaced by Portuguese, and the missionaries themselves restricted to evangelical work with still uncontacted tribes.[7]

Missionary activity in the gold and diamond mining areas – the present-day states of Minas Gerais, Goiás and Mato Grosso do Sul – during the first half of the eighteenth century was unique in that it was restricted to the secular clergy. This was due to specific policies developed by the crown. Strict controls on the export of gold and diamonds to Portugal, and on all official trade, had to be maintained and smuggling had to be effectively stamped out. This largely explains the ban on the entry of missionaries into Minas (1711) and the withdrawal of the Jesuits who had established themselves at Ribeirão do Carmo (now Mariana) in 1721. The Portuguese state feared the independence of the religious orders. For this reason, the religious activity of the mining period was restricted to the secular clergy and lay organizations, the so-called 'tertiary orders'. The mining area was, therefore, characterized by churches and not convents. The Jesuits had no tertiary order, which explains why the more radical and less traditionalist influence of the Jesuits was minimal in the mining areas.

In the south both Jesuits and Franciscans were active in the area of São Vicente in the mid-sixteenth century. Secular priests founded the first Casa de Misericordia in Brazil, a social welfare organization which was to spread throughout the country. The founding of a Jesuit college at São Paulo de Piritininga in January 1554 marked the beginning of expansion inland. The college, built on the banks of the Rio Anhembi was far removed from the coast where the Indian was enslaved and forced to work on sugar plantations. Many Indian settlements were built in the vicinity of the township of São Paulo, and there was an attempt

[7] See Hemming, *CHLA*, II, ch. 13.

on the part of the Jesuits to create something along the lines of their Paraguay missions. In the ensuing conflicts the Benedictines, whose monastery was built with the money of a slave hunter, Fernão Dias Paes Leme, sided with the colonists and the Jesuits with the Indians. The Franciscans and Carmelites later appeared on the scene and sided with the colonists. At the beginning of the seventeenth century, São Paulo was a poor town, with a mixed European/Indian population, speaking mainly Tupi. There were no export products, the only economic activities being subsistence agriculture, some cattle raising and the trade in Indian slaves. The conflict between colonists and Jesuits became public, and the latter were expelled in 1640, only returning in 1653 on condition that they would not get involved in 'Indian affairs', but limit themselves to their 'pastoral role'.

Chaplains accompanied many of the great slave hunting expeditions of the *bandeirantes*, including the one led by Antônio Raposo Tavares which moved west and south from São Paulo. It was, however, Spanish Jesuits (from Asunción) who took the lead in missionary activities in the region between São Paulo and the Río de la Plata in the early to mid-sixteenth century and again in the late seventeenth and early eigl ?enth centuries.[8]

The regular orders whose members were European, or at least European in cultural orientation, were thus responsible for the opening up of successive new areas for evangelization. They received their financial backing from the *Padroado*, but attempted to become more independent by creating their own sources of income in the shape of farms, plantations, cattle ranches, sugar mills and slaves, often obtained through donation, inheritance, or the promises of the faithful. Religious holdings occupied considerable space in the towns, where the 'patrimony of the saints' usually constituted part of the original nucleus of settlement, as well as in the interior. The wealth of the religious orders in Brazil was manifested in the magnitude of their convents and monasteries and in the sumptuousness of their Baroque churches richly ornamented with gold. The clergy devoted themselves, to a large degree, to money matters, buying and selling, and using the interest on loans to good avail. The spacious corridors of some convents were like banking halls. Only a minority of priests in fact engaged themselves in missionary activities. In 1765, for example, there were 89 Carmelite

[8] See Schwartz, *CHLA*, II, ch. 12 and Hemming, *CHLA*, II, ch. 13.

priests distributed in five religious houses in Amazonia. Of this number only eight lived and worked as 'vicars of the Negro and Solimões Rivers occupied in the service of the Church and His Majesty the King'.[9] From the end of the eighteenth century the number of regular clergy declined, but the property of the religious orders (except for the Jesuits and to a lesser extent the Mercedarians) remained intact. In a report of 1870, it was discovered that the Benedictines, with only 41 monks in eleven monasteries, possessed seven sugar mills, more than 40 plantations, 230 houses and 1,265 slaves; the Carmelites, with 49 friars in fourteen convents, possessed more than 40 plantations, 136 buildings and 1,050 slaves; the Franciscans, however, with 85 friars in 25 convents, possessed only 40 slaves.[10]

The organization of the secular church in Brazil came under the *Padroado Real*. The right of patronage had been ceded to the Portuguese crown by the papacy, with the proviso that the king would actively encourage and protect the rights and organization of the church in any lands to be discovered. It was therefore through the intermediary of the Padroado and the royal tithes (the 10 per cent levy on whatever the land produced) that the expansion of Catholicism in Brazil was financed. The Portuguese state also disposed of other means by which to control the church. The *Mesa de Consciência e Ordens*, for example, made all ecclesiastical appointments in the Portuguese empire. Because of the predominance of the Padroado, the influence of Rome on Brazil was modest. The ordinances of the Council of Trent were only applied to the country in the nineteenth century.

The organization of dioceses and parishes was slow and their influence on Catholic practice in Brazil for a long time minimal. Between 1551 and 1676 there was only one diocese in Brazil, at Salvador da Bahia. In 1676/7, three more were created, at Pernambuco, Rio de Janeiro (which was responsible for Minas Gerais, Mato Grosso and Goiás, as well as São Paulo) and São Luís do Maranhão. The latter was directly dependent on Lisbon. During the first half of the eighteenth century three further dioceses were created at Pará (1719) also dependent on Lisbon, Mariana (1745) and São Paulo (1745). The birth of these dioceses corresponded to the opening up of the interior and its

---

[9] A. Prat, *Notas históricas sobre as missões carmelitas* (Recife, 1940), 139.

[10] H. Fragoso, 'A igreja na formação do estado liberal: 1840–1875', *História da Igreja no Brasil* (Petrópolis, 1980), 201.

incorporation into the colonial system. The number of dioceses then remained the same until Independence in 1822. The dioceses, prelacies and parishes remained vacant for long periods of time. Few bishops undertook the pastoral visits recommended by the Council of Trent, not least because of the distances involved and the hazards of travel.[11] The actual practice of Catholicism was not therefore affected to any great extent by the ecclesiastical hierarchy. One synod was held in Salvador in 1707, and the 'First Constitutions of the Archbishopric of Bahia' constituted the only piece of ecclesiastical legislation drawn up in Brazil during the colonial period.

The secular clergy attended to the administration of the sacraments, such as baptism, marriage, annual Easter confession, funeral rites and Seventh Day Mass. These sacraments were administered to the whole population, not only to those groups which freely accepted them. They were, in other words, considered compulsory. Part of the secular clergy ran the chapels of the different confraternities in the towns, while the other part looked after the parishes in the towns and in the interior of the country. Parishes were organized, particularly after Pombal's legislation of 1755, to coincide with old Indian mission settlements, the encampments of the *bandeirantes*, sugar mills and landed estates. The parish priest would pay regular visits to the different chapels throughout his usually vast territory. He would travel on horseback, or sometimes in a hammock carried by slaves, in order to administer the sacraments to the population. Preaching was normally reserved for missionaries of the regular clergy, while the parish priests looked after problems of discipline and administered the sacraments. The secular clergy was divided into the higher clergy, including the archbishop, bishops and other dignatories, who were paid out of the ecclesiastical purse of the Padroado, and the lower clergy, including parish priests and chaplains, who lived closer to the people and shared their privations. Literature on the secular clergy in Brazil during the first three centuries is sparse to say the least. There are severe gaps in our knowledge of the life of the clergy, its observance of the rules of celibacy, its involvement in political rivalries and popular struggle and its financial resources and general situation. As many of its members were mestizos, it was the victim of racial and culture prejudice and this again has hindered the keeping of any records of its activities.

Laymen managed to infiltrate the Brazilian church through the

[11] On the early bishops in colonial Brazil see Johnson, *CHLA*, I, ch. 8.

confraternities, brotherhoods and tertiary orders which Brazil had
inherited from Portugal and which flourished especially in Minas
Gerais. The brotherhoods corresponded to the racial, social and
ideological characteristics of the different strata of society. There were
black brotherhoods (Rosário, São Benedito, Santa Ifigênia), mestizo
brotherhoods (Conceição, Amparo, Livramento, Patrocínio) and white
brotherhoods (Santíssimo Sacramento, São Francisco, Nossa Senhora
do Carmo, Santa Casa de Misericórdia). There were brotherhoods of
landowners, merchants, soldiers, artisans and slaves. The brotherhoods
revealed their own particular personalities and aspirations during their
festivals, processions and through the promises they made. There is
no doubt that Catholic tradition in Brazil was essentially lay in its
characteristics.

In order to understand the process by which a Christian society
developed in Brazil it is important to recognize the problems faced by
Portugal when undertaking its colonial enterprise in America. There
were enemies, both outside and inside, against which Catholic Brazil
had to be defended. Other European states, especially France, Holland
and England, competed with Portugal for hegemony in the South
Atlantic. During this long period of rivalry, Catholicism helped to
define Portuguese policy, which was considered orthodox and even
apostolic, while the designs of Portugal's competitors were qualified as
heretical, depraved and impure, because those competitors were
Protestant. The passport for entry into the colony was a religious one:
only Catholics were allowed in. Priests desiring to work in Brazil were
carefully scrutinized: no cleric left Portugal without the explicit
authority of the king which was given only after personal interview and
an oath of allegiance. Missionaries were required to assemble in Lisbon
and were transported exclusively on Portuguese ships. The same
formalities were required of foreign missionaries. Bishops who resided
in Brazil could not correspond directly with Rome and in practice never
made the traditional pastoral visit to the Vatican because of distance
and cost. There was practically no communication between Rome and
the church in Brazil. Everything passed through Lisbon in obedience
to the Portuguese policy of monopolizing commerce and communications with its colony.

Within the Portuguese empire itself there were New Christians (Jews who had been converted by force and their descendants) against whom discriminatory legislation was directed.[12] Moreover, although the Inquisition was never permanently established in Brazil repressive measures were carried out by visiting officers of the Inquisition in cities where there was thought to be the most likelihood of danger: Salvador, Olinda, Rio de Janeiro, Belém. Suspects were taken to Portugal for trial before the Tribunal of the Holy Office. However, the Portuguese authorities generally preferred methods of manipulation rather than direct repression, and to this end they relied to a large extent on ecclesiastical institutions. Catholicism was the only official religion in Brazil and religious devotion virtually compulsory. 'Enforced devotion', as Antônio Vieira called it, was useful to the Portuguese state because it controlled the accumulation of capital by the local bourgeoisie and channelled money into harmless displays of religious ostentation. The governing bodies of many *irmandades*, lay religious brotherhoods or confraternities, in Brazilian towns became more or less bureaucratic entities whose function it was to raise money from the landed and commercial class for religious ends. (A typical product of this type of activity was the famous Triunfo Eucarístico celebrated at Ouro Preto in 1733.) On the other hand, the Santa Casa de Misericórdia, which existed in all the main towns was at the same time chaplaincy, hospital, orphanage, hostel for marriageable girls, medical school, pharmacy, mortuary, artists' home, as well as proprietor of buildings, plantations and mills. It could equally be said to have been the first bank in the city, offering an interest rate of 6 per cent.

The church was an agent of social control in colonial Brazil in a number of important ways. Take, for example, the role of the nunneries, which were financed by the *Padroado*. Many landowners sought to maintain their daughters in convents, as marriage threatened the integrity of their estates. According to research carried out in the archive of the Convent of Desterro at Salvador, 77 per cent of the daughters of 53 Bahian families during the period 1680–1797 entered the convent, 8 per cent remained at home without marrying and only 14 per cent married. There was even a case of one *fidalgo*, José Pires de Carvalho, who managed to place all six of his daughters in the convent. The social division between free and slave was transferred intact to these convents. At Desterro in 1764, for example, each white

[12] On the New Christians in colonial Brazilian society, see Schwartz, *CHLA*, II, ch. 12.

nun with a black veil was served by two or more 'white veiled nuns', who were in fact black slaves.[13]

The church was called upon to create a general climate of agreement in favour of slavery. A theological justification for slavery was devised, for example, by Antônio Vieira, who compared Africa to Hell, where the black was a slave in both body and spirit, and Brazil to Purgatory, where the soul of the black was freed through baptism and destined to enter Heaven at death. The Jesuits put this 'transmigration of the soul' theory into practice by participating in the slave trade. Apart from theological devices, moral teaching also served the interests of the slave-owners: slaves were instilled with the ideal of resignation, and slave-owners taught the benefits to themselves of charity and paternalism. The system whereby the sacraments were given also regulated and legitimized the institution of slavery: before embarking for Brazil, recently purchased slaves had to be baptized. As for marriage, conjugal links contracted in Africa were broken without hesitation and slaves were condemned in theory to a life of celibacy in Brazil.[14] It must be stressed that, apart from individual priests, slaves found no support or defence of their interests within the church.

The Jesuits, although defending and profiting from African slavery, managed almost alone to maintain some degree of independence from the state and, in their successful attempt to create an alternative ecclesiastical model, to offer some challenge to the colonial system. In a society in which education received no stimulus from the state, in which religious devotion held priority over education, and in which there was no printing press, university, or free circulation of books, the Jesuits succeeded in creating an important educational network through their college seminaries, missions and villages. The colleges trained candidates for entry into the Society of Jesus, the secular clergy and even lay occupations. In the sixteenth century, five colleges were founded at Salvador, Rio de Janeiro, Olinda, São Paulo and Vitória. The eighteenth century witnessed the creation of three more at Recife, São Luís do Maranhão and Belém do Pará. A second initiative of the Jesuits was the creation of smaller seminaries at Belém da Cachoeira (1686), Aquiraz (1727) and Paranaguá (1729). Finally, the Jesuits were responsible for the creation of six tridentine or diocesan seminaries at

13 See Susan Soeiro, 'The social and economic role of the convent women and nuns in colonial Bahia, 1677–1800', *HAHR*, 54 (1974), 209–32.
14 Pope Gregory XIII decreed in 1585 that African marriages could be annulled (Canon Law, Code of 1917, Canon 1125, Document VI of Appendix).

São Paulo (1746), Salvador (1747), Paraíba and Mariana (1748), Belém do Pará (1749) and São Luís do Maranhão (1752). Two other diocesan seminaries were founded, apparently without Jesuit influence, at Rio de Janeiro (1740) and Olinda (1800). Apart from this, the Jesuits devoted considerable time and energy to the task of catechizing the Indians. For this they devised methods of teaching which included vocabularies and grammars of Tupi. With regard to the Africans, the Jesuit Pedro Dias published an 'Introduction to the Language of Angola' in 1697.

Luís dos Santos Vilhena, Bahian chronicler of the late eighteenth century, relates how the crown spent 26 times more on the cathedral at Salvador than on the missions in the interior, and twenty times more on priests looking after the spiritual welfare of the settlers than on missionaries.[15] The Jesuits, however, succeeded, particularly in Amazonia between 1652 and 1759, in putting to good use their own financial resources acquired from their cattle ranches, their sugar, cotton and cacao plantations and their control of the trade in natural forest products. They created an economy which was independent of the state and by so doing aggravated the feelings of those in the state of Maranhão as well as in the state of Brazil, who increasingly came to resent the temporal power of the missions. At the same time the Jesuits had produced during the seventeenth century a number of outspoken defenders of the Indians, like João Felipe Bettendorff, Pedro de Pedrosa and, above all, Antônio Vieira. Situated as they were, far from the towns, plantations and sugar mills, the missions highlighted a whole series of problems related to colonialism. They, therefore, became subversive to the system, and this culminated in the famous expulsion of the Jesuits in 1759. There were, of course, other contributing factors such as Enlightenment ideology, the absolutism of the Portuguese monarchy, as well as certain financial abuses for which the missions were blamed. However, it cannot be doubted that the alliance between church and state was thrown into question and even contested by Jesuits and, for this, they paid the price.[16]

In the long run, however, the activities of the popular religious organizations perhaps constituted a more effective challenge to the colonial system than those of the Jesuits. Such organizations were of

[15] Quoted in Hoornaert, 'A evangelização', 36.
[16] For further discussion of the reasons behind the expulsion of the Jesuits from Brazil, see Mansuy-Diniz Silva, CHLA, I, ch. 13, and Alden, CHLA, II, ch. 15.

the most diverse kind: the *quilombos*, communities of runaway slaves, which fulfilled such an important evangelizing role throughout vast areas of Brazil, since the religion commonly practised was Catholicism; the clandestine cults of African or Indian origin, in which old forms of religious worship and organization, antedating European colonization, were preserved; the black brotherhoods in the towns; the festivals, whether in celebration of Carnival or the saints' days; religious movements among poorer classes built around *beatas* (women who chose celibacy and therefore freedom in a male-dominated society without entering a convent), and, of course, the religious pilgrimages and visits to shrines. These manifestations of popular religious belief required considerable organizational ability, a good measure of stealth, cunning and, above all, that particular Brazilian quality of spontaneous improvization. They were never openly subversive, at least on a religious level. Nevertheless, such practices meant that the Catholicism imposed by the colonizer was gradually redefined by a Brazilian people imbued with a strong will to resist. The fact that they never succeeded in creating an alternative model for the development of the church in Brazil can be attributed, among other things, to the unwillingness or inability of the hierarchy to respond.

BIBLIOGRAPHICAL ESSAYS

I. MESOAMERICA BEFORE 1519

A comprehensive bibliography dealing with the archaeology and ethnohistory of Mesoamerica and the north of Mexico, from 1514 to 1960, has been prepared by Ignacio Bernal, *Bibliografía de arqueología y etnografía de Mesoamérica y norte de México, 1514–1960* (Mexico, 1962). Descriptions of many of the extant indigenous sources, i.e., pictorial manuscripts and others in the native historical tradition, are provided by John B. Glass, Donald Robertson, Charles Gibson and Henry B. Nicholson in a series of articles in Volumes XIV and XV (1975), edited by Howard F. Cline, of the *Handbook of Middle American Indians*, ed. Robert Wauchope (16 vols., Austin, Texas, 1964–76).

The works of the sixteenth and seventeenth-century Spanish, mestizo and Indian chroniclers containing basic references to the pre-Columbian epoch have been the subject of various analyses and critical appraisals, although there is no comprehensive study which examines them all systematically. A general survey can be found in *Historiografía Indiana*, by Francisco Esteve Barba (Madrid, 1964). A number of studies about the works of authors like Bernardino de Sahagún, Antonio de Herrera and Juan de Torquemada are included in 'The guide to ethnohistorical sources', *Handbook of Middle American Indians*, XII (1973). The National University of Mexico is currently publishing critical editions of some of the indigenous sources and of the sixteenth-century chronicles, the *Textos de los informantes indígenas de Sahagún*, *Códices Matritenses*, edited by Angel María Garibay and Miguel León-Portilla, 4 vols. (Mexico, 1958–1969); *Poesía Náhuatl*, edited by A. M. Garibay, 3 vols. (Mexico, 1964, 1965 and 1968); the *Apologética Historia Sumaria*, by Bartolomé de Las Casas, 2 vols. (Mexico, 1967); *Memoriales*, by Toribio de

Benavente Motolinía (Mexico, 1971); *Obras Históricas*, by Fernando de
Alva Ixtlilxóchitl, 2 vols. (Mexico, 1975–7), edited by Edmundo
O'Gorman *et al.*, and the *Monarquía Indiana*, by Juan de Torquemada,
edited by M. León-Portilla *et al.*, 7 vols. (Mexico, 1975–80).

A contribution deserving particular attention is the edition and
translation into English prepared by Arthur J. O. Anderson and
Charles E. Dibble of the encyclopaedic source for the study of the
cultures of central Mexico, the *Florentine Codex*, 12 vols. (Santa Fe, N.M.,
1950–82). In the case of the Maya, no recent edition has surpassed the
work of Alfred M. Tozzer as editor, translator and commentator of
the chronicle by Diego de Landa, *Relación de las Cosas de Yucatán*
(Cambridge, Mass., 1941).

The achievements of archaeological research in Mesoamerica are
recorded and described by Gordon R. Willey and Jeremy A. Sabloff in
A History of American archaeology (San Francisco, 1974), and by Ignacio
Bernal, *Historia de la arqueología en México* (Mexico, 1979). A volume
edited by Norman Hammond includes various papers dealing with some
of the more recent research programmes, *Mesoamerican Archaeology. New
approaches* (Austin, Texas, 1974). Volumes II, III, IV, X and XI of *The
Handbook of Middle American Indians* (1965, 1966 and 1971) include
several excellent syntheses about the archaeology of the various areas
of northern and southern Mesoamerica. The first volume of a new series
entitled 'Supplement to the Handbook of Middle American Indians',
has been published to cover recent research in the area: *Archaeology*,
edited by Jeremy A. Sabloff, assisted by Patricia A. Andrews (Austin,
Texas, 1981).

A few reliable surveys of the cultural evolution of Mesoamerica in
its entirety have appeared during recent decades. Wigberto Jiménez
Moreno has revised a previously published work that throws considerable light on the subject, 'Mesoamerica Before the Toltecs', in
Ancient Oaxaca, edited by John Paddock (Stanford, 1968). The joint
effort of several specialists co-ordinated by José Luis Lorenzo, Alberto
Ruz, Ignacio Bernal and Miguel León-Portilla has resulted in an ample
section devoted to the Mesoamerican past in the first three volumes of
the *Historia de México*, 11 vols. (Mexico, 1974). Amongst the contributions made in terms of theory may be mentioned the small volume
prepared by William T. Sanders and Barbara J. Price to demonstrate
that civilization can be understood as a result of ecological adaptation:
Mesoamerica: the evolution of a civilization (New York, 1968).

During recent decades, publications about particular areas, periods or aspects within the cultural evolution of Mesoamerica have been extremely abundant but of uneven quality. For the origins, development and diffusion of Oltec culture, see Michael D. Coe, *America's First Civilization* (New York, 1968), and Ignacio Bernal, *The Olmec World* (Berkeley, 1969). Michael D. Coe has published a well-documented synthesis about *The Maya* (London, 1966; rev. ed. 1980). See also the classic contributions of J. Eric S. Thompson: *The rise and fall of Maya civilization* (1954; 2nd edn Norman, Oklahoma, 1967); *Maya hieroglyphic writing: an introduction* (Norman, Oklahoma, 1970); *A catalog of Maya hieroglyphs* (Norman, Oklahoma, 1962); and *Maya history and religion* (Norman, Oklahoma, 1970). Also two recent works: John S. Henderson, *The world of the Ancient Maya* (Ithaca, 1981), and Norman Hammond, *Ancient Maya civilization* (Cambridge, 1982). *Ancient Oaxaca*, edited by John Paddock (Stanford, 1968), includes important contributions about the Zapotec and Mixtec cultures.

Several excellent facsimile reproductions of indigenous books or 'codices', both pre-Columbian and early colonial of native Mesoamerican origin, facilitate the study of these primary sources: *Codex Cospi, Codex Borbonicus, Codex Borgia,* with a commentary by K. A. Novotny (Graz, 1968, 1974, 1978); *Codex Egerton, Codex Land, Codex Fejervary Mayer,* with an introduction by C. A. Burland (Graz, 1965, 1966, 1971); *Codice Xolotl,* with an introductory study by Charles E. Dibble, 2 vols. (Mexico, 1980).

The cultures of Central Mexico, in particular those which succeeded in building the metropoli of Teotihuacan, Tula and Mexico-Tenochtitlan, have been the object of increasing attention. The proceedings of the XI Round Table of the Sociedad Mexicana de Antropología include various important papers about the classic metropolis, *Teotihuacan,* 2 vols. (Mexico, 1966–72). Concerning the development of urbanism in the Teotihuacan period, the mapping project headed by René Millon has resulted in several contributions. See, for instance, his 'Teotihuacan: completion of map of giant ancient city in the Valley of Mexico', *Science,* 170 (Washington, D.C., 1970), 1077–82, and 'The study of urbanism in Teotihuacan', in Norman Hammond (ed.), *Mesoamerican archaeology. New approaches* (London, 1974), 313–34. For comprehensive ethnohistorical studies on the Toltecs, see Nigel Davies, *The Toltecs: until the fall of Tula* (Norman, Oklahoma, 1977), and *The Toltec Heritage* (Norman, 1980).

On the socio-economic and political structures prevalent in central Mesoamerica at the time of the contact with the Spaniards, Manuel M. Moreno, *La Organización política y social de los Aztecas* (Mexico, 1962); Friedrich Katz, *Situación social y económica de los Aztecas durante los Siglos XV y XVI* (Mexico, 1966); Pedro Carrasco, 'Social organisation in Ancient Mexico', *Handbook of Middle American Indians*, x, 349–75; Johanna Broda, Pedro Carrasco, *et al.*, *Estratificación social en la Mesoamérica Prehispánica* (Mexico, 1976); Pedro Carrasco and Johanna Broda (eds.), *Economía política e ideología en el México Prehispánico* (Mexico, 1978); Pedro Carrasco, 'La economía prehispánica de México', in Enrique Florescano (ed.), *Ensayos sobre el desarrollo económico de México y América Latina (1500–1950)* (Mexico, 1979). Angel Palerm, in *Obras hidráulicas prehispánicas* (Mexico, 1973), stresses the role of irrigation in Mesoamerican development, making use of the ideas expressed by Karl A. Wittfogel. See also Warwick Bray, 'Land use, settlement patterns and politics in Prehispanic Mesoamerica, a review', in *Man, settlement and urbanism* (London, 1970).

Alfonso Caso, in addition to his archaeological research in the Oaxaca area and his facsimile editions with the 'lecture' of several Mixtec codices, has written many studies on the Aztecs and on the calendaric systems of central Mesoamerica, including *Los calendarios prehispánicos* (Mexico, 1967). Eduardo Noguera's many pioneering contributions in the field of ceramics culminated in a basic work of reference, *La cerámica arqueológica de Mesoamérica* (Mexico, 1975). Ignacio Marquina's volume on the *Arquitectura prehispánica* (Mexico, 1960) provides the classic treatment of this subject.

The literary creations of the Nahuatl-speaking groups have been researched by Angel María Garibay, whose *Historia de la literatura Nahuatl*, 2 vols. (Mexico, 1953–4), remains a landmark in these studies. A general guide to the indigenous literary productions of the Maya, Nahua and Mixtec peoples is provided by M. León-Portilla, *Precolumbian literatures of Mexico* (Norman, Oklahoma, 1969). A collection of texts of the native Mesoamerican tradition, translated from Nahuatl, Maya, Quiche and Mixtec, including creation myths, examples of the 'ancient word', poetry and the saga of Quetzalcoatl, has been edited by Miguel León-Portilla, J. O. A. Anderson, C. E. Dibble and M. Edmonson, *Native Mesoamerican spirituality* (New York, 1980).

Religion and world view in Mesoamerica have been better approached during the two last decades through the analysis of the indigenous manuscripts and the findings of archaeology. A pioneering paper in this field is that of J. Eric S. Thompson on the *Sky bearers, colors and directions in Maya and Mexican religion* (Washington, D.C., 1934). Alfonso Caso's *The Aztecs: people of the sun* (Norman, Oklahoma, 1958), keeps its value as an introduction to the religion of the Aztecs. Several writings of the great Mexicanist, Eduard Seler, included in his *Gesammelte Abhandlungen*, 5 vols. (Berlin, 1902–23), are also of considerable importance for the study of Mesoamerican religion and world view. *Aztec thought and culture. A study of the ancient Nahuatl mind* (Norman, Oklahoma, 1963), and *Time and reality in the thought of the Maya* (Boston, 1972), by M. León-Portilla, provide analysis of texts considered of primary importance to approach the world view of these two peoples. Papers rich in new insights are those of Thomas S. Barthel, 'Algunos principios de ordenación en el panteón azteca', *Traducciones Mesoamericanísticas*, II, 45–78 (Mexico, 1968), and the classificatory attempt of the various deities prepared by Henry B. Nicholson, 'Religion in pre-Hispanic Central Mexico', in *Handbook of Middle American Indians* (1972), X, 305–446. An excellent survey of the culture of the inhabitants of Central Mexico before the arrival of the Spaniards is available in Warwick Bray, *Everyday life of the Aztecs* (London, 1968). For a fine general synthesis, see Nigel Davies, *The Aztecs* (London, 1973).

2. THE INDIANS OF THE CARIBBEAN AND CIRCUM-CARIBBEAN AT THE END OF THE FIFTEENTH CENTURY

Several of the major sixteenth-century European chroniclers of Spanish exploration and settlement in the New World provide primary material concerning the native customs of the Greater Antilles, northern Venezuela, the northern half of Colombia, and lower Central America. The following sources are, therefore, fundamental to any ethnohistorical research concerning the Caribbean and circum-Caribbean: Pietro Martire d'Anghiera, *De Orbe Novo*, available in two volumes in English translation by Francis Augustus MacNutt under the title *De Orbe Novo, the eight decades of Peter Martyr d'Anghera* (New York, 1912); Bartolomé de Las Casas, *Historia de las Indias*, edited in three volumes by Agustín Millares Carlo (Mexico, 1951); Gonzalo Fernández de Oviedo y Valdéz, *Historia general y natural de las Indias* [Madrid, 1851–5], 5 vols. (Madrid, 1959), and, by the same author, *Sumario de la natural historia de las Indias* [1526] (Mexico, 1950), translated into English and edited by Sterling

A. Stoudemire as *Natural History of the West Indies* (Chapel Hill, 1959). The *Historie del S. D. Fernando Colombo* [Venice, 1571], also published by Ramón Iglesia as *Vida del Almirante Don Cristóbal Colón* (Mexico, 1947), should also be consulted, particularly for the Greater Antilles and lower Central America. This record of Columbus' voyages has been translated into English by Benjamin Keen as *The life of the Admiral Christopher Columbus by his son, Ferdinand* (New Brunswick, N.J., 1959).

Luis Duque Gómez's two-volume work on Colombian prehistory provides a basic introduction to that country's indigenous peoples at the time of the Conquest. Both volumes, *Prehistoria*, I: *Etnohistoria y arqueológia* (1965) and II: *Tribus indigenas y sitios arqueológicos* (1967), have been published as volume I of *Historia extensa de Colombia* (Bogotá, 1965, 1967). *Prehistoria*, II, chap. 1 contains a useful discussion of the various chroniclers whose works provide much primary data. Of these, Pedro de Aquado's *Recopilación historial* is particularly significant, for many well-known later writers rested heavily on this source. The four-volume edition by Juan Friede (Bogotá, 1956–7) is definitive. Another exceptional sixteenth-century observer, Pedro de Cieza de León, left an excellent description of his travels through the Cauca Valley. This material is contained in the first part of his well-known chronicle of Peru [1554] and has been translated into English by Clements R. Markham as *The Travels of Pedro de Cieza de Leon, A.D. 1532–1550* (London, 1864).

Turning to contemporary scholars, much data concerning Cauca valley peoples has been compiled by Hermann Trimborn in his *Vergessene Königreiche* (Brunswick, 1948). This work, however, is seriously flawed by outmoded theories and questionable generalizations, and must be used with care. More recently Luis Duque Gómez has focused specifically on the indigenous peoples of the Quindío region in *Los Quimbayas* (Bogotá, 1970). An excellent discussion of traditional settlements and agricultural adaptations is provided by Thomas S. Schorr, 'Cauca Valley settlements, a culture ecological interpretation', in *Actas y Memorias*, I, 37th Congreso Internacional de Americanistas (Buenos Aires, 1968), 449–66.

On the Cenú region of the north Colombian lowlands, two studies merit particular mention. B. LeRoy Gordon's *Human geography and ecology in the Sinú country of Colombia* (Berkeley, 1957) includes a reconstruction of native cultures at the time of contact. James J. Parsons and William A. Bowen discuss evidence for intensive agricultural techniques in

'Ancient ridged fields of the San Jorge river floodplain, Colombia', *The Geographical Review*, 56 (1966), 317–43.

The traditional cultures of the Santa Marta region have been discussed in detail by Gerardo Reichel-Dolmatoff, *Datos historicos-culturales sobre las tribus de la antigua Gobernacion de Santa Marta* (Bogotá, 1951). Henning Bischof's excellent work, *Die Spanisch-Indianische Auseinandersetzung in der nördlichen Sierra Nevada de Santa Marta (1501–1600)* (Bonn, 1971), builds on Reichel-Dolmatoff's earlier volume.

Much has been written on the Muisca or Chibcha. From among the numerous studies the following provide good introductions, particularly to questions of pre-Columbian ecology and socio-political organization: Robert C. Eidt, 'Aboriginal Chibcha settlement in Colombia', *Annals of the Association of American Geographers*, 49 (1959), 374–92; Sylvia M. Broadbent, 'A prehistoric field system in Chibcha territory, Colombia', *Ñawpa Pacha*, 6 (1968), 135–47, and *Los Chibchas; organizacion socio-politica* (Bogotá, 1964); Juan A. and Judith E. Villamarin, 'Kinship and inheritance among the Sabana de Bogotá Chibcha at the time of Spanish conquest', *Ethnology*, 14 (1975), 173–9. On a broader note, Gerardo Reichel-Dolmatoff presents a general survey of pre-conquest agricultural features in 'The agricultural basis of the sub-Andean chiefdoms of Colombia', in *The evolution of horticultural systems in native South America, causes and consequences*, edited by Johannes Wilbert (Caracas, 1961), 83–100. Regional and long-distance exchange in native Colombia is discussed by S. Henry Wassén, 'Algunos datos del comercio preColombino [sic] en Colombia', *Revista colombiana de Antropologia*, 4 (1955), 87–110.

Although the fullest accounts of the indigenous cultures of Panama are contained in Oviedo y Valdéz's *Historia general* and his *Sumario*, valuable data concerning eastern Panama and north-western Colombia are to be found in the letter of 1513 to King Ferdinand written by Vasco Núñez de Balboa. This missive has been published with others by Martín Fernández de Navarrete in his *Colección de los viages y descubrimientos que hicieron por mar los Españoles* (Madrid, 1829), III, 358–76. An English translation can be found in the report by Pascual de Andagoya translated as *Narrative of the Proceedings of Pedrarias Davila in the provinces of Tierra Firme* by Clements R. Markham (London, 1865), i–xix. Andagoya's narrative is itself another important source.

Using these and other records, Samuel Lothrop presents a general summary of the pre-Columbian societies of western Panama in *Coclé, an archaeological study of central Panama* (Cambridge, 1937), part I, 1–48. An earlier and little known history by C. L. G. Anderson, *Old Panama and Castilla del Oro* (Boston, 1914), is also useful. More recently Carl Sauer has discussed such topics as subsistence, settlement pattern and metallurgy in *The early Spanish Main* (Berkeley, 1966). Mary W. Helms has analysed procedures for succession to chiefship in 'Competition, power, and succession to office in Pre-Columbian Panama', in *Frontier adaptations in lower Central America*, edited by Mary W. Helms and Franklin O. Loveland (Philadelphia, 1976), 25–35. In another study entitled *Ancient Panama: chiefs in search of power* (Austin, Texas, 1979), she has offered a general anthropological interpretation of the operation of Panamanian polities at the time of conquest with particular emphasis on long-distance contacts.

The standard introduction to Costa Rican materials is Ricardo Fernández Guardia, *Historia de Costa Rica* (San José, 1905), also available in an English translation by Harry Weston Van Dyke as *History of the discovery and conquest of Costa Rica* (New York, 1913). Considerable ethnohistoric data are also found in the *Cartas de Juan Vazquez de Coronado*, also published by Fernández Guardia (Barcelona, 1908). The first chapter of his *Reseña histórica de Talamanca* (San José, 1918) provides information from early missionary reports regarding this isolated region. Of this genre, the memorial written by Fr Agustín de Zevallos in 1610 regarding the Talamancan natives is particularly informative. It appears in volume V of the *Colección de documentos para la historia de Costa Rica* published by León Fernández (Paris, 1886), 156–61.

Turning to north-western Venezuela, Federico Brito Figueroa's *Población y economía en el pasado indígena venezolano* (Caracas, 1962) provides an excellent reconstruction and overview of late fifteenth-century indigenous demographic patterns and socio-economic characteristics. It is particularly useful for the northern mountain and coastal regions. The ethnographically complex region surrounding Lake Maracaibo has been analysed by Mario Sanoja O. in 'Datos etnohistóricos del Lago de Maracaibo', *Economia y Ciencias Sociales*, 2nd ser., 8 (1966), 221–51. Erika Wagner's 'The Mucuchíes phase: an extension of the Andean cultural pattern into western Venezuela', *American Anthropologist*, 75 (1973), 195–213 reconstructs with archaeological evidence aspects of the culture pattern characteristic of the *tierra fría* region of the nearby Venezuelan Andes.

The most detailed primary account of the indigenous customs of the

Greater Antilles is found in Bartolomé de Las Casas, *Apologética historia de las Indias*, published as volume 1 of *Historiadores de Indias*, by M. Serrano y Sanz (Madrid, 1909). Additional information on the ideology and religious practices of the natives of Hispaniola can be found in the report of Friar Ramón Pané. An English translation of this account appears in Edward Gaylord Bourne, 'Columbus, Ramon Pane and the beginnings of American anthropology', *Proceedings of the American Antiquarian Society*, N.S. 17 (1907), 310–48 and in Keen's *Life of the Admiral*, 153–69. Turning to secondary sources, a valuable contribution to demographic studies has been made by Ángel Rosenblat, 'The population of Hispaniola at the time of Columbus' in *The native population of the Americas in 1492*, edited by William M. Denevan (Madison, 1976), 43–66. Indigenous agricultural practices in the Greater Antilles are discussed in 'Taino agriculture' by William C. Sturtevant, in J. Wilbert, ed., *The evolution of horticultural Systems*, 69–82. Insights into the association of plant and animal forms with art and ritual are offered by Adolfo de Hostos in his *Anthropological papers* (San Juan, 1941).

On a more general level, the extensive compilation by Sven Lovén, *Origins of the Tainan culture, West Indies* (Göteborg, 1935) contains much information, but must be used carefully because of a tendency for unreliability in quotes and in interpretations. Although written almost a century ago, the paper by Hy. Ling Roth, 'The aborigines of Hispaniola', *Journal of the Anthropological Institute of Great Britain and Ireland*, 16 (1887), 247–86, remains an excellent summary of, and introduction to, the subject. Another basic work concerned with Cuba is Felipe Pichardo Moya's *Los Indios de Cuba en sus tiempos historicos* (Havana, 1945). Sauer's *Spanish Main* devotes considerable space to discussion of indigenous mainland relationships in the Greater Antilles.

The most authoritative observations concerning the native population of the Lesser Antilles were made by the seventeenth-century missionary, Father Raymond Breton. Although Breton's own ethnographic record is apparently lost, much information is contained in his *Dictionnaire Caraïbe-Français* (Leipzig, 1892). Breton also provided material for a report written by his superior, Armand de La Paix, entitled *Relation de l'Isle de la Guadeloupe* which appears in *Les Caraïbes, la Guadeloupe: 1635–1656* edited by Joseph Rennard (Paris, 1929), 23–127.

Douglas Taylor, the foremost ethnohistorian of the Island Carib, has written many articles, including 'Kinship and social structure of the

Island Carib', *Southwestern Journal of Anthropology*, 2 (1946), 180–212, 'The meaning of dietary and occupational restrictions among the Island Carib', *American Anthropologist*, 52 (1950), 343–9, and 'Diachronic note on the Carib contribution to Island Carib', *International Journal of American Linguistics*, 20 (1954), 28–33. See also Taylor and Walter H. Hodge, 'The ethnobotany of the Island Carib of Dominica', *Webbia*, 12 (1957), 513–644. Richard Moore has presented a reasoned, if somewhat impassioned, critique of Island Carib cannibalism in his 'Carib "cannibalism": a study in anthropological stereotyping', *Caribbean Studies*, 13 (1973), 117–35. Jacques Petitjean-Roget has published an ethnographic reconstruction of Island Carib culture based on Breton's works. The English version is titled 'The Caribs as seen through the dictionary of the Reverend Father Breton', *First International Convention for the study of pre-Columbian culture in the Lesser Antilles, Part I* (Fort-de-France, Martinique, 1961), 43–68. The same report is published in French in the same source, pp. 16–42.

For the cultures of the coastal mountains and interior llanos of north-eastern Venezuela, see Paul Kirchhoff, 'The tribes north of the Orinoco River' in *Handbook of South American Indians* ed. Julian H. Steward (6 vols., Washington D.C., 1946–50), IV, 481–93. Kirchhoff relies on a notable late seventeenth-century work, *Conversión en Pirití de Indios Cumanagotas y Palenques* (Madrid, 1892) by Fray Matías Ruiz Blanco. Another missionary, Padre José Gumilla, produced a major ethnographic report on the central and western Venezuelan *llanos*, *El Orinoco ilustrado y defendido* (Caracas, 1963). Utilizing Gumilla's data and information from numerous other sources, ethnohistorians Nancy and Robert Morey have described and analysed the culture patterns of the *llanos* in *Relaciones comerciales en el pasado en los llanos de Colombia y Venezuela* (Caracas, 1975) and 'Foragers and farmers: differential consequences of Spanish contact', *Ethnohistory*, 20 (1973), 229–46.

3. ANDEAN SOCIETIES BEFORE 1532

An early inventory of the sources for Andean ethnohistory in English was prepared by Phillip A. Means, *Biblioteca Andina* (1928) in Transactions, Connecticut Academy of Arts and Sciences, vol. 29, 271–525. It is still a useful discussion of the eyewitness accounts of the European invasion. More recently, Peruvian historians have prepared a *Manual de estudios Peruanistas* (5th edn, Lima, 1959) by Rubén Vargas Ugarte and *Los cronistas del Perú* (Lima, 1962) by Raúl Porras Barrenechea.

Beginning in 1956, the Biblioteca de Autores Españoles, published in Madrid by the Real Academia, undertook new editions of many of the European chronicles: for example, Bernabé Cobo's *Historia del Neuvo Mundo* [1653] (Madrid, 1956). Each work has a new introduction, if of unequal value; the texts themselves are carefully reproduced. No one, so far has replaced Marcos Jiménez de la Espada as a locator of primary sources; a new edition of his *Relaciones Geográficas de Indias* [1586] (4 vols., 1881–97; reprinted in 3, Madrid, 1965), is particularly useful.

In some cases the familiar texts are based on copies of the original manuscripts, now lost; the copyists were frequently unfamiliar with the Andean languages, so the names of places and of individuals are misspelt and sometimes unrecognizable. The search for the originals has led to new, much improved editions of, for example, Juan de Matienzo's *Gobierno del Peru* [1567] published by the Institut Français d'Études Andines (Lima, 1967).

Texts in the Andean languages are catalogued in Paul Rivet and G. de Créqui-Montfort's *Bibliographie Aymara et Kichua*, 4 vols. (Travaux et Mémoires, Institut d'Éthnologie, Paris, 1951–6). Most of these texts are quite late: so far, many fewer have been located for Quechua and Aymara than we have in Mexico for Nahuatl. One significant exception is the oral tradition of the Yauyu people of Huarochiri, published in a bilingual edition by Hermann Trimborn (*Quellen und Forschungen zur Geschichte der Geographie und Völkerkunde*, IV (Leipzig, 1939)). Since this edition was almost completely destroyed during the war, Trimborn, in collaboration with Antje Kelm, brought out a retranslation, *Francisco de Avila*, an annotated bilingual edition of the text (Quellenwerke zur alten Geschichte Amerikas aufgezeichnet in den Sprachen der Eingeborenen, VIII (Berlin, 1967)). A Spanish translation was undertaken by José María Arguedas, *Dioses y hombres de Huarochiri* (Instituto de Estudios Peruanos (Lima, 1966)), and a French edition by Gerald Taylor, *Rites et traditions de Huarochiri* (Paris, 1980). An English version is being prepared by Donald Solá.

We also owe to Rivet the first, facsimile edition of the first book known to have been written by an Andean author, Felipe Guaman Poma de Ayala, *Nueva Corónica y Buen Gobierno* [1615] (Institut d'Éthnologie, Paris, 1936; reprinted 1968). A critical edition, with indexes, translations of the material in Quechua and a transcription of the entire manuscript, came out in 1980 in Mexico, edited by J. V. Murra and Rolena Adorno.

María Rostworowski de Diez Canseco has pioneered the publication and interpretation of administrative and litigation records from the sixteenth century (for example, studies of weights and measures, of land tenure, the coastal ethnic lords). In recent years she has stressed the accessibility of Andean materials from coastal regions which have been published by the Instituto de Estudios Peruanos, Lima: *Señoríos indígenas de Lima y Canta* (1978); *Recursos naturales renovables y pesca, siglos XVI y XVII* (1981). Waldemar Espinoza Soriano has edited a series of useful regional texts which he had culled from the Archivo de Indias, Seville: for example, 'Los Huancas, aliados de la conquista: tres informaciones inéditas sobre la participación indígena en la conquista del Perú [1558–61]', in the *Anales Científicos* of the University of Huancayo, Peru, 1971–2. Journals which have published such administrative texts include the *Revista del Museo Nacional*, the *Bulletin* of the Institut Français d'Etudes Andines, *Historia y Cultura* and *Histórica*, all of Lima. J. V. Murra has edited two sixteenth-century inspections of Andean ethnic groups, both published in Peru and analysed in his collection, *Formaciones económicas y políticas del mundo andino* (Lima, 1975). Similar sources for the northern Andes have been selected and published by Segundo Moreno Yañez for the Colección Pendoneros of Otavalo, Ecuador: for example, Udo Oberem, *Los Quijos* (1980), and Frank Salomon, *Ethnic lords of Quito in the age of the Incas: the political economy of north Andean chiefdoms* (Cornell, 1978; Spanish trans. 1980). In the south, the former Audiencia de Charcas, this role has been played by Ramiro Condarco Morales, Tristan Platt, Silvia Rivera Cusicanqui, Thérèse Bouysse-Cassagne and Thierry Saignes, who have published administrative and census records in *Historia y Cultura* and *Avances* of La Paz and *Historia Boliviana* of Cochabamba.

Structural analyses of symbolic and religious materials from the Andes have been offered by R. T. Zuidema, *The Ceque system of Cuzco: the social organization of the capital of the Incas* (Leiden, 1964), as well as by Pierre Duviols and Nathan Wachtel (see below). J. V. Murra and N. Wachtel have edited a special issue of *AESC*, 33/5–6 (1978), on the 'historical anthropology' of the Andes.

Beyond the older analyses of Inka society such as Heinrich Cunow, 'Das Peruanische Verwandschaftsystem und die Geschlechtsverbaende der Inka', in *Das Ausland* (Berlin, 1891), Sir Clements Markham, *The*

Incas of Peru (London, 1912), Louis Baudin, *L'Empire socialiste des Incas* (Paris, 1928), John H. Rowe, 'Inca culture at the time of the Spanish conquest', in *Handbook of South American Indians*, II (Washington, 1946) or J. V. Murra, *The economic organization of the Inka state* (1955; Greenwich, Conn., 1980), there are also recent studies using new sources or asking new questions. Notable among them are Franklin Pease García Yrigoyen's *El dios creador andino* (Lima, 1973) and Juergen Golte's *La racionalidad de la organización andina* (Lima, 1980). Waldemar Espinoza has edited a collection of many, diverse points of view in *Modos de producción en el imperio de los incas* (Lima, 1978) – among them Emilio Choy's view that it was a slave system, and Virgilio Roel's argument that there was a separate Inka mode of production.

The archaeology of the Andean area is summarized by Luis G. Lumbreras, *The people and cultures of ancient Peru* (Washington, D.C., 1974). An early but still useful guide to the artifacts is Wendell C. Bennett and Junius B. Bird, *Andean culture history* (New York, 1949), based on the collections of the American Museum in New York. A comprehensive reader has been prepared by John H. Rowe and Dorothy Menzel, *Peruvian archaeology* (Palo Alto, Calif., 1967), which includes Rowe's essay on Chavin art. In 1968, the Dumbarton Oaks Library sponsored a conference on Chavin, the proceedings of which were published in 1971 and represent a major effort to interpret the Early or Formative 'horizon' in Andean civilization. At various times Dumbarton Oaks has published other conference reports, with an emphasis on the art of coastal Peru.

John H. Rowe wrote his *Introduction to the archaeology of Cuzco* in 1944. Since then he has devoted most of his time to unravelling the position of Cusco, both in time and as an urban centre. He edits *Ñawpa Pacha*, the journal of the Institute of Andean Studies at Berkeley, California, which publishes technical reports but also general work about the Andean past; most of the articles are in English.

Architects have recently made major advances in the description, measurement and interpretation of Andean urbanism. Jorge Hardoy published *Ciudades Precolombinas* (Buenos Aires, 1964), which has gone through several editions in various languages. With Richard Schaedel, Hardoy has frequently produced readers bringing the subject up to date; see, for example, *El proceso de urbanización en América desde sus orígenes hasta nuestros días* (Buenos Aires, 1969). Graziano Gasparini and Luise Margolies, *Arquitectura Inka* (Caracas, 1977), is a major survey of the

monuments and cities, based on new plans and photographs. An
English translation was published in 1980 by the University of Indiana.
Craig Morris, of the American Museum in New York, has begun
publishing about Huanuco Pampa, the best preserved of the Inka
administrative centres, with close to 5,000 buildings of which 497 were
warehouses. John Hyslop has made a field study of the Inka road
system; he thinks it was the largest public works in the pre-industrial
world – at least 20,000 km. Heather Lechtman and Ana María Soldi have
published the first volume of a reader on Andean technology: *Runakunap
Kawsayninkupaq Rurasqankunaqa* (Mexico, 1981).

A special feature of Andean historiography is the search for explana-
tions of the rapid collapse of the Inka state after 1532. See John
Hemming, *The conquest of the Incas* (London, 1970) and Nathan Wachtel,
Vision des vaincus (Paris, 1971), translated as *The vision of the vanquished*
(Sussex, 1977). In Peru, the stress has been on the assistance the
Europeans had received from Andean polities rebelling against the Inka.
Waldemar Espinoza, *La destrucción del imperio de los incas* (Lima, 1973)
and Edmundo Guillén Guillén, *Versión inca de la conquista* (Lima, 1974)
are the works most readily available.

Early colonial institutions and their effect on the Andean population
were surveyed in 1946 by George Kubler, 'The Quechua in the Colonial
World', in *Handbook of South American Indians*, II (Washington, D.C.,
1946). James Lockhart, *Spanish Peru (1532–60), a colonial society* (Wisconsin, 1968) and Josep Barnadas, *Charcas (1535–65)* (La Paz, 1972) are
modern introductions to early European rule. Karen Spalding is the
author of an influential thesis, 'Indian rural society in colonial Peru'
(Berkeley, 1967), which remains unpublished, but articles based on it
were included in her *De indio a campesino* (Lima, 1974). See also her article
'The colonial Indian: past and future research perspectives', *Latin
American Research Review*, 6/1 (1972), 47–76. The economic processes
affecting the Andean population are analysed in C. Sempat Assadourian,
'La producción de la mercancía dinero en la formación del mercado
interno colonial', included in Enrique Florescano, *Ensayos sobre el
desarrollo económico de México y América Latina (1500–1975)*, published in
Mexico, 1979. With Cecilia Rabell, Assadourian has also attempted to
explain self-regulating mechanisms in Inka demography in *Proceedings*,
International Population Conference, Mexico, 1977. The colonial
demography of the Andean population was studied in Nicolás Sánchez-
Albornoz, *Indios y tributos en el Alto Perú* (Lima, 1978).

The most notable primary sources on changes in the Andes to surface in recent years are the records of the seventeenth-century campaign to 'extirpate idolatry', analysed by Pierre Duviols, *La lutte contre les réligions autochtones dans le Pérou colonial* (Lima–Paris, 1971). The protocols of these campaigns, more than 6,000 pages, were located in the archbishop's archives in Lima and are being prepared for publication by the Instituto de Estudios Peruanos.

Incorporating the Andean millennia into the national histories of Ecuador, Bolivia and Peru was a task that did not seem so alien in the 1920s to scholars like Domingo Angulo, Romeo Cúneo-Vidal, Jacinto Jijón y Caamaño, Rigoberto Paredes or Luis E. Valcárcel. In later decades the continuities before and after 1532 became less obvious. More recently, the idea of an Andean historiography which would encompass both pre-Columbian civilizations and the post-European centuries has been surfacing again in the work of Jorge Basadre, Ramiro Condarco, Alberto Crespo, Pablo Macera and Silvia Rivera. This Andean dimension of national history is the subject of Franklin Pease's recent volume of essays, *Del Tawantinsuyu a la historia del Perú* (Lima, 1978).

Since 1967, the *Handbook of Latin American Studies* (Library of Congress, Washington, D.C.), has included a section surveying Andean ethnohistory in the Humanities volume published every two years.

4. THE INDIANS OF SOUTHERN SOUTH AMERICA IN THE MIDDLE OF THE SIXTEENTH CENTURY

The quantity and the quality of early material on the southern cone of South America varies from area to area according to the period. First observers rarely confined their writings to a single ethnic group, but chroniclers, military poets and priests were attracted at once by Mapuche resistance to the conquest. However, similarly worthwhile accounts about other places on either side of the Andes are scarce, and our knowledge of some sixteenth- and seventeenth-century documents is based entirely on references to them in eighteenth-century chronicles.

There is useful information on the northern section of the southern Andes in the region's earliest chronicle, the *Crónica y relación copiosa y verdadera de los reinos de Chile*, completed in 1558 by Gerónimo de Bibar. Bibar not only accompanied Pedro de Valdivia on his conquest of Chile but also ventured from the northern deserts to the southern archipelago, besides further travels east of the Andes. His account, which has chapters on the geography and ethnography of the provinces he visited, has been widely used by ethnohistorians since its rediscovery and publication in Santiago in 1966. Other interesting works on the northern section include the *Relación del descubrimiento y conquista de los reinos del Perú* [1571] by Pedro Pizarro, an encomendero of Tarapacá; and the collection of chronicles which document Diego de Almagro's 1535 expedition to Chile, including Fernández de Oviedo's *Historia general y natural de las Indias*, an anonymous *Relación* attributed to the 'Almagrist' Cristóbal de Molina, and Mariño de Lovera's *Crónica del Reino de Chile* [1595]. Moreover, the three volumes of Father Barriga's *Documentos para la historia de Arequipa, 1534–1580* are an abundantly rich source of information. Brief but useful accounts of north-west Argentina, compiled by Marcos Jiménez de la Espada in the *Relaciones geográficas de Indias. Peru* [1881–97], 3 vols. (Madrid, 1965) are those of Diego Pacheco [1569], Gerónimo Luis de Cabrera [1573] and Pedro Sotelo Narváez [1583], as well as the letters of Juan de Matienzo [1566], Juan Lozano Machuca [1581], and Father Alonso de Barzana [1594]. Both Friar Reginaldo de Lizárraga's *Descripción breve de toda la tierra del Perú, Tucumán, Río de la Plata y Chile* (1603–9) (Madrid, 1968), and Antonio Vázquez de Espinoza's *Compendio y descripción de las Indias Occidentales* [1629] (Washington, D.C., 1948) reflect the social changes which were taking place as a result of the conquest. Documentary collections such as those edited by Robert Levillier, *La Audiencia de Charcas. Correspondencia de presidentes y oidores (1561–79)* (Madrid, 1918); *Gobernación del Tucuman. Probanzas de méritos y servicios de los conquistadores* (Madrid, 1919), and *Gobernantes del Perú. Cartas y papeles, siglo XVI: documentos del Archivo de Indias*, 14 vols. (Madrid, 1921–6); Pedro de Angelis, *Colección de obras y documentos relativos a la historia antigua y moderna de las provincias del Río de la Plata*, 5 vols. (2nd edn, Buenos Aires, 1910); and, especially, José Toribio Medina (*Colección de documentos inéditos para la historia de Chile desde el viaje de Magallanes hasta la batalla de Maipú, 1518–1818*, 30 vols. (Santiago, 1888–1902) – to cite but three historians in this field – are indispensable for studies in the historical reconstruction of the peoples of the southern cone.

Although published documentary evidence is limited, there are vast resources in European and New World archives, which must be given the specialist attention which they deserve. At the same time, there is no doubt that ethnohistorical research in the area must go hand in hand with the contributions of archaeology and social anthropology. As regards the study of the central southern Andes, in particular, the *Handbook of South American Indians* [*HSAI*], edited by Julian H. Steward, 6 vols. (Washington, D.C., 1949), has been surpassed to a large extent by research which has been done in the last two decades.

There is greater wealth of documentary material on Mapuche history than there is for other societies, but the Mapuche material is itself a source of information about adjacent groups – notably, the letters of Pedro de Valdivia (1545–52); Alonso de Ercilla's epic poem *La Araucana* [1569]; chronicles by Bibar [1558], Góngora Marmolejo [1575] and Mariño de Lovera [1595], in addition to Miguel de Olavarría's *Informe* [1594]. We have seventeenth-century grammars and vocabularies of the Huarpe and Mapuche languages written by Father Luis de Valdivia, *Arte, vocabulario y confesionario de la lengua de Chile* ([Lima, 1606], Leipzig, 1887), and Diego de Rosales, *Historia general del reino de Chile* [1674], 3 vols. (Valparaiso, 1877). As regards Spanish policy towards the Indians Alonso González de Nájera, *Desengaño y reparo de la guerra de Chile* [1614] (Santiago, 1889), and Francisco Nuñez de Pineda y Bascuñan, *Cautiverio feliz ... y razón de las guerras dilatadas de Chile* [1673] (Santiago, 1863) – soldiers who had direct experience of frontier life and of the Araucanian War – reflect opposite attitudes. Nuñez de Pineda y Bascuñan, who had been the Mapuche's captive as a youth in 1629, abandoned an early ethnocentric attitude towards their way of life and adopted a position of understanding and sympathy. The Araucanian War continued to motivate lengthy annals of events in Chile in the eighteenth and nineteenth centuries, including among others those by Pietas [1729], Sors [1765], Olivares [1767], Febrés [1767], Havestadt [1777], Bueno [1777], Usauro Martínez de Bernabé [1782], Molina [1787], Gómez de Vidaurre [1789], González de Agüeros [1791], Carvallo y Goyeneche [1796], Martínez [1806] and Pérez García [1810]. Nineteenth-century travellers from Europe and North America – Azara [1809], Stevenson [1825], Poepping [1826–9], Darwin [1832], Dessalines D'Orbigny [1835], Domeyko [1845], Smith [1853], Treutler [1861], etc. – extend the list, to which can be added Chilean authors writing before and after the pacification of Araucania. For a commentary on the ethnographic value of the writings of these authors, see Horacio Zapater, *Los aborígenes chilenos a través de cronistas y viajeros* (Santiago, 1973).

The basin of the Río de la Plata lacks the documentation which is typical of Spanish exploration in other parts of the Americas in the sixteenth century. First-hand observations on the regional population are available, nevertheless, both in Pedro Hernandez, ' *Los Comentarios*' *de Alvar Núñez Cabeza de Vaca* [1545] (Madrid, 1852) and in the chronicle of a journey to La Plata and Paraguay rivers by the German soldier Ulrich Schmidt, published in German in Frankfurt in 1567. In the seventeenth century, the *Cartas anuas de la Provincia del Paraguay, Chile y Tucumán* of the Society of Jesus are a valuable source of ethnographic information, and were used as such by Father Nicolás del Techo in his *Historia Provincial Paraquariae* [1673]. By far the most important contribution to the ethnography of the area, however, are works written by Jesuits who, through their missionary activities in the eighteenth century, had become familiar with a number of autochthonous societies. Outstanding are the works of Father Pedro Lozano, *Descripción coro-gráfica del Gran Chaco Gualamba* [1736] (Tucumán, 1941), *Historia de la Compañia de Jesús en la Provincia del Paraguay*, 2 vols. (Madrid, 1754–5), and *Historia de la conquista del Paraguay, Río de la Plata y Tucumán*, 5 vols. (Buenos Aires, 1873–5). Further essential sources for the study of the peoples of the Chaco are François Xavier de Charlevoix, *Histoire du Paraguay*, 6 vols. (Paris, 1757) and Martín Dobritzhoffer, *Historia de Abiponibus* (Vienna, 1784). To the south, Father Sánchez Labrador, *El Paraguay Católico* (1770) and Father Thomas Falkner, *A Description of Patagonia, and the adjoining parts of South America* (Hereford, 1774) return us to the Mapuche, this time in connection with their eastward expansion. The early nineteenth century is characterized by travellers' accounts: José Guevara, *Historia del Paraguay, Río de la Plata y Tucumán*, and Felix de Azara, *Voyages dans l' Amérique Méridionale* (1809), which, according to Alfred Métraux, is marked by an attitude of hostility towards the Indians. For the twentieth century, the works of Métraux in the *HSAI* – his 'Ethnography of the Chaco' (1, 1946), in particular – and Branislava Susnik, *El Indio colonial del Paraguay* (Asunción, 1971), the third volume of which draws both on published and on unpublished documents to show the operation of economic and political relations among Chaco societies in the sixteenth century, deserve mention.

Only at a late stage did the societies of the Pampa, Patagonia and the southern archipelago receive ethnographic attention. Since the sixteenth century references to them had arisen from attempts to conquer and colonize the Río de la Plata, from maritime expeditions to the Magellan Straits and from expeditions across the Andes (expeditions which initially set out to explore, and thereafter went in search of the legendary City of the Caesars). Juan Schobinger, in 'Conquistadores, misioneros y exploradores en el Neuquen. Antecedentes para el conocimiento etnográfico del noroeste Patagónico' (*Runa*, Buenos Aires, 9/1–2 (1958–9), 107–23), reviews the available ethnographic material on north-west Patagonia between the sixteenth and nineteenth centuries; John M. Cooper's 'The Patagonian and Pampean hunters', *HSAI* (1, 1946, 127–68) gives a general bibliography for the whole of the Pampa and Patagonia; but the ethnohistorical account of these areas in this chapter has been guided mainly by Rodolfo M. Casamiquela's ethnological reinterpretation of the sources, *Un nuevo panorama etnológico del área Pampeana y Patagónica adyacente. Pruebas etnohistóricas de la filiación Tehuelche septentrional de los Querandíes* (Santiago, 1969).

The southern fishing societies are mentioned by countless sailors who made the passage up the Magellan Straits and into the archipelago. See also John M. Cooper's reviews of the Ona and Yahgan sources in *HSAI* (1, 1946). The Alacaluf are the subject of Joseph Emperaire, *Los nómades del mar* (Santiago, 1963), but, overall, the greatest contribution to the historical and anthropological study of the peoples of the southern archipelago is to be found in Martín Gusinde, *Hombres primitivos en la Tierra del Fuego; de investigador a compañero de tribu* (translated from the German by Diego Bemúdez Camacho, Seville, 1951).

5. THE INDIANS OF BRAZIL IN 1500

Many of the most important sixteenth-century authors have been discussed in the text. The first Portuguese to write on Brazil was Pero Vaz de Caminha in his famous letter to King Manoel, 1 May 1500 (translated in *The voyages of Pedro Alvares Cabral to Brazil and India*, Hakluyt Society, 2nd ser., LXXXI, 1937, 3–33). Later in the century we have the valuable chronicles of Gabriel Soares de Sousa, *Tratado descriptivo do Brasil em 1587* (São Paulo, 1938), and Pero de Magalhães de Gandavo's *Tratado da terra do Brasil* and *Historia da Provincia de Santa Cruz* (1576, translated by John B. Stetson Jr., *The Histories of Brazil*, 2 vols., Cortes Society, New York, 1922). Essential material is in letters from Nóbrega, Anchieta and other Jesuits, best consulted in Serafim Leite's excellent collection *Cartas dos primeiros Jesuitas do Brasil*, 3 vols. (São Paulo, 1954–8, or, with a fourth volume, *Monumenta Brasiliae* (*Monumenta Historica Societatis Jesu*, 79–81, 87), Rome, 1956–60); for the entire period, the same author's monumental ten-volume *Historia da Companhia de Jesus no Brasil* (Lisbon–Rio de Janeiro, 1938–50) is of fundamental importance, and he published a good summary of this in *Suma histórica da Companhia de Jesus no Brasil* (Lisbon, 1965); there are also anthologies of José de Anchieta's writings, of which the best is edited by António de Alcântara Machado (Rio de Janeiro, 1933). A good Jesuit chronicler is Fernão Cardim, whose *Do clima e terra do Brasil* and *Do principio e origem dos Indios do Brasil* (*c.* 1584) survived only in Richard Hakluyt's English translation of the captured originals, in Samuel Purchas, *Hakluytus Posthumus or Purchas His Pilgrimes* (London, 1625). For a modern edition, see *Tratados do terra e gente do Brasil*, ed. Capistrano de Abreu (Rio, 1925). An anonymous Jesuit wrote a good account of Portuguese campaigns to extend their frontier north from Pernambuco, *Sumário das armadas que so fizeram...na conquista do Rio Paraíba* (*c.* 1587, in *Revista do Instituto Histórico e Geográfico Brasileiro*, 36/1 (1873)). The two most important early histories of Brazil are the Franciscan Vicente do Salvador's *Historia do Brasil* (1627, various modern editions since that in *Anais da Biblioteca Nacional do Rio de Janeiro*, 13 (1885–6)) which is particularly good for the north and Pará; and the Jesuit Simão de Vasconcellos, *Chronica das cousas do Brasil* and *Chronica da Companhia de Jesus do Estado do Brasil* (Lisbon, 1663), which is marred by being somewhat too hagiographic. Mem de Sá's letters and record of service are also important: *Anais da Biblioteca Nacional*, etc., 27 (1905).

It has often been said that other Europeans were more perceptive observers of Brazilian Indians than were the Portuguese. Outstanding are two French missionaries and a German mercenary, all of whom were with the Tupinamba or Tamoio of Rio de Janeiro in mid-sixteenth century: the Franciscan André Thevet, *Les Singularitez de la France Antarctique* [Paris, 1558] and *La Cosmographie universelle* [1575], both in Suzanne Lussagnet, *Les Français en Amérique pendant la deuxième moitié du XVIe siècle: le Brésil et les brésiliens* (Paris, 1953); Jean de Léry, *Histoire d'un voyage faict en la Terre du Brésil* (La Rochelle, 1578, and modern editions and translations); Hans Staden, *Wahrhaftige Historie und Beschriebung eyner Landtschafft der wilden, nacketen, grimmigen, menschfresser Leuten, in der newen Welt America gelegen...* ([Marburg, 1557] and modern editions and translations, including two into English: Hakluyt Soc., 1st ser., LI, 1874, and London, 1928). Another German provided interesting information on tribes of southern Brazil: Ulrich Schmidel, *Wahrhaftige Historie einer wunderbaren Schiffart* ([Frankfurt-am-Main, 1567] and recent editions of which the best is Graz, 1962, and translation in Hakluyt Soc., 1st ser., LXXXI, 1889). The English corsair, Anthonie Knivet, gives much information on tribes and slaving at the end of the century: his *Admirable Adventures and Strange Fortunes*...are in *Purchas His Pilgrimes*, pt 2, bk 6, ch. 7. The Spanish Dominican friar, Gaspar de Carvajal, provides essential information on the tribes encountered on the Amazon during Francisco de Orellana's first descent in 1542, *Descubrimiento del Río de las Amazonas* (many modern editions, and the best English translation in the New York, 1934 edition); Spaniards such as Toribio de Ortigüera and Francisco Vázquez, Custódio Hernandez, López Vaz and many others gave some information in their accounts of the Ursúa–Aguirre descent of 1561; and Cristóbal de Acuña complements this earlier information in his *Nuevo descubrimiento del gran río de las Amazonas* (1641, many modern editions and English translation in Hakluyt Soc., 1st ser., XXIV, 1859). Two other admirable French observers described the Indians of Maranhão during the brief French colony there (1612–15): Claude d'Abbeville, *Histoire de la mission des Pères Capucin en l'Isle de Maragnan*...[Paris, 1614]; and Yves d'Evreux, *Voyage dans le nord du Brésil* [1614], and Paris, 1864).

There are relatively few modern interpretations of Indians on the eve of the conquest. The most important are the books by Alfred Métraux, *La Civilisation matérielle des tribus Tupi-Guaraní* (Paris, 1928) and *La Religion des Tupinambá et ses rapports avec celle des autres tribus Tupi-Guaraní* (Paris, 1928), together with his papers on the Tupi and other tribes in the *Journal de la Société des Américanistes de Paris* and his contributions to the *HSAI*, I and III, and, more particularly, Florestan Fernandes' studies of Tupinamba society and the role of warfare in it, *Organização social dos Tupinambá* (1948; São Paulo, 1963) and *A função social de guerra na sociedade Tupinambá* (São Paulo, 1952). For the archaeology of the Amazon, the outstanding scholars are Betty J. Meggers, Clifford Evans and Curt Nimuendajú. More recently, some challenging theories have been put forward in Donald W. Lathrap, *The Upper Amazon* (London, 1970). On the Indian population of Brazil around 1500, see William M. Denevan, 'The aboriginal population of Amazonia', in W. M. Denevan (ed.), *The native population of the Americas in 1492* (Madison, 1977), and John Hemming, *Red gold. The conquest of the Brazilian Indians* (London, 1978), appendix.

The history of Indians during the period immediately after the conquest appears to some extent in the classic works of Robert Southey

(1810–19), Francisco Adolpho de Varnhagen, João Capistrano de
Abreu, Sérgio Buarque de Holanda, Caio Prado Júnior and João
Fernando de Almeida Prado. More particularly, see Alexander Marchant,
From barter to slavery (Baltimore, 1942), and Georg Thomas, *Die
Portugiesische Indianerpolitik in Brasilien, 1500–1640* (Berlin, 1968).
Hemming, *Red gold*, seeks to present a coherent and comprehensive
history of the treatment of the Brazilian Indians from 1500 to 1760.

The social anthropology of the tribes before the European conquest
should be deduced by reference to studies of modern tribes. There is
an immense literature of such studies, with monographs on the
ethnography of all the important surviving tribes. The *Handbook of South
American Indians [HSAI]*, ed. Julian Steward (6 vols., Washington,
D.C., 1946–50) is still useful though published in the 1940s. The most
relevant volumes are I on 'Marginal tribes', III on tropical forest tribes
and the later VI (1963) on such topics as linguistics and social geography.
There are important essays or listings of tribes in *Indians of Brazil in the
twentieth century*, edited by Janice H. Hopper (Washington, 1967). Artur
Ramos, *Introdução à antropologia brasileira: as culturas indígenas* (Rio de
Janeiro, 1971), and Julio César Melatti, *Indios do Brasil* (Brasília, 1970),
provide good introductions to Brazil's tribes, and the problem of
acculturation and assimilation is tackled by Egon Schaden, *Aculturação
indigena* (São Paulo, 1969) and Darcy Ribeiro, *Os índios e a civilização* (Rio
de Janeiro, 1970). Herbert Baldus' *Bibliografia critica da etnologia brasileira*,
2 vols. (São Paulo, 1954; Hanover, 1968) is useful although now out
of date.

Among the many anthropological monographs on modern tribes
shedding light on pre-conquest conditions, the works of Curt (Unkel)
Nimuendajú are outstanding because of his long practical experience
of living with tribes and his knowledge of their history and archaeology:
for example, *The Apinayé*, translated by Robert H. Lowie (Washington,
D.C., 1939); *The Serente*, translated by Lowie (Los Angeles, 1942); *The
Eastern Timbira*, translated by Lowie (Berkeley, 1946); *The Tukuna*,
translated by William D. Hohenthal (Berkeley, 1952) and his contributions to vol. III of the *HSAI*. A few other scholars might be
mentioned: on the Bororo, Cesar Albisetti and Angelo Jayme Venturelli,
Enciclopédia Bororo, 2 vols. (Campo Grande, 1962); on the tribes of the
Tocantins, Roberto da Mata and Roque de Barros Laraia, *Indios e
castanheiros: a emprêsa extrativa e os índios no Médio Tocantins* (São Paulo,
1967); on the Terêna and Tukúna, Roberto Cardoso de Oliveira, *O*

Processo de assimilização dos Terêna (Rio de Janeiro, 1960) and *O índio e o mundo dos brancos: a situação dos Tukúna do Alto Solimões* (São Paulo, 1964); on the Canela, the Tirió and the tribes of the Rio Negro, essays by William H. Crocker, Protásio Frickel and Eduardo Galvão respectively in the *Boletim do Museo Paraense Emílio Goeldi* (Belém); on the Chavante, David Maybury-Lewis, *Akwê-Shavante Society* (Oxford, 1967), and G. Giaccaria and A. Heide, *Auwê uptabi – uomine veri – vita Xavante* (Turin, 1971; Portuguese translation, São Paulo, 1972); on the Kain-gang, Jules Henry, *Jungle People: a Kaingang tribe of the highlands of Brazil* (New York, 1941); on the Indians of the north-east, Estevão Pinto, *Os indigenas do Nordeste* (São Paulo, 1935); on the Urubu, Francis Huxley, *Affable savages. An anthropologist among the Urubu Indians of Brazil* (New York, 1957); on the Mundurucú, Robert Francis Murphy, *Headhunter's heritage: social and economic change among the Mundurucú Indians* (Berkeley, 1960); on the Tapirapé, Charles Wagley, *Welcome of tears: the Tapirapé Indians of Central Brazil* (New York, 1978); Thomas Gregor, *Mehinaku* (Chicago, 1977).

6. THE SPANISH CONQUEST AND SETTLEMENT OF AMERICA

Charles Julian Bishko, 'The Iberian background of Latin American history: recent progress and continuing problems', *HAHR*, 36 (1956), 50–80, is an admirable introduction to the essential bibliographical tools and identifies the areas in which more research is needed, as well as those in which valuable work has been done. The *Indice histórico español* (Barcelona, 1953–), which may be regarded as a sequel to Benito Sánchez Alonso's indispensable *Fuentes de la historia española e hispano-americana*, 3 vols. (3rd edn, Madrid, 1952), with the additional advantage of including brief comments on the books and articles which it lists, has unfortunately shown signs of flagging in recent years. There is now a good selection of general books on the Iberian peninsula in the later Middle Ages and the Early Modern period, although Spain is much better served in this respect than Portugal. The classic work of Roger B. Merriman, *The rise of the Spanish Empire in the Old World and the New*, 4 vols. (New York, 1918–34, reprinted 1962) is still useful, particularly for political and institutional history, but has at many points been superseded by more recent work. It is weakest in the areas of economic and social history, where it should be supplemented by Jaime Vicens Vives, *An economic history of Spain* (Princeton, 1969), and vols. II and

III of the *Historia social y económica de España y América* (Barcelona, 1957), a collaborative enterprise edited by Vicens Vives. Medieval Spain as a frontier society is surveyed by A. MacKay, *Spain in the Middle Ages* (London, 1977), and later medieval Spain is examined in much greater detail by J. N. Hillgarth, *The Spanish kingdoms, 1250–1516*, 2 vols. (Oxford, 1976–8). For the sixteenth and seventeenth centuries, see Antonio Domínguez Ortiz, *The Golden Age of Spain, 1516–1659* (London, 1971); J. H. Elliott, *Imperial Spain, 1469–1716* (London, 1963); John Lynch, *Spain under the Habsburgs*, 2 vols. (2nd edn, Oxford, 1981). *Spain. A companion to Spanish studies*, ed. P. E. Russell (London, 1973) offers a useful up-to-date introduction to Spanish history and civilization.

There exist a number of good surveys of the colonial period in Spanish America which begin with the conquest and early settlement and which offer helpful bibliographical guidance: C. H. Haring, *The Spanish Empire in America* (New York, 1947); J. H. Parry, *The Spanish Seaborne Empire* (London, 1966); Charles Gibson, *Spain in America* (New York, 1966); Richard Konetzke, *Süd- und Mittelamarika, 1. Die Indianerkulturen Altamerikas und die spanisch-portugiesische Kolonialherrschaft* (Fischer Weltgeschichte, XXII, Frankfurt, 1965); Francisco Morales Padrón, *Historia general de América* (2nd edn, Madrid, 1975); Guillermo Céspedes, *Latin America: the early years* (New York, 1974).

To these general works should be added more specialized studies of particular aspects of the relationship between Spain and America. In the area of law and institutions, J. M. Ots Capdequí, *El estado español en las Indias* (3rd edn, Mexico, 1957), and Silvio Zavala, *Las instituciones jurídicas en la conquista de América* (Madrid, 1935), remain very useful investigations of the juridical foundations of Spanish rule. The same theme is explored with great richness of detail by Mario Góngora, *El estado en el derecho indiano* (Santiago de Chile, 1951). Mario Góngora's *Studies in the colonial history of Spanish America* (Cambridge, 1975) brings together a number of his essays on different aspects of Spain in the Indies and reveals how much the understanding of Spanish society and institutions can add to the understanding of the historical development of Spanish America. For many years, Earl J. Hamilton, *American treasure and the price revolution in Spain, 1501–1650* (Cambridge, Mass., 1934) was the starting-point for all discussion of the economic relationship between Spain and America, and, in spite of criticisms which reflect changing trends in the study of economic history, it remains a work of fundamental importance. Its theme, however, has been amplified and in many respects transformed by the massive study of Pierre and Huguette Chaunu on Seville's Atlantic trade, *Séville et l'Atlantique, 1504–1650* (8 vols., Paris, 1955–9). Different aspects of the relationship between Spain and the Indies are briefly examined and summarized in J. H. Elliott, *The Old World and the New, 1492–1650* (Cambridge, 1970), which pays particular attention to the cultural interplay between the two. Some of the themes discussed in this book, along with many others, were explored at an international conference held at the University of California in Los Angeles in 1975. The conference papers, which include some important pioneering essays, were published under the title of *First images of America*, edited by Fredi Chiappelli, 2 vols. (Los Angeles, 1976).

The literature on the discovery and conquest of America is enormous. One possible way of approaching it is through two volumes by Pierre Chaunu, *L'Expansion européenne du XIIIe au XVe siècle*, and *Conquête et exploitation des Nouveaux Mondes* ('Nouvelle Clio', vols. 26 and 26 *bis*, Paris, 1969). These not only contain long bibliographies, but also discuss some of the problems which have dominated recent historical debate. The Iberian maritime empires are set into the general context of European overseas expansion in G. V. Scammell, *The world encompassed* (London–Berkeley, 1980). See also the works of J. H. Parry, most recently *The discovery of South America* (London, 1979).

A great deal of time and energy was invested, especially in the nineteenth century, in the publication of documentary collections of material on the discovery, conquest and colonization of America. A great corpus of documentation is therefore available in print, although the editing of it often leaves much to be desired. Major collections include *Colección de documentos inéditos relativos al descubrimiento, conquista y organización de las antiguas posesiones españolas de América y Oceania*, ed. Pacheco, Cárdenas and Torres de Mendoza, 42 vols. (Madrid, 1863–84), and its sequel, *Colección de documentos inéditos relativos al descubrimiento, conquista y organización de las antiguas posesiones españolas de Ultramar*, 25 vols. (Madrid, 1885–1932). For both of these series, Ernst Schäfer, *Indice de la colección de documentos inéditos de Indias…*(Madrid, 1946), is an indispensable guide. Another great Spanish series, the *Colección de documentos inéditos para la historia de España*, 112 vols. (Madrid, 1842–95), also contains important American material, which is best located through Julián Paz, *Catálogo de la colección de documentos inéditos para la historia de España*, 2 vols. (Madrid, 1930–1). Richard Konetzke, *Colección de documentos para la historia de la formación social de Hispanoamerica*,

1493–1810, 3 vols. (Madrid, 1953–62), is an extremely valuable selection of documents relating to the theme of government and society in the Spanish colonial world.

The discovery, conquest and colonization of the New World can also be approached through printed contemporary accounts. An important new bibliographical guide to this material is now being prepared at the John Carter Brown Library of Brown University, Providence, which contains extensive holdings of early works on the Americas: *European Americana: a chronological guide to works printed in Europe relating to the Americas, 1493–1776*, ed. John Alden. Vol. I, covering the period 1493–1600, was published in 1980, and vol II, covering 1600–1650, in 1982. Many of the early histories and descriptions of the Americas are discussed in Francisco Esteve Barba, *Historiografía Indiana* (Madrid, 1964), while Colin Steele, *English interpreters of the Iberian New World from Purchas to Stevens, 1603–1726* (Oxford, 1975) is a bibliographical study which lists and describes English translations of Spanish and Portuguese books on the New World.

During the nineteenth and early twentieth centuries a great deal of scholarly effort was devoted to narrative and descriptive accounts of the discovery and conquest of America and to biographical studies of individual explorers and *conquistadores*. In the second half of the twentieth century interest has tended to shift towards such questions as the social background of the *conquistadores* as a collective group, and the organization and financing of voyages of discovery and colonization. But the old tradition was maintained in particular by Samuel Eliot Morison, both in his classic biography of Columbus, *Admiral of the Ocean Sea*, 2 vols. (Boston, 1942), and his *The European discovery of America*, of which the volume dealing with the southern voyages (New York and Oxford, 1974) is concerned with the Iberian New World. J. H. Parry, *The age of reconnaissance* (London, 1963) is a comprehensive survey of the history of European overseas discovery and colonization, and the collection of essays by Charles Verlinden, *The beginnings of modern colonization* (Ithaca and London, 1970) contains important information on the transfer of colonial techniques from the Mediterranean to the Atlantic, and on the role of the Genoese in the early stages of colonization. Further useful information on the role of the entrepreneur in colonial enterprises can be found in Guillermo Lohmann Villena, *Les Espinosa. Une famille d'hommes d'affaires en Espagne et aux Indes à l'époque de la colonisation* (Paris, 1968).

Wilcomb E. Washburn, 'The Meaning of "Discovery" in the Fifteenth and Sixteenth Centuries', *HAHR*, 68 (1962), 1–21, is a suggestive exploration of what discovery meant to contemporary Europeans. A somewhat similar inquiry was undertaken by Edmundo O'Gorman in his controversial work, *The invention of America* (Bloomington, 1961), which, as its title suggests, replaces the concept of 'discovery' by that of 'invention'.

The best introduction to the 'island' period of discovery is Carl O. Sauer, *The early Spanish Main* (Berkeley, Los Angeles and Cambridge, 1966). Ursula Lamb, *Frey Nicolás de Ovando, gobernador de las Indias, 1501–1509* (Madrid, 1956), is an important study of trial and error in the first Spanish attempts at settlement in the New World. The later story of the Caribbean is admirably told by Kenneth R. Andrews, *The Spanish Caribbean. Trade and plunder, 1530–1630* (New Haven–London, 1978); and, as always, much fascinating information can be gleaned from the Chaunus' *Séville et l'Atlantique*, cited above.

For the Spanish movement into mainland America, Mario Góngora, *Los grupos de conquistadores en Tierra Firme, 1509–1530* (Santiago de Chile, 1962) is an important examination of the background and composition of bands of *conquistadores*. Juan Friede, *Los Welser en la conquista de Venezuela* (Caracas–Madrid, 1961) looks at the role of commercial considerations in the process of conquest and colonization, as also does Enrique Otte, *Las perlas del Caribe: Nueva Cádiz de Cubagua* (Caracas, 1977). Murdo J. MacLeod, *Spanish Central America. A socioeconomic history, 1520–1720* (Berkeley, 1973), traces similar themes far into the colonial period.

Richard Konetzke, *Descubridores y conquistadores de América* (Madrid, 1968), leads up to the conquest of Mexico by way of the Caribbean and the first probing of the mainland. For the conquest of Mexico itself the letters of Cortés, and Bernal Díaz del Castillo's *Conquest of New Spain*, provide a superb record of events from the Spanish point of view, but need to be read with caution. The most convenient compilation of Cortés' letters and papers is Hernán Cortés, *Cartas y documentos*, ed. Mario Hernández Sánchez-Barba (Mexico, 1963), but a critical edition is badly needed. Hernán Cortés, *Letters from Mexico*, translated and edited by A. R. Pagden (Oxford, 1972) is a modern unabridged English translation, and has the advantage of notes and commentary. In recent years there has been a growing interest in the conquest from the standpoint of the conquered, stimulated by Miguel León-Portilla's anthology of texts compiled from indigenous sources, *Visión de los vencidos* (Mexico, 1959; translated as *The broken spears*, London, 1962). As yet, there is no comprehensive study of the conquest of Mexico from this standpoint comparable to Nathan Wachtel's *La Vision des vaincus. Les Indiens du Pérou devant la conquête espagnole, 1530–1570* (Paris, 1971; translated as *The vision of the vanquished*, London, 1977). For a full discussion of this theme, see *CHLA*, I, bibliographical essay 7. As far as the military aspects of conquest are concerned, Alberto Mario Salas, *Las armas de la conquista* (Buenos Aires, 1950) provides a detailed discussion of the weapons and methods of warfare of conquerors and conquered, while C. H. Gardiner examines the important theme of *Naval power in the conquest of Mexico* (Austin, 1956).

For warfare and conquest in other parts of Mexico and Central America, the following works are particularly useful: Robert S. Chamberlain, *The conquest and colonization of Yucatán* (Washington, D.C., 1948), and, by the same author, *The conquest and colonization of Honduras* (Washington, D.C., 1953); and for northern and north-western New Spain, Philip Wayne Powell, *Soldiers, Indians and silver. The northward advance of New Spain, 1550–1600* (Berkeley and Los Angeles, 1952), and Edward H. Spicer, *Cycles of conquest. The impact of Spain, Mexico and the United States on the Indians of the South-west, 1533–1960* (Tucson, 1962).

The literature on the conquest of Peru is on the whole less satisfactory than that on the conquest of Mexico, but two contributions to volume II of the *Handbook of South American Indians* (Washington, D.C., 1946), provide an admirable starting-point: J. H. Rowe, 'Inca Culture at the time of the Spanish Conquest', and G. Kubler, 'The Quechua in the colonial world'. John Hemming, *The conquest of the Incas* (London, 1970) is a splendid narrative in the tradition of Prescott, and is particularly good on the continuation of Inca resistance once the 'conquest' was over. James Lockhart provides a prosopography of the conquerors in *The men of Cajamarca* (Austin, 1972), which may be regarded as a prelude to his *Spanish Peru, 1532–1560* (Madison, 1968). For the Araucanian wars in Chile, see Alvaro Jara, *Guerre et société au Chili. Essai de sociologie coloniale* (Paris, 1961). See also *CHLA* I, bibliographical essays 5 and 7.

George M. Foster, *Culture and conquest* (Chicago, 1960) is a suggestive anthropological study of problems of acculturation in the Spanish colonial world, a theme which is impressively pursued for the Indian population of Mexico by Charles Gibson in his *The Aztecs under Spanish rule* (Stanford, 1964). José Durand studies the transformation of conqueror into colonist in *La transformación social del conquistador*, 2 vols. (Mexico, 1953). The hopes, fears and concerns of the early colonists are vividly revealed in their letters, selected, edited and translated by James Lockhart and Enrique Otte, *Letters and people of the Spanish Indies. The sixteenth century* (Cambridge, 1976). Richard Konetzke, 'La Formación de la nobleza de Indias', *Estudios Americanos*, 3 (1951), 329–57, is fundamental for the evolution of a new social elite in the Spanish Indies.

On population, land and towns in the immediate post-conquest period, see *CHLA* II, bibliographical essays 1, 5, 6 and 3, and on the church, see *CHLA* I, bibliographical essay 14. For the theme of 'spiritual conquest' Robert Ricard, *La 'Conquête spirituelle' du Mexique* (Paris, 1933) and John L. Phelan, *The Millennial Kingdom of the Franciscans in the New World* (2nd edn, Berkeley and Los Angeles, 1970), deserve special mention.

7. INDIANS AND THE SPANISH CONQUEST

Western historiography, for a long time dominated by a Eurocentric view of historical development, has devoted considerable attention to the exploits of the *conquistadores*, but has only recently begun to examine the 'vision of the vanquished'. Still useful however, in spite of being more than a century old, are the works of William H. Prescott, *History of the conquest of Mexico*, 3 vols. (New York, 1843), and *History of the conquest of Peru*, 2 vols. (London, 1847). The same is true of other classic works by Georg Friederici, *Der Charakter der Entdeckung und Eroberung Amerikas durch die Völker der alten Welt*, 3 vols. (Stuttgart, 1925–36), and by Robert Ricard, *La Conquête spirituelle du Mexique. Essai sur l'apostolat et les méthodes missionnaires des ordres mendiants en Nouvelle-Espagne de 1523–24 à 1572* (Paris, 1933). For a full discussion of work published on the conquest, see *CHLA* I, bibliographical essay 6. An important revisionist work might be mentioned here: Ruggiero Romano, *Les mécanismes de la conquête coloniale: les conquistadores* (Paris, 1972).

In the last two decades ethnohistorical research has made remarkable progress both on Mesoamerica and the Andes. The work of Angel M. Garibay, Miguel León-Portilla, Gonzalo Aguirre Beltran, Pedro Carrasco and others on the one hand, and of John V. Murra, Maria

Rostworowski de Diez Canseco, Tom Zuidema and others on the other, has transformed our knowledge of American societies before and after the conquest: we now have completely new perspectives on the Indian reaction to the European invasion. The two anthologies of Miguel León-Portilla, in particular, *Visión de los vencidos. Relaciones indigenas de la conquista* (Mexico, 1959) (translated as *The Broken Spears* (London, 1962)), and *El reverso de la conquista. Relaciones aztecas, mayas e incas* (Mexico, 1964), have been complete revelations. Nathan Wachtel's *La Vision des vaincus. Les Indiens du Pérou devant la conquête espagnole, 1530–1570* (Paris, 1971) (translated as *The Vision of the Vanquished* (Sussex, 1977)), has continued in the same vein.

Works of synthesis, with a comparative perspective, such as Alberto Mario Salas, *Las armas de la conquista* (Buenos Aires, 1950), or Friedrich Katz, *The ancient American civilizations* (New York, 1972), are unfortunately only too rare. Most current research is restricted to limited areas, usually at the regional level. To the well-known works of Charles Gibson, *Tlaxcala in the sixteenth century* (New Haven, 1952) and *The Aztecs under Spanish rule. A history of the Indians of the valley of Mexico, 1519–1810* (Stanford, 1964), Juan Friede, *Los Quimbayas bajo la dominación española, 1559–1810* (Bogotá, 1963) and Jean Borde and Mario Góngora, *Evolución de la propiedad rural en el valle de Puanque* (Santiago, 1956), can now be added, for Mexico, William B. Taylor, *Landlord and peasant in colonial Oaxaca* (Stanford, 1972), John K. Chance, *Race and class in Colonial Oaxaca* (Stanford, 1978), and Ida Altman and James Lockhart (eds.), *Provinces of early Mexico* (Los Angeles, 1976). For the Andes one should mention the numerous articles of Waldemar Espinoza Soriano, especially on the *mitma*, his publicatin of the *Memorial de Charcas. 'Chrónica' inédita de 1582* (Lima, 1969), and his study of the alliance of the Huancas with the Spanish invaders, *La destrucción del Imperio de los Incas. La rivalidad politica y señorial de los curacazgos andinos* (Lima, 1973). For the Ecuadorian region, the excellent works of Udo Oberem: 'Don Sancho Hacho, ein cacique mayor des 16. Jahrhunderts', *JGSWGL*, 4 (1967), 199–225; 'Trade and trade goods in the Ecuadorian montaña'; in Patricia J. Lyon (ed.), *Native South Americans* (Boston, 1974); *Los Quijos. Historia de la transculturación de un grupo indígena en el oriente ecuatoriano, 1538–1958*, 2 vols. (Madrid, 1971); and *Notas y documentos sobre miembros de la familia del Inca Atahuallpa en el siglo XVI. Estudios etnohistóricos del Ecuador* (Guayaquil, 1976). Finally, the recent, pathbreaking study of Frank Salomon, *Los señores étnicos de Quito en la época de los Incas* (Otavalo, 1980). For the southern Andes, Josep M. Barnadas, *Charcas. Orígenes históricos de una sociedad colonial* (La Paz, 1973). At a more general level, there are important contributions from Franklin Pease, *Los últimos incas del Cuzco* (Lima, 1972), and *Del Tawantinsuyu a la historia del Perú* (Lima, 1978); also from Karen Spalding, *De indio a campesino. Cambios en la estructura social del Perú colonial* (Lima, 1978), and Nicolás Sánchez-Albornoz, *Indios y tributo en el Alto Perú* (Lima, 1978). The remarkable work by Teresa Gisbert, *Iconografía y mitos indígenas en el arte* (La Paz, 1980), which links iconographical material, both pre-Colombian and colonial, with an examination of indigenous myths and beliefs also deserves mention: it opens up completely new perspectives on the historical anthropology of art. Finally, a special number of *AESC* (September–December 1978) edited by John V. Murra and Nathan Wachtel, is devoted to 'l'anthropologie historique des sociétés andines'.

This flowering of ethnohistorical research has stimulated, both for Mesoamerica and the Andes, numerous publications of sources, with full scholarly apparatus: for example, *Beyond the codices*, edited by Arthur J. O. Anderson, Frances Berdan and James Lockhart (Berkeley–Los Angeles, 1976); Garci Diez De San Miguel, *Visita hecha a la provincia de Chucuito (1567)*, edited by John V. Murra and Waldemar Espinosa Soriano (Lima, 1964); Inigo Ortiz De Zúñiga, *Visita de la Provincia de León de Huánuco (1562)*, edited by John V. Murra, 2 vols. (Huánuco, 1967–72); *Tasa de la visita general Francisco de Toledo*, edited by Noble D. Cook (Lima, 1975); *Visita general de Perú por el virrey don Francisco de Toledo. Arequipa, 1570–1575*, edited by Alejandro Malaga Medina (Arequipa, 1974); *Collaguas I*, edited by Franklin Pease (Lima, 1977). See also critical editions of *Rites et traditions de Huarochiri: manuscrit quechua du début du 17e siècle*, edited by Gerald Taylor (Paris, 1980), and Felipe Guaman Poma de Ayala, *El primer nueva coronica y buen gobierno*, edited by John V. Murra and Rolena Adorno, 3 vols. (Mexico, 1980). Under the same rubric can be classified an admirable publication by Silvio Zavala, *El servicio personal de los indios en el Perú (extractos del siglo XVI)*, I (Mexico, 1978).

On the 'frontiers', besides the comparative study of Edward H. Spicer, *Cycles of conquest. The impact of Spain, Mexico and the United States on the Indians of the Southwest, 1533–1960* (Tucson, 1962), there are a number of more specific studies: Philip Wayne Powell, *Soldiers, Indians and Silver. The Northward advance of New Spain, 1550–1600* (Berkeley, 1952); Jack D. Forbes, *Apache, Navaho, and Spaniard* (Norman, 1960);

R. E. Latcham, *La Capacidad guerrera de los Araucanos: sus armas y métodos militares* (Santiago, 1915) and *La Organisación social y las creencias religiosas de los antiguos Araucanos* (Santiago, 1922); Robert C. Padden, 'Cultural change and military resistance in Araucanian Chile, 1550–1730', *South-Western Journal of Anthropology* (1957), 103–21; Alvaro Jara, *Guerre et société au Chili. Essai de sociologie coloniale. La transformation de la guerre d'Araucanie et l'esclavage des Indiens du début de la Conquête espagnole aux débuts de l'esclavage légal (1612)* (Paris, 1961); and also the work in preparation by Thierry Saignes on the Chiriguanos. Further works on this topic can be found in *CHLA* 1, bibliographical essay 5.

8. THE PORTUGUESE SETTLEMENT OF BRAZIL, 1500–80

The best overall introduction to the sources and the literature of colonial Brazilian history is provided in José Honório Rodrigues' *História da história do Brasil, 1ª parte: historiografia colonial* (2nd edn, São Paulo, 1979); his more detailed but older *Historiografía del brasil, siglo XVI* (Mexico, 1957) deals exclusively with the sixteenth century. Also useful is Rubens Borba de Moraes, *Bibliografia Brasileira do período colonial* (São Paulo, 1969), a 'catalog with commentaries of works published before 1808 by authors born in Brazil'. Many important sources have been transcribed and published as appendixes to the various chapters of Carlos Malheiro Dias (ed.), *História da colonização Portuguesa do Brasil* (hereafter cited as *HCPB*), 3 vols. (Porto, 1921–4). Other major collections of source material can be found scattered throughout the *Anais da Biblioteca Nacional do Rio de Janeiro* (Rio de Janeiro, 1876–) and the volumes of the series *Documentos Históricos* (Rio de Janeiro, 1928–) published by the same institution. Many relevant documents have also appeared scattered throughout the volumes of *As gavetas da Torre do Tombo*, 11 vols. to date (Lisbon, 1960–).

Standard accounts of Brazilian history all treat, in varying degrees, the subjects touched upon in the chapter. Among the more useful are Pedro Calmon, *História do Brasil*, 7 vols. (Rio de Janeiro, 1959); Sérgio Buarque de Holanda (ed.), *História geral da civilização Brasileira*, I, 2 vols. (São Paulo, 1960); and Francisco Adolfo Varnhagen's nineteenth-century classic (enriched with notes by Capistrano de Abreu and Rodolfo Garcia): *História geral do Brasil*, 5 vols. (5th edn, São Paulo, 1948). *HCPB*, Carlos Malheiro Dias (ed.), a collaborative work that reflects the best Portuguese scholarship of its generation, stops at the year 1580; while João Capistrano de Abreu's classic, *Capítulos de história colonial* (4th edn, Rio de Janeiro, 1954) goes up to 1800. A survey of the period to 1580 with emphasis on the economic relations between settlers and Indians is provided by Alexander Marchant in *From barter to slavery* (Baltimore, 1942). Eulália M. L. Lobo has written an excellent overview of Brazilian colonial administration and enriched it by comparison with Spanish examples: *Processo administrativo ibero-americano* (Rio de Janeiro, 1962). Sérgio B. de Holanda gives an attractive account of one aspect of imperial ideology in his *Visão do Paraíso; os motivos edênicos no descobrimento e colonização do Brasil* (Rio de Janeiro, 1959), and Eduardo Hoornaert has edited a collection of studies of the colonial Brazilian church: *História da igreja no Brasil, primeira época* (Petropolis, 1977).

Portugal's thrust into the Atlantic during the fifteenth century has generated a large literature, separate from that of colonial Brazil and too vast to cover in detail. For a general introduction to the field, see Vitorino Magalhães Godinho, *A economia dos descobrimentos henriquinos* (Lisbon, 1962) with an excellent critical bibliography; this may be supplemented by the more exhaustive list provided in Bailey W. Diffie and George D. Winius, *Foundations of the Portuguese Empire, 1415–1580* (Minneapolis, 1977), 480–516. The essential facts of the expansion are given in Damião Peres' standard work, *História dos descobrimentos Portugueses* (2nd edn, Coimbra, 1960), and in Luís de Albuquerque, *Introdução a história dos descobrimentos* (Coimbra, 1962). Contrasting poles of interpretation are offered by Duarte Leite's *História dos descobrimentos* (2 vols., Lisbon, 1958–61) – critical, sceptical and debunking – and by Jaime Cortesão's two-volume synthesis, *Os descobrimentos Portugueses* (Lisbon, 1958–61), which gives greater rein to the historical imagination with sometimes dubious results. The various studies of Teixeira da Mota, dispersed in many journals, are valuable, as is Manuel Nuno Dias' *O capitalismo monárquico Português*, 2 vols. (Coimbra, 1963–4), for its wealth of data, not always fully digested. A stimulating essay that attempts to define some fundamental characteristics of colonial Brazilian life and discover their Iberian provenance has been written by Sérgio B. de Holanda, *Raízes do Brasil* (6th edn, Rio de Janeiro, 1971).

Metropolitan events during the sixteenth century can be approached via A. H. de Oliveira Marques' excellent and interpretive *História de Portugal*, 2 vols. (Lisbon, 1973) – to be preferred to the earlier edition in English – as well as through an older collaborative work edited by

Damião Peres, *et al.*, *História de Portugal*, 7 vols. (Barcelos, 1931–5); most recent is Joaquim Veríssimo Serrão, *História de Portugal, III (1498–1580)* (Lisbon, 1978), of value primarily for its wealth of bibliographical citations. For the reign of King Manuel 'The Fortunate', a good secondary study is lacking, but earlier accounts are fundamental: Damião de Góis, *Crónica do Felicíssimo Rei D. Manuel*, edited by David Lopes, 4 vols. (Coimbra, 1949–55) and Jerónimo Osório, *Da vida e feitos d'El Rey D. Manuel*, 3 vols. (Lisbon, 1804–6), a translation of his *De rebus Emmanuelis gestis* (Lisbon, 1571). For the reign of Manuel's successor we have Alfredo Pimenta's *D. João III* (Porto, 1936) as well as two seventeenth-century accounts: Fr. Luís de Sousa, *Anais de D. João III*, edited by M. Rodrigues Lapa, 2 vols. (Lisbon, 1938), and Francisco d'Andrada, *Chronica de... Dom João III...* 4 vols. (Coimbra, 1796). In addition much of the correspondence about imperial affairs between João III and the count of Castanheira has been edited and published (in the original Portuguese) by J. D. M. Ford and L. G. Moffatt, *Letters of John III, King of Portugal, 1521–1557* (Cambridge, Mass., 1931). King Sebastião and his successor, cardinal-King Henrique, have found their biographer in Queiroz Velloso, whose *D. Sebastião, 1554–1578* (3rd edn, Lisbon, 1945) and *O reinado do Cardeal D. Henrique* (Lisbon, 1946) give the essential story.

Vitorino Magalhães Godinho has examined the structure and functioning of the empire, taken as a whole, in various articles printed in his collected *Ensaios II: Sobre a história de Portugal*, 2nd edn (Lisbon, 1978), and more comprehensively in his *Os descobrimentos e a economia mundial*, 2 vols. (Lisbon, 1963), while José Sebastião da Silva Dias has dealt with sixteenth-century Portuguese culture and intellectual life in an excellent study, *A polítícia cultural da época de D. João III*, 2 vols. (Coimbra, 1969). An older work by Hernani Cidade, *A literatura Portuguesa e a expansão ultramarina*, 1 (2nd edn, Coimbra, 1963), is still useful.

Cabral's discovery of Brazil has generated much controversy cogently summarized by the late Samuel Eliot Morison in *The European discovery of America: the southern voyages 1492–1616* (New York, 1974), 210–35; the voyages that followed Cabral's have been carefully sorted out by Max Justo Guedes in the *História naval Brasileira* (hereafter cited as *HNB*), 2 vols. (Rio de Janeiro, 1975–9), 1: 1, 179–245. Both Marchant, *From barter to slavery*, and the *HCPB* provide good accounts of the voyage of the *Bretoa*, while Rolando Laguarda Trías clarifies the

Spanish–Portuguese conflict over the La Plata region in the *HNB*, 1: 1, 249–348. His account of the voyages of Christóvão Jaques revises the earlier account of António Baião and C. Malheiro Dias in the *HCPB*, III, 59–94. He is also responsible for the best recent account of the expedition of Martim Afonso da Sousa, the primary source for which – a diary of the voyage by Martim's brother, Pero Lopes de Sousa – has been lavishly edited with supplementary documentation by Eugénio Castro (ed.), *Diario da navegação de Pero Lopes de Sousa (1530–1532)*, 2 vols. (Rio de Janeiro, 1940).

The period of settlement is probably the least well studied of the various phases of Brazil's sixteenth-century history and good analyses are lacking. Some of the donatarial grants are printed in the *HCPB*, III, 257–83, 309–423, and competently analysed by Paulo Merêa in an accompanying chapter; the subsequent histories of the captaincies are touched upon in all the general accounts, but the topic still lacks an up-to-date synthesis. One can meanwhile consult the works of João Fernando de Almeida Prado, *Primeiros povoadores do Brasil, 1500–1530* (São Paulo, 1935); *Pernambuco e as capitanias do nordeste do Brasil*, 4 vols. (São Paulo, 1941); *Bahía e as capitanias do centro do Brasil, 1530–1626*, 3 vols. (São Paulo, 1945–50); *São Vicente e as capitanias do sul do Brasil, 1501–1531* (São Paulo, 1961); *A conquista da Paraíba* (São Paulo, 1964). An uncritical, but competent, general account is Elaine Sanceu, *Captains of Brazil* (Barcelos, 1965). Of the earlier writers, Vicente do Salvador, Soares de Sousa and Fernão Cardim give the most information on the post-settlement development of the various captaincies. José António Gonçalves de Melo has re-edited (in collaboration with Cleonir Xavier de Albuquerque) the letters of Duarte Coelho, donatary of Pernambuco: *Cartas de Duarte Coelho a el Rei* (Recife, 1967) with a valuable introductory study, while many of the other letters about the early settlements that were sent back to Portugal have been published as appendixes to various chapters of the *HCPB*, III, 257–83, 309–23.

Post-discovery relations between Indians and Portuguese can now be followed in the excellent and detailed survey (with full bibliography) of John Hemming, *Red gold: the conquest of the Brazilian Indians, 1500–1760* (London, 1978), while the evolution of Portuguese policy toward the Brazilian natives is outlined by Georg Thomas, *Die portugiesische Indianerpolitik in Brasilien, 1500–1640* (Berlin, 1968). The Jesuits' role in the conversion and acculturation of the Tupi is related in detail by Serafim Leite, *História da Companhia de Jesus no Brasil*, 10 vols.

(Lisbon–Rio de Janeiro, 1938–50), while the principal sources – the Jesuit missionaries' letters – have been edited in four volumes by the same scholar: *Monumenta Brasiliae* (Rome, 1956–60). This prolific historian has also given us (*inter alia*) Nóbrega's *corpus* in *Cartas do Brasil e mais escritos do P. Manuel da Nóbrega* (Coimbra, 1955), as well as a study of the foundation and early history of São Paulo, so closely linked to Jesuit activity: *Nóbrega e a fundação de São Paulo* (Lisbon, 1953). More references to the Jesuits will be found in *CHLA* I, bibliographical essay 15. Other works on the early history of São Paulo are Jaime Cortesão, *A fundação de São Paulo – capital geográfica do Brasil* (Rio de Janeiro, 1955), and Vitorino Nemésio, *O campo de São Paulo. A Companhia de Jesus e o plano Português do Brasil, 1528–1563* (Lisbon, 1954).

A short, introductory overview is Michel Mollat's 'As primeiras relações entre a França e o Brasil: dos Verrazano a Villegagnon', *Revista de História* (São Paulo), 24 (1967), 343–58. More detail is given in Paul Gaffarel, *Histoire de Brésil français au XVIe siècle* (Paris, 1878), and, recently, in Charles-André Julien, *Les Voyages de découverte et les premiers établissements (XV–XVI siècles)* (Paris, 1948). For the rise and fall of Villegaignon's settlement at Rio de Janeiro, we now have a comprehensive, up-to-date study from Philipe Bonnichon and Gilberto Ferrez, 'A França Antártica', *HNB*, II, 402–71. Two famous contemporary accounts of the colony (which also provide much first-hand information about the Indians) are the Calvinist, Jean de Léry's *Histoire d'un Voyage faict en la terre du Brésil* (La Rochelle, 1578) and *Les Singularitéz de la France Antartique autrement nommée Amérique* (Paris and Antwerp, 1558) by the Franciscan, André Thevet, who sailed out with Villegaignon in 1555.

In addition to the contemporary sources mentioned in the footnotes to the chapter, valuable information on Brazilian society and economy, *c.* 1580, is given in Frédéric Mauro's classic study of the 'sugar cycle', *Le Portugal et l'Atlantique au xviie siècle, 1570–1670* (Paris, 1960), and in Roberto Simonsen's pioneering *História econômica do Brasil, 1550–1820* (4th edn, São Paulo, 1962). A. J. R. Russell-Wood's *Fidalgos and Philanthropists: the Santa Casa da Misericordia of Bahía, 1550–1755* (Berkeley, 1968), and Arnold Wiznitzer's, *Jews in colonial Brazil* (New York, 1960), deal with important aspects of early Brazilian society. Stuart B. Schwartz has examined the composition of the labour force and work practices on some late sixteenth-century sugar plantations in his article, 'Indian labor and New World plantations: European demands and Indian responses in northeastern Brazil', *American Historical Review*, 83/1 (1978), 43–79.

9. SPAIN AND AMERICA IN THE SIXTEENTH AND SEVENTEENTH CENTURIES

In addition to the general studies by Domínguez Ortiz, Elliott and Lynch, listed in *CHLA* I, bibliographical essay 6, there are a number of more specialized studies of Spanish government and society which ought to be taken into account by anyone interested in following the relationship between Spain and its American possessions in the sixteenth and seventeenth centuries. The best brief account of the reign of Charles V is by H. G. Koenigsberger, 'The empire of Charles V in Europe', in vol. II of *The New Cambridge Modern History* (Cambridge, 1958). There are two recent biographies of Philip II: Peter Pierson, *Philip II of Spain* (London, 1975) and Geoffrey Parker, *Philip II* (Boston and Toronto, 1978). But incomparably the most important study of the age of Philip II is by Fernand Braudel, *La Méditerranée et le monde méditerranéen à l'époque de Philippe II*, 2 vols. (2nd edn, Paris, 1966); translated as *The Mediterranean and the Mediterranean world in the age of Philip II*, 2 vols. (London, 1972–3), which is especially useful for tracing the shift in the centre of gravity of Spanish power from the Mediterranean to the Atlantic during the course of Philip's reign. I. A. A. Thompson, *War and government in Habsburg Spain, 1560–1620* (London, 1976), is a pioneering piece of research into Spain's organization for war, and the strains imposed by warfare on the Spanish administrative system.

Problems relating to the decline of Spain are discussed by J. H. Elliott, 'The decline of Spain', and 'Self-perception and decline in seventeenth-century Spain', in *Past and Present*, 19 (1961) and 74 (1977) respectively, and there is a brilliant treatment of this theme by Pierre Vilar, 'Le Temps du Quichotte', *Europe*, 34 (1956). The reign of Charles II, the least-known period in the history of Habsburg Spain, is discussed by Henry Kamen in *Spain in the later seventeenth century* (London, 1980), while R. A. Stradling surveys the vicissitudes of Spanish power in *Europe and the decline of Spain* (London, 1981). Vol. II of John Lynch, *Spain under the Habsburgs*, 2 vols. (2nd edn, Oxford, 1981), has the great merit of relating the history of seventeenth-century Spain to that of Spanish

America, but there is a crying need for a systematic and comprehensive study of this relationship over the sixteenth and seventeenth centuries as a whole. Pierre and Huguette Chaunu's *Séville et l'Atlantique*, 8 vols. (Paris, 1958–9), does this on a massive scale for the commercial relationship, but many other aspects of the relationship, at both the institutional and the personal level, have scarcely begun to be explored. Some indication of the possibilities is suggested by the uncompleted, and in many respects flawed, work of Manuel Giménez Fernández, *Bartolomé de Las Casas*, 2 vols. (Seville, 1953–60), which places under a microscope the crown's policies towards the Indies between 1516 and 1523 and the role of its advisers and officials in formulating and implementing those policies, but which is distorted by its obsessive hatred of Ferdinand the Catholic and his men. For the reign of Philip II, the title of José Miranda's *España y Nueva España en la época de Felipe II* (Mexico, 1962) promises well, but the book consists of two separate sections, one on Spain and the other on New Spain, and while each constitutes an excellent essay in itself, the connection between the two is never developed.

In view of the dearth of studies examining simultaneous developments in the metropolis and the colonies, the bibliographical suggestions which follow will include works on both Spain and Spanish America.

J. H. Parry, *The Spanish theory of empire in the sixteenth century* (Cambridge, 1940) and Silvio Zavala, *La filosofía política en la conquista de América* (Mexico, 1947) are helpful introductions to the Spanish theory of empire, as also is chapter 2 of Mario Góngora's *Studies in the colonial history of Spanish America* (Cambridge, 1975). J. A. Fernández-Santamaria, *The state, war and peace* (Cambridge, 1977) is a close examination of Spanish political theory in the first half of the sixteenth century, which includes discussions of attitudes to the Indies, while Venancio Carro, *La teología y los teólogo-juristas españoles ante la conquista de Indias* (Seville, 1945), directly addresses the problem of the conquest of America in scholastic thought.

H. G. Koenigsberger, *The practice of empire* (Ithaca, 1969), although concerned with the government of Sicily under Philip II, raises issues of general importance for the understanding of Spanish administrative practice. The most important organ for the administration of the Spanish New World was the Council of the Indies, and the composition and institutional history of this council are examined in detail in the classic work by Ernesto Schäfer, *El Consejo Real y Supremo de las Indias*,

2 vols. (Seville, 1935–47), to which should be added the volume of essays by D. Ramos and others, *El Consejo de las Indias en el siglo XVI* (Valladolid, 1970). Aspects of financial administration are discussed by Ismael Sánchez-Bella, *La organización financiera de las Indias, siglo XVI* (Seville, 1968).

A splendid mass of documentation for the study of the viceroys of Mexico and Peru during the Habsburg period has now been made available by Lewis Hanke, in his *Los virreyes españoles en América durante el gobierno de la casa de Austria*, Biblioteca de Autores Españoles, vols. 233–7 (Madrid, 1976–8) for Mexico, and vols. 280–5 (Madrid, 1978–80) for Peru. A number of viceroys have received individual studies, of which the following are especially noteworthy: Arthur S. Aiton, *Antonio de Mendoza, first viceroy of New Spain* (Durham, N.C., 1927); Roberto Levillier, *Don Francisco de Toledo, supremo organizador del Perú*, 2 vols. (Buenos Aires, 1935–40); María Justina Sarabia Viejo, *Don Luís de Velasco, virrey de Nueva España 1550–1564* (Seville, 1978).

The best study of an *audiencia* is J. H. Parry, *The Audiencia of New Galicia in the sixteenth century* (Cambridge, 1948), but in general far too little is known about Spanish judges and officials in the Indies. Peggy K. Liss, *Mexico under Spain, 1521–1556* (Chicago, 1975), besides synthesizing a complicated period in the history of Mexico, shows how the crown gradually imposed its authority on *conquistador* society. Richard L. Kagan, *Students and society in early modern Spain* (Baltimore, 1974) is a pioneering study of the educational background of the men who administered Spain and America, but too few of these men are yet known as individual personalities. This makes all the more valuable John Leddy Phelan's *The kingdom of Quito in the seventeenth century* (Madison, 1967), which examines the contrasts between the ideals and the practice of the Spanish bureaucracy through a study of the career of Dr Antonio de Morga, president of the *audiencia* of Quito from 1615 to 1636. Another approach to these judges and officials is by way of their own writings, of which Alonso de Zorita's *The lords of New Spain*, translated and edited by Benjamin Keen (London, 1965) and Juan de Matienzo's *Gobierno del Perú*, edited by Guillermo Lohmann Villena (Paris and Lima, 1967) are especially revealing.

Other useful studies of different aspects of Spanish colonial administration are Guillermo Lohmann Villena, *El corregidor de Indios en el Perú bajo los Austrias* (Madrid, 1957), and J. H. Parry's examination of *The sale of public office in the Spanish Indies under the Hapsburgs* (Berkeley, 1953), a theme which is also considered in Mark A. Burkholder and D. S. Chandler, *From impotence to authority. The Spanish crown and the American Audiencias, 1687–1808* (Columbia, Mo., 1977). For a fuller discussion of the literature on urban development and municipal administration, see *CHLA* ii, bibliographical essay 3, and, on the church, see *CHLA*, i, bibliographical essay 14.

The Spanish treatment of the Indians was a source of controversy to contemporaries and has remained so ever since. As Sverker Arnoldsson showed in his *La leyenda negra. Estudios sobre sus orígenes* (Göteborg, 1960), the 'black legend' of Spanish cruelty pre-dated the conquest of America, but the reports of the massacres and maltreatment of the Indians did much to determine the image of Spain in the European consciousness. This in turn called forth from Spain and its defenders a 'white legend'. Charles Gibson examines both in his anthology, *The black legend: Anti-Spanish attitudes in the Old World and the New* (New York, 1971).

Spanish theory and practice as regards the treatment of the indigenous peoples of America has been the source of intense study and heated debate in the historiography of the past 50 years, a debate focused particularly, although not exclusively, on the controversial figure of Bartolomé de Las Casas. The bibliography on Las Casas is now enormous, as can be seen from the selection of titles at the end of Juan Friede and Benjamin Keen, *Bartolomé de Las Casas in history* (DeKalb, 1971), a selection of essays on different aspects of his career and reputation. A central figure in the Las Casas controversy has been Lewis Hanke, who has done more than anyone else to bring the aspirations and achievements of Las Casas to the attention of the English-speaking world, and whose *The Spanish struggle for justice in the conquest of America* (Philadelphia, 1949), and *Aristotle and the American Indians* (London, 1959) have breathed new life into the sixteenth-century debate for twentieth-century readers. The great French Hispanist, Marcel Bataillon, whose monumental study of the influence of Erasmus in Spain, *Erasmo y España*, 2 vols. (Mexico, 1950) also has important implications for sixteenth-century America, wrote a number of carefully argued essays on Las Casas and his writings, which were collected under a single cover in his *Études sur Bartolomé de Las Casas* (Paris, 1965). Out of a massive bibliography two other books besides the work of Giménez Fernandez (*B. de Las Casas*) deserve special mention: Juan Friede, *Bartolomé de Las*

Casas; precursor del anticolonialismo (Mexico, 1974), which pays close attention to the context in which Las Casas was operating, and Angel Losada, *Fray Bartolomé de Las Casas a la luz de la moderna crítica histórica* (Madrid, 1970). A recent biography which takes account of modern research is Philippe-Ignace André-Vicent, *Bartolomé de Las Casas. Prophète du Nouveau Monde* (Paris, 1980). Angel Losada also devoted himself to studying and editing the works of Las Casas' rival, Sepúlveda. Las Casas and Sepúlveda, however, are only two of the many sixteenth-century Spaniards, some well known and others scarcely known at all, who discussed the capacities and status of the Indians and the treatment they deserved. The works of some of these figures are only now becoming accessible for study, thanks to the efforts of scholars like Ernest J. Burrus, whose *The writings of Alonso de la Vera Cruz*, 5 vols. (Rome, St Louis and Tucson, 1968–76) shows the possibilities. Other contemporary documents of great interest are published by José A. Llaguno in *La personalidad jurídica del indio y el III Concilio Provincial Mexicano (1585)* (Mexico, 1963). Joseph Höffner, *Christentum und Menschenwürde. Das Anliegen der Spanischen Kolonialethik im goldenen Zeitalter* (Trier, 1947), remains a useful survey of sixteenth-century Spanish theories about the Indians, but the source material and studies that have appeared in recent years suggest the need for a new synthesis.

One of the major problems in the study of the controversy over the Indians is to determine what effects, if any, the theorizing had on colonial practice; and here a work like that by Juan A. and Judith E. Villamarin, *Indian labor in mainland colonial Spanish America* (Newark, Delaware, 1975) serves as a salutary reminder of the gulf that separated ideals from reality. The effectiveness, or otherwise, of theory and legislation on behaviour in the Indies and the general question of the relationship between settler society and the *república de los indios* still requires much study at the local level, of the type undertaken by Juan Friede in his *Vida y luchas de don Juan del Valle, primer obispo de Popayán y protector de indios* (Popayán, 1961), or Eugene E. Korth, *Spanish policy in colonial Chile. The struggle for social justice, 1535–1700* (Stanford, 1968).

On the sea link between Spain and the Indies, the *carrera de Indias*, and colonial trade, see *CHLA* i, bibliographical essay 10.

Problems of war, defence and taxation must loom large in any attempt to chart the changing relationship between metropolitan Spain and the Indies in the later sixteenth and seventeenth centuries. A. P. Newton,

The European nations in the West Indies, 1493–1688 (London, 1933; reprinted 1966), remains a useful outline survey of the incursions of North Europeans into the Spanish colonial world. This should be supplemented by Kenneth R. Andrews, *The Spanish Caribbean. Trade and plunder, 1580–1630* (New Haven and London, 1978) and by the same author's excellent re-assessment of *Drake's voyages* (London, 1967). Peter Gerhard, *Pirates on the West Coast of New Spain, 1575–1742* (Glendale, 1960) examines the growing threat posed by piracy in the Pacific. For reactions to these attacks, Roland D. Hussey, 'Spanish reaction to foreign aggression in the Caribbean to about 1680', *HAHR*, 9 (1929), 286–302 is still of value. The defence of the Panama isthmus is examined by Guillermo Céspedes del Castillo, 'La defensa militar del istmo de Panamá a fines del siglo XVII y cominezos del XVIII', *Anuario de Estudios Americanos*, 9 (1952), 235–75, while Günter Kahle, 'Die Encomienda als militärische Institution im kolonialen Hispanoamerika', *JGSWGL*, 2 (1965), 88–105, traces the decline and fall of the military role of the *encomendero*. Detailed examinations of defence problems at a local level, and also of the consequences of enemy attack, may be found in J. A. Calderón Quijano, *História de las fortificaciones en Nueva España* (Seville, 1957); Enriqueta Vila Vilar, *Historia de Puerto Rico, 1600–1650* (Seville, 1974); Frank Moya Pons, *Historia colonial de Santo Domingo* (3rd edn, Santiago, Dominican Republic, 1977); and C. R. Boxer, *Salvador de Sá and the struggle for Brazil and Angola, 1602–1688* (London, 1952). Olivares' scheme for the Union of Arms is briefly discussed in J. H. Elliott, *The revolt of the Catalans* (Cambridge, 1963), ch. 7, while Fred Bronner examines attempts to introduce it in Peru in 'La Unión de Armas en el Perú. Aspectos político-legales', *Anuario de Estudios Americanos*, 24 (1967), 1133–71, but the scheme still requires a comprehensive treatment. For the introduction of the *alcabala* into the Indies, Robert S. Smith, 'Sales taxes in New Spain, 1575–1770', *HAHR*, 28 (1948), 2–37, is fundamental.

The seventeenth century is the least well known, and the least studied, of any century of Spanish-American history. Thanks to the pioneering work of Woodrow Borah, *New Spain's century of depression* (Berkeley and Los Angeles, 1951), the more sombre aspects of the century have tended to be emphasized, at the expense of its more creative and formative characteristics. The Borah thesis is examined in the light of more recent research by P. J. Bakewell in his introduction to the Spanish translation, *El siglo de la depresión en Nueva España* (Mexico, 1975). J. I. Israel, *Race, class and politics in colonial Mexico, 1610–1670* (Oxford, 1975), discusses some of the processes at work in seventeenth-century Mexican society, as does José F. de la Peña, *Oligarquía y propiedad en Nueva España, 1550–1624* (Mexico, 1983), which examines the important theme of the consolidation of an elite, on the basis of rich new documentation. An important aspect of the creole question is analysed by A. Tibesar in 'The Alternativa: a study in Spanish–Creole relations in seventeenth-century Peru', *The Americas*, 11 (1955), 229–83, but in general more work has been done for New Spain than for Peru on the formation of a settler society with its own growing sense of identity. Irving A. Leonard, *Baroque times in Old Mexico* (Ann Arbor, 1959) and Jacques Lafaye, *Quetzalcóatl and Guadalupe. The formation of Mexican national consciousness, 1531–1813* (Chicago, 1976) are the outstanding recent contributions to a subject of fundamental importance for understanding the eventual break with Spain.

10. SPAIN AND AMERICA: THE ATLANTIC TRADE, 1492–1720

In spite of a great quantity of recent literature the history of Spanish and Spanish American oceanic navigation and trade before 1720 is very uneven in its availability and level of sophistication. Some aspects, eras and episodes are well known; others, such as the connections between certain specific areas and the *carrera*, have been studied hardly at all. Yet others, such as the dimensions and significance of smuggling, can never be known accurately. The subject has also suffered from a tug-of-war between romance and statistics. Some writers have emphasized treasure, pirates, hurricanes, galleons and derring-do on the Spanish Main. The other school has counted the ships, the crews, the crossings, the prices, the cargoes, until the graphs and tables reduce the whole epic to banality.

The literature on the expansion of Europe is immense and there are many approaches. One of the most imaginative and comprehensive surveys is Pierre Chaunu, *L'éxpansion européenne du XIIIe au XVe siècle* (Paris, 1969), a fine example of the author's emphasis on economics and geography. Another general survey, more closely tied to men and events, is Boies Penrose, *Travel and discovery in the Renaissance, 1420–1620* (Cambridge, Mass., 1952). Carlo Cipolla in his entertaining *Guns, sails and empires: technological innovation and the early phases of European expansion, 1400–1700* (New York, 1966), summarizes what we know about the role of material advantages in Europe's advance overseas. John H. Parry, *Europe and a wider world, 1415–1715* (London, 1959), explains early routes, ships, navigation and trades.

The Portuguese explorations have produced an enormous amount of scholarship, as can be appreciated by scrutinizing the bibliography in Bailey W. Diffie and George D. Winius' excellent survey, *Foundations of the Portuguese empire, 1415–1580* (Minneapolis, 1977). The Portuguese writings of the age of discovery are listed and briefly discussed in Joaquim Barradas de Carvalho, 'A Literatura portuguesa de viagems (século XV, XVI, XVII)', *Revista de Historia* (São Paulo), 40/81 (1970), 51–74.

Samuel Eliot Morison's biography of Columbus, *Admiral of the Ocean Sea; a life of Christopher Columbus*, 2 vols. (Boston, 1942), is the standard account. The same author's *The European discovery of America*, 2 vols. (New York, 1971, 1974), especially volume II on the southern voyages, contains a wealth of material on early voyages of discovery, ships, crews, navigational methods and life at sea. (See especially chap. 8, 'The mariner's day'.)

Two manuals of navigation of that era have been published: Pedro de Medina, *Libro de Cosmographía*, first published in 1538, translated into many languages, and superbly edited and translated in a modern and facsimile edition as *A navigator's universe: the Libro de Cosmographía of 1538*, by Ursula Lamb (Chicago, 1972); and Diego García de Palacio, *Instrucción náutica para navegar*, which first appeared in Mexico in 1587 and in Madrid in facsimile in 1944.

For the sixteenth-century Spanish background, see *CHLA* 1, bibliographical essays 9 and, especially, the works of Fernand Braudel, John H. Elliott and John Lynch.

The best succinct analysis of the pre-eminence of Iberia's south-west corner, and of the role played by the stepping-stone islands, is by Pierre Chaunu, in his *Conquête et exploitation des nouveaux mondes (XVIe siècle)* (Paris, 1969). John H. Parry, *The Spanish seaborne empire* (New York, 1966), is a convenient, clearly explained account of the same determinants. The map on p. 40 is eloquent. Chapter 2 explains how Seville came to dominate as the American port, both in the Spanish and the Andalusian contexts. It also contains the early history of the *Casa de Contratación*, and much else on the history of the Indies. The early and continuing importance of the Canaries is covered in Francisco Morales Padrón, *El comercio canario-americano (siglos XVI, XVII y XVIII)*

(Seville, 1955). A more recent work is Felipe Fernández-Armesto, *The Canary Islands after the Conquest. The making of a colonial society in the early sixteenth century* (New York, 1982). There are many accounts of voyages. Tomás de la Torre's amusing yet harrowing account has been published several times, most recently as, *Desde Salamanca, España, hasta Ciudad Real, Chiapas; diario de viaje, 1544–1545* (Mexico, 1945).

The Atlantic sea link between Spain and the New World up to the middle of the seventeenth century has been examined at length and in overwhelming detail by Pierre and Huguette Chaunu. Their massive *Séville et l'Atlantique, 1504–1650*, 13 vols. in 8 (Paris, 1955–60) is the one indispensable source for the carrera. Volume VII, *Construction Graphique*, is enormously informative in its visual impact as it discusses winds, currents, voyages, distances in time, ships, gross movements of ships, cargoes, and origins and destinations of cargoes. Volume VIII: 1 studies the evolution of ship types; navigation; once again and at length the reasons for the Andalusian–Guadalquivir ports complex and its predominance; the stepping-stone islands; and the role of the carrera in the development of each part of Spanish America. Volume VIII: 2, which is in fact two volumes, discusses macro-movements, the great cycles of Spanish Atlantic commerce, and the inflation in prices. Throughout, and in a variety of ways, the authors discuss the determinants of ship size and speed, the length of voyages, and the weight, bulk and profitability of cargoes.

These determinants are discussed more compactly by L. Denoix in 'Caractéristiques des navires de l'époque des grandes découvertes', in *Ve Colloque d'Histoire Maritime* (Paris, 1966). Another basic text on Spain, the carrera and Spanish America is Clarence H. Haring's *Trade and navigation between Spain and the Indies in the time of the Hapsburgs* (Cambridge, Mass., 1918; reprinted Gloucester, Mass., 1964). Works by J. Everaert, Antonio García-Baquero González, Lutgardo García Fuentes, Henry Kamen and Michel Morineau, which continue the story of the carrera beyond 1650 until its demise in the late eighteenth century, are discussed in context below.

Other aspects of Seville and the carrera mentioned in this chapter may be found in Ruth Pike, *Enterprise and Adventure: the Genoese in Seville and the opening of the New World* (Ithaca, 1966), which may overstate its case, and in the work of a contemporary, Joseph de Veitia Linaje, *Norte de la contratación de las Indias Occidentales*, first published in Seville in 1672 and reprinted in Buenos Aires in 1945. An English translation was published by Captain John Stevens in 1702, republished in facsimile in 1977. The laws governing the early *flota* system are to be found in Volume IV of Diego Encinas, *Cedulario Indiano*, 4 vols. [first published in 1596] (facsimile, Madrid, 1945).

On the island period of discovery and settlement and the gold cycle, see, beside the Chaunus, the works of Carl O. Sauer and Kenneth R. Andrews cited in *CHLA* II, bibliographical essay 6.

On early Spanish migration to the New World, see the work of Peter Boyd-Bowman and Magnus Mörner cited in *CHLA* II, bibliographical essay 1.

The slave trade in Nicaraguan Indians is discussed by David R. Radell in 'The Indian slave trade and population of Nicaragua during the sixteenth century', *The Native Population of the Americas in 1492*, William M. Denevan (ed.) (Madison, 1976), 67–76. William L. Sherman in *Forced native labor in sixteenth-century Central America* (Lincoln, Nebraska, 1979), would disagree with Radell, and with the present author, on the extent of the trade and the numbers involved.

The following give a general account of the encomienda and the tribute: Lesley Byrd Simpson, *Exploitation of land in Central Mexico in the sixteenth century* (Berkeley and Los Angeles, 1952); Silvio Zavala, *La Encomienda indiana* (Madrid, 1945); and José Miranda, *El tributo indígena en la Nueva España* (Mexico, 1951). See also *CHLA* II, bibliographical essays 5 and 6. On the collapse of the Indian population, see *CHLA* II, bibliographical essay 1 and, on silver mining, *CHLA* II, bibliographical essay 4.

Woodrow Borah and Sherburne Cook began the study of price inflation in Mexico in their *Price trends of some basic commodities in Central Mexico, 1531–1570* (Berkeley and Los Angeles, 1958), while Earl J. Hamilton's classic *American treasure and the price revolution in Spain, 1501–1650* (Cambridge, Mass., 1934), did the same for Spain. A modern study of American bullion and of the price revolution is by Pierre Vilar, *Oro y moneda en la historia (1450–1900)* (Barcelona, 1969; English translation, London, 1976).

Cochineal as a product in Atlantic commerce is the subject of Raymond L. Lee, 'American cochineal in European commerce, 1526–1625', *Journal of Modern History* [*JMH*], 23 (1951), 205–24. For indigo, see Mario Rubio Sánchez, *Historia del añil o xiquilite en Centro América*, 2 vols. (San Salvador, 1976, 1978). For pearling, see Enrique Otte, *Las perlas del Caribe* (Caracas, 1977). The work of the Chaunus has much information on these and the lesser Atlantic cargoes.

Woodrow Borah studied the first links between Mexico and Peru in *Early colonial trade between Mexico and Peru* (Berkeley and Los Angeles, 1954). For Venezuela's small trades with Cartagena and much larger cacao trade with Veracruz, see the two books by Eduardo Arcila Farías, *Economía colonial de Venezuela* (Mexico, 1956), and *Comercio entre Venezuela y México en los siglos xvi y xvii* (Mexico, 1950). Havana's trade patterns are described in detail in Levi Marrero, *Cuba, economía y sociedad*, 8 vols. to date (San Juan, P.R. and Madrid, 1972–80). William Lytle Schurz, *The Manila Galleon* (New York, 1959), is a classic story of the Philippine link. Pierre Chaunu, *Les Philippines et le Pacifique des Ibériques (xvie, xviie, xviiie siècles); introduction méthodologique et indices* (Paris, 1960), emphasizes the economic and the quantifiable in this trade.

On the defence of the Indies against the incursions of North Europeans, see *CHLA* 1, bibliographical essay 9.

For the literature on the slave trade to Spanish America, see *CHLA* 11, bibliographical essay 10. The classic work is Georges Scelle, *La Traite négrière aux Indes de Castille*, 2 vols. (Paris, 1906). The rise of smuggling in its various aspects can be followed in Curtis Nettels, 'England and the Spanish American trade, 1680–1715', *JMH*, 3 (1931), 1–32; A. P. Thornton, 'Spanish slave-ships in the English West Indies, 1660–85', *HAHR*, 35 (1955), 374–85; Sergio Villalobos R., 'Contrabando francés en el Pacífico, 1700–1724', *Revista de Historia de América*, 51 (1961), 49–80; and Vera Lee Brown, 'Contraband trade as a factor in the decline of Spain's empire in America', *HAHR*, 8 (1928), 178–89. It is interesting that there is little recent work on the topic of contraband. This and other trends of that period in the Caribbean have been skilfully summarized in the early chapters of Geoffrey J. Walker, *Spanish politics and imperial trade, 1700–1789* (London, 1979).

John H. Elliott examined 'The decline of Spain', in *Crisis in Europe, 1560–1660*, Trevor Aston (ed.) (New York, 1967). Whether there was a coincidental or related decline in the colonies, or any decline at all, has been the subject of debate. For opposite views, see, for example, Woodrow Borah, *New Spain's century of depression* (Berkeley and Los Angeles, 1951), and Vol. 11 of John Lynch's *Spain under the Hapsburgs*, 2 vols. (2nd edn, Oxford, 1981). Pierre and Huguette Chaunu, *Séville et l'Atlantique*, show conclusively that the carrera declined from the 1620s to mid-century and perhaps beyond.

Two authors, using different consular reports and interpretations, have found a dramatic rise in Spanish imports of American bullion after about 1670 until the end of the century. They are J. Everaert, *De internationale en koloniale Handel der Vlaamse Firma's te Cadiz, 1670–1700* (Bruges, 1973), especially p. 395, and Michel Morineau, 'D'Amsterdam à Séville: de quelle realité l'histoire des prix est-elle le miroir?', *AESC*, 23 (1968), 178–205, and especially pp. 196–7. Henry Kamen discusses the findings of these writers, and the stages of Spain's demographic, economic and commercial recovery in *Spain in the Later Seventeenth Century, 1665–1700* (London and New York, 1980). The official carrera's decline to even lower levels, 1650–1700, and its ephemeral slight revivals, are traced in Lutgardo García Fuentes, *El comercio Español con América, 1650–1700* (Seville, 1980). Those who wish to follow Spain's Atlantic career still further in time should read Antonio García-Baquero González, *Cádiz y el Atlántico, 1717–1778, el comercio colonial español bajo el monopolio gaditano*, 2 vols. (Seville, 1976).

Changes in English shipping and trading patterns can be followed in Ralph Davis, *The rise of the English shipping industry in the 17th and 18th Centuries* (London, 1962), in the same author's *The rise of the Atlantic economies* (Ithaca, 1973), and in his two articles on English foreign trade between 1660 and 1775 in *The growth of English overseas trade in the 17th and 18th centuries*, W. E. Minchington (ed.) (London, 1969).

Theories on the role of the Spanish carrera in European and American history are numerous, and all cannot be listed here. For some of these long-term impacts the following are suggestive: Stanley J. and Barbara H. Stein, *The colonial heritage of Latin America: essays in economic dependence in perspective* (New York, 1970) and the provocative Immanuel Wallerstein, *The Modern World System*, 2 vols. to date (New York and London, 1976, 1980). Fernand Braudel's latest massive opus, *Civilisation matérielle, économie et capitalisme, XVe–XVIIIe siècle*, 3 vols. (Paris, 1979), is long, repetitious and disorganized, but it has many brilliant passages, including several discussions of the larger, worldwide implications of the carrera and of American colonial bullion.

11. BOURBON SPAIN AND ITS AMERICAN EMPIRE

For Spain at the start of the Bourbon period there is John Lynch, *Spain under the Habsburgs*, 2 vols. (2nd edn, Oxford, 1981) and two works by Henry Kamen, *Spain in the Later Seventeenth Century* (London, 1980), and *The War of Succession in Spain 1700–15* (London, 1969). The best general accounts of the eighteenth century are Gonzalo Anes, *El antiguo régimen: los Borbones* (Historia de España Alfaguara IV, Madrid, 1975) and

Antonio Domínguez Ortiz, *Sociedad y estado en el siglo XVIII español* (Madrid, 1976). The impact of the Enlightenment is discussed in Richard Herr, *The eighteenth-century revolution in Spain* (Princeton, 1958), Luis Sánchez Agesta, *El pensamiento político del despotismo ilustrado* (Madrid, 1953) and Jean Sarrailh, *L'Espagne éclairée de la seconde moitié du XVIIIe siècle* (Paris, 1954). On Jansenism read Joël Saugnieux, *Le Jansénisme espagnol du XVIIIe siècle, ses composantes et ses sources* (Oviedo, 1975). On the economy there is Jordi Nadal and Gabriel Tortella (eds.), *Agricultura, comercio colonial y crecimiento económico en la España contemporánea* (Barcelona, 1974), Gonzalo Anes, *Las crisis agrarias en la España moderna* (Madrid, 1970) and David R. Ringrose, *Transportation and economic stagnation in Spain 1750–1850* (Durham, N.C., 1970), and his 'Perspectives on the economy of eighteenth century Spain' in *Historia Ibérica* (1973), I, 59–102. Trade with the American empire is dealt with by Geoffrey J. Walker, *Spanish politics and imperial trade 1707–1789* (London, 1979), and Antonio García-Baquero González, *Cádiz y el Atlántico 1717–1778*, 2 vols. (Seville, 1976), and his *Comercio colonial y guerras revolucionarias* (Seville, 1972). See also Barbara H. and Stanley J. Stein, 'Concepts and realities of Spanish economic growth 1759–1789', *Historia Ibérica*, 1 (1973), 103–19.

For the Revolution of Government see the first part of D. A. Brading, *Miners and merchants in Bourbon Mexico 1763–1810* (Cambridge, 1971). Other studies are Luis Navarro García, *Intendencias de Indias* (Seville, 1959), John Lynch, *Spanish colonial administration 1782–1810. The intendant system in the viceroyalty of the Río de la Plata* (London, 1958), and J. R. Fisher, *Government and society in colonial Peru. The intendant system 1784–1814* (London, 1970). For its impact in New Granada see John Leddy Phelan, *The people and the king. The Comunero Revolution in Colombia, 1781* (Madison, 1978). Céspedes del Castillo, *Lima y Buenos Aires* (Sevilla, 1956), is still useful. On creole participation in *audiencias*, see Mark A. Burkholder and D. S. Chandler, *From impotence to authority. The Spanish crown and the American audiencias 1787–1808* (Columbia, Miss., 1977). The campaign against the Church is dealt with by Nancy M. Farriss, *Crown and clergy in colonial Mexico 1759–1821. The crisis of ecclesiastical privilege* (London, 1968). No less than three books are available on the military: Christon I. Archer, *The army in Bourbon Mexico 1760–1810* (Albuquerque, 1977), Leon G. Campbell, *The military and society in colonial Peru 1750–1810* (Philadelphia, 1978) and Allan J. Kuethe, *Military reform and society in New Granada, 1773–1808* (Gainesville, 1978).

On the colonial economy the starting point must always be Alexander
von Humboldt, *Essai politique sur le Royaume de la Nouvelle-Espagne*, 2
vols. (Paris, 1807–11), and *Voyage aux régions equinoxiales de Nouveau
Continent fait en 1799, 1801, 1802, 1803 et 1804* (Paris, 1807). Both these
works present a mass of information and have been translated into both
English and Spanish. For Mexico there is E. Arcila Farías, *El siglo
ilustrado en América. Reformas económicas del siglo XVII en Nueva España*
(Caracas, 1955). Brian R. Hamnett, *Politics and trade in southern Mexico
1750–1821* (Cambridge, 1971) covers repartimientos de comercio and
D. A. Brading, *Miners and merchants in Bourbon Mexico*, the export
economy.

For Cuba, apart from Humboldt's *Voyage*, there is Manuel Moreno
Fraginals, *The sugar mill. The socioeconomic complex of sugar in Cuba
1760–1860* (New York, 1976), but see also Javier Ortiz de la Tabla
Ducasse, *Comercio exterior de Veracruz 1778–1821* (Seville, 1978). On
Central America, consult Robert S. Smith, 'Indigo production and trade
in colonial Guatemala', *HAHR*, 39 (1959), 181–211; and Troy S. Floyd,
'Bourbon palliatives and the Central American mining industry
1765–1800', *The Americas*, 18 (1961), 103–25 and his 'The indigo
merchant: promoter of Central American economic development
1700–1808', *Business History Review*, 39 (1965), 466–88. For Venezuela,
E. Arcila Farías, *Comercio entre Venezuela y Mexico en los siglos XVII y
XVIII* (Mexico, 1950) is all-important. On Colombia, see John Leddy
Phelan, *The people and the king. The Comunero revolution in Colombia, 1781*
and A. D. Macfarlane, 'Economic change in the viceroyalty of New
Granada with special reference to overseas trade 1739–1810' (Ph.D.
dissertation, London University, 1977). On Ecuador, the coast is
covered by Michael T. Hammerly, *Historia social y económica de la antigua
provincia de Guayaquil 1763–1842* (Guayaquil, 1973).

On silver-mining in Peru, J. R. Fisher, *Silver mines and silver miners in
colonial Peru 1776–1824* (Liverpool, 1977), gives the chief series of
production. For a comparative view see D. A. Brading and Harry
E. Cross, 'Colonial silver mining: Mexico and Peru', *HAHR*, 52
(1972), 545–79. For a fuller discussion of the literature on eighteenth-
century mining, see *CHLA* II, bibliographical essay 4. For Chile the
best introduction is Marcello Carmagnani, *Les Mécanismes de la vie
économique dans une société coloniale: le Chili 1680–1830* (Paris, 1973).
Equally important are Sergio Villalobos, *El comercio y la crisis colonial*
(Santiago de Chile, 1968), and Mario Góngora, *Origen de los 'inquilinos'*

de Chile central (Santiago de Chile, 1960). For the Río de la Plata area the introductory chapter of Tulio Halperin-Donghi, *Politics, economics and society in Argentina in the revolutionary period* (Cambridge, 1975), is invaluable; a supplement is Susan Midgen Socolow, *The merchants of Buenos Aires 1778–1810. Family and commerce* (Cambridge, 1978). For the literature on eighteenth-century population growth, see *CHLA* II, bibliographical essay 1. Similarly, on urban growth *CHLA*, II, essay 3, on agriculture *CHLA*, II, essays 5 and 6, and on the internal economy, including the *obrajes*, *CHLA*, II, essay 7.

12. PORTUGAL AND BRAZIL: POLITICAL AND ECONOMIC STRUCTURES OF EMPIRE, 1580–1750

The following general histories of Portugal are indispensable: in English, H. V. Livermore, *A new history of Portugal* (London, 1966); in Portuguese, A. de Oliveira Marques, *Historia de Portugal*, 2 vols. (Lisbon, 1972–3) (trans. into English and French), and J. Verissimo Serrão, *Historia de Portugal*, 5 vols. (Lisbon, 1980); in French, A. A. Bourdon, *Histoire de Portugal* (Paris, 1970), short but very good, and Y. Bottineau, *Le Portugal et sa vocation maritime. Histoire et civilisation d'une nation* (Paris, 1977), written with style and subtlety, preserving the balance between underlying structures and events. Mention must also be made of the very useful *Dicionario de historia de Portugal*, ed. Joel Serrão, 4 vols. (Lisbon, 1961–71), Damião Peres' great *Historia de Portugal*, 8 vols. (Barcelos, 1929–35), and vols. I and v of Fortunato de Almeida, *Historia de Portugal* (Coimbra, 1922–31), which consist of a description of Portuguese institutions and their development. A. Silbert, *Le Portugal méditerranéen à la fin de l'Ancien Régime*, 2 vols. (Paris, 1966) is very useful for the study of agrarian and social structures. On the Portuguese empire, a start can be made with C. R. Boxer, *The Portuguese seaborne empire 1415–1825* (London, 1973), and *Four centuries of Portuguese expansion 1415–1825: a succinct survey* (Johannesburg, 1965). V. Magalhães Godinho, *L'Économie de l'empire portuguais aux XVe et XVIe siècles* (Paris, 1969), has been expanded from the Portuguese, *Os descobrimentos e a economia mundial*, 2 vols. (Lisbon, 1963–5; 2nd edn, 4 vols., 1983). See also V. Magalhães Godinho's contributions to the *New Cambridge Modern History*: 'Portugal and her empire', *NCMH*, v, 384–97, and 'Portugal and her empire 1680–1720', *NCMH*, vI (1970), 509–40. F. Mauro, *Le Portugal et l'Atlantique au XVIIe siècle 1570–1670. Étude économique* (Paris, 1960; 2nd edn, 1983) is fundamental and has a convenient bibliography to which reference can be made. See also V. Magalhães Godinho, 'Le Portugal – les flottes du sucre et les flottes de l'or (1670–1770)', *AESC*, April–June (1950), 184–97, reprinted in *Ensaios*, II (Lisbon, 1968), 293–315. For complementary material, see B. T. Duncan, *Atlantic Islands...in the XVIIth century* (Chicago, 1972). João Lúcio de Azevedo, *Épocas de Portugal económico* (2nd edn, Lisbon, 1973) remains very useful. For Brazil, F. Mauro, *Le Brésil du XVe à la fin du XVIIIe siècle* (Paris, 1977), brings the subject up to date and gives bibliographical information. See also F. Mauro's brief *Histoire du Brésil* (2nd edn, Paris, 1978).

There are also a number of monographs essential for an understanding of Portugal's role in America and its repercussions in the Old World. For Portugal's Atlantic policy, see C. R. Boxer, *Salvador de Sá and the struggle for Brazil and Angola 1602–1686* (2nd edn, Westport, 1975), and *The Golden Age of Brazil, 1695–1750* (Berkeley, 1962), and Dauril Alden, *Royal government in colonial Brazil* (Berkeley, 1968), a major part of which is devoted to matters of diplomacy and war. For a study of Portuguese administration in America, see Stuart B. Schwartz, *Sovereignty and society in colonial Brazil: the judges of the High Court of Bahia, 1586–1750* (Berkeley, 1974); also J. N. Joyce, 'Spanish influence on Portuguese administration: a study of the Conselho da Fazenda and Habsburg Brazil' (University of South California, Ph.D., 1974). On Portuguese political economy and the part played in it by Brazil, J. B. de Macedo, *Problemas de historia da industria Portuguesa no seculo XVIII* (Lisbon, 1963) is important. Also the new edition of V. M. Godinho, *Ensaios II. Sobre historia de Portugal* (Lisbon, 1978). An important recent contribution is Carl Hanson, *Economy and society in Baroque Portugal, 1668–1703* (Minneapolis, 1981). On Portuguese diplomacy in America, the following should be consulted: A. P. Canabrava, *O comércio português no Río da Prata 1580–1640* (São Paulo, 1944), Luis Ferrand de Almeida, *A diplomacia portuguesa e os limites meridionais do Brasil*, I, 1493–1700 (Coimbra, 1957), J. Cortesão, *Raposo Tavares e a formação territorial do Brasil* (Rio de Janeiro, 1958), and J. Cortesão, *Alexandre de Gusmão e o Tratado de Madrid* (8 vols., Rio de Janeiro, 1950–9). For the north, see H. C. Palmatory, *The river of the Amazonas. Its discovery and early exploration 1500–1743* (New York, 1965), and Mario Meireles, *Historia do Maranhão* (São Luis, 1960).

On nautical questions, see the sundry publications of the various

Portuguese congresses, such as the Congresso da Historia da Expansão Portuguesa no Mundo, Congresso do Mundo Português, Congresso dos Descobrimentos Henriquinos; also A. Marques Esparteiro, *Galeotas e bergantins reais* (Lisbon, 1965); N. Steensgaard, *Carracks, caravans and companies* (Copenhagen, 1973), a new edition of which has appeared under the title: *The Asian trade revolution of the seventeenth century. The East India companies and the decline of the caravan trade* (Chicago, 1974); Sousa Viterbo, *Trabalhos nauticos dos Portugueses nos seculos XVI e XVII* (Lisbon, 1900); H. Leitão and J. V. Lopes, *Dicionario da linguagem de Marinha Antiga e Actual* (2nd edn, Lisbon, 1974); Fontoura da Costa, *A marinharia dos Descobrimentos* (Lisbon, 1933); the work of Virginia Rau on foreign merchants in Lisbon, for example, 'Os mercadores e banqueiros estrangeiros em Portugal no tempo de D. João III (1521–1587)', in *Estudios de Historia Economica* (Lisbon, 1961), 35–62; finally, all the studies which have appeared in the publications of the *Junta de Investigações Cientificas do Ultramar*, particularly those of the Centro de Estudos de Cartografia Antiga, Secção de Coimbra e Secção de Lisboa.

On the exports from Brazil, especially sugar and gold, see *CHLA* II, bibliographical essays 12 and 14.

On the slave trade to Brazil the following should be noted: M. Goulart, *Escravidão africana no Brasil* (São Paulo, 1950); G. Scelle, *Histoire politique de la traite négrière aux Indes de Castille*, 2 vols. (Paris, 1906); Philip Curtin, *The Atlantic slave trade* (Madison, 1969); H. S. Klein, 'The Portuguese slave trade from Angola in the 18th century', *Journal of Economic History*, 33/4 (1972), 894–917, and *The Middle Passage. Comparative studies in the Atlantic slave trade* (Princeton, 1978); E. G. Peralta Rivera, *Les Mécanismes du commerce esclavagiste XVIIe siècle* (3rd cycle thesis EHESS, Paris, 1977); P. Verger, *Flux et reflux de la traite des nègres entre le golfe du Bénin et Bahia de Todos os Santos du XVIIe au XIXe siècle* (Paris, 1968), and 'Mouvements de navires entre Bahia et le Golfe de Bénin XVIIe–XIXe siècles', *Revue Française d'Histoire d'Outre-Mer* (Paris), 55 (1968), 5–36; E. Vila Vilar, *Hispano-America y el comercio de esclavos. Los asientos portugueses* (Seville, 1977); finally, K. Polanyi, *Dahomey and the slave trade: an analysis of an archaic economy* (Washington, 1966).

On money, see Teixeira de Aragão, *Descripção geral e historica das moedas cunhadas em nome dos reis de Portugal*, 3 vols. (Lisbon, 1874–80), and, among others, N. C. da Costa, *Historia das moedas do Brasil* (Porto Alegre,

1973). On wars at sea, Botelho de Sousa, *Subsidios para a historia das guerras da Restauração no Mar e no Alem Mar*, I, (Lisbon, 1940), and W. J. van Hoboken, *Witte de With in Brazilie 1648–1649* (Amsterdam, 1955). For institutions, Marcelo Caetano, *Do Conselho Ultramarino ao Conselho do Imperio colonial* (Lisbon, 1943); *Regimento das Casas das Indias e Minas*, ed. Damião Peres (Coimbra, 1947); Gustavo de Freitas, *A Companhia Geral do Comercio do Brasil* (São Paulo, 1951).

For foreign relations, the two classic works are E. Prestage, *The diplomatic relations of Portugal with France, England and Holland from 1640 to 1668* (Watford, 1925), and E. Brasâo, *A Restauração. Relacões diplomaticas de Portugal de 1640 à 1668* (Lisbon, 1939). See also Charles Verlinden, *Les Origines de la civilisation atlantique* (Paris, 1966), and F. Mauro, *Études économiques sur l'expansion portugaise 1500–1900* (Paris, 1970). For Spain and the Spanish empire, see the works of E. J. Hamilton, P. and H. Chaunu, and others, cited in *CHLA* I, bibliographical essays 6, 9 and 10. As regards France, there is no comprehensive work, only chapters or articles in various publications. See, in particular, the numerous articles by J. Soares de Azevedo on French trade in Lisbon. I. S. Revah, *Le Cardinal de Richelieu at la Restauration de Portugal* (Lisbon, 1950) also deserves mention.

On the relations of Portugal with England, many works are available: V. M. Shillington and A. B. Wallis Chapman, *The commercial relations of England and Portugal* (London, 1908; reprinted New York, 1970), the standard work; Sir Richard Lodge, 'The English factory at Lisbon', *Transactions of the Royal Historical Society* (4th ser., 16 (1933), 210–47; A. R. Walford, *The British factory in Lisbon* (Lisbon, 1940); Alan K. Manchester, *British preeminence in Brazil, its rise and decline* (Chapel Hill, 1933); R. Davis, 'English foreign trade 1660–1700', *Economic History Review*, VII (1954), 150–66, and 'English foreign trade, 1700–1774', *EconHR*, xv (1962), 285–303; Elizabeth Boody Schumpeter, *English overseas trade statistics (1697–1808)* (Oxford, 1960); H. E. S. Fisher, *The Portugal trade: a study of Anglo-Portuguese commerce 1700–1770* (London, 1971); A. D. Francis, *The Methuens and Portugal 1691–1708* (Cambridge, 1966); S. Sideri, *Trade and Power: informal colonialism in Anglo-Portuguese relations* (Rotterdam, 1970); C. R. Boxer, 'Brazilian gold and British traders in the first half of the eighteenth century', *HAHR*, 49/3 (1969), 454–72; and, most recently, Virgílio Noya Pinto, *O ouro brasileiro e o comercio anglo-português (uma contribuicão aos estudos de economia atlantica no seculo XVIII* (São Paulo, 1979).

As regards the Dutch, their trade with Portugal can be studied in J. Nanninga Uitterdijk, *Een Kamper Handelshuis te Lisabon 1572–1594* (Zwolle, 1904); A. E. Christensen, *Dutch trade to the Baltic about 1600* (The Hague, 1941); and N. W. Posthumus, *Inquiry into the history of prices in Holland* (Leiden, 1946). For the diplomatic and political aspects of the Dutch presence in Brazil, see C. R. Boxer, *The Dutch in Brazil* (2nd edn, Hamden, 1973); P. Agostinho, 'A politica Vieira e a entrega de Pernambuco', *Espiral* (January–March 1965), 122–34; C. R. Boxer, 'Portuguese and Dutch colonial rivalry', *Studia*, 2 (1958), 7–42; J. M. Campos, *A restauração em Portugal e no Brasil* (Lisbon, 1962); V. Rau, 'A embaixada de Tristão de Mendonça Furtado e os arquivos holandeses', *Anais da Academia Portuguesa de Historia*, 2nd ser., 8 (1958), 93–160; G. D. Winius, 'India or Brazil. Priority for imperial survival during the wars of the Restoration', *Journal of the American-Portuguese Cultural Society*, 1/4–5 (1967), 34–42. Finally, A. Wiznitzer, *Jews in Colonial Brazil* (New York, 1960), deserves mention.

13. PORTUGAL AND BRAZIL: IMPERIAL RE-ORGANIZATION, 1750–1808

For a general approach to the Portuguese empire during the period 1750–1808, there are two fundamental works by C. R. Boxer, *The Portuguese seaborne empire, 1415–1815* (London, 1969), chapters VI and VII, and *The Golden Age of Brazil 1695–1750. Growing pains of a colonial society* (Berkeley, 1962), the last chapter. Useful textbooks include A. H. Oliveira Marques, *História de Portugal desde os tempos mais remotos até ao governo do Sr. Marcelo Caetano*, 2 vols. (Lisbon, 1972), I, chapters VIII and IX, and *História geral da civilização Brasileira*, ed. Sérgio Buarque de Holanda (São Paulo, 1960–), I: *A época colonial* (2 vols., 1960), and II: *O Brasil monárquico*, 1, *O processo de emancipação* (1962). There are also certain studies of individual reigns which, despite the limitations of their time and genre, deserve mention: Simão José da Luz Soriano, *História do reinado de El-Rei D. José e da administrado do Marquès de Pombal*, 2 vols. (Lisbon, 1867); João Lúcio d'Azevedo, *O Marquês de Pombal e sua época* (2nd edn, Lisbon, 1922), an early critical study; Alfredo Duarte Rodrigues, *O Marquês de Pombal e os seus biógrafos* (Lisbon, 1947), which summarizes the early literature; Caetano Beirão, *Dona Maria I (1777–1792)* (4th edn, Lisbon, 1944), still unfortunately the best work on the post-Pombal years; and Angelo Pereira, *D. João VI Principe e Rei*,

4 vols. (Lisbon, 1953–7), I: *A retirada da família real para o Brasil (1807)*.
More recently, there are several excellent works based on extremely
important archival research. Dauril Alden, *Royal government in colonial
Brazil, with special reference to the administration of the Marquis of Lavradio,
viceroy, 1769–1779* (Berkeley, 1968) is particularly concerned with the
structure of royal power in Brazil in the Pombal era and the activities
of an enlightened administrator, and, more generally, with the political,
military and economic history of the captaincies of the South. Kenneth
R. Maxwell, *Conflicts and conspiracies: Brazil and Portugal 1750–1808*
(Cambridge, 1973), makes a new contribution to the study of the
tensions between the metropolis and the colony and of the first moves
towards Brazilian independence, notably in 1789. Fernando A. Novais,
Portugal e Brasil na crise do antigo sistema colonial (1777–1808) (São Paulo,
1979), gives us an important survey of mercantilist colonialism and of
the economic policies of the Portuguese government at the end of the
eighteenth and beginning of the nineteenth century. Like Boxer's *Golden
Age* for the preceding period, these last three penetrating analyses are
a landmark in the historiography of Brazil.

More specifically, on the territorial redefinition of Brazil, J. Cortesão,
Alexandre de Gusmão e o Tratado de Madrid (1750), 10 vols. (Rio de
Janeiro, 1952–63), gives an extremely full documentation for the Treaty
of Madrid, its antecedents and some of its consequences, together with
a commentary which is often polemical. Alden, *Royal government*, already
cited, pp. 59–275, makes an extremely lucid and detached analysis of
the same subject, especially concerned with all the negotiations and
military operations from the Treaty of Madrid to the Treaty of San
Ildefonso (1778) and after. On the occupation, defence and colonization
of the Amazon region and the government's Indian policy, the
fundamental documents were published in Marcos Carneiro de
Mendonça, *A Amazônia na era pombalina (correspondência inédita do
Governador e Capitão General do Estado do Grão Pará e Maranhão, Francisco
Xavier de Mendonça Furtado, 1751–1759*, 3 vols. (Rio de Janeiro, 1963);
see also João Lúcio de Azevedo, *Os Jesuítas no Grão Pará* (Lisbon, 1901),
and 'Política de Pombal relativa ao Brasil', in *Novas Epanáforas. Estudos
de história e literatura* (Lisbon, 1932), 7–62; more recently, Manuel Nunes
Dias, 'Política pombalina na colonização da Amazonia 1755–1777',
Studia, 23 (1968), 7–32, together with his exhaustive study of one of the
instruments of Pombal's policy, the commercial company of Grão Pará

e Maranhão (see below). Among the works of Arthur Cezar Ferreira Reis, see especially *A política de Portugal no valle amazônico* (Belém, 1940).

On the reorganization of political institutions, a good general study is lacking. This is a major lacuna in Portuguese historiography and there is no alternative to recourse to the sources. The best general essay is the chapter on administration, justice and the army in Caio Prado Júnior, *Formação do Brasil contemporâneo: Colônia* (8th edn, São Paulo, 1965), translated by Suzette Macedo, as *The colonial background of modern Brazil* (Berkeley, 1967). See also the works by Alden and Maxwell cited above. Despite its many omissions so far as the description and analysis of administrative structures are concerned, the *Dicionário de História de Portugal* (ed. Joel Serrão), 4 vols. (Lisbon, 1961–71) has its uses. There are also the articles of Marcelo Caetano, 'As Reformas pombalinas e post-pombalinas respeitantes ao Ultramar. O novo espírito em que são concebidas', *História da expansão Portuguesa no mundo*, 3 vols. (Lisbon, 1940), III, 251–60, and José Gonçalo de Santa Ritta, 'Organização da administração ultramarina no século XVIII', *Congresso do mundo Português* (Lisbon, 1940), VIII, 123–53.

The fundamental importance of the texts of laws and decrees, of which much use has been made in this chapter, should be underlined. In the absence of a complete edition, it is necessary to turn to compilations such as: *Collecção das Leys, Decretos e Alvarás que comprehende o feliz Reinado del Rey Fidelissimo D. José I Nosso Senhor, desde o anno de 1750 até o de 1777*, 4 vols. (Lisbon, 1777), and Antônio Delgado da Silva, *Collecção da Legislação Portugueza desde a ultima compilação das Ordenações. Legislação de 1756 a 1820*, 6 vols. (Lisbon, 1830–5).

On the reorganization of the economy, besides consulting manuscript sources it is indispensable to go to contemporary accounts, among which, see especially the following: *Memorias Economicas da Academia Real das Sciencias de Lisboa para o adiantamento da Agricultura, das Artes e da Industria em Portugal e suas Conquistas*, 5 vols. (Lisbon, 1789–1815), analysed by Abílio Carlos d'Ascensão Diniz Silva, 'La Formulation d'une politique de développement économique au Portugal à la fin du XVIIIe siècle' (Mémoire for the Diploma in Sciences Économiques, University of Paris 1, 1969); *Obras Econômicas de J. J. da Cunha de Azeredo Coutinho* (1794–1804), edited by Sérgio Buarque de Holanda (São Paulo, 1966); Jacome Ratton, *Recordaçoens de... sobre occurrencias do seu tempo em Portugal... de Maio 1744 a Setembro de 1810* (London, 1813); Dom

Rodrigo de Souza Coutinho, speeches, memoranda, reports and letters, published by the Marquis of Funchal, *O Conde de Linhares, Dom Rodrigo Domingos Antonio de Souza Coutinho* (Lisbon, 1908), and by Marcos Carneiro de Mendonça, *O Intendente Câmara, Manoel Ferreira da Câmara Bethencourt e Sá, Intendente Geral das Minas e dos Diamantes, 1764–1835* (Rio de Janeiro, 1933); Adrien Balbi, *Essai statistique sur le Royaume de Portugal et d'Algarve*, 2 vols. (Paris, 1822); José Accursio das Neves, *Noções historicas, economicas e administrativas sobre a produção e manufactura das sedas em Portugal*...(Lisbon, 1827), and *Variedades sobre objectos relativos às artes, commercio e manufacturas*, 2 vols. (Lisbon, 1814–17).

Among the studies of economic history dating from the first half of the twentieth century, two classics should not be forgotten: João Lúcio de Azevedo, *Epocas de Portugal económico* (2nd edn, Lisbon, 1973), and Roberto C. Simonsen, *História econômica do Brasil 1500–1820* (6th edn, São Paulo, 1969).

Among recent works dealing with the whole period, two well-documented studies have made a fundamental contribution: the pioneering work of quantitative history, Vitorino Magalhães Godinho, *Prix et monnaies au Portugal 1750–1850* (Paris, 1955), and Kenneth R. Maxwell, *Conflicts and conspiracies* (cited above).

Apart from these, it is necessary to have recourse to books dealing with specific subjects and specific periods, of which the Pombal era is by far the most thoroughly studied, notably by Jorge Borges de Macedo, *A situacão económica no tempo de Pombal.* (1951; 2nd edn, Lisbon, 1982), a suggestive and well-documented work, and by the Viscount of Carnaxide, *O Brasil na administração pombalina* (*Economia e política externa*) (São Paulo, 1940), a controversial study. See also J. Borges de Macedo, 'Portugal e a economia "pombalina". Temas e hipoteses', *Revista de História* (São Paulo), 19 (1954), 81–99. On the fleet system, see V. Magalhães Godinho, 'Portugal, as frotas do açúcar e as frotas do ouro 1670–1770', *Ensaios*, II (Lisbon, 1968), 293–315 (original in French in *AESC* (1950), 184–97). See also Eulália Maria Lahmeyer Lobo, 'As frotas do Brasil', *JGSWGL*, 4 (1967), 465–88; Albert-Alain Bourdon, 'Le Marquis de Pombal et la réorganisation des flottes de commerce entre le Portugal et le Brésil (1753–1766)', Universidade de Lisboa, *Revista da Faculdade de Letras*, 3rd ser., 6 (1962), 182–97; and especially Virgílio Noya Pinto, *O ouro brasileiro e o comércio anglo-portugûes* (*Uma contribução aos estudos de economia atlântica no século XVIII*) (São Paulo, 1979). For the post-Pombal period, there is now Fernando

A. Novais, *Portugal e Brasil na crise do antigo sistema colonial* (cited above), as well as José Jobson de A. Arruda, *O Brasil no comércio colonial* (São Paulo, 1980), which is a detailed analysis of the trade balances of the last years of the period.

On commercial companies and monopolies, besides the exhaustive studies by Manuel Nunes Dias, *Fomento e mercantilismo. A Companhia Geral de Comércio do Grão Pará e Maranhão (1755–1778)* (São Paulo, 1971), and José Ribeiro Júnior, *Colonização e monopólio no Nordeste Brasileiro. A Companhia Geral de Pernambuco e Paraíba (1759–1780)* (São Paulo, 1976), see the article by Jorge Borges de Macedo, 'Companhias commerciais', in *Dicionário de História de Portugal*, 1, 637–44, which provides both a synthesis and a good bibliography, and two penetrating studies by Myriam Ellis: *O monopólio do sal nos Estados do Brasil (1631–1801)* (Universidade de São Paulo, 1955) and *A Baleia no Brasil colonial* (São Paulo, 1969). For the slave trade, see the works cited in *CHLA* 1, bibliographical essay 12, and, more particularly for the late eighteenth century, Antonio Carreira, *As companhias pombalinas de Grão-Pará e Maranhão e Pernambuco e Paraíba* (2nd edn, Lisbon, 1983).

On industrial policy, Jorge Borges de Macedo, *Problemas de história da indústria portuguesa no século XVIII* (1963; 2nd edn, Lisbon, 1982), and the analysis of Fernando A. Novais, 'A Proibição das manufacturas no Brasil e a política econômica portuguesa do fim do século XVIII', *Revista de História* (São Paulo), XXXIII, 67 (1966), 145–66. On the' policy of developing traditional and new colonial products, see *CHLA* 11, bibliographical essay 15.

Portugal's international trade, notably with England, has been the object of several good analyses, such as H. E. S. Fisher, *The Portugal trade. A study of Anglo-Portuguese commerce, 1700–1770* (London, 1971), whose statistics may be supplemented, for the years 1770–1808, with those in E. B. Schumpeter, *English overseas trade statistics (1697–1808)* (Oxford, 1962), 17–18; see also Sandro Sideri, *Trade and power. Informal colonialism in Anglo-Portuguese relations* (Rotterdam, 1970), and the very recent study of Virgílio Noya Pinto, *O ouro brasileiro e o comércio anglo-português* (cited above). For reference, José de Almada, *A aliança inglesa. Subsídios para o seu estudo*, 2 vols. (Lisbon, 1946). The short- and long-term consequences of the famous Methuen Treaty have been the subject of violent controversy. See the solid study by A. D. Francis, *The Methuens and Portugal 1691–1708* (Cambridge, 1966), and the survey by Jorge Borges de Macedo, 'Methuen', in *Dicionário de história de Portugal*,

III, 49–55. On Franco-Portuguese trade, which has been studied less intensively, Vitorino Magalhães Godinho, *Prix et monnaies* (cited above), 321–71, and Frédéric Mauro, 'L'Empire portugais et le commerce franco-portugais au milieu du XVIIIe siècle', in his *Études économiques sur l'expansion portugaise* (Paris, 1970), 81–95. On the very end of the period, Jorge Borges de Macedo, *O bloqueio continental. Economia e guerra peninsular* (Lisbon, 1962).

As regards quantitative history, besides the work of Magalhães Godinho, Novais and Arruda, there are three conference papers published in *L'Histoire quantitative du Brésil de 1800 à 1930* (Colloques Internationaux du C.N.R.S., Paris, 11–15 Octobre 1971) (Paris, 1973): Fernando A. Novais, 'Notas para o estudo do Brasil no comércio internacional do fim do século XVIII e início do século XIX (1796–1808)', 59–75, Harold B. Johnson, Jr, 'Money and prices in Rio de Janeiro (1760–1820)', 39–57, and Kátia M. de Queirós Mattoso, 'Os preços na Bahia de 1750 a 1930', 167–82. Queiriós Mattoso has also written 'Conjoncture et société au Brésil à la fin du XVIIIe siècle', *Cahiers des Amériques Latines*, 5 (1970), 33–53, while Johnson is also the author of 'A preliminary enquiry into money, prices and wages 1763–1823', in *The colonial roots of modern Brazil*, edited by Dauril Alden (Berkeley, 1972).

On Pombal the majority of the works already mentioned have something to say. See also Francisco José Calazans Falcon, *A Epoca pombalina* (*Política econômica e Monarquia ilustrada*) (São Paulo, 1982). A number of valuable publications appeared on the occasion of the two hundredth anniversary of Pombal's death in 1982, notably: *O Marquês de Pombal e o seu tempo*, edited by the Instituto de História e Teoria das Ideias of the Faculdade de Letras de Coimbra (*Revista de História das Ideias*, IV, 1982); *Como interpretar Pombal? No bicentenário da sua morte*, edited by *Brotéria* (Lisbon, 1983), and Joaquim Veríssimo Serrão, *O Marquês de Pombal: o homem, o diplomata e o estadista* (Lisbon, 1982). Martinho de Mello e Castro has not been the subject of any monograph, but Dom Rodrigo de Souza Coutinho is currently being studied by Andrée Mansuy-Diniz Silva.

14. THE CATHOLIC CHURCH IN COLONIAL SPANISH AMERICA

The historiography of the Church in colonial Spanish America is in a far more primitive state than the historiography of colonial Spanish

America in general. Only in recent years has it emerged from some of its accumulated backwardness, giving promise of a better future.

A number of general histories of the Church world-wide include chapters, more or less generous in scope, devoted to Latin America: volumes XVI to XIX of the *Histoire de l'Église depuis les origines jusqu'à nos jours* (Paris, 1948–60), edited by Augustin Fliche and others; volumes V to VIII of·Hubert Jedin's *Manual de historia de la Iglesia* (Barcelona, 1974–8); volume III of *The Christian centuries: a new history of the Catholic Church*, edited by Louis-Jacques Rogier, R. Aubert and M. D. Knowles (London, 1964–); and volumes III and IV of the *Historia de la Iglesia católica* (Madrid, 1954–63) by Bernardino Llorca, Ricardo García Villoslada and Francisco Javier Montalbán. From the Protestant point of view there is K. S. Latourette's *A history of the expansion of Christianity* (New York and London, 1938–53). A student can also turn to volumes II, III and IV of Simon Delacroix' *Histoire universelle des missions catholiques* (Paris, 1956–9).

There are also a number of works specifically Latin American in scope: Leandro Tormo Sanz, *Historia de la Iglesia en América Latina*, volumes I and III (Madrid, 1962–3), A. Ybot León, *La Iglesia y los eclesiásticos en la empresa de Indias*, 2 vols. (Barcelona, 1954–63), and León Lopétegui, Félix Zubillaga and Antonio de Egaña, *Historia de la Iglesia en la América española desde el descubrimiento hasta comienzos del siglo XIX*, 2 vols. (Madrid, 1965–6) confine themselves to the colonial period, though in some cases stretching it to cover the period of the Wars of Independence. For its part, Richard Pattee, *El Catolicismo contemporáneo hispanoamericano* (Buenos Aires, 1951) offers us the most extensive chronological range. Enrique D. Dussel's *Hipótesis para una historia de la Iglesia en América Latina* (Barcelona, 1967) which was transformed – and expanded – into *Historia de la Iglesia en América Latina* (Barcelona, 1972), shows a marked preference for the twentieth century. C. R. Boxer, *The Church Militant and Iberian Expansion, 1440–1770* (Baltimore, 1978) deals selectively with a number of historical problems and includes Asia and Africa as well as Latin America. Hans Jürgen Prien's *Die Geschichte des Christentums in Lateinamerika* (Göttingen, 1978) is the only work that can be considered fully comprehensive. However, the ambitious project that the Comision de Estudios de Historia de la Iglesia en América Latina has been advancing since 1973 – the publication simultaneously in Spanish (Salamanca), in Portuguese (Petrópolis) and in English (New York), of 11 volumes of a *Historia General de la Iglesia en América Latina* under the general editorship of E. D. Dussel – deserves mention. Latin

American ecclesiastical history lacks a basic bibliographical work of reference and historical journal. Anyone wishing to venture among the islands of this archipelago has to consult the general learned journals, such as the *Revue d'Histoire Écclésiastique* (Louvain), the *Indice Histórico Español* (Barcelona), the *Hispanic American Historical Review* (Durham, North Carolina) and the *Revista de História de America* (Mexico).

There are a number of studies devoted to the history of the Church in particular countries, but they are unfortunately variable in their range and sources of information. Outstanding among them are Mariano Cuevas, *Historia de la Iglesia en México*, 5 vols. (El Paso, 1921–8); Rubén Vargas Ugarte, *Historia de la Iglesia en el Perú*, 5 vols. (Lima and Burgos, 1953–62); Cayetano Bruno, *Historia de la Iglesia en la Argentina*, 8 vols. so far (Buenos Aires, 1966–71); C. Jilva Cotapos, *Historia Eclesiástica de Chile* (Santiago, 1925); and José María Vargas, *Historia de la Iglesia en el Ecuador durante el Patronato Español* (Quito, 1962).

There are also histories of the religious orders who worked in Spain's American colonies. Here, too, the historiographical quality is most unequal, ranging from irreproachable critical works such as the Mexican, Peruvian and Brazilian series of the *Monumenta Historica Societatis Jesu* on the one hand, to the literature of edification and apologias for home-grown glory on the other. Outstanding are M. I. Pérez Alonso, *La Compañía de Jesús en Mexico; cuatro siglos de labor cultural, 1572–1972* (Mexico, 1975); Serafim Leite, *Historia da Companhia de Jesus no Brasil*, 10 vols. (Rio de Janeiro and Lisbon, 1938–50); Juan Manuel Pacheco, *Los Jesuitas en Colombia* (Bogotá, 1959–62), with two volumes so far; Alberto E. Arizas, *Los Dominicos en Venezuela* (Bogotá, 1971); Avencio Villarejo, *Los Agustinos en el Perú, 1548–1965* (Lima, 1965); Andrés Millé, *La Orden de la Merced en la conquista del Perú, Chile y Tucumán, 1218–1804* (Buenos Aires, 1958); E. de Palacio and J. Brunet, *Los Mercedarios en Bolivia* (La Paz, 1976).

For easily comprehensible reasons, evangelization has proved powerfully attractive as a subject. Robert Ricard, *La conquête spirituelle du Mexique: essai sur l'apostolat et les méthodes missionaires des Ordres Mendiants en Nouvelle Éspagne, de 1523 à 1572* (Paris, 1933) opened up a wide field of research in relation to the transfer of Christianity from Europe to America. One aspect of the phenomenon was pursued by John Leddy Phelan, *The millennial kingdom of the Franciscans in the New World* (Berkeley, 1956). Another pathbreaking work is Fernando de Armas Medina, *La Cristianización del Peru, 1532–1600* (Seville, 1953), in which there is much important information on ecclesiastical organization and practice. Johann Specker, *Die Missionsmethode in Spanisch-Amerika im 16. Jahrhundert mit besonderer Berücksichtigung der Konzilien und Synoden* (Schöneck-Beckenried, 1953), sets out to systematize the earliest Latin American conciliar enactments. See also, Pedro Borges, *Métodos misionales en la cristianización de America* (Madrid, 1960), Constantino Bayle, *El clero secular y la evangelización de America* (Madrid, 1950) and E. D. Dussel, *El episcopado hispano americano, defensor y evangelizador del indio 1504–1620,* 9 vols. (Cuernavaca, 1964–71), and *Les Évêques hispano-americains, defenseurs et évangelisateurs de l'indien 1503–1620* (Wiesbaden, 1970).

On Bartolomé de Las Casas and the cultural, theological and religious significance of the controversies surrounding his life, see the works cited in *CHLA* I, bibliographical essay 9.

The bibliography available on the Jesuit Reductions is formidable, reflecting an age-old polemic. See, for example, Magnus Mörner's pioneering study, *The political and economic activities of the Jesuits in the La Plata region: the Habsburg era* (Stockholm, 1953), Bartomeu Melía's *La Création d'un langage chrétien dans les reductions des Guarani au Paraguay* (Strasbourg, 1969) and, among Melía's articles, 'La reducciones jesuiticas del Paraguay: un espacio para una utopia colonial', *Estudios Paraguayos*, 6 (1978), 157–68. Most recently Louis Necker, *Indiens Guaranis et chamanes franciscaines: les premières réductions du Paraguay, 1580–1800* (Paris, 1979) has assessed the continuity between Franciscan missionary efforts and the general application of their method by the Jesuits.

For the growing literature on nunneries, see *CHLA* II, bibliographical essay 9.

The recent interest in ethno-historical exploration has had some effect upon the image we can perceive of the religious acculturation of the Indian population. Such works as Pierre Duviols, *La Lutte contre les religions autochtones dans le Pérou colonial: l'extirpation de l'idolatrie entre 1532 et 1660* (Lima and Paris, 1971), Nathan Wachtel, *La Vision des vaincus: les indiens du Pérou devant la conquête espagnole* (Paris, 1971, English translation, 1977), and Jacques Lafaye, *Quetzalcoatl et Guadalupe* (Paris, 1974, English translation, 1977) have illuminated obscure and neglected areas in the history of a native population that was officially Christianized, but which remained for centuries in revolt against its indoctrination.

On the Inquisition, Henry Kamen, *The Spanish Inquisition* (London, 1976) is a recent general study, while Richard E. Greenleaf examines the Mexican Inquisition in *Zumárraga and the Mexican Inquisition 1536–1543* (Washington, D.C., 1961), and *The Mexican Inquisition in the Sixteenth Century* (Albuquerque, 1969).

On the *Patronato Real* and its source, the papal bulls of donation, we must consider as classics the works of Manuel Giménez Fernández, for instance his *Nuevas consideraciones sobre la historia, sentido y valor de las bulas alejandrinas de 1493 referentes a las Indias* (Seville, 1943), and those of Alfonso García Gallo, for example his study 'Las bulas de Alejandro VI y el ordenamiento jurídico de la expansión portuguesa y castellana en Africa e Indias', in the *Anuario de Historia del Derecho Español*, volumes 27 and 28 (1957–8). See also the important studies of Pedro de Leturia, collected in volume 1 of his *Relaciones entre la Santa Sede y Hispanoamerica*, 3 vols. (Rome and Caracas, 1959), and the work of his disciple, Antonio de Egana, *La teoría del Regio Vicariato español de Indias* (Rome, 1958), for the seventeenth century, and also, so far as the regalist and gallican developments in the eighteenth century are concerned, Alberto de La Hera, *El regalismo borbónico* (Madrid, 1963).

An important monograph on the Church in late colonial Mexico, and especially the attack by the crown on the *fuero eclesiastico*, is Nancy M. Farris, *Crown and clergy in colonial Mexico 1759–1821. The crisis of ecclesiastical privilege* (London, 1968). The best overall view of the relations between state and church remains William Eugene Shiels, *King and Church: the rise and fall of the Patronato Real* (Chicago, 1961).

15. THE CATHOLIC CHURCH IN COLONIAL BRAZIL

Two volumes of the *História da Igreja no Brasil* (Petrópolis, 1977–80) have been published. They contain two studies on the colonial period: E. Hoornaert, 'A Evangelização e a cristandade durante o primeiro período colonial' (1977), and R. Azzi, 'A Instituição eclesiástica durante o primeiro período colonial (1977). Equally important is the comprehensive and well-documented study by Hans-Jürgen Prien, *Die Geschichte des Christentums in Lateinamerika* (Göttingen, 1978).

Certain sources are of particular importance to an understanding of the basic themes of church history in Brazil between 1500 and 1800. Claude d'Abbeville, *Histoire de la mission des Pères Capucins de l'Ile de Maragnon et terres circonvoisines* [Paris, 1614] (Rio de Janeiro, 1975); João Daniel, 'Tesouro descoberto do máximo rio Amazonas, 1757–1776', *Anais da Biblioteca Nacional*, 2 vols. (Rio de Janeiro, 1976); Miguel

Garcia, 'Carta ao Pe. Geral Aquiviva, da Bahia: sobre graus e ressaibos da universidade do colégio da Bahia; sobre a liberdade dos índios, de que era defensor, tornando-se-lhe intoleráveis as confissões dos moradores, 1583', excerpts in Serafim Leite, *Historia da Companhia de Jesus no Brasil*, 10 vols. (Rio de Janeiro, 1938–50) (hereafter cited as *HCJB*), I, 98; II, 227, 440; Gonçalo Leite, 'Carta ao Pe. Geral contra as homicidas e roubadores da liberdade dos índios do Brasil' [Lisboa, 1586], excerpts in *HCJB*, II, 229; Martin de Nantes, 'Relation succinte de la mission du père Martin de Nantes, predicateur capucin, missionaire apostolique dans le Brésil, parmi les indiens appellés Cariris' [Quimper, 1705] (Rio de Janeiro, 1979); Manuel da Nóbrega, 'Diálogo sobre a conversão do Gentio, 1556–1557', in Serafim Leite, *Monumentae Brasiliae*, 4 vols. (Rome, 1956–60) (hereafter cited as *MB*), II, 317–44; Dom Sebastiao Monteiro da Vide, 'Constituições primeiras do Arcebispado da Bahia, propostas e aceitas em o Sinodo diocesano que o dito Senhor celebrou em 12 de junho de 1707' [Lisboa, 1719, Coimbra, 1720] (São Paulo, 1853); António Vieira, 'Informação que por ordem do Conselho Ultramarino deu sobre as coisas do Maranhão ao mesmo Conselho o Padre António Vieira' [Lisbon, 1678], in *Revista do Instituto Histórico e Geográfico Brasileiro* (hereafter cited as *RIHGB*), 72/1 (1910), 72; 'Regulamento das aldeias do Pará e Maranhão ou "visita" do P. António Vieira', *HCJB*, IV, 106–24.

With regard to the process of evangelization, the Jesuit missionary movement has been recorded by Serafim Leite in the *HCJB* and *MB* already cited. For the missionary activities of other religious orders we have only partial studies. For the Franciscans, there is V. Willeke, *Missões franciscanas no Brasil* (Petrópolis, 1974); for the Carmelites, A. Prat, *Notas históricas sobre as missões carmelitas* (Recife, 1940), and M. M. Wermers, 'O Estabelecimento das missões carmelitanas no Rio Negro e no Solimões 1695–1711' in *Vᵒ Colóquio Internacional de Estudos Luso-Brasileiros* (Coimbra, 1965); for the Capuchins, M. Nembro, *Storia dell'attivitá missionária dei Minori Cappuccini nel Brasile 1538–1889* (Institutum Historicum Ordinis Fratrum Minorum Cappuccinorum, Rome, 1958); for the Benedictines, J. G. de Luna, *Os monges beneditinos no Brasil* (Rio de Janeiro, 1974); for the Oratorians, A. Rupert, 'A ação missionária do Oratório no Brasil e a Propaganda' in *S.C. de Propaganda Fide Memoria Rerum, 1622–1972* (Rome, 1972), II, 1121–30.

The expulsion of the Jesuits is discussed, albeit only partially, in the work by Serafim Leite. The question, with particular reference to its impact on Grão Pará and Maranhão, is discussed in D. Alden, 'Economic aspects of the expulsion of the Jesuits from Brazil. A preliminary report', in *Conflict and continuity in Brazilian Society*, edited by Henry H. Keith and S. F. Edwards (Columbia, S. Carolina, 1969), 25–65.

On the Church itself, apart from the *Historia da Igreja no Brasil*, already cited, P. F. da Silveira Camargo, *História eclesiástica do Brasil* (Petrópolis, 1955), F. de Macedo, *O Brasil religioso* (Salvador, 1920), M. Barbosa, *A Igreja no Brasil* (Rio de Janeiro, 1945) and J. C. de Macedo Soares, 'Fontes da história da Igreja Católica no Brasil', *RIHGB*, 220 (1952), 7–338 are worthy of note.

The *Padroado* has been studied by Ch. de Witte in 'Les bulles pontificales et l'expansion portugaise au XVe siècle', *Revue d'Histoire Écclésiastique*, 48 (1953), 683–718. A good examination of the effect of the *Padroado* on church finances is O. de Oliveira, *Os dízimos eclesiásticos do Brasil nos períodos da colônia e do império* (Belo Horizonte, Minas Gerais, 1964). However, the best study is still the famous 'Introduction' to Cândido Mendes de Almeida's *Direito civil eclesiástico brasileiro* (Imprensa Oficial, Rio de Janeiro, 1860–73). On the specific theme of cultural repression in Brazil, see E. Frieiro, *O diabo na livraria do cônego* (Belo Horizonte, 1957).

On the question of the New Christians in Portugal, the student should consult A. Saraiva, *Inquisição e cristãos-novos* (Oporto, 1969). For Brazil, see A. Novinsky, *Cristãos-novos na Bahia* (São Paulo, 1972). A further study written at the beginning of the century shows how the system of repression worked, even against the missionaries: Barão de Studart, 'O Padre Martin de Nantes e o Coronel Dias d'Avila', *Revista da Academia Cearense*, 7 (1902), 41–55.

The Indian policy of the Church has been comprehensively studied by John Hemming in *Red gold, the conquest of the Brazilian Indians* (London, 1978), while church policy towards the blacks is mentioned at various points in Pierre Verger's voluminous study, *Flux et reflux de la traite des nègres entre le golfe de Benin et Bahia de Todos os Santos du 17e au 19e siècle* (Paris, 1968). See also A. J. Saraiva, 'Le Père Antoine Vieira SJ et la question de l'esclavage des noirs au 17e siècle', *AESC* (1967), 1289–309.

The life and thought of António Vieira, the most famous Jesuit of the period, has been the subject of two interesting studies: M. Haubert, *L'Église et la défense des 'sauvages'* (Bruxelles, 1964), and R. Cantel,

Prophétisme et messianisme dans l'oeuvre d'António Vieira (Paris, 1960).
José Honório Rodrigues' lucid article on 'Vieira, doutrinador do
colonialismo português' is reprinted in his *História e historiografia*
(Petrópolis, 1970), 34–55.

There are one or two good monographs on the religious brotherhoods
such as that of F. Teixeira de Salles, *Associações religiosas no circlo de ouro*
(Belo Horizonte, 1953). Also, J. Scarano, *Devoção e escravidão: a Irmandade
de N.S. do Rosário dos Pretos no distrito diamantino no século 18* (São Paulo,
1976). On the Santa Casa de Misericórdia, there is the study by C. B. Ott,
A Santa Casa de Misericórdia da cidade do Salvador (Rio de Janeiro, 1960)
and A. J. R. Russell-Wood, *Fidalgos and philanthropists* (London, 1968).

The social and economic role of the convents was the subject of a
study by Wanderley Pinho entitled 'Costumes monásticos na Bahia',
Revista do Instituto Histórico da Bahia, 25 (1918). See also Susan Soeiro,
'The social and economic role of the convent: women and nuns in
colonial Bahia, 1677–1800', *HAHR*, 54 (1974), 209–32.

Finally, on the religious, including missionary, dimension of popular
movements during the colonial period see E. Hoornaert, *Formação do
catolicismo brasileiro 1500–1800* (Petrópolis, 1974).

INDEX